August 13–15, 2018
Espoo, Finland

I0047549

**Association for
Computing Machinery**

Advancing Computing as a Science & Profession

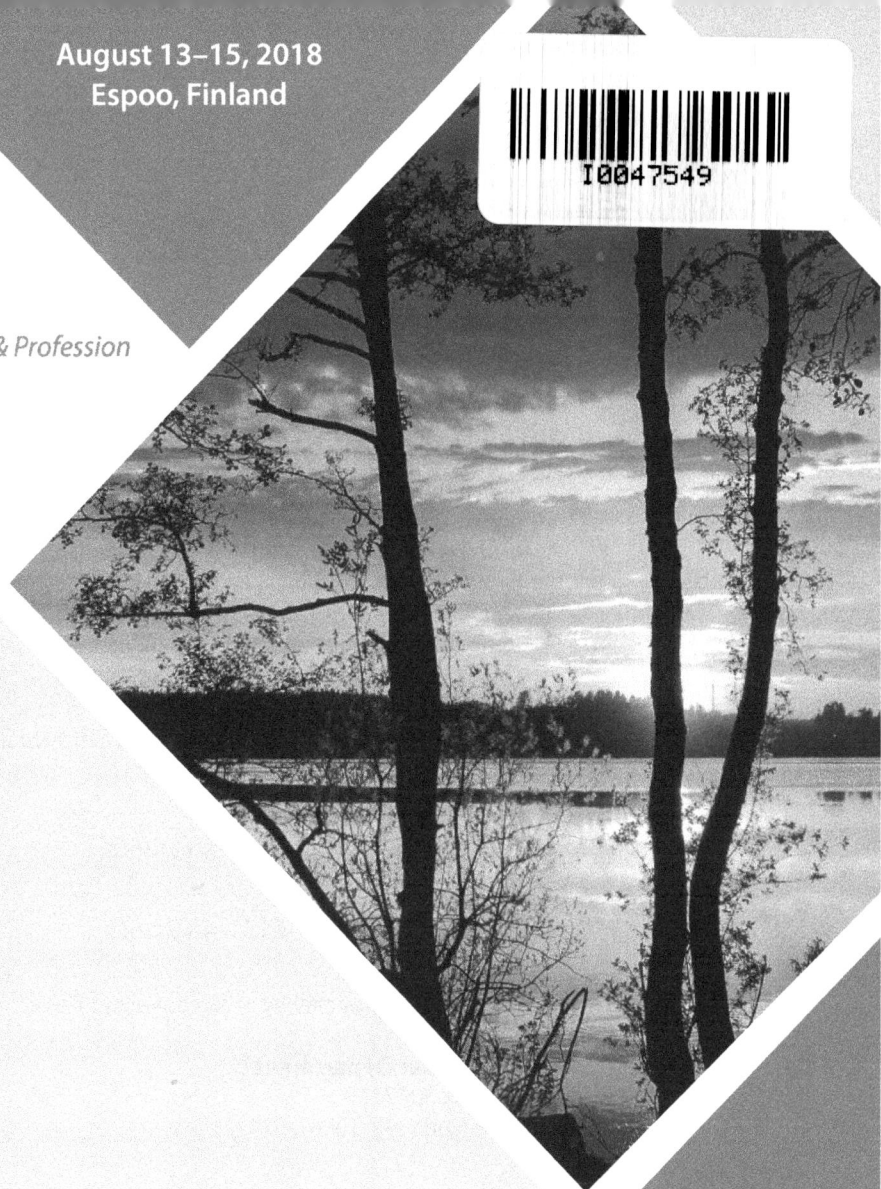

ICER'18

Proceedings of the 2018 ACM Conference on
International Computing Education Research

Sponsored by:
ACM SIGCSE

Supported by:
Oracle Academy, Aalto University, Helsinki Institute for Information Technology, and Federation of Finnish Learned Societies

**Association for
Computing Machinery**

Advancing Computing as a Science & Profession

The Association for Computing Machinery
2 Penn Plaza, Suite 701
New York, New York 10121-0701

ISBN: 978-1-4503-5628-2 (Digital)

ISBN: 978-1-4503-6151-4 (Print)

Additional copies may be ordered prepaid from:

ACM Order Department
PO Box 30777
New York, NY 10087-0777, USA

Phone: 1-800-342-6626 (USA and Canada)
+1-212-626-0500 (Global)
Fax: +1-212-944-1318
E-mail: acmhelp@acm.org
Hours of Operation: 8:30 am – 4:30 pm ET

ICER 2018 Chairs' Welcome

We welcome you to the fourteenth annual International Computing Education Research Conference, ICER 2018, sponsored by the ACM Special Interest Group on Computer Science Education (SIGCSE). Espoo, Finland is the host city for this year's conference, with sessions taking place on the Aalto University campus.

ICER stands as the premier ACM forum for dissemination and discussion of the latest findings in computing education research across the globe. ICER research papers represent significant, rigorous contributions to the field. One hundred twenty-five research papers were submitted, with twenty-eight papers accepted for publication (a 22% acceptance rate) in the conference proceedings in the ACM Digital Library. All papers were double-blind peer reviewed by three members of the program committee. In addition, each paper received a meta-review by a member of the senior program committee, with the two Program Co-Chairs making final acceptance decisions.

In addition to the research paper presentations, ICER includes Lightning Talk and Poster sessions as a way for ICER attendees to present early results, gain feedback from conference attendees, find collaborators on a topic, and/or spark discussion among conference participants. The conference also serves a vital mentoring and advising role for upcoming discipline-based computing education researchers through the Doctoral Consortium. The Work in Progress workshop is a dedicated one-day workshop for ICER attendees to provide and receive friendly, constructive feedback on research during formative stages of development.

Associated co-located workshops with external sponsorship at ICER 2018 include Building Your Team of Change Champions and Computing Science Educational Infrastructure: Crossing the Borders.

We are honored to welcome Kirsti Lonka, the Professor of Educational Psychology in the Faculty of Education at the University of Helsinki, Finland to present the ICER 2018 keynote address. For the past 30 years, she has been investigating various aspects of learning in higher education, medical education, teacher education, and postgraduate education (PhD students). In the area of academic writing, her work has focused around conceptions of writing, note taking, process writing, portfolios and writing across curriculum (writing as a learning tool). Professor Lonka's keynote, *Growing minds - 21st century competences and digitalization among Finnish youth?*, discusses her recent research concerning the digital technology background among Finnish school children and its relation to their activities and attitudes. The keynote addresses the intensive reforms, both in research-based teacher education and at school that are going on in Finland. In addition to the new Finnish curricula, the latest developments in education, innovative pedagogical methods, technologies in education and new learning environments will be presented.

ICER's diverse program is the result of the program committee, senior program committee and conference organizing team's combined effort. We thank all of our volunteers for their hard work in making this year a success. We particularly thank those reviewers willing to step in at the last minute to take on additional reviews. Lastly, we thank our supporters for their generous contributions that will help ensure ICER 2018 will be both successful and memorable for all.

Lauri Malmi, Ari Korhonen, Robert McCartney, Andrew Petersen

Table of Contents

Session 10: Case Studies of Assessment and Studying

Doctoral Consortium

ICER 2018 Conference Organization

General Chairs: Lauri Malmi *(Aalto University, Finland)*
Ari Korhonen *(Aalto University, Finland)*
Robert McCartney *(University of Connecticut, USA)*
Andrew Petersen *(University of Toronto Mississauga, Canada)*

Program Chairs: Lauri Malmi *(Aalto University, Finland)*
Robert McCartney *(University of Connecticut, USA)*

Site Chairs: Ari Korhonen *(Aalto University, Finland)*
Andrew Petersen *(University of Toronto Mississauga, Canada)*

Lightning Talks and Posters Chairs: Anna Eckerdal *(Uppsala University, Sweden)*
Kate Sanders *(Rhode Island College, USA)*

Doctoral Consortium Chairs: Jan Vahrenhold *(Westfälische Wilhelms-Universität Münster, Germany)*
Andrew J. Ko *(University of Washington, Seattle, USA)*

Doctoral Consortium Discussants: Brian Dorn *(University of Nebraska Omaha, USA)*
Anna Eckerdal *(Uppsala University, Sweden)*
Kate Sanders *(Rhode Island College, USA)*
David Weintrop *(University of Maryland, USA)*
Aman Yadav *(Michigan State University, USA)*

Work in Progress Workshop Chairs: Colleen Lewis *(Harvey Mudd College, USA)*
Mark Guzdial *(Georgia Institute of Technology/University of Michigan, USA)*

Submission Chair: Simon *(University of Newcastle, Australia)*

Website: Jan Erik Moström *(Umeå University, Sweden)*

Senior Program Committee: Michal Armoni *(Weizmann Institute of Science, Israel)*
Andrew Begel *(Microsoft Research, USA)*
Tony Clear *(Auckland University of Technology, New Zealand)*
Brian Dorn *(University of Nebraska Omaha, USA)*
Katrina Falkner *(University of Adelaide, Australia)*
Mark Guzdial *(Georgia Institute of Technology/University of Michigan, USA)*
Maria Knobelsdorf *(University of Vienna, Austria)*
Andrew J. Ko *(University of Washington, Seattle, USA)*
Colleen Lewis *(Harvey Mudd College, USA)*
Andrew Luxton-Reilly *(University of Auckland, New Zealand)*
Laurie Murphy *(Pacific Lutheran University, USA)*

Senior Program Committee
(continued): Kate Sanders *(Rhode Island College, USA)*
R. Benjamin Shapiro *(University of Colorado, Boulder, USA)*
Beth Simon *(University of California, San Diego, USA)*
Juha Sorva *(Aalto University, Finland)*
Josh Tenenberg *(University of Washington Tacoma, USA)*

Program Committee: Ruth Anderson *(University of Washington, USA)*
Christine Alvarado *(University of California, San Diego, USA)*
Brett Becker *(University College Dublin, Ireland)*
Moti Ben-Ari *(Weizmann Institute of Science, Israel)*
Jonas Boustedt *(University of Gävle, Sweden)*
Dennis Bouvier *(Southern Illinois University, USA)*
Kristy Elizabeth Boyer *(University of Florida, USA)*
Neil Brown *(King's College London, UK)*
Matthew Butler *(Monash University, Australia)*
Tzu-Yi Chen *(Pomona College, USA)*
Donald Chinn *(University of Washington Tacoma, USA)*
Michelle Craig *(University of Toronto, Canada)*
Quintin Cutts *(University of Glasgow, UK)*
Adrienne Decker *(Rochester Institute of Technology, USA)*
Leigh Ann DeLyser *(CSforALL, USA)*
Philip East *(University of Northern Iowa, USA)*
Nick Falkner *(The University of Adelaide, Australia)*
Sally Fincher *(University of Kent, UK)*
Kathi Fisler *(Brown University, USA)*
Sue Fitzgerald *(Metropolitan State University, USA)*
Diana Franklin *(University of Chicago, USA)*
Judith Gal-Ezer *(The Open University of Israel, Israel)*
Margaret Hamilton *(RMIT University, Australia)*
Orit Hazzan *(Technion - Israel Institute of Technology, Israel)*
Arto Hellas *(University of Helsinki, Finland)*
Geoffrey Herman *(University of Illinois, USA)*
Michael Hewner *(Rose-Hulman Institute of Technology, USA)*
Petri Ihantola *(University of Helsinki, Finland)*
Matthew Jadud *(Bates College, USA)*
Ilkka Jormanainen *(University of Eastern Finland, Finland)*
Mike Joy *(University of Warwick, UK)*
Yasmin Kafai *(University of Pennsylvania, USA)*
Päivi Kinnunen *(Aalto University, Finland)*
Cynthia Lee *(Stanford University, USA)*
Michael J. Lee *(New Jersey Institute of Technology, USA)*

ICER 2018 Sponsors & Supporters

Sponsor:

Supporters:

 TIETEELLISTEN SEURAIN VALTUUSKUNTA
VETENSKAPLIGA SAMFUNDENS DELEGATION
FEDERATION OF FINNISH LEARNED SOCIETIES

Support for the Doctoral Consortium provided by researchers from

Michigan State University,

Rhode Island College,

University of Maryland,

University of Nebraska Omaha, and

Uppsala University

Self-Efficacy, Cognitive Load, and Emotional Reactions in Collaborative Algorithms Labs – A Case Study

Laura Toma
Department of Computer Science
Bowdoin College
Brunswick, ME 04011, USA
ltoma@bowdoin.edu

Jan Vahrenhold
Department of Computer Science
Westfälische Wilhelms-Universität Münster, Einsteinstr. 62,
48149 Münster, Germany
jan.vahrenhold@uni-muenster.de

ABSTRACT

While previous research has investigated psychological factors in introductory programming courses, only little is known about their impact in algorithms courses. Similarly, despite the importance of collaborative problem solving in both academic and non-academic settings, only a small number of studies reports on group work in domains other than programming.

In our case study, we focused on the labs of an introductory algorithms course. We measured the cognitive load of the lab assignments as well as the students' emotional reaction to them. We connect these observations to self-efficacy, performance, psychological traits, and help-seeking behavior as well as to the insights gained from a comprehensive set of follow-up interviews.

Even though our study is a small-scale study, the results from applying both quantitative and qualitative methods frame directions for both pedagogic interventions and further (revalidation) studies related to the connection of non-cognitive factors, learning experiences, and performance in collaborative algorithms labs.

CCS CONCEPTS

• **Social and professional topics** → **Computer science education**; *Student assessment*;

KEYWORDS

Computer Science Education; Self-Efficacy; Algorithms

ACM Reference Format:
Laura Toma and Jan Vahrenhold. 2018. Self-Efficacy, Cognitive Load, and Emotional Reactions in Collaborative Algorithms Labs – A Case Study. In *ICER '18: 2018 International Computing Education Research Conference, August 13–15, 2018, Espoo, Finland*. ACM, New York, NY, USA, 10 pages. https://doi.org/10.1145/3230977.3230980

1 INTRODUCTION

Enrollments in introductory Computer Science courses and the number of Computer Science majors have risen significantly in the past 10 years at most universities and colleges. While growth in the introductory-level classes is the most dramatic, growth is present

at all levels of the curriculum. Resources—faculty time, TAs, classroom space—are becoming overwhelmed [45] and need to be used efficiently. While many studies in Computing Education Research have focused on introductory, programming-related courses, less is known about effective teaching and learning of courses further down the pipeline. With the success of initiatives such as CS4All and ComputingAtSchool, it is reasonable to expect introductory programming courses to trickle down to high school, and classes that are now later in the sequence, will be the "new" introductory classes. Hence, understanding and addressing learning barriers and utilizing teaching resources for non-programming courses will be instrumental to maintaining enrollment and retention numbers.

Bomotti summarizes evidences from literature that "[it] has been estimated that freshmen and sophomores spend from 30 to 50 percent of their undergraduate classroom hours in contact with TAs in some institutions" [11, p. 371] and recent research has looked into formal training for teaching assistants [16, 23, 26, 51].

In the case study reported upon in this paper we focused on students' experiences during the labs of an introductory algorithms course. At Bowdoin College, the institution where this study was conducted, the course has been full and wait-listed for the past several years, and the department has moved from offering it once a year to offering it every semester, and soon will need to offer more than one section at a time. The surge in enrollments has brought along greater breadth of backgrounds, broader interests, more diverse learning styles and affective experiences. Hence, we also looked into self-efficacy and other psychological factors.

Extending instruments from previous research and combining quantitative and qualitative methods, our research questions sought to understand and connect the cognitive load of lab assignments, emotional reactions, perceived benefits of collaboration, inclusiveness, and self-efficacy, in an introductory algorithms course.

> **RQ1:** Can we revalidate / extend the previous findings on algorithms self-efficacy for a small, diverse student population?
>
> **RQ2:** What type and (relative) amounts of cognitive load are reported for the labs?
>
> **RQ3:** Are there labs that induce negative emotional responses? If so, does this correspond to cognitive load / other factors?
>
> **RQ3':** Can we identify learning barriers in algorithms labs?
>
> **RQ4:** What are the students' perceived benefits of collaborative algorithms lab? Are they inclusive?

2 RELATED WORK

Self-efficacy is the self-reported expectation of efficacy, and determines "whether coping behavior will be initiated, how much effort will be expended, and how long it will be sustained in the fact of obstacles and aversive experiences" [3]. It is well known that self-efficacy influences academic achievement and learning outcomes—see, e.g., Pajares and Schunk [50] and the references therein. In Computing Education Research self-efficacy has been assessed mainly in introductory programming courses. Several quantitative studies [18, 55, 66] use the general instrument developed by Ramalingam and Wiedenbeck [56] while others use an instrument geared towards the focus of the respective research study [7, 10, 54]. A generic scale from the Motivated Strategies for Learning Questionnaire (MSLQ) was used by Lishinski et al. [39], and another study [38] used a single generic item ("Considering the difficulty of this course, the teacher, and my skills, I think I will do well in this course."). A qualitative study [31, 32] reports on both self-efficacy for and emotional reactions to programming assignments. Also, Lishinski et al. [38] found emotional reactions while learning to program influence academic outcomes, self-regulation, and self-efficacy; thus understanding emotional reactions can be an important tool to improve self-efficacy.

Two recent studies [18, 22] have investigated self-efficacy in algorithms courses. Elström and Kann [22] used action research for a multiple-year, interactive refinement of an algorithms and complexity course. As part of their study, and starting from the assumption that dynamic programming and NP-completeness are the two topics that pose most problems for students, they developed questionnaires related to self-efficacy for these topics. The authors, however, do not report on an assessment of the construct validity of their instrument. The instrument we use in our study was developed by Danielsiek et al. [18]. In this study, we developed an instrument directed at self-efficacy for an introductory algorithms course and provided an initial assessment of the instrument's construct validity. This instrument as well as the other instruments used in our previous study can be obtained from https://algo-git.uni-muenster.de/self-efficacy-cs2/questionnaires where the instruments used in this study can be found as well.

Cognitive load theory is concerned with how the learning processes are affected by the restrictions on the learner's working memory. As presented originally, cognitive load can be factored into intrinsic load (induced by the natural complexity of the concept to be understood and the learner's knowledge), extraneous load (induced by the complexity of instruction or exposition), and germane load (concerned with the learner's characteristics and independent of the information presented) [62]. Recent work in cognitive load theory suggests that intrinsic load includes germane load and thus only two factors, intrinsic and extrinsic load, should be measured [1, 35, 63]. In Computing Education Research cognitive load has been investigated primarily in introductory programming courses to assess instructional methods and programming assignments, see, e.g., [41, 42, 44]. We used an adaptation of Morrison et al.'s instrument [43] to measure cognitive load.

There are few studies on emotional reactions in introductory computing courses. Kinnunen and Simon [31] and Lishinski et al. [38] assessed the influence of emotional reaction on programming assignment. In contrast to popular belief, Bennedsen and Caspersen [5] could not show a correlation between various factors related to optimism and academic success in an introductory computing course. To the best of our knowledge, emotional reactions have not been assessed for (theory-based) assignments in an

introductory algorithms course. Similarly, help-seeking behavior is mainly assessed in online or interactive learning environments, see, e.g., [46, 53] and the survey by Aleven et al. [2].

Studies that aim at detecting learning barriers usually fall into one of three categories: analyses of the literature (e.g., [22]), approaches through the analysis of artifacts and/or interviews (e.g., [17]), or educational data mining approaches (e.g., [21]). While the approaches in the first category are limited to reconfirmation studies, the approaches in the second category are time- and cost-intensive, and the approaches in the third category require large sample sizes. It this thus desirable to have a time and cost-efficient approach that works with small sample sizes and has the potential of detecting learning barriers previously unknown.

The benefits of collaboration (see Dillenbourg [20] for a discourse on different interpretations of this term) have been assessed widely for introductory programming courses, mainly in the context of pair programming, see, e.g., [4, 12, 19, 27, 37, 57]. Israel et al. [30] present an instrument for assessing collaborative computing. Chowdhury et al. [13] discuss the advantages of a collaborative cohort model for teaching Computational Thinking to a multidisciplinary audience. Coleman and Lang [15] provide insights into an intradisciplinary cohort approach across a full curriculum. An early study by Hübscher-Younger and Narayanan [28] discusses how an interactive CSCL environment can be used to explore algorithms. A phenomenographic study by Falkner et al. [24] cautions that collaborative activities can induce anxiety if groups are assembled randomly or students have conflicting perceptions of expected learning outcomes. While collaboration in Mathematics classrooms is a well-researched subject, see, e.g., [33] and the references therein, Danielsiek et al. [18] point out substantial differences between "problem solving" in Mathematics and in Algorithms.

3 PARTICIPANTS AND ADMINISTRATION

The Algorithms course is the second course in the core sequence required for the Computer Science Major at Bowdoin College. The prerequisite for the course is Data Structures. Algorithms does not currently have any Mathematics course as a prerequisite. Students who want to major in Computer Science take Algorithms in their sophomore year right after Data Structures. The course is capped at 22 students and occasionally allows a small number of students over the cap in case of compelling reasons. In the recent years, due to enrollment surges, the course has filled and has been wait-listed.

Algorithms is a theoretical course which gives an introduction to the analysis and design of algorithms. The class has three parts: (1) analysis tools; (2) design techniques; and (3) graphs. The first two weeks of the class give an accelerated introduction to asymptotic notation, summations and recurrences. Sorting algorithms, which students have seen in Data Structures, are used as case studies to demonstrate analysis and use of $\Theta()$, $\Omega()$, $O()$, summations and recurrences. Linear-time sorting and sorting lower bound are introduced at the end of this module. The second, longest part of the class focuses on design techniques: divide-and-conquer, dynamic programming, and greedy. The last part covers some elements of graph theory and graph search, topological sorting, strongly connected components, shortest paths, and minimum spanning trees, and presents examples of dynamic programing and greedy algorithms.

Week	Lab	Topics covered	Type
1	1	Asymptotics/Summations	theory
2	2	Recurrences	theory
3	3	Sorting and heaps	theory
4	4	Sorting	theory + programming
5	5	Selection	theory
6		Exam 1: On Labs 1–4	in class, theory
7	6	Divide-and-conquer	theory

Week	Lab	Topics covered	Type
8	7	Dynamic programming	theory
9	8	Dynamic programming	theory + programming
10		Exam 2: Emphasis on selection and techniques	in class, theory
11	9	Graphs basics	theory
13	10	Graphs (shortest paths)	theory
		Exam 3: Graphs	in class, theory

Table 1: Timeline of labs and exams.

Overall, the Algorithms course requires a significant jump in abstraction from Data Structures. The goal of the class is not only to present fundamental algorithms, but to give the conceptual tools to enable students to analyze and design new algorithms for new problems. Although Algorithms is not traditionally a lab-based class, in order to support the learning goals, the department introduced a few years ago a weekly lab. The motivation behind the labs is that they allow students to work though the examples from lectures and work on additional problems at their own pace and style.

Lab attendance is by default required as per college policy. However, attendance was not taken and not part of the grade. Despite this, almost all of the students in our study population (see below) did not miss a single lab. Each lab consists of an in-class part and a homework part. Students are expected to work on all in-lab problems during the lab in groups; answers must be turned in by all students, even those not attending the labs, but are not graded.

The in-class part of the lab usually consists of simpler, foundation exercises that practice the concepts from lecture (for, e.g., simulating an algorithm, answering questions about specific algorithms covered, etc.). The homework part of the lab consists of an average of four problems, which are usually hard and require applying the concepts from class in a novel way. Solving the homework part of the lab is usually a process that involves bouncing ideas, seeking help at office hours and attending study groups. The course has four to six hours a week of study groups and often some individual tutors who work individually with students.

The students are encouraged to work in groups for both the in-class and the homework part of the lab. A few years ago the department fine-tuned its collaboration policy introducing several levels of collaboration: in collaboration level-1 students can work together sharing everything; in collaboration level-2 students can bounce ideas but without sharing pseudocode, and must write individual solutions. The in-lab work (which is not graded) is at collaboration level 1, and the homework is at collaboration level 2.

This study was conducted in Fall 2017, when the algorithms course was taught by the first author twice a week (Mon/Wed), in 85 minute sessions; with a weekly, mandatory lab (Fri), also 85 minutes long. Two in-class exams were administered in week 5 and 10 of the semester, and a final in the designated exam-period at the end of the semester (Table 1). The study population consisted of 23 students (15 male, 6 female, 2 who did not not identify as either). Six students belonged to ethnic minorities. Three female students had declared dual majors (Computer Science and Mathematics), one female student had declared a Mathematics minor.

Throughout the study, we administered a variety of questionnaires/surveys; these were pseudonymous, as matching of the answers was done using one-way hashcodes based upon information privy to the students only. Participation was voluntary, but almost all of the students participated at all data collection points (one student dropped the class) thus giving almost complete coverage.

After the end of the course, we followed up by semi-structured interviews in which we sought to gain more information regarding those labs which the quantitative data had revealed to be of particular interest. Also, we elicited responses regarding the perceived benefits of the collaborative labs and their inclusiveness. Participation in the interviews was voluntary, seven students (all but one of them male and only one of them belonging to an ethnic minority) chose to not to participate. Weighing advantages and disadvantages, we decided to let the first author, i.e., the instructor of the course conduct the interviews. First, the interviewer had both an "understanding of the context of the project" and had developed "rapport with the interviewee[s]"—factors that are known to facilitate conducting semi-structured interviews [47, p. 80]. Also, as the interviews also touched upon aspects of inclusiveness and equity, we expected the fact that the instructor is a female professor to make students more comfortable to openly speak about these topics. The concern that students might not be willing to address negative experiences in the presence of a faculty member was mitigated by the fact that all grades had been finalized before the students were invited to participate in the interviews. Also, the instructor/student roles helped avoiding the pitfall of "going native" [25, p. 655] and becoming an member of the group of interviewees.

4 ANALYSES

We start with the results obtained quantitatively[1] and then discuss how the follow-up interviews helped refine our understanding. While we are aware of the limitations of our study due to the small sample size, we use quantitative analyses to provide a fuller picture of the study conditions. As our research was a case study detailing the analysis of the labs of one particular course offering, the quantitative description are intended to facilitate other instantiations of such an analyses and the comparison of their results.

While the qualitative data gathered could be used as a starting point for developing a grounded theory, we used it to follow up on and to complement the quantitative data. We transcribed all interviews and then performed an exhaustive, generative-coding analysis. According to Seale's recommendations [59], we present all qualitative data as low-inference descriptors.

4.1 Self-Efficacy (RQ1)

As one part of our study, we were interested to see whether we could replicate the findings of our previous study [18]. In this study,

---

[1] Analyses were performed using IBM SPSS^{TM} 25 with 95% confidence intervals.

we had evaluated our instrument in four institutions, a larger German public university and three U.S. institutions for which the demographics and sizes of the respective groups of subjects were very similar to ours (the institution in our study was one of the three U.S. institutions in the previous study). The main restriction of our previous study with respect to the U.S. institutions was that the factor analysis of their instrument's scores could only be performed on the full study population ($n = 362$) as the Kaiser-Meyer-Olkin measure for the U.S. subpopulation was too small to allow for a factor analysis of this subpopulation's scores. As we did not look at the individual factors, this did not impact our current study.

The fact that the algorithms course at the German institution in our previous study did not require a midterm exam, restricted our finer analysis of changes in algorithms self-efficacy to the three U.S. institution. As the course in our study did require a midterm exam, we sought to replicate our previous findings regarding changes in self-efficacy for our study population.

We also followed up on our earlier hypothesis regarding the fact that, in contrast to well-documented gender differences in programming self-efficacy, we did not see any such differences in algorithms self-efficacy. We had hypothesized that self-selection and the math-oriented focus of the algorithms course could significantly decrease if not eliminate these differences. Preempting the results from Sections 4.1.1 and 4.1.3 and the demographics reported during the interviews, our study corroborates this hypothesis. As these effects, however, may also be due to the limitations of our study, we defer the discussion of gender-related findings to Section 5.

4.1.1 Pre-Course Self-Efficacy By Gender. Following the setup of our previous study, we started by assessing the subjects' programming self-efficacy as a baseline measure. Data are mean ± standard deviation, unless otherwise stated. There were 15 male and 6 female participants (two participants did not identify as either male or female). An independent-samples t-test was run to determine if there were differences in programming self-efficacy (as measured by Ramalingam and Wiedenbeck's instrument [56]) between males and females. There were no outliers in the data, as assessed by inspection of a boxplot. Programming self-efficacy scores for each level of gender were normally distributed, as assessed by Shapiro-Wilk's test ($p > 0.05$), and there was homogeneity of variances, as assessed by Levene's test for equality of variances ($p = 0.457$). Male students reported a higher programming self-efficacy ($5.71 ± 0.83$) than female students ($5.42 ± 0.75$), but this difference was not statistically significant (95% CI, $−0.52$ to 1.11), $t(19) = 0.748, p = 0.464$.

We also ran an independent-samples t-test to determine if there were differences in pre-course algorithms self-efficacy (as measured by our instrument [18]) between males and females. There were no outliers in the data, as assessed by inspection of a boxplot. Algorithms self-efficacy scores for each level of gender were normally distributed, as assessed by Shapiro-Wilk's test ($p > 0.05$), and there was homogeneity of variances, as assessed by Levene's test for equality of variances ($p = 0.845$). Male and female students reported almost identical self-efficacy values ($4.33 ± 1.19$ for male students, $4.33 ± 1.23$ for female students), the difference was not statistically significant (95% CI, $−1.21$ to 1.22), $t(19) = 0.01, p = 1.000$.

4.1.2 Changes in Self-Efficacy. As part of revalidating our previous observations, we assessed algorithms self-efficacy at the same

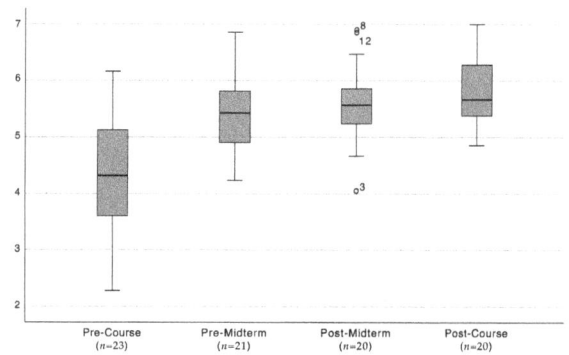

Figure 1: Distributions of algorithms self-efficacy scores.

four points in time: pre-course, pre-midterm, post-midterm, and post-course. Figure 1 shows the boxplots of the corresponding self-efficacy scores. We assessed the differences between consecutive measurements and between pre- and post-course measurements.

We used a paired-samples t-test to determine whether there was a statistically significant mean difference between algorithms self-efficacy measured pre-course and pre-midterm ($n_{matched} = 21$). Visual inspection of the boxplot did not reveal any outliers, the assumption of normality was not violated, as assessed by Shapiro-Wilk's test ($p = 0.571$). As observed in our previous study and consistent with general self-efficacy theory, we saw a statistically significant increase of 0.947 (95% CI, 0.454 to 1.439), $t(20) = 4.009$, $p = 0.001$, from pre-course ($4.379 ± 1.145$) to pre-midterm ($5.326 ± 0.792$). The effect size was large ($d = 0.875$), the sample size was large enough to reliably detect such an effect [14].

When examining the differences between pre- and post-midterm algorithms self-efficacy ($n_{matched} = 19$), we detected three outliers that were more than 1.5 box-lengths from the edge of the box in a boxplot. One of these (data point 3 in Figure 1) was a student who reported a very low self-efficacy immediately post-midterm but later self-reported a very high grade (between 91% and 100%) for the midterm exam. As we could not ignore these outliers, we compared the self-efficacy scores used a related-samples Wilcoxon signed rank test. Eleven participants saw an increase in self-efficacy, six a decrease, and there were two ties. The mean increased from pre-midterm ($5.421 ± 0.154$) to post-midterm ($5.547 ± 0.163$), but this change was not statistically significant ($z = 1.256, p = 0.209$). This observation is consistent with general self-efficacy theory that states that an exam (or feedback in general) serves as a calibration point in either direction—see also [18, 39].

For the next phase, comparing the algorithms self-efficacy post-midterm and post-course, we again used a paired-samples t-test to determine whether there was a statistically significant mean difference ($n_{matched} = 18$). Visual inspection of the boxplot did not reveal any outliers, the assumption of normality was not violated, as assessed by Shapiro-Wilk's test ($p = 0.520$). Again, as observed in our previous study and consistent with general self-efficacy theory, we saw a statistically significant increase of 0.289 (95% CI, 0.053 to 0.524), $t(17) = 2.588, p = 0.019$, from post-midterm ($5.519 ± 0.768$) to post-course ($5.808 ± 0.701$). Cohen's d was calculated as $d = 0.610$, however, the sample size was not large enough to reliably confirm that this was medium effect size [14].

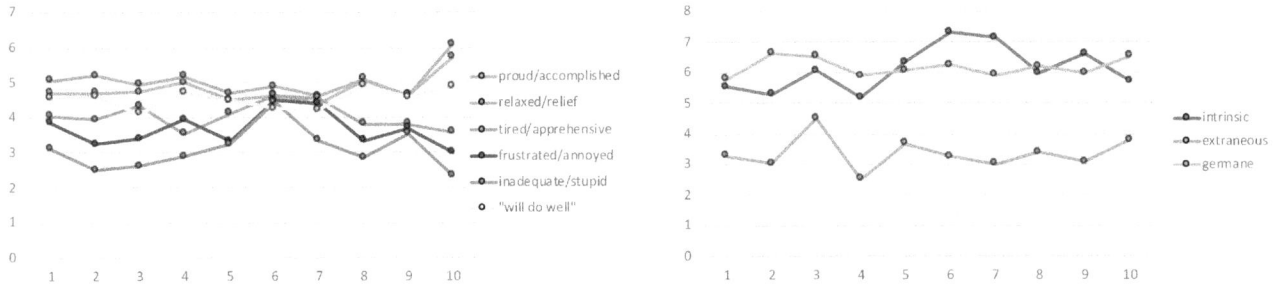

Figure 2: Emotional responses (left) and cognitive load (right) per lab, averaged over all responses ($n \in [16, 21]$).

Finally, the change in algorithms pre- and post-course was analyzed. For this, we used a paired-samples t-test as well ($n_{matched} = 20$). Visual inspection of the boxplot did not reveal any outliers, the assumption of normality was not violated (Shapiro-Wilk's test, $p = 0.720$). Consistent with previous results and self-efficacy theory, we saw a statistically significant increase of 1.391 (95% CI, 1.012 to 1.969), $t(19) = 6.524, p < 0.001$, from post-midterm (4.258 ± 1.113) to post-course (5.749 ± 0.793). The effect size was large ($d = 1.459$), the sample size was large enough to reliably detect such an effect [14].

4.1.3 Post-Course Self-Efficacy By Gender. When analyzing the algorithms self-efficacy values at the end of the course, there was one outlier in the data (a female student with a reported self-efficacy above the boxplot) that prevented running an independent samples t-test. Asserting the similarity of distributions using visual inspection of the respective histograms, we ran an independent-samples Kruskal-Wallis test. Its outcome suggested to retain the null hypothesis that the distribution of the self-efficacy scores was the same for male and female students at the end of the course ($p = .759$).

4.2 Cognitive Load (RQ2), Emotional Reactions (RQ3), and Learning Barriers (RQ3')

For assessing the cognitive load (RQ2) of the labs, we used the CS Cognitive Load Component Survey (CS CLCS) [43] which asks for agreement with given statements on a scale from 0 ("Not at all the case") to 10 ("Completely the case"). We merged three pairs of items that had distinguished between concepts and their implementation and used the question ordering C from [43].

In their work on emotional responses to programming assignments, Lishinski et al. [38] asked students to respond to a subset of three out of five statements derived from the work of Kinnunen and Simon [31] plus a generic self-efficacy statement. To be more comprehensive in assessing the emotional reactions of the labs (RQ3), we used all statements plus the generic statement:

(1) "Upon completing the project lab, I felt proud/accomplished."
(2) "Upon completing the project lab, I felt relaxed/relief."
(3) "Upon completing the project lab, I felt tired/apprehensive."
(4) "While working on the project lab, I often felt frustrated/annoyed."
(5) "While working on the project lab, I felt inadequate/stupid."
(6) "Considering the difficulty of this course, the teacher, and my skills, I think I will do well in this course."

All statements were responded to on a scale from 1 ("Not true of me at all") to 7 ("Extremely true of me").

In contrast to the work of Lishinski et al. [38], our study did not aim at distinguishing emotional reactions by gender or at deriving a path model. Instead, we sought to use averaged cognitive load components (RQ2) and emotional reactions (RQ3) to identify labs that pose particular learning barriers (RQ3') and to better understand these during the follow-up interviews. By design, the small number of data points (10 labs) did not allow for meaningful quantitative analyses of cognitive load and emotional responses. Instead, we proceeded by visual inspection of the charts depicted in Figure 2.

First of all, we see (Figure 2, left) that proudness and relief (omitted by Lishinski et al.) are felt in unison. Also, with the notable exceptions of Lab 3 and Labs 10, the generic self-efficacy statement is responded to in the same way. Regarding tiredness/apprehensiveness, Labs 4 and 8 show drops with respect to the preceding labs; the same holds for the intrinsic load reported for these labs. This can be explained by the fact that these two were the only labs with programming assignments (see Table 1); assignments asked to implement algorithms the students had seen in the preceding labs.

Reported tiredness/apprehensiveness, frustration/annoyance, inadequacy/stupidity, and intrinsic load peaked for Lab 6 even though extraneous load was relatively moderate. We followed up on the reasons (RQ3') by explicitly asking for a comment on Lab 6 (and 10). All but two students immediately mentioned one particular problem, sometimes even before Lab 6 was addressed by the interviewer:

[Student 1:] *The skyline problem is very memorable in terms of being difficult. […] That's the one that stands out the most.*

In a nutshell, the "Skyline" problem asks to develop a divide-and-conquer algorithm for computing the union of rectangles anchored at the x-axis. The solution using divide-and-conquer requires a non-trivial merge step with several cases to distinguish:

[Student 7:] *It had a lot of very different cases, it was hard to visualize. I remember drawing a bunch of diagrams. I remember having difficulty not necessarily how to solve it, but how to understand what it was asking and how to approach the problem.*

When probed further, one student explained:

[Student 5:] *It was how meticulous you had to be. In a lot of these algorithms you can abstract a lot, and you can say, sort this, but in this one, when you're combining, you have to say: if this point is above this, and if…I don't remember exactly, but there's a lot of ifs in there and figuring out exactly what to do in each case was very hard, because you had to almost think down to the level of almost implementing it, not necessarily implementation, but definitely closer. So that was difficult.*

This exactly in line with the following quote by Knuth [65]:

[The] psychological profiling [of a programmer] is mostly the ability to shift levels of abstraction, from low level to high level. To see something in the small and to see something in the large.

The intrinsic load (RQ2) was also high for Lab 7, the first lab on Dynamic Programming. In line with previous research [17, 22], students mentioned Dynamic Programming as a difficult topic:

[Student 9:] So I think for me dynamic programming is the hardest. It's just a concept hard to wrap my head around I guess, understanding it is separate from the actual programs we're doing.

[Student 11:] The idea of keeping a table, I don't know, it got a little abstract and scary.

With respect to the labs (RQ3), however, the emotional responses show that students did not feel too inadequate/stupid. Also, students eventually considered Dynamic Programming manageable.

[Student 6:] Setting up the whole [DP] problem in a big grid and realizing that there was this whole structure that emerges, was really hard to see the first couple of times, like what was going on, and why you get so much overlap. So that was confusing to begin with. But once I did a number of problems. I think it became straightforward in the sense that there is a straightforward approach on how to turn a problem that is suitable for it into a DP solution. As opposed to divide and conquer, you have to more case by case break everything down and think about it.

The germane load (RQ2) was almost constant—thus, our earlier discussions based on changes in intrinsic load are not affected by whether or not it includes germane loads (see Section 2)—and showed moderate increases for Lab 2 and Lab 10.

[Student 5:] The hardest topic I think it was recurrences [Lab 2] because I hadn't done math and I've been rusty for a while, and just figuring out how to do the steps it was difficult.

Lab 10, the last lab prior to the exam, was about a variety of graph problem, each of which required a different algorithmic approach.

[Student 1:] One thing I remember being confused about in this last unit was keeping straight all the different like SSSP, Dijkstra, and Bellman-Ford and that kind of stuff In the end, I had to sit down and look at the differences in my mind at least they all got blurred together and it took a long time to separate them and see exactly how they worked.

[Student 5:] I remember that once I figured out [problem] 3, I found [problem] 4 not as challenging. But I found [problem] 3 challenging because understanding the basis of the graph problems and how to solve them was kinda difficult, But then, once I understood it, then from one problem to the next, it seemed not too bad.

Extraneous load (RQ2) peaked for Lab 3. We conjecture this to be due to STOOGESORT, an algorithm that sorts an array by recursively sorting its first two-thirds, then its last two-thirds, and then again its first two-thirds. The algorithm is designed to be a complicated algorithm leading to a rather simple recurrence relation.

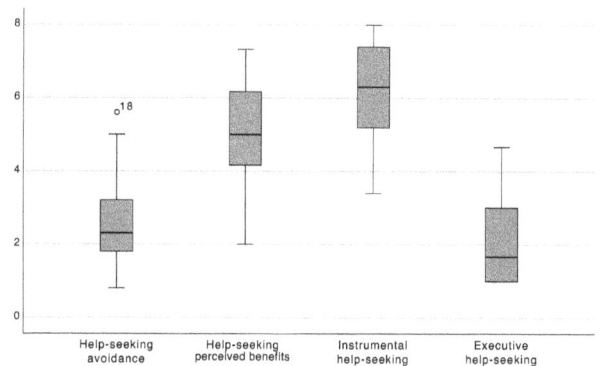

Figure 3: Help-seeking behavior (pre-course, $n = 22$).

4.3 Collaborative Labs (RQ4)

As discussed in Section 3, the department had recently changed the course to include labs and refined the collaboration policy. We thus sought to understand the students' perceived benefits of collaboration, the inclusiveness of the labs, and factors that might be related to these experiences. In particular, we looked at help-seeking behavior, personality traits, and motivation as possible factors influencing the perceived benefits of collaborative work.

4.3.1 Help Seeking. Help-seeking behavior was measured using a scale developed by Pajares et al. [49] for computer science courses. The scale contained 19 items that measured instrumental help-seeking (5 items), executive help-seeking (3 items), perceived benefits of help-seeking (6 items), and avoidance of help-seeking (5 items). Each item presented a statement and asked for agreement on a scale from 1 ("Not true of me at all") to 8 ("Extremely true of me"). The boxplots in Figure 3 can be interpreted as follows: There was a large variation in how beneficial help-seeking was perceived to be, with a slight tendency towards a positive perception. The population in our study was much more prone to instrumental help-seeking, i.e., to asking for just enough help to be able to solve a problem on their own, than to executive help-seeking, i.e., to asking for somebody else to solve that problem. This was confirmed by one student during the interviews:

[Student 14:] Working in groups outside of class: I think all of the TAs were really good at NOT telling you the answer and guiding you through, I appreciated it.

We conclude that with the exception of one person (data point 18, discussed below), the population was not avoiding to seek help.

4.3.2 Traits and Motivation. For assessing psychological factors that might affect collaborative work, we used scales from from the NEO personality inventory [40] and determined scores for the "Openness to Experience" (eight items) and "Conscientiousness" personality traits scores (sixteen items) that had been used in our previous study. Similarly, we reused the scales for "Autonomous Motivation" and "Controlled Motivation" from the Self-Regulation Questionnaire for Learning (SRQ-L) [9]. These instruments were applied pre-course.

The descriptive statistics shown in Figure 4 can be interpreted as follows. The students in our student population showed varying

Please consider the following completions of: "In partner or group work during the labs or for the assignments..."

(1) ...I got to know other solutions.
(2) ...the explanations of my peers helped me.
(3) ...I realized things I did not understand before.
(4) ...the other students had ideas that I could think about further.
(5) ...we could solve problems that were too difficult for me alone.
(6) ...I understood things better by explaining them.
(7) ...I benefited from the way other students approached the problems.
(8) ...it was exciting to think along the other people's lines of thought.

Table 2: Instrument for assessing the perceived benefits of group work [60].

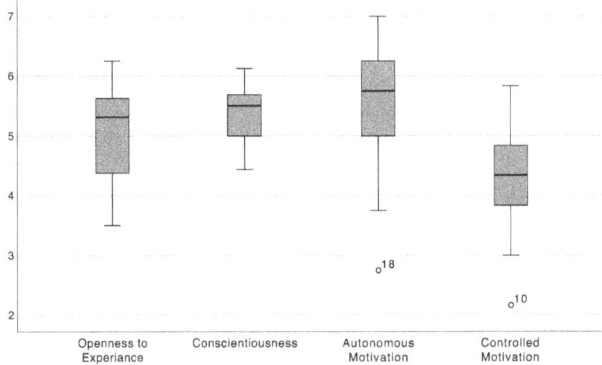

Figure 4: Personality traits / motivation (pre-course, $n = 22$).

degrees of openness to experience but with a higher-than-average mean and were found to be rather conscientious. Given the positive association between these two factors and academic success [48] and the academic requirements of the institution, this observation is not surprising. Turning to the descriptive statistics regarding motivation, we see that, as a group, the students in the study population were motivated more autonomously (intrinsic) than controlled (extrinsic). This was assessed, given the outliers visible in Figure 4, by a related-samples Wilcoxon signed rank test ($z = -3.599$, $p < 0.001$). We note that the student who showed the highest help-seeking avoidance showed the least intrinsic motivation (data point 18).

4.3.3 Perceived Usefulness. After the follow-up interviews, we asked the participants to pseudonymously fill out a questionnaire regarding the perceived usefulness of the labs; we did not give this questionnaire prior to the interviews to avoid a priming bias. The scale used for this was an adapted form of a scale by Stebler and Reusser [60] that was used as part of the Swiss extensions of the Third International Mathematics and Science Study (TIMSS 1995). This validated scale asks to rate the statements shown in Table 2 on a scale from 1 ("strongly disagree") to 4 ("strongly agree"). The scores of the 15 students who participated in the interviews were normally distributed, as assessed by Shapiro-Wilk's test ($p = 0.983$), with a mean of 3.283 ± 0.092 (95% CI, 3.086 to 3.480). By and large, these descriptive statistics show that students perceived the labs as useful; this had become evident from the interviews as well:

[Student 1:] *At least for me working with other people was really helpful. You don't get to that point where you get stuck and can't go any further.*

[Student 12:] *Towards the end we got on a flow: We'd write on the board, helping each other out, and we could move faster so*

we'd get more work done without focus on few small mistakes you made here and there.

The usefulness of collaboration in labs was acknowledged even by a student who declared to prefer working independently:

[Student 2:] *Most of the time, I worked independent on my own. [...] I think the aspect of me not knowing a part and him not knowing a part was key to me wanting to be in that group, because I need to understand the part that I didn't. So if there is ever a lab in which you give half the students a different component of the lab, and gave the other half the students another component, and then they could pair up with someone from the other side, so that they could figure out both sides together; that would be something advantageous to me because I would not be able to go out on my own and figure out both parts. Something in which I need the other person would motivate me, and then I'd probably realize the group aspect of it is definitely beneficial as well.*

However, there were two outliers, one student more than 1.5 box-lengths above the edge of the box in a boxplot and one below. This latter student was the same student (data point 18) who had shown highest help-avoidance and least intrinsic motivation. We concede that a follow-up interview regarding these characteristics would have been of high interest not only from a research perspective but also from the point of study counseling, but as the interviews were detached from the pseudonymous surveys, we had no means of discovering this student's identity and to follow up in person.

We examined the results obtained from this scale for correlation with the traits and motivational factors measured pre-course. However, given the small sample size of 15 data points for the perceived usefulness would have required a correlation coefficient of $r = 0.670$ to be determinable with $\alpha = 0.05$ (two-tailed) and $\beta = 0.20$ [29]. The correlation coefficients closest to this were determined by "Controlled Regulation" ($r = 0.501$; not significant, $p = 0.051$) and "Autonomous Regulation" ($r = 0.647$, $p = 0.012$; the assumption of normality as assessed by Shapiro-Wilk's test, however, was not quite satisfied, $p = 0.044$). Our findings are thus inconclusive. Nonetheless, we hypothesize that students with a strong intrinsic motivation actively participate in collaborative labs and perceive them as more beneficial. This hypothesis is supported by statements from the follow-up interviews (see above) but asks for a quantitative study with a larger study population.

4.3.4 Inclusiveness of the Labs. As part of the interviews, we asked participants to fill out a questionnaire regarding the inclusiveness of the labs (RQ4). The scale used for this was an adapted form of a scale by Prenzel et al. [52] that was used as part of a

Swiss-German study on the quality of learning in mathematics classrooms [33]. This validated scale asks to rate the following statements on a scale from 1 ("never") to 4 ("always"):

(1) "During labs, I was treated by other students in the lab as a peer."
(2) "During labs, I felt that the other students in the lab would help me if it were necessary."
(3) "During labs, I felt understood by the others in the lab."
(4) "During labs, I had the feeling of belonging to the group."

The responses of the 15 students participating in the interviews indicated strongly positive experiences (mean 3.550 ± 0.147; 95% CI, 3.235 to 3.864). In addition to gaining quantitative insights about the inclusiveness, however, we used this as a deliberate priming for the following interview question:

Do you have any positive or negative experiences to report about your collaboration in the lab and in the homework?

While most responses referred to the effectiveness of groupwork (discussed above), some students addressed inclusiveness:

[Student 8 (male, african-american):] *Positive, I will say that it was very dynamic, so whenever I would work I was able to jump in. So I wasn't put aside. [...] The TA sessions were really inclusive.*

[Student 10 (female, white):] *The fact that we started doing the labs in class on Friday made me more comfortable approaching those people outside of class and say "Hey, do you want to meet up and work on this later?". I thought that was very beneficial.*

One student mentioned an equity issue (discussed in Section 5):

[Student 11 (female, white):] *I always feel that in Computer Science classes I'm not happy with how I'm treated in group work, in general, just because I think people underestimate me. And like I remember it took me a while, even with [names male collaborator], he's such a nice guy, and we got like to a point where he would like listen to me if I'd told him "No, I don't think that is right", but I remember in the first few weeks, being so frustrated with him, because he wouldn't... because he just like assumed that his thing was right. I think it's probably a gender thing; also, the way I come off, as a person, I'm quiet, I don't know, it's hard for me to be forceful about an idea.*

5 DISCUSSION AND LIMITATIONS

By nature of being a case study, obvious limitations apply to our research. Given the small sample sizes, the insights obtained from quantitative data can only be used "for purposes of fuller descriptions, rather than to draw statistical inferences" [58, p. 183].

In contrast to previous studies related to inclusiveness (RQ4), e.g., [34, 36], our interviews revealed only one self-reported occurrence of gender-based inequity and no self-reported occurrence of ethnic-based inequity. We offer the following possible explanations:

- The selectiveness of the institution in which our study was undertaken might have led to less variation in status than in other environments. According to Berger et al.'s *status characteristic theory*, "in certain circumstances, if subjects are equal in status, the effect of a status characteristic that discriminates between them is reduced" [6, p. 254].

- The course, being an algorithms course, had a much stronger focus on mathematics and formal methods than the introductory programming courses in which previous research had been conducted. As summarized by Beyer [8], the underrepresentation of female students in introductory computer science courses is not at all due to a lack of mathematics ability. In fact, all but one female student reported to be a mathematics minor or major. Again, this is likely to have counteracted negative stereotypes.

- The instructor of the course was a female CS professor. As Stout et al. [61] point out, a female role model is an important factor in enhancing women's self-concept in STEM.

- Finally, the groups were not (deliberately) balanced towards being representative of either gender or ethnicity [24]. As the class was a mixed-ethnic group, Wilkinson and Fung's conclusions that the "findings [from literature] suggest that ethnic background moderates the effects of gender on interaction and learning on mixed-gender groups" [64, p. 435] may have played a role here as well.

We note that our findings do not contradict the results from Beyer's large-scale study [7] on gender differences in, among others, self-efficacy as Beyer investigated *computer* self-efficacy, i.e., a technology-oriented construct. In fact, her conclusion that only female students with high (computer) self-efficacy take future computer science courses implies that the female students in the population of our study had predominantly high self-efficacy and explains the non-significant differences in programming self-efficacy reported in Section 4.1.1. The above observations about mathematics ability [8] are also suited to explain the non-significant differences for algorithms self-efficacy (RQ1) throughout the course.

6 CONCLUSIONS

In our case study we showed how a combination of instruments can be assembled to gain insights into which factors affect self-efficacy and emotional responses in collaborative algorithms labs. We found students to perceive the labs as highly beneficial, in particular given the collaboration policies that explicitly allowed for sharing ideas (qualitative details omitted due to space constraints). We suggest to use low-cost instruments to assess perceived benefits and inclusiveness of lab sessions. Future research includes investigating a break-down of self-efficacy and emotional responses by demographic groups (see Section 5) for larger study populations.

The methodological contributions of our study include a low-cost quantitative instrument based on cognitive load and emotional responses for detecting learning barriers which gave us a starting point for a qualitative follow-up. Our study population was more challenged by an assignment involving a rather simple algorithmic concept having multiple levels of abstraction than by dynamic programming problems which had been the focus of earlier research. Even though we are reluctant to generalize this particular finding, using our combination of instruments may help instructors and researchers alike to understand the learning barriers students in different environments face.

Acknowledgements. We thank M. Evers for her help with entering the data. This work was partially supported by the German Federal Ministry of Education and Research (grant 01PB14007A).

REFERENCES

[1] S. Aldekhyl, R. B. Cavalcanti, and L. M. Naismith. Cognitive load predicts point-of-care ultrasound simulator performance. *Perspectives in Medical Education*, 7(1):23–32, Feb. 2018.

[2] V. Aleven, E. Stahl, S. Schworm, F. Fischer, and R. Wallace. Help seeking and help design in interactive learning environments. *Review of Educational Research*, 73(3):277–320, 2003.

[3] A. Bandura. Self-efficacy: Toward a unifying theory of behavioral change. *Psychological Review*, 84(2):191–215, 1977.

[4] L. Battestilli, A. Awasthi, and Y. Cao. Two-stage programming projects: Individual work followed by peer collaboration. In T. Barnes, D. D. Garcia, E. K. Hawthorne, and M. A. Pérez-Quiñones, editors, *Proceedings of the 49th ACM Technical Symposium on Computer Science Education, SIGCSE 2018*, pages 479–484. ACM Press, 2018.

[5] J. Bennedsen and M. E. Caspersen. Optimists have more fun, but do they learn better? On the influence of emotional and social factors on learning introductory computer science. *Computer Science Education*, 18(1):1–16, 2008.

[6] J. Berger, B. P. Cohen, and M. Zelditch, Jr. Status characteristics and social interaction. *American Sociological Review*, 37(3):241–255, June 1972.

[7] S. Beyer. Why are women underrepresented in computer science? Gender differences in stereotypes, self-efficacy, values, and interests and predictors of future CS course-taking and grades. *Computer Science Education*, 24(2–3):153–192, 2014.

[8] S. Beyer. Women in computer science: Deterrents. In P. A. Laplante, editor, *Encyclopedia of Computer Science and Technology*, pages 871–879. CRC Press, second edition, 2017.

[9] A. E. Black and E. L. Deci. The effects of instructors' autonomy support and students' autonomous motivation on learning organic chemistry: A self-determination theory perspective. *Science Education*, 84(6):740–756, Nov. 2000.

[10] J. M. Blaney and J. G. Stout. Examining the relationship between introductory computing course experiences, self-efficacy, and belonging among first-generation college women. In M. E. Caspersen, S. H. Edwards, T. Barnes, and D. D. Garcia, editors, *Proceedings of the 2017 ACM SIGCSE Technical Symposium on Computer Science Education*, pages 69–74. ACM Press, 2017.

[11] S. S. Bomotti. Teaching assistant attitudes towards college teaching. *The Review of Higher Education*, 17(4):371–393, 1994.

[12] M. Celepkolu and K. E. Boyer. Thematic analysis of students' reflections on pair programming in cs1. In T. Barnes, D. D. Garcia, E. K. Hawthorne, and M. A. Pérez-Quiñones, editors, *Proceedings of the 49th ACM Technical Symposium on Computer Science Education, SIGCSE 2018*, pages 771–776. ACM Press, 2018.

[13] B. Chowdhury, A. C. Bart, and D. Kafura. Analysis of collaborative learning in a computational thinking class. In T. Barnes, D. D. Garcia, E. K. Hawthorne, and M. A. Pérez-Quiñones, editors, *Proceedings of the 49th ACM Technical Symposium on Computer Science Education, SIGCSE 2018*, pages 143–148. ACM Press, 2018.

[14] J. Cohen. A power primer. *Psychological Bulletin*, 112(1):155–159, July 1992.

[15] B. Coleman and M. Lang. Collaboration across the curriculum: A disciplined approach to developing team skills. In L. A. S. King, D. R. Musicant, T. Camp, and P. T. Tymann, editors, *Proceedings of the 43rd ACM technical symposium on Computer science education, SIGCSE 2012*, pages 277–282. ACM Press, 2012.

[16] H. Danielsiek, P. Hubwieser, J. Krugel, J. Magenheim, L. Ohrndorf, D. Ossenschmidt, N. Schaper, and J. Vahrenhold. Undergraduate teaching assistants in computer science: Teaching-related beliefs, tasks, and competences. In *Proceedings of the 2017 IEEE Global Engineering Education Conference (EDUCON)*, pages 718–725, 2017.

[17] H. Danielsiek, W. Paul, and J. Vahrenhold. Detecting and understanding students' misconceptions related to algorithms and data structures. In L. A. S. King, D. R. Musicant, T. Camp, and P. T. Tymann, editors, *Proceedings of the 43rd ACM technical symposium on Computer science education, SIGCSE 2012*, pages 21–26. ACM Press, 2012.

[18] H. Danielsiek, L. Toma, and J. Vahrenhold. An instrument to assess self-efficacy in introductory algorithms courses. In J. Tenenberg, D. Chinn, J. Sheard, and L. Malmi, editors, *Proceedings of the 2017 ACM Conference on International Computing Education Research, ICER 2017*, pages 257–265. ACM Press, 2017.

[19] E. Deitrick, M. H. Wilkerson, and E. Simoneau. Understanding student collaboration in interdisciplinary computing activities. In J. Tenenberg, D. Chinn, J. Sheard, and L. Malmi, editors, *Proceedings of the 2017 ACM Conference on International Computing Education Research, ICER 2017*, pages 118–126. ACM Press, 2017.

[20] P. Dillenbourg. What do you man by collaborative learning? In P. Dillenbourg, editor, *Collaborative Learning: Cognitive and Computational Approaches*, pages 1–19. Elsevier, Oxford, 1999.

[21] S. H. Edwards, N. Kandru, and M. B. M. Rajagopal. Investigating static analysis errors in student Java programs. In J. Tenenberg, D. Chinn, J. Sheard, and L. Malmi, editors, *Proceedings of the 2017 ACM Conference on International Computing Education Research, ICER 2017*, pages 65–72. ACM Press, 2017.

[22] E. Enström and V. Kann. Iteratively intervening with the "most difficult" topics of an algorithms and complexity course. *ACM Transactions on Computing Education*, 17(1), Jan. 2017. Article 4, 38 pages.

[23] F. J. Estrada and A. Tafliovich. Bridging the gap between desired and actual qualifications of teaching assistants: An experience report. In R. Davoli, M. Goldweber, G. Rößling, and I. Polycarpou, editors, *Proceedings of the 2017 ACM Conference on Innovation and Technology in Computer Science Education, ITiCSE 2017*, pages 134–139, New York City, 2017. ACM.

[24] K. Falkner, N. J. G. Falkner, and R. Vivian. Collaborative learning and anxiety. In T. Camp, P. T. Tymann, J. D. Dougherty, and K. Nagel, editors, *The 44th ACM Technical Symposium on Computer Science Education, SIGCSE '13*, pages 227–232. ACM Press, 2013.

[25] A. Fontana and J. H. Frey. The interview: From structured questions to negotiated text. In N. K. Denzin and Y. S. Lincoln, editors, *Handbook of Qualitative Research*, pages 645–672. SAGE Publications, second edition, 2000.

[26] J. Forbes, D. J. Malan, H. Pon-Barry, S. Reges, and M. Sahami. Scaling introductory courses using undergraduate teaching assistants. In M. E. Caspersen, S. H. Edwards, T. Barnes, and D. D. Garcia, editors, *Proceedings of the 2017 ACM SIGCSE Technical Symposium on Computer Science Education*, pages 657–658. ACM Press, 2017.

[27] A. Hellas, J. Leinonen, and P. Ihantola. Plagiarism in take-home exams: Help-seeking, collaboration, and systematic cheating. In R. Davoli, M. Goldweber, G. Rößling, and I. Polycarpou, editors, *Proceedings of the 2017 ACM Conference on Innovation and Technology in Computer Science Education, ITiCSE 2017*, pages 238–243, New York City, 2017. ACM.

[28] T. Hübscher-Younger and N. H. Narayanan. Constructive and collaborative learning of algorithms. In S. Grissom, D. Knox, D. Joyce, and W. Dann, editors, *Proceedings of the 34th SIGCSE Technical Symposium on Computer Science Education*, pages 6–10. ACM Press, 2003.

[29] S. B. Hulley, S. R. Cummings, W. S. Browner, D. G. Grady, and T. B. Newman. *Designing Clinical Research*. Lippincott Williams & Wilkins, fourth edition, 2013.

[30] M. Israel, Q. M. Wherfel, S. Shehab, E. A. Ramos, A. Metzger, and G. C. Reese. Assessing collaborative computing: development of the collaborative-computing observation instrument (C-COI). *Computer Science Education*, 26(2–3):208–233, 2016.

[31] P. Kinnunen and B. Simon. Experiencing programming assignments in CS1: the emotional toll. In M. E. Caspersen, M. J. Clancy, and K. Sanders, editors, *Proceedings of the 6th International Workshop on Computing Education Research (ICER 2010)*, pages 77–86. ACM Press, 2010.

[32] P. Kinnunen and B. Simon. CS majors' self-efficacy perceptions in CS1: Results in light of social cognitive theory. In M. E. Caspersen, A. Clear, and K. Sanders, editors, *Proceedings of the 7th International Workshop on Computing Education Research (ICER 2011)*, pages 19–26. ACM Press, 2011.

[33] E. Klieme and K. Reusser. Unterrichtsqualität und mathematisches Verständnis im internationalen Vergleich – Ein Forschungsprojekt und erste Schritte zur Realisierung [Teaching quality and conceptual understanding in international comparison]. *Unterrichtswissenschaft*, 31(3):194–205, 2003. In German.

[34] A. N. Kumar. A study of stereotype threat in computer science. In T. Lapidot, J. Gal-Ezer, M. E. Caspersen, and O. Hazzan, editors, *Annual Conference on Innovation and Technology in Computer Science Education, ITiCSE '12*, pages 273–278, New York City, 2012. ACM.

[35] J. Leppink and A. van den Heuvel. The evolution of cognitive load theory and its application to medical education. *Perspectives in Medical Education*, 4(3):119–127, June 2015.

[36] C. M. Lewis and N. Shah. How equity and inequity can emerge in pair programming. In B. Dorn, J. Sheard, and Q. I. Cutts, editors, *Proceedings of the eleventh annual International Conference on International Computing Education Research, ICER 2015*, pages 41–50. ACM Press, 2015.

[37] C. M. Lewis, N. Titterton, and M. Clancy. Using collaboration to overcome disparities in Java experience. In A. Clear, K. Sanders, and B. Simon, editors, *International Computing Education Research Conference, ICER '12*, pages 79–86. ACM Press, 2012.

[38] A. Lishinski, A. Yadav, and R. Enbody. Students' emotional reactions to programming projects in introduction to programming: Measurement approach and influence on learning outcomes. In J. Tenenberg, D. Chinn, J. Sheard, and L. Malmi, editors, *Proceedings of the 2017 ACM Conference on International Computing Education Research, ICER 2017*, pages 30–38. ACM Press, 2017.

[39] A. Lishinski, A. Yadav, J. Good, and R. Enbody. Learning to program: Gender differences and interactive effects of students' motivation, goals, and self-efficacy on performance. In J. Sheard, J. Tenenberg, D. Chinn, and B. Dorn, editors, *Proceedings of the 2016 ACM Conference on International Computing Education Research (ICER 2016)*, pages 221–220. ACM Press, 2016.

[40] J. L. Maples, L. Guan, N. T. Carter, and J. D. Miller. A test of the international personality item pool representation of the revised NEO personality inventory and development of a 120-item IPIP-based measure of the five-factor model. *Psychological Assessment*, 26(4):1070–1084, Dec. 2014.

[41] R. Mason, Simon, G. Cooper, and B. Wilks. Flipping the assessment of cognitive load: Why and how. In J. Sheard, J. Tenenberg, D. Chinn, and B. Dorn, editors, *Proceedings of the 2016 ACM Conference on International Computing Education Research, ICER 2016*, pages 43–52. ACM Press, 2016.

[42] B. B. Morrison. Dual modality code explanations for novices: Unexpected results. In J. Tenenberg, D. Chinn, J. Sheard, and L. Malmi, editors, *Proceedings of the 2017 ACM Conference on International Computing Education Research, ICER 2017*,

pages 225–235. ACM Press, 2017.

[43] B. B. Morrison, B. Dorn, and M. Guzdial. Measuring cognitive load in introductory CS: Adaptation of an instrument. In Q. I. Cutts, B. Simon, and B. Dorn, editors, *International Computing Education Research Conference, ICER 2014*, pages 131–138. ACM Press, 2014.

[44] B. B. Morrison, L. E. Margulieux, and M. Guzdial. Subgoals, context, and worked examples in learning computing problem solving. In B. Dorn, J. Sheard, and Q. I. Cutts, editors, *Proceedings of the eleventh annual International Conference on International Computing Education Research, ICER 2015*, pages 21–29. ACM Press, 2015.

[45] National Academies of Sciences Engineering and Medicine. *Assessing and Responding to the Growth of Computer Science Undergraduate Enrollments*. The National Academies Press, Washington, DC, 2018.

[46] M. Nelimarkka and A. Hellas. Social help-seeking strategies in a programming MOOC. In T. Barnes, D. D. Garcia, E. K. Hawthorne, and M. A. Pérez-Quiñones, editors, *Proceedings of the 49th ACM Technical Symposium on Computer Science Education, SIGCSE 2018*, pages 116–121. ACM Press, 2018.

[47] L. Noaks and E. Wincup. *Criminological Research: Understanding Qualitative Methods*. SAGE Publications, 2004.

[48] M. C. O'Connor and S. V. Paunonen. Big five personality predictors of post-secondary academic performance. *Personality and Individual Differences*, 43(5):971–990, 2007.

[49] F. Pajares, Y. F. Cheon, and P. Oberman. Psychometric analysis of computer science help-seeking scales. *Educational and Psychological Measurement*, 64(3):496–513, 2004.

[50] F. Pajares and D. H. Schunk. Self-beliefs and school success: Self-efficacy, self-concept, and school achievement. In R. Riding and S. Rayner, editors, *Perception*, pages 239–266. Ablex Publishing, London, 2001.

[51] E. Patitsas. A case study of the development of CS teaching assistants and their experiences with team teaching. In *Proceedings of the 13th Koli Calling International Conference on Computing Education Research*, Koli Calling '13, pages 115–124, New York, NY, USA, 2013. ACM.

[52] M. Prenzel, A. Kirsten, P. Dengler, and T. Beer. Selbstbestimmt motiviertes und interessiertes Lernen in der kaufmännischen Erstausbildung. *Zeitschrift fuer Berufs- und Wirtschaftspädagogik, Beiheft*, 13:108–127, 1996. In German.

[53] T. W. Price, R. Zhi, and T. Barnes. Hint generation under uncertainty: The effect of hint quality on help-seeking behavior. In E. André, R. Baker, X. Hu, M. M. T. Rodrigo, and B. du Boulay, editors, *Artificial Intelligence in Education, AIED 2017*, volume 10331 of *Lecture Notes in Computer Science*, pages 311–322. Springer, 2017.

[54] A. Quade. Development and validation of a computer science self-efficacy scale for CS0 courses and the group analysis of CS0 student self-efficacy. In *Proceedings of the International Conference on Information Technology: Computers and Communications (ITCC'03)*, pages 60–64. IEEE Computer Society, 2003.

[55] V. Ramalingam, D. LaBelle, and S. Wiedenbeck. Self-efficacy and mental models in learning to program. In R. D. Boyle, M. Clark, and A. Kumar, editors, *Proceedings of the 9th Annual SIGCSE Conference on Innovation and Technology in Computer Science Education (ITiCSE 2004)*, pages 171–175, New York City, 2004. ACM.

[56] V. Ramalingam and S. Wiedenbeck. Development and validation of scores on a computer programming self-efficacy scale and groups analyses of novice programmer self-efficacy. *Journal of Educational Computing Research*, 19(4):367–381, Dec. 1998.

[57] F. J. Rodrígues, K. M. Price, and K. E. Boyer. Exploring the pair programming process: Characteristics of effective collaboration. In M. E. Caspersen, S. H. Edwards, T. Barnes, and D. D. Garcia, editors, *Proceedings of the 2017 ACM SIGCSE Technical Symposium on Computer Science Education*, pages 507–512. ACM Press, 2017.

[58] M. Sandelowski. Sample size in qualitative research. *Research in Nursing & Health*, 18(2):179–183, Apr. 1995.

[59] C. Seale. Quality in qualitative research. *Qualitative Inquiry*, 5(4):465–478, 1999.

[60] R. Stebler and K. Reusser. Skalendokumentation der Schweizerischen Zusatzerhebungen zu TIMSS. Technical report, University of Zurich, Department of Educational Studies, 1995. In German.

[61] J. G. Stout, N. Dasgupta, M. Hunsinger, and M. A. McManus. STEMing the tide: Using ingroup experts to inoculate women's self-concept in science, technology, engineering, and mathematics (STEM). *Journal of Personality and Social Psychology*, 100(2):255–270, 2011.

[62] J. Sweller. Element interactivity and intrinsic, extraneous, and germane cognitive load. *Educational Psychological Review*, 22(2):123–138, June 2010.

[63] J. Sweller. Measuring cognitive load. *Perspectives in Medical Education*, 7(1):1–2, Feb. 2018.

[64] I. A. G. Wilkinson and I. Y. Y. Fung. Small-group composition and peer effects. *International Journal of Educational Research*, 37(5):425–447, 2002.

[65] J. Woehr. An interview with Donald Knuth. Dr Dobbs Journal, Apr. 1996. http://www.drdobbs.com/an-interview-with-donald-knuth/184409858.

[66] D. Zingaro. Peer instruction contributes to self-efficacy in CS1. In J. D. Dougherty, K. Nagel, A. Decker, and K. Eiselt, editors, *Proceedings of the 45th SIGCSE Technical Symposium on Computer Science Education (SICGSE 2014)*, pages 373–378. ACM Press, 2014.

Fixed versus Growth Mindset Does not Seem to Matter Much

A Prospective Observational Study in Two Late Bachelor level Computer Science Courses

Antti-Juhani Kaijanaho
antti-juhani.kaijanaho@jyu.fi
University of Jyväskylä
Faculty of Information Technology
Jyväskylä, Finland

Ville Tirronen
ville.e.t.tirronen@jyu.fi
University of Jyväskylä
Faculty of Information Technology
Jyväskylä, Finland

ABSTRACT

Psychology predicts that a student's mindset—their implicit theory of intelligence—has an effect on their academic performance. We attempted to corroborate this in the computer science education context by asking the students on two bachelor-level courses, typically taken in the third year of studies, to fill out a standard mindset questionnaire, and analyzing their answers in relation to their grades on those courses. In a sample of 133 students, with only 24 (18 %) students with a clear fixed mindset, there is no detectable correlation between the students' mindsets and their course grades. An ordinal logistic regression estimates, at the 95 % confidence level, a statistically nonsignificant effect between a decrease by a factor of 0.46 and an increase by a factor of 2.03 in the odds of achieving a better course grade when moving from a strong fixed mindset to neutral mindset, or when moving from a moderate fixed mindset to a moderate growth mindset. This suggests that any effect the mindset has on the outcomes of these courses is small. We conclude that educational interventions targeting students' mindsets may not be worth the effort in late bachelor-level CS education, possibly because students who suffer from their fixed mindset have already dropped out by the third year.

CCS CONCEPTS

• **Social and professional topics** → **Computer science education**; **Adult education**;

KEYWORDS

mindsets, growth mindset, fixed mindset, implicit theories, entity theory, incremental theory, psychology

ACM Reference Format:
Antti-Juhani Kaijanaho and Ville Tirronen. 2018. Fixed versus Growth Mindset Does not Seem to Matter Much: A Prospective Observational Study in Two Late Bachelor level Computer Science Courses. In *ICER '18: 2018 International Computing Education Research Conference, August 13-15, 2018, Espoo, Finland.* ACM, New York, NY, USA, 10 pages. https://doi.org/10.1145/3230977.3230982

1 INTRODUCTION

We, like many other teachers, are intuitively inclined to adopt the stance that *mindsets matter* and act accordingly in our teaching [2, 37, 40]. Here, *mindset* refers to Carol Dweck and colleagues' psychological theory [10, 11, 13] according to which one's *implicit theory* of one's own intelligence—either an *entity theory* (a *fixed mindset*) or an *incremental theory* (a *growth mindset*)—influences how one reacts to difficulties, leading to different levels of academic achievement. However, is it worth our time and effort to try to change our students' mindset? In this paper we investigate, in an observational setting, the size of any effect mindsets have on student achievement in late bachelor-level courses, and find, to our surprise, that this effect is too small for us to measure. We also find a relatively small number of students with a fixed mindset in our courses.

The context of our study is two core bachelor-level computer science courses at the University of Jyväskylä, Finland, targeting second and third year students but usually taken in the third year of studies: one on the theory of computing and one on functional programming. Both courses are essential for the field, but many students struggle with them. The subject matter in these courses is challenging and seems to require deep understanding only obtainable through long hours of practice causing students to face both *motivational* and *affective* difficulties (cf. Kinnunen and Malmi [20]). This highlighted to us the potential importance of the correct mindset as enabler of persistence.

The effect of mindset on student achievement has been experimentally demonstrated, but there are relatively few studies on the magnitude of such an effect, especially in the context of computer science education. We thus set out to investigate the size of the effect mindsets have on outcomes in our own courses. Knowing the effect size estimate is important in practice: the larger the effect, the more important it is for us to try to influence student mindset, while a small effect would make such interventions mostly irrelevant. Our research question then became:

RQ Assuming a causal connection between a student's implicit self-theory of intelligence and their academic achievement, how large is its contribution in the context of late bachelor-level computer science courses?

Notice that we make a causal assumption here; it is, we think, well established by prior research.

Table 1: Features associated with fixed and growth mindset (summarizing Dweck and Leggett [13]).

Category	Fixed mindset	Growth mindset
Implicit theory of intelligence	*Entity:* intelligence is something one was born with and cannot be changed	*Incremental:* intelligence can be developed by conscious action
Goals	*Performance:* trying to achieve the recognition of one's preexisting abilities and to hide one's preexisting weaknesses	*Learning:* trying to improve one's abilities
Behavior pattern	*Helpless:* difficulties are insurmountable barriers	*Mastery:* difficulties are challenges to be overcome
View of high required effort	A sign of lack of talent	A sign of learning
Task choice with low perceived ability	Seek easy tasks	Seek challenging tasks
Effect of difficulties on …		
…affect	Negative emotions	Neutral or positive emotions
…problem-solving performance	Decrease	Neutral or increase

2 MINDSETS

2.1 Basic theory

The psychological theory of *mindsets* [10, 11, 13] posits that people can be roughly sorted into two categories based on their (current) view on the nature of their own intelligence:

- People holding the *fixed mindset* believe that (their own) intelligence is something they were born with in a certain amount that they cannot affect.
- People holding the *growth mindset* believe that (their own) intelligence is something they can develop by conscious action.

We use here terminology apparently first used in a popular exposition published in 2006 [11]. The seminal article [13], along with much of the older literature, used the general term *implicit theories* together with the specific terms *entity theory* (fixed mindset) and *incremental theory* (growth mindset). Other terms seen in the literature include *self-theories*, *lay theories* and *naive theories*.

The theory of mindsets predicts a number of differences between individuals based on their mindset, as summarized in Table 1. The educational import of the theory is the prediction that a fixed mindset leads one to suboptimal study strategies and to give up studying a topic early, as challenges start to appear, resulting in worse educational outcomes, while a growth mindset encourages working through difficulties, resulting in better educational outcomes.

Lüftenegger and Chen [25] recommend using the *implicit theories* terminology in academic publications. However, as mindsets are more familiar for the nonpsychologist audience, we continue to use them. In our usage, mindsets are (mutable) categories of people, and the implicit theories of intelligence are psychological constructs measured by specific instruments, which— according to the theory— determine mindsets.

Intelligence is not the only thing that people have implicit theories of. Dweck [10] mentions studies on implicit theories of other people's personality and morality as well as of the malleability of the world. Researchers have also studied implicit theories of programming aptitude [35, 36, 37]. However, our interest is in the original theory of mindsets, involving the claim that the implicit theory of intelligence predicts particular behaviors and thus influences outcomes; for our purposes, then, these alternative constructs are beside the point.

2.2 Empirical evidence

The theory of mindsets grew out of experimental phenomena. Carol Dweck and colleagues showed in psychological experiments in the 1970s that children's ability to persist in the face of failures depends on whether they take responsibility for their own success and failure, and that training children to take such responsibility improves persistence [9, 14]. Subsequent experiments uncovered much of the associated features summarized in Table 1, and eventually it was noticed that the theory of intelligence that a person holds (often without realizing it) is a reliable predictor of these two categories. Dweck and Leggett [13] summarize these developments and the associated experiments up to the late 1980s, by which time the theory was largely complete and experimentally corroborated in many contexts. Dweck further published at the turn of the century an academic monograph [10] on the theory, and later another book for the popular audience [11].

Since the seminal work by Dweck, the theory has been examined in field conditions and in specific contexts such as mathematics or in transitions between educational levels. This research has discovered new associations, such as the association between self-esteem and growth mindset [33] in young adults.

Although field research has provided some evidence supporting the theory in real world context [4], there are a number of studies that cast doubt on using mindsets as predictors of academic success. For example, Macnamara and Rupani [27] found no evidence that growth mindset would predict higher academic achievement in their study of first year psychology students. Instead, the authors observed the opposite, though non-significant, association. Likewise, Clevenger [7] finds in her thesis no apparent association between mindset and academic achievement in K12 students and their parents. However, growth mindset did predict performance goals in the way described by Dweck [10].

Similar results were also obtained in context of mathematics by Priess-Groben and Hyde [30], who studied mindsets during transition from high school to college. They found that, although growth mindset was a significantly associated with achievement, controlling factors such as prior success effectively eliminated this association. They suspect that mindset is just one factor of many affecting success in this field. Relatedly, Zonnefeld [45] studied mindsets connected to learning university level statistics. Here also, the result hints that student mindset does not affect the measured learning outcome.

Regardless of several negative studies, a meta-analysis of experimental and observational studies by Burnette et al. [1] shows a small positive association of a growth mindset with goal achievement.

In the context of computer science education, mindsets have been studied fairly little. Experiments involving mindset interventions on first year university students [8, 40] show mixed results in changes of mindset and no measurable effect in course outcomes. Observational studies, mainly in the CS1 context, have found either weak or unmeasurable effect of mindsets on course outcomes [15, 24, 38, 41].

All of the above mentioned studies have been conducted in a WEIRD (Western, Educated, Industrialized, Rich, and Democratic) context [17], mostly in the United States and mostly with college and university level students. Although the original theory does not posit a cultural dependency on the effect of mindset, it is possible that one exists. For example Chen and Wong [5] has studied the mindset theory within Chinese culture, finding that their results were consistent some of the time with some differences the authors identify as cultural.

2.3 Measurement

The standard instruments for measuring implicit theories (mindsets) are given in an appendix to Dweck's monograph [10]. We focus on her self-theories of intelligence form for adults (on p. 178), as it is the most relevant for this study. It consists of eight items scored from 1 (strongly agree) to 6 (strongly disagree) with no neutral option. Four items are assertions consistent with an entity theory of intelligence (fixed mindset), e. g.,

> *1. You have a certain amount of intelligence, and you can't really do much to change it.*

and the rest are assertions consistent with an incremental theory (growth mindset), e. g.,

> *5. You can always substantially change how intelligent you are.*

Dweck [10] advises (p. 176) that the entity theory items can be used alone; in such a case, a rejection of the entity theory would be taken as the acceptance of the incremental theory.

The entity theory and the incremental theory item responses can be straightforwardly summed or averaged separately. This creates two scores, the entity theory score and the incremental theory score. Most empirical studies tend to either use the entity theory score alone or a combined score where the incremental theory items have been reverse scored [1, 25], considering in both cases a low score as indicating an entity theory. This seems logical, as the entity theory and the incremental theory appear to be logically inconsistent, and it seems difficult to see how one can endorse both

of the example items quoted above. However, Chen and Tutwiler [4], Lüftenegger and Chen [25], and Tempelaar et al. [42] argue that there is not sufficient correlation between the two scores to justify combining them; in effect, they say, the entity theory and the incremental theory appear to be separate constructs that are highly related instead of two faces of the same coin.

Older studies seem to simplify their analyses by dichotomizing the scores. For example, Dweck et al. [12, p. 269] created two groups by categorizing all participants with a score of at most 3 as entity theorists and all participants with a score of at least 4 as incremental theorists. The remaining participants—with a score between 3 and 4—were then excluded from analysis. They reported that only 15 % of their participants were thus excluded. However, dichotomization of scores is generally disfavored by methodologists (see, e. g., MacCallum et al. [26] and Rucker et al. [34]).

Dweck and Leggett [13, fn. 5 on p. 263] reported that she and her colleagues have obtained bimodal distributions for scores measuring implicit theories of intelligence. In other works [12, 22], Dweck and colleagues have reported various distributions of dichotomized implicit theory variables, with both incremental and entity theories having substantial (but not always equal) support, and a fairly low exclusion rate; this indirectly suggests a fairly bimodal distribution of the underlying scores. More recently, Tempelaar et al. [42] found a roughly normal distribution of implicit theory scores, with 64 % of their sample lying within a one deviation around the mean; however, both theories were approximately equally endorsed. Most reports of studies that we are aware of do not give sufficient detail on their score distributions for similar analyses. There thus is some doubt on whether there actually is a bimodal underlying distribution that would justify classifying people into two groups in this manner; however, both theories seem to be generally endorsed in the population.

3 METHOD

3.1 Participants

We recruited participants in two bachelor-level computer science courses typically taken in the third year—one in functional programming (TIEA341 Functional Programming 1, henceforth FP1) and the other in the theory of computing (TIEA241 Automatons and Formal Languages, henceforth TCS)—taught in Fall 2017 at the Faculty of Information Technology of the University of Jyväskylä, Finland. In one course (FP1), completion of the informed consent form form (either giving or refusing consent) was presented as required though not enforced, and in the other course (TCS), completion of the form counted as one of 59 exercises that together could contribute to the final grade up to two grade points out of five.

As to demographic data, we obtained the age, the number of credits attained, and the number of years enrolled in our department for each student enrolled in our courses as part of course completion data. They thus represent a snapshot after the courses had been completed. We had no ready access to students' sex or gender: legal sex would have only been available by derivation from each students' national personal identity code, but we had no legal or moral basis to access this information, which is legally considered sensitive data; and neither the course completion data nor our questionnaire data included self-reported gender.

Our sampling stopping rule [39] was simple: we recruited only from the aforementioned two courses, and we included all consenting students who answered all questions in our questionnaire. Thus, there was no need to set any arbitrary sample size, and no need for pre-data power calculations.

3.2 Measurements

The implicit theories of the students were measured using the self-theories of intelligence scale as described by Dweck [10]. In addition to the original English, a Finnish version translated by one of us and checked by the other was used. We scored each item on the implicit theory form on an ordinal scale of 1–6 with *strongly agree* as 1 or, when reverse scoring, with *strongly disagree* as 1.

We created three scores, which we treat as interval data, for each student: the *entity theory score* averages the entity theory items; the *incremental theory score* averages the reverse-scored incremental theory items; and the *combined theories score* averages the entity theory items and the reverse-scored incremental theory items. All scores were then rescaled to range between −1 and 1, so that a one-unit change corresponds to a move from a strongly held theory to ambivalence (or vice versa), or from one weakly held theory to another. A high score indicates an incremental theory and a low score indicates an entity theory.

The FP1 course awarded passing students a whole number of 1–5 study credits with a vacuous grade ("pass"), and TCS awarded passing students exactly 5 credits and a grade on the ordinal scale 1–5. The FP1 course was assessed based on homework exercises successfully completed, with a mandatory brief oral interview at the end to discourage fraudulent submissions. There was no final exam in FP1. The general deadline for submitting work for this course was January 15, 2018.

The TCS course could be completed by taking a written final exam, or by completing three course topics separately. Each of the three topics could be completed separately by taking a written partial exam soon after the relevant material was covered in lectures; alternatively, two of the topics could be completed separately by a programming project and the third topic by submitting satisfactory answers to a specific set of homework exercises. In all cases, if a student attempted more than one way of completion, the best results prevailed. For all passing students in TCS, the successful completion of homework exercises counted toward the grade, up to two grade points. The general deadline for the programming project and homework exercises was January 8, 2018; and the first opportunity to take the final exam was January 19, 2018.

3.3 Procedure

The informed consent form and the implicit theories form were administered together as an online questionnaire that was open for the students throughout the course period (from October 23 to December 15, 2017). The questionnaire was offered in Finnish or English based on the student's language preference.

We took a snapshot of course completion data for both courses on January 26, 2018. Thus, our completion data is based on the FP1 and TCS credits and grades as they stood in the official registry on that date. Any grades and credits later awarded are ignored by our analysis.

Throughout the courses and the grading period (until January 26, 2018), we deliberately kept ourselves ignorant of the students' answers to both the informed consent form and the implicit theories form; we only obtained a list of students who had answered the questionnaire, so that we could mark the corresponding exercises as completed. We acquired the full data on the answers after taking the snapshot of the completion data.

3.4 Analyses

We excluded from analysis students who did not answer the informed consent form or expressedly declined consent. We further excluded from analysis those students who did not answer all items on the implicit theory form.

We assessed the internal reliability of these scores by computing Coefficient Alpha for each. Nunnally and Bernstein [29, p. 265] consider values near $\alpha = .70$ acceptable only for early stages of measure development, while $\alpha \approx 0.80$ is sufficient for group-based basic research, and $\alpha > 0.90$ is necessary only for individual testing affecting decisions of importance.

We examined the resulting scores in a scatter plot of entity theory score versus incremental theory score. We expected to find a visually apparent correlation, and perhaps two visually obvious distinct clusters; we further computed the Pearson product–moment correlation for these two scores. Given the strong correlation we observed (as discussed later) and the difficulties collinearity gives to regression analysis, we elected to pursue our analyses with the combined theories score.

We grouped students into three groups: those who registered only for FP1, those who registered only for TCS, and those who registered for both courses. For the FP1 group, we used as the outcome variable the number of credits awarded, treating noncompletion (for whatever reason) as a zero credit outcome; since credits nominally measure hours worked, we treat this as an interval variable. For the TCS group, we used as the outcome variable the grade awarded, treating noncompletion (for whatever reason) as a zero grade outcome. Grades are most naturally modeled as ordinal variables, though treating them as interval variables is not uncommon.

The outcome variable for the both-courses group necessarily is a combination of the outcomes of both courses. Both FP1 credits and TCS grades range from 0 to 5 and both can be regarded as measuring educational achievement. Thus, we can combine them into a single interval variable by averaging them. For analyses better done using an ordinal variable, we rounded the result upward so that passing one course is counted as 1.

Since the outcome can be treated as an interval variable, we tried to use linear regression with the course group as well as the combined theory score as the explanatory variables and the outcome variable as the response variable. We expected the course group to be needed because each course was graded using course-specific criteria, potentially introducing statistical dependence among group members; however, we also tried an analysis without the group variable. Model misspecification was tested (see, e. g., Chatterjee and Simonoff [3], p. 15) by using

Table 2: Enrollment in the courses and exclusions from the study. The FP1 and TCS rows in this table include the overlap; thus, the total equals the sum of FP1 and TCS minus the overlap.

	Students	No answer	Refused consent	Missing data	Included participants
FP1	214	94	10	11	99
TCS	139	44	21	6	68
overlap	59	14	8	3	34
Total	294	124	23	14	133

- a scatter plot of residuals versus predictors or fitted values to detect nonlinearity, heteroscedasticity, and outliers; and
- a normal probability plot for residuals to detect nonnormal errors.

An alternative, should the linear regression not be satisfactory, was ordinal logistic regression. Here, the explanatory variables would be the same as in the linear regression, and the response variable would be the ordinal version of the outcome variable. This has the proportional odds assumption; this can be checked by running separate binary outcome logits for each threshold.

We should briefly note that we considered the use of structural equation modeling (SEM) to analyze our data; however, our sample size is too small for a worth-while SEM model of our data, especially considering the ordinal nature of our data.

We generally report confidence intervals (CIs) at the 95 % level instead of statistical significance tests and p values, because we feel that CIs are more informative. However, CIs correspond to significance tests in a very simple manner: a 95 % CI consists of exactly those values for which the hypothesis that the true value equals that value is not rejected at $\alpha = 0.05$; in particular, a null hypothesis is rejected if and only if the null value is outside the CI. Thus, we are licensed to rule out any value that is outside a CI to the same extent that rejection of a hypothesis licenses us to rule out the value specified by the hypothesis. We do not conduct post-data power analyses, as they add nothing useful to confidence intervals [18, 19].

All statistical analyses were conducted using the statistical programming language R [31], with the aid of the packages moments [21], ordinal [6], plyr [43], and psych [32]. All plots were produced using pgfplots in LaTeX.

4 RESULTS

Course enrollment, exclusions due to missing informed consent or incomplete questionnaire data, and the number of students included in this study are summarized in Table 2. In addition, one student was not registered in either course (and thus is not included in this study) yet had granted informed consent; they must have been registered to at least one of the courses earlier.

Basic demographic information available to us is shown in Table 3. Credits are nominally a measure of time spent in studies, with 60 credits nominally equaling one year of study. Thus, 138 credits are consistent with a student on their third full-time study year.

Table 3: Demographic profile of the participants, reported as means and standard deviations. The FP1 and TCS rows in this table include the overlap.

	Age	Credits	Year
Consenting students	25 (4.3)	138 (95.8)	3 (2.6)
Included participants			
— all	25 (4.4)	138 (97.6)	3 (2.6)
— FP1	24 (3.5)	137 (95.1)	3 (2.6)
— TCS	25 (5.1)	136 (96.3)	4 (2.5)

Table 4: Odds ratios (and their 95 % CIs) given by successive logistic regressions with various outcome thresholds, where the combined theory score is the explanatory variable and the outcome is dichotomized at each successive level.

≤ 0	≤ 1	≤ 2	≤ 3	≤ 4
0.79	0.96	1.02	1.39	1.72
[0.34, 1.82]	[0.41, 2.23]	[0.42, 2.52]	[0.49, 4.13]	[0.47, 6.86]

However, credits are attached to courses and do not directly correspond to an individual student's time use.

The Cronbach coefficient alpha is, over the whole sample, for the entity theory score $\alpha = 0.92$, 95 % CI [0.88, 0.94], for the incremental theory score $\alpha = 0.94$, 95 % CI [0.91, 0.96], and for the combined theory score $\alpha = 0.95$, 95 % CI [0.92, 0.97]. The entity and incremental theory scores are plotted against each other in Figure 1. The distribution of the combined scores is shown in Figure 2; it has a mean of 0.16, a standard deviation of 0.41, a skewness of −0.36, and a kurtosis of 3.24. Attempting a Dweck et al. [12, p. 269] dichotomization, using the thresholds −0.2 and 0.2, leads to a highly problematic result: in our sample, there are 24 clear entity theorists and 60 clear incremental theorists, while 49 participants would be excluded as ambivalent.

The distributions of the course outcomes are plotted in Figure 3.

Course outcomes plotted against the combined theory score, see Figure 4, reveal no apparent functional relationship. Thus, it seems doubtful that an association is present in this data. We corroborate this by attempting to demonstrate one using regression analysis.

A linear regression with the group and the combined theory score as explanatory variables and the averaged outcome as the response variables results in diagnostic plots indicating both non-normality of residuals and heteroscedasticity, thus, a misspecification. Respecifying the model without the group as an explanatory variable gives better residuals, but even here, the distribution of residuals is far from normal. The pattern suggests that a logistic regression might be more appropriate.

Successive logistic regressions with the combined theory score as the explanatory variable and the binary response variable of under/over a threshold result with the odds ratios for the theory score given in Table 4; the confidence intervals have a large overlap, and the point estimates all fit inside the intersection of the confidence intervals. Thus, it seems that the assumption of proportional odds is approximately met. Thus, we adopt a proportional-odds model

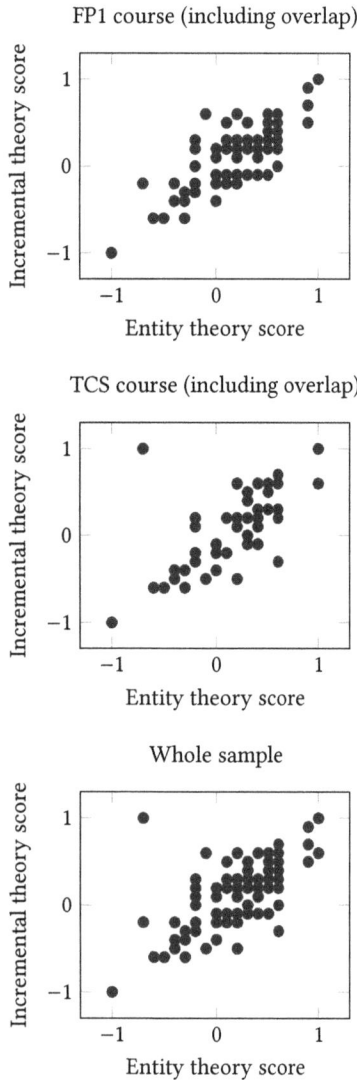

Figure 1: Scatter plot of entity and incremental theory scores. Note that a low entity score indicates an entity theory, and a high incremental theory score indicates an incremental theory; thus, the positive correlation is expected. The Pearson product-moment correlation coefficient is $r = 0.79$ for the whole sample, $r = 0.87$ for the FP1 attendees (including overlap), and $r = 0.76$ for the TCS attendees (including overlap).

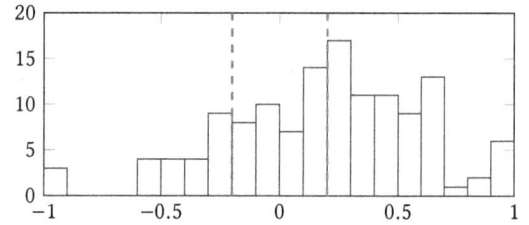

Figure 2: Histogram of combined theory scores across the sample. The dashed vertical lines indicate the cutoff points for Dweck et al. [12, p. 269] dichotomization (see Subsection 2.3).

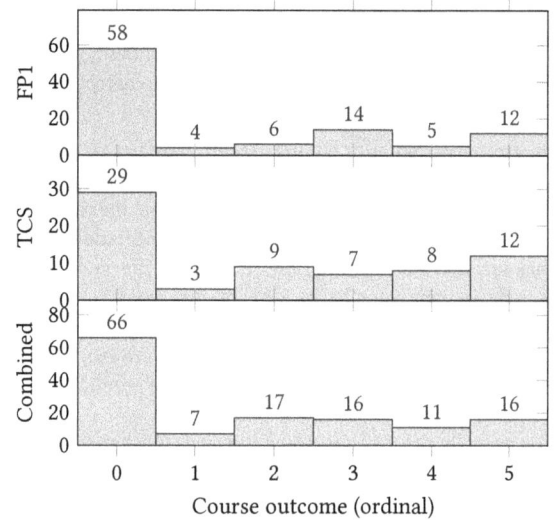

Figure 3: Distribution of course outcomes on FP1 only, TCS only, and in the whole sample. In the combined case, the outcomes of both courses have been averaged and rounded up.

Table 5: Coefficients in ordinal logistic regression with the combined theory score as the explanatory variable.

	Coefficient	95 % CI
Combined theory score	−0.04	[−0.78, 0.71]
Threshold 0 | 1	−0.02	[−0.38, 0.34]
Threshold 1 | 2	0.19	[−0.17, 0.55]
Threshold 2 | 3	0.73	[0.36, 1.11]
Threshold 3 | 4	1.36	[0.93, 1.80]
Threshold 4 | 5	1.98	[1.45, 2.52]

(ordinal logistic regression) with the combined theory score as the explanatory variable and the ordinal outcome as the response variable; it results in a non-significant odds ratio of 0.96, 95 % CI [0.46, 2.03], for the theory score. The model coefficients (which are logarithms of either odds or odds ratios, depending on the coefficient) are shown in Table 5.

Figure 5 is an simple effect display inspired by Fox and Andersen [16], visualizing the behavior of the proportional-odds model we chose. It shows, for each ordinal outcome, the 95 % confidence interval (as a gray band) for the predicted probability of a student to achieve that particular outcome, conditional on and as a function of that student's combined theory score. It also superimposes the corresponding empirical conditional probability (as a bar graph) derived from our data; note that the distribution is somewhat influenced by the choice of bins, and the choice here was influenced by a balance between avoiding small bins where individual data points dominate and avoiding too few bins.

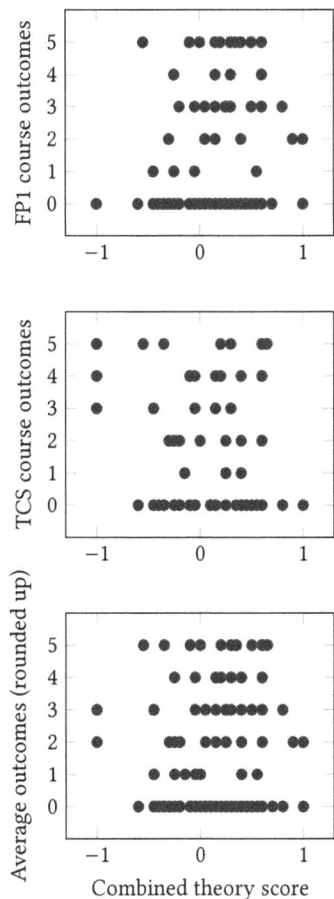

Figure 4: Scatter plot of combined theory score with ordinal course outcomes. The Spearman rank correlation coefficient is $\rho = 0.03$ ($p = 0.76$) for the whole sample, $\rho = 0.11$ ($p = 0.27$) for the FP1 attendees (including overlap), and $\rho = -0.02$ ($p = 0.89$) for the TCS attendees (including overlap). The p values are bootstrapped.

As final corroboration, we categorized each student as entity theorist, incremental theorist, or ambivalent, based on the dichotomization proposed by Dweck et al. [12, p. 269], as discussed in Subsection 2.3. A Kruskal-Wallis rank sum test fails to see any difference in the three groups' averaged outcomes ($\chi^2(2) = 0.133$, $p = 0.936$).

5 DISCUSSION

We can detect no association between a student's mindset and their course outcomes in this study with 133 participants. Assuming, as we do, a causal relationship between them, this means that the effect of mindset on outcomes is too small to be measured using this sample size and study design. Our results are as consistent with a decrease in odds down to roughly one third as with an increase of odds up to roughly doubling them, associated with a one unit of difference in mindset. In the mindset scale we used, one unit difference means moving from a strongly held mindset to a neutral

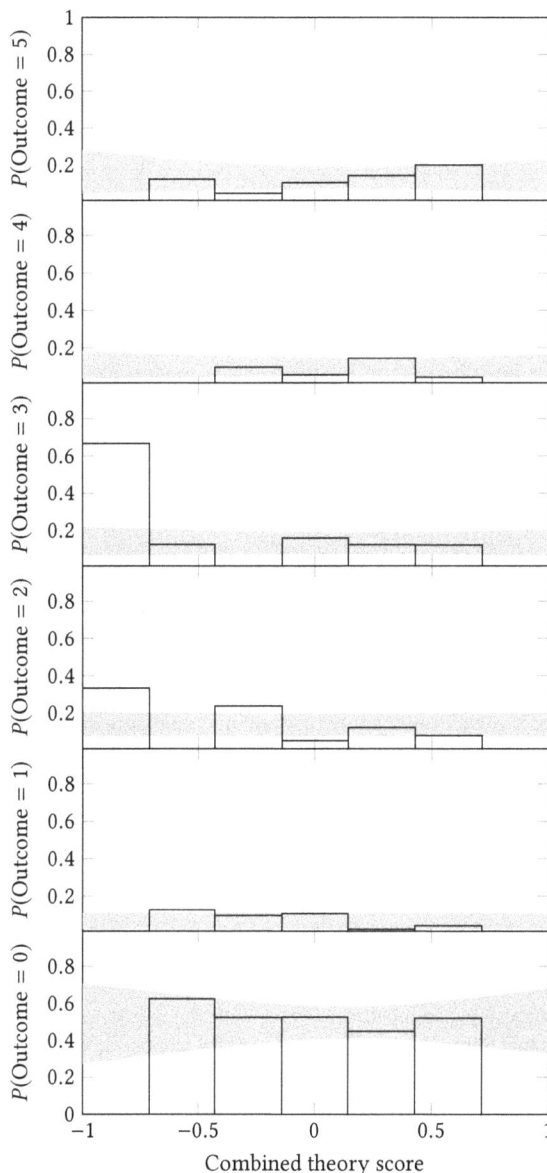

Figure 5: Confidence intervals of fitted probabilities (gray areas) and empirical probabilities (bars) of each outcome level conditional on each combined theory score. The model is an ordinal logistic regression with the combined theory score as the explanatory variable and the ordinal outcomes as the response.

one or vice versa, or moving from one weakly held mindset to another.

The main source of this uncertainty appears to be the pronounced normal distribution of theory of intelligence scores in our data set, contrary to what Dweck et al. suggest: using the Dweck et al. [12, p. 269] dichotomization—which in their study resulted in only 15 % of their participants being categorized as neutral—would discard 49 (37 %) of our participants because they do not endorse either theory clearly. In our data set, we have only 24 (18 %) entity theorists (students with a fixed mindset) by this criterion.

Similarly, there was a large number of noncompletions in our data set, which means that only a small number of students receive any particular passing grade; thus, the amount of data for fixed mindset students who pass our courses is fairly limited—only 13 fixed mindset students passed at least one course. Accordingly, there are very few events per variable in the ordinal regression. However, the events per variable count is adequate in the binary logistic regression with fail/pass as the response variable. As our regressions aim to verify that there is no detectable association in our data, we regard these problems as noncritical.

The key observation is that even our modest data set is able to reject most effect sizes at the conventional $\alpha = 0.05$ level. We are justified in rejecting odds ratios below 0.46 and above 2.03 for a unit change in the combined theory score. Thus, we can say with confidence that the odds of increasing one grade point are not lower than 0.46 times as low, and not higher than 2.03 times as high, with a moderate incremental theory (growth mindset) as with a moderate entity theory (fixed mindset). The remaining effect sizes, which we are unable to reject here, are not trivial, but they are small. This result is consistent with the results of previous observational studies in both computing and other fields.

We do not believe our study to suffer from construct validity issues. We used a well known instrument to measure mindsets, one that has been in use for decades and that has a record of no serious validity issues. While our Finnish translation is new, we have no reason to suspect it to have caused problems. Further, our own data exhibit excellent Coefficient Alpha reliability. Similarly, our measure of course outcomes is the gold standard (grades and credits awarded): while it can be argued, with good reason, that grades and credits do not accurately reflect true skill and knowledge, they do reflect academic achievement at this level by definition. Our course designs do not provide more precise measures of academic success.

Our study also mostly complies with the requirements for authors that Simmons et al. [39] proposed for mitigating the problems of false positive reports. We report our stopping rule; we report all variables that we measured; we report all experimental conditions performed (there were none); we did not eliminate observations based on an analysis of our data; and we report covariate-less analyses. The only problem this study has is in the cell size: our data includes only 11 clear entity theorists who did not complete either course, while Simmons et al. recommend a cell size of at least 20.

The greatest limitation of this study is its observational nature. We cannot rule out the possibility that another factor, not controlled for in this study, acts to counterbalance the effect of the mindset and thus masks it from our view. A properly conducted experiment would be able to eliminate any such confounding. We think such confounding is unlikely, however; far more likely is that the effect of mindsets are simply too low to stand out from the noise with this sample size.

A related limitation of this study is that we did not generate more psychological measurements beyond the implicit theory data. For example, the mindset literature suggests that a high confidence in one's intelligence, which we did not measure, makes one's mindset irrelevant in determining goal orientation. Thus, it is possible that our entity theorists had high self-confidence, removing the disadvantage of their mindset. In future studies, we suggest that researchers always measure self-confidence in intelligence as well as implicit theories; we plan to follow our own suggestion.

It is possible that there is a causal effect of changing mindsets that goes beyond the simple difference in preexisting mindsets; thus, while we could not demonstrate a large effect, we cannot rule out the possibility that an intervention experiment would see effect sizes in the range that we rule out in this study.

One of our coworkers, having heard us discuss these results at the coffee table, suggested an explanation for our results: both of our courses discussed in this paper occur typically in the third year of study, and it is possible that those students who tend to choose to avoid challenges (due to their mindset or for other reasons) have already dropped out of our degree program before they encounter either of those courses. However, Macnamara and Rupani [27] found no influence of mindsets to education levels achieved. Still, even if that explanation was true, it would only mean that our results may not be applicable to first-year student populations.

Taking all that into account, we conclude that mindsets do not seem to matter much. Certainly, our results cast doubt on the wisdom of subjecting all students at the late-stage bachelor level to mindset interventions. The expected payoff is simply not large enough to justify it. In contrast, addressing other student self-beliefs may have a larger effect. For example, self-efficacy interventions have a stronger basis in the literature [28] and their effect is established in context of computer science [23, 44].

Our participants are Finnish students and thus WEIRD (Western, Educated, Industrialized, Rich, and Democratic) people [17]. One should be cautious about transferring our results to a different population. Likewise, it should be noted that there are important differences in educational systems between Finland and, for example, the United States. Nevertheless, our results are, for the most part, compatible with those reported in the prior research, which was primarily based on American participants.

Our conclusion only applies to mass interventions at a single-course context. As another of our colleagues pointed out to us in private conversation, our results say nothing about the usefulness of targeted interventions based on a teacher's expert assessment that a particular student might be hampered specifically by their fixed mindset. Similarly, it may be that mindsets only affect the level at which one stops studying altogether, not the level of achievement at a particular course.

Indeed, we feel that further study of this topic can still be fruitful. We think it may be worthwhile to study the effect of student mindsets on peak achievement (such as dropping out versus graduating from a degree program) in computing. It may also be useful for studies to aim for identifying student subpopulations for which mindset interventions might be worthwhile, and design and evaluate effective interventions for the population of computing student population at various education levels.

ACKNOWLEDGMENTS

We thank Jukka-Pekka Santanen and Ville Isomöttönen for discussions, and Jonne Itkonen for maintaining the questionnaire while we were keeping ourselves ignorant of its results during the courses. We also thank the anonymous reviewers for their useful feedback.

REFERENCES

[1] Jeni L. Burnette, Ernest H. O'Boyle, Eric M. VanEpps, Jeffrey M. Pollack, and Eli J. Finkel. 2013. Mind-sets matter. A meta-analytic review of implicit theories and self-regulation. *Psychological Bulletin*, 139, 3, 655–701. DOI: 10.1037/a0029531.

[2] John Cato. 2011. Mindset matters. *The Physics Teacher*, 49, 1, 60–60. DOI: 10.1119/1.3527763.

[3] Samprit Chatterjee and Jeffrey S. Simonoff. 2013. *Handbook of Regression Analysis*. Wiley, Hoboken, NJ.

[4] Jason A. Chen and M. Shane Tutwiler. 2017. Implicit theories of ability and self-efficacy. *Zeitschrift für Psychologie*, 225, 2, 127–136. DOI: 10.1027/2151-2604/a000289.

[5] Wei-Wen Chen and Yi-Lee Wong. 2015. Chinese mindset. Theories of intelligence, goal orientation and academic achievement in hong kong students. *Educational Psychology*, 35, 6, 714–725. DOI: 10.1080/01443410.2014.893559.

[6] R. H. B. Christensen. 2015. Ordinal: regression models for ordinal data. R package version 2015.6-28. (2015). https://cran.r-project.org/web/packages/ordinal/.

[7] Erin Clevenger. 2013. *The relation of theory of intelligence to academic motivation and academic outcomes*. PhD thesis. The Florida State University. http://purl.flvc.org/fsu/fd/FSU_migr_etd-7331.

[8] Quintin Cutts, Emily Cutts, Stephen Draper, Patrick O'Donnell, and Peter Saffrey. 2010. Manipulating mindset to positively influence introductory programming performance. In *SIGCSE '10 Proceedings of the 41st ACM Technical Symposium on Computer Science Education*, 431–435. DOI: 10.1145/1734263.1734409.

[9] Carol S. Dweck. 1975. The role of expectations and attributions in the alleviation of learned helplessness. *Journal of Personality and Social Psychology*, 31, 4, 674–685. DOI: 10.1037/h0077149.

[10] Carol S. Dweck. 2000. *Self-theories. Their Role in Motivation, Personality, and Development*. Psychology Press, New York.

[11] Carol S. Dweck. 2016. *Mindset. The New Psychology of Success*. (Updated edition). Random House, New York.

[12] Carol S. Dweck, Chi-yue Chiu, and Ying-yi Hong. 1995. Implicit theories and their role in judgments and reactions. A world from two perspectives. *Psychological Inquiry*, 6, 4, 267–285. DOI: 10.1207/s15327965pli0604_1. http://www.jstor.org/stable/1448940.

[13] Carol S. Dweck and Ellen L. Leggett. 1988. A social–cognitive approach to motivation and personality. *Psychological Review*, 95, 2, 256–273. DOI: 10.1037/0033-295X.95.2.256.

[14] Carol S. Dweck and N. Nickon Reppucci. 1973. Learned helplessness and reinforcement responsibility in children. *Journal of Personality and Social Psychology*, 25, 1, 109–116. DOI: 10.1037/h0034248.

[15] Abraham E. Flanigan, Markeya S. Peteranetz, Duane F. Shell, and Leen-Kiat Soh. 2015. Exploring changes in computer science students' implicit theories of intelligence across the semester. In *ICER '15 Proceedings of the Eleventh Annual International Conference on International Computing Education Research*, 161–168. DOI: 10.1145/2787622.2787722.

[16] John Fox and Robert Andersen. 2006. Effect displays for multinomial and proportional-odds logit models. *Sociological Methodology*, 36, 1, 225–255. DOI: 10.1111/j.1467-9531.2006.00180.x.

[17] Joseph Henrich, Steven J. Heine, and Ara Norenzayan. 2010. The weirdest people in the world? *Behavioral and Brain Sciences*, 33, 2–3, 61–135. DOI: 10.1017/S0140525X0999152X.

[18] John M. Hoenig and Dennis M. Heisey. 2001. The abuse of power. The pervasive fallacy of power calculations for data analysis. *American Statistician*, 55, 1, 19–24. DOI: 10.1198/000313001300339897.

[19] Michael R. Jiroutek and J. Rick Turner. 2018. Why it is nonsensical to use retrospective power analyses to conduct a postmortem on your study. editorial. *Journal of Clinical Hypertension*, 20, 2, 408–410. DOI: 10.1111/jch.13173.

[20] Päivi Kinnunen and Lauri Malmi. 2006. Why students drop out cs1 course? In *ICER '06 Proceedings of the second international workshop on Computing education research*, 97–108. DOI: 10.1145/1151588.1151604.

[21] Lukasz Komsta and Frederick Novomestky. 2015. *moments: Moments, cumulants, skewness, kurtosis and related tests*. R package version 0.14. https://cran.r-project.org/web/packages/moments.

[22] Sheri R. Levy, Steven J. Stroessner, and Carol S. Dweck. 1998. Stereotype formation and endorsement. The role of implicit theories. *Journal of Personality and Social Psychology*, 74, 6, 1421–1436. DOI: 10.1037/0022-3514.74.6.1421.

[23] Alex Lishinski, Aman Yadav, Jon Good, and Richard Enbody. 2016. Learning to program. Gender differences and interactive effects of students' motivation, goals, and self-efficacy on performance. In *Proceedings of the 2016 ACM Conference on International Computing Education Research* (ICER '16). ACM, New York, NY, USA, 211–220. DOI: 10.1145/2960310.2960329.

[24] Dastyni Loksa, Andrew J. Ko, Will Jernigan, Alannah Oleson, Christopher J. Mendez, and Margaret M. Burnett. 2016. Programming, problem solving, and self-awareness. Effects of explicit guidance. In *CHI '16 Proceedings of the 2016 CHI Conference on Human Factors in Computing Systems*, 1449–1461. DOI: 10.1145/2858036.2858252.

[25] Marko Lüftenegger and Jason A. Chen. 2017. Conceptual issues and assessment of implicit theories. *Zeitschrift für Psychologie*, 225, 2, 99–106. DOI: 10.1027/2151-2604/a000286.

[26] Robert C. MacCallum, Shaobo Zhang, Kristopher J. Preacher, and Derek D. Rucker. 2002. On the practice of dichotomization of quantitative variables. *Psychological Methods*, 7, 1, 19–40. DOI: 10.1037/1082-989X.7.1.19.

[27] Brooke N. Macnamara and Natasha S. Rupani. 2017. The relationship between intelligence and mindset. *Intelligence*, 64, 52–59. DOI: 10.1016/j.intell.2017.07.003.

[28] Karen D. Multon, Steven D. Brown, and Robert W. Lent. 1991. Relation of self-efficacy beliefs to academic outcomes. A meta-analytic investigation. *Journal of Counseling Psychology*, 38, 1, 30–38. DOI: 10.1037/0022-0167.38.1.30.

[29] Jum C. Nunnally and Ira H. Bernstein. 1994. *Psychometriic Theory*. (3rd edition). McGraw-Hill, New York.

[30] Heather A. Priess-Groben and Janet Shibley Hyde. 2017. Implicit theories, expectancies, and values predict mathematics motivation and behavior across high school and college. *Journal of youth and adolescence*, 46, 6, 1318–1332. DOI: 10.1007/s10964-016-0579-y.

[31] R Core Team. 2017. *R: A Language and Environment for Statistical Computing*. R Foundation for Statistical Computing. Vienna, Austria. https://www.R-project.org/.

[32] William Revelle. 2017. *psych: Procedures for Psychological, Psychometric, and Personality Research*. R package version 1.7.8. Northwestern University. Evanston, Illinois. https://cran.r-project.org/web/packages/psych.

[33] Richard W. Robins and Jennifer L. Pals. 2002. Implicit self-theories in the academic domain. Implications for goal orientation, attributions, affect, and self-esteem change. *Self and identity*, 1, 4, 313–336. DOI: 10.1080/1529886029010680.

[34] Derek D. Rucker, Blakeley B. McShane, and Kristopher J. Preacher. 2015. A researcher's guide to regression, discretization, and median splits of continuous variables. *Journal of Consumer Psychology*, 25, 4, 666–678. DOI: 10.1016/j.jcps.2015.04.004.

[35] Michael J. Scott and Gheorgita Ghinea. 2014. On the domain-specificity of mindsets. The relationship between aptitude beliefs and programming practice. *IEEE Transactions on Education*, 57, 3, 169–174. DOI: 10.1109/TE.2013.2288700.

[36] Michael James Scott and Gheorghita Ghinea. 2013. Implicit theories of programming aptitude as a barrier to learning to code. Are they distinct from intelligence. In *ITiCSE '13 Proceedings of the 18th ACM conference on Innovation and technology in computer science education*. ACM, New York, 347. DOI: 10.1145/2462476.2462515.

[37] Michael James Scott and Gheorghita Ghinea. 2014. Measuring enrichment. The assembly and validation of an instrument to assess student self-beliefs in cs1. In *ICER '14 Proceedings of the tenth annual conference on International computing education research*, 123–130. DOI: 10.1145/2632320.2632350.

[38] Duane F. Shell, Leen-Kiat Soh, Abraham E. Flanigan, and Markeya S. Peteranetz. 2016. Students' initial course motivation and their achievement and retention in college cs1 courses. In *SIGCSE '16 Proceedings of the 47th ACM Technical Symposium on Computing Science Education*, 639–644. DOI: 10.1145/2839509.2844606.

[39] Joseph P. Simmons, Leif D. Nelson, and Uri Simonsohn. 2011. False-positive psychology. Undisclosed flexibility in data collection and analysis allows presenting anything as significant. *Psychological Science*, 22, 11, 1359–1366. DOI: 10.1177/0956797611417632.

[40] Beth Simon, Brian Hanks, Laurie Murphy, Sue Fitzgerald, Renée McCauley, Lynda Thomas, and Carol Zander. 2008. Saying isn't necessarily believing. Influencing self-theories in computing. In *ICER '08 Proceedings of the Fourth International Workshop on Computing Education Research*, 173–184. DOI: 10.1145/1404520.1404537.

[41] F. Boray Tek, Kristin S. Benli, and Ezgi Deveci. 2018. Implicit theories and self-efficacy in an introductory programming course. *IEEE Transactions on Education*. DOI: 10.1109/TE.2017.2789183.

[42] Dirk T. Tempelaar, Bart Rienties, Bas Giesbers, and Wim H. Gijselaers. 2015. The pivotal role of effort beliefs in mediating implicit theories of intelligence and achievement goals and academic motivations. *Social Psychology of Education*, 18, 1, 101–120. DOI: 10.1007/s11218-014-9281-7.

[43] Hadley Wickham. 2011. The split-apply-combine strategy for data analysis. *Journal of Statistical Software*, 40, 1, 1–29. http://www.jstatsoft.org/v40/i01/.

[44] Daniel Zingaro and Leo Porter. 2016. Impact of student achievement goals on cs1 outcomes. In *Proceedings of the 47th ACM Technical Symposium on Computing Science Education* (SIGCSE '16). ACM, New York, NY, USA, 279–296. DOI: 10.1145/2839509.2844553.

[45] Valorie L Zonnefeld. 2015. *Mindsets, attitudes, and achievement in undergraduate statistics courses*. PhD thesis. University of South Dakota. https://digitalcollections.dordt.edu/faculty_work/199.

Towards an Analysis of Program Complexity From a Cognitive Perspective

Rodrigo Duran
Aalto University, Finland
rodrigo.duran@aalto.fi

Juha Sorva
Aalto University, Finland
juha.sorva@aalto.fi

Sofia Leite
University of Porto, Portugal
lpsi05114@fe.up.pt

ABSTRACT

Instructional designers, examiners, and researchers frequently need to assess the complexity of computer programs in their work. However, there is a dearth of established methodologies for assessing the complexity of a program from a learning point of view. In this article, we explore theories and methods for describing programs in terms of the demands they place on human cognition. More specifically, we draw on Cognitive Load Theory and the Model of Hierarchical Complexity in order to extend Soloway's plan-based analysis of programs and apply it at a fine level of granularity. The resulting framework of Cognitive Complexity of Computer Programs (CCCP) generates metrics for two aspects of a program: *plan depth* and *maximal plan interactivity*. Plan depth reflects the overall complexity of the cognitive schemas that are required for reasoning about the program, and maximal plan interactivity reflects the complexity of interactions between schemas that arise from program composition. Using a number of short programs as case studies, we apply the CCCP to illustrate why one program or construct is more complex than another, to identify dependencies between constructs that a novice programmer needs to learn and to contrast the complexity of different strategies for program composition. Finally, we highlight some areas in computing education and computing education research in which the CCCP could be applied and discuss the upcoming work to validate and refine the CCCP and associated methodology beyond this initial exploration.

CCS CONCEPTS

• **Social and professional topics** → **Computer science education**; *Model curricula*; Student assessment;

KEYWORDS

Model of Hierarchical Complexity; Cognitive Load Theory; Program Cognitive Complexity; Complexity; Plan-Composition Strategies

ACM Reference Format:
Rodrigo Duran, Juha Sorva, and Sofia Leite. 2018. Towards an Analysis of Program Complexity From a Cognitive Perspective. In *ICER '18: 2018 International Computing Education Research Conference, August 13–15, 2018, Espoo, Finland.* ACM, New York, NY, USA, 10 pages. https://doi.org/10.1145/3230977.3230986

1 INTRODUCTION

For instructional design to be successful, the designer must consider the trajectories that students move along as they learn. Ideally, learners engage in activities that are neither too hard nor too easy for them; with growing expertise, each learner can eventually tackle increasingly complex tasks. This goal was famously captured by Vygotsky in the concept of *zone of proximal development*, which continues to inspire developments in instructional design [e.g., 68].

Teachers routinely assess the complexity of the tasks they give to their students and seek to sequence those tasks in an effective manner. As a part of this effort, a programming teacher assesses the complexity of the programs that feature in examples and assessments and the programs they expect their students to write.

So, how does one tell how complex a program is, or whether one program is more complex than another? Typically, the teacher draws on their intuition and experience to make an informal assessment. If the teacher's luck aligns with their ability, it works.

To assist teachers in instructional design, research in educational psychology has produced frameworks such as 4C/ID [84] that sequence classes of activities by increasing complexity. Establishing a theoretically motivated, empirically sustainable, and pedagogically feasible methodology for sequencing topics by complexity is one of the major goals in curriculum development [64]. Within computing education research (CER), scholars have explored the relationships between programming concepts and suggested a number of learning trajectories for introductory programming [e.g., 35, 55, 62]. However, there exists no well-established methodology for evaluating complexity or tracing such trajectories in programming.

In this article, we set our sights on a more solid theoretical and methodological footing for assessing the complexity of programs. We focus on a facet of complexity that can be extracted, with the help of theory, from concrete programs: the cognitive structures that are required to mentally manipulate a program as one studies or writes it. Recognizing (like [46]) that programming requires the programmer to think about low-level elements of code (the trees) as well as how those elements combine to achieve a higher-level purpose (the forest), we seek a model that attends to both aspects.

Our primary contribution is to suggest *a theoretical framework for reasoning about the complexity of computer programs*. The framework is meant for analyzing the cognitive schemas present in the design of a given program and the way those schemas are intertwined. In addition to providing a more nuanced analysis, our framework can be used to generate two numerical metrics that summarize program complexity; unlike the more technical metrics from software engineering and algorithm analysis, our metrics reflect a cognitive perspective which is meaningful for instructional design and CER and which can be applied to the sort of short programs that are common in introductory-level programming. To illustrate the application of our model, and as a preliminary proof-of-concept evaluation of it, we discuss three programs as case studies.

Our framework derives from two main sources. The first is schema theory and the related Cognitive Load Theory (CLT) [2, 10, 80], which are concerned with the limitations of working memory and the growth of expertise as schemas in long-term memory; here we extend the earlier work in CER by Soloway, Rist, and others who have analyzed schemas as reflected in programs [63, 73, 77]. Our other main influence is the Model of Hierarchical Complexity (MHC) [16], a neo-Piagetian theory concerned with the relative complexities of tasks; to the best of our knowledge, the MHC has not been previously applied in computing education.

Section 2, below, explains the theoretical background. Section 3 then presents our framework for analyzing programs as well as the case studies that illustrate it. In Section 4, we discuss how the present work relates to, and differs from, earlier efforts in CER, and consider its applications of our framework. Finally, in Section 5, we review the contributions and limitations of this article and consider the future work of empirically validating our theoretical model.

2 THEORETICAL BACKGROUND

2.1 Schemas and Cognitive Load

Cognitive Load Theory (CLT) [2, 10, 68, 80] is a framework for investigating the effects of the human cognitive apparatus on task performance and learning; the primary goal of CLT is to improve instructional design. CLT has its foundation in studies of human cognition. Its basic premise is that cognition and learning are constrained by a bottleneck created by *working memory*, in which we humans can hold only a handful of elements at a time for active processing. What enables us to carry out complex tasks is our virtually unlimited *long-term memory*. We learn by chunking related elements into domain-specific *schemas* that are stored in long-term memory and retrieved for processing in working memory as a single element. As our experience grows, we construct hierarchies of increasingly complex higher-level schemas that encompass numerous low-lever schemas. Even though an expert's working memory, too, is very limited, the expert can occupy it with high-level schemas they have previously constructed, which enables them to process vast amounts of information that a beginner could not hope to cope with. For example, a novice programmer will be overwhelmed by a "basic" loop that uses expressions, assignment, variables, and selection to process inputs unless they are sufficiently practiced with the lower-level schemas involved; a more experienced programmer will perceive the entire loop as a single instance of a familiar pattern.

Cognitive load is the demand that a situation places on a person's working memory. It is determined by *element interactivity*, which is the degree of interconnectedness between the elements of information that one needs to hold in working memory simultaneously in order to perform successfully [37]. Element interactivity, in turn, depends on prior knowledge in the form of existing schemas: someone who can represent the situation with higher-level schemas will require fewer of them as elements in working memory. An estimate of element interactivity can be obtained by identifying interacting elements in learning materials [2, 80]; such estimates necessarily rely on assumptions about learners' existing schemas [10].

According to CLT, cognitive load can be analytically separated into two components: intrinsic and extraneous [81]. *Intrinsic load* is caused by interacting elements that are necessary for task performance and learning. *Extraneous load* is caused by elements that "don't need to be there," but are, whether because of ineffective instructional design, external interference while learning, or some other reason. What counts as intrinsic depends on the learning objectives. For example, in a programming task, syntax can be intrinsic (if the goal is to learn a programming language) or extraneous (if the goal is to learn to solve a problem). Instructional design based on CLT generally seeks to minimize extraneous load, encourages schema formation through practice, and sequences tasks such that intrinsic load is kept in check [e.g., 84].

Cognitive load is an idealistic construct in that it assumes the full attention of a motivated learner. The amount of working memory capacity that a learner actually dedicates to germane processing depends on external factors such as engagement [40, 81].

2.2 Plans: Schemas in Programs

Schema theory has influenced studies of program construction and comprehension. In their seminal work, Soloway and his colleagues [e.g., 73, 74, 77] broke down programs in goal-plan trees: such a tree recorded a hierarchical structure of *goals* and subgoals and the corresponding *plans* and subplans that provide solutions to those goals. What Soloway's group termed "plans" are essentially schemas in the programming domain: a plan represents a stereotypical solution to a programming problem. Building on Soloway's work, Rist [63] showed how schemas affect programming strategy: both novices and experts program top-down when they can but resort to constructing solutions bottom-up where their existing schemas fail them. The key difference between novices and experts is that experts have a much more extensive "library" of programming schemas in long-term memory.

Within CER, these cognitive theories have inspired pedagogies that explicitly teach plan-like patterns to students [20, 34, 66].

Recently, several studies have examined how students prefer to compose their overall solution from a number of interrelated subplans [25–27]. For instance, one might sequence the subplans (perhaps using separate functions for each) or interleave them (perhaps using a single loop associated with multiple subplans); such decisions may impact on readability and error rates [25, 27, 33, 74]. Plan composition is a potentially significant determinant of cognitive load since it impacts on which elements (i.e., schemas) the writer or reader of a program needs to keep in mind simultaneously; this is something we will explore later in this article.

An established measure of cognitive load for *programs* does not exist. However, there is an instrument for estimating cognitive load from learners' ratings of perceived mental effort after a learning task [42], which has been adapted for programming tasks [57].

2.3 Complexity vs. Difficulty

As illustrated in a survey by Liu and Li [47], complexity means different to different people. Following Liu and Li (ibid.), we use the word *complexity* for the "objective," learner-independent characteristics of a task, whereas the *difficulty* of a task additionally depends on the characteristics of the person who engages in the task, such as prior knowledge and motivation, as well as on contextual factors.

We consider element interactivity to be a key aspect of both complexity and difficulty. The inherent *complexity* of any task is determined by the interconnectedness of the elements present in the task. It reflects the need to process multiple elements simultaneously in working memory, assuming no prior knowledge in the domain. Existing schemas mediate complexity by helping the learner deal with it in larger chunks, thereby reducing the element interactivity — and, by extension, the *difficulty* — of a complex task. The more complex a task is, the more schemas the learner must possess so that the task is not too difficult for them.

In this article, we are primarily concerned with complexity — the unmediated element interactivity inherent in a task. More specifically, we are interested in the complexity inherent in *programs*. That complexity, we argue, accounts for a substantial part of the complexity of any activity in which the learner has to mentally manipulate those programs, such as writing or comprehending them. Of course, complexity alone does not account for real-world learning outcomes; we will say more about difficulty in later sections.

2.4 The Model of Hierarchical Complexity

The *Model of Hierarchical Complexity* (MHC) [16] is a neo-Piagetian theoretical model for analyzing the complexity of actions within a domain. Moreover, the MHC seeks to characterize the domain-specific stages of development that a learner goes through as they gain expertise in the domain and become capable of successful performance on increasingly complex actions.

According to the MHC, an *action* is an exhibited behavior with a particular sort of input and a particular sort of output; a person employs cognition to perform an action but the specific cognitive processes that occur are not explained by the MHC. Instead, the MHC is concerned with the structural relationships between actions, in particular, the "recursive" relationships between a more complex action and its less complex sub-actions.

The MHC posits that actions within a domain can be organized in a hierarchy. How high a particular action appears in such a hierarchy reflects its intrinsic complexity and is determined by its recursive relationships with other actions. Not just any dependency between actions is enough for a difference in complexity, however: an action is only more complex than another if it *coordinates* less complex actions according to the MHC axioms or *rules*.

The MHC distinguishes between two kinds of actions: 1) primary actions at the lowest level of complexity, and 2) composite actions that organize other actions according to a rule that may or may not imply higher complexity. There are three rules [12]:

- The *prerequisite rule* applies where succeeding at action A requires successful performance of exactly one other action at the same level of complexity as A. However, this does not mean that A is more complex than its prerequisite, only that successful performance on A is preceded by successful performance on it.
- The *chain rule* applies where a higher-level action A requires the organization of two or more lower-level actions in an arbitrary way: the lower-level actions are parts of A but can be carried out in any order and the whole is no greater than the sum of its chained parts. For example, the action of calculating $1 + 2 - 4$

links the actions of addition and subtraction with the chain rule, as one may carry out those sub-actions in either order.
- Finally, and most importantly, the *coordination rule* applies where a higher-level action A organizes two or more actions at a lower level of complexity *in a non-arbitrary way*. This means that the lower-level actions must serve distinct roles within the higher-level action; they cannot be simply swapped for each other or performed in an arbitrary order [13]. The distributive law is an example: computing $2 \times (5 + 3) = (2 \times 5) + (2 \times 3)$ displays more complex behavior by giving addition and multiplication distinct roles rather than just performing the sub-actions separately.

For an action to be more complex than another, it must organize a minimum of two lower-level actions as per the coordination rule. Every primary (lowest-level) action A_0 within a domain has the complexity level $h(A_0) = 0$. Every more complex action A_k coordinates at least two lower-level actions $A_{i...j}$ and has a higher level of complexity than any of them: $h(A_k) = max(h(A_i), ..., h(A_j)) + 1$.

The MHC characterizes each level of complexity in terms of lower-level actions. In doing so, it postulates that someone who is able to perform at level n is also able to perform at level $n - 1$; this implies a learning trajectory from less complex actions to more complex ones. According to the MHC, the developmental level of a learner in a domain equals the level of the highest action that the learner is able to carry out successfully [15].

The MHC has been empirically validated in several educational disciplines. For instance, Commons [12] applied Rasch analysis to show a positive correlation between the predicted complexity of equations in physics (the pendulum test) and measured student performance. In another study, Dawson [19] compared an MHC-based metric of learner development to other developmental scoring systems and found that it measured the same latent variables and was more internally consistent than the other metrics. The MHC has been used for complexity analysis in diverse domains such as physics [78], bias in forensics [14], chemistry [3], and student competence in graduate courses [56].

3 THE COGNITIVE COMPLEXITY OF COMPUTER PROGRAMS

The *Cognitive Complexity of Computer Programs* (CCCP) framework is a theoretical model for reasoning about the complexity of computer programs and generating metrics that summarize aspects of complexity. The CCCP characterizes the complexity of a program from a cognitive perspective: it describes and quantifies the cognitive constructs that are present in the program design and that are required for mentally manipulating the program.

Building on the analyses of Soloway and Rist cited above, we examine not only abstract, language-agnostic plans but also the lower-level plans that implement the higher-level plans as individual instructions in a concrete program written in a particular language. The CCCP also extends existing plan-based approaches to program analysis by adapting the hierarchy-building rules of the MHC to the study of computer programs. The formal rules of the MHC structure the study of the relationships between plans and provide a foundation for claims about the relative complexity of different plans and the programs the plans appear in.

Taking our cue from Rist [63], we distinguish between plan schemas and plans. A *plan schema* is a cognitive structure that a programmer mentally manipulates, while a *plan* is the concrete realization of a plan schema in a program. The CCCP assumes that there is a direct mapping between plans in code and plan schemas in the memory of the programmer who successfully works on the program; therefore, our analysis of plans in a program can be said to provide a cognitive perspective on the plan schemas that the program calls for. Moreover, we posit that applying a plan schema can be viewed in terms of the MHC as an action; therefore, we can adopt the MHC rules for the analysis of plan hierarchies.

We define the cognitive complexity of a program in terms of the hierarchical structure of plans present in the program. The CCCP is concerned with two aspects of this complexity: 1) the complexity level of each plan in the hierarchy, and 2) any interactions between plans that demand simultaneous processing of the plans in working memory, thus contributing to higher intrinsic load. Correspondingly, the CCCP can be used for two types of analysis, which we term *hierarchical analysis* and *interactivity analysis*, respectively. A full CCCP analysis of a program starts with the concrete code (or detailed pseudocode) and produces a plan hierarchy as well as the associated metrics of *plan depth* and *maximal plan interactivity*.

The subsections below introduce hierarchical analysis and interactivity analysis in turn, demonstrating them with case studies of programs. Our intention here is not to provide an unambiguous algorithm for thoroughly analyzing any given program. We merely seek to illustrate what complexity is in terms of the CCCP, to provide a few proof-of-concept examples of the sort of output that a CCCP-based analysis can produce, and to tentatively explore methods that can generate that output.

All the case studies were analyzed in iterations by the first author, with feedback from the other authors.

3.1 Hierarchical Analysis

Hierarchical analysis of a program produces a description of the program as a tree of plans; Figure 1 shows an abstract example. Each plan appears in the tree at a particular level of complexity, with the primary plans at the lowest level of zero and the more complex plans at increasingly high levels. The plan that corresponds to the entire program is at the top (root) of the hierarchy.

The level of a plan is known as its *plan depth* (PD); this is our programming-domain equivalent of what is termed an action's "order" or "level" by the MHC. The plan depth of the top-level plan is the plan depth of the entire program; this is one of the two main numerical metrics of complexity that the CCCP can generate. Programs can be compared in terms of their plan depth. In addition to this summary metric, the plan tree provides a comprehensive look at the plans involved in reading or writing the program.

Following the application of the MHC in other domains, we start hierarchical analysis from the primary plans at the bottom. These elements are chosen so that they represent primitive operations of a *notional machine* [22, 75] that the programmer instructs. We did not use an explicit specification of a notional machine; instead, we started with system capabilities for which we could identify no coordination of other plans without introducing low-level concepts outside of the target notional machine implied by the program. (E.g., the capability to store a value is a primary notional-machine

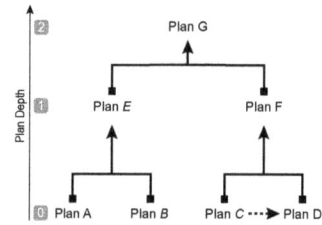

Figure 1: A generic plan tree. Solid arrows indicate that a higher-level plan *coordinates* lower-level plans, as per the MHC axioms. Dotted arrows indicate a *prerequisite*. The plan depths of each level are shown in the blue boxes.

element, as is the capability to jump to a different part of the code; bit-level operations are not, as they are unnecessary for understanding the programs in our case studies.)

To build the upper levels of the hierarchy, we considered how the plans depend on each other. Specifically, we sought instances of the MHC rules of coordination (i.e., lower-level plans serve distinct roles in a higher-level one) and prerequisites (i.e., a plan depends on one other plan at the same depth). The chain rule (i.e., applying simpler plans in an arbitrary sequence) does not contribute to higher complexity in the MHC/CCCP sense; to avoid unnecessarily complicating our plan trees, we chose to ignore chaining.

3.1.1 Case Study 1: Summing Program. We analyze a program that sums a fixed sequence of numbers using an explicit loop control variable; the code is shown below and the plan tree in Figure 2.

```
1  int i, input, sum;
2  sum = 0;
3  for (i = 1; i <= 10; i++) {
4      read(input);
5      sum = sum + input; }
```

The summing program features four primary plans (P1–P4) at the lowest level. The *define literals* plan (P1) represents the use of numerical data in the program. P1 is a prerequisite for the *declare variable* plan (P2), an abstraction of the linking of names to storage in computer memory. The *arithmetic operator* plan (P3) signifies the use of arithmetic operations such as addition. The *jump to code* plan (P4) represents the unconditional transition of control to a different part of the code, as at the end of the loop.

The *initialize variable* plan (P5) represents the assignment of a literal value to a variable. It organizes two lower-level plans (P1 and P2) using a coordination rule. (The order of the assignment matters; $1 = i$ would be an error.) $PD(P5) = max(PD(P1), PD(P2)) + 1 = max(0, 0) + 1 = 1$. The *evaluate an expression* plan (P6) organizes P2 and P3, so expressions are evaluated over variables. Thus, $PD(P6) = max(PD(P2), PD(P3)) + 1 = 1$. The *accumulate in a variable (P8)* plan coordinates the assignment of a literal to a variable (P5) and the evaluation of the expression to be assigned (P6). Therefore, $PD(P8) = max(PD(P5), PD(P6)) + 1 = 2$. The *test for termination* plan (P9) is a selection plan that coordinates P6 and P4, evaluating an expression and branching to the appropriate part of the code. $PD(P9) = max(PD(P4), PD(P6)) + 1 = 2$. The *read input* plan (P7) represents a library function call. To apply P7, it is only necessary

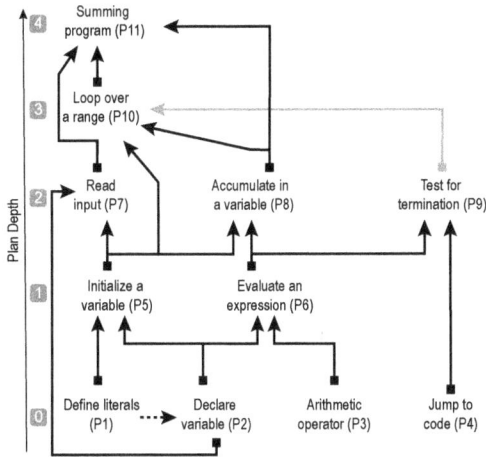

Figure 2: Plan tree for Case Study 1.

to comprehend the purpose of the function and consider its input [41], a variable (P2); P7 coordinates P2 and the return value that is assigned to a variable with P5. (While the assignment of the return value and an initialization plan have different goals, they coordinate the same plans and have the same plan structure.) Thus, $PD(P7) = max(PD(P5), PD(P2)) + 1 = 2$.

Loop over a range (P10) coordinates the initialization (P5), test for termination (P9) and increment (P8) plans in a non-arbitrary order defined by the desired control flow. Thus, $PD(P10) = max(PD(P5), PD(P8), PD(P9)) + 1 = 3$. Finally, the entire *summing program* (P11) coordinates the loop (P10), input (P7), and accumulation (P8). $PD(P11) = max(PD(P10), PD(P7), PD(P8)) + 1 = 4$.

3.1.2 Case Study 2: Averaging Program. While presenting the hierarchical analysis of the following program, we only discuss what is new compared to the first case study.

```
1  def average(collection):
2      return sum(collection) / len(collection)
3  l = [1, 2, 3 ,4]
4  average(l)
```

As shown in Figure 3, the primary plan *declare variable* (P2) is a prerequisite for the *declare collections* plan (P3). *Initialize a collection* (P9) assigns a sequence of literals to a collection, coordinating P5 and P3, thus having a $PD(P9) = 1$. *Assign a literal to a variable* (P8) similarly coordinates P2 and P5.

The library-function-calling plans *sum/size of a collection* (P7) coordinate the input of the function, a collection (P3), and the assignment of the return value to memory (P8), where $PD(P7) = max(PD(3), PD(8)) + 1 = 2$. The *call average function* plan (P6) has a similar structure, adding a jump to code plan (P1) and activating the user-defined function. $PD(P6) = max(PD(P3), PD(P8), PD(P1)) + 1 = 2$. The *assign an expression to a variable (P12)* plan coordinates the evaluation of an expression (P10) and the assignment of its result to a variable (P8). $PD(P12) = max(PD(P8), PD(P10)) + 1 = 2$. The *pass a parameter (P11)* plan is the use of a collection as a parameter (P9), which is later instantiated within the function activation (P3). Therefore, $PD(P11) = max(PD(P3), PD(P9)) + 1 = 2$.

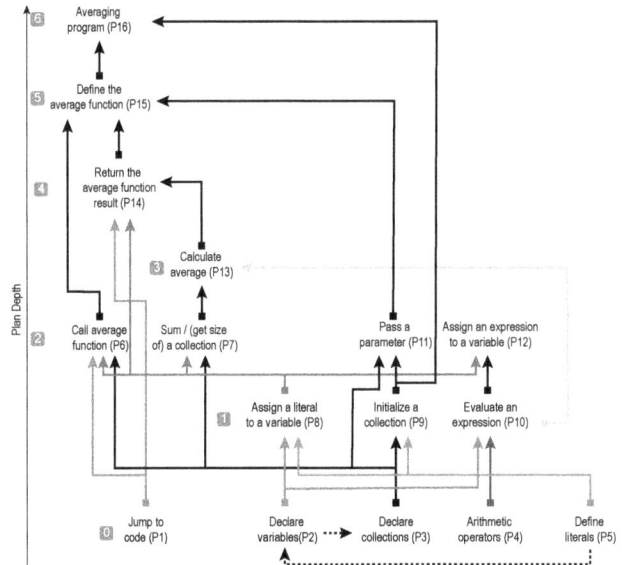

Figure 3: Plan tree for Case Study 2. The arrow colors are for visual clarity only.

The *calculate average* plan (P13) coordinates the results of the sum and size function calls (P7) and the evaluation of an expression (P10). $PD(P13) = max(PD(P7), PD(P10)) + 1 = 3$. The *return the average function result* plan (P14) takes as input the result of the average calculation of P13 and terminates the function activation, performing a jump to the main program (P1) and assigning its result to memory in the global scope (P8). Therefore $PD(P14) = max(PD(P1), PD(P8), PD(P13)) + 1 = 4$. The *define the average function* plan (P15) encapsulates the whole function activation, coordinating its return statement (P14), its parameters (P11), and the function invocation (P6). $PD(P15) = max(PD(P6), PD(P11), PD(P14)) + 1 = 5$. The whole *averaging program* (P16) coordinates the function definition (P14) and the initialization of the collection (P9). $PD(P16) = max(PD(P9), PD(P15)) + 1 = 6$.

3.2 Interactivity Analysis

We have shown how hierarchical analysis (HA) gives an overall sense of the complexity of a program. It also suggests how learning to understand a particular aspect of the program (plan) is predicated on first learning to understand other aspects. HA does not, however, attend to simultaneous processing in working memory, which is central to element interactivity and cognitive load. For this purpose, the CCCP extends HA with interactivity analysis (IA).

Plans are again our basic unit of analysis; IA examines how plans are put together in a program. Specifically, we estimate which plans must be kept in mind simultaneously as the programmer mentally manipulates the (higher-level) plans of the program.

Whereas HA was concerned with complexity alone, IA additionally deals with difficulty: we must consider the programmer's prior knowledge and the chunking of multiple subplans into larger wholes that is processed as a single element. As a starting point for IA, we take the program code and the plan tree produced by HA, and state our assumptions about the prior knowledge of the programmer: which plans do we expect the programmer to be able to deal with as single elements because they are sufficiently familiar with that plan's individual subplans? We can then use IA to estimate the plan interactivity for programmers that meet the assumption.

We build on the concept of *focus of attention* (FoA) [18, 60], which we have adapted to a programming context. At any given time while a programmer works on a program, the FoA is a single plan that has been activated in working memory for immediate processing. It is linked to a subset of other plans in the program that need to be considered simultaneously with the FoA; these other plans form a *region of direct access* (RDA)[60] that must also be stored in working memory. As a programmer processes a program, their FoA will shift from one plan to another at which point they will also rearrange the RDA in working memory as required.

To conduct IA, we examine the control and data flow of the program. We trace the execution of the program step by step, considering how the program flow and (we posit) the FoA shift from one plan to another. We ignore the lower-level plans that the programmer is expected to have abstracted away from working memory. At each FoA shift, we compute a *plan interactivity* (PI) metric that equals the number of plans inside the RDA; PI is essentially a programming-domain estimate of element interactivity as defined by CLT [cf. 2]. *Maximal plan interactivity* (MPI) is the highest PI value at any FoA in the program.[1]

Which plans fall within the RDA of a particular FoA depends on the way plans are merged, sequenced, and nested. We consider a plan A to be in the RDA of another plan B if A is directly nested within B or vice versa, or if the execution of A interleaves with that of B. If A's execution is done before B's starts, the plans can be considered non-simultaneously and are not in each other's RDA.[2]

3.2.1 Case Study 1 revisited for IA.
For the IA of Case Study 1, we color-coded the Summing Program so that each color maps to a relatively high-level plan: loop (P10) in blue; accumulate (P8) in red; and reading (P7) in green. In this example of IA, we assume that the programmer has sufficient prior knowledge that they can process each of these schemas as a chunk. The control and data flow of these three plans are interleaved. It is difficult to isolate the control flow of the reading plan from the accumulate and loop plans: the shared iterative control structure dictates when the plans start and end. The data flow also suggests an interaction between reading and summing plans (a shared input variable). This means that all three plans need to be active in the RDA in order to process any one of them as the FoA, which yields an MPI of 3.

3.2.2 Case Study 2 (Averaging Program) revisited for IA.
In the IA of Case Study 2, we assume the programmer can process the initialization (P9, cyan), average function definition (P15, purple), sum (P7, red) and size (P7, brown) plans as single chunks. The initialization of a collection plan can be processed in isolation in the RDA, with a PI of 1. Calling the average function (line 4) activates the function-definition plan in the RDA. The sequenced plan-composition strategy enables the programmer to evaluate

plans in isolation and later compose only the *results* of the plans. They can shift the FoA to a specific plan, compute its result, and shift to the next FoA with the result of the previous FoA as input. For example, the FoA shifts from the summing plan (nested inside the average plan, PI 2) to the size plan (nested with the average plan, PI 2). Shifting the FoA back to the function definition plan, activated in the RDA, we compute the average by activating the *results* of the function calls (not all their constituent parts) and evaluate an expression (from the average plan), computing the return value of the function. The MPI for case study 2 is therefore 2.

3.2.3 Case Study 3: Averaging Rainfall.
In this case study, we consider a version of the Rainfall Problem [69, 73]. We compare two solutions that differ in plan composition: a merged-plans solution (Figure 4) and a sequenced-plans solution (Figure 5), both adapted from [76]. Each color corresponds to one of the main high-level plans identified in other work on the same problem [26, 69]: iteration (light blue), a sum (red), read (light green), average (purple), count (brown), guard against negative (dark blue), guard against division by zero (orange) and sentinel (light green). We assume the programmer can deal with each highlighted plan as a single chunk. With the exception of the exit-in-the-middle loop with a while (true) statement (which coordinates a literal and a jump-to-code plan), we already analyzed the other plans (or their close variants) in the previous case studies.

```
1    var count = 0
2    var sum = 0
3    var average = 0
4    while (true) {
5        val input = readInt()
6        if (input >= 0) {
7            if (input >= 999999) {
8                if (count == 0) { println("No data!"); break }
9                println(average);
10               break }
11           count += 1
12           sum += input
13           average = sum / count } }
```

Figure 4: A color-coded merged-plans solution for Rainfall.

The merged-plans program and sequence-plans program employ different plans and therefore yield different PD scores. We will leave that aside, however, since our present purpose is to explore the interactivity between plans in each program.

Analyzing the merged-plans program in Figure 4, we observe that all plans share the same control flow through the loop plan (using the while (true) loop) and some plans share the same data flow. For instance, the variable *input* is shared among the input, negative, sentinel and sum plans, while count is shared by the count and guard plans. This interleaving of control and data flow forces the activation of all these subplans in working memory for every FoA shift. In order to be able to process the program and extract its meaning (or write it), the programmer needs to evaluate the impact of each plan on the data and control flow. Therefore, for the merged-plans program in Figure 4 all plans must interact in the RDA, yielding an MPI of 8.

The sequenced-plans approach in Figure 5 uses, where possible, a compartmentalization strategy by making extensive use of

---

[1]IA is loosely related to the work of Letovsky and Soloway [43], who studied delocalized plans scattered in the program text. However, IA is based on program flow rather than the textual organization of program code.

[2]Since programs are generally written down, the program text can in practice serve as a tool for external cognition [65], reducing working memory load. IA, as presented, does not account for this and may overestimate load in some cases.

```
1   def isNotSentinel (input : Int) = input < 999999
2   def isValid (input : Int) = input >= 0
3   def average (numbers : List [Int]) =
4       if (numbers.nonEmpty)
5           numbers.sum / numbers.size
6       else 0
7   val validInputs = inputs.takeWhile(isNotSentinel).filter(isValid)
8   val averageRainfall = average(validInputs)
```

Figure 5: A sequenced-plans solution for Rainfall.

functions. By switching the FoA at each function call (or function evaluation), sequenced plans composition induces a *switch-process-store-output (SPSO)* processing pattern, reducing the number of simultaneously activated plans in the RDA.

To process the reading plan (line 7), the FoA switches to the sentinel plan, composed with the loop plan, with both simultaneously in the RDA (PI 2). At the end of the input plan (sentinel found), the plans collapse to a single result (a collection), stored in the RDA. The FoA switches to the negative plan (also line 7), which is processed using (only) the result of the previous step as input and which outputs a collection to the reading plan (PI 1, processing just the negative plan). The reading plan is then processed with its inputs and stored for later composition.

At line 8, a function call switches the FoA to the averaging plan of line 3. The averaging plan activates the guard-against-zero plan (lines 4 and 6) and the computation of the average itself. To compute the average (with guard and average active in the RDA), the FoA switches to the sum plan (using an SPSO pattern), which makes the sum plan the only active plan in the RDA for now. After another switch to the count plan (SPSO again) we are back to the first RDA in order to compute the averaging expression. Having the average and guard plans activated yields a PI of 2. Overall, the sequenced-plans Rainfall program of Figure 5 has an MPI of 2.

4   RELATED WORK AND DISCUSSION

Of the theoretical tools that have been used in CER for categorizing activities by complexity, Bloom's Taxonomy [5] is probably the most common [7, 29, 52]. Meanwhile, the SOLO taxonomy [4] has been used for analyzing students' responses to code-reading tasks [71], the structure of students' code [11], and aspects of program design such as testing and abstraction [9]. In addition to classifying skills such as tracing and writing code in taxonomies, researchers have investigated the dependencies between the skills and the way the skills evolve with growing expertise [17, 44, 48, 82]

The studies cited above emphasize the general types of activities that programmers engage in (Bloom) and/or the general degree of structuredness in learning outcomes (SOLO). Our work on the CCCP differs from them in that we seek to characterize the *content* of the programming activities—the programs themselves—and to do so at a relatively fine level of detail. We believe that this is a useful complement to the existing work that examines the complexity of different programming activities and the relationships between them. For example, to establish a progression of skills, some studies have sought to compare student performance on reading code vs. writing code of "similar complexity" [45, 72] and would benefit from a better definition of program complexity than is currently

available. Simon et al. [72] ask: "Is an assignment statement easier or harder to read and understand than a print statement? Is a nested loop easier or harder than an if-then-else? Is the difficulty of a piece of code simply the linear sum of the difficulties of its constituent parts?" By adopting the axioms of complexity from the MHC, the CCCP provides a theoretical grounding for claims about the relative complexity of different programming constructs; by further considering the shifting focus of attention and cognitive load, the CCCP suggests that difficulty is not simply a linear sum of the entire code.

We are not the first to propose a set of cognitive complexity metrics for programming. Cant et al. [8, 32] conceptualized *CCM*, a tentative framework for measuring complexity, which resembles ours in its goals and in that it, too, draws on schema theory and related findings from cognitive psychology. Our present work overlaps that of Cant et al.: we focus on a narrower set of metrics, operationalize them, and bring them to bear on actual programs.

The MHC has been applied in other domains to define learning trajectories of increasingly complex tasks [e.g., 3]. The CCCP similarly suggests a progression from the concepts required at the leaves of the plan trees towards the higher-level roots. In this respect, our work shares some goals with earlier work that has proposed learning trajectories for introductory programming. The proposal of Mead et al. [55] links concepts in intuitively-constructed "anchor graphs," in which learning an earlier concept ought to carry some of the cognitive load of later concepts; the most obvious difference between their work and ours is that they focused on generic programming concepts whereas we analyze plans in individual programs. Rich et al. [62] created a set of K-8 learning trajectories for three concepts: sequencing, repetition, and conditionals; they identified challenges in basing the trajectories on a heterogeneous and sparse set of prior reports of concept difficulty. Izu et al. [35] suggested an intuitive, SOLO-inspired learning trajectory in which the learner abstracts increasingly complex "building blocks" (language constructs and plan-like "templates") in order to tackle the next concepts; the CCCP differs from this work, and the other research just cited, in its use of MHC to structure the plan hierarchy.

The CCCP may also help interpret some earlier results in CER. For instance, Mühling et al. [58] gave students a psychometric test whose items featured different programming constructs. Contrasting student performance on different items, Mühling et al. found that simple sequences were easy for the participants and that loops with a fixed number of iterations were easier than all items involving conditionals. Their most surprising result, the authors suggest, was that nested control structures were easier than a loop with an exit condition. The CCCP predicts these findings (albeit with the proviso that the CCCP deals with complexity, whereas measured difficulty is affected by prior exposure to different constructs). For example, nesting fixed-iteration loops does not increase plan depth beyond that of a conditional loop exit. As another example, Ajami et al. [1] measured the performance of professional developers on program-comprehension tasks that were otherwise similar but featured different programming constructs. Their findings suggest that conditionals were less complex than for loops, that the size of the expressions used as inputs for constructs had an impact on performance, and that flat structures are slightly easier than nested ones; these results match what is predicted by our plan depth metric.

It has been suggested that students find merged, interleaved plans difficult and that sequential plan composition is easier to deal with [73, 76]. There is also evidence that students mistakenly concatenate plans instead of merging and generally struggle with plans which interact in complex ways [28], that students sometimes read merged plans as if they were composed sequentially [30], and that a student's plan composition strategy interacts with the likelihood they will write defective code [25, 74]; a sequenced-plans approach may lead to better outcomes [25]. The CCCP offers a partial explanation for these findings — merged plan composition demands more plans simultaneously in the region of direct access, which may result in cognitive overload — and puts forward the plan interactivity metric as an indicator of program complexity.

Student performance on code-writing and code-reading questions has been assessed in a number of multi-institutional studies, usually to the conclusion that introductory-level students commonly perform at a level below their teachers' expectations [45, 54, 83]. In order for measurable progress to be made and reasonable expectations set, the complexity of the programs in such assessment instruments should be evaluated. Simon et al. [72] argue: "If we are to have a reliable measure of students' abilities at reading and writing code, we would need to consider a minute analysis of the difficulty levels of code-reading and code-writing questions at the micro level." We expect that a tool like the CCCP could contribute towards such a "micro-level" analysis.

A number of studies over the past few decades have investigated bugs in student code and mapped the bugs to the plans in which they appear [23, 25, 36, 59, 69]. As the CCCP extends Soloway's plan-based analysis by introducing the MHC rule set, it may contribute to the methodology of future studies in this vein.

Another point of reference for our work is the use of program metrics in CER. Luxton-Reilly et al., like ourselves, analyzed individual programs in order to characterize their structure [50, 51]; their analysis and metrics are fundamentally different from ours in that they focused exclusively on syntactic features whereas we have focused on cognitive plans. In a related line of CER, surface-level metrics from Software Engineering such as Cyclomatic Complexity [53], lines of code, and block depth have been applied to code-comprehension tasks [38], code-writing tasks [24], and multiple-choice questions [67]. Such metrics provide one perspective on software complexity but do not indicate how different constructs and plans affect complexity [1], have a low correlation with perceived complexity [39], and disregard the role of prior knowledge.

Finally, a different sort of metric was validated by Morrison et al. [57], who estimated cognitive load by asking students for their subjective perceptions of mental effort after the students had engaged in various types of CS study. We certainly see such post-activity surveys as being valuable, too, but at the same time we hope that the CCCP will mature into a complementary tool for the analytical *a-priori* assessment of individual *programs* during instructional design [cf. 2, 61, 81].

5 CONTRIBUTIONS AND LIMITATIONS

We have outlined a theoretical framework, the CCCP, for assessing the cognitive complexity that is manifested in computer programs.

We have explored how to analyze plan hierarchies and the interactions between plans in terms of the CCCP and demonstrated the complexity metrics of plan depth and plan interactivity. Moreover, we have discussed how such analyses can contribute to debates about the relative merits of curricular decisions as well as the design and interpretation of research on student programming.

Our methodological exploration so far has been tentative. We have a goal, a framework, and examples of plausible analyses of programs in terms of the framework; we do not yet have a well-defined analysis process. Before the CCCP can be applied more easily and transparently, we must further refine the steps that an analyst must take in order to delimit plans and apply the MHC-derived rules of the CCCP to them. Even so, our work lends preliminary support to the idea that the MHC, which has not been previously applied to CER, can provide structure to analyses of program complexity.

The CCCP is built on general theoretical models for which there is empirical support. Nevertheless, if the CCCP is to be more than an idealistic construct that fails in practice, it must be directly evaluated and refined based on empirical findings. Each of our case studies reflects one possible breakdown of an example program in terms of the CCCP, and while we have provided a rationale for this analysis in theoretical terms, it remains to be seen whether it aligns with student performance, for instance. Since student performance reflects the *difficulty* of a task, any empirical evaluations will need to account for prior knowledge [cf. 10, 64].

We have limited our analysis of complexity to a particular facet: the cognitive complexity present in program designs. We believe this to be a very significant aspect of complexity in programming tasks, but it is not the only one. Another significant facet of task complexity is what the learner is expected to do with the program. We envision that the CCCP could be used in combination with other frameworks that emphasize the activity aspect: for instance, in the 4C/ID model of instructional design [84], students engage in different activities within a task class (e.g., worked examples followed by completion tasks followed by problem solving) before proceeding to another task class with more complex content. The CCCP could help in identifying and ordering task classes.

The complexity of a programming task is additionally influenced by factors such as task presentation [70], contextualization [6, 49] and syntax [21, 79], which are not covered by the CCCP as presented. In the future, we may expand the framework by adapting a generic task model from the literature [e.g., 47] to programming education.

Violating programmers' expectations of code structure leads to poorer comprehension, as existing schemas fail to apply [e.g., 31]. In the present work, we have only considered programs that are "planlike" and unsurprising.

Our example programs cover only a handful of basic plans. Additional work is required in order to extend the present work to other content (e.g. recursion, objects) and more complex plans.

In the future, we intend to adopt a mixed-methods approach to evaluating the CCCP and developing the analysis process. The evaluation may incorporate elements such as expert validation, empirical measurements of prior knowledge (cf. earlier work in estimating cognitive load [2]), correlation of predicted complexity with task performance through Rasch analysis (cf. how the MHC has been validated in other domains [13]), and triangulation against mental effort ratings [57].

REFERENCES

[1] Shulamyt Ajami, Yonatan Woodbridge, and Dror G Feitelson. 2017. Syntax, predicates, idioms: what really affects code complexity?. In *Proceedings of the 25th International Conference on Program Comprehension*. IEEE Press, 66–76.

[2] Jens F Beckmann. 2010. Taming a beast of burden–On some issues with the conceptualisation and operationalisation of cognitive load. *Learning and instruction* 20, 3 (2010), 250–264.

[3] Sascha Bernholt and Ilka Parchmann. 2011. Assessing the complexity of students' knowledge in chemistry. *Chemistry Education Research and Practice* 12, 2 (2011), 167–173.

[4] John B Biggs and Kevin F Collis. 2014. *Evaluating the quality of learning: The SOLO taxonomy (Structure of the Observed Learning Outcome)*. Academic Press.

[5] Benjamin S Bloom et al. 1956. Taxonomy of educational objectives. Vol. 1: Cognitive domain. *New York: McKay* (1956), 20–24.

[6] Dennis Bouvier, Ellie Lovellette, John Matta, Bedour Alshaigy, Brett A. Becker, Michelle Craig, Jana Jackova, Robert McCartney, Kate Sanders, and Mark Zarb. 2016. Novice Programmers and the Problem Description Effect. In *Proceedings of the 2016 ITiCSE Working Group Reports (ITiCSE '16)*. ACM, New York, NY, USA, 103–118. https://doi.org/10.1145/3024906.3024912

[7] Duane Buck and David J. Stucki. 2000. Design early considered harmful: Graduated exposure to complexity and structure based on levels of cognitive development. *SIGCSE Bulletin* 32, 1 (2000), 75–79. https://doi.org/10.1145/331795.331817

[8] SN Cant, DR Jeffery, and B Henderson-Sellers. 1995. A conceptual model of cognitive complexity of elements of the programming process. *Information and Software Technology* 37, 7 (1995), 351 – 362. https://doi.org/10.1016/0950-5849(95)91491-H

[9] Francisco Enrique Vicente Castro and Kathi Fisler. 2017. Designing a multi-faceted SOLO taxonomy to track program design skills through an entire course. In *Proceedings of the 17th Koli Calling Conference on Computing Education Research*. ACM, 10–19.

[10] Hwan-Hee Choi, Jeroen JG Van Merriënboer, and Fred Paas. 2014. Effects of the physical environment on cognitive load and learning: towards a new model of cognitive load. *Educational Psychology Review* 26, 2 (2014), 225–244.

[11] Tony Clear, Anne Philpott, Phil Robbins, and Simon. 2009. Report on the Eighth BRACElet Workshop: BRACElet Technical Report 01/08. *Bulletin of Applied Computing and Information Technology* 7, 1 (2009).

[12] Michael Lamport Commons. 2008. Introduction to the model of hierarchical complexity and its relationship to postformal action. *World Futures* 64, 5-7 (2008), 305–320.

[13] Michael Lamport Commons, Eric Andrew Goodheart, Alexander Pekker, Theo Linda Dawson, Karen Draney, and Kathryn Marie Adams. 2008. Using Rasch scaled stage scores to validate orders of hierarchical complexity of balance beam task sequences. *Journal of Applied Measurement* 9, 2 (2008), 182.

[14] Michael Lamport Commons, Patrice Marie Miller, Eva Yujia Li, and Thomas Gordon Gutheil. 2012. Forensic experts' perceptions of expert bias. *International journal of law and psychiatry* 35, 5-6 (2012), 362–371.

[15] Michael Lamport Commons, JA Rodriguez, PM Miller, SN Ross, A LoCicero, EA Goodheart, and D Danaher-Gilpin. 2007. Applying the model of hierarchical complexity. *Unpublished manuscript* (2007).

[16] Michael Lamport Commons, Edward James Trudeau, Sharon Anne Stein, Francis Asbury Richards, and Sharon R Krause. 1998. Hierarchical complexity of tasks shows the existence of developmental stages. *Developmental Review* 18, 3 (1998), 237–278.

[17] Malcolm Corney, Donna Teague, Alireza Ahadi, and Raymond Lister. 2012. Some empirical results for neo-Piagetian reasoning in novice programmers and the relationship to code explanation questions. In *Proceedings of the Fourteenth Australasian Computing Education Conference-Volume 123*. Australian Computer Society, Inc., 77–86.

[18] Nelson Cowan, Emily M Elliott, J Scott Saults, Candice C Morey, Sam Mattox, Anna Hismjatullina, and Andrew RA Conway. 2005. On the capacity of attention: Its estimation and its role in working memory and cognitive aptitudes. *Cognitive psychology* 51, 1 (2005), 42–100.

[19] Theo Linda Dawson. 2002. A comparison of three developmental stage scoring systems. *Journal of applied measurement* 3, 2 (2002), 146–189.

[20] Michael de Raadt. 2008. *Teaching programming strategies explicitly to novice programmers*. Ph.D. Dissertation. University of Southern Queensland.

[21] Paul Denny, Andrew Luxton-Reilly, Ewan Tempero, and Jacob Hendrickx. 2011. Understanding the Syntax Barrier for Novices. In *Proceedings of the 16th Annual Joint Conference on Innovation and Technology in Computer Science Education (ITiCSE '11)*. ACM, New York, NY, USA, 208–212. https://doi.org/10.1145/1999747.1999807

[22] Benedict du Boulay. 1986. Some difficulties of learning to program. *Journal of Educational Computing Research* 2, 1 (1986), 57–73.

[23] Alireza Ebrahimi. 1994. Novice programmer errors: Language constructs and plan composition. *International Journal of Human-Computer Studies* 41, 4 (1994), 457–480.

[24] Said Elnaffar. 2016. Using Software Metrics to Predict the Difficulty of Code Writing Questions. In *2016 IEEE Global Engineering Education Conference*. 513–518.

[25] Kathi Fisler. 2014. The recurring rainfall problem. In *Proceedings of the tenth annual conference on International computing education research*. ACM, 35–42.

[26] Kathi Fisler and Francisco Enrique Vicente Castro. 2017. Sometimes, Rainfall Accumulates: Talk-Alouds with Novice Functional Programmers. In *Proceedings of the 2017 ACM Conference on International Computing Education Research*. ACM, 12–20.

[27] Kathi Fisler, Shriram Krishnamurthi, and Janet Siegmund. 2016. Modernizing plan-composition studies. In *Proceedings of the 47th ACM Technical Symposium on Computing Science Education*. ACM, 211–216.

[28] David Ginat, Eti Menashe, and Amal Taya. 2013. Novice difficulties with interleaved pattern composition. *Lecture Notes in Computer Science* 7780 LNCS (2013), 57–67. https://doi.org/10.1007/978-3-642-36617-8_5

[29] Richard Gluga, Judy Kay, Raymond Lister, and Sabina Kleitman. 2013. Mastering cognitive development theory in computer science education. *Computer Science Education* 23, 1 (2013), 24–57.

[30] Shuchi Grover and Satabdi Basu. 2017. Measuring student learning in introductory block-based programming: Examining misconceptions of loops, variables, and boolean logic. In *Proceedings of the 2017 ACM SIGCSE Technical Symposium on Computer Science Education*. ACM, 267–272.

[31] Michael Hansen, Robert L Goldstone, and Andrew Lumsdaine. 2013. What makes code hard to understand? *arXiv preprint arXiv:1304.5257* (2013).

[32] Michael E Hansen, Andrew Lumsdaine, and Robert L Goldstone. 2012. Cognitive architectures: A way forward for the psychology of programming. In *Proceedings of the ACM international symposium on New ideas, new paradigms, and reflections on programming and software*. ACM, 27–38.

[33] Felienne Hermans and Efthimia Aivaloglou. 2016. Do code smells hamper novice programming? A controlled experiment on Scratch programs. In *Program Comprehension (ICPC), 2016 IEEE 24th International Conference on*. IEEE, 1–10.

[34] Minjie Hu, Michael Winikoff, and Stephen Cranefield. 2012. Teaching novice programming using goals and plans in a visual notation. In *Proceedings of the Fourteenth Australasian Computing Education Conference-Volume 123*. Australian Computer Society, Inc., 43–52.

[35] Cruz Izu, Amali Weerasinghe, and Cheryl Pope. 2016. A study of code design skills in novice programmers using the SOLO taxonomy. In *Proceedings of the 2016 ACM Conference on International Computing Education Research*. ACM, 251–259.

[36] W. Lewis Johnson, Elliot Soloway, Benjamin Cutler, and Steven Draper. 1983. *Bug Catalogue: I*. Technical Report. Yale University, YaleU/CSD/RR \#286.

[37] Slava Kalyuga. 2011. Cognitive load theory: How many types of load does it really need? *Educational Psychology Review* 23, 1 (2011), 1–19.

[38] Nadia Kasto and Jacqueline Whalley. 2013. Measuring the difficulty of code comprehension tasks using software metrics. In *The 15th Australasian Computer Education Conference*, Vol. 136. 59–65.

[39] Bernhard Katzmarski and Rainer Koschke. 2012. Program complexity metrics and programmer opinions. In *Program Comprehension (ICPC), 2012 IEEE 20th International Conference on*. IEEE, 17–26.

[40] Andreas Korbach, Roland Brünken, and Babette Park. 2017. Differentiating Different Types of Cognitive Load: a Comparison of Different Measures. *Educational Psychology Review* (2017), 1–27.

[41] Sofia Leite, Jose Carlos Principe, Antonio Carlos Silva, Joao Marques-Teixeira, Michael L Commons, and Pedro Rodrigues. In Review. Connectionist models capture hierarchical complexity transitions in development: discrimination between memory-based and operationally-based transitions. (In Review).

[42] Jimmie Leppink, Fred Paas, Cees PM Van der Vleuten, Tamara Van Gog, and Jeroen JG Van Merriënboer. 2013. Development of an instrument for measuring different types of cognitive load. *Behavior research methods* 45, 4 (2013), 1058–1072.

[43] Stanley Letovsky and Elliot Soloway. 1986. Delocalized plans and program comprehension. *IEEE Software* 3, 3 (1986), 41.

[44] Raymond Lister. 2011. Concrete and Other Neo-Piagetian Forms of Reasoning in the Novice Programmer. *Proceedings of the Thirteenth Australasian Computing Education Conference* Ace (2011), 9–18.

[45] Raymond Lister, Elizabeth S Adams, Sue Fitzgerald, William Fone, John Hamer, Morten Lindholm, Robert McCartney, Jan Erik Moström, Kate Sanders, Otto Seppälä, et al. 2004. A multi-national study of reading and tracing skills in novice programmers. In *ACM SIGCSE Bulletin*, Vol. 36. ACM, 119–150.

[46] Raymond Lister, Beth Simon, Errol Thompson, Jacqueline L. Whalley, and Christine Prasad. 2006. Not seeing the forest for the trees: Novice programmers and the SOLO taxonomy. In *Proceedings of the 11th annual SIGCSE conference on Innovation and Technology in Computer Science Education*. 118–122. https://doi.org/10.1145/1140123.1140157

[47] Peng Liu and Zhizhong Li. 2012. Task complexity: A review and conceptualization framework. *International Journal of Industrial Ergonomics* 42, 6 (2012), 553–568.

[48] Mike Lopez, Jacqueline Whalley, Phil Robbins, and Raymond Lister. 2008. Relationships between reading, tracing and writing skills in introductory programming. *Proceedings of the Fourth International Workshop on Computing Education Research* (2008), 101–112. https://doi.org/10.1145/1404520.1404531

[49] Aleksi Lukkarinen and Juha Sorva. 2016. Classifying the Tools of Contextualized Programming Education and Forms of Media Computation. In *Proceedings of the 16th Koli Calling International Conference on Computing Education Research (Koli Calling '16)*. ACM, New York, NY, USA, 51–60. https://doi.org/10.1145/2999541. 2999551

[50] Andrew Luxton-Reilly, Brett A Becker, Yingjun Cao, Roger McDermott, Claudio Mirolo, Andreas Mühling, Andrew Petersen, Kate Sanders, Jacqueline Whalley, et al. 2018. Developing Assessments to Determine Mastery of Programming Fundamentals. In *Proceedings of the 2017 ITiCSE Conference on Working Group Reports*. ACM, 47–69.

[51] Andrew Luxton-Reilly and Andrew Petersen. 2017. The Compound Nature of Novice Programming Assessments. In *Proceedings of the Nineteenth Australasian Computing Education Conference*. ACM, 26–35.

[52] Susana Masapanta-Carrión and J. Ángel Velázquez-Iturbide. 2018. A systematic review of the use of Bloom's Taxonomy in computer science education. In *Proceedings of the 49h ACM Technical Symposium on Computer Science Education (SIGCSE '18)*. ACM, 441–446.

[53] Thomas J McCabe. 1976. A complexity measure. *IEEE Transactions on software Engineering* 4 (1976), 308–320.

[54] Michael McCracken, Vicki Almstrum, Danny Diaz, Mark Guzdial, Dianne Hagan, Yifat Ben-David Kolikant, Cary Laxer, Lynda Thomas, Ian Utting, and Tadeusz Wilusz. 2001. A Multi-national, Multi-institutional Study of Assessment of Programming Skills of First-year CS Students. *SIGCSE Bull.* 33, 4 (2001), 125 – 180. https://doi.org/10.1145/572139.572181

[55] Jerry Mead, Simon Gray, John Hamer, Richard James, Juha Sorva, Caroline St. Clair, and Lynda Thomas. 2006. A Cognitive Approach to Identifying Measurable Milestones for Programming Skill Acquisition. *SIGCSE Bull.* 38, 4 (June 2006), 182–194. https://doi.org/10.1145/1189136.1189185

[56] Patrice Marie Miller and Darlene Crone-Todd. 2016. Comparing different ways of using the model of hierarchical complexity to evaluate graduate students. *Behavioral Development Bulletin* 21, 2 (2016), 223.

[57] Briana B Morrison, Brian Dorn, and Mark Guzdial. 2014. Measuring cognitive load in introductory CS: adaptation of an instrument. In *Proceedings of the tenth annual conference on International computing education research*. ACM, 131–138.

[58] Andreas Mühling, Alexander Ruf, and Peter Hubwieser. 2015. Design and first results of a psychometric test for measuring basic programming abilities. In *Proceedings of the Workshop in Primary and Secondary Computing Education*. ACM, 2–10.

[59] Laurie Murphy, Sue Fitzgerald, and Scott Grissom. 2015. Bug infestation! A goal-plan analysis of CS2 students' recursive binary tree solutions. In *Sigcse '15*. 482–487. https://doi.org/10.1145/2676723.2677232

[60] Klaus Oberauer. 2002. Access to information in working memory: exploring the focus of attention. *Journal of Experimental Psychology: Learning, Memory, and Cognition* 28, 3 (2002), 411.

[61] Fred Paas, Juhani E Tuovinen, Huib Tabbers, and Pascal WM Van Gerven. 2003. Cognitive load measurement as a means to advance cognitive load theory. *Educational psychologist* 38, 1 (2003), 63–71.

[62] Kathryn M. Rich, Carla Strickland, T. Andrew Binkowski, Cheryl Moran, and Diana Franklin. 2017. K-8 Learning Trajectories Derived from Research Literature: Sequence, Repetition, Conditionals. In *Proceedings of the 2017 ACM Conference on International Computing Education Research (ICER '17)*. ACM, New York, NY, USA, 182–190. https://doi.org/10.1145/3105726.3106166

[63] Robert S Rist. 1989. Schema creation in programming. *Cognitive Science* 13, 3 (1989), 389–414.

[64] Peter Robinson. 2001. Task complexity, task difficulty, and task production: Exploring interactions in a componential framework. *Applied linguistics* 22, 1 (2001), 27–57.

[65] Yvonne Rogers. 2004. New theoretical approaches for HCI. *Annual review of information science and technology* 38, 1 (2004), 87–143.

[66] Jorma Sajaniemi and Marja Kuittinen. 2005. An experiment on using roles of variables in teaching introductory programming. *Computer Science Education* 15, 1 (2005), 59–82.

[67] Kate Sanders, Marzieh Ahmadzadeh, Tony Clear, Stephen H. Edwards, Mikey Goldweber, Chris Johnson, Raymond Lister, Robert McCartney, Elizabeth Patitsas, and Jaime Spacco. 2013. The Canterbury QuestionBank: Building a repository of multiple-choice CS1 and CS2 questions. In *ITICSE'13 Working Group Reports (ITiCSE WGR '13)*. 33–51. https://doi.org/10.1145/2543882.2543885

[68] Wolfgang Schnotz and Christian Kürschner. 2007. A reconsideration of cognitive load theory. *Educational psychology review* 19, 4 (2007), 469–508.

[69] Otto Seppälä, Petri Ihantola, Essi Isohanni, Juha Sorva, and Arto Vihavainen. 2015. Do we know how difficult the Rainfall Problem is?. In *Proceedings of the 15th Koli Calling Conference on Computing Education Research (Koli Calling '15)*. ACM, 87–96. https://doi.org/10.1145/2828959.2828963

[70] Judy Sheard, Angela Carbone, Donald Chinn, Tony Clear, Malcolm Corney, Daryl D'Souza, Joel Fenwick, James Harland, Mikko-Jussi Laakso, Donna Teague, et al. 2013. How difficult are exams?: a framework for assessing the complexity of introductory programming exams. In *Proceedings of the Fifteenth Australasian Computing Education Conference-Volume 136*. Australian Computer Society, Inc., 145–154.

[71] Judy Sheard, Angela Carbone, Raymond Lister, Beth Simon, Errol Thompson, and Jacqueline L Whalley. 2008. Going SOLO to assess novice programmers. In *ACM SIGCSE Bulletin*, Vol. 40. ACM, 209–213.

[72] Simon, Mike Lopez, Ken Sutton, and Tony Clear. 2009. Surely we must learn to read before we learn to write!. In *Conferences in Research and Practice in Information Technology Series (ACE '09)*, Margaret Hamilton and Tony Clear (Eds.), Vol. 95. Australian Computer Society, 165–170.

[73] Elliot Soloway. 1986. Learning to program = Learning to construct mechanisms and explanations. *Commun. ACM* 29, 9 (1986), 850–858.

[74] Elliot Soloway, Jeffrey Bonar, and Kate Ehrlich. 1983. Cognitive strategies and looping constructs: An empirical study. *Commun. ACM* 26, 11 (1983), 853–860.

[75] Juha Sorva. 2013. Notional machines and introductory programming education. *ACM Transactions on Computing Education* 13, 2 (2013), 1–31. https://doi.org/10.1145/2483710.2483713

[76] Juha Sorva and Arto Vihavainen. 2016. Break Statement Considered. *ACM Inroads* 7, 3 (Aug. 2016), 36–41. https://doi.org/10.1145/2950065

[77] James C Spohrer, Elliot Soloway, and Edgar Pope. 1985. A goal/plan analysis of buggy Pascal programs. *Human–Computer Interaction* 1, 2 (1985), 163–207.

[78] Kristian Stålne, Michael Lamport Commons, and Eva Yujia Li. 2014. Hierarchical complexity in physics. *Behavioral Development Bulletin* 19, 3 (2014), 62.

[79] Andreas Stefik and Susanna Siebert. 2013. An empirical investigation into programming language syntax. *ACM Transactions on Computing Education (TOCE)* 13, 4 (2013), 19.

[80] John Sweller. 1988. Cognitive load during problem solving: Effects on learning. *Cognitive science* 12, 2 (1988), 257–285.

[81] John Sweller. 2010. Element interactivity and intrinsic, extraneous, and germane cognitive load. *Educational psychology review* 22, 2 (2010), 123–138.

[82] Donna Teague and Raymond Lister. 2014. Programming: reading, writing and reversing. In *Proceedings of the 2014 conference on Innovation & technology in computer science education*. ACM, 285–290.

[83] Ian Utting, Dennis J. Bouvier, Michael E. Caspersen, Allison Elliott Tew, Roger Frye, Yifat Ben-David Kolikant, Mike McCracken, James Paterson, Juha Sorva, Lynda Thomas, and Ta Wilusz. 2013. A fresh look at novice programmers' performance and their teachers' expectations. In *Proceedings of the 2013 ITiCSE working group reports (ITiCSE -WGR '13)*. ACM, 15–32. https://doi.org/10.1145/2543882.2543884

[84] Jeroen JG Van Merriënboer and Paul A Kirschner. 2017. *Ten steps to complex learning: A systematic approach to four-component instructional design*. Routledge.

On Use of Theory in Computing Education Research

Greg L. Nelson
University of Washington
Allen School, DUB Group
Seattle, Washington
glnelson@uw.edu

Andrew J. Ko
University of Washington
The Information School, DUB Group
Seattle, Washington
ajko@uw.edu

ABSTRACT

A primary goal of computing education research is to discover designs that produce better learning of computing. In this pursuit, we have increasingly drawn upon theories from learning science and education research, recognizing the potential benefits of optimizing our search for better designs by leveraging the predictions of general theories of learning. In this paper, we contribute an argument that theory can also inhibit our community's search for better designs. We present three inhibitions: 1) our desire to both advance explanatory theory and advance design splits our attention, which prevents us from excelling at both; 2) our emphasis on applying and refining general theories of learning is done at the expense of domain-specific theories of computer science knowledge, and 3) our use of theory as a critical lens in peer review prevents the publication of designs that may accelerate design progress. We present several recommendations for how to improve our use of theory, viewing it as just one of many sources of design insight in pursuit of improving learning of computing.

CCS CONCEPTS

• **Social and professional topics** → **Computing education**;

KEYWORDS

Theory, cognitive load theory, design, design science, domain-specific theory, peer review, publication bias

ACM Reference Format:
Greg L. Nelson and Andrew J. Ko. 2018. On Use of Theory in Computing Education Research. In *Proceedings of 2018 International Computing Education Research Conference (ICER '18)*. ACM, New York, NY, USA, 9 pages. https://doi.org/10.1145/3230977.3230992

1 INTRODUCTION

As a field of inquiry, computing education is broadly concerned with searching for designs that improve both the learning of computing and broader effects of that learning. Our community investigates a wide range of design ideas including programming IDEs [25], tutorials [28], learning trajectories [52], curricula [4], pedagogy

[51], teacher training [15] and more. Our community also considers diverse broader effects of learning, from gaining knowledge measured by tests [60], developing identity [23], improving task performance [31], and gaining expertise [29], to more humanistic and social concerns such as motivation [33], self-efficacy [10], improved quality of life [20], and equity in outcomes and society [47].

To achieve these design goals, our field is increasingly using theory, both to help find better designs and to help interpret their effects on the world. For example, in the 2017 ACM International Computing Education Research Conference (ICER) proceedings, papers drew upon theories of identity development [24], affect [30], cognitive load theory [34], distributed cognition [9], and collaborative learning [19]. This rich body of theoretical work from other disciplines has offered a foundation upon which to derive hypotheses about the classes we teach, the tools we build, and the explanations of computing we form, and to help us interpret what happens when we share them with learners. In addition, in principle, if a theory correctly predicts that a design will be poor, we can avoid building and evaluating it, and instead pursue designs predicted to be better.

Simultaneously, we are also increasing the role of theory in peer reviewing of our research. The reviewing guidelines for most of the major computing education research conferences and journals (for example, ICER, ACM Transactions on Computing Education, and the Computer Science Education journal) explicitly assess the application of theory in both empirical studies and designs. As criterion, the incorporation of theory in our field's design inquiry has great potential to increase the scientific rigor of our discoveries.

In this paper, we argue that while theory *can* accelerate our field's progress and increase its rigor, if not used carefully, it can also inhibit progress in subtle but important ways. We will focus on three ways that theory can inhibit design progress:

- By using theory to explain learning phenomena *and* pursue better designs, we may create tensions between breadth and depth that limit our impact in both pursuits.
- By focusing on general theories of learning, we may overlook the need for domain-specific theory about the content of computing that is so critical to accelerating design progress.
- By using theory as a critical lens in peer review of designs, we may create a publication bias that inhibits both theory evaluation and our search for better designs.

In the rest of this paper, we will outline what theory is, how we use it in computing education for explanation and design, and then examine our three critiques of its use in detail. Throughout, we will use Cognitive Load Theory [57] as an example of a theory that our field has used to provide clear benefits to our search for better problem solving instruction, but that may also be impeding progress. We end with a series of concrete recommendations for how to better use theory[1] in computing education research in our shared pursuit of better learning.

2 USES OF THEORY IN COMPUTING EDUCATION

In academic research broadly, a theory may include terms, framing, causal mechanisms [18], arguments (a collection of related claims), and a body of evidence that supports or contradicts those arguments [53]. For this paper we define a *descriptive* theory as including terms that name and describe phenomena (called "analysis" theory by [16] and [7]). We also define an *operational* theory as one with procedures for measurement of some terms as well as arguments and evidence for their validity. For example, Danielsiek et al. [10] operationalizes self-efficacy for an algorithms class by creating a survey and studying the survey to validate that it measures self-efficacy.

In computing education research, we use both kinds of theory for design inquiry to describe, generate, and predict the effects of designs. Theory can help *describe* designs; for example, we might summarize the role and content of a UI element in a design by calling it a "sub-goal label" and referencing the worked examples and cognitive load theory literature that created that term [2, 56]. Theory can help characterize *design spaces* that describe many possible designs, as in how Kafai and Resnick use constructionism to illustrate a whole landscape of learning settings and tools [22]. Theories can be also be used to *generate* designs and *predict* their effects. For example, in recent years, computing education researchers have leveraged Cognitive Load Theory (CLT) for genres of design and their effects [2]. For example, Morrison et al. adapted worked examples from other domains (such as physics [2, 56]) to worked examples for computing, adding sub-goal labels such as "initialize variables" and "determine loop condition" to convey programming problem solving [42]. Figure 1 summarizes how we may use theory during design inquiry to describe and generate designs.

Predictions based on theory are also used to provide *rationale* for design, by arguing for some design choices based on a (usually qualitative) prediction of the design's effects. For example, the design of the Gidget coding tutorial drew upon social psychological theories of in-group relation to reason that manipulating animal elements would engage learners more compared to inanimate objects; this provided a rationale for that design choice [27].

As Figure 2 depicts, theories can also help us explore design alternatives. If theories can make reliable predictions about designs we have not yet fully built, they can help us evaluate designs without having to test them empirically. They provide this value by providing some explanation of the *mechanisms* behind a phenomenon that are useful for a design. For example, CLT is valuable in principle because it helps a designer reason about different types of

---

[1]We are writing this paper to the philosophy of science prior knowledge we expect most readers to have. This overlooks important and varied philosophical and epistemelogical issues; for example, Hedstrom et al. review the mechanism-based approach to explanatory theory [18], which is a major but only one among several approaches. We believe considering these issues would lead to stronger critical views on use of theory and higher standards for use of explanatory theory in our field (i.e. beyond the "we should consider falsifiability when choosing theories" we later argue).

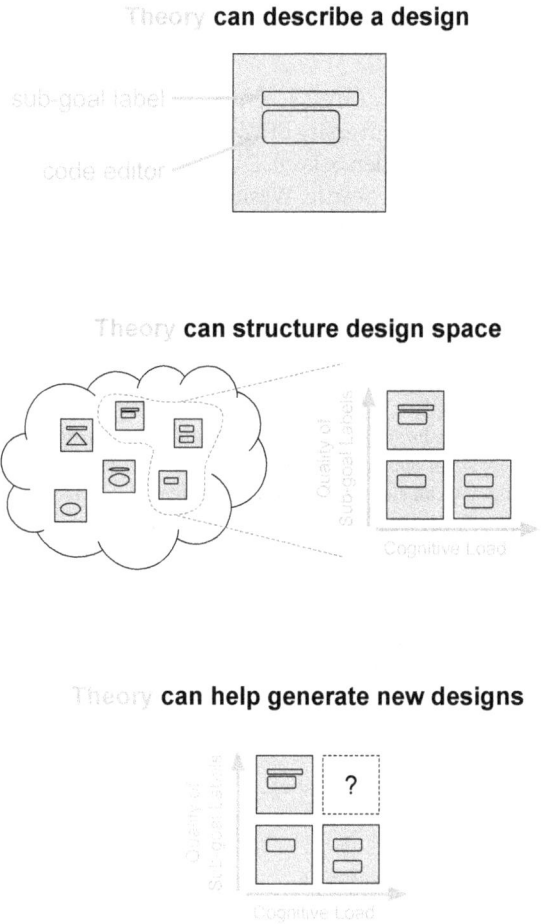

can describe a design

can structure design space

can help generate new designs

Figure 1: Theory aids design inquiry by helping us describe designs, structure the design space, and generate new designs.

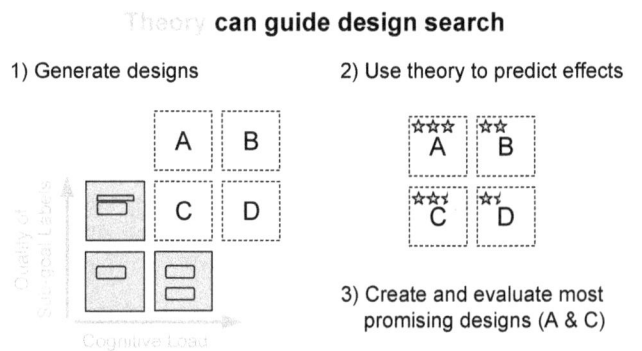

can guide design search

1) Generate designs   2) Use theory to predict effects

3) Create and evaluate most promising designs (A & C)

Figure 2: Our field may speed up our design search by prioritizing which designs to build and test based on theoretical predictions of their effects (if the predictions are accurate).

load (e.g., intrinsic, extraneous, and germane) and make predictions about which type of load a design is imposing. If CLT's predictions are correct in general, and a designer's interpretation of a design's various kinds of load are sound with respect to the theory, a designer may predict their design's effects on load without empirically testing their design's effects. Thus, a designer should be able to more rapidly refine the instructional materials they design, as they don't need to wait for empirical testing as they iterate. Recent applications of CLT do exactly this, proposing more rapid methods of instructional design through theory [39].

Theories can also be useful to interpret why a design has failed. For example, CLT provides the concepts necessary to explain why the split attention effect [6] (in which multiple types of information presented in the same modality) interferes with learning. In the same way, when we test new designs for worked examples that have mixed benefits, CLT can offer useful concepts in interpreting why those benefits were mixed.

Within computing education, the use of CLT has offered all of these benefits to our collective search for effective worked examples of programming. It has helped us name and generate new points in a design space of worked examples for computing (e.g., [17, 35]) and it has helped us explain the outcomes of evaluations of worked example designs[2] (e.g., [13, 42]). In these respects, it has focused our community's design efforts, it has helped us build upon our own work, and it has helped us build upon more general theories of learning and education.

3 HOW THEORY CAN INHIBIT DESIGN PROGRESS

While theory has clearly been useful in computing education research, we have observed three ways in which it may also inhibit our search for effective designs for learning. In this section, we present these three forms of inhibition, then in the next section, provide concrete recommendations for how to avoid them.

3.1 Tensions between explanation and design

Ultimately, the goal of design exploration is *breadth* of investigation: by considering many design alternatives, and their numerous tradeoffs, designers are better positioned to find optimal ways for people to learn computing. In contrast, the pursuit of explanatory theory such as CLT promotes *depth* of investigation of design, identifying and measuring the causal mechanisms that explain learning outcomes and broader effects[3] of learning. Achieving this depth of explanation essentially requires holding designs more fixed, so we may deeply understand the mechanisms behind their benefits. Our community's joint interest in breadth and depth creates tensions and trade-offs in research. We will consider these tensions from both perspectives.

3.1.1 Design goals undermine explanation goals. To make high-quality tests of explanations, we need to make high-quality validated measures for them. The time we spend broadly exploring innovative designs takes resources away from building these validated measures. Consider, for example, the series of papers by

Morrison et al. on worked examples. This work began with some investment in measurement depth by building a validated measure of cognitive load [44], but it was largely followed by broad design explorations [37, 42], at the expense of addressing the measurement issues that may have led to some of the inconclusive explanatory results reported in their papers (learning outcomes varied for the designs but their cognitive load had little to no difference). This balance of design and explanation that Morrison et al. chose is not inherently good or bad; rather, it is an example of the inherent tradeoff between pursuing deep explanations and innovative designs.

This tradeoff can also lead to problematic split attention. To properly build upon the bodies of evidence related to design and explanation, we must apply limited resources to reading papers about both domain-specific design innovations we publish in our own community, but also papers on the general theories being refined in learning and education research. Because our time to read is limited, every paper we read about design is a paper we do not read about the explanatory theories that inform design. While as researchers we might hope we take time to read deeply, the fact that we need to read two bodies of knowledge can change what we even perceive as sufficient depth, given the reality of our limited resources.

One concrete manifestation of this split attention on reading is that we miss ongoing critical debates about the theories we choose to use. For example, there is active debate about CLT in the learning science community about CLT's falsifiability. (A theory is falsifiable if someone can conduct an experiment and, in principle, observe outcomes that contradict predictions by the theory, thus demonstrating the causal mechanisms cannot explain those outcomes [50]). Recent work in the learning science community argues that cognitive load theory is actually not falsifiable[4] [11, 41]. If a theory is unfalsifiable, experiments with explanatory goals may always appear to validate the theory, because an unfalsifiable theory cannot be disproved (at most, results might appear inconclusive). Falsifiability should thus be an important factor in choosing which theories we use[5]. We have found no papers from our community that cite or discuss CLT's falsifiability debate among the 22 papers published

---

[2]Ericson et al. [13] is also an example of design-based research, a research method that tries to balance iterative design exploration and theory.
[3]See introduction paragraph 1, e.g. identity development, equity, self-efficacy.

[4]CLT (which can only measure *total* cognitive load with independent validity) is unfalsifiable because it can explain any observed outcome (see [11, 14, 41] for fuller arguments and other difficulties). To illustrate, if an experiment compares two designs and observes higher cognitive load and higher learning outcomes for one design, a researcher can suggest that there was higher intrinsic load to explain outcomes. If the observation was higher load and lower outcomes, one can suggest there was higher extraneous load to explain outcomes. For lower load and lower outcomes, one suggests there was lower intrinsic load, and for lower load and higher outcomes, one suggests there was less extraneous load. Thus, CLT can explain any observable outcomes of total cognitive load and learning outcomes. If a measure could distinguish between the components, the theory could be falsified; however, all validated ways of measuring cognitive load components assume their relationship with learning outcomes during their development and validation [14].
[5]Popper's notion of falsifiability is seen as problematic among most present-day philosophers of science; for example, the Duhem-Quine thesis argues that even if an experiment's results contradict a theory's prediction, one cannot deduce the theory is flawed (perhaps the design used was not analyzed properly with the theory, perhaps the experimental design was flawed, etc.). Beyond falsification, more nuanced sociocultural perspectives have richer notions of scientific practice [26]. We leaves as important future work deeper engagement with these philosophical issues (including explanatory theory and issues with naive empiricism), which is critical for informing recommendations on appropriate theory use in our field. For an example in another community, the papers criticizing CLT engage with these issues and use more modern perspectives [11, 14, 41]. On the limits of falsifiability, see [21] as an accessible example.

Research with:	Fixed Resources for:			Contribution to:	
	Design	Explanation	Experiment	Explanation	Design
Explanatory Goals Only	Reuse a prior design	*Make design variations to test theory *Rigorous experimental design	Measure designs and theory factors	⬤	○
Explanatory & Design Goals	Generate 2 designs inspired by theory	Design experiment to test tiny part of theory	Measure design 1 and theory factors	◯	◯
Design Goals Only	*Generate 4 designs *Describe systematic design refinement	Reuse prior theory	Measure design 1 & 4	○	⬤

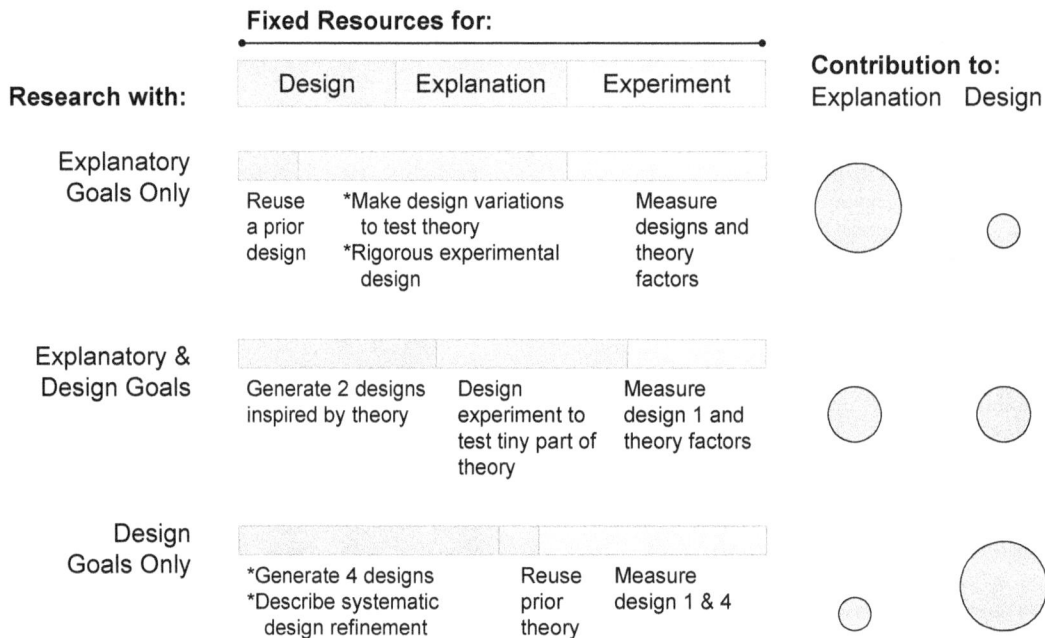

Figure 3: Splitting attention between design goals and explanation goals may lead to work with shallower contributions and less overall contribution.

in our community on CLT (counted via a search of the ACM Digital Library under SIGCSE's conferences for "cognitive load").

Splitting our attention between design and explanation goals may also lead to missed opportunities to do deeper explanatory work, as our community also has not engaged in such debates. Compared to the 22 papers published in our community on CLT, we only found two papers by computing education researchers who published in the learning science communities about CLT [35, 37] and two in the educational psychology community[36, 38]. This engagement has come mostly in the form of confirming CLT, and not in sharing contradictory evidence with the broader learning science or educational psychology community to inform the broader falsifiability debate. For example, CLT generally explains differences in learning outcomes via differences in cognitive load; it generally predicts higher cognitive load will reduce learning. However, in our community, three studies measured learning outcomes and cognitive load with a validated instrument for different designs [44]. They saw differences in learning gains with little to no difference in cognitive load, and reported those to our community, with some potential theoretical explanations framed within CLT [34, 42, 43]. We are unaware of work sharing these conflicting results with the broader learning sciences community, nor the educational psychology community.

Again, we are not arguing that these authors' individual choices of how and whether to engage in this debate are inherently good or bad. Rather, it reveals a fundamental tension between the goals of design and explanation, and how that tension leads to missed opportunities for deeper explanatory work on CLT.

3.1.2 Explanation goals undermine design goals. Taking the opposite view, when we pursue deeper theoretical explanations, we

tend to limit our design exploration. This occurs for a few reasons. First, because the pursuit of deeper theoretical accounts of a design's effects can be done with *sufficiently effective* designs, there is no incentive to pursue *optimally effective* designs. For example, the community's work on CLT *can* be done with the worked example designs originally published by Morrison et al. [42], and so it largely has been, at the expense of more radical interpretations of what constitutes a worked example for programming problems.

A second way that explanatory goals inhibit design exploration is that we may not explore designs because it is unclear theoretically why they might work. This deters the exploration of designs that do not yet have a theoretical justification, even though those designs might be objectively better in a way we cannot yet explain.

In summary, our community's joint interest in breadth for design and depth for explanation creates tensions and trade-offs in research, given our fixed resources. Figure 3 illustrates these tensions by contrasting hypothetical research examples with explanatory or design goals only, and a mix of both.

3.2 Less effort towards domain-specific theory
One effect of our community grappling with the tensions between explanation and design is that we may contribute less time to advancing our own domain-specific theories of computer science learning. For example, these theories might include theories of what it means to know a programming language, what it means to know how to program, what it means to be an expert software engineer, what it means to have computer science literacy, and numerous other unanswered and yet foundational questions that are specific to computing education. These theories are critical to design progress in our field, because, without them, we cannot

know if we are making progress on our shared goal of helping people acquire and use such knowledge and expertise.

This lack of attention on domain-specific theory is particularly acute because of our community's limited research resources. While we have applied resources to making domain-specific validated measures for constructs from general theories like cognitive load [44], the volume of this work, in past decades, shows we have mostly applied resources towards general theories of learning and identity, while overlooking major gaps in our domain-specific theories of the content of computing knowledge. This trend is clear in Malmi et al.'s literature review of theory use covering 2005-2011, which found that we use external theories frequently [32]: of papers referencing theory, 60% reference theory from Education, Psychology, or other parent disciplines, compared to 16% using theories created from within computing education.

While some use of general theory may help us, it may also divert resources from one of the most critical gaps in our field: domain-specific theories of the knowledge of computing we want people to learn. Little work has proposed such theories; only recently, Nelson et al. have proposed one for program tracing knowledge [45], and Loksa et al. have proposed one for programming problem solving [31]. Some theoretical work (such as [54]) has considered program dynamics as a threshold concept, proposing a mechanism to explain the large variation in outcomes for learning programming; this kind of nascent theory of knowledge may develop with more work into part of a theory relating conceptual knowledge and the ability to learn programming skills. Other partial work towards a theory of knowledge includes work on learning trajectories (paths from initial knowledge to deeper knowledge), though recent work still lacks direct observations and instead is based on aggregating results from the scholarly literature [52].

Not only do we lack theories of computing knowledge, but critical for evaluating designs, we also lack robust, validated measurements of this knowledge. Some work has advanced towards concept inventories for computer science [12, 46], drawing inspiration from work in other domain-specific research communities such as physics [58]. Concept inventories attempt to validly assess core topics rather than covering a broad theory of knowledge in an area, so they might also act as steps towards broader theories of knowledge. Within this genre the FCS1 [12] and SCS1 [46] are major points of progress, as they show some feasibility for language-independent validated assessments. Their validity argument extended a classic approach in education research to model knowledge that builds on existing teaching practices - 1) start with how a subject is taught today (here, CS1 textbooks), 2) synthesize a conceptual theory of the knowledge [59], and 3) validate the theory and a test specification for it with a panel of experts. This socially validates that the FCS1 and SCS1 measure something like what CS1 textbooks cover and CS1 finals and midterms measure, and represents a sophisticated validity argument and methodology that education researchers have taken years to develop.

While our community can make progress by using such methods and conceptual domain-specific theories of CS knowledge, when we build conceptual theory starting from existing practice, we somewhat assume that current practice actually works. However, it might be that some learners "figure out" tacit unsaid knowledge to succeed (for example, in CS1), which is not actually covered in textbooks or the class itself. This can lead to gaps in our domain-specific knowledge theories that are hard to see.

As CER researchers we might lead education research by representing knowledge beyond the conceptual level, as programs or with other formal representations; these more formal domain-specific theories might potentially lead to better assessments and designs for learning. For example, we have tried building a nascent formal theory of program tracing knowledge as knowing all paths through the compiler program for a language [45]; this uses a formal programming language to represent the knowledge. One can argue for validity of a formal knowledge theory by showing a computer can use that representation to perform tasks that require that knowledge (for example, we know that a compiler program can trace programs because we use them all the time to execute programs). This forces the knowledge theory to be complete and potentially more decomposable; it is less clear when a conceptual theory is truly complete. Formal domain-specific theory might inform assessment creation; for example, our nascent formal theory of program tracing knowledge could inform a more complete assessment for program tracing by requiring test questions that cover each path. Formal domain-specific theory may also inform design; for example, we also used our nascent formal theory to gain insight into what knowledge needs to be shown to learners, leading to a new design for teaching tracing that shows more detailed connections between AST tokens and program execution [45]. These examples are just for tracing, and we hope the community will work on others as well.

Ultimately, without domain-specific theories of computing knowledge, we cannot know when we are making progress on design. We need these theories and measurements to compare the designs we create across standard measurements. We need validated measurements to be confident in our results. And we need theories of the knowledge to make clear to both researchers and teachers precisely what knowledge we are helping learners acquire. With our community's limited resources, when we choose to advance non-domain specific theories, we make less progress on our critically necessary domain-specific theories.

3.3 Publication bias in peer review

While theory can bias what work we choose to do and what work we read, it can also bias how we evaluate each others' work. In particular, we argue that when theory is used as a critical lens in reviewing publications about innovative designs, we are at risk of rejecting papers that describe designs that may be valuable but cannot yet be explained theoretically. This ultimately reduces the breadth of design exploration as well as the base of published evidence for building and testing new or alternative explanatory theories.

To substantiate this publication bias, let us consider one case of a paper being rejected for its use of CLT as a theoretical framework. Because these are the critiques of just one case, we are *not* arguing that these peer review criteria are pervasive in our community. Rather we use this case to highlight the potential for more widespread publication bias, if such rationales were to become prevalent. We will show that the negative consequences of such bias are sufficiently severe that a single case of the review and meta-reviewing process failing to catch this is cause for concern and discussion.

In our original submission, we shared excerpts from reviews that an anonymous author had shared with us for use in this analysis; none of the authors of our paper were on or involved in that work. However, the ICER program chairs would not let us list quotes from these reviews or paraphrased quotes out of concerns for the potential impact on reviewers, and so we explain the reviews' arguments here in our own words.

The reviews concern a paper contributing a system that used a design genre from CLT (worked examples), prototyped a new design, and performed two studies: 1) a randomized comparison with a large sample size of the system vs. existing practice materials that had mixed results and 2) a large in-the-wild self-selected "open to students to use" evaluation showing positive effects. This paper was submitted as a CS education research paper to ICER twice, SIGCSE once, and rejected each time. There were not substantive issues with the paper's evaluation, in fact one meta-review noted a consensus among the reviewers that the experimental design was good, with random assignment and a large sample size.

This paper was rejected for several reasons, many of these reasons using CLT as a critical lens. One CLT critique in the reviews was that *a theoretically-framed design evaluation must produce results that support the theory*. More specifically, in this case CLT predicted a design with worked examples should do better, but instead the empirical results of the paper were mixed. Reviews praised the study design and the paper's aims to build on theory, noted the paper would have been a good "reproducing" experiment if it had positive results, and ultimately emphasized the results were only promising and that the system's design seemed different from work that had found positive results.

Rejecting work with this rationale impedes both design and theory progress. First, if peer review requires that a design framed from a CLT perspective must produce positive results in support of CLT, we will never share evidence about designs that provide evidence *against* CLT, losing insight about how the theory might be refined. Second, if we do not publish designs that work poorly, our community risks wasting resources on re-implementing and re-evaluating designs that have already been explored. Third, sharing novel designs with non-optimal effects also may inspire designs with improved effects. Finally, this critique undervalues studies that compare existing designs, even when those comparisons reveal no differences.

A second CLT critique was that *a design should be consistent with the recommendations of the theory*. More specifically, in this case the logic was that, since the design followed some recommendations from CLT, but it had mixed results, the design should be revised to follow all the recommendations and re-evaluated. Reviews noted the system's design lacked sub-goals and self-explanation steps and did not seem to fit recommendations that prior research made for designing worked examples. Reviews went so far as questioning if the system's "worked examples" met theoretical criteria for being a worked example, and raised issues with interpreting the results as related to CLT and worked examples.

If we were to follow this criteria in peer review, we would not publish designs that contradict theories, which would otherwise allow us to refine or reject theories via new evidence. Additionally, rejecting papers that explore new design variations that go beyond a theory's current recommendations prevents us from discovering designs that might be superior to existing ones and from generating new and improved theories. This policy thus shrinks the space of design search to only designs compatible with existing theories, and precludes the refinement of CLT. In fact, the critique that *a design should be consistent with the recommendations of the theory* means that a design must exhaustively meet the recommendations of theory in order for negative results to be publishable (otherwise, the reviews will say to "improve your design and resubmit"); this creates a potentially insurmountable burden of proof for publishing conflicting evidence.

A third critique was that *an evaluation that does not provide a causal account of positive results is not worth sharing*. Reviews generally praised the methodology for the randomized part of the evaluation with mixed results, which had a stronger causal interpretation. In contrast, reviews criticized that the positive results in the observational evaluation came from a self-selected group of learners, while acknowledging the paper highlighted that fact in its discussion. Reviews expressed concerns focusing on potential confounders to causal interpretations of results: 1) learners opted-in to using the system for extra practice, making it vulnerable to self-selection bias, and 2) observed differences might come from the system or other factors, such as from unmeasured individual factors such as prior knowledge or field of study. Reviews also wanted more causal interpretability for the evaluation as a whole, criticizing that the system was only studied at one institution with its own potential contextual factors, the analysis explained little of the overall variation in exam scores, and the potential for a ceiling effect in the evaluation tasks. The potential for misinterpretation of the observational results by readers was also raised in the reviews.

This critique inhibits design exploration in several ways. First, it prevents the sharing of designs that may produce real effects of learning, but that cannot yet be explained by existing theories[6]. This biases our evidence base toward only designs with well-explained effects. Second, only publishing designs with a clear benefit (rather than just promise) creates a harmful incentive to design simpler interventions with measurable but incremental gains, rather than exploring more radical, innovative designs that have the potential to improve learning, but may take multiple publications to refine and systematically measure benefits. Third, many designs may actually be deployed for discretionary use (a self-selected setting) or even designed specifically for discretionary use; devaluing empirical studies of discretionary use creates barriers to building design knowledge on how to improve the effects of learning in discretionary contexts.

These three uses of theory in peer review —reviewers judging that a) a theoretically-framed design evaluation must produce results that support the theory, b) a design should be consistent with the recommendations of the theory, and/or c) an evaluation that does not provide a causal account of positive results is not worth sharing — ultimately inhibit the breadth of design exploration, which, in turn, may inhibit the learning gains and broader effects of learning we can achieve through better design. They also severely limit our ability to falsify theories that are actually inaccurate and

---

[6]This is particularly an issue for broader effects of learning, see introduction paragraph 1, e.g. identity development, equity, self-efficacy.

impede our ability to evaluate, refine, and build new theory by restricting the available evidence.

Fundamentally, these peer review critiques confuse the relationship between theory and a body of evidence: a body of evidence tells us if a theory is meaningful and useful, not the other way around. Observations of designs and their immediate and broader effects are *inherently* valuable to progress on improved designs, whether they are consistent with existing theories or not.

While we present only one actual paper here (as we cannot sample or search all peer reviews), unless we resist these uses of theory in peer review, they have the potential to seriously restrict and bias the base of evidence used for creating and evaluating theories, as well as our community's search for better designs.

4 IMPLICATIONS

While theory can help our search for effective designs, we have argued that it can also inhibit design progress by creating tensions between design and explanation, lowering investment in domain-specific theories of computing knowledge, and biasing peer review. In this section we make recommendations for how to avoid these problems.

4.1 Focus on design and use theory as a guide

First, we believe our community should wholeheartedly commit to focusing on design and not on refining general theories of learning. First, general learning researchers will be best at refining general theories of learning. Second, our community has carefully cultivated skills and knowledge for creating domain-specific designs that improve computing learning outcomes and broader effects of learning computing. Third, other learning research communities lack these skills, and are therefore unlikely to make design advances in computing. In summary, our skills uniquely position us to make designs to improve effects[7] of learning in our domain; others cannot do this work.

By committing to design, we can focus our use of theory on guiding design. We should use theory as a guide for selecting designs to explore, as just one of many sources of insight to guide design. These sources include: prior designs (even in other domains), theory, intuition, experience, learner and teacher insights, and iterative and qualitative methods. Design-based research methods from the learning sciences use theory as a guide and include iterative testing of design hypotheses [1, 3, 5, 8]; these methods may also help bridge domain-specific education research and broader education research [48]. However, this method can favor starting with existing theory, which may limit radical design exploration and the creation of new theories. As our community explores these and other methods [40, 49, 55], we should not privilege conformance with or explanation via theory, as this reduces the potential positive impact of other ways to guide design. If someone made an argument based on strong evidence that theory performs better as a guide, perhaps we should privilege it relative to other ways to guide design, but not before we consider and debate that argument as a community, and not at the expense of other valuable sources of insight.

In our use of theory as a guide, we should explicitly read ongoing debates about theory in their communities of origin, so that we use theory with full awareness of its strengths and weaknesses. We should incentivize deeper reading by encouraging papers that take a large body of work on one or more theories and distills it to make it accessible and actionable for our research on designs and to guide design search. We should extend the page lengths of our archival venues to allow for discussion of such nuance.

4.2 Invest in CER-specific theories and validated measures for effects of learning

In addition to focusing our use of theory as a guide, we should recognize that improved effects of learning are the ultimate guide and indicator of progress for our community's design search. Therefore, we should invest significant resources in building domain-specific theories and measures of those effects (especially computing knowledge) so that we may use them as indicators of progress. These theories include: 1) domain-specific theories and validated measures of what people want to learn about computing, providing a map for the community's design efforts, 2) domain-specific theories and measures of effects of learning like self-efficacy, motivation, identity development, improved quality of life, and equity in outcomes and society (even when they are more difficult to measure and evaluate), and 3) theories of external validity, relating these measures to professional performance and achievement of wider goals that learners have, within and beyond computer science. Better measures of all of these effects (such as learning gains) may even help us gather more resources as a community, providing a return on invested effort.

4.3 Do not use theory or evaluation results as a barrier to publishing novel designs

As we use theory as a guide in design exploration, we should not use theory as a barrier to publication. We should at least publish novel designs with objectively promising benefits, regardless of their theoretical framing. This practice prioritizes building a broad design body of knowledge faster by removing publication barriers. There are three important reasons to do this. First, more radical, innovative designs that have the potential to improve learning may take multiple publications to refine and systematically measure benefits. Second, sharing novel designs with non-optimal effects also may inspire designs with improved effects. Third, if we do not publish designs, our community risks wasting resources on re-implementing and re-evaluating designs that have already been explored.

The same three reasons above actually support publishing *all* novel designs, not just those with measurable benefits. We should trust that our community will not try to game the system and make up novel designs for the sole sake of publication; those strategies will not work well in the long term anyway, as they will not result in convincing letters for tenure cases, job applications, or other career advancement. We might *worry* that such abuse will happen, but we *know* real harms occur from not publishing designs, as we argued above and as we showed in our section on publication bias.

Even more radical than publishing all novel designs, we believe we should not require all designs to have theoretical framing or

---

[7]Broadly defined, see introduction paragraph 1, e.g. identity development, equity, self-efficacy.

rationale. Requiring these actually inhibits both design exploration as well as the development and evaluation of theory, by restricting what designs we share. Moreover, it encourages researchers to generate unhelpful post-hoc design rationale just to satisfy a design rationale requirement. This can also cloud our understanding of how we actually design and what helps design in practice, which limits our ability to improve how we design.

One way to implement these recommendations is to create new tracks for work at publication venues. The publication threshold already varies by publication venue and track; for example, the "Experience Reports and Tools" track at SIGCSE and the "Innovative Practice" track at Frontiers in Education (FIE) invite work without formal experimental evaluations.

However, multiple tracks alone is not a solution to the issues raised in this paper. First, even within a track, the publication threshold may vary in an ad hoc way among reviewers, creating unseen publication bias that may harm our community's design progress. Second, even if we had consistent reviewing within tracks, separate tracks can encourage rejecting work that pushes boundaries or tries to improve an aspect of their contribution without meeting the bar for high quality work in that area; for example, having a non-randomized quantitative evaluation (instead of a "student's liked it" evaluation [61]) may make an experience report seem more like a research paper with a lower-quality evaluation. Third, reviewers may reject work for "being in the wrong track", authors may revise then submit it to another track, only to have it rejected there again for "being in the wrong track". While it is only one case, this actually happened to the worked examples paper we discussed in our peer review section (it was rejected from the Experience Report track at SIGCSE, and ICER twice). In summary, our community should discuss publication thresholds and how to help reviewers achieve consistency pragmatically, in order to improve design progress and build a broader unbiased evidence base.

4.4 Improve support for and audit peer review

We hope that these peer-reviewing biases in the previous section and in section 3.3 are not prevalent in our community, but, upon reflection, our community has little way to know this because peer reviews are not shared widely. Moreover, individual peer reviewers cannot see the aggregate effects of their critiques on our field. Therefore, to gain awareness of biases in our empirical knowledge base, our journal editorial boards and conference steering committees should conduct qualitative studies of the reasons that papers are rejected for publication, using best practices for such studies (such as multiple raters, calculating inter-rater reliability, and blinding each review's author and the paper under review). The results should also be given to individual reviewers for each specific paper they review, to check the results and so they can reflect on their reviewing process. The final anonymized data (and any conflicts) should be published publicly along with a paper interpreting the data.

In summary, we strongly recommend the computing education research community:

(1) Focus on design, domain-specific theories of learning, and validated measures of effects of learning.

(2) Publish work that distills theory from other fields to make it actionable for design and guiding design search.

(3) Publish all novel designs with some promise of improving outcomes.

(4) Publish all novel designs that future work might build on to then actually improve learning.

(5) Publish all novel designs that appear not to work well that other researchers might recreate, to avoid wasted effort.

(6) Conduct a periodic qualitative study of the critiques used in peer review in our community to detect and mitigate bias.

We face an urgent need to scale learning of computing in a changing world. While CLT and other theories have greatly matured computing education research, it is time to view theory as just one powerful way among many to guide our community's design inquiry.

5 ACKNOWLEDGEMENTS

This material is based upon work supported by Microsoft, Google, Adobe, and the National Science Foundation (Grant No. 12566082, 1539179, 1314399, 1314399, and 1153625). We thank the anonymous authors of the rejected worked examples paper and their candor in discussing their paper. We thank the reviewers for their deep engagement and constructive feedback, which we hope to incorporate more of in future work. We thank Briana Morrison and Mark Guzdial for discussions and doing some of the highest quality theory-based work in our field. We recognize the benefit researchers have brought to our community when using theory well and thank them for their contributions. Likewise, we thank you, the reader, for your time and care in reading (and critical discussion).

REFERENCES

[1] Terry Anderson and Julie Shattuck. 2012. Design-Based Research: A Decade of Progress in Education Research? *Educational Researcher* 41, 1 (2012), 16–25. https://doi.org/10.3102/0013189X11428813 arXiv:https://doi.org/10.3102/0013189X11428813

[2] Robert K. Atkinson, Sharon J. Derry, Alexander Renkl, and Donald Wortham. 2000. Learning from Examples: Instructional Principles from the Worked Examples Research. *Review of Educational Research* 70, 2 (2000), 181–214.

[3] Sasha Barab and Kurt Squire. 2004. Design-Based Research: Putting a Stake in the Ground. *Journal of the Learning Sciences* 13, 1 (2004), 1–14. https://doi.org/10.1207/s15327809jls1301_1 arXiv:https://doi.org/10.1207/s15327809jls1301_1

[4] Julian M Bass, Roger McDermott, and JT Lalchandani. 2015. Virtual teams and employability in global software engineering education. In *Global Software Engineering (ICGSE), 2015 IEEE 10th International Conference on*. IEEE, 115–124.

[5] Philip Bell. 2004. On the Theoretical Breadth of Design-Based Research in Education. *Educational Psychologist* 39, 4 (2004), 243–253. https://doi.org/10.1207/s15326985ep3904_6 arXiv:https://doi.org/10.1207/s15326985ep3904_6

[6] Paul Chandler and John Sweller. 1992. The split-attention effect as a factor in the design of instruction. *British Journal of Educational Psychology* 62, 2 (1992), 233–246.

[7] Tony Clear. 2011. Doctoral work in computing education research. *ACM Inroads* 4, 2 (jun 2011), 28. https://doi.org/10.1145/2465085.2465092

[8] Allan Collins, Diana Joseph, and Katerine Bielaczyc. 2004. Design Research: Theoretical and Methodological Issues. *Journal of the Learning Sciences* 13, 1 (2004), 15–42. https://doi.org/10.1207/s15327809jls1301_2 arXiv:https://doi.org/10.1207/s15327809jls1301_2

[9] Kathryn Cunningham, Sarah Blanchard, Barbara Ericson, and Mark Guzdial. 2017. Using Tracing and Sketching to Solve Programming Problems: Replicating and Extending an Analysis of What Students Draw. In *2017 ACM Conference on International Computing Education Research*. ACM, 164–172.

[10] Holger Danielsiek, Laura Toma, and Jan Vahrenhold. 2017. An Instrument to Assess Self-Efficacy in Introductory Algorithms Courses. In *2017 ACM Conference on International Computing Education Research*. ACM, 217–225.

[11] Ton de Jong. 2010. Cognitive load theory, educational research, and instructional design: Some food for thought. *Instructional Science* 38, 2 (2010), 105–134.

[12] Allison Elliott Tew. 2010. Assessing fundamental introductory computing concept knowledge in a language independent manner. December 2010 (2010), 147. http://search.proquest.com/docview/873212789?accountid=14696

[13] Barbara J Ericson, Kantwon Rogers, Miranda C Parker, Briana B Morrison, and Mark Guzdial. 2016. Identifying Design Principles for CS Teacher Ebooks through Design-Based Research.. In *ICER*. 191–200.

[14] Peter Gerjets, Katharina Scheiter, and Gabriele Cierniak. 2009. The scientific value of cognitive load theory: A research agenda based on the structuralist view of theories. *Educational Psychology Review* 21, 1 (2009), 43–54. https://doi.org/10.1007/s10648-008-9096-1 arXiv:arXiv:astro-ph/0507464v2

[15] Susannah Go and Brian Dorn. 2016. Thanks for Sharing: CS Pedagogical Content Knowledge Sharing in Online Environments. In *WiPSCE '16 (WiPSCE '16)*. ACM, New York, NY, USA, 27–36. https://doi.org/10.1145/2978249.2978253

[16] Shirley Gregor. 2006. The nature of theory in Information Systems. *MIS Quarterly: Management Information Systems* 30, 3 (2006), 611–642. https://doi.org/10.2307/25148742

[17] Jean M Griffin. 2016. Learning by taking apart: deconstructing code by reading, tracing, and debugging. In *Conference on Information Technology Education*. ACM, 148–153.

[18] Peter Hedström and Petri Ylikoski. 2010. Causal Mechanisms in the Social Sciences. *Annual Review of Sociology* 36, 1 (2010), 49–67. https://doi.org/10.1146/annurev.soc.012809.102632

[19] Maya Israel, Quentin M Wherfel, Saadeddine Shehab, Oliver Melvin, and Todd Lash. 2017. Describing Elementary Students' Interactions in K-5 Puzzle-based Computer Science Environments using the Collaborative Computing Observation Instrument (C-COI). In *2017 ACM Conference on International Computing Education Research*. ACM, 110–117.

[20] Betsy James DiSalvo, Sarita Yardi, Mark Guzdial, Tom McKlin, Charles Meadows, Kenneth Perry, and Amy Bruckman. 2011. African American men constructing computing identity. In *CHI '11*. ACM, 2967–2970.

[21] Ashutosh Jogalekar. 2014. Falsification and its discontents. *Scientific American* (2014). https://blogs.scientificamerican.com/the-curious-wavefunction/falsification-and-its-discontents/

[22] Yasmin B Kafai and Mitchel Resnick. 1996. *Constructionism in practice: Designing, thinking, and learning in a digital world*. Routledge.

[23] Andrew J Ko. 2009. Attitudes and self-efficacy in young adults' computing autobiographies. In *IEEE Symposium on Visual Languages and Human-Centric Computing*. IEEE, IEEE, New Jersey, 67–74.

[24] Andrew J Ko and Katie Davis. 2017. Computing Mentorship in a Software Boom-town: Relationships to Adolescent Interest and Beliefs. In *2017 ACM Conference on International Computing Education Research*. ACM, 236–244.

[25] Michael Kölling. 2010. The greenfoot programming environment. *ACM Transactions on Computing Education (TOCE)* 10, 4 (2010), 14.

[26] T.S. Kuhn. 1962. *The Structure of Scientific Revolutions*. University of Chicago Press. https://books.google.com/books?id=E6MJuAAACAAJ

[27] Michael J Lee and Andrew J Ko. 2012. Investigating the role of purposeful goals on novices' engagement in a programming game. In *Visual Languages and Human-Centric Computing (VL/HCC), 2012 IEEE Symposium on*. IEEE, 163–166.

[28] Michael J Lee, Andrew J Ko, and Irwin Kwan. 2013. In-game assessments increase novice programmers' engagement and level completion speed. In *ICER '13*. ACM, 153–160.

[29] Paul Luo Li, Andrew J Ko, and Jiamin Zhu. 2015. What makes a great software engineer?. In *37th International Conference on Software Engineering-Volume 1*. IEEE Press, 700–710.

[30] Alex Lishinski, Aman Yadav, and Richard Enbody. 2017. Students' Emotional Reactions to Programming Projects in Introduction to Programming: Measurement Approach and Influence on Learning Outcomes. In *2017 ACM Conference on International Computing Education Research*. ACM, 30–38.

[31] Dastyni Loksa, Andrew J Ko, Will Jernigan, Alannah Oleson, Christopher J Mendez, and Margaret M Burnett. 2016. Programming, Problem Solving, and Self-Awareness: Effects of Explicit Guidance. In *2016 CHI Conference on Human Factors in Computing Systems*. ACM, 1449–1461.

[32] Lauri Malmi, Ahmad Taherkhani, Judy Sheard, Roman Bednarik, Juha Helminen, Päivi Kinnunen, Ari Korhonen, Niko Myller, and Juha Sorva. 2014. Theoretical underpinnings of computing education research. *ICER '14* (2014), 27–34. https://doi.org/10.1145/2632320.2632358

[33] Jane Margolis and Allan Fisher. 2003. *Unlocking the clubhouse: Women in computing*. MIT press, Cambridge, MA.

[34] Lauren Margulieux and Richard Catrambone. 2017. Using Learners' Self-Explanations of Subgoals to Guide Initial Problem Solving in App Inventor. In *ICER '17*. ACM, 21–29.

[35] Lauren E. Margulieux and Richard Catrambone. 2016. Improving problem solving with subgoal labels in expository text and worked examples. *Learning and Instruction* 42, 2016 (apr 2016), 58–71.

[36] Lauren E. Margulieux, R. Catrambone, and M. Guzdial. 2013. Subgoal labeled worked examples improve K-12 teacher performance in computer programming training. *Proceedings of the 35th Annual Conference of the Cognitive Science Society*

[37] Lauren E. Margulieux, B.B. Morrison, M. Guzdial, and R. Catrambone. 2016. Training Learners to Self-Explain: Designing Instructions and Examples to Improve Problem Solving. *Proceedings of International Conference of the Learning Sciences* 1 (2016), 98–105.

[38] M. Margulieux, L. E., Catrambone, R., & Guzdial. 2012. Subgoals improve performance in computer programming construction tasks. In *Proceedings of the EARLI SIG 6&7 Conference*. 60–62.

[39] Raina Mason, Graham Cooper, Barry Wilks, et al. 2016. Flipping the Assessment of Cognitive Load: Why and How. In *ICER '16*. ACM, 43–52.

[40] Mary J. Melrose. 2001. Maximizing the Rigor of Action Research: Why Would You Want To? How Could You? *Field Methods* 13, 2 (2001), 160–180. https://doi.org/10.1177/1525822X0101300203 arXiv:https://doi.org/10.1177/1525822X0101300203

[41] Roxana Moreno. 2010. Cognitive load theory: more food for thought. *Instructional Science* 38, 2 (2010), 135–141. https://doi.org/10.1007/s11251-009-9122-9

[42] Briana Morrison, Lauren Margulieux, and Mark Guzdial. 2015. Subgoals, Context, and Worked Examples in Learning Computing Problem Solving. In *Proceedings of the eleventh annual International Conference on International Computing Education Research - ICER '15*. ACM Press, 267–268. https://doi.org/10.1145/2787622.2787744

[43] Briana B. Morrison. 2017. Dual Modality Code Explanations for Novices. *ICER '17* (2017), 226–235. https://doi.org/10.1145/3105726.3106191

[44] Briana B. Morrison, Brian Dorn, and Mark Guzdial. 2014. Measuring cognitive load in introductory CS. *ICER '14* (2014), 131–138. https://doi.org/10.1145/2632320.2632348

[45] Greg L Nelson, Benjamin Xie, and Andrew J Ko. 2017. Comprehension First: Evaluating a Novel Pedagogy and Tutoring System for Program Tracing in CS1. *thirteenth International Workshop on Computing Education Research Workshop (ICER '17)* (2017), 42–51.

[46] Miranda C Parker and Mark Guzdial. 2016. Replication, validation, and use of a language independent CS1 knowledge assessment. *ICER* (2016), 93–101. https://doi.org/10.1145/2960310.2960316

[47] Hadi Partovi. 2015. A comprehensive effort to expand access and diversity in computer science. *ACM Inroads* 6, 3 (2015), 67–72.

[48] Melanie Peffer, Maggie Renken, and Debra Tomanek. 2016. Practical Strategies for Collaboration across Discipline-Based Education Research and the Learning Sciences. *CBEâĂŤLife Sciences Education* 15, 4 (2016), es11. https://doi.org/10.1187/cbe.15-12-0252 arXiv:https://doi.org/10.1187/cbe.15-12-0252 PMID: 27881446.

[49] Ken Peffers, Tuure Tuunanen, Marcus Rothenberger, and Samir Chatterjee. 2007. A Design Science Research Methodology for Information Systems Research. *J. Manage. Inf. Syst.* 24, 3 (Dec. 2007), 45–77. https://doi.org/10.2753/MIS0742-1222240302

[50] Karl R Popper. 1959. The logic of scientific discovery. (1959).

[51] Leo Porter, Dennis Bouvier, Quintin Cutts, Scott Grissom, Cynthia Lee, Robert McCartney, Daniel Zingaro, and Beth Simon. 2016. A multi-institutional study of peer instruction in introductory computing. *ACM Inroads* 7, 2 (2016), 76–81.

[52] Kathryn M. Rich, Carla Strickland, T. Andrew Binkowski, Cheryl Moran, and Diana Franklin. 2017. K-8 Learning Trajectories Derived from Research Literature: Sequence, Repetition, Conditionals. In *ICER '17*. ACM, 182–190. https://doi.org/10.1145/3105726.3106166

[53] Yvonne Rogers. 2012. HCI Theory: Classical, Modern, and Contemporary. *Synthesis Lectures on Human-Centered Informatics* 5, 2 (2012), 1–129. https://doi.org/10.2200/S00418ED1V01Y201205HCI014

[54] Juha Sorva. 2010. Reflections on threshold concepts in computer programming and beyond. *Koli Calling '10* (2010), 21–30. https://doi.org/10.1145/1930464.1930467

[55] Daniel Stokols. 2006. Toward a Science of Transdisciplinary Action Research. *American Journal of Community Psychology* 38, 1 (01 Sep 2006), 63–77. https://doi.org/10.1007/s10464-006-9060-5

[56] John Sweller. 2010. Element interactivity and intrinsic, extraneous, and germane cognitive load. *Educational Psychology Review* 22, 2 (2010), 123–138. https://doi.org/10.1007/s10648-010-9128-5 arXiv:arXiv:1002.2562v1

[57] John Sweller, Paul Ayres, and Slava Kalyuga. 2011. *Cognitive load theory*. Vol. 1. Springer.

[58] C. Taylor, D. Zingaro, L. Porter, K.C. Webb, C.B. Lee, and M. Clancy. 2014. Computer science concept inventories: past and future. *Computer Science Education* 24, 4 (2014), 253–276. https://doi.org/10.1080/08993408.2014.970779

[59] Allison Elliott Tew and Mark Guzdial. 2010. Developing a Validated Assessment of Fundamental CS1 Concepts. In *Proceedings of the 41st ACM Technical Symposium on Computer Science Education (SIGCSE '10)*. ACM, New York, NY, USA, 97–101. https://doi.org/10.1145/1734263.1734297

[60] Allison Elliott Tew and Mark Guzdial. 2011. The FCS1: a language independent assessment of CS1 knowledge. In *42nd ACM technical symposium on Computer science education*. ACM, 111–116.

[61] David W Valentine. 2004. CS educational research: a meta-analysis of SIGCSE technical symposium proceedings. *ACM SIGCSE Bulletin* 36, 1 (2004), 255–259. https://doi.org/10.1145/1028174.971391

Metacognitive Difficulties Faced by Novice Programmers in Automated Assessment Tools

James Prather
Abilene Christian University
Abilene, TX
jrp09a@acu.edu

Raymond Pettit
University of Virginia
Charlottesville, VA
raymond.pettit@gmail.com

Kayla McMurry, Alani Peters
USAA
San Antonio, TX
kayla.mcmurry,alani.peters@usaa.com

John Homer
Abilene Christian University
Abilene, TX
jdh08a@acu.edu

Maxine Cohen
Nova Southeastern University
Ft. Lauderdale, FL
cohenm@nova.edu

ABSTRACT

Most novice programmers are not explicitly aware of the problem-solving process used to approach programming problems and cannot articulate to an instructor where they are in that process. Many are now arguing that this skill, called metacognitive awareness, is crucial for novice learning. However, novices frequently learn in university CS1 courses that employ automated assessment tools (AATs), which are not typically designed to provide the cognitive scaffolding necessary for novices to develop metacognitive awareness. This paper reports on an experiment designed to understand what difficulties novice programmers currently face when learning to code with an AAT. We describe the experiences of CS1 students who participated in a think-aloud study where they were observed solving a programming problem with an AAT. Our observations show that some students mentally augmented the tool when it did not explicitly support their metacognitive awareness, while others stumbled due to the tool's lack of such support. We use these observations to formulate difficulties faced by novices that lack metacognitive awareness, compare these results to other related studies, and look toward future work in modifying AATs.

CCS CONCEPTS

• **Social and professional topics** → **CS1**; • **Human-centered computing** → **User studies**;

KEYWORDS

Education, CS1, automated assessment tools, HCI, human factors, metacognitive awareness

ACM Reference Format:
James Prather, Raymond Pettit, Kayla McMurry, Alani Peters, John Homer, and Maxine Cohen. 2018. Metacognitive Difficulties Faced by Novice Programmers in Automated Assessment Tools. In *ICER '18: 2018 International*

Computing Education Research Conference, August 13-15, 2018, Espoo, Finland.
ACM, New York, NY, USA, 10 pages. https://doi.org/10.1145/3230977.3230981

1 INTRODUCTION

Learning how to code involves more than just syntax and data structures; it also requires a mental scaffold around which a learner can correctly place knowledge and begin developing metacognitive awareness [19, 42, 53]. Metacognitive awareness is the ability not only to understand the problem but also to understand where one is in the problem-solving process and to reflect on that state. In his seminal 1945 book, *How To Solve It*, Polya identified four stages that learners move through while solving a math problem, hoping to make learners more explicitly aware of their movement [51]. When Dijkstra attempted to effect this four-stage process in his students, he told them, "Beautiful proofs are not 'found' by trial and error but are the result of a consciously applied design discipline" [13]. In order to be successful in the task of learning programming, novices must adapt these metacognitive strategies [57]. Despite this, most novice programmers lack metacognitive awareness [19], though sometimes the highest-performing novices display some aspects of metacognitive awareness, which could be a clue to their success in such a difficult discipline [8]. Most recently, Loksa et al. [40] investigated metacognitive awareness in novice programmers using a framework similar to Polya's. They identified six specific stages in learning to solve programming problems of which students should be aware: (1) *reinterpret the prompt*, (2) *search for analogous problems*, (3) *search for solutions*, (4) *evaluate a potential solution*, (5) *implement a solution*, (6) *evaluate implemented solution*. Loksa et al's approach was to explicitly coach students on these stages and help them identify which stage they were in when they became stuck. In this paper, we investigate the theoretical foundation of Loksa et al.'s proposal in an online learning setting via an automated assessment tool (AAT), looking for ways in which the tool itself could be built to support and help implicitly build a novice's metacognitive awareness. We report on a think-aloud study with CS1 students to observe their interactions with an AAT in order to better understand where AATs presently fail - and where AATs could be augmented - to help novice students build metacognitive awareness in CS1. Therefore, our research question is:

- **RQ:** What difficulties do novices who may lack metacognitive awareness face when using an AAT?

2 RELATED WORK

2.1 Automated Assessment Tools

Because this study's intervention centers on automated assessment tools, it is important to first consider their history and how they are currently designed with regard to supporting metacognitive awareness. In 1960, Hollingsworth created one of the first tools to automatically assess student programming assignments on punch cards [26]. Several hundred automated assessment tools have been created since then with varying levels of adoption [1, 14, 28, 29, 49]. Different tools focus on different aspects of automated assessment: some focus strictly on assessment, others are explicitly built to help novice students, and still others focus on test-driven development [17].

One feature consistently present in AATs that could cause novices to reflect on their location in the problem-solving process, and therefore help to build metacognitive awareness, is compiler error messages (CEMs). CEMs have long been documented as a recurrent source of confusion and frustration to students, and many AATs have been created to address this problem. Traver addresses problems with CEMs, highlighting some of the challenges in improving messages and showing many actual examples of the misleading messages that compilers produce [60]. Murphy et al. were part of a large multi-institution group analyzing debugging strategies of novice programmers [46]. Their observations from class sessions and one-on-one interviews make apparent the frustrations caused by misunderstanding errors in programming code. Finally, Marceau et al. discuss how poor error messages lead to student frustrations, which led Marceau et al. to create their AAT, DrRacket [43]. Furthermore, Marceau observes that some languages used to teach introductory programming, such as Alice [34] and Scratch [41] were created with a goal of protecting students from any possibility of creating syntax errors in their early programs. The rate of error messages has been tied to success through Jadud's EQ measurement [31] and enhanced compiler error messages (ECEMs) have been shown to reduce EQ and similar measures of error rates [6].

Since students so often struggle with understanding CEMs, many creators of automated assessment tools have attempted to enhance the standard CEMs that students receive. One of the earliest examples of an ECEM is seen in CAP, developed by Schorsh in 1995. The intent of CAP was to provide students in an introductory programming course with user-friendly feedback pertaining to syntax, logic, and style errors [55]. In 2012, Watson discussed the tool BlueFix, which applied his principle of adapting the compiler messages to the level of the students [62]. Other examples of enhancing CEMs for novice students include Thetis [22], HiC [24], Expresso [27], Gauntlet [21], a tool by Dy [15], LearnCS! [39], an IDE by Barik [4], and ITS-Debug [11].

A few researchers have reported empirical results on the efficacy of ECEMs. In 2014, Denny et al. reported that there was no statistically significant difference in students' behavior between control and experimental groups [12]. These results seem non-intuitive. In contrast, Becker similarly enhanced CEMs in the automated assessment tool, Decaf, also used for Java programming and found that the enhanced messages actually did change student behavior: after viewing an ECEM, students were less likely to generate the same error in the future [5]. Pettit et al. enhanced CEMs in an automated assessment tool, Athene, used for C++ programming and did not find conclusive results that the ECEMs were more helpful than standard CEMs [50]. Prather et al. took a human-factors approach to redesign the ECEMs in Athene, conducted a mixed-methods experiment, and found that the newly redesigned ECEMs were more helpful than the standard CEMs [52], showing that human-centered design of ECEMs is highly important. Finally, Becker et al. returned to the problem, examined these conflicting results, and found that previous studies were measuring different phenomena. They found a consistent way to explain the seemingly different results on efficacy of ECEMs and reported on another experiment which supported their explanation [7].

Despite the importance of useful feedback messages as cognitive scaffolding to implicitly create metacognitive awareness in novices, and its empirically confirmed helpfulness, most AATs provide only rudimentary feedback for submissions [1, 2]. Reporting on 69 different tools and how they provide feedback, Keuning et al. report that most feedback is on failed test cases, some on failure to compile, and very little about anything else [35]. Most of this feedback is binary in nature (pass/fail). Kyrilov and Noelle report that only providing binary feedback to students leads to lower engagement and higher rates of cheating [37]. It therefore seems that feedback must be enhanced beyond binary pass/fail, but the existing literature has yet to establish a standard design for this feedback.

Hartmann et al. [23] created HelpMeOut, an automated assessment tool that provides students with feedback similar to Denny et al. [12]. HelpMeOut queries a database of similar errors and presents users with examples and how to fix them. This approach contrasts with many others that implement enhanced feedback via expert opinion and not user observation [21, 30]. Furthermore, HelpMeOut's top suggestion is accomplished through crowdsourced voting by students. Hartmann et al. did not attempt to measure whether their AAT helped novice programmers create a better conceptual model of the errors they received or whether it increased learnability for novice programmers. Marceau et al. took a human factors approach to creating DrRacket [44]. They ran mixed-methods experiment and discovered that students were grossly misinterpreting the feedback messages and were confused by DrRacket's highly specialized vocabulary. Marceau et al. postulated that perhaps students do not take the time to read the messages but rather use the presence of CEMs only as an "oracle" that somehow knows how to fix their code; Marceau et al. also suggested that students may read only the code highlights that indicate the necessary change. In following work, they provided a rubric for evaluating the effectiveness of error messages based on student behavior after encountering them [43]. Marceau et al. recommended changes to error messages: simplify vocabulary, be more explicit in pointing to the problem, help students match terms in the error message to parts of their code (e.g. using color coded highlighting), design the programming course with error messages in mind (rather than an afterthought), and teach students how to read and understand error messages during class time.

Several other recent studies utilize aspects of a human factors approach to an automated assessment tool such as the theroy behind error message design [60], design and personification of feedback [38], and eye-tracking to determine if novices read error messages and what they are reading when they do [3].

2.2 Metacognition in Novice Programmers

Introductory courses in programming often focus solely on syntax and data structures, but there is a growing consensus among computer science education researchers that it should also focus on assisting the novice in building a mental scaffold around which they can correctly place knowledge and develop metacognitive awareness [8, 19, 25, 40, 42, 53, 56]. Metacognitive awareness is, simply put, knowing about knowing. Applied to programming, it is not just knowledge of the problem, but knowledge of where one is in the problem-solving process and self-reflection on that state [45].

Incorporating metacognitive awareness into the instruction of novice programmers is rather uncommon, but the subject appears more often in literature regarding intelligent tutoring systems. In 2000, Vizcaíno et al. described the intelligent tutoring system HabiPro [61]. HabiPro included four exercises intended to help students develop good programming habits. The exercises in intelligent tutors can help build mental scaffolding in novices [53], but HabiPro was not designed to build metacognitive awareness. HabiPro is also not an automated assessment tool. A more recent study by Cao et al. reports on Idea Garden, an integrated development environment (IDE) that helps novices by providing mental scaffolding through just-in-time contextual hints [10]. A follow-up study by Jernigan et al. implemented these concepts into a larger prototype and reported that novices in the experimental group required substantially less help than the control group, which did not use the prototype [32]. Finally, Nelson et al. proposed a comprehension-first pedagogy paired with PLTutor, an intelligent tutoring system that aims to help novices better learn meta-programming skills such as code-tracing [47].

Falkner et al. [20] carried out a mixed-methods study that observed self-awareness of learning strategies, such as metacognitive awareness, in novice students in an introductory programming course. Participants engaged in a multi-part reflection process as they worked on programming assessments. Falkner et al. reported that only a few students were able to articulate metacognitive awareness; they therefore recommend instructors engage in targeted explicit cognitive scaffolding to help students develop this skill.

Hauswirth and Adamoli [25] studied CS2 students' metacognitive awareness in two courses by observing what they did in response to explicit coaching on help-seeking and self-assessment behaviors. They found that students engaged in metacognitive activities to varying degrees, but they largely explained this variation as connected to the setup of the CS2 courses. However, they did discover some instances of deeper self-reflection among students in unexpected ways, such as student revision of mastery self-assessments, indicating a student first thought they had mastered a skill and then realized they hadn't. Hauswirth's and Adamoli's study is limited by their data collection method, which was observation of what students did, as opposed to what students thought, even though the study was trying to measure metacognitive awareness. They call for additional work to complement their study by investigating what students are thinking. We attempt to fill this gap through our study's think-aloud protocol.

The most relevant study on promoting metacognitive awareness in novice programmers is by Loksa et al. [40]. As listed above, they identified six distinct problem-solving stages that learners usually progress through sequentially. They reported on an intervention at a code camp where the control group was taught how to code and the experimental group was additionally trained in these six problem-solving stages and the use of an IDE with an Idea Garden. They reported that students with this training were significantly more productive and required less help. As the literature indicates, then, modified pedagogical approaches and coding environments warrant development. Some successful modifications, however, are difficult to scale or hard to implement for online learning technologies, such as massively open online courses, which Loksa et al. acknowledged as a limitation of their work. Our intention with the present study is to adapt the spirit of these interventions to automated assessment tools that can span this gap.

3 METHODOLOGY

In this paper, we investigate novice programmers' problem-solving abilities by observing them complete a programming assignment using an AAT in order to better understand how an AAT could be built to implicitly increase student metacognitive awareness. In order to understand how AATs might help improve metacognitive awareness in novices, we looked at existing literature for anything that might fit into one of the six stages used by Loksa et al. Only the discussions of feedback in AATs fit that criteria and, when done correctly, could help with stage 5, *implement a solution*. For this study, we chose to use the AAT Athene because of the extensive research already done to enhance its CEMs [48, 50, 52, 59] and its availability for the researchers to further modify. In our previous work [52], we iteratively refined the design of the ECEMs in Athene through two pilot studies and a larger mixed-methods study and reported that the newly-refined ECEMs had a positive impact on student performance. From this work, we are confident that Athene successfully attends to stage 5 by providing helpful and useful feedback to students while they try to write code that can compile. We therefore conducted a think-aloud study [54, 58, 63] to watch novice programmers use Athene and qualitatively analyzed the data in order to understand what difficulties they faced in building metacognitive awareness and how that tool could be further augmented to support users through Loksa et al.'s other five problem-solving stages.

Instead of the regular three hours of classes during week six of the semester in CS1, the primary researcher canceled class and held hour-long one-on-one sessions with each student to provide individualized feedback about their programming process. While meeting for the one-on-one sessions was mandatory, release of information was opt-in, and a different professor than the primary researcher handed out and collected the IRB signature forms while the primary researcher was not in the room. Students were clearly told by the other professor that choosing not to opt-in would not have any effect on their grade and the researchers did not know who had opted in during the one-on-one sessions, as per IRB requirements. All 31 students chose to release their data for this research. Each student met one-on-one with a researcher where the student was observed completing a practical quiz. Students received a programming problem in Athene and had to solve it in a proctored 35-minute time window. Students were asked to verbalize their thoughts while they solved the problem. In an effort to control for differing development environments and the help students might or might not receive from certain IDEs, students were only allowed to type their code in the default Windows notepad application and could only access compilation and runtime error checking via submission to Athene. After the practical quiz had been successfully completed, or the time had expired, students received detailed feedback on their programming skills and problem-solving process from the researcher.

The general format of the think-aloud study follows the usability testing guidelines found in Rubin and Chisnell [54], including pre- and post-testing checklists and scripts. At the beginning of each think-aloud session, the evaluator read from a script outlining the reason for the session, the goal of the session, and what was expected of the student. Students were then given a very simple task and asked to think aloud so they could get used to verbalizing their thoughts, the observer, and the process, as suggested by [58] and [63]. This simple task was to write a program that would output "Hello, world." This particular task was chosen because it was cognitively easy code to write for any level of student at that point in the semester, so practicing the think-aloud protocol would be manageable.

After completing the warm-up exercise, students were asked to complete the practical quiz within a time limit of 35 minutes. The task was this: given *n* integers, compute whether there were more positive or negative integer numbers provided as input. For this problem, students would need to understand the following concepts: console input, console output, conditionals, and loops. This problem was selected because it correlated with course topics at the time and therefore should have been moderately challenging. An additional reason for selecting this problem was that it has been used as an in-class assessment in previous semesters, also with a 35-minute time limit, and a majority of students from those previous semesters completed the problem within the limit. While each student worked to solve the problem, a researcher took extensive notes on what the student did and said. Interactions during the practical quiz between the researcher and student were kept to a minimum per Ericsson and Simon [18].

Participant observation allowed us to record the participants' actions, apparent thought and problem-solving process, and external reactions to error messages and other feedback. Participant-specific data were separately recorded and then moved into ATLAS.ti, a qualitative software analysis package. Tags for the data included Loksa et al.'s six problem-solving stages, users' external reactions to feedback from the AAT, and outward expressions of emotion (verbalizing or demonstrating through body language feeling encouraged, happy, frustrated, or angry). ATLAS.ti determines groundedness as a measure of the relevance of a code within the dataset.

4 RESULTS

In this section, we describe from observation during the think-aloud study how students working in Athene moved through Loksa et al.'s six learning stages. This qualitative data from the think-aloud study will highlight the relevant ways in which AATs, like Athene, fail to help students build metacognitive awareness. We tagged, coded, and grouped the observation notes and interview transcripts

into categories by the collaborative agreement of two researchers. This approach allowed larger trends to emerge from the natural groupings of the qualitative data. Specifically, we tagged data in 433 places and from that identified 39 recurring themes as first-order concepts that emerged from our ground-level observations. We then built these 39 themes into five second-order concepts, which are summarized below in the Discussion. To show how we arrived at the second-order concepts, we begin with the raw data of participant experience broken into two categories: students who successfully completed the program within the 35-minute time limit and students who did not. This is followed by a discussion of the data that groups these experiences into broader concepts by using [40] as our theoretical foundation. Student names in this section were changed for the sake of anonymity.

4.1 Students that Completed the Quiz

In the group that completed the quiz, several students finished in under 10 minutes and displayed a similar set of traits. The first trait was a consistent approach to starting the problem. Observation notes report that at the outset, these students, "interpreted the instructions for the problem," and "immediately verbalized a clear conceptual model for the problem." Next, these students followed a similar pattern of thinking through the problem, thinking about how to solve it, choosing a solution (in this case, using a while loop), implementing a solution, and tracing their code with specific test cases in mind. Several students in this group were observed pausing multiple times to think about their chosen solution and their process to solve the problem. Only one student in this group received an ECEM. The student who received this message, Bill, did not read the enhanced portion at first, but read the standard portion, successfully edited his code, and then double-checked his edit by opening the enhanced portion, reading it, and agreeing that his fix was correct. Bill's experience is ideal. Still, by the time these particular students were receiving feedback regarding test cases, they had successfully moved through Loksa et al.'s first five stages of problem-solving and therefore they quickly interpreted any failed test cases and fixed the offending code.

Jane, who took 14 minutes to finish the quiz, first thought through the problem, immediately decided on a solution, and proceeded to create comments about what she planned to do throughout the file and then filled it out with code. This student received one ECEM, did not read the enhanced portion, and immediately successfully edited the code. Her next submission compiled, passed two of the test cases, and failed on the third. She made an edit to her code and resubmitted, receiving the same failed test case message, and then repeated this pattern once more. Finally, after receiving the same test case failure three times, she stopped and carefully walked through her code with specific test cases in mind, found the issue, fixed the code, and finished.

Another student, Patricia, who finished in 18 minutes, read the problem prompt quickly and immediately began attempting to solve it as if it was a different problem students in CS1 had previously encountered that semester ("Even or Odd?": given *n* numbers, compute whether there were more even or odd integer numbers provided as input). She seems to have failed initially to correctly move through problem-solving stage 1, *reinterpret problem prompt*, before moving on to stage 2, *search for analogous problems*. She correctly chose the "Even or Odd?" problem as analogous, but when moving onto stage 3, *search for solutions*, she chose to use the solution for the "Even or Odd?" problem itself instead of using the problem as the basis from which to form a new solution to a different problem. However, as Patricia began to write her solution, this approach made apparently less and less sense, and she verbalized realizing something was off. She checked the instructions again, but she still didn't seem to understand what was wrong-providing a fascinating case of how forming the wrong conceptual model early on can make it difficult to fundamentally change how one views the programming problem at hand. Finally, after being stuck for a few more minutes, she re-read the instructions a third time and apparently understood. After this, Patricia solved the problem very quickly.

Another interesting group of students who completed the quiz were those who took 30-35 minutes, coming right up against the time limit. Adam, completing the quiz in 30 minutes, read the prompt and immediately verbalized a clear conceptual model of what the problem required and how to solve it. However, Adam ran into extensive issues with syntax and therefore became stuck on stage 5, *implement a solution*. His spoken narration demonstrated that he recognized his deficiency in the particulars of syntax correctness and utilized the enhanced portion of the ECEMs to his advantage, finally solving it on the seventh submission.

Finally, Wayne, who completed the problem in 33 minutes, ran into the same issue as Patricia, confusing the problem for "Even or Odd?" However, Wayne did not recognize his mistake early on. At multiple points in the session, he carefully talked through his algorithm, revealing his incorrect conceptual model. After writing his solution, built for the "Even or Odd?" problem, he encountered one ECEM, fixed the error, and moved on to the final stage, *evaluate implemented solution*, where he failed the first test case. Wayne looked at the expected output compared to the actual output of his program, made an edit, and then passed the next test case. He continued failing test cases, adding to his code to create the right output, and failing the next test case. His code grew longer until he had passed 10 test cases, a process that took just over 30 minutes during which he showed increasing frustration. Finally, at 31 minutes, he re-read the problem prompt and exclaimed, "Oh! Wait! This just hit me that it's doing positive and negative rather than evens and odds. I don't know why that happened," and he very quickly solved the problem. In this case, failing to correctly navigate Loksa et al.'s first few stages of problem-solving apparently led to an incorrect interpretation of the AAT's error messages and an incorrect conception of location in the problem-solving process. By solving compilation problems and working through multiple test cases, Wayne described feeling that he was very close to solving the problem, when he was actually very far away. This story highlights how a lack of metacognitive awareness *almost* kept an otherwise-capable student from succeeding.

4.2 Students that Did Not Complete the Quiz

The 11 students who did not complete the quiz all failed to successfully move through at least one of the problem-solving stages. If the way to a correct solution can be thought of like a path from stage to stage, these students often diverged very early, backtracked

frequently, and never returned to the crucial juncture to take the correct path. The most frequent issue these students encountered was a failure to build a correct conceptual model of the problem. Unable or unwilling to spend the time to successfully navigate stage 1, *reinterpret problem prompt*, many of these students searched for analogous problems and solutions to the wrong problem. And, unlike Wayne above, these students never demonstrated recognition that they had the wrong conceptual model. The AAT was not able to alert these students to this failure of metacognitive awareness, allowing them to meander down the wrong path, totally lost until the quiz time had expired.

The most obvious example of a failure to create a correct conceptual model can be seen in the experience of Theo, who spent nearly a third of his quiz time reading and re-reading the quiz prompt. At one point, halfway into the quiz time, the researcher noted that he "just keeps repeating the same phrase from the instructions, 'if the number of positive is greater than the number of negative,' over and over again." Eventually, Theo wrote some code and submitted it, and he received a standard CEM. He spent the rest of his time trying to understand this message. Since the CEM was only responding to a syntax error, if Theo had corrected and submitted his code again, Athene would have begun running his code against the set of test cases. The feedback Theo received was not the feedback that he needed in order to succeed. His time expired while he was re-reading the prompt for the eighth time.

Neil provides a good example of what happens when one fails to navigate each of Loksa et al.'s stages. After skimming the problem prompt, Neil immediately began coding without stopping to think through stage 2, *search for analogous problems*, stage 3, *search for solutions*, or stage 4, *evaluate a potential solution*, jumping right to stage 5, *implement a solution*. This leap was evidenced by his statement after a few minutes, "What I'm wondering is if I need the prompt for input to be in the loop or not," followed quickly by removing that prompt entirely. A minute later, he created two variables and said, "Somehow I'm going to let those represent positive and negative values. I think I'll have to do that in my while loop." At that point in the quiz, his code was structured to accept two integer values and report if they were positive or negative, which is not code appropriate to the correct problem. Minutes later, he said, "I'm going to mentally run through it now," but he did so without any specific test cases. All of these actions show a lack of understanding about what problem he was trying to solve and how to solve the problem he thought it was, as well as an inability to evaluate his own solution. Finally, he submitted his code to Athene and spent the rest of his quiz time working through compiler errors. Slowly working through seven CEMs/ECEMs seems to have provided a false sense of progress to Neil, because his program, even without syntax errors, was very far away from a correct solution.

Thomas successfully navigated stages 1-2, failed to solve stage 3, and was subsequently totally unprepared to move into stages 4-6. Early on, Thomas said things like, "I'm trying to figure out how to . . . that's not going to work," and, "I'm trying to figure out how to make it count the positive ones. I don't know how to . . . that's going to be my issue." He continued tinkering with his code and said, "I just don't know how to see if there's more positive or negative." Thomas' comments reveal that he understood what he needed to do but had great difficulty successfully getting through stage 3, *search for solutions.* Apparently frustrated and eager for some feedback, Thomas submitted his code, saying, "I guess I'll run it just to see what it will say." His code was syntactically valid and so Athene began running test cases. Once in stage 6, *evaluate implemented solution*, Thomas struggled with the first test case for the remainder of the time, unsure as to how to convert the specified input into the correct output. Near the end of his quiz time, Thomas said, "I feel like I'm close, but I just don't know how to count up positive and negatives. Why is this not working?" The feedback from Athene seems to have given Thomas a false sense of progression through the problem. He described feeling very close, but without finding a solution in stage 3 from which to build his own solution, he was actually quite far from completion. Thomas' experience was almost exactly repeated in the experience of two other students; one, for example, said , "really close to finishing this, I think," when he was quite far away.

Several other observations are worth mentioning as well. A few students said that they usually solve the problem through trial and error. This behavior shows that AATs, such as Athene, allow for submission of code immediately without any assurances that the student understands the problem-they are focused solely on correctness via syntax and test cases. Another issue researchers noticed is that several students seemed to become very frustrated during the quiz, with one student even calling herself and her code "stupid." This suggests that an absence of appropriate feedback from an AAT can contribute to students' feeling lost and frustrated, and potentially forming negative opinions of their work and the discipline. Finally, one positive behavior in this group was displayed by Jenny, who successfully navigated stages 1-3, stalled in stage 4, *evaluate a potential solution*, and finally got out a piece of scratch paper and sketched the flow of the program. This action helped her immensely, and she was able to immediately move on to stage 5, *implement a solution*. Unfortunately, by the time Jenny verbalized the idea to sketch out her solution, her quiz time was nearly over.

5 DISCUSSION

In this section, we will contrast the two groups above in order to answer the RQ: *What difficulties do novices who may lack metacognitive awareness face when using an AAT?* The most glaring inconsistency between those who completed the quiz and those who did not is in the initial formation of a correct conceptual model for the problem, which corresponds to Loksa et al.'s stage 1, *reinterpret problem prompt*. This breakdown shows perhaps the single greatest weakness in modern AATs: the tools merely present the problem and assume that the successful student will eventually conceptualize the problem correctly. Furthermore, there are no measures between viewing the problem and submitting source code to ensure that the student understands what they're being asked to do. As it is, tools like Athene treat every student submission the same, as a solution properly designed and requiring only syntactic corrections for completion. Wayne and Patricia, who both realized their incorrect conceptual model, saw feedback that paralleled the feedback given to multiple students who did not complete the quiz, only these others were not fortunate enough to realize their conceptual errors. It's very possible that these students would have completed the quiz if Athene had somehow prompted them to form the correct

conceptual model at the outset. Such a modification would not only benefit the poorer performing students; after all, Wayne completed the quiz, but just barely. It is likely that Wayne would not have taken 33 minutes to solve the problem had he been operating under the correct conceptual model the entire time. Both Patricia and Wayne also illustrate that simply re-reading the problem prompt may not help a student who has formed an incorrect conceptual model, due to the difficulty in dislodging a model once formed.

After forming a correct conceptual model, Jane and several other students who completed the quiz took the time at the outset to build out some scaffolding inside their code by placing comments about how they intended to solve the problem. These students used this technique to navigate stage 2, *search for analogous problems*, by thinking back to similar problems they had encountered, and stage 3, *search for solutions*, by thinking through how they had solved those previous problems, and finally stage 4, *evaluate a potential solution*, by sketching the solution in comments before actually implementing it. This strategy proved to be a helpful way of thinking through an approach before committing to any code. Jenny, who did not complete the quiz, also employed this strategy, but she did so far too late into the quiz time. Meanwhile, many of the students who did not complete the quiz read the prompt (often briefly) and jumped directly to coding, skipping stages 1-4 entirely. This proved disastrous for them as they wandered aimlessly, seeming to hope they would eventually stumble on a solution.

Another important distinction can be drawn in stage 5, *implement a solution*, when considering how some in the incomplete group attempted to work through the received CEMs/ECEMs though they had no idea they had incorrectly navigated all previous stages. Having used Athene for the assigned homework problems in weeks 1-5 of CS1 thus far, these students associated receiving CEMs/ECEMs with being mostly complete, a finding that became obvious during the think-aloud session or in the interviews afterward. This poor sense of location in the problem-solving process ultimately distracted them from the real issue at hand: even if they could get their code to be syntactically correct, their code was not going to solve the problem.

The most-repeated theme in the data also appears in stage 5, *implement a solution*, which was the amount of ECEMs read by students. The participants who did not complete the quiz read nine of the 29 enhanced messages encountered, while the participants that completed the quiz read 23 of the 31 enhanced messages encountered. From the quiz data, reading the enhanced messages seems to correlate with quiz completion among all students that completed the quiz, though it correlates especially strongly for the several students who might not have completed the quiz otherwise. However, we did not control for the so-called "diligent student effect" in this experiment. Students such as Adam, who correctly navigated stages 1-4 but became stuck on stage 5 with syntax errors, heavily relied upon and successfully utilized the enhanced messages to reach a correct solution. Most perplexing is the general behavior of the students who didn't utilize the enhanced messages. One student in particular saw the same ECEM 15 times but never clicked on the enhanced message to expand and read it.

Finally, the experiences of Neil and Thomas can be juxtaposed with the experience of Jane to offer a window into stage 6, *evaluate implemented solution*. When Jane began receiving test case feedback

Table 1: Observed difficulties to metacognitive awareness by novices using AATs

Metacognitive Difficulty	Explanation
Forming	Forming the wrong conceptual model about the right problem
Dislodging	Dislodging an incorrect conceptual model of the problem may not be solved by re-reading the prompt
Assumption	Forming the correct conceptual model for the wrong problem
Location	Moving too quickly through one or more stages incorrectly leads to a false sense of accomplishment and poor conception of location in the problem-solving process
Achievement	Unwillingness to abandon a wrong solution due to a false sense of being nearly done

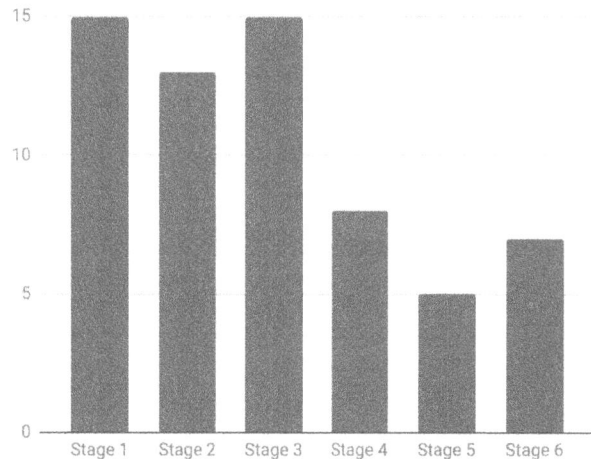

Figure 1: Groundedness of each learning stage within the full dataset.

from Athene, she had already successfully navigated stages 1-5 and was therefore ready to incorporate the feedback accordingly. Because she was solving the right problem, had chosen an approach that could solve the problem, and had correctly implemented the code for her solution, the feedback about failed test cases that she received enabled her to tweak her code and quickly arrive at a correct solution. Both Neil and Thomas, on the other hand, also reached stage 6, but because they had incorrectly navigated stages 1-5, the feedback they received was misleading. Because Athene told them which test cases they had failed, Neil and Thomas expressed that they assumed they should evaluate these feedback messages and that doing so would lead them to a correct solution. Unfortunately, no amount of failed test case feedback would have helped them correct their fundamental misunderstanding of the problem. Reporting that they felt so close to finishing, these two participants apparently never considered that the real issue was their chosen solution.

As noted above, we tagged the data from all 31 student talk-aloud sessions and identified 39 recurring themes as first-order concepts. Six of those themes were Loksa et al.'s six stages, and we used ATLAS.ti to analyze the groundedness of each stage within the full dataset. For reference, the highest level of groundedness of any theme ("helpfulness of ECEMs") was 33, which represents the theme of students reading an ECEM and immediately correcting a compile error. Out of all 39 first-order concepts that showed some level of groundedness, only eight had a higher level of groundedness than the first and third learning stages (which each had groundedness levels of 15); as Figure 1 shows, stage 2 was the next saturated (with a groundedness level of 13). This observation is particularly interesting because "helpfulness of ECEMs" should happen in stage five, implement a solution (groundedness: 5).

In moving from first-order to second-order concepts, we discovered that students often encountered ECEMs when, unbeknownst to them, they were stuck in the first few learning stages by regressing back to an earlier stage from a later stage. Recognizing this pattern helped us to identify the trends in the data leading towards

the final two second-order concepts in Table 1, where students encountered ECEMs and mistook it for progress, did not understand feedback that could point them to their incorrect approach to a solution, or were unwilling to backtrack after incorrectly feeling close to a solution.

We went on to group the 39 themes into five second-order concepts that emerged from this research, as summarized in Table 1. The first few difficulties in Table 1 all center around the first three learning stages, which is not surprising given the level of groundedness of the earlier stages compared with the later stages, as shown in Figure 1.

Our results support previous research on metacognitive awareness in novice programmers. Bergin et al. [8] showed that higher-performing students tend to display some metacognitive awareness while lower-performing students display lower or no metacognitive awareness. In our results, students who completed the quiz tended to display some metacognitive awareness, while those who did not complete the quiz tended to lack that awareness. Obviously, determining whether or not a student has some metacognitive awareness depends on whether or not they display it, either verbally or with some behavior. A few students that completed the quiz did so very quickly without saying anything or showing any metacognitive behaviors, such as planning out a solution with comments before coding. However, most students who completed the quiz displayed at least some metacognitive awareness to the researchers. Some students who did not complete the quiz, such as Jenny, displayed some metacognitive awareness but did not do so early enough or consistently enough. Bergin et al. also showed that students with higher intrinsic motivation were more likely to display metacognitive awareness. Our research also confirms this finding. The students who did not complete the quiz showed far less motivation, in part because they seemed to think much less of their programming skills. Several students in the group repeatedly berated themselves out of frustration.

The results of our study should also be brought into conversation with those of Falkner et al. [20]. They found that when teachers included specific exercises in CS1 classes such as design activities, task difficulty assessments, and expectation of iterative coding practices, and when teachers encouraged students to explore alternative designs, students were more likely to develop self-regulated learning strategies such as metacognitive awareness. We found that students who were already aware of their need to practice these skills were more likely to be in the group completing the assessment. Falkner et al. also noted that students in their study frequently skipped design and problem exploration in favor of jumping right into coding. We noted this behavior as well, among both successful and unsuccessful groups, though it was far more frequent among unsuccessful students. The positive scaffolding that Falkner et al. propose and the negative behaviors they observed could be supported and prevented, respectively, if the programming environment that was used implicitly supported metacognitive awareness, which in combination with our research suggests potential direction for modifying AATs to improve student performance.

Finally, Loksa et al. [40] categorize the learning barriers that learners might encounter at a particular stage using the classification system provided by Ko et al. [36]. This classification system describes the different cognitive, environmental, and programming systems barriers that can prevent programming students from finding a solution and solving a given problem. However, only one barrier, *design*, is described as specifically cognitive, while the rest are environmental, programming systems, API interface, or user interface related. The description of the *design* barrier seems to contain several of the metacognitive difficulties we noted above in Table 1, including Forming and Assumption. Ko et al. did not describe the other metacognitive difficulties we found. While the learning barriers presented by Ko et al. can be a useful classification system, it is not particularly equipped to understand the specifically metacognitive difficulties faced by novice programmers. The metacognitive difficulties presented above in Table 1, however, seem to extend the work of Ko et al. by expanding and unpacking their *design* barrier, as well as to offer new insights into the matter.

6 CONCLUSION

In this paper, we have presented a think-aloud study of CS1 students in order to understand the difficulties faced by novices in forming metacognitive awareness when using an AAT. Our analysis shows how successful students mentally augmented Athene while exploring how and why unsuccessful students faltered from Athene's lack of cognitive scaffolding. Unfortunately, this lack of cognitive scaffolding with regard to each of Loksa et al.'s stages is common in most AATs, and so our observations should apply more broadly to a wide range of AATs. The only exception occurs in relation to stage 5, where some tools are already moving to enhance the default CEMs, but even those that have done so are still often lacking in effective human-centered design. The primary contribution of this paper is the identification of metacognitive difficulties that novice programming students often face as shown in Table 1, which can serve to inform future AAT development.

The present study has shown the need for AATs to provide implicit support of metacognitive awareness. Prior research has shown that explicit teaching of metacognitive skills has a positive impact on learning, self-regulation, and growth mindset [40]. In our study, we did not explicitly train students on metacognition because we wanted to determine where AATs presently fail to provide adequate cognitive scaffolding such that a novice can implicitly learn metacognitive programming skills. In this case, we consider metacognitive training implicit because it is built into the tool itself and requires no explicit instruction on learning strategies or stages, and students who use an AAT with built-in metacognitive support would largely be unaware that they were being trained to develop that skill. Our results call for AATs to evolve significantly and move somewhere between their present form and that of intelligent tutoring systems. So what would such an AAT look like?

From the discussion above, it seems that AATs should be modified to provide more comprehensive cognitive scaffolding for novices around which they can appropriately locate their knowledge as they learn. Since a student at a university that uses an AAT will typically complete dozens of problems in a semester, the AAT that is designed to overcome the issues described above will implicitly build metacognitive awareness in novices as they use it over and over again. Such an AAT should help novices work through each of Loksa et al.'s learning stages [40] by confirming that students understand the problem before proceeding, helping them think through previous problems they have encountered, asking them to outline their solution via something like Parsons Problems [33], and requiring students to write their own test cases to submit alongside their code [9, 16], in addition to enhancing the compiler error messages [23, 44, 52]. A more thorough discussion of these suggestions, including empirically testing of each one individually and also testing all of them together, is presently underway and will be reported on in future work.

There are several threats to the validity of this study. First, our observations took place in a laboratory setting and may not reflect actual student behavior and experience. Second, students in the think-aloud study were in a one-on-one setting, were asked to think-aloud, and did not have access to previous code. It is possible that all of these factors increased student cognitive load and, therefore, skewed the results. We attempted to offset the cognitive load concern by adding in the warm-up exercise as suggested by Teague et al. [58]. Third, we acknowledge that coming to firm conclusions in think-aloud studies can be perilous as it can seem like the researchers are narrating the thoughts of participants. However, we only tagged data from students' verbalizations and concrete actions, tying the two together as often as possible, in order to avoid this trap. Finally, the low number of student participants (n=31) is another possible threat to validity. Still, although it is helpful in quantitative studies to increase the number of participants, a higher number would have been prohibitive in conducting an in-depth experiment such as this.

7 ACKNOWLEDGMENTS

Special thanks to Heidi Nobles for her editorial support in preparing this manuscript.

REFERENCES

[1] Kirsti M Ala-Mutka. 2005. A survey of automated assessment approaches for programming assignments. *Computer science education* 15, 2 (2005), 83–102.

[2] José Luis Fernández Alemán. 2011. Automated assessment in a programming tools course. *IEEE Transactions on Education* 54, 4 (2011), 576–581.

[3] Titus Barik, Justin Smith, Kevin Lubick, Elisabeth Holmes, Jing Feng, Emerson Murphy-Hill, and Chris Parnin. 2017. Do Developers Read Compiler Error Messages?. In *Proceedings of the International Conference of Software Engineering*. ACM.

[4] Titus Barik, Jim Witschey, Brittany Johnson, and Emerson Murphy-Hill. 2014. Compiler error notifications revisited: an interaction-first approach for helping developers more effectively comprehend and resolve error notifications. In *Companion Proceedings of the 36th International Conference on Software Engineering*. ACM, 536–539.

[5] Brett A Becker. 2016. An effective approach to enhancing compiler error messages. In *Proceedings of the 47th ACM Technical Symposium on Computing Science Education*. ACM, 126–131.

[6] Brett A Becker. 2016. A new metric to quantify repeated compiler errors for novice programmers. In *Proceedings of the 2016 ACM Conference on Innovation and Technology in Computer Science Education*. ACM, 296–301.

[7] B. A. Becker, K. Goslin, and G. Glanville. 2018. The Effects of Enhanced Compiler Error Messages on a Syntax Error Debugging Test. In *Proceedings of the 2018 ACM Conference on Innovation and Technology in Computer Science Education*. ACM, 640–645.

[8] Susan Bergin, Ronan Reilly, and Desmond Traynor. 2005. Examining the role of self-regulated learning on introductory programming performance. In *Proceedings of the first international workshop on Computing education research*. ACM, 81–86.

[9] Kevin Buffardi and Stephen H Edwards. 2015. Reconsidering Automated Feedback: A Test-Driven Approach. In *Proceedings of the 46th ACM Technical Symposium on Computer Science Education*. ACM, 416–420.

[10] Jill Cao, Scott D Fleming, Margaret Burnett, and Christopher Scaffidi. 2014. Idea Garden: Situated support for problem solving by end-user programmers. *Interacting with Computers* 27, 6 (2014), 640–660.

[11] Elizabeth Carter. 2015. Its debug: practical results. *Journal of Computing Sciences in Colleges* 30, 3 (2015), 9–15.

[12] Paul Denny, Andrew Luxton-Reilly, and Dave Carpenter. 2014. Enhancing syntax error messages appears ineffectual. In *Proceedings of the 2014 conference on Innovation & technology in computer science education*. ACM, 273–278.

[13] Edsger W. Dijkstra. 1995. Introducing a course on calculi. https://www.cs.utexas.edu/users/EWD/transcriptions/EWD12xx/EWD1213.html Remarks by Edsger Dijkstra at Department of Computer Sciences, The University of Texas at Austin [Accessed: 2017 08 25].

[14] Christopher Douce, David Livingstone, and James Orwell. 2005. Automatic test-based assessment of programming: A review. *Journal on Educational Resources in Computing (JERIC)* 5, 3 (2005), 4.

[15] Thomas Dy and Ma Mercedes Rodrigo. 2010. A detector for non-literal Java errors. In *Proceedings of the 10th Koli Calling International Conference on Computing Education Research*. ACM, 118–122.

[16] Stephen H Edwards. 2003. Rethinking computer science education from a test-first perspective. In *Companion of the 18th annual ACM SIGPLAN conference on Object-oriented programming, systems, languages, and applications*. ACM, 148–155.

[17] Stephen H Edwards and Manuel A Perez-Quinones. 2008. Web-CAT: automatically grading programming assignments. In *ACM SIGCSE Bulletin*, Vol. 40. ACM, 328–328.

[18] Karl Anders Ericsson and Herbert Alexander Simon. 1993. *Protocol analysis*. MIT press Cambridge, MA.

[19] Anneli Eteläpelto. 1993. Metacognition and the expertise of computer program comprehension. *Scandinavian Journal of Educational Research* 37, 3 (1993), 243–254.

[20] Katrina Falkner, Rebecca Vivian, and Nickolas JG Falkner. 2014. Identifying computer science self-regulated learning strategies. In *Proceedings of the 2014 conference on Innovation & technology in computer science education*. ACM, 291–296.

[21] Thomas Flowers, Curtis A Carver, and James Jackson. 2004. Empowering students and building confidence in novice programmers through Gauntlet. In *Frontiers in Education, 2004. FIE 2004. 34th Annual*. IEEE, T3H–10.

[22] Stephen N Freund and Eric S Roberts. 1996. Thetis: an ANSI C programming environment designed for introductory use. In *SIGCSE*, Vol. 96. 300–304.

[23] Björn Hartmann, Daniel MacDougall, Joel Brandt, and Scott R Klemmer. 2010. What would other programmers do: suggesting solutions to error messages. In *Proceedings of the SIGCHI Conference on Human Factors in Computing Systems*. ACM, 1019–1028.

[24] Robert W Hasker. 2002. HiC: a C++ compiler for CS1. *Journal of Computing Sciences in Colleges* 18, 1 (2002), 56–64.

[25] Matthias Hauswirth and Andrea Adamoli. 2017. Metacognitive calibration when learning to program. In *Proceedings of the 17th Koli Calling Conference on Computing Education Research*. ACM, 50–59.

[26] Jack Hollingsworth. 1960. Automatic graders for programming classes. *Commun. ACM* 3, 10 (1960), 528–529.

[27] Maria Hristova, Ananya Misra, Megan Rutter, and Rebecca Mercuri. 2003. Identifying and correcting Java programming errors for introductory computer science

students. In *ACM SIGCSE Bulletin*, Vol. 35. ACM, 153–156.

[28] Petri Ihantola, Tuukka Ahoniemi, Ville Karavirta, and Otto Seppälä. 2010. Review of recent systems for automatic assessment of programming assignments. In *Proceedings of the 10th Koli Calling International Conference on Computing Education Research*. ACM, 86–93.

[29] Petri Ihantola, Arto Vihavainen, Alireza Ahadi, Matthew Butler, Jürgen Börstler, Stephen H Edwards, Essi Isohanni, Ari Korhonen, Andrew Petersen, Kelly Rivers, et al. 2015. Educational data mining and learning analytics in programming: Literature review and case studies. In *Proceedings of the 2015 ITiCSE on Working Group Reports*. ACM, 41–63.

[30] James Jackson, Michael Cobb, and Curtis Carver. 2005. Identifying top Java errors for novice programmers. In *Frontiers in Education, 2005. FIE'05. Proceedings 35th Annual Conference*. IEEE, T4C–T4C.

[31] Matthew C Jadud. 2006. *An exploration of novice compilation behaviour in BlueJ*. Ph.D. Dissertation. University of Kent.

[32] Will Jernigan, Amber Horvath, Michael Lee, Margaret Burnett, Taylor Cuilty, Sandeep Kuttal, Anicia Peters, Irwin Kwan, Faezeh Bahmani, and Andrew Ko. 2015. A principled evaluation for a principled Idea Garden. In *Visual Languages and Human-Centric Computing (VL/HCC), 2015 IEEE Symposium on*. IEEE, 235–243.

[33] Ville Karavirta, Juha Helminen, and Petri Ihantola. 2012. A mobile learning application for parsons problems with automatic feedback. In *Proceedings of the 12th Koli Calling International Conference on Computing Education Research*. ACM, 11–18.

[34] Caitlin Kelleher, Randy Pausch, and Sara Kiesler. 2007. Storytelling Alice motivates middle school girls to learn computer programming. In *Proceedings of the SIGCHI conference on Human factors in computing systems*. ACM, 1455–1464.

[35] Hieke Keuning, Johan Jeuring, and Bastiaan Heeren. 2016. Towards a systematic review of automated feedback generation for programming exercises. In *Proceedings of the 2016 ACM Conference on Innovation and Technology in Computer Science Education*. ACM, 41–46.

[36] Andrew J Ko, Brad A Myers, and Htet Htet Aung. 2004. Six learning barriers in end-user programming systems. In *Visual Languages and Human Centric Computing, 2004 IEEE Symposium on*. IEEE, 199–206.

[37] Angelo Kyrilov and David C Noelle. 2015. Binary instant feedback on programming exercises can reduce student engagement and promote cheating. In *Proceedings of the 15th Koli Calling Conference on Computing Education Research*. ACM, 122–126.

[38] Michael J Lee and Andrew J Ko. 2011. Personifying programming tool feedback improves novice programmers' learning. In *Proceedings of the seventh international workshop on Computing education research*. ACM, 109–116.

[39] Derrell Lipman. 2014. LearnCS!: a new, browser-based C programming environment for CS1. *Journal of Computing Sciences in Colleges* 29, 6 (2014), 144–150.

[40] Dastyni Loksa, Andrew J Ko, Will Jernigan, Alannah Oleson, Christopher J Mendez, and Margaret M Burnett. 2016. Programming, Problem Solving, and Self-Awareness: Effects of Explicit Guidance. In *Proceedings of the 2016 CHI Conference on Human Factors in Computing Systems*. ACM, 1449–1461.

[41] John Maloney, Mitchel Resnick, Natalie Rusk, Brian Silverman, and Evelyn Eastmond. 2010. The scratch programming language and environment. *ACM Transactions on Computing Education (TOCE)* 10, 4 (2010), 16.

[42] Murali Mani and Quamrul Mazumder. 2013. Incorporating metacognition into learning. In *Proceeding of the 44th ACM technical symposium on Computer science education*. ACM, 53–58.

[43] Guillaume Marceau, Kathi Fisler, and Shriram Krishnamurthi. 2011. Measuring the effectiveness of error messages designed for novice programmers. In *Proceedings of the 42nd ACM technical symposium on Computer science education*. ACM, 499–504.

[44] Guillaume Marceau, Kathi Fisler, and Shriram Krishnamurthi. 2011. Mind your language: on novices' interactions with error messages. In *Proceedings of the 10th SIGPLAN symposium on New ideas, new paradigms, and reflections on programming and software*. ACM, 3–18.

[45] Janet Metcalfe and Arthur P Shimamura. 1994. *Metacognition: Knowing about knowing*. MIT press.

[46] Laurie Murphy, Gary Lewandowski, Renée McCauley, Beth Simon, Lynda Thomas, and Carol Zander. 2008. Debugging: the good, the bad, and the quirky–a qualitative analysis of novices' strategies. In *ACM SIGCSE Bulletin*, Vol. 40. ACM, 163–167.

[47] Greg L Nelson, Benjamin Xie, and Andrew J Ko. 2017. Comprehension First: Evaluating a Novel Pedagogy and Tutoring System for Program Tracing in CS1. In *Proceedings of the 2017 ACM Conference on International Computing Education Research*. ACM, 2–11.

[48] Raymond Pettit, John Homer, Roger Gee, Susan Mengel, and Adam Starbuck. 2015. An empirical study of iterative improvement in programming assignments. In *Proceedings of the 46th ACM Technical Symposium on Computer Science Education*. ACM, 410–415.

[49] Raymond Pettit and James Prather. 2017. Automated Assessment Tools: Too Many Cooks, Not Enough Collaboration. *J. Comput. Sci. Coll.* 32, 4 (April 2017),

113–121. http://dl.acm.org/citation.cfm?id=3055338.3079060

[50] Raymond S Pettit, John Homer, and Roger Gee. 2017. Do Enhanced Compiler Error Messages Help Students?: Results Inconclusive. In *Proceedings of the 2017 ACM SIGCSE Technical Symposium on Computer Science Education*. ACM, 465–470.

[51] George Polya. 1945. *How to solve it: A new aspect of mathematical method* (2014 reprint ed.). Princeton university press.

[52] James Prather, Raymond Pettit, Kayla Holcomb McMurry, Alani Peters, John Homer, Nevan Simone, and Maxine Cohen. 2017. On Novices' Interaction with Compiler Error Messages: A Human Factors Approach. In *Proceedings of the 2017 ACM Conference on International Computing Education Research*. ACM, 74–82.

[53] Ido Roll, Natasha G Holmes, James Day, and Doug Bonn. 2012. Evaluating metacognitive scaffolding in guided invention activities. *Instructional science* 40, 4 (2012), 691–710.

[54] Jeffrey Rubin and Dana Chisnell. 2008. *Handbook of usability testing: how to plan, design and conduct effective tests* (2 ed.). John Wiley & Sons.

[55] Tom Schorsch. 1995. CAP: an automated self-assessment tool to check Pascal programs for syntax, logic and style errors. In *ACM SIGCSE Bulletin*, Vol. 27. ACM, 168–172.

[56] Teresa M Shaft. 1995. Helping programmers understand computer programs: the use of metacognition. *ACM SIGMIS Database* 26, 4 (1995), 25–46.

[57] Judy Sheard, S Simon, Margaret Hamilton, and Jan Lönnberg. 2009. Analysis of research into the teaching and learning of programming. In *Proceedings of the fifth international workshop on Computing education research workshop*. ACM, 93–104.

[58] Donna Teague, Malcolm Corney, Alireza Ahadi, and Raymond Lister. 2013. A qualitative think aloud study of the early neo-piagetian stages of reasoning in novice programmers. In *Proceedings of the Fifteenth Australasian Computing Education Conference-Volume 136*. Australian Computer Society, Inc., 87–95.

[59] Dwayne Towell and Brent Reeves. 2009. From Walls to Steps: Using online automatic homework checking tools to improve learning in introductory programming courses. (2009).

[60] V Javier Traver. 2010. On compiler error messages: what they say and what they mean. *Advances in Human-Computer Interaction* 2010 (2010).

[61] Aurora Vizcaíno, Juan Contreras, Jesús Favela, and Manuel Prieto. 2000. An adaptive, collaborative environment to develop good habits in programming. In *Intelligent Tutoring Systems*. Springer, 262–271.

[62] Christopher Watson, Frederick WB Li, and Jamie L Godwin. 2012. Bluefix: Using crowd-sourced feedback to support programming students in error diagnosis and repair. In *International Conference on Web-Based Learning*. Springer, 228–239.

[63] Jacqueline Whalley and Nadia Kasto. 2014. A qualitative think-aloud study of novice programmers' code writing strategies. In *Proceedings of the 2014 conference on Innovation & technology in computer science education*. ACM, 279–284.

Who Tests the Testers?*

Avoiding the Perils of Automated Testing

John Wrenn
Computer Science
Brown University
USA
jswrenn@cs.brown.edu

Shriram Krishnamurthi
Computer Science
Brown University
USA
sk@cs.brown.edu

Kathi Fisler
Computer Science
Brown University
USA
kfisler@cs.brown.edu

ABSTRACT

Instructors routinely use automated assessment methods to evaluate the semantic qualities of student implementations and, sometimes, test suites. In this work, we distill a variety of automated assessment methods in the literature down to a pair of assessment models. We identify pathological assessment outcomes in each model that point to underlying methodological flaws. These theoretical flaws broadly threaten the validity of the techniques, and we actually observe them in multiple assignments of an introductory programming course. We propose adjustments that remedy these flaws and then demonstrate, on these same assignments, that our interventions improve the accuracy of assessment. We believe that with these adjustments, instructors can greatly improve the accuracy of automated assessment.

CCS CONCEPTS

• **Social and professional topics** → **Student assessment**; CS1;
• **Software and its engineering** → **Software defect analysis**;

ACM Reference Format:
John Wrenn, Shriram Krishnamurthi, and Kathi Fisler. 2018. Who Tests the Testers?: Avoiding the Perils of Automated Testing. In *ICER '18: 2018 International Computing Education Research Conference, August 13–15, 2018, Espoo, Finland.* ACM, New York, NY, USA, 9 pages. https://doi.org/10.1145/3230977.3230999

1 INTRODUCTION

Instructors routinely rely on automated assessment methods to evaluate student work on programming assignments. In principle, automated techniques improve the scalability and reproducibility of assessment. However, while more reproducible than non-automated methods, automated techniques are not, ipso facto, more accurate. Automated techniques also make it easy to perform *flawed* assessments at scale, with little feedback to warn the instructor. Not only does this affect students, it can also affect the reliability of research that uses it (e.g., that correlates against assessment scores).

*This work was partially supported by the US National Science Foundation.

In this work, we explore methods for assessing implementations and test suites submitted in response to programming problems. In particular, we consider how student-submitted artifacts may be used to enhance instructor-provided ones within the context of automated assessment. This is hardly a new question: as discussed in section 2, many authors use student artifacts to assess other students' work. However, we find that the models in the literature for doing this can have significant flaws that can unfairly reward or penalize students.

As we will show, the key to including student artifacts in a fair way builds on screening them with particular kinds of instructor-provided artifacts, both implementations and test suites, both correct and incorrect. Concretely, we analyze two common methods for assessing student implementations. We explore the methods both foundationally and experimentally, using data from an introductory course. We highlight the perils of these approaches, and present an improved model and technique with which instructors can immunize their assessments from these perils.

The contributions of this paper are:

(1) identification of conceptual pathologies in existing methods for automated assessment,
(2) experimental evidence that these issues arise in practice, and
(3) a new method for assessing implementations and test suites that mitigates these pathologies.

After reviewing related work (section 2) and defining terminology (section 3), we present (section 4) three models for assessing implementations (one of them novel). Section 5 describes a process for instructors by which our novel model can be combined with another in a manner that iteratively improves the outcomes of both until they are identical, and section 6 evaluates these models and this process experimentally in the context of assessing both implementations and test suites. Section 7 discusses implications for those who develop or use automated assessments for programming assignments.

2 RELATED WORK

Automatic assessment of student implementations and test suites is typically done by testing their behavior against a reference artifact (rather than through proof-based formal methods [31]). We focus our work (and thus this section) on assignments for which the inputs and outputs are data values (as opposed to, say, GUIs which require their own style of testing techniques [12, 17, 35]).

There are multiple choices for both the form of the reference artifact(s) and the corresponding testing methodology, depending on which student artifact one wishes to test.

2.1 Evaluating Implementation Correctness

Goldwasser [18] asked students to submit a collection of interesting inputs. He then ran each input through each of the student implementations and an instructor-written one, checking whether the two agreed on their computed output. He notes the challenge of this approach when the outputs are non-deterministic.

Many testing frameworks support assertions that consist of conditions to check against the run-time behavior of an implementation. While such assertions can be embedded in the implementation itself, we focus here on ones that are provided as a standalone artifact (as this is a better fit for automated testing). These assertions can check that a specific input yields a specific output, or that the output of a given function always satisfies a stated predicate (such as lying within a range of numbers). Assertions are part of most unit-testing frameworks; some languages even include constructs for these assertions directly in the language itself (e.g., Pyret [5], the Racket student languages [14], and Rust [6]).

Some forms of assertion-based testing generate the inputs to use in testing, rather than require students or instructors to provide them manually. Tools such as QuickCheck [3] generate test cases from formal specifications of a program's expected behavior (then test the program against the same formal specification).

Many instructors assess student implementations using a test suite of their own creation [2, 15, 16, 19, 21, 22, 24, 27, 36]). This approach is supported by major automatic assessment tools, such as ASSYST [23], Web-CAT [7], and Marmoset [34]. Some instructors also leverage student-written tests for testing other students' implementations. In the literature, this approach is most closely associated with all-pairs style evaluations, in which student test suites and implementations are assessed by running every test suite against every implementation [11, 18, 25]. This approach also appears in research on students' testing abilities, such as Edwards' proposed metric of "bug revealing capability" [8–10]. Broadly, student test suites can be appropriated for the task of assessing *any* corpus of implementations whose correctness is unknown—not just those of students. For instance, Shams and Edwards [30] use student test suites to filter out mutations of an initially-correct reference implementation whose faultiness is not detectable by any student or instructor test suite.

2.2 Evaluating Test Suites

Student test suites are typically assessed against two metrics: whether the tests conform to the specification (*correctness*), and whether the tests cover the interesting inputs to a problem (*thoroughness*) [27]. Assessing correctness of a test suite typically entails running it against an instructor-written implementation [2, 8–10, 27, 32]. This check is particularly important when using student tests to assess each others' implementations [8–10, 25].

Code coverage is often used as a proxy for thoroughness; ASSYST [23], Web-CAT [7], and Marmoset [34] all take this approach. Code coverage is attractive because it reflects professional software engineering practice [26] and is not labor-intensive [8]. However, a growing body of evidence challenges the appropriateness of coverage as a measure of thoroughness [1, 9, 20], in both professional and pedagogic contexts. Alternatively, instructors may run student

test suites against a corpus of incorrect implementations, checking what fraction of these a test suite rejects. This corpus may be sourced from students [10, 11, 18, 25, 33], from machine-generated mutations of a reference implementation [1, 30, 33], or crafted by the instructor [2, 27].

3 ASSUMPTIONS AND TERMINOLOGY

We assume that instructors assess implementations by running tests against them, where each test indicates both an input to the program and the expected output (whether directly or via some sort of assertion). We do not assume that instructors are trying to handle all forms of assessment automatically; style and design assessments, for example, may be handled through separate processes and are out of the scope of this paper. This paper focuses on automated assessment for functional correctness. We further assume that instructors are willing to perform some manual inspection of some testing results as part of calibrating the artifacts against which automation will assess student work.

We will use the term *conforms* to describe test suites or implementations that are consistent with a given specification (usually provided by the problem statement). For a test suite to accurately flag non-conformant implementations, it needs to be fairly thorough (a term we introduced in section 2.2). Our definition of thoroughness suggests that it targets a relative, rather than absolute, standard. Completely thorough test suites are generally not achievable in practice: most programs have an infinite number of behaviors, which cannot be covered in a finite number of tests. Nevertheless, we assume that instructors are trying to be thorough relative to the bugs that are likely in student implementations. We call tests that are nonconformant (either because they assert something nonsensical, or they mis-represent the specification) *invalid*.

When assessing an implementation against a test suite, we say that the test suite *accepts* the implementation if every individual test in the suite passes on the implementation. If even one test fails, we will say that the test suite *rejects* the implementation.

Given a set of test suites to check an implementation, we will say (par abus de langage) that the implementation is *correct* (relative to those suites) if every test suite accepts the implementation. Otherwise, we will say that the implementation is *faulty*.

4 MODELS OF ASSESSMENT

In this paper we study and contrast three models for assessing student implementations, the first two of which are commonly used in prior work. We give each a name and describe its general form, though of course individual uses of each model may differ slightly. Figure 1 pictorially summarizes our models and the workflows that define them. The upper part shows a student implementation running against one or more test suites. The lower part shows which implementations a student test suite must pass to be run against other student implementations.

We study these models in two contexts: (1) assessing student implementations, and (2) assessing student test suites. Each model outputs a judgment of whether each student implementation is faulty or not. Having established the correctness of implementations, an instructor may then evaluate the accuracy of each student's test suite by checking how closely its judgments of implementation correctness match the judgments made by the model.

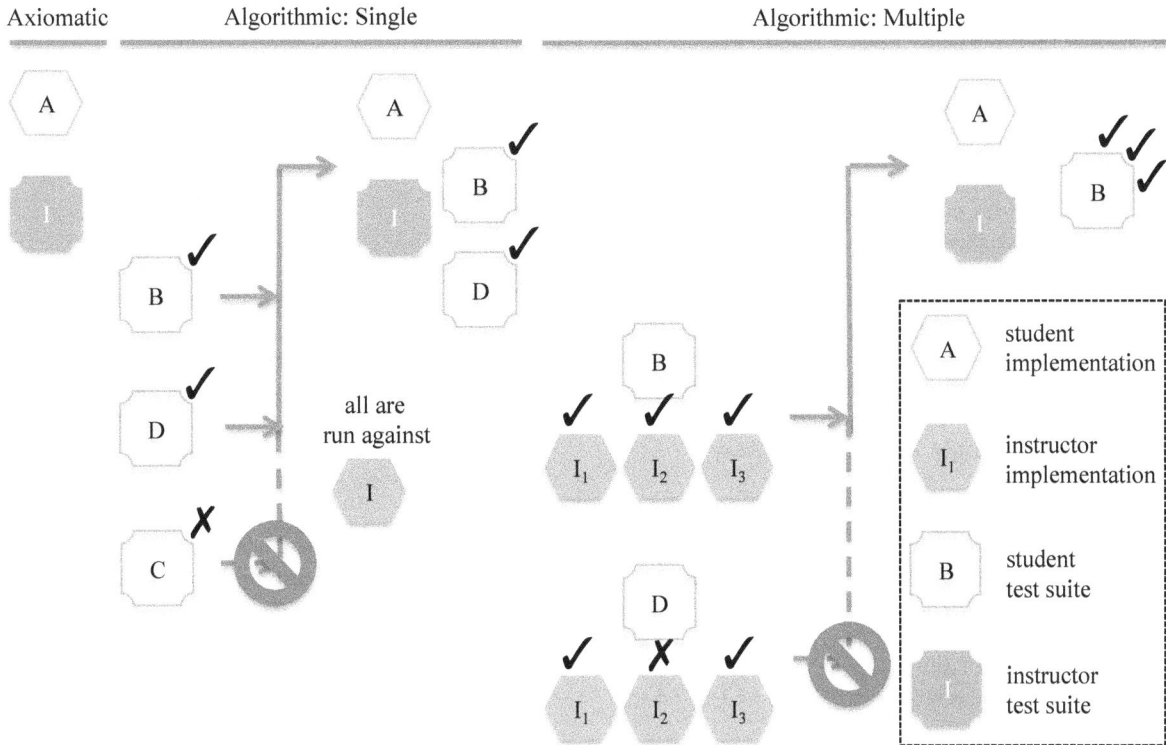

Figure 1: Three models of assessing implementations, each based on a different collection of test suites. Hexagons are implementations, squares with concave corners are test suites. Solid artifacts (labeled I) are instructor-provided while hollow ones are from students, with letters and numbers differentiating them as needed.

```
import number_sort from impl

check:
    number_sort([3,2,1,0]))
        is [0,1,2,3]
end
```
Instructor Test Suite

```
import number_sort from impl

check:
    number_sort([3,2,2,1]))
        is [1,2,2,3]
end
```
A Clever Test Suite

```
import number_sort from impl

check:
    number_sort([0,1,2,3]))
        is [3,2,1,0]
end
```
A Faulty Test Suite

Figure 2: Three contrived test suites for (ascending) `number_sort`: (1) an instructor test suite; (2) a student test suite that, by checking with an input that includes duplicate elements, can catch a bug that the instructor test suite cannot; and (3) a student test suite that, by expecting the sort to occur in descending order, is invalid with respect to the assignment specification.

4.1 Axiomatic (Axm)

The *axiomatic* approach, shown at the top left of fig. 1, is the simplest and most common:

> **Model Summary:** Each student implementation is assessed against a single instructor-written test suite.

In the figure, student A's implementation is being assessed against the instructor test suite.

Pitfall. This method relies solely on the judgment of the instructor test suite. If this test suite is incorrect (which it usually isn't, but could be in subtle ways), conformant student implementations may be labeled as faulty. What is even more likely, we contend, is that the instructor test suite may be insufficiently thorough, in which case student implementations that are actually nonconformant may be wrongly labeled correct.

As a simplistic but illustrative example, assume that students have been asked to implement a function, `number_sort`, that sorts its input in ascending order. Figure 2 shows a rudimentary instructor test suite (left). Another test suite (center) tests something beyond the instructor suite (in this case, correct handling of duplicate elements); we call such test suites *clever*. If a student implementation did not handle duplicate elements, the instructor test suite will accept it while the clever suite rejects it. The test suite on the right violates the specification by expecting descending order; such a test suite is invalid (as defined in section 3).

Instructors might assume (based on their experience with the material) that their test suites are correct and fairly thorough (especially for assignments they have given multiple times), but this model provides no inherent mechanism for validating this belief. The authors of this paper, in particular, were victims of this hubris (we return to this in section 6.1).

Assessment Impact. If the instructor test suite is insufficiently thorough, faulty implementations may be labeled as correct. These students would not receive feedback about these undetected flaws. Furthermore, if these labels are used as a basis to assess student test suites, students who manage to detect bugs the instructor does not will be penalized, since their suite's judgments about correctness disagree with the judgments of the instructor's suite.

4.2 Algorithmic: Single Implementation (ALGSING)

How might we raise the thoroughness of the test suite used for assessing student implementations? Numerous existing tools and methodologies augment instructor test suites with student-written ones (e.g., [8–10, 18, 30]). Of course, student test suites could be incorrect, so this approach needs a method to determine which ones can be trusted for this task. Validating students' test suites against an instructor implementation is a obvious (and oft-taken) approach:

> **Model Summary:** Each student implementation is assessed against the instructor test suite as well as student test-suites that are correct relative to the instructor implementation.

In the first test-suite assessment in fig. 1 (lower left), B's, C's, and D's test suites are evaluated against the instructor implementation. B's and D's are consistent with the implementation—the check marks on them indicate that they have passed this check—but C's is not. C's test suite is subsequently ignored, but B's and D's are added to the pool of test suites against which A's implementation is tested. The instructor test suite has presumably already been checked for correctness against the instructor implementation, or is axiomatically taken as correct.

Note that this model does not consider thoroughness as a criterion for including a student test suite. A test suite that is not thorough might not add much testing power, but it won't inaccurately mark an implementation as faulty. The other authors cited in section 2 include student tests at the granularity of a single test case. For simplicity sake, our work considers only entire test suites. Note that this does not change the flaws we identify, only the potential magnitude of our measurements.

A First Experiment. When we tried this technique on submissions for one of our assignments, the number of faulty implementations skyrocketed, from 28% of implementations identified as faulty by the instructor test suite alone, to 89% when student tests were also used. (We discuss details in section 6.) What happened?

This drastically different assessment outcome resulted from trusting tests that made assertions beyond the bounds of the specification. We illustrate the issue using two succinct example problems (that are simpler than those from our real data):

(1) Implement a function that computes a distance metric between two non-empty lists of values.
(2) Implement a function that transforms a list of numbers into a binary search tree. (The assignment does not specify in which branch duplicates should be placed.)

Each of these specifications, as given, admits multiple, functionally-distinguishable implementations. Respectively, the student implementations

(1) may do *anything* if either of the inputs are empty;
(2) may place equal values in either the left or right subtree.

The authors of these implementations are likely to write tests that assert whichever particular behavior they happened to choose. These tests, while correct with respect to the student's *own* implementation, are not appropriate tests of *all* implementations.

In general, such tests, which we term *over-zealous*, can exceed the bounds of the specification in two ways:

- *Be overly liberal in what they supply for inputs*; e.g., if the specification asks for a function that is only defined on non-empty lists, then a test that supplies the function with an empty list is over-zealous.
- *Be overly conservative in what they accept as outputs*; e.g., if the specification does not dictate to which side of the binary search tree duplicate elements should be placed, a test that assumes duplicates go to a particular side is over-zealous.

Pitfall of Over-Zealous Tests. Consider a student test suite whose over-zealous test cases *coincidentally* conform to the specific behavior of the instructor implementation. Since that suite will pass the instructor implementation, it will be labeled correct and then used to judge whether *other* student implementations are correct. Consequently, any other student implementations that behave differently (even if they satisfy the specification) will be marked faulty by that over-zealous test suite.

If two student test suites over-zealously test *different* aspects of the specification, and are both incorporated into the implementation assessment process, it can be virtually impossible for any implementation to be deemed correct. Both forms arose in our experiment, resulting in the dramatic increase in the percentage of implementations that were deemed faulty. This experiment illustrates why *eliminating over-zealous test cases from the implementation labeling process is crucial.*

Assessment Impact. If over-zealous tests are not eliminated, any conformant implementation that diverges even slightly from the instructor implementation may be wrongly judged as faulty. Furthermore, if this flawed labeling is used to assess student test suites, students will "fail" to identify these "faulty" implementations, and will be penalized for apparently having un-thorough test suites.

4.3 Algorithmic: Multiple Implementation (ALGMULT)

Fundamentally, the problem created by over-zealous tests is one of over-fitting: while the specification describes a *space* of implementations, just *one* sample from that space (a single instructor implementation) is used to determine whether all other implementations conform to that specification. To mitigate this flaw, an instructor can craft *multiple* correct implementations in a manner to be defined shortly. When assessing implementations, only test suites that are deemed correct against *all* of the instructor implementation are used in assessing other student implementations.

> **Model Summary:** Each student implementation is assessed against the instructor test suite as well as student test-suites that are correct relative to multiple instructor implementations.

In fig. 1, B's and D's test suites are checked against three instructor implementations. B's is consistent with all three, but D's appears to be over-zealous, failing implementation 2. Therefore, D's test suite is no longer considered, whereas B's test suite (whose checks denote passed instructor implementations) can be added to the pool of test suites for assessing A's implementation.

How should instructor implementations be different? Different instructor implementations should reflect different scenarios allowed by the specification (e.g., guarding against different kinds of over-zealous tests). In particular, different implementations might admit more inputs than the specification requires, or might produce outputs that are consistent with the specification in different ways. For example:

(1) If the specification only dictates how a function behaves on non-empty lists, then given an empty list, one instructor implementation might throw an exception while another returns an innocuous value.

(2) If the specification does not dictate to which side of a binary search tree duplicate elements should be placed, one instructor implementation might place them on the left, while another places them on the right.

Such implementations are *adversarial* in that they check for violations of the robustness principle.[1] A good set of adversarial implementations would be diverse enough that an over-zealous test suite would reject at least one of them. If this happens, over-zealous test suites would be ruled out before being used to assess other student implementations.

These restrictions against over-zealousness may appear to pose a high bar on student tests. Indeed they do, but the bar is not unattainable: in another experiment (section 6.1), the addition of adversarial instructor implementations reduced the fraction of student test suites trusted for assessing implementations from 79% to 35%. It is important to remember, however, that this high bar is for a test suite *to assess other student implementations*; it is not necessarily the bar we would use to grade the test suite itself.

We observe in passing that nothing in our description limits adversarial implementations to screening *student* tests. The fruits of labor to obtain additional tests by any means—from colleagues, by crowdsourcing, by the instructors themselves, etc.—should all pass through the same adversarial process before being used to assess student work. This burden is nevertheless worth bearing due to the problems created by the two more common methods of assessment (Axm and AlgSing).

---

[1]This principle is also known as *Postel's Law*, after Jon Postel's formulation of the principle in an early specification of TCP: "TCP implementations should follow a general principle of robustness: be conservative in what you do, be liberal in what you accept from others." [28]

Assessment Impact. Through crafting multiple adversarial implementations, an instructor can defend against the risk of incorporating over-zealous tests. However, the consequences of misplacing trust in even a single over-zealous test are the same (and no less dire) than those described for the AlgSing method.

5 TESTING THE TESTER

A common flaw underlies the vulnerabilities of all three models: if an instructor does not adequately consider some aspect of the problem, their assessments of students may suffer. Taken individually, they provide neither a resolution nor a means to detect this flaw. While AlgMult partially defends against against the severe threat of mistrusting a student test, its defense relies on instructors' sufficient development of adversarial implementations. Instructors can avoid this risk entirely by using Axm instead of an algorithmic model to grade student implementations, but that leaves Axm's risk of penalizing students who detect bugs that the instructor failed to write tests for.

By leveraging *both* axiomatic and algorithmic labeling, an instructor can detect and resolve this flaw. Consider that for an assignment with an adequate set of adversarial implementations and an instructor test suite that is not out-matched by any valid student test, Axm and AlgMult must result in an *identical* correctness labeling of student implementations. If either of these conditions is false, there must exist an incorporated student's test that identifies some implementation as faulty that the instructor's test suite identified as correct. In this event, one of two possibilities must be true: (1) that the student test is, in fact, nonconformant, but there was not an adversarial implementation to identify it as such, or (2) that the student test is, in fact, conformant, and captures a behavior not explored by any test in the instructor's suite. The instructor should examine the test case in question, identify whether it is conformant, and either create an adversarial implementation that rules it out, or incorporate it into their test suite. In section 6, we apply this process to quantify the impact of these assessment flaws on a number of assignments in an introductory programming course.

6 EVALUATION ON COURSE DATA

To assess the extent to which these perils may *actually* impact the robustness of course assessment, we applied the models to re-assess the submitted programs and test suites of students from a semester-long accelerated introduction to computer science course at a highly-selective private US university. The course is primarily taken by students with prior programming experience; students place into it based on a series of programming assignments over the summer. In one semester, the course covers most of the same material as the department's year-long introductory sequences (fundamentals of programming, data structures, core algorithms, and big-O algorithm analysis).

The course teaches functional programming (many students who place into it have prior experience with object-oriented programming), following techniques from the *How to Design Programs* [13] curriculum. Both this curriculum and the course emphasize testing. Students are required to submit test suites for every assignment. Test suites are graded for both correctness and thoroughness, and are weighted similarly to implementations in determining final

Assignment	% of Student Implementations Labled Faulty		
	AXM	ALGSING	ALGMULT
DOCDIFF	34%	98%	46%
NILE	35%	97%	35%
FILESYSTEM	22%	52%	26%
MAPREDUCE	28%	89%	57%

Table 1: Percent of student implementations labeled faulty by each model.

Assignment	% of Student Test Suites Incorporated	
	ALGSING	ALGMULT
DOCDIFF	90%	81%
NILE	28%	0%
FILESYSTEM	94%	71%
MAPREDUCE	79%	35%

Table 2: Percent of student test suites incorporated by each algorithmic model.

course grades. On some assignments, students submit test suites a few days before submitting implementations, receiving feedback on test-suite correctness in time to make modifications to their implementations and test suites.

For each assignment under study, we assessed student implementations under: (i) AXM, using the instructor test suite that was used during the semester to grade student implementations; (ii) ALGSING, using the instructor implementation that was used during the semester to grade the validity of student test suites; and then (iii) ALGMULT, using the criterion specified in section 5 to develop adversarial implementations. We quantify the impact of AXM's and ALGSING's vulnerabilities by contrasting their outcomes to that of ALGMULT.

Assignments Under Study. For the analysis for this paper, we selected four assignments that are quite different from each other and representative of the course overall:

- DOCDIFF, where 91 students implemented and tested programs computing a document similarity metric using a bag-of-words model [29].
- NILE, where 70 students implemented and tested a rudimentary recommendation system.
- FILESYSTEM, where 76 students implemented and tested rudimentary Unix-style commands for traversing a (in-memory) file structure with mutually-dependent datatypes [13].
- MAPREDUCE, where 38 pairs of students implemented and tested the essence of MapReduce [4] (implemented sequentially), and applied it to multiple problems. This included re-doing some previous assignments (including NILE) in terms of the MapReduce paradigm, using their implementation.

We explored only four assignments because constructing multiple adversarial implementations is a potentially time-consuming process. For each assignment we constructed between two (for NILE) and seven (for MAPREDUCE) adversarial implementations.

The differing number of students submitting for each assignment reflects students dropping the course (after DOCDIFF), then working in pairs (on MAPREDUCE); the assignments are listed in the order in which they were assigned. On each assignment, there were a few (2-3, though 9 for NILE) submissions that were not included in the analysis (and are not reflected in the above counts): these assignments either had compile-time errors or threw run-time exceptions that we were not able to resolve with a few minutes of work.

6.1 Impact on Implementation Assessment

The models produced drastically different assessments of implementation correctness. Table 1 summarizes the percentage of student

implementations that were deemed faulty under each of the three models (the MAPREDUCE data were mentioned in section 4). Very few implementations are deemed faulty under AXM, the majority are deemed faulty under ALGSING, and ALGMULT lies in between (that the ALGMULT percentages are no smaller than those for AXM matches our expectation based on their definitions).

With the AXM model, we noted that an insufficiently thorough instructor test suite may fail to detect all faulty implementations. We assumed that our test suites for these assignments were thorough, but had not validated this belief. Contrasting the first and third columns of table 1, we find that a substantial proportion of students who were notified that their implementations were correct *actually* had faults in their submissions. These data confirm that there is significant room to improve the thoroughness of our tests: both DOCDIFF and MAPREDUCE show notable differences in the percentage of faulty implementations flagged between AXM and ALGMULT.

With the algorithmic models, instructors bolster their own test suites with student tests but, we noted, face the risk and consequences of inadvertently mis-trusting an over-zealous student test. In the case of ALGSING, instructors rely on just *one* known-correct implementation to filter out invalid tests. Contrasting the second and third columns of table 1, we find that an substantial proportion of the implementations marked faulty by ALGSING were, in fact, correct[2]. These data show that a single implementation was not sufficient for filtering student tests. Table 2 shows the percentage of students whose tests were incorporated by ALGSING and ALGMULT. Contrasting its two columns, we find that ALGSING consistently over-trusted student tests.

6.2 Impact on Assessing Test Suites

Next, we explore the impact of these perils on test-suite assessment, working with our MAPREDUCE data.

Methodology: The models in this paper classify implementations as correct or faulty. As we mention in section 4, we can then use this classification as a ground truth to assess the accuracy of student tests. We do this by applying each test suite to a collection of (assessed) implementations, and comparing the test suite's classification of their correctness against that provided by the model.

We perform this analysis on a collection of 53 MAPREDUCE implementations. This collection contains all 38 student implementations,

---

[2]We do not report statistical significance, because the nature of these analyses introduce considerable nuance and difficulty in designing a statistical test. Regardless, for students, these differences have *personal* significance.

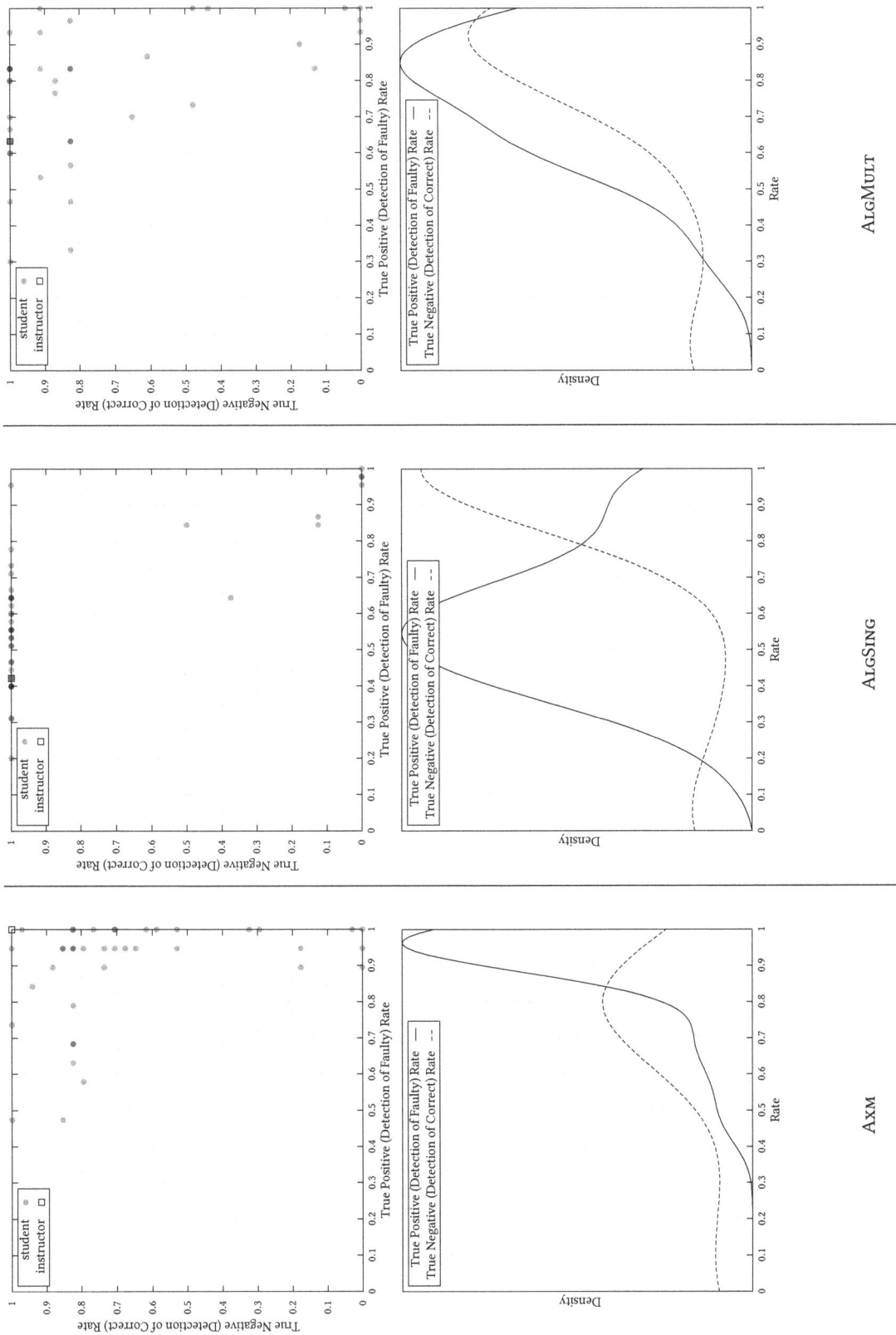

Figure 3: Assessment of test suites on MapReduce. In the top row, each dot represents a test suite; its location encodes its respective true-positive rate (the % of faulty implementations it accepted) and true-negative rate (the % of correct implementations that it rejected). Below, a kernel density estimation plot shows the relative commonality of true-positive and true-negative rates.

as well as seven (adversarial) correct and eight faulty specially-crafted implementations. These latter implementations were included to make sure that the corpus contained a handful of each kind of implementation (since we could not predict where the student implementations would fall).

We quantify the closeness of each student test suite's classification to the classification of the underlying models using the standard metrics of binary classifiers:

- *true-positive rate*, the fraction of faulty implementations that the test suite appropriately identifies as *faulty*;[3]
- *true-negative rate*, the fraction of correct implementations that the test suite appropriately identifies as *correct*.

Figure 3 depicts the resulting true-positive and true-negative rates of each test suite relative to the classifications produced by Axm, AlgSing, and AlgMult (one column each, respectively). These graphs illustrate, from the perspective of assessing student test suites, the drastically different outcomes that can arise depending on which model is used to label implementations.

Axm *Perils:* In the Axm model, a student that writes a test that identifies a bug missed by the instructor test suite is *penalized* for their thoroughness, as their test suite's judgment of correctness is observed as disagreeing with the judgment of the instructor's test suite. In the context of test suite assessment, this is reflected as a decrease in true-negative rate.

This pathology significantly impacted the outcomes of our test suite assessments performed atop Axm. The gaps in our test suites were accessible enough for *many* students to find (even though we had refined these test suites over several years). On DocDiff, Filesystem, and MapReduce, respectively, 63%, 9% and 29% of students identified at least one faulty implementation that instructor test suite missed. (Only on Nile did *no* student test more cleverly than the instructor had.) A contrast of the Axm and AlgMult columns of fig. 3 bears this pathology out in the context of test suite assessment. The true-negative density curve of Axm is shifted slightly to the left of that of AlgMult, indicating that Axm assessed students as having lower true-negative rates than AlgMult did. Furthermore, we note that Axm penalizes equally students who write invalid tests and students who test more cleverly than the instuctor. Thus, an instructor using Axm might incorrectly conclude that their best students failed to understand the problem specification.

AlgSing *Perils:* In theory, AlgSing and AlgMult (which acknowledge that students may find bugs the instructor does not) remedy this pathology. However, as discussed in section 6.1, incorrectly incorporating student tests can easily give rise to a catastrophically inaccurate assessment of implementations, which in turn leads to inaccurate assessment of test suites. Under AlgSing, most students have very high true-negative rates and very low true-positive rates. This came about in part because so few implementations were labeled correct by AlgMult (see the middle column of table 1). Thus, there is much less nuance in the true-negative rates, as reflected in the horizontal bands of points in the scatter plot.

6.3 Takeaway

The theoretical flaws of the standard models had real, substantial impacts on our assessments. Using the technique in section 5 to develop an AlgMult assessment, we identified and corrected numerous shortcomings in our grading artifacts. This process required close examination of each assignment statement, and we also encountered ways in which our assignments could be made clearer. Thus, in addition to improving our grading system with this process, we have improved the assignments themselves.

7 DISCUSSION

In an era of growing enrollments and on-line courses, it is essential to understand the nuances of automated assessment, especially since it seems to naturally fit some aspects of computing. In particular, this fit can mask worrisome weaknesses. With automated assessment widespread in everything from K-12 and tertiary courses to MOOCs to programming competitions to job placement sites and more, its foundations require greater scrutiny.

In this paper we look closely at automated assessment of programs and of their first-cousins, test suites. Through pure reasoning, we show that the standard models (sections 4.1 and 4.2) can suffer from significant measurement flaws. We present a new model of assessment (section 4.3) and a corrective technique that utilizes it (section 5). The results of section 6 validate all these claims in practice when assessing both implementation and test suite quality.

The problems we find in these models are disturbing in two ways. First, the flaws can be subtle, so instructors and students many never notice them. Indeed, as we have noted, in some cases the assessment results in students appearing to do better than their true performance. This may give students a false sense of confidence in their abilities. Second, it is not trivial to extrapolate from the feedback of these models to identifying a systemic flaw in students' work. Especially in massive or disconnected settings, it may be difficult to identify the problems we raise. The sheer volume of data available may blind some people to the true quality of the data.

On a personal note, we can relate how easy these flaws are to overlook. Like many others educators, we had used the two flawed methods for nearly two decades, growing increasingly dependent on them with growing class sizes (a widespread phenomenon in the US). The initial purpose of this study was simply to test the quality of student tests, in comparison to an earlier study by Edwards and Shams [10]. As we began to perform our measurements, we wondered how *stable* they were, and started to use different methods to evaluate stability. When we noticed wild fluctuations—which made our analyses highly unreliable—we began to investigate why small changes to the implementation set would have large effects, which led to unearthing the problems reported in this paper.

We therefore conclude with a salutary warning. While automated assessments are valuable and have their place, their use—as with any machine-generated artifact that draws on a large set of data—requires significant reflection. Happily, we demonstrate that the method of multiple adversarial implementations (section 4.3) avoids the pathologies we have found in automated assessment, enabling us to draw on a larger pool of inputs (namely, to consider student test suites and implementations as well), which in turn results in better evaluation of student implementations and test suites.

[3]While associating "positive" with "faulty" may seem backwards, the goal of thoroughness is to accurately identify faulty implementations.

REFERENCES

[1] Kalle Aaltonen, Petri Ihantola, and Otto Seppälä. 2010. Mutation Analysis vs. Code Coverage in Automated Assessment of Students' Testing Skills. In *Proceedings of the ACM International Conference Companion on Object Oriented Programming Systems Languages and Applications Companion (OOPSLA '10)*. ACM, New York, NY, USA, 153–160. http://doi.acm.org/10.1145/1869542.1869567

[2] Michael K. Bradshaw. 2015. Ante Up: A Framework to Strengthen Student-Based Testing of Assignments. In *Proceedings of the 46th ACM Technical Symposium on Computer Science Education (SIGCSE '15)*. ACM, New York, NY, USA, 488–493. http://doi.acm.org/10.1145/2676723.2677247

[3] Koen Claessen and John Hughes. 2000. QuickCheck: A Lightweight Tool for Random Testing of Haskell Programs. In *Proceedings of the Fifth ACM SIGPLAN International Conference on Functional Programming (ICFP '00)*. ACM, New York, NY, USA, 268–279. http://doi.acm.org/10.1145/351240.351266

[4] Jeffrey Dean and Sanjay Ghemawat. 2008. MapReduce: Simplified Data Processing on Large Clusters. *Commun. ACM* 51, 1 (Jan. 2008), 107–113. http://doi.acm.org/10.1145/1327452.1327492

[5] The Pyret Project Developers. 2018. *The Pyret Programming Language*. Chapter 2.2. https://www.pyret.org/docs/latest/testing.html

[6] The Rust Project Developers. 2018. *The Rust Programming Language*. Chapter 11. https://doc.rust-lang.org/book/second-edition/ch11-00-testing.html

[7] Stephen H. Edwards. 2003. Improving Student Performance by Evaluating How Well Students Test Their Own Programs. *Journal on Educational Resources in Computing* 3, 3, Article 1 (Sept. 2003). http://doi.acm.org/10.1145/1029994.1029995

[8] Stephen H. Edwards. 2003. Improving Student Performance by Evaluating How Well Students Test Their Own Programs. *J. Educ. Resour. Comput.* 3, 3, Article 1 (Sept. 2003). http://doi.acm.org/10.1145/1029994.1029995

[9] Stephen H. Edwards and Zalia Shams. 2014. Comparing Test Quality Measures for Assessing Student-written Tests. In *Companion Proceedings of the 36th International Conference on Software Engineering (ICSE Companion 2014)*. ACM, New York, NY, USA, 354–363. http://doi.acm.org/10.1145/2591062.2591164

[10] Stephen H. Edwards and Zalia Shams. 2014. Do Student Programmers All Tend to Write the Same Software Tests? In *ITiCSE*. ACM, New York, NY, USA, 171–176. http://doi.acm.org/10.1145/2591708.2591757

[11] Stephen H. Edwards, Zalia Shams, Michael Cogswell, and Robert C. Senkbeil. 2012. Running Students' Software Tests Against Each Others' Code: New Life for an Old "Gimmick". In *Proceedings of the 43rd ACM Technical Symposium on Computer Science Education (SIGCSE '12)*. ACM, New York, NY, USA, 221–226. http://doi.acm.org/10.1145/2157136.2157202

[12] John English. 2004. Automated Assessment of GUI Programs Using JEWL. In *Proceedings of the 9th Annual SIGCSE Conference on Innovation and Technology in Computer Science Education (ITiCSE '04)*. ACM, New York, NY, USA, 137–141. http://doi.acm.org/10.1145/1007996.1008033

[13] Matthias Felleisen, Robert Bruce Findler, Matthew Flatt, and Shriram Krishnamurthi. 2001. *How to Design Programs*. MIT Press.

[14] Matthias Felleisen, Robert Bruce Findler, Matthew Flatt, and Shriram Krishnamurthi. 2018. *How to Design Programs* (second ed.). MIT Press.

[15] George E. Forsythe and Niklaus Wirth. 1965. Automatic Grading Programs. *Commun. ACM* 8, 5 (May 1965), 275–278. http://doi.acm.org/10.1145/364914.364937

[16] Eric Foxley, Omar Salman, and Zarina Shukur. 1997. The Automatic Assessment of Z Specifications. In *The Supplemental Proceedings of the Conference on Integrating Technology into Computer Science Education: Working Group Reports and Supplemental Proceedings (ITiCSE-WGR '97)*. ACM, New York, NY, USA, 129–131. http://doi.acm.org/10.1145/266057.266141

[17] Xiang Fu, Boris Peltsverger, Kai Qian, Lixin Tao, and Jigang Liu. 2008. APOGEE: Automated Project Grading and Instant Feedback System for Web Based Computing. In *Proceedings of the 39th SIGCSE Technical Symposium on Computer Science Education (SIGCSE '08)*. ACM, New York, NY, USA, 77–81. http://doi.acm.org/10.1145/1352135.1352163

[18] Michael H. Goldwasser. 2002. A Gimmick to Integrate Software Testing Throughout the Curriculum. In *Proceedings of the 33rd SIGCSE Technical Symposium on Computer Science Education (SIGCSE '02)*. ACM, New York, NY, USA, 271–275. http://doi.acm.org/10.1145/563340.563446

[19] J. B. Hext and J. W. Winings. 1969. An Automatic Grading Scheme for Simple Programming Exercises. *Commun. ACM* 12, 5 (May 1969), 272–275. http://doi.acm.org/10.1145/362946.362981

[20] Laura Inozemtseva and Reid Holmes. 2014. Coverage is Not Strongly Correlated with Test Suite Effectiveness. In *Proceedings of the 36th International Conference on Software Engineering (ICSE 2014)*. ACM, New York, NY, USA, 435–445. http://doi.acm.org/10.1145/2568225.2568271

[21] Peter C. Isaacson and Terry A. Scott. 1989. Automating the Execution of Student Programs. *SIGCSE Bull.* 21, 2 (June 1989), 15–22. http://doi.acm.org/10.1145/65738.65741

[22] David Jackson. 2000. A Semi-automated Approach to Online Assessment. In *Proceedings of the 5th Annual SIGCSE/SIGCUE ITiCSEconference on Innovation and Technology in Computer Science Education (ITiCSE '00)*. ACM, New York, NY, USA, 164–167. http://doi.acm.org/10.1145/343048.343160

[23] David Jackson and Michelle Usher. 1997. Grading Student Programs Using ASSYST. In *Proceedings of the Twenty-eighth SIGCSE Technical Symposium on Computer Science Education (SIGCSE '97)*. ACM, New York, NY, USA, 335–339. http://doi.acm.org/10.1145/268084.268210

[24] David G. Kay, Terry Scott, Peter Isaacson, and Kenneth A. Reek. 1994. Automated Grading Assistance for Student Programs. In *Proceedings of the Twenty-fifth SIGCSE Symposium on Computer Science Education (SIGCSE '94)*. ACM, New York, NY, USA, 381–382. http://doi.acm.org/10.1145/191029.191184

[25] Will Marrero and Amber Settle. 2005. Testing First: Emphasizing Testing in Early Programming Courses. In *Proceedings of the 10th Annual SIGCSE Conference on Innovation and Technology in Computer Science Education (ITiCSE '05)*. ACM, New York, NY, USA, 4–8. http://doi.acm.org/10.1145/1067445.1067451

[26] Sebastian Pape, Julian Flake, Andreas Beckmann, and Jan Jürjens. 2016. STAGE: A Software Tool for Automatic Grading of Testing Exercises: Case Study Paper. In *Proceedings of the 38th International Conference on Software Engineering Companion (ICSE '16)*. ACM, New York, NY, USA, 491–500. http://doi.acm.org/10.1145/2889160.2889203

[27] Joe Gibbs Politz, Shriram Krishnamurthi, and Kathi Fisler. 2014. In-flow Peer-review of Tests in Test-first Programming. In *ICER*. ACM, New York, NY, USA, 11–18. http://doi.acm.org/10.1145/2632320.2632347

[28] Jon Postel. 1980. *Transmission Control Protocol*. Internet-Draft. Internet Engineering Task Force. https://tools.ietf.org/html/rfc761

[29] Gerard Salton, Anita Wong, and Chung-Shu Yang. 1975. A Vector Space Model for Automatic Indexing. *Commun. ACM* 18, 11 (Nov. 1975), 613–620. http://doi.acm.org/10.1145/361219.361220

[30] Zalia Shams and Stephen H. Edwards. 2013. Toward Practical Mutation Analysis for Evaluating the Quality of Student-written Software Tests. In *Proceedings of the Ninth Annual International ACM Conference on International Computing Education Research (ICER '13)*. ACM, New York, NY, USA, 53–58. http://doi.acm.org/10.1145/2493394.2493402

[31] K. K. Sharma, Kunal Banerjee, and Chittaranjan Mandal. 2014. A Scheme for Automated Evaluation of Programming Assignments Using FSMD Based Equivalence Checking. In *Proceedings of the 6th IBM Collaborative Academia Research Exchange Conference (I-CARE) on I-CARE 2014 (I-CARE 2014)*. ACM, New York, NY, USA, Article 10, 4 pages. http://doi.acm.org/10.1145/2662117.2662127

[32] Joanna Smith, Joe Tessler, Elliot Kramer, and Calvin Lin. 2012. Using Peer Review to Teach Software Testing. In *Proceedings of the Ninth Annual International Conference on International Computing Education Research (ICER '12)*. ACM, New York, NY, USA, 93–98. http://doi.acm.org/10.1145/2361276.2361295

[33] Rebecca Smith, Terry Tang, Joe Warren, and Scott Rixner. 2017. An Automated System for Interactively Learning Software Testing. In *Proceedings of the 2017 ACM Conference on Innovation and Technology in Computer Science Education (ITiCSE '17)*. ACM, New York, NY, USA, 98–103. http://doi.acm.org/10.1145/3059009.3059022

[34] Jaime Spacco, Jaymie Strecker, David Hovemeyer, and William Pugh. 2005. Software Repository Mining with Marmoset: An Automated Programming Project Snapshot and Testing System. In *Proceedings of the 2005 International Workshop on Mining Software Repositories (MSR '05)*. ACM, New York, NY, USA, 1–5. http://doi.acm.org/10.1145/1082983.1083149

[35] Matthew Thornton, Stephen H. Edwards, Roy P. Tan, and Manuel A. Pérez-Quiñones. 2008. Supporting Student-written Tests of Gui Programs. In *Proceedings of the 39th SIGCSE Technical Symposium on Computer Science Education (SIGCSE '08)*. ACM, New York, NY, USA, 537–541. http://doi.acm.org/10.1145/1352135.1352316

[36] Urs von Matt. 1994. Kassandra: The Automatic Grading System. *SIGCUE Outlook* 22, 1 (Jan. 1994), 26–40. http://doi.acm.org/10.1145/182107.182101

Evaluating the Efficiency and Effectiveness of Adaptive Parsons Problems

Barbara J. Ericson
Georgia Institute of Technology
Atlanta, Georgia
ericson@cc.gatech.edu

James D. Foley
Georgia Institute of Technology
Atlanta, Georgia
jim.foley@cc.gatech.edu

Jochen Rick
Georgia Institute of Technology
Atlanta, Georgia
jochen.rick@gatech.edu

ABSTRACT

Practice is essential for learning. There is evidence that solving Parsons problems (putting mixed up code blocks in order) is a more efficient, but just as effective, form of practice than writing code from scratch. However, not all students successfully solve every Parsons problem. Making the problems adaptive, so that the difficulty changes based on the learner's performance, should keep the learner in Vygotsky's zone of proximal development and maximize learning gains. This paper reports on a study comparing the efficiency and effectiveness of learning from solving adaptive Parsons problems vs non-adaptive Parsons problem vs writing the equivalent code. The adaptive Parsons problems used both intra-problem and inter-problem adaptation. Intra-problem adaptation means that if the learner is struggling to solve the current problem, the problem can dynamically be made easier. Inter-problem adaptation means that the difficulty of the next problem is modified based on the learner's performance on the previous problem. This study provides evidence that solving intra-problem and inter-problem adaptive Parsons problems is a more efficient, but just as effective, form of practice as writing the equivalent code.

CCS CONCEPTS

• **Social and professional topics** → **Computing education**; **Student assessment**;

KEYWORDS

Parsons problems; adaptive Parsons problems; Parsons puzzles; Parson's problems; zone of proximal development; cognitive load

ACM Reference Format:
Barbara J. Ericson, James D. Foley, and Jochen Rick. 2018. Evaluating the Efficiency and Effectiveness of Adaptive Parsons Problems. In *ICER '18: 2018 International Computing Education Research Conference, August 13–15, 2018, Espoo, Finland.* ACM, New York, NY, USA, 9 pages. https://doi.org/10.1145/3230977.3231000

1 INTRODUCTION

Several countries, including the United States, want to increase computing in K-12 [3, 5, 11, 12, 17, 24]. To accomplish this goal,

thousands of teachers with no programming experience need to learn programming [18, 31]. However, learning to program can be difficult [7, 10, 39]. Novice programmers spend hours trying to fix errors in their programs, like unmatched parentheses [6]. Most introductory programming courses require novices to learn by writing many small programs [29, 35]. However, writing programs, even short ones, is a complex cognitive task, which can easily overwhelm novices and impede learning [40, 44]. Busy teachers need a more efficient way to learn programming.

One recommended way to reduce cognitive load is to use a completion task rather than a whole task [43]. Parsons problems are a type of code completion task in which the correct code to solve a problem is provided, but is broken into mixed up code blocks, and the user must place the blocks in the correct order [34].

Ericson, Margulieux, and Rick provided evidence that solving non-adaptive Parsons problems is more efficient (with respect to completion time), and just as effective (with respect to learning gains) as fixing the same code with errors or writing the equivalent code [22]. However, that study did not include a control group to verify that the learning gains were due to the instructional practice condition, rather than from answering the same or similar questions with feedback. Also, some students struggle to solve Parsons problems and some never solve them [21], which means that Parsons problems could be improved.

This study compared the efficiency and effectiveness of adaptive (both intra-problem and inter-problem) Parsons problems vs non-adaptive Parsons problems vs writing the equivalent code. It also included a control group that solved off-task adaptive Parsons problems. This study tested the following three hypotheses:

- **H1**: Learners who solve adaptive and non-adaptive Parsons problems will finish the instructional problems significantly faster than the learners who write code.

- **H2**: Learners who solve adaptive Parsons problems will have similar learning gains from pretest to immediate posttest as those who solve non-adaptive Parsons problems and write code.

- **H3**: Learners who solve off-task (not related to the pretest questions) adaptive Parsons problems (the control group) will have lower learning gains than those who solve on-task problems.

This paper contributes to research on adaptive learning and Parsons problem. It is the first study of the efficiency and effectiveness of intra-problem and inter-problem adaptive Parsons problems.

2 RELATED WORK

This research is based on cognitive load theory. The study was informed by prior research on adaptive learning and Parsons problems.

2.1 Cognitive Load Theory

Cognitive Load Theory (CLT) was developed by John Sweller in the late 1980s [40]. It can be used to improve the design of instructional material. Three types of cognitive load are described in the theory: intrinsic cognitive load, germane cognitive load, and extraneous cognitive load. Intrinsic cognitive load is the amount of load due to the difficulty of the problem being solved. Extraneous cognitive load is the load added by the complexity of the instructional materials. Germane cognitive load is the load devoted to the processing, construction and automation of schemas in long-term memory. Schemas are cognitive frameworks for organizing and interpreting information.

Instructional materials should be designed to free up working memory to allow learning to occur by reducing the extraneous load and focusing resources on the germane load to allow for the construction of schemas. If the instructional material overloads working memory then learning is impeded. If the intrinsic load is too high then the problem should be broken into smaller and simpler sub problems. It is important to note that the amount of cognitive load that a learner experiences is based on the learner's prior knowledge. This implies that learning should be enhanced if the task is adapted based on the learner's prior performance.

2.2 Research on Adaptive Learning

Corbalan, Kester, and van Merrienboer found that dynamically adaptive practice, where the practice problems are adapted based on the learners prior performance, improves learning, takes less time, and increases engagement [15]. This is not surprising since adaptive practice is more likely to keep the learner in Vygotsky's zone of proximal development [8], which is what the learner can accomplish with support versus independently.

Soloway, Guzdial, and Hay called for more scaffolding to support learners as they try to accomplish new tasks [36]. To be most effective, scaffolding should fade as the learner develops expertise. In other words, the system should adapt to the learner's performance to reduce the cognitive load of the task.

Intelligent Tutoring Systems (ITS) provide scaffolding on the current problem in the form of explicit hints if the learner is struggling to solve the problem. They also use selection adaptation, which means that after the learner finishes a problem the system selects the next problem based on the learner's performance and a model of what the student has mastered. ITS take a great deal of time to build [16] and are not widely used [2]. Parsons problems are relatively easy to create and Parsons problems are already supported in several free online learning environments [21, 30].

2.3 Research on Parsons Problems

Parsons problems should have lower cognitive load than code writing problems, since they are a type of code completion problem. There are several variants on Parsons problems. Some include distractor blocks which include syntactic or semantic errors and should

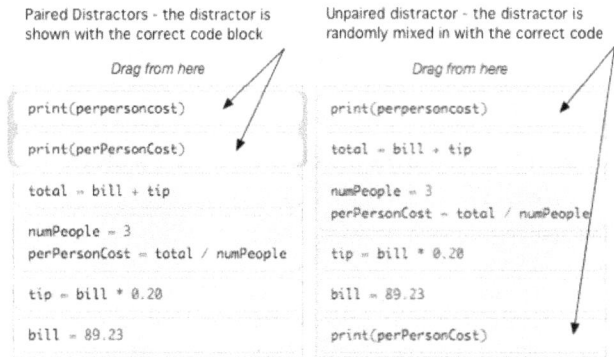

Figure 1: Paired distractor and correct code on the left and an unpaired distractor randomly mixed in with the correct code on the right

not be used in a correct solution. In some Parsons problems, a distractor block is shown either above or below the correct code block as shown on the left in Figure 1. These are called paired distractors. In unpaired distractors, shown on the right in Figure 1, the distractor blocks are randomly mixed in with the correct code blocks. Some Parsons problems require the learner to indent the code horizontally. These are called two-dimensional Parsons problems.

Research has shown that Parsons problems with only the correct code (no distractors) are the easiest to solve [25, 26], while conversely, increasing the number of distractors in a Parsons problem increases the difficulty of the problem [19]. Parsons problems with visually paired distractors are easier to solve than those with unpaired distractors [19]. Parsons problems that require the learner to provide indentation are harder than those that do not [19, 28]. Parsons problems with more blocks tend to be harder to solve than those with fewer blocks [21], especially if students are just randomly trying different combinations of blocks [27]. While many students find solving Parsons problems engaging [34], students sometimes struggle to solve the problems, and some students give up without ever solving them [21]. Since learning gains are based on the number of practice problems that students solve and understand [1], scaffolding that allows students to solve more problems should improve learning. However, it is also important that practice problems challenge the learner. Bjork and Bjork found that making practice too easy reduced learning gains [9]. They advocate for *desirable difficulties* during learning to improve long-term retention. Our adaptive Parsons problems were designed to scaffold learners that need help solving the current problem while providing desirable difficulties to learners who found the last problem too easy.

Kumar created a web-based tool for adaptive Parsons problems called Epplets [30]. Epplets uses selection adaptation, similar to what is used in Intelligent Tutoring Systems. This means that the next Parsons problem to solve is selected based on the learner's performance on the previous problem. This is the same approach used in Intelligent Tutoring Systems. Similar problems are presented until the user has demonstrated mastery on a particular concept. He reported that students get faster at solving similar Parsons problems, but did not compare solving selection-based adaptive Parsons problems with other forms of practice, such as writing code. His approach also requires a valid student model to track mastery.

3 INTRA-PROBLEM AND INTER-PROBLEM ADAPTIVE PARSONS PROBLEMS

This study used two new types of adaptation: intra-problem adaptation and inter-problem adaptation. In *intra-problem adaptation* if the learner is struggling to solve the current Parsons problem, then the problem can be made easier by removing distractors, providing indentation, or combining blocks. These changes are implicit hints which should guide the learner to the correct solution, compared to the explicit hints offered by Intelligent Tutoring Systems.

Each time the user asks for help by clicking the "Help Me" button one action is taken to make the problem easier. Help is only provided if the user has made at least three full attempts, otherwise an alert is shown explaining that help is not yet available. A full attempt contains at least the required number of blocks.

After three full unsuccessful attempts an alert is shown to inform the user that help is available. If the user asks for help, and a distractor block has been used in the solution area on the right side, then the distractor block animates moving back from the solution area to the source area on the left and then grays out to show that it is disabled. Animation is useful for grabbing attending and conveying a change over time [4, 13]. If the distractor block was originally shown paired with its correct code block and the correct code block is still in the source area on the left, then the distractor moves below the correct code and the purple edge decorations shown in Figure 1 are drawn to again show that the blocks are paired. If there are no distractors in the solution area, and the solution requires indentation, then space is slowly added to the code blocks to provide the indentation. Finally, if there are no distractors in the solution and indentation is not needed, the system will animate moving one block below another and then redraw the two blocks as one block. If the user asks for help, and there are only three blocks left in the correct solution, the user is told that they should be able to solve the problem.

In *inter-problem adaptation*, the difficulty of the next problem is modified based on the learner's performance on the previous problem. While this is somewhat similar to selection adaptation, it differs in that it does not require a model of the learner's mastery of concepts and it does not affect which problem the learner solves next. If the learner solved the last Parsons problem in only one attempt, then the next Parsons problem is made more difficult by un-pairing distractors (randomly mixing them in with the correct code) and by using all available distractors. If it took the learner four or five attempts to solve the last Parsons problem, then on the next problem the distractors are shown paired with the correct code blocks. If it took the learner 6-7 attempts to solve the last problem, then 50% percent of the available distractors are removed and the remaining distractors are shown paired with the correct code blocks on the next problem. If it took the learner 8 or more attempts to solve the last problem, then all distractors are removed from the next problem. The goal is to keep the learner in Vygotsky's zone of proximal development to optimize learning.

4 METHODS

This was a between-subjects study to test the efficiency (time to complete the practice problems) and effectiveness (learning gains) from solving intra-problem and inter-problem adaptive Parsons problems versus non-adaptive Parsons problem versus writing the equivalent code.

4.1 Participants

Undergraduate students were recruited from two sections of an introductory computer science course for computing majors at a research-intensive university in the United States. The sections had the same instructor and followed the same curriculum with the same homework and assessments. This course covers introductory programming concepts in Python including variables, selection, iteration, and lists. At the time of the study, the course had covered all of these topics and was covering files and dictionaries. Ericson visited the course during lecture to recruit participants and also sent an announcement to all of the students enrolled in the course. Participants earned 2.5 points of extra credit for completing the first session and another 2.5 points of extra credit for completing the second session one week later. Students who did not participate in the study could alternatively earn up to 5 points of extra credit by writing a paper on a computing innovation, which Ericson graded and that grade was submitted to the course instructors. None of the authors were involved in the teaching of the course.

4.2 Study Design

The first of two sessions took 2.5 hours and included consent, a demographic survey, pretest, instructional material, and an immediate posttest. The second session, lasting an hour one week later, was a delayed posttest to measure retention of the instructional material.

The instructional material in the first session contained four worked-example plus practice pairs. A worked example is a worked out expert solution to a problem [41]. Research has found that interleaving worked-examples with similar practice problems improves learning gains [42]. Students were randomly assigned to one of four practice conditions for the instructional material: 1) solving on-task adaptive Parsons problems with distractors, 2) solving on-task non-adaptive Parsons problems with distractors, 3) writing the equivalent code as the Parsons problems, or 4) a control group that solved off-task adaptive Parsons problems with distractors.

4.3 Study Procedure

Both sessions were held in a closed classroom with all participants attending at the same time. Students were instructed to bring their laptops and were provided with scratch paper and a pen. All of the study materials were online and students were asked to only use those materials, even though they had access to the Internet. Proctors checked that the students were on task.

In the first session, the procedure was 1) provide consent and randomly be placed into one of the four practice conditions, 2) complete the demographic survey, 3) complete the practice problems which familiarized the students with the online environment and problem types, 4) complete the pretest, 5) complete four worked examples plus practice pairs, where the type of practice problem differed based on the condition, and 6) complete the immediate posttest.

At the second session, a week later, participants completed the delayed posttest, which was isomorphic to the first posttest. Only the variable names and some values were changed, but the structure of the problems was the same, meaning that they required near transfer to solve. Near transfer is being able to solve a new problem in a similar context to one that you have already solved. The delayed posttest tested for retention of the material one week later.

4.4 Study Materials

The study materials include a demographic survey, familiarization (practice) materials, a pretest, instructional material, an immediate posttest, and a delayed posttest.

4.4.1 Demographic Survey. The survey asked the participant's age, gender, race, first spoken language, comfort level with reading English, high school grade point average, college grade point average, current major, expected grade in the course, and prior programming experience. If participants reported prior programming experience, they were also asked what courses, where they took them, and how many years they had been programming.

4.4.2 Familiarization Activities. The participants in this study had not previously used the online study environment, so materials were developed to introduce them to the types of problems they would see in the pretest. This included instruction on how to start and finish a timed section (a section that must be completed in a given amount of time), how to move to the next page, how to answer multiple-choice questions, how to check the solution for a fix code or write code problem, and how to drag blocks and check the solution on a Parsons problem.

The familiarization activities also include two easy practice multiple-choice questions, a practice fix code problem, a practice Parsons problem, and a practice write code problem. The fix code problem included instructions on how to fix the code. The correct solution was displayed above both the Parsons and write code problems.

4.4.3 Pretest. The participants had 15 minutes to complete the first section of five multiple-choice questions and 10 minutes to complete each of the other three sections (fix code, Parsons problem, and write code). If the participant ran out of time, the current answer(s) were automatically recorded. The goal was to control the amount of time the learner had for each section.

The five multiple-choice questions required tracing code with lists, ranges, selection, and iteration. The questions included code to find the minimum value in a list between a range of indices as shown in Figure 2, compare values in two sorted lists, return the count of the number of times a target value appeared in a range of indices in a list, trace the values of variables in a complex for loop, and return the average of values in a range of indices in a list. The question that compared the values in two lists had been used in prior research with 65% of the those students getting it correct [32].

The fix code problem was intended to calculate and return the average of a list of numbers, but double the highest value. However, it had errors that the learner had to find and fix, as shown in Figure

```
2-1-1: What does the following function return from mystery([2, 5, 8, 3, -1],1,3)?

def mystery(numList, start, end):
    save = numList[start]
    for index in range(start,end+1):
        value = numList[index]
        if value < save:
            save = value
    return save

A. -1
B. 2
C. 3
D. 5
E. 8
```

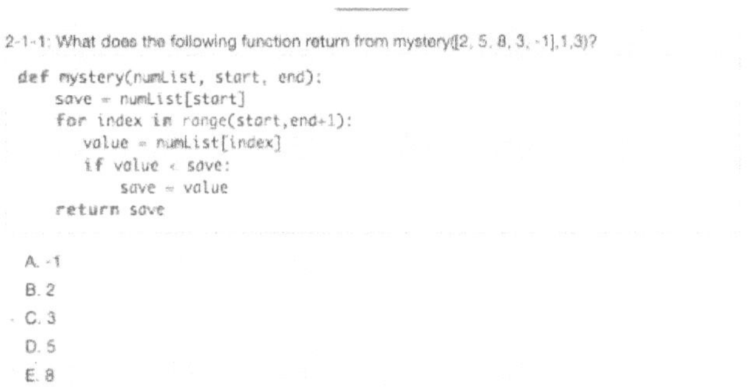

Figure 2: The first multiple-choice question in the pretest and immediate posttest

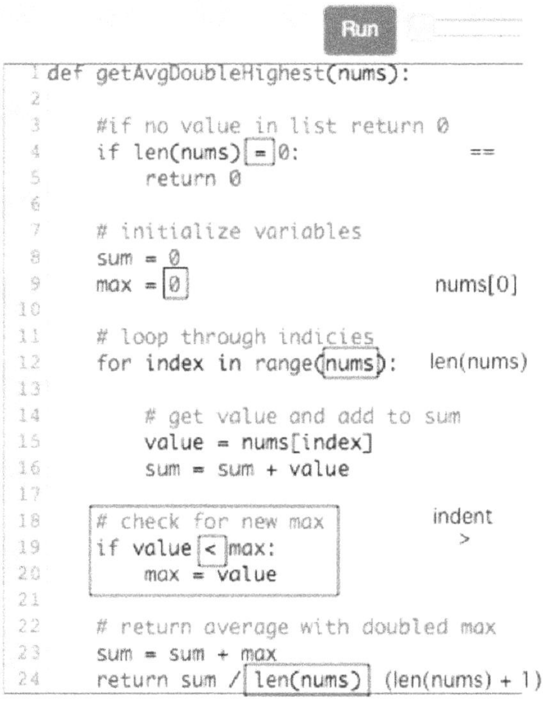

Figure 3: Pretest fix code problem with the errors boxed and the correct code to the right

Result	Actual Value	Expected Value	Notes
Pass	2	2	Test of getAvgDoubleHighest([1,1,3])
Pass	0	0	Test of getAvgDoubleHighest([])
Pass	3.0	3.0	Test of getAvgDoubleHighest([3.0,5.0,2.0,0])
Pass	-3.5	-3.5	Test of getAvgDoubleHighest([-3,-3,-5])

You passed: 100.0% of the tests

Figure 4: The unit test results when all the errors in the fix code problem have been corrected

3. The problem included unit tests, to verify the correctness of the code as shown in Figure 4.

Drop blocks here

```
def isLevel(elList, start, end):

    max = elList[start]

    min = max

    for index in range(start,end+1):

        value = elList[index]
        if value > max:

            max = value

        if value < min:

            min = value

    return (max - min) <= 10
```

Figure 5: The solution to the pretest Parsons problem

The Parsons problem asked the participant to order the code for a function, *isLevel*, which should return true if the difference between the maximum and minimum value between a given start and end index (inclusive) was 10 or less. This problem included five unpaired distractor code blocks, in which the distractor blocks were randomly mixed in with the correct code blocks. The solution to this problem is shown in Figure 5. Note that the user had to order the blocks vertically as well as indent the blocks horizontally to achieve a correct solution.

The write code problem was a modified version of Soloway's rainfall problem [10], which has been studied by several researchers [20, 23, 37, 38]. The original problem totals the non-negative values in an input loop until a sentinel value is reached and then outputs the average. The solution must avoid a division by zero. The problem was modified to loop through a list of numbers rather than read input until a sentinel value was reached as shown in Figure 6. Simon found that students still perform poorly on this problem and that students are not used to reading input in a loop until a sentinel value is reached [38]. The instructions explained the algorithm in English, provided example input and output, and provided unit tests.

4.4.4 Instructional Material (Worked Example + Practice). There were four worked examples with interleaved practice problems in the instructional material. The type of practice problem depended on the condition: adaptive Parsons problems, non-adaptive Parsons problems, write code problems, or the control group which solved off-task adaptive Parsons problems on turtle graphics.

Each worked example contained an algorithm in English and example input and output. It also included runnable code with comments as shown in Figure 7. When the user ran the example code it displayed the results from running the unit tests.

```
1 # Write the getAverageRainfall function below
2 # It should sum all the non-negative values in
3 # the list rain and return the average which is
4 # the sum divided by the count of non-negative values
5 # if there are no non-negative values it should
6 # return 0
7 def getAverageRainfall(rain):
8     sum = 0
9     count = 0
10    for value in rain:
11        if value >= 0:
12            sum = sum + value
13            count = count + 1
14    if count > 0:
15        return sum / count
16    return 0
17
```

Figure 6: The write code problem with a correct solution

Run Code

Click the [ ] button to run the tests that check that this code is working correctly. All tests should print [Pass] since this is correct code. Scroll down to try to solve the practice problem below.

[Run]

```
1 # define the function
2 def getAverage(numList):
3
4     # prevent a divide by zero
5     if len(numList) == 0:
6         return 0
7
8     # init sum
9     sum = 0
10
11    # loop through indicies
12    for index in range(len(numList)):
13
14        # get value at index
15        value = numList[index]
16
17        # add value to sum
18        sum = sum + value
19
20    # return the average
21    return sum / len(numList)
22
23
```

Figure 7: A worked example with runnable code

Each of the practice problems also contained an algorithm in English, example input and output, and unit tests to verify the user's solution. The user had 10 minutes to complete each problem. The user answer was saved if the user ran out of time.

The first worked example returned a count of the number of times a target value appeared in a list using a loop that looped through all the indices. The associated practice question was to return the count of a target value in a given range of indices (inclusive). The second worked example returned the maximum value from a list and the associated practice problem was to return the minimum value. The third worked example returned the average of the values in a list and protected against a divide by zero error as shown in Figure 7. The associated practice problem returned the average but did not include the lowest value in the list in the average and also guarded against a divide by zero error as shown in Figure 8. The fourth worked example returned the minimum value in a given range of indices (inclusive). The associated practice

Drop blocks here

```
def getAverageDropLowest(numList):
    if len(numList) == 0:
        return 0
    sum = 0

    lowest = numList[0]

    for index in range(len(numList)):

        value = numList[index]
        sum = sum + value

        if value < lowest:

            lowest = value

    return (sum - lowest) /
            (len(numList) - 1))
```

Figure 8: The correct solution to the third instructional Parsons problem

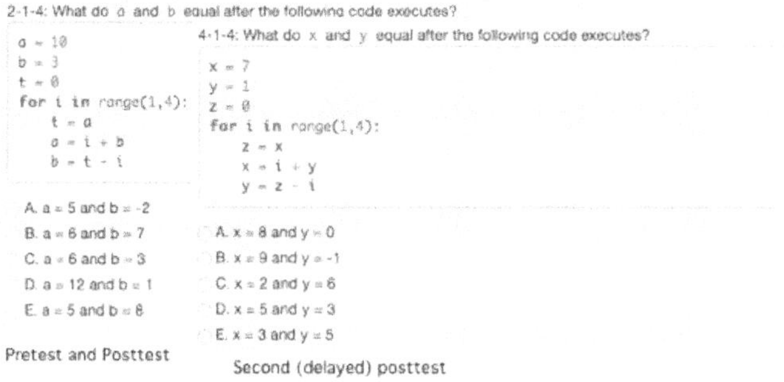

Figure 9: One of the multiple-choice questions from the pretest, first posttest, and second (delayed) posttest. Note that the second posttest changed the variable names and values.

problem returned the maximum value in a given range of indices (inclusive).

4.4.5 Posttests. The immediate posttest, which was administered at the end of the first session, had the exact same questions as the pretest. The delayed posttest, administered one week later, was isomorphic to the immediate posttest, meaning that the problems to be solved had the same structure, but different surface level features, like variable names as shown in Figure 9.

5 ANALYSIS

A total of 163 students participated in the first session. However, 37 of these students did not answer at least one question during the session or spent less than 30 seconds answering a question without

Table 1: Mean time in seconds and standard deviation for each of the four practice problems by group (condition)

Group	P1 secs (std dev)	P2 secs (std dev)	P3 secs (std dev)	P4 secs (std dev)
1. ($n=32$) A. Parsons	115.65 (50.1)	97.88 (34.3)	191.88 (130.5)	74.63 (23.5)
2. ($n=34$) Parsons	114.29 (56.3)	92.85 (31.0)	190.79 (91.2)	72.94 (26.8)
3. ($n=27$) Write	177.44 (152.0)	118.07 (113.3)	270.48 (152.0)	102 (63.6)
4. ($n=33$) Control	252.24 (100.9)	176.70 (79.6)	178.12 (107.13)	325.06 (160.3)

getting the question correct. This paper reports on the data from the remaining 126 students (32 in the adaptive Parsons condition, 34 in the non-adaptive Parsons condition, 27 in the write condition, and 33 in the control group that solved off-task adaptive Parsons problems) from the first session.

Students were not required to come back for the second session one week later, but earned an additional 2.5 points of extra credit for completing this session. A total of 126 students returned for the second session. Of these, 100 students completed all the questions in both the first session and second session and spent at least 30 seconds on each question or got the question correct in under 30 seconds (27 in the adaptive Parsons condition, 30 in the non-adaptive Parsons condition, 19 in the write condition, and 24 in the control group that solved off-task adaptive Parsons problems). These 100 students were used to study the retention of the material one week later.

5.1 Testing for Efficiency

The mean time in seconds to complete each practice problem and the standard deviation is shown in Table 1 for each condition. Note that the adaptive Parsons (group 1) and non-adaptive Parsons (group 2) had similar mean completion times. In an observational study of teachers solving both adaptive and non-adaptive Parsons problems, the adaptive problems sometimes took longer to solve than the non-adaptive because the teacher checked their solution after each change. With inter-problem adaptation, if the learner struggled on the previous problem then the next problem was made easier and if the learner solved the previous problem in one attempt the next problem was made harder, which probably kept the total completion times similar. The Cohen's d for the write code group mean total time to solve the practice problems in seconds compared to the adaptive Parsons group is ($d=0.756$) and for the non-adaptive Parsons group is ($d=0.845$). Cohen describes 0.2 as a small effect size, 0.5 as a medium effect size, and 0.8 as a large effect size [14]. There was a large effect between the non-adaptive Parsons and the write code group and a medium effect between the adaptive Parsons and write code group.

To test if the time differences were significant, outliers were removed (values more than three standard deviations from the mean) to normalize the data so that z-scores could be calculated.

Z-scores allow for different size groups to be compared. A test for skew (a test to indicate whether or not the data falls in a normal distribution) revealed that the values were all in the acceptable range (under 2). Removing outliers left 31 students in the adaptive Parsons group, 33 in the non-adaptive Parsons group, and 22 in the write group. Z-scores were created from the total time in seconds to solve the four practice problems minus the mean and divided by the standard deviation. A Least Squares Difference test (LSD) was used to compare the three on-task groups (Adaptive Parsons, Parsons, and Write). The fourth condition was the control group, which was solving off-task problems, so it was not included in the test for efficiency. There was no significant difference in completion time between the adaptive Parsons group and non-adaptive Parsons group. The time was significantly different between the adaptive Parsons group and the write group (mean difference of -.33 and p=.025) as well as the non-adaptive Parsons group and the write group (mean difference of -.32 and p=.025).

5.2 Testing for Effectiveness

Grading rubrics were created for the pretest and posttest write and fix code problems. Two people graded each problem independently and then met to resolve any differences in scores. The hand graded scores correlated with the unit test results. A factor analysis showed that the hand graded scores and unit test scores appeared to be measuring the same construct.

The Parsons problems were graded automatically. Each correct line in the correct order starting from the beginning of the solution received a half point. If the correct line was also indented correctly it received an additional half point. If the line was incorrect, but was the paired distractor and was indented correctly, it received a half point. Grading continued until a line was found that was neither the correct line nor its paired distractor (i.e. a line out of order). Grading then continued from the end of the solution back towards the first line that had been found to be incorrect.

This grading approach was based on an observation that learners had the most difficulty in the middle of the solution. We also wanted the grading to be similar to the grading of the fix code problems, and the fix code problems had the advantage that the code was already in the correct order.

The mean and standard deviation for each pretest and immediate posttest are shown by condition in Table 2. The pretest and posttest both contained four sections. One section had five multiple-choice (MC) questions which a maximum score of five, one had a fix code problem with a maximum score of 11, one had a Parsons with a maximum score of 10, and one had a write code problem with a maximum score of 10. The Cohen's d for the differences in the gains from pretest to immediate posttest by condition versus the control group were: *(d=0.799)* for the adaptive Parsons group, *(d = 0.311)* for the non-adaptive Parsons, and *(d=0.133)* for the code writing group. This is a medium effect size for the adaptive Parsons group and a small effect size for the non-adaptive Parsons group.

Remember that not all of the students took the delayed (2nd) posttest one week later. The mean score and standard deviation for the pretest, immediate (1st) posttest, and delayed (2nd) posttest for just the students who attended both sessions is shown in Table 3.

Table 2: Mean score and standard deviation for the pretest and immediate posttest (first posttest) by group

	Group 1 A. Parsons (n=32)	Group 2 Parsons (n=34)	Group 3 Write (n=27)	Group 4 Control (n=33)
Pre MC	2.7 (1.5)	3 (1.1)	3.8 (1.4)	3.6 (1.4)
Post MC	3.8 (1.1)	3.4 (.17)	4.3 (1.3)	4.2 (1.2)
Pre Fix	8.1 (1.6)	8.9 (2.0)	9.0 (1.6)	8.8 (1.8)
Post Fix	9.2 (1.8)	9.6 (2.0)	9.8 (1.8)	8.8 (2.1)
Pre Order	7.3 (3.3)	8.6 (3.0)	7.7 (3.4)	7.4 (3.6)
Post Order	8.5 (3.0)	9.5 (1.8)	8.0 (3.3)	7.9 (3.5)
Pre Write	8.6 (2.3)	9.3 (1.3)	9.0 (1.7)	9.2 (1.2)
Post Write	9.3 (1.3)	9.4 (1.0)	9.0 (1.9)	9.2 (1.4)

Table 3: Mean score and standard deviation for the pretest, immediate posttest (first posttest), and delayed posttest (2nd posttest) by group

	Group 1 A. Parsons (n=27)	Group 2 Parsons (n=30)	Group 3 Write (n=19)	Group 4 Control (n=24)
Pre MC	2.7 (1.5)	2.9 (1.1)	3.8 (1.3)	3.8 (1.5)
1st Post	3.9 (1.0)	3.7 (1.6)	4.2 (1.5)	4.3 (1.3)
2nd Post	3.8 (1.1)	3.7 (1.2)	4.3 (1.1)	3.8 (1.2)
Pre Fix	8.1 (1.6)	8.9 (2.0)	8.9 (1.6)	8.6 (1.9)
1st Post	9.3 (1.7)	9.6 (2.0)	9.4 (2.0)	8.8 (2.2)
2nd Post	9.1 (1.8)	9.7 (1.9)	9.5 (1.8)	9.3 (1.6)
Pre Order	7.7 (3.1)	8.1 (3.3)	6.8 (3.7)	7.2 (3.8)
1st Post	8.2 (3.1)	9.4 (2.0)	7.1 (3.7)	7.4 (3.7)
2nd Post	8.7 (2.4)	9.7 (1.4)	9.2 (2.0)	8.3 (2.9)
Pre Write	8.9 (1.9)	9.4 (1.4)	8.7 (2.0)	9.1 (1.3)
1st Post	9.4 (1.2)	9.5 (1.1)	8.7 (2.2)	9.0 (1.5)
2nd Post	9.3 (1.1)	9.7 (1.0)	9.0 (2.1)	9.3 (1.3)

There was a statistically significant change from pretest to the immediate posttest using a multivariate analysis of variance (MANOVA) with Pillai's trace *(F=2.36 and p=.031)*. A MANOVA was used since there were four conditions in this study. The Bonferroni post-hoc test does not indicate a statistically significant difference by condition from the pretest to the immediate posttest, which means that no condition seemed to have done better or worse than the others.

The differences in the scores from pretest to immediate posttest were compared for all the on-task conditions compared to the control group. Twenty-seven results were chosen at random from each condition in order to compare equal size samples. A Mann-Whitney U test was used, which does not assume that the data follows a normal distribution. The difference between the pretest score and the posttest score was significant *(p=.007882)* for the adaptive condition versus the control group (who solved turtle graphics problems). There was not a significant difference for any of the other on-task

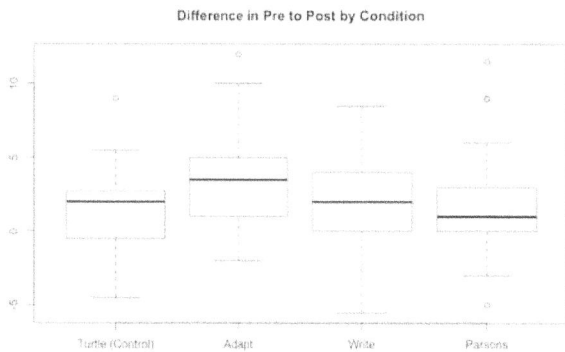

Figure 10: Results from a Mann-Whitney U test comparing the pretest score to the immediate posttest score by condition

conditions compared to the control group. See Figure 10 for a box and whisker plot by condition.

Kurtosis was high on the pretest write and posttest write problems which indicates that the scores fall in a narrow range. This means there was likely a ceiling effect on the write code problem. The mean scores on the pretest write problem ranged from 8.7 to 9.4 out of a maximum of 10 as shown in Table 3.

5.3 Analysis of the Demographic Information

Of the 126 students who completed all questions in the first session, 73 (58%) self-identified as male and 51 (40%) as female and two (2%) students did not answer the question.

An analysis of the demographic information showed a strong positive correlation with the student's actual grade in the course $(p < .001)$. There was a moderate negative correlation between the pretest score and the student's age $r(121) = -.413, p < .001$, which means that older students did worse than younger. This course is intended to be a first course for majors, so older students may be retaking the course after failing it in the past, or be weaker students who delayed taking the course. We found a moderate negative correlation for gender with males performing better than females on the delayed posttest $\rho(99) = -.362, p < .001$.

There was no interaction between condition and any of the demographic characteristics that affected performance. This means that the groups were comparable.

6 DISCUSSION

The on-task Parsons groups (both the adaptive and non-adaptive) solved the four practice problems in significantly $(p=.025)$ less time than the write code group with medium (adaptive Parsons group) $(d=0.756)$ to large (non-adaptive Parsons group) $(d=0.845)$ effect sizes. This supports hypothesis **H1**.

There was a significant improvement in composite scores from pretest to immediate posttest. However, there was no significant difference between the three on-task conditions. This means that learners solving both adaptive and non-adaptive Parsons problems

had equivalent learning gains as those in the write code condition. This supports hypothesis **H2**.

The learners in the control group who solved off-task turtle graphics adaptive Parsons problems had a significantly $(p=.007882)$ lower learning gain from pretest to immediate posttest than the on-task adaptive Parsons group and there was a medium effect size $(d=0.799)$, which supports hypothesis **H3**. However, there was no significant difference between the control group and the non-adaptive Parsons group or between the control group and the write code group. This means that hypothesis **H3** was not fully supported.

7 LIMITATIONS

There was not any significant difference for the learning gains from the pretest to the immediate posttest between the control group and the non-adaptive Parsons group or the write code group. This implies that at least some of the learning gains were from answering the same or similar problems with correctness feedback.

This study used both intra-problem and inter-problem adaptation. We do not know the relative effectiveness of each type of adaptation. Further studies should be done to test this.

The results are only from undergraduates from one research intensive university in the United States. The results would be strengthened by replication at other universities around the world and by similar studies with teachers.

8 CONCLUSIONS

This study provides evidence that solving either adaptive Parsons problems or non-adaptive Parsons problems is a more efficient, but just as effective, form of practice than writing the equivalent code. It also found that solving adaptive Parsons problems led to a significant learning gain compared to the control group. However, there was no significant difference in learning gains between the control group and either the non-adaptive Parsons problems group or the write code group. This means that at least some of the learning gains were likely due to repeated exposure to the same problems with correctness feedback. Further studies are needed to verify the learning gains from solving adaptive Parsons problems versus non-adaptive Parsons problems versus writing the equivalent code. If solving adaptive Parsons problems is a more efficient, but just as effective form of low cognitive load practice, they could be used to help prepare thousands of new computing teachers and reduce the time that it takes to learn to program. The Parsons software is freely available as part of the Runestone Interactive platform [33].

ACKNOWLEDGMENTS

This study was supported by the National Science Foundation under grants 1138378 and 1432300. Any opinions, findings, and conclusions expressed in this material are those of the authors and do not necessarily reflect the views of the National Science Foundation. We thank all the people who assisted in this research. Lauren Margulieux conducted most of the statistical tests. Matthew Guzdial ran the Mann-Whitney U test. Matt Lord graded the fix and write code problems. We also thank the reviewers for their helpful comments.

REFERENCES

[1] John R. Anderson, Frederick G. Conrad, and Albert T. Corbett. 1989. Skill Acquisition and the LISP Tutor. *Cognitive Science* 13 (1989), 467–505.

[2] John R. Anderson, Albert T. Corbett, Kenneth R. Koedinger, and Ray Pelletier. 1995. Cognitive Tutors: Lessons Learned. *Journal of the Learning Sciences* 4, 2 (1995), 167–207. https://doi.org/10.1207/s15327809jls0402_2

[3] Owen Astrachan, Jan Cuny, Chris Stephenson, and Cameron Wilson. 2011. The CS10K project: mobilizing the community to transform high school computing. In *Proceedings of the 42nd ACM technical symposium on Computer science education.* ACM, 85–86.

[4] Ronald Baecker and Ian Small. 1990. Animation at the interface. *The art of human-computer interface design* (1990), 251–267.

[5] Tim Bell, Peter Andreae, and Lynn Lambert. 2010. Computer science in New Zealand high schools. In *Proceedings of the Twelfth Australasian Conference on Computing Education-Volume 103.* Australian Computer Society, Inc., 15–22.

[6] Klara Benda, Amy Bruckman, and Mark Guzdial. 2012. When Life and Learning Do Not Fit: Challenges of Workload and Communication in Introductory Computer Science Online. *Trans. Comput. Educ.* 12, 4 (2012), 1–38. https://doi.org/10.1145/2382564.2382567

[7] Jens Bennedsen and Michael E. Caspersen. 2007. Failure rates in introductory programming. *SIGCSE Bull.* 39, 2 (2007), 32–36. https://doi.org/10.1145/1272848.1272879

[8] Laura E. Berk and Adam Winsler. 1995. *Scaffolding Children's Learning: Vygotsky and Early Childhood Education.* National Association for the Education of Young Children.

[9] Elizabeth L Bjork and Robert A. Bjork. 2011. Making things hard on yourself, but in a good way: Creating desirable difficulties to enhance learning. *Psychology and the real world: Essays illustrating fundamental contributions to society* (2011), 56–64.

[10] Benedict Du Boulay. 1988. *Some Difficulties of Learning to Program.* Lawrence Erlbaum Associates, 283–299.

[11] Neil C. C. Brown, Sue Sentance, Tom Crick, and Simon Humphreys. 2014. Restart: The Resurgence of Computer Science in UK Schools. *Trans. Comput. Educ.* 14, 2 (2014), 1–22. https://doi.org/10.1145/2602484

[12] Michael E Caspersen and Palle Nowack. 2013. Computational thinking and practice: A generic approach to computing in Danish high schools. In *Proceedings of the Fifteenth Australasian Computing Education Conference-Volume 136.* Australian Computer Society, Inc., 137–143.

[13] Fanny Chevalier, Nathalie Henry Riche, Catherine Plaisant, Amira Chalbi, and Christophe Hurter. 2016. Animations 25 years later: new roles and opportunities. In *Proceedings of the International Working Conference on Advanced Visual Interfaces.* ACM, 280–287.

[14] Jacob Cohen. 1988. Statistical power analysis for the behavioral sciences. 2nd.

[15] Gemma Corbalan, Liesbeth Kester, and Jeroen JG Van Merriënboer. 2008. Selecting learning tasks: Effects of adaptation and shared control on learning efficiency and task involvement. *Contemporary Educational Psychology* 33, 4 (2008), 733–756.

[16] Albert T Corbett, Kenneth R Koedinger, and John R Anderson. 1997. Intelligent tutoring systems. *Handbook of human-computer interaction* 5 (1997), 849–874.

[17] Tom Crick and Sue Sentance. 2011. Computing at school: stimulating computing education in the UK. In *Proceedings of the 11th Koli Calling International Conference on Computing Education Research.* ACM, 122–123.

[18] Jan Cuny, Diane A Baxter, Daniel D Garcia, Jeff Gray, and Ralph Morelli. 2014. CS principles professional development: only 9,500 to go!. In *Proceedings of the 45th ACM technical symposium on Computer science education.* ACM, 543–544.

[19] Paul Denny, Andrew Luxton-Reilly, and Beth Simon. 2008. Evaluating a new exam question: Parsons problems. In *Proceedings of the fourth international workshop on computing education research.* ACM, 113–124.

[20] Alireza Ebrahimi. 1994. Novice programmer errors: language constructs and plan composition. *International Journal of Human-Computer Studies* 41 (1994), 457–480.

[21] Barbara J Ericson, Mark J Guzdial, and Briana B Morrison. 2015. Analysis of interactive features designed to enhance learning in an ebook. In *Proceedings of the eleventh annual International Conference on International Computing Education Research.* ACM, 169–178.

[22] Barbara J Ericson, Lauren E Margulieux, and Jochen Rick. 2017. Solving parsons problems versus fixing and writing code. In *Proceedings of the 17th Koli Calling Conference on Computing Education Research.* ACM, 20–29.

[23] Kathi Fisler. 2014. The recurring rainfall problem. In *Proceedings of the tenth annual conference on International computing education research.* ACM, 35–42.

[24] Judith Gal-Ezer, Catriel Beeri, David Harel, and Amiram Yehudai. 1995. A high school program in computer science. *Computer* 28, 10 (1995), 73–80.

[25] Stuart Garner. 2007. An Exploration of How a Technology-Facilitated Part-Complete Solution Method Supports the Learning of Computer Programming. *Journal of Issues in Informing Science and Information Technology* 4 (2007), 491–501. https://doi.org/10.28945/966

[26] Kyle James Harms, Jason Chen, and Caitlin L Kelleher. 2016. Distractors in Parsons Problems Decrease Learning Efficiency for Young Novice Programmers.

In *Proceedings of the 2016 ACM Conference on International Computing Education Research.* ACM, 241–250.

[27] Juha Helminen, Petri Ihantola, Ville Karavirta, and Lauri Malmi. 2012. How do students solve parsons programming problems?: an analysis of interaction traces. In *Proceedings of the ninth annual international conference on International computing education research.* ACM, 119–126.

[28] Petri Ihantola and Ville Karavirta. 2011. Two-Dimensional Parson's Puzzles: The Concept, Tools, and First Observations. *Journal of Information Technology Education* 10 (2011), 119–132. https://doi.org/10.28945/1394

[29] Paivi Kinnunen and Beth Simon. 2010. Experiencing programming assignments in CS1: the emotional toll. In *Proceedings of the Sixth international workshop on Computing education research.* ACM, 77–86.

[30] Amruth N Kumar. 2018. Epplets: A Tool for Solving Parsons Puzzles. In *Proceedings of the 49th ACM Technical Symposium on Computer Science Education.* ACM, 527–532.

[31] Karen Lang, Ria Galanos, Joanna Goode, Deborah Seehorn, Fran Trees, Pat Phillips, and Chris Stephenson. 2013. *Bugs in the System: Computer Science Teacher Certification in the U.S.* Report. The Computer Science Teachers Association The Association for Computing Machinery.

[32] Raymond Lister, Elizabeth S Adams, Sue Fitzgerald, William Fone, John Hamer, Morten Lindholm, Robert McCartney, Jan Erik Moström, Kate Sanders, Otto Seppälä, et al. 2004. A multi-national study of reading and tracing skills in novice programmers. In *ACM SIGCSE Bulletin,* Vol. 36. ACM, 119–150.

[33] Brad Miller and David Ranum. 2014. Runestone interactive: tools for creating interactive course materials. In *Proceedings of the first ACM conference on Learning@ scale conference.* ACM, 213–214.

[34] Dale Parsons and Patricia Haden. 2006. Parson's programming puzzles: a fun and effective learning tool for first programming courses. In *Proceedings of the 8th Australasian Conference on Computing Education-Volume 52.* Australian Computer Society, Inc., 157–163.

[35] Andrew Petersen, Michelle Craig, and Daniel Zingaro. 2011. Reviewing CS1 exam question content. In *Proceedings of the 42nd ACM technical symposium on Computer science education.* ACM, 631–636.

[36] Barbara Rogoff. 1990. *Apprenticeship in thinking: Cognitive development in sociocultural activity.* Oxford University Press, New York, NY, USA.

[37] Otto Seppälä, Petri Ihantola, Essi Isohanni, Juha Sorva, and Arto Vihavainen. 2015. Do we know how difficult the rainfall problem is?. In *Proceedings of the 15th Koli Calling Conference on Computing Education Research.* ACM, 87–96.

[38] Simon. 2013. Soloway's Rainfall Problem has become Harder. In *Learning and Teaching in Computing and Engineering.* IEEE Computer Society, Washington DC, USA, 130–135.

[39] Elliot Soloway. 1986. Learning to program = learning to construct mechanisms and explanations. *Commun. ACM* 29, 9 (1986), 850–858. http://dl.acm.org/citation.cfm?doid=6592.6594

[40] John Sweller. 1988. Cognitive load during problem solving: Effects on learning. *Cognitive science* 12, 2 (1988), 257–285.

[41] John Sweller and Graham Cooper. 1985. The Use of Worked Examples as a Substitute for Problem Solving in Learning Algebra. *Cognition and Instruction* 2, 1 (1985), 59–89.

[42] John Gregory Trafton and Brian J. Reiser. 1993. The contributions of studying examples and solving problems to skill acquisition. In *15th Annual Conference of the Cognitive Science Society.* Lawrence Erlbaum Associates, Inc., 1017–1022. http://citeseerx.ist.psu.edu/viewdoc/download?doi=10.1.1.52.9933&rep=rep1&type=pdf

[43] Jeroen JG Van Merriënboer and Marcel BM De Croock. 1992. Strategies for computer-based programming instruction: Program completion vs. program generation. *Journal of Educational Computing Research* 8, 3 (1992), 365–394.

[44] Jeroen JG Van Merriënboer, Paul A Kirschner, and Liesbeth Kester. 2003. Taking the load off a learner's mind: Instructional design for complex learning. *Educational psychologist* 38, 1 (2003), 5–13.

Pedagogical Content Knowledge for Teaching Inclusive Design

Alannah Oleson, Christopher Mendez, Zoe
Steine-Hanson, Claudia Hilderbrand,
Christopher Perdriau, Margaret Burnett
School of Electrical Engineering and Computer Science
Oregon State University
Corvallis, Oregon
[olesona,mendezc,steinehz,minic,perdriac,burnett]@eecs.
oregonstate.edu

Andrew J. Ko
The Information School
University of Washington
Seattle, Washington
ajko@uw.edu

ABSTRACT

Inclusive design is important in today's software industry, but there is little research about how to teach it. In collaboration with 9 teacher-researchers across 8 U.S. universities and more than 400 computer and information science students, we embarked upon an Action Research investigation to gather insights into the pedagogical content knowledge (PCK) that teachers need to teach a particular inclusive design method called GenderMag. Analysis of the teachers' observations and experiences, the materials they used, direct observations of students' behaviors, and multiple data on the students' own reflections on their learning revealed 11 components of inclusive design PCK. These include strategies for anticipating and addressing resistance to the topic of inclusion, strategies for modeling and scaffolding perspective taking, and strategies for tailoring instruction to students' prior beliefs and biases.

CCS CONCEPTS

• **Human-centered computing → HCI design and evaluation methods**; • **Applied computing → Education**;

KEYWORDS

Inclusive design; pedagogical content knowledge; design methods

ACM Reference Format:
Alannah Oleson, Christopher Mendez, Zoe Steine-Hanson, Claudia Hilderbrand, Christopher Perdriau, Margaret Burnett and Andrew J. Ko. 2018. Pedagogical Content Knowledge for Teaching Inclusive Design. In *ICER '18: 2018 International Computing Education Research Conference, August 13–15, 2018, Espoo, Finland.* ACM, New York, NY, USA, 9 pages. https://doi.org/10.1145/3230977.3230998

1 INTRODUCTION

Although most computer science classes in higher education focus on the *engineering* of software, an increasing number of students take human-computer interaction (HCI) classes, learning the *design* of software as well. These two distinct skills—deciding what to make (design) and deciding how to make it (engineering)—are both critical to being an effective software professional. In companies without designers (e.g., small startups or companies lacking a design culture), engineers are often responsible for user interface design [23]. In many open source projects, software engineers are the gatekeepers to user experience design decisions [24]. In large software companies, engineers manage and collaborate with designers to make design decisions [26]. In all of these settings, a robust understanding of user experience design is key.

In today's software industry, however, a grasp of design is not enough: software professionals must also understand *inclusive* design*. Numerous issues exist today with gender and diversity in software companies: software has repeatedly shown failures to be accessible, usable, and/or functional for diverse populations (e.g., [1, 3, 5, 25]). With many software companies exploring ways to improve their cultures and the inclusiveness of what they design, understanding how to teach inclusive design to the students who will design tomorrow's software has never been more important.

Unfortunately, inclusion aside, teaching even basic design skills is hard. Some HCI teachers simply avoid teaching design, focusing instead on the theoretical and formal foundations of HCI research that are well-described in textbooks, but providing little connection to the broader skills involved in design [9]. Research exploring ways to engage students in design practice reports significant challenges in knowing how to teach these methods. For example, Reimer [30] incorporated hands-on, studio-based learning and found that students rated the class as more difficult, more confusing, and more work-intensive than traditionally-taught CS classes. McCrickard et al. [28] used case studies to teach design in a way that students reported as more enjoyable, but the teachers in the study struggled to motivate students to engage with the cases. Hundhausen et al. [21] investigated using a "prototype walkthrough" method in class, finding that students were able to ground their critiques in evidence, but that much of students' learning might be explained by teacher expertise. Studies like these reveal that not only is teaching design hard, but that we do not yet know why it is hard, or even what knowledge is required to teach it successfully. We know even less about teaching *inclusive* design to computer science students.

In education research, this missing knowledge is referred to as *pedagogical content knowledge* (PCK). Originally introduced by Shulman [32], PCK is the intersection of pedagogical knowledge

ICER '18, August 13–15, 2018, Espoo, Finland
© 2018 Association for Computing Machinery.
ACM ISBN 978-1-4503-5628-2/18/08...$15.00
https://doi.org/10.1145/3230977.3230998

---

* Inclusive design differs subtly from accessibility in that accessibility is about designing for a particular underserved population (e.g., Facebook for blind users) whereas inclusive design is about designing for a broad spectrum of populations (e.g., Facebook for both sighted and blind users).

(background in effective teaching techniques and practices) and content knowledge (background in the subject being taught). Shulman examined teachers' experiences through the lens of how their knowledge set contributed to their successes or failures. When expert teachers possessed some knowledge about how to teach specific course content that novices did not, and when the novice teacher was less successful in their teaching efforts, Shulman called the knowledge PCK for the topic.

PCK is not general. To the contrary: prior work shows that PCK is specific to the topic at hand (e.g., photosynthesis, quadratic equations) and to the audience [14]. In past research on PCK in a range of fields (including literature and geography [32], chemical and biological sciences [14, 22], math [19, 32], and computer science [20]), results show that even measuring PCK is domain-specific [18].

Recent surveys of research on PCK in STEM fields shows that teachers with better-developed PCK for their topic often see evidence of better learning in their students [7]. PCK is critical even when teachers have exceptionally high content expertise: Fernandez-Balboa and Stiehl's study of PCK in higher education found that even the most exceptional teachers needed PCK [10].

For this exploration into PCK for teaching inclusive design, we chose to investigate as many issues as we could for teaching one inclusive design method rather than a broad but more shallow coverage of multiple methods. The inclusive design method we used as our lens into the PCK of teaching inclusive design is GenderMag [5]. GenderMag allows us to explicitly focus on inclusivity (in this case, gender inclusivity), rests on well-established foundations, and has been shown to be effective at uncovering inclusiveness issues that affect all genders in software, with the most success in finding issues that disproportionately affect women [2, 3, 8].

To investigate PCK necessary for this topic, we followed methods of prior work, looking to both novice and expert teachers to identify the PCK required [14, 22, 32] to answer the following research question: *what PCK do teachers need to teach GenderMag effectively?*

This paper contributes:

(1) An analysis of risks to student learning that teachers may encounter when teaching inclusive software design methods in higher education, and a set of mitigations to address these risks.
(2) Evidence for the existence of *resistant learners* in inclusive design courses and strategies to reduce resistance.
(3) An explicit set of inclusive design PCK.

2 BACKGROUND: GENDERMAG

In HCI, there are a range of methods for finding usability problems in designs. Some are empirical, including usability testing and A/B testing, gathering problems as they occur during use. Others are analytical, using principles and argumentation to predict issues that may occur during future use. The GenderMag [3, 5] inclusive design inspection method falls into the analytical category.

GenderMag integrates specialized personas [17] that cover an array of cognitive characteristics together with a specialized Cognitive Walkthrough (CW) [27, 35]. To evaluate a system's gender inclusiveness using GenderMag, a small group of software professionals (e.g., software developers, HCI experts, software managers, etc.) walk through a scenario in their system, step by step, through the eyes of one of the GenderMag personas. At each step, they

decide whether their persona (e.g., "Abby") will (1) know what to do and, (2) if Abby performs the action, whether she will know that she is progressing toward her goal. Multiple real-world technology teams have used GenderMag to identify gender-inclusiveness issues in a wide array of systems, with useful results [2, 3, 8].

To use GenderMag correctly, learners must understand both the process described above and the four personas. The GenderMag personas—Abby, Patricia, Patrick, and Tim—rest on five *facets* related to technological problem-solving styles: *motivations* for using tech; *information processing style (IPS)*; computer *self-efficacy*; *learning style (by process or by tinkering)*; and *attitude toward risk* (Figure 1). For example, on the facet "learning style," Tim loves to tinker with software features and sometimes forgoes finishing a task in favor of exploring software, whereas Abby likes to learn a process first and then fill in with details of the features to carry it out.

Each persona has different facet values to reflect the segment of the population that they represent. Abby represents the facet values whose proportions disproportionately skew towards females, Tim represents the facet values that disproportionately skew towards males, and the two "identical twins" Pat(ricia) and Pat(rick) fill in values near the middle of the spectra of facet values [5, 6]. Of the four personas, the Abby persona provides the strongest lens to unearth gender-inclusiveness issues in the user experience because, as prior work has shown, software is often inadvertently designed around the way males tend to use software [2, 3].

3 METHOD: ACTION RESEARCH

Unlike prior work on PCK [14], we chose Action Research as the research method for our investigation into inclusive design PCK. Action Research is a form of longitudinal field study conducted by a group facing a problem (in our case, teachers wanting to effectively teach inclusive design). Field work in Action Research involves continuous reflection on the nature of that problem while also trying to address it [15, 33]. Action Research is unlike other empirical studies in that it does not attempt to "control" the setting being observed; instead, the goal is to intervene and learn through

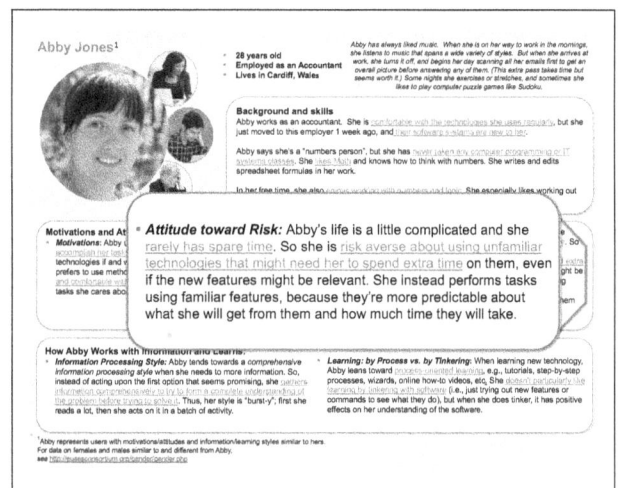

Figure 1: Abby is a "multi-persona," meaning that she has multiple appearances and her demographic portions are customizable [17]. One of the facets is blown up for legibility.

that intervention. Participants often act as researchers themselves, using data to refine theories of the problem, which in turn informs interventions and further data gathering. Action Research has been used in education research for decades [36].

This cycle of theoretical refinement relies on *triangulation*—assessing the extent to which multiple sources of evidence suggest the same explanation of a problem—to establish credibility and validity of interpretations. Toward this end, we collected data across six sources: (1) interviews with the teacher-researchers about their experiences, (2) emails from teacher-researchers with additional observations, (3) materials the teacher-researchers created to teach their courses, (4) observations in the teacher-researchers' courses, (5) individual students' feedback about the content, and (6) students' responses on course evaluation surveys.

3.1 The participants

We had two types of participants: (1) "teacher-researchers," higher education faculty who incorporated gender-inclusive design into their courses and reflected on their practices and (2) students in the teacher-researchers' classrooms. We engaged nine teacher-researchers. Only two had experience teaching GenderMag in college courses. This enabled us to investigate both the novice discovery of PCK and the expert reflection on PCK. One teacher-researcher self-identified as an expert at teaching GenderMag, while the others identified as novices. We designate expertise with "X" or "N" in participant identifiers. The nine teacher-researchers integrated GenderMag into 12 courses overall (Table 1). Courses were located in eight different U.S. states, reaching more than 400 students.

3.2 The on-line community

Prior work shows that community enhances teachers' acquisition of PCK, fostering relationships through which to share knowledge and materials [13]. To facilitate sharing, we created a wiki (Figure 2) and invited the teacher-researchers to contribute to it. The wiki contained diverse materials: slide decks with lecture modules on various portions of the GenderMag method, homework assignments that scaffolded practice of GenderMag walkthroughs on example websites, suggested readings, in-class activities such

Table 1: Teacher-researchers and students by course. The six courses in which students performed a GenderMag walkthrough are marked with asterisks.

Teacher	Course topic	Level	# Students
T1N	HCI	Undergrad	61
T1N	HCI	Graduate	15
T2N	HCI: Design*	Undergrad	37
T3X	HCI: Design*	Mixed	35
T3X	Seminar: Diversity in Tech	Graduate	16
T3X	Seminar: Ethics of Tech	Undergrad	59
T4N	HCI: Usability*	Undergrad	59
T5N	HCI: Usability	Graduate	29
T6N	SE: Capstone Project*	Undergrad	27
T7N	SE: Fundamentals	Undergrad	83
T8N	SE: Game Dev*	Mixed	21
T9N	SE: Internet Dev*	Graduate	25

as an interactive GenderMag walkthrough activity to be done in class, the current version of the GenderMag kit [4], and test questions. We built some of the wiki's materials ourselves; the rest were contributed over time by teacher-researchers in this study and by other teachers who have taught GenderMag.

3.3 The data

Of our six data types, three came from the teacher-researchers. First, we conducted interviews with the teacher-researchers just after they had finished preparing for their class but *before class* (usually a day before or the day of class). We interviewed them again as soon *after class* as possible, also collecting any teaching materials they had created. If the teacher-researchers taught GenderMag over multiple classes, we held multiple interview sessions. One teacher-researcher was not available for interviews, and instead sent us an open-ended email with experiences and reflections.

Prior work shows that teachers often have difficulty verbalizing PCK [32]. Thus, we focused the interviews on the gaps that teachers perceived between their preparation for the course and the outcome of that preparation, based on their perceptions of student reactions to the material. (The complete set of interview questions is available at https://sites.google.com/site/gendermagteach/appendix-a-interview-questions.) We suspected these gaps would be particularly salient for those who were teaching GenderMag for the first time. We video- and audio-recorded interviews for later transcription and analysis. In total, the interviews and email produced 141 responses to interview questions.

Three data sources came from students: class observations, student-written feedback, and student surveys. For two courses, researchers observed pedagogy and student behavior, for a total of 230 observations. In six courses across four universities, teacher-researchers provided an anonymous free-form questionnaire asking students to reflect on their learning of GenderMag, producing 260 comments. Two teacher-researchers also gathered end-of-term impressions about GenderMag, producing 12 comments and 132 five-point Likert-style responses.

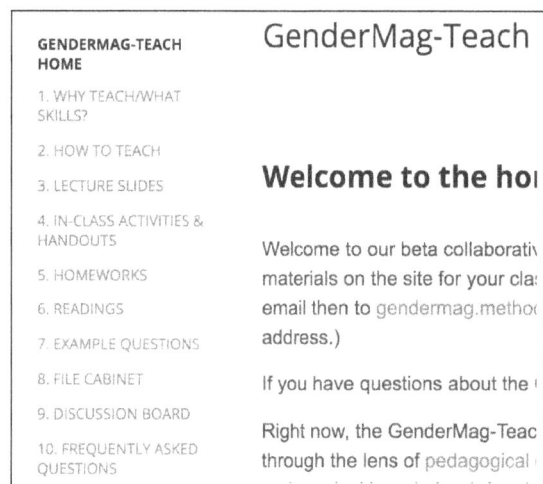

Figure 2: Structure of the GenderMag-Teach community wiki. Available in full at the GenderMag site (http://gendermag.org/).

3.4 Analysis

We began by analyzing the student behavior data, since teacher-researchers' reflections were relative to student behavior. We performed affinity diagramming on the 502 observations and student reflections in these data to inductively generate categories of issues with students' learning of inclusive design. This resulted in the seven issues shown in Table 2. Two researchers then qualitatively coded the reflections and observations, reaching 97.6% agreement on 21.24% of the data (Jaccard index). We then coded the 141 teachers' interview responses using these same issue types, to align the teacher data with the student data. Finally, we derived the PCK from the teacher-researchers' reflections about each issue, drawing upon their judgments of students' difficulties and the pedagogy that helped students overcome them.

4 RESULTS

Two of the courses collected 5-point Likert-scale questions as part of their universities' end-of-term student teaching evaluations, enabling us to measure those students' own perceptions of their learning. Their 132 responses are summarized in Figure 3.

Qualitative data from other courses corroborate these data, with teachers and students commenting upon the students' engagement, understanding, and reflections upon GenderMag:

T5N: *"People were interested, I think people understood why I integrated GenderMag when I teach personas."*

T2N: *"Some ... were visibly excited about the idea that there was a method that had anything at all to do with inclusion. ... Something about the idea that there's a well-defined skill or process ... "*

T2N-Student (quiz response): *"GenderMag makes use of predefined personas in order to see how your design functions according to a variety of users. These personas vary in both experience and motivation, analyzing your design from many perspectives."*

T4N-Student (on handout): *"Do persona facets ever conflict so greatly that an interface cannot be made?"*

T9N: *"She [a student] is enthusiastic ... kind of using it as an excuse to brainstorm and show how she could think through other applications of this ... "*

These results provide a context for the PCK results that follow, which are summarized and evaluated in Table 3 in the Discussion. We can view positive learning outcomes such as those in Figure 3

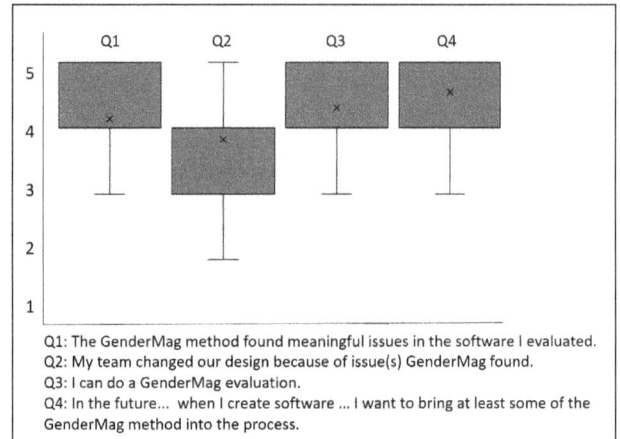

Q1: The GenderMag method found meaningful issues in the software I evaluated.
Q2: My team changed our design because of issue(s) GenderMag found.
Q3: I can do a GenderMag evaluation.
Q4: In the future... when I create software ... I want to bring at least some of the GenderMag method into the process.

Figure 3: Student evaluations of their own learning (1=strongly disagree, 5=strongly agree), with 132 responses. On all four questions, students rated their understanding and application of the material positively.

and in the above qualitative data as being due in part to teachers' mastery of requisite PCK, and we can view learning difficulties in the sections to follow as being due in part to teachers' PCK gaps.

4.1 PCK for teaching the foundations

Risk and Prevalence: One risk is that some students can be uncertain about the effectiveness and utility of GenderMag unless they know there are foundational data backing the method. For example:

T2N-Student: *"How do the personas account for diverse users? i.e., not 'normal' users."*

T2N-Student: *"Why is GenderMag different? What makes it unique besides 4 personas compared to any other cognitive walkthrough for a product?"*

Foundations issues appeared in nine of the twelve courses (Table 2), and they were the most prevalent risk encountered. Some of the mitigations in upcoming sections rest upon solid foundations.

Mitigation and PCK: To mitigate this risk, teacher T3X described a strategy s/he used: first introduce the GenderMag personas including the foundations and evidence base behind them, then have students build analogous personas, and only after these

Table 2: Data instances and courses in which each learning issue was observed. Denominators are the number of instances or courses in which that issue could have arisen. The six courses are the same marked in Table 1 as having done walkthroughs.

Problem	Description	Data Instances	Courses
Research foundations	Students asked questions about the research foundations of GenderMag or whether other inclusive design methods exist.	121/643	9/12
Persona & facets	Students did not understand the personas' facets, how the facets apply to interface features beyond examples provided, or used facets incorrectly.	25/643	5/12
Walkthrough process	Student incorrectly executed the walkthrough methodology, or reported the walkthrough as pointless or tedious.	49/482	4/6
Theory of Mind	Students had trouble taking the perspective of the persona or viewing the persona holistically (e.g. using one example from the description to define the persona).	19/482	4/6
"I" methodology	Students conducted a walkthrough as if *they* were using the interface, not the persona.	7/482	1/6
Bias	Students stereotyped use of technology, e.g., "all men" or "all women."	13/643	8/12
Resistance	Students expressed disengagement or disinterest in GenderMag.	55/643	9/12

activities move on to introducing the GenderMag process. Teacher T3X used this PCK to plan for later sessions:

T3X: *"When I finally do present GenderMag, which is probably about a month from now, the students will be so used to Abby and her facets, and other facets of personas (the ones they've been developing), that there's not going to be any pushback... they're just going to be really bought into it at that point."*

PCK1-Framing: Providing foundations first can give students the capacity to understand and engage with inclusive design methods.

Other PCK related to foundations came from resources that teachers used to build students' conceptual foundations of inclusive design. Teacher T5N found it useful both personally and for their students to read research papers about GenderMag before practicing the method in class, as the papers clearly argued the rationale and need for the method. Experiences like this about where the "best knowledge" about GenderMag resided was also critical PCK:

T5N: *"First I read, and if there are specific research papers associated with it I will also read those research papers. Also I go to YouTube, because some people put up video lectures on a particular topic, and those are very efficient ways of learning ... some of those videos I share with my students."*

T5N: *"It was really helpful to assign the CHI paper [17] as reading before today's lecture because students were definitely ready to talk about it and they really understood why I am using this."*

PCK2-Credibility: Providing students credible resources can convince them inclusive design methods are valid and useful.

4.2 PCK for teaching the personas and facets

Risk and Prevalence: Another risk was students misunderstanding the problem-solving facets that defined the GenderMag personas. Persona and facet issues appeared in five out of the twelve courses (Table 2). For example:

T2N-Student: *"Why were these five facets the ones picked? (More specifically what insight do they offer?)"*

T5N also encountered issues explaining the differences between personas' *Information Processing Style* and *Learning Style*:

T5N: *"I thought those five facets were orthogonal in a sense ... but as I explained to students, they are very related to one another. For example, information processing style and their learning style, I feel like they are very related ... I think students understood why we use GenderMag, but I am not confident that they understood those five facets..."*

Mitigations and PCK: These issues suggest two PCK gaps: a gap in deep enough content knowledge about the facets to help students understand the relationships among them, and a gap in strategies for presenting these relationships.

One instance of the content depth gap was revealed when T5N requested a deeper understanding of the facets. In response, an expert researcher in the GenderMag method provided a detailed explanation of the nuanced relationships among the facets and examples of how people with these facets might act for use in teaching (Figure 4). The clarifications in that message aimed at the PCK gaps that T5N had experienced.

PCK3-ContentKnowledge: Content knowledge of the facets can help teachers explain to students each facet's impacts on how a user might interact with software.

For PCK on how to *convey* the distinctiveness of each facet, T3X's presentation strategy showed promise. As class observation data showed, every time T3X introduced a new problem-solving facet, s/he immediately followed the facet's name with a concrete description. For example, T3X began describing the *Motivations* facet by naming it and then reframing it as *"Why is the persona sitting in this chair [in front of the computer with this software]?"*

Such "concretizations" may have helped students to ground the further elaboration that followed. For example, later in the course as T3X's students performed a GenderMag walkthrough, researchers observed the students successfully identifying design issues relating directly to the personas' facets, such as the persona Tim's propensity to tinker with software:

T3X-student: *"I was Tim [for the walkthrough], and would like to tinker, but there was no back button [to recover from failed tinkering]."*

PCK4-Concretization: Reframing facets in concrete ways to explain persona behavior can model how students should use the facets to predict persona behavior.

4.3 PCK for teaching the process itself

Risk and Prevalence: Students performed the GenderMag process (known as GenderMag walkthroughs) as in-class exercises in six courses. In four of these courses, students became confused about how to perform the walkthrough correctly (Table 2, row *Walkthrough processes*). Confused students may not be able to finish their walkthroughs successfully, which could translate into reluctance to use inclusive methods in the future.

For example, in T2N's course, instead of following the sequence of actions the designer intended, a group of students drifted into a sequence they thought Abby might pursue. This led to a "dead end" in being able to fulfill the subgoal they had started with, so they were unsure how to proceed:

T2N-Student: *"What should we do if we end up on a different page?"*

Researcher's notes: *"This team had stopped following the walkthrough steps and decided Abby would do something else. Ended up on the wrong [website] page and unsure how to proceed."*

T3X's course also showed confusion about the correct process:

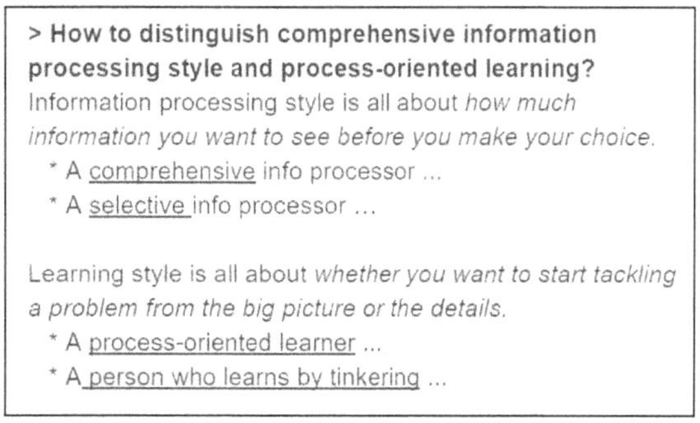
> How to distinguish comprehensive information processing style and process-oriented learning?

Information processing style is all about *how much information you want to see before you make your choice.*

* A comprehensive info processor ...
* A selective info processor ...

Learning style is all about *whether you want to start tackling a problem from the big picture or the details.*

* A process-oriented learner ...
* A person who learns by tinkering ...

Figure 4: Snippets of the message sent to T5N describing distinctions between facets. The email also contained concrete examples of how users with the facets might use software.

Researcher's notes: *"At both tables with multiple teams, one team would follow the other team's lead. Such as flipping or changing forms, or [one team] would listen in to the other's conversation as a launching point for their own [conversation]."*

Mitigation and PCK: T3X's mitigation strategy for this risk relied on the student foundations, prompting students with questions and coaching them during their hands-on activity to help them understand the walkthrough components. For example, as one team attempted to come up with a scenario, subgoals, and actions for their walkthrough, T3X provided corrective clarifying feedback:

T3X: *"Why are they in this app? What is their motivation for sitting in front of their screen?"*

Researcher notes later during the class: *"Trouble generating subgoal ...If <T3X> didn't intervene this would have gone poorly."*

T3X-Student: *"Can we use subgoal or the scenario when answering the action question?"*

T3X: *"Yes you can reference both if it applies to your reasoning."*

T3X-Student: *"So is the 'right thing' the action? [Referring to wording on the walkthrough forms]"*

T3X: *"Yes, it is what <student> defined to us as the action."*

> *PCK5-Modeling:* Modeling correct process for students both before and during hands-on practice can help students improve their use of an inclusive design process.

4.4 PCK for increasing students' application of "Theory of Mind"

Risk and Prevalence: Four of the six courses that performed GenderMag walkthroughs revealed PCK gaps relating to Theory of Mind. Theory of Mind is the human ability to reason and make inferences about another's feelings, desires, intentions, and goals [29, 31]. Methods like GenderMag leverage this ability to help evaluators predict the usability of a product by people different from themselves. Thus, learning how to apply GenderMag depended on the degree to which students could take on the perspective of the persona. But some students had difficulties doing so.

For example, ten T2N students wrote comments about Theory of Mind difficulties "channeling" the persona, such as:

T2N-Student: *"It was difficult to determine what I would do vs what Abby would do."*

T2N-Student: *"Really hard to put yourself in others shoes."*

T2N-Student: *"Intuitively I was considering the general understanding of users and it is difficult to consider the persona if it doesn't make sense based on personal experience."*

Another way Theory of Mind issues manifested was students using a single example from the facet description to entirely define the persona, such as the *Learning Styles* example of Abby preferring tutorials over tinkering to learn technology. For example:

T3X-Student: *"No, she wants to watch a tutorial."*

T3X-Student: *"I don't think she would be here. She likes wizards and this isn't that."*

Mitigation and PCK: To mitigate risks like these, T3X repeatedly emphasized that students should immerse themselves in the persona's perspectives. For example, during T3X's class activity with students doing GenderMag walkthroughs on example software prototypes, researchers observed T3X telling different groups of students...:

T3X: *"Your job at this table is to become Abby. Your job [at another table] is to become Tim. Don't think about anyone but Tim. ... Your brain becomes that person's brain—absorb everything about that person."*

> *PCK6-TheoryOfMind:* Coaching students to immerse themselves in the persona can help them with their "Theory of Mind" abilities to see software through the eyes of a persona.

4.5 PCK for reducing "I" methodology

Risk and Prevalence: One way specific failures of perspective taking manifested was when students performed a GenderMag walkthrough not as the persona, but instead as themselves: *"I would know to click this button to advance to the next page, so of course Abby would do that too."* Some teacher-researchers described this as *"I" methodology.* All seven instances observed of "I" methodology (Table 2) occurred in T2N's course. For example:

T2N-Student: *"It is a little difficult to walkthrough based on a persona. At multiple parts I was thinking what I would do in this situation."*

Use of "I" methodology has also been reported in GenderMag work in industry [16], so a few suggestions for warding it off had been posted to the GenderMag-Teach community wiki. For example, following one of these suggestions, T2N cautioned their class to "stay true to the persona." Even so, some of T2N's students had more difficulty than others with stepping into another's cognitive shoes. T2N reflected on their students' range of success staying clear of "I" methodology pitfalls:

T2N: *"Some students seem to have no problem just slipping right into that mindset of 'Abby's a different person, I understand that different people have different ways of thinking about things, I'm going to speculate from her perspective.' And other students ... [at least] recognize that their perspectives aren't the only ones, and that they don't understand other people's perspectives. But there are still students that don't."*

Mitigation and PCK: T3X had run into "I" methodology issues before in prior courses, and had found a way to mitigate it. T3X's method was to watch for it to arise during class GenderMag walkthroughs. As soon as an instance arose, T3X would intervene to ask the student to rephrase what they had just said, replacing "I" with the name of the persona they were using (e.g., "Abby"). As T3X explained in one of their pre-teaching interviews just before a class in which students would run GenderMag walkthroughs:

T3X: *"I'll remind them of the rules, such as they're never allowed to say "I" or "you" or "the user," they have to say Abby ... or Tim [the GenderMag personas]."*

> *PCK7-Averting"I":* Listening for uses of "I" during in-class activities and prompting students to use the personas' names can reduce use of "I" methodology and increase perspective-taking.

Another mitigation strategy, used by T6N, was to task their students with writing persona "backstories" for the persona they used. For example, one team modified the Abby persona, turning her into "Jenn." Part of the backstory they devised for her was:

T6N-Student: *"Jenn needs to find housing for her 18 years old son who is deaf and transferring to <University>."*

There were no "I" methodology instances observed in either of the courses that used these interventions.

PCK8-Engagement: Tasking students to modify non-essential parts of inclusive design method materials, such as background information, can increase engagement with the materials through a heightened sense of ownership.

4.6 PCK for addressing gender biases

Risk and Prevalence: Biases in the form of gender stereotyping arose in eight of the twelve courses (Table 2). These arose when a student overgeneralized or gender-stereotyped a persona's ability to use technology or to problem-solve.

For example, one of T4N's students wrote the following on their handout after learning about the GenderMag personas:

T4N-Student: *"Why are boys reckless?"*

We interpreted this student's comment to be about the Tim persona (whose problem-solving traits are statistically more common in males than in females). Tim likes to learn by tinkering with software and also tolerates risk in software. These two traits may have informed this student's characterization of males as "reckless".

Mitigation and PCK: Stereotyping is an ingrained human characteristic [34] that is difficult to eliminate entirely. Furthermore, framing GenderMag as a way to find gender-inclusiveness issues makes the concept of gender highly salient. This salience of gender automatically leads to gender stereotype activation [11]. Thus, teachers reported either *proactively* finding ways to reduce its number of instances or *reactively* explicitly addressing it head-on.

T4N pointed out one reactive mitigation strategy, observing some students asking about the evidence base behind gender differences in problem-solving. Evidence (e.g., a qualitative study showing how different problem-solving strategies can result in equally effective solutions [12]) helped students ground their decisions in solid foundations rather than stereotypes. One instance of this strategy occurred in teacher T3X's lecture on GenderMag's foundations:

T3X: *"This [pattern of data] holds strongest for male versus female developers. Why do you think this is?"*

T3X-Student: *"Women are more emotional, they don't like technology."*

T3X: *"Not true, they [in these data] are software developers."*

PCK9-RefutingStereotypes: Pointing students to the evidence underlying inclusive design methods can help students connect their work to foundations rather than stereotypes.

As for proactive strategies to address stereotyping, our data showed that practicing an actual GenderMag walkthrough, rather than just learning about it conceptually, had fewer instances of stereotyping. In fact, all but one of the instances occurred in courses without a walkthrough activity or before the walkthrough activity. These data are corroborated by a prior study investigating stereotyping in the presence of the GenderMag inclusive design method, which found that groups that performed a GenderMag walkthrough gender-stereotyped personas less than those who did not do a walkthrough—and both groups gender-stereotyped the personas less than empirical norms of how much people gender-stereotype actual people [17].

PCK10-ReducingStereotypes: Having students perform the inclusive design process can reduce tendencies to stereotype members of populations unlike themselves.

4.7 PCK for addressing resistant learners

Risk and Prevalence: Stereotyping (or fears of it) also manifested in students as resistance to learning about inclusive methods. Some of the teachers foresaw this resistance:

T5N: *"I really hope the students don't take it as a way of stereotyping genders ... From previous experience, I found that when students create personas that are very shallow level, that's what they do, they stereotype a particular gender or a particular age group. "*

Other teachers predicted that GenderMag's explicit focus on gender might elicit a negative response. T8N, who taught GenderMag in their undergraduate-level game design course, predicted that the name "GenderMag" would generate resistance:

T8N: *"[The] title for the project ... will turn people off before they understand how valuable it is."*

In nine of the twelve courses, these teachers' fears came to pass. One type of resistance came from some students concerns that GenderMag might promote gender stereotyping:

T1N: *"Some women [in the class] felt that the personas exaggerated the differences between genders, and created a perception that women were technologically helpless ... while it succeeded in drawing engineers' attention to the shortcomings of the software, it also reinforced unhelpful stereotypes ... This was not the first time in my teaching that students were alarmed by an intervention that highlighted differences between genders."*

A second kind of resistance involved students who overtly stereotyped the personas:

T7N: *"People were not taking Abby seriously 'she is scared of pressing a button' ... trivializing the facets."*

Some teachers did not have a ready strategy to mitigate this risk:

T7N: *"I didn't know how to make them be serious ... There were a bunch of people who were not even trying. "*

A third type of resistance was students not seeing the point of learning about GenderMag and inclusive design methods. One student in T3X's course showed evidence of this kind of resistance on an evaluation response: when asked what could be done to improve instruction, T3X-Student simply replied "Less GenderMag."

These examples show the existence of *resistant learners* in inclusive design classrooms: students who not only are unmotivated to learn the material, but who actively dispute or trivialize the concepts of inclusive design.

Mitigation and PCK: Teachers responded to resistance in three ways. One mitigation was to simply avoid talking about gender, using language of inclusion instead. When T1N taught GenderMag in their undergraduate HCI course the following term, s/he modified their approach to include an active-learning, in-class activity that allowed students time to get their questions answered. S/he elected to remove any mention of gender from their second lesson and focus solely on the persona's software usage styles as a lens for inclusivity. T1N found that this intervention helped students understand the importance of inclusiveness in software without potentially getting caught up on the gendered nature of the topic. T1N also observed, however, that this came at the cost of not fully leveraging GenderMag's foundations, because to do so would require bringing up gender.

A second strategy involved situating gender in the broader goal of inclusion and discussing the primary benefits of inclusion. For example, T3X spoke to the benefits of inclusive design when a student doubted its efficacy:

T3X: *"Somebody else doubted whether you could have a 100 percent perfect interface for everyone, and I totally agreed, and said we're not aiming for 100 percent here, we're just aiming for 'better.' He bought that."*

T3X reported that after that interaction, the student was enthusiastic and engaged in the rest of the lecture. Focusing on inclusiveness for its own sake may thus motivate an otherwise resistant subset of students.

A third strategy was to mitigate resistance by focusing on the secondary benefits of inclusion. In their courses on GenderMag, T7N mentioned that designing inclusive software can increase a product's user base:

T7N: *"50% of people are women, it's better economics."*

T6N made a similar point to their class:

T6N: *"They like the idea that we have to design software for everyone. I used the illustration that if only half the market wants to buy your software, that's not going to be a very successful product."*

> *PCK11-HandlingResistance:* Relating inclusive design methods' utility to the broader goal of inclusive appeal and/or to greater market share can mitigate the risk of students' resistance and motivate them to learn inclusive design.

5 DISCUSSION AND CONCLUDING REMARKS

The goal of our study was to uncover what PCK teachers need to teach inclusive design through the lens of GenderMag. We found at least four major categories of PCK:

- Students can be skeptical about gender differences in problem-solving, which can impede willingness to learn, but are often convinced by research evidence (PCK 1 and 2).

Table 3: Triangulation: Each new PCK was supported by three or more different data sources. (Numbers refer to sections showing instances of the data source.)

PCK #	Interview & Emails	Class Obs	Student Feedback	Teaching Materials	Prior Work
PCK1-Framing	✓4.1	✓	✓		
PCK2-Credibility	✓	✓	✓	✓4.2	
PCK3-Content Knowledge	✓Fig 4	✓	✓4.2		
PCK4-Concretization	✓	✓4.2	✓4.2		
PCK5-Modeling	✓	✓	✓4.3		
PCK6-TheoryOfMind	✓	✓	✓4.4		
PCK7-Averting"I"	✓4.5	✓4.5	✓4.5		
PCK8-Engagement		✓	✓	✓4.5	
PCK9-Refuting Stereotypes	✓	✓4.6	✓4.6		[11, 34]
PCK10-Reducing Stereotypes	✓	✓	✓		[17]
PCK11-Handling Resistance	✓4.7	✓	✓		

- Learning GenderMag's persona facets and walkthrough process requires careful scaffolding before and during active practice of the method. Generalizing to other inclusive design methods, the PCK for leveraging personas should also be useful for considering real people in a target population (PCK 3, 4, and 5).
- Some students struggle with perspective-taking and stereotyping, but prescriptive rules such as avoiding the word "I", corrective feedback, and student production of materials can engage students in more facet-based reasoning (PCK 6, 7, and 8).
- Some students hold gender biases, political stances, and interpersonal fears of discussing gender in a classroom, but connecting goals to evidence, engaging students in practicing a walkthrough, and situating discussion of gender under a broader goal of inclusion can mitigate resistance (PCK 9, 10, and 11).

Although our data was rich, some aspects of our study design limit the internal and external validity of these interpretations. As an Action Research study, we did not attempt to control for teachers' pedagogical knowledge or content knowledge; even had we wanted to, there is a lack of robust measurements for either. Teachers varied in their ability to reflect on their PCK, and both students and teachers varied in their ability to reflect on students' learning, which led to variation in the level of detail in our data across courses. There were also several factors that may have determined what we did and did not observe, such as teachers' existing pedagogical knowledge, whether courses were required or electives, and the teachers' varying degrees of preparation and classroom management skills. Therefore, some of the interpretations we made from the data might be different had we studied other teachers or students. Consistent with Action Research methods, we safeguarded against these limitations through extensive use of triangulation, which we enumerate in Table 3.

Despite the limitations, our results have important implications for research. For example, our data suggest a testable hypothesis: that teachers need a robust understanding of their students' existing perspectives on inclusion in order to successfully connect conceptual content to their prior knowledge, to answer questions during active learning, and to facilitate discussions about inclusive design. Our data also suggest a hypothesis that perspective taking is a critical prerequisite skill for conducting a successful GenderMag walkthrough and that without it, students may struggle or fail to become proficient in inclusive design. Future work should develop ways of measuring the factors and outcomes in these hypotheses so that we may rigorously test them.

Although our research on how to teach inclusive design is just beginning, our results also have implications for teachers. The PCK we present in this paper suggests that with a careful orientation to inclusion, highly scaffolded practice for persona-based walkthroughs, and corrective feedback on this practice, students can successfully perform inclusive design processes, identifying inclusion issues in user experience designs. Through these efforts and further progress in effective teaching of inclusive design, future generations of designers and engineers can be empowered to shape not only novel user experiences, but inclusive ones.

ACKNOWLEDGMENTS

This work is supported in part by the National Science Foundation under Grants 1735123, 1314399, 1703304, 1314384, and 1528061.

REFERENCES

[1] Engin Bozdag. 2013. Bias in algorithmic filtering and personalization. *Ethics and information technology* 15, 3 (2013), 209–227. https://doi.org/10.1007/s10676-013-9321-6

[2] M. Burnett, R. Counts, R. Lawrence, and H. Hanson. 2017. Gender HCI and microsoft: Highlights from a longitudinal study. In *2017 IEEE Symposium on Visual Languages and Human-Centric Computing (VL/HCC)*. 139–143. https://doi.org/10.1109/VLHCC.2017.8103461

[3] Margaret Burnett, Anicia Peters, Charles Hill, and Noha Elarief. 2016. Finding gender-inclusiveness software issues with GenderMag: A field investigation. In *Proceedings of the 2016 CHI conference on human factors in computing systems (CHI '16)*. ACM, New York, NY, USA, 2586–2598. https://doi.org/10.1145/2858036.2858274

[4] Margaret Burnett, Simone Stumpf, Laura Beckwith, and Anicia Peters. 2018. The GenderMag Kit: How to use the GenderMag Method to find inclusiveness issues through a gender lens. (February 2018). http://gendermag.org

[5] Margaret Burnett, Simone Stumpf, Jamie Macbeth, Stephann Makri, Laura Beckwith, Irwin Kwan, Anicia Peters, and William Jernigan. 2016. GenderMag: A method for evaluating software's gender inclusiveness. *Interacting with Computers* 28, 6 (2016), 760–787. https://doi.org/10.1093/iwc/iwv046

[6] Margaret M. Burnett, Laura Beckwith, Susan Wiedenbeck, Scott D. Fleming, Jill Cao, Thomas H. Park, Valentina Grigoreanu, and Kyle Rector. 2011. Gender pluralism in problem-solving software. *Interacting with Computers* 23, 5 (2011), 450–460. https://doi.org/10.1016/j.intcom.2011.06.004

[7] Rebecca Cooper, John Loughran, and Amanda Berry. 2015. Science Teachers' PCK. *Berry, A., Friedrichsen, P. & Loughran, J., Re-examining Pedagogical Content Knowledge in Science Education* (2015), 60–74.

[8] Sally Jo Cunningham, Annika Hinze, and David M Nichols. 2016. Supporting gender-neutral digital library creation: A case study using the GenderMag toolkit. In *International Conference on Asian Digital Libraries*. Springer, 45–50. https://doi.org/10.1007/978-3-319-49304-6_6

[9] Anthony Faiola. 2007. The design enterprise: Rethinking the HCI education paradigm. *Design Issues* 23, 3 (2007), 30–45. https://doi.org/10.1162/desi.2007.23.3.30

[10] Juan-Miguel Fernandez-Balboa and Jim Stiehl. 1995. The generic nature of pedagogical content knowledge among college professors. 11 (05 1995), 293–306. https://doi.org/10.1016/0742-051X(94)00030-A

[11] Anthony G Greenwald and Mahzarin R Banaji. 1995. Implicit social cognition: attitudes, self-esteem, and stereotypes. *Psychological review* 102, 1 (1995), 4. https://doi.org/doi:10.1037/0033-295X.102.1.4

[12] Valentina Grigoreanu, Margaret Burnett, Susan Wiedenbeck, Jill Cao, Kyle Rector, and Irwin Kwan. 2012. End-user debugging strategies: A sensemaking perspective. *ACM Transactions on Computer-Human Interaction (TOCHI)* 19, 1 (2012), 5. https://doi.org/10.1145/2147783.2147788

[13] Allison Gulamhussein. 2013. Teaching the Teachers: Effective professional development. (Sep 2013). http://www.centerforpubliceducation.org/research/teaching-teachers-effective-professional-development

[14] Jan H. van Driel, Nico Verloop, and Wobbe de Vos. 1998. Developing science teachers' pedagogical content knowledge. 35 (08 1998), 673–695. https://doi.org/10.1002/(SICI)1098-2736(199808)35:6<673::AID-TEA5>3.0.CO;2-J

[15] Gillian R Hayes. 2014. Knowing by doing: Action Research as an approach to HCI. In *Ways of Knowing in HCI*. Springer, 49–68.

[16] C. Hill, S. Ernst, A. Oleson, A. Horvath, and M. Burnett. 2016. GenderMag experiences in the field: The whole, the parts, and the workload. In *2016 IEEE Symposium on Visual Languages and Human-Centric Computing (VL/HCC)*. 199–207. https://doi.org/10.1109/VLHCC.2016.7739685

[17] Charles G. Hill, Maren Haag, Alannah Oleson, Chris Mendez, Nicola Marsden, Anita Sarma, and Margaret Burnett. 2017. Gender-inclusiveness personas vs. stereotyping: Can we have it both ways?. In *Proceedings of the 2017 CHI conference on human factors in computing systems (CHI '17)*. ACM, New York, NY, USA, 6658–6671. https://doi.org/10.1145/3025453.3025609

[18] Heather C. Hill, Deborah Loewenberg Ball, and Stephen Schilling. 2008. Unpacking pedagogical content knowledge: Conceptualizing and measuring teachers' topic-specific knowledge of students. 39 (07 2008), 372–400. https://doi.org/10.1145/3025453.3025609

[19] Heather C. Hill, Brian Rowan, and Deborah Loewenberg Ball. 2005. Effects of teachers' mathematical knowledge for teaching on student achievement. *American Educational Research Journal* 42, 2 (2005), 371–406. https://doi.org/10.3102/00028312042002371 arXiv:https://doi.org/10.3102/00028312042002371

[20] Peter Hubwieser, Johannes Magenheim, Andreas Mühling, and Alexander Ruf. 2013. Towards a conceptualization of pedagogical content knowledge for computer science. In *Proceedings of the ninth annual international ACM conference on international computing education research (ICER '13)*. ACM, New York, NY, USA, 1–8. https://doi.org/10.1145/2493394.2493395

[21] C. D. Hundhausen, D. Fairbrother, and M. Petre. 2012. An Empirical Study of the "Prototype Walkthrough": A Studio-Based Activity for HCI Education. *ACM Trans. Comput.-Hum. Interact.* 19, 4, Article 26 (Dec. 2012), 36 pages. https://doi.org/10.1145/2395131.2395133

[22] N. H. Ibrahim, J. Surif, A. H. Abdullah, and N. A. S. Sabtu. 2014. Comparison of pedagogical content knowledge between expert and novice lecturers in teaching and learning process. In *2014 International Conference on Teaching and Learning in Computing and Engineering*. 240–246. https://doi.org/10.1109/LaTiCE.2014.53

[23] Andrew J Ko. 2017. A three-year participant observation of software startup software evolution. In *Proceedings of the 39th International Conference on Software Engineering: Software Engineering in Practice Track*. IEEE Press, 3–12. https://doi.org/10.1109/ICSE-SEIP.2017.29

[24] Andrew J Ko and Parmit K Chilana. 2011. Design, discussion, and dissent in open bug reports. In *Proceedings of the 2011 iConference*. ACM, 106–113. https://doi.org/10.1145/1940761.1940776

[25] Andrew J Ko and Richard E Ladner. 2016. AccessComputing promotes teaching accessibility. *ACM Inroads* 7, 4 (2016), 65–68. https://doi.org/10.1145/2968453

[26] Paul Luo Li, Andrew J Ko, and Andrew Begel. 2017. Cross-disciplinary perspectives on collaborations with software engineers. In *Cooperative and Human Aspects of Software Engineering (CHASE), 2017 IEEE/ACM 10th International Workshop on*. IEEE, 2–8. https://doi.org/10.1109/CHASE.2017.3

[27] Thomas Mahatody, Mouldi Sagar, and Christophe Kolski. 2010. State of the art on the cognitive walkthrough method, its variants and evolutions. *Intl. Journal of human–computer interaction* 26, 8 (2010), 741–785. https://doi.org/10.1080/10447311003781409

[28] D. Scott McCrickard, C. M. Chewar, and Jacob Somervell. 2004. Design, science, and engineering topics?: teaching HCI with a unified method. In *Proceedings of the 35th SIGCSE technical symposium on computer science education (SIGCSE '04)*. ACM, New York, NY, USA, 31–35. https://doi.org/10.1145/971300.971314

[29] David Premack and Guy Woodruff. 1978. Does the chimpanzee have a theory of mind? *Behavioral and Brain Sciences* 1, 4 (1978), 515–526. https://doi.org/10.1017/S0140525X00076512

[30] Yolanda Jacobs Reimer and Sarah A Douglas. 2003. Teaching HCI design with the studio approach. *Computer science education* 13, 3 (2003), 191–205.

[31] Dana Schneider, Rebecca Lam, Andrew P Bayliss, and Paul E Dux. 2012. Cognitive load disrupts implicit theory-of-mind processing. *Psychological Science* 23, 8 (2012), 842–847. https://doi.org/10.1177/0956797612439070

[32] Lee Shulman. 1987. Knowledge and teaching: Foundations of the new reform. *Harvard educational review* 57, 1 (1987), 1–23. https://doi.org/10.17763/haer.57.1.j463w79r56455411

[33] Ernest T Stringer. 2007. Action Research (3e éd.). (2007).

[34] Phil Turner and Susan Turner. 2011. Is stereotyping inevitable when designing with personas? *Design studies* 32, 1 (2011), 30–44. https://doi.org/10.1016/j.destud.2010.06.002

[35] Cathleen Wharton. 1994. The cognitive walkthrough method: A practitioner's guide. *Usability inspection methods* (1994).

[36] Ortrun Zuber-Skerritt. 1992. *Action research in higher education: examples and reflections*. ERIC.

Digital Competence, Teacher Self-Efficacy and Training Needs

Linda Mannila
Aalto Univ. & Linköping Univ.
Espoo, Finland & Linköping, Sweden
linda.mannila@aalto.fi

Lars-Åke Nordén
Uppsala University
Uppsala, Sweden
lars-ake.norden@it.uu.se

Arnold Pears
Uppsala University
Uppsala, Sweden
arnold.pears@it.uu.se

ABSTRACT

Computing related content is introduced in school curricula all over the world, placing new requirements on school teachers and their knowledge. Little attention has been paid to fostering the skills and attitudes required to teach the new content. This involves not only traditional computing topics, such as algorithms or programming, but also the role of technology in society as well as questions related to ethics, safety and integrity. As technology develops at a fast rate, so does the content to be taught. Learning computing content through isolated in-service training initiatives is by no means enough, but rather, teachers need to develop confidence to independently and continuously explore what is new, what is relevant and how to include digital competence in their teaching. Teachers' self-efficacy is hence of crucial importance.

In a previous article [13] we described the development of a self-efficacy scale for teachers, focusing on digital competence as described in EU's framework DigComp 2.0. In this paper, we extend that work by analysing 530 teachers' responses collected in Autumn 2017 during a series of workshops and other professional development events. Our goal was to collect baseline data, painting a picture of teachers' current self-efficacy levels in order to facilitate follow-up studies. In addition, our results also point out challenging areas, consequently providing important insight into what topics and themes should be emphasized in professional development initiatives.

KEYWORDS

Digital competence, self-efficacy, teacher training, K-9 education, professional development

ACM Reference Format:
Linda Mannila, Lars-Åke Nordén, and Arnold Pears. 2018. Digital Competence, Teacher Self-Efficacy and Training Needs. In *ICER '18: 2018 International Computing Education Research Conference, August 13–15, 2018, Espoo, Finland.* ACM, New York, NY, USA, 8 pages. https://doi.org/10.1145/3230977.3230993

1 INTRODUCTION

As computing related topics are introduced in school curricula a range of new challenges arise. While teaching and learning computing content at university level has been the focus of research

for quite some time, most questions still need to be formulated and empirically studied in primary and high school education. One of the most important questions concerns teacher preparation; how can teachers prepare for teaching the new content and integrate computing and digital competences in different subjects into their everyday classroom practice. As technology develops rapidly, so does the content to be taught. Learning new content through isolated in-service training initiatives is not sufficient, rather, teachers need to develop the confidence to independently and continuously explore what is new, what is relevant and develop methods through which they can include digital competence in their teaching [14].

Teacher self-efficacy is a key factor in this process, as it is strongly correlated to an individual's perseverance and resilience in the face of difficulty. A low self-efficacy is more likely to result in lower levels of persistence, and ultimately failure to deal effectively with the task at hand. The higher the sense of efficacy, the greater the effort, persistence, and resilience of the individual [7, 22]. These are factors that are crucial to problem solving endeavours in computing, self-regulated learning, and lifelong learning. There are also studies indicating that teachers with high self-efficacy positively affect student learning and building of new competences [11, 17, 19]. These arguments underpin the important contribution strong self-efficacy in digital competences can make, and emphasise its necessity in supporting teachers as they start to involve themselves in an evolving curricula that include computing and digital competences.

In [13] we described the development of a self-efficacy scale for teachers, focusing on digital competence as described in the European Commission's DigComp 2.0 framework. DigComp is highly influential and affects how computing and digital competences are viewed in national school curricula within the European Union (EU). For instance, revised curricula in Sweden and Finland have seen the introduction of digital competence as a transverse collection of knowledge and skills. The Finnish curriculum came into force in fall 2016, while the Swedish revisions will take effect in July 2018. The DigComp standard can however also be considered relevant to countries outside the EU. The items included in our instrument are directly derived from the key dimensions of the DigiComp framework.

In this paper, we extend our previous work by analysing responses collected from 530 teachers in Autumn 2017 during a series of workshops and professional development events. In a situation like this one, where an entire profession is affected, it is important — both for individual teachers and for decision makers — to be able to evaluate and follow-up on competence levels over time. For this we need both a suitable instrument and comparison data. The goal of this study was therefore to provide data that can be used as a basis for future studies. The results describe teachers' current digital competences and self efficacy. We also identify challenging areas, consequently providing important insight into what topics

Table 1: Listing of competences included in the DigComp 2.0 framework.

Competence area	Competence
Information and data literacy	1.1 Browsing, searching and filtering data, information and digital content
	1.2 Evaluating data, information and digital content
	1.3 Managing data, information and digital content
Communication and collaboration	2.1 Interacting through digital technologies
	2.2 Sharing through digital technologies
	2.3 Engaging in citizenship through digital technologies
	2.4 Collaborating through digital technologies
	2.5 Netiquette
	2.6 Managing digital identity
Digital content creation	3.1 Developing digital content
	3.2 Integrating and re-elaborating digital content
	3.3 Copyright and licenses
	3.4 Programming
Safety	4.1 Protecting devices
	4.2 Protecting personal data and privacy
	4.3 Protecting health and well-being
	4.4 Protecting the environment
Problem solving	5.1 Solving technical problems
	5.2 Identifying needs and technological responses
	5.3 Creatively using digital technologies
	5.4 Identifying digital competence gaps

and themes should be emphasized in professional development initiatives.

The study focuses on two main questions:

- What is the current level of teachers' self-efficacy in digital competence?
- What areas need to be emphasized in teacher training efforts?

The paper is organized as follows. We begin by briefly describing the theory underlying the notion of self-efficacy. Next we present the DigComp framework and our self-efficacy instrument. We then present the study setting and methodology, and provide the details of our results. We conclude the paper with a discussion of these results and their implications for in-service and pre-service teacher training.

2 THE DIGCOMP FRAMEWORK

The European Commission defines digital competence in terms of five main competence areas in their framework DigComp 2.0. These competence areas are: 1) information and data literacy, 2) communication and collaboration, 3) digital content creation, 4) safety and 5) problem solving. Each competence area is accompanied by 3-6 competences, describing the skills and knowledge seen as essential for the component at hand (Table 1) [4].

3 SELF-EFFICACY

Self-efficacy theory is used in educational research, training and other activities where a person is to attain a new, or develop a higher, level of skill. Self-efficacy is defined as a belief in personal agency, for instance one's ability to successfully perform a particular behaviour or task [6]. Bandura discusses self-efficacy in terms of belief in one's capabilities to organize and execute the course of action required to attain a goal [2]. Self-efficacy beliefs exert a palpable influence on behaviour, in particular how long individuals persevere when confronted with difficult tasks and how resilient they will be in the face of difficulty or failure. A low self-efficacy is more likely to result in less persistent efforts in relation to a task, and may ultimately result in failure to complete the task at hand. Attainment of a high sense of self-efficacy is at least as important as possessing the skills themselves. Studies have shown that a person that lacks a certain skill still can complete a task requiring that skill successfully if their self-efficacy regarding the skill is high. Self-efficacy beliefs are also malleable and can affect a person's intellectual performance.

Research on teacher self-efficacy identifies a positive correlation between teacher self-efficacy and students' motivation, achievements and building of competences [11, 17, 19, 24]. Teacher self-efficacy also affects students indirectly via the instructional strategies, planning and a willingness to try out new material and approaches to teaching a subject [20]. Teacher self-efficacy seems to be a rather strong predictor of the way teachers shape their teaching practices in order to foster students' motivation to learn [19] and is thus relevant in education as well as other activities where skill development is a primary focus [16].

The perceived self-efficacy of an individual refers to an identified strength [7] which is measured by degrees of certainty that one can perform specific tasks [27]. As a consequence, self-efficacy is typically measured directly by the subject of the study using a self-reporting scale. Preparation of a self-efficacy scale that properly measures the behaviour in question requires careful design.

A self-efficacy scale consists of a number of statements (items) that express a personal position in relation to different skills and competences related to the subject in question. Respondents are asked to express to what extent they believe that they could do what is described in the statement based on their current level of knowledge. Answers are recorded on a Likert scale. Statements are positively-worded and express actions rather than expressing specific knowledge. In the case of testing whether a person knows how to turn on a computer, an appropriate statement in a self-efficacy scale might be *I could turn on a computer* rather than *I know how to turn on a computer*.

4 SELF-EFFICACY IN DIGITAL COMPETENCES

As we observed in the previous section, there is an extensive body of literature on self-efficacy [1, 10, 26]. However, this literature, while providing a scholarly foundation for our work, is not sufficiently specific as to be directly applicable to the evaluation of self-efficacy in relation to the teaching of digital competences.

Several self-efficacy scales have been developed for computing skills and sub-areas of digital competence, e.g. [3, 5, 12, 15, 21, 25]. While relevant, these scales focus primarily on core computing skills, in contrast to the broader set of skills that DigComp identifies. In [13] we developed a scale aimed at evaluating the self-efficacy of practising school teachers in the context of computing and/or digital competence being added to national school curricula in Europe. The approach being taken by European national authorities affects not only teachers in programming and computing, but also in many other school subjects including mathematics, natural sciences, technology and craft.

As a first step in deriving a self-efficacy scale, we created a list of 74 statements to cover the competence areas and competences specified in DigComp 2.0. The majority of the statements were directly inspired by examples provided by the framework. In addition to the items we extracted from the framework documents we formulated a small number of additional statements to provide specific coverage of competences and knowledge that our prior research and development work has identified are relevant for school teachers. The 74-statement scale was converted into an online questionnaire, where teachers were asked to rate their own confidence in relation to each of the 74 statements on a scale of 1 (very uncertain) to 7 (very confident). In addition, we asked some background questions related to their teaching background and subjects. The scale was distributed online to teachers and school leaders in Finland and Sweden using a combination of social media, mailing lists and group communication tools. The questionnaire was administered

in Swedish. Given that the curriculum content related to digital competence is rather similar in Finland and Sweden, these two countries they seemed a natural choice for our pilot study. In addition, there are Swedish speaking teachers in both countries, making it possible to avoid potential ambiguity arising from a need to translate the statements into several languages. Based on 107 responses the 74 items were reduced to 27 statements through removal of redundant items as well as items with poor discriminatory power. This was done by computing discrimination indexes for all items and performing cross correlation between all responses. A more detailed description of the process of developing the instrument can be found in [13].

5 METHODOLOGY
5.1 Data collection

The data were collected using the 27-statement instrument during professional development initiatives in Sweden during a three-month period (September - November) in 2017. The workshops were 1-3 hours long and discussed digital competence from a school perspective building on the questions why, what and how: why is this area introduced in the curriculum, what does it mean in practice and how can the new content be taught? The workshops were interactive and the participants were expected to share ideas and experiences with each other. As Sweden is only about to renew their curriculum it is likely that most respondents had not participated in any large scale professional development programs before attending the workshops.

The instrument was distributed as an online questionnaire during workshops and seminars, giving the respondents the opportunity to ask questions and discuss the instrument right after filling it out. No discussions took place while the respondents answered the questionnaire, and no changes were made to the responses once submitted.

Just as when developing the instrument, we used a 7-point Likert scale when asking respondents to rate the 27 statements based on how certain they felt that they could carry out the activity described in each statement. The response options ranged from 1 (very uncertain) to 7 (very confident).

In addition to the 27 statements, the instrument also asked for background information (years of teaching, experience of technology in teaching, age, gender, grade levels taught, subjects taught, comments on the statements).

The respondents were in one way or another involved in teaching at kindergarten or primary school (grades 1-9) in Sweden. All in all we received 530 responses (80.6 % female, 16.0 % male, 3.4 % would rather not say). Almost 80% of the respondents were teachers, whereas the rest were either principals or had a specific area of expertise (for instance, IT, extracurricular activities or special education). Over a fifth (22%) of the teachers had less than 5 years of teaching experience, 39% had taught for 5-15 years, 26% for 16-25 years and 13% had more than 25 years of teaching experience.

The largest age group was those reporting to be 40 - 49 years of age (31.5 %). Roughly one fifth of the respondents were aged under 30 years (16.8 %), 30 - 39 years (21.3 %) and 50 - 59 years (22.3 %). Only 6.0 % were over 59 years old, while 2.1 % did not want to state their age. Technology use varied greatly, as some respondents stated that they used no technology at all, whereas others listed a long set of tools and approaches for integrating technology in the classroom.

5.2 Analysis

Responses were collected using an online form, from which the data were downloaded for statistical analysis. Self-efficacy scores were summed for each respondent across the 27 instrument and the sum was mapped onto the scale 1-7. In this way a composite self-efficacy measure (CSE) was created, making it possible to compare the overall self-efficacy scores of the respondents. The corresponding analysis was also conducted for each competence area separately, in order to make it possible to compare teachers' CSE for the five areas. In addition, we also summed the scores for each of the 27 statements, in order to gain insight into the experienced difficulty level of individual competences. By creating a composite measure, the data were transformed from ordinal into quantitative, making it possible to also calculate descriptive statistics such as medians, means and standard deviations.

In a situation where professional development initiatives are discussed and planned, it is important to have insight into what the actual needs are. To address this question, we describe three general CSE levels (low, moderate and strong self-efficacy) in order to paint a picture of the broad and diverse need for training efforts. A CSE of 1-3 was decided to represent *low self-efficacy*, 4-5 *moderate self-efficacy* and 6-7 *strong self-efficacy*.

Each of the 27 competences in the test relate to one of the competence areas presented in table 1. The cumulative distribution for each competence area was computed to describe differences in distributions of perceived self efficacy for each area.

6 RESULTS

The composite self-efficacy (CSE) scores can be analysed both on a respondent and a statement basis. When treating the data on a respondent basis we computed a cumulative self-efficacy for the individual by summing the scale values for all items in the instrument. In this case, the lowest possible summed self-efficacy was 27 and the highest possible 189 (27 statements with minimum score 1 and maximum score 7). When conducting the corresponding analysis for individual scale items considering the entire population of respondents, the lowest possible summed score was 530 and the highest possible 3710 (530 responses with minimum score 1 and maximum score 7).

6.1 Respondent CSE scores

Individuals with a summed score of 27 points (corresponding to 1 on all statements) were categorized as a CSE of 1, those with a score in the range 28-54 were categorized as a CSE of 2, and so forth.

For our sample the mean overall CSE for all respondents was 4.65, with a standard deviation of 1.22. The median CSE was 5. The distribution of CSE scores among the 530 respondents is presented in Figure 1.

When conducting the corresponding analysis separately for the five competence areas, we arrived at scores between 5-35 (for areas with five statements) and 6-42 (for areas with six statements). For areas with five statements a CSE of 1 consequently corresponded to

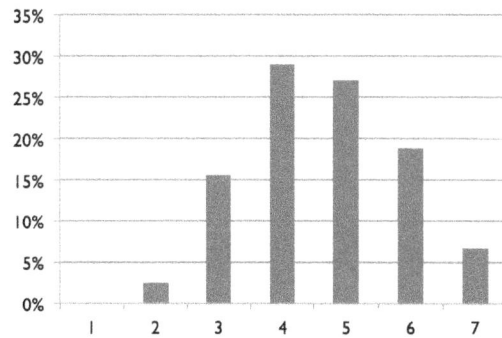

Figure 1: Distribution of CSE (1-7) among the 530 respondents

a summed up score of 5, a CSE of 2 to a summed up score between 6-10, and so on. For areas with six statements, on the other hand, a CSE of 1 corresponded to a summed up score of 6, a CSE of 2 to a summed up score between 7-12, and so forth. The CDF plot in Figure 2 illustrates the distribution of CSE scores for the five competence areas (CA1..CA5) respectively.

As the diagram illustrates, teachers' CSE score is the highest (mostly 5 and 6) for the first competence area (CA1: Information and data literacy), while the lowest CSE scores are found in the third competence area (CA3: Digital content creation).

6.2 CSE scores for individual competences

Analysis of competence components is based on the cumulative value attributed to the scale statements by the 530 respondents. After sorting the statements according to their score and then categorizing them onto the scale 1-7 (CSE 1 = score 530, CSE 2 = scores in the range 531-1060, and so on), we obtained the results shown in the column "Overall CSE" in Table 2.

The mean overall CSE for all statements is 4.59 with a standard deviation of 0.80. The median is 5. None of the individual statements or competences has one of the lowest (1-2) or highest (7) CSE scores. The specific competences with the highest overall CSE score (6) are related to using search engines, storing and organizing digital content and recognizing hate speech online. Correspondingly, the competences with lowest self-efficacy (3) are choosing a suitable creative commons licence and writing a program that accomplishes a certain task.

The distribution of CSE scores for each of the competence areas is shown in Figure 2. We observe a substantial difference between the first and the third competence areas, represented by the top and bottom curves in Figure 2. A closer look at competence area 3 is presented in Figure 3, in which the competences labelled C1..C6 correspond to the 6 competences in competence area 3 presented in Table 2. This closer examination reveals, for instance, that over 60% of all respondents had a weak CSE (1-3) on the statement "I could write a program that accomplishes a certain task provided I had sufficient time".

In addition to looking at the overall CSE scores, we also analysed the scores based on the CSE level (low, moderate or strong). A *low self-efficacy* is defined as an overall CSE of 1,2 or 3, and was the

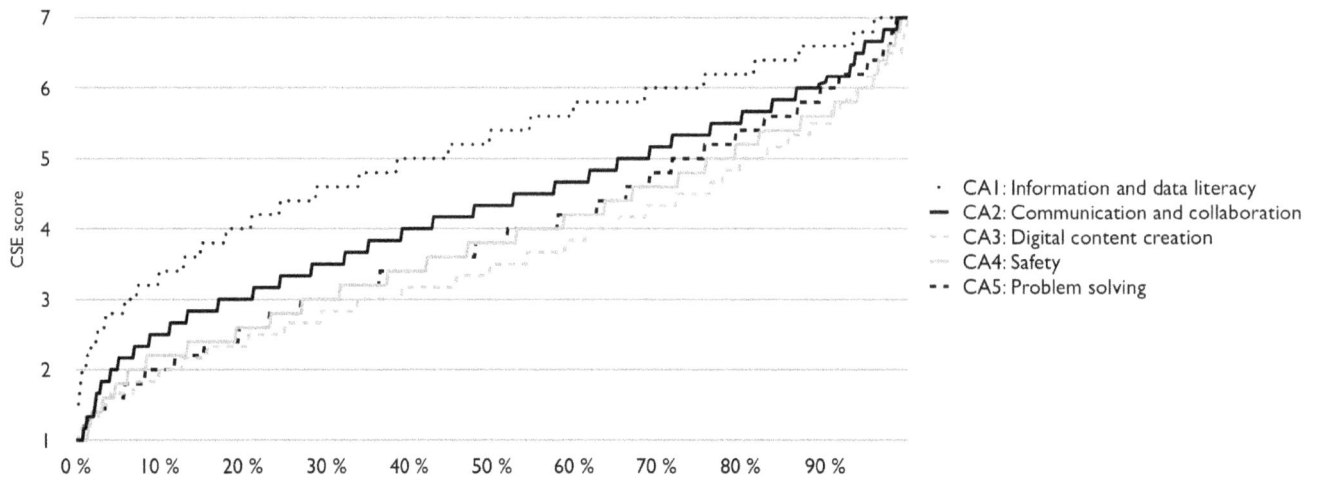

Figure 2: CDF plot showing the CSE score distribution (1-7) among the 530 respondents and the five competence areas

Table 2: CSE of individual competences

Competence area	I could...	Overall CSE	Low CSE	Mod. CSE	Strong CSE
Information and data literacy	... adapt my searches based on knowledge about how search engines produce results	5	4	5	7
	... use search engines to find a given type of information, e.g. images, videos or maps	6	5	6	7
	... determine whether a news story being disseminated online is false	5	4	5	6
	... store and organize digital content in a way so I can later find it	6	4	6	7
	... choose a safe and lasting storage place for digital content	5	4	5	7
Communication and collaboration	... communicate with someone online without exposing my identity	4	2	4	6
	... correctly cite the creator when using or disseminating other people's material	5	3	4	6
	... find a relevant online meeting place for a specific area of interest	5	3	5	7
	... arrange an online meeting as a replacement for a physical meeting	5	3	5	7
	... recognize hate speech in discussions online	6	4	6	7
	... manage and delete my digital traces	4	2	3	5
Digital content creation	... combine tools in order to create digital content	5	3	5	7
	... summarize information from different sources in a representative manner	5	4	5	7
	... choose a suitable creative commons license for material I have created	3	2	3	5
	... write a program that accomplishes a certain task provided I had sufficient time	3	2	3	5
	... plan and design a solution to a problem in the form of step-by-step instructions	4	2	4	6
	... identify when and how programming can be used in different subject areas	4	2	3	5
Safety	... protect digital equipment from undesired access online	4	2	3	5
	... detect when someone is trying to trick me into sharing personal information	5	3	5	6
	... identify web sites that can be used for fraud or other types of unwanted activity	4	3	4	6
	... help prevent online bullying	5	3	4	6
	... estimate the impact of my use of digital equipment on the environment	4	3	4	6
Problem solving	... find solutions to technical problems by searching online	5	3	5	7
	... adapt and adjust the behaviour and functionality of a program through its settings	4	2	4	6
	... construct a product with the support of digital technology	4	2	3	6
	... learn a new programming language on my own	4	2	3	5
	... adapt my ways of working based on new digital tools	5	3	5	7

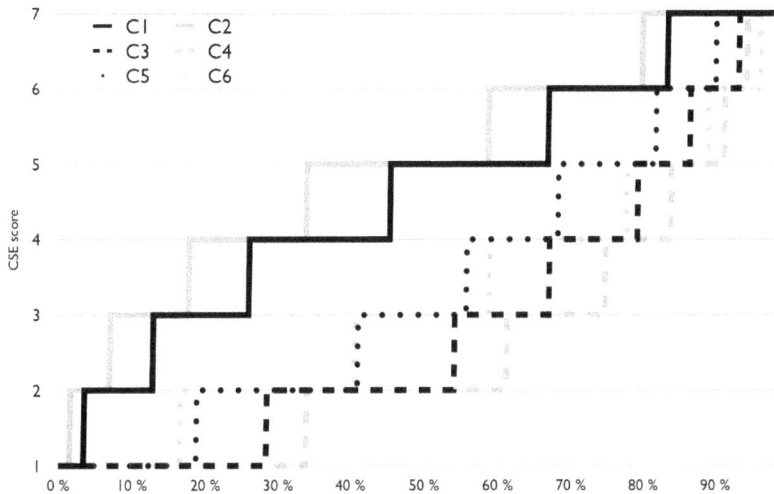

Figure 3: CDF plot of the CSE scores for the individual statements in competence area 3 (Digital content creation)

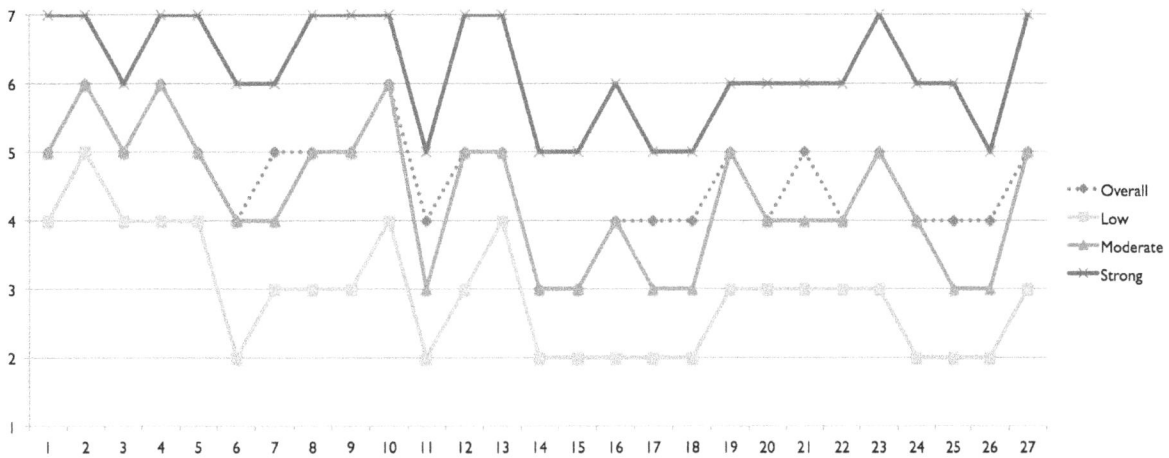

Figure 4: CSE scores plotted for the 27 individual statements

result for 18% of the respondents (Figure 1). These cases had a mean CSE of 2.86 and a standard deviation of 0.34. No teacher had the lowest CSE score (1). Over half (56%) of the teachers exhibited a *moderate self-efficacy*, that is, an overall CSE of 4-5, with a mean CSE of 4.48 and a standard deviation of 0.50. Finally, a *strong self-efficacy* is defined as a CSE of 6-7. In our study, 26% of the teachers ended up at this CSE level. These cases had a mean CSE of 6.26 and a standard deviation of 0.44.

The three columns to the right in Table 2 show the corresponding CSE score for each statement and CSE level. Similarly, the diagram in Figure 4 visualizes the differences in CSE scores between the three levels and the overall result for the 27 statements. The results pinpoint large differences overall for most statements. The gap between a low and strong self-efficacy score is the largest for statement 6 ("I could communicate with someone online without exposing my identity") and smallest for the first competence area (Information and data literacy, statements 1-5).

7 DISCUSSION

The results presented above show a large spread in teachers' self-efficacy levels. The competences with the highest overall CSE were those in competence area 1, that is, skills related to information and data literacy. This finding is in line with our pilot study when developing the self-efficacy instrument [13], where we found that the respondents, in general, felt most confident in this area. This can, however, be considered an expected result, as handling data and information is something we all do on a regular basis in our everyday life. Similar results have also been found in other studies, for instance in a survey of school teachers' engagement in computational thinking practices [9].

Overall, teachers seem to be least confident with regard to competences related to programming and copyright/licenses. Sixty percent of the respondents felt very insecure (CSE 1-3) when it came to solving problems using programming. Similar results have been found elsewhere, for instance in England, where the new subject

Computing was introduced in the curriculum in 2014. At that point, 60% of the teachers felt that they were not ready for teaching the new content [23]. In a report from 2017 [18], 48% of the teachers participating in a survey still were not confident in teaching Computing, due to, for instance, lacking "theoretical and technical knowledge of computing", including aspects of programming.

The large spread becomes particularly obvious when looking at the situation for low, moderate and strong self-efficacy respectively (Table 2 and Figure 4). Teachers with a *strong self-efficacy* had a CSE of 6 or 7 on almost all competences. The only exceptions were the competences related to digital traces, creative commons, programming and digital protection, which all had a CSE of 5. Nevertheless teachers with a strong self-efficacy feel quite or very confident in all competence areas. For teachers with a *moderate self-efficacy* three competences were rated as strong (CSE of 6-7), while most competences fell in the moderate interval (CSE of 4-5). The competences where the respondents felt most insecure (CSE of 3) were the same as those for the respondents with a strong self-efficacy mentioned above (digital traces, creative commons, programming and protection from undesired access) in addition to using technology as a means of constructing a product. Finally, teachers with a *low self-efficacy* did not have a strong self-efficacy score for any competence. A minority of the competences (7/27) had a moderate score (all competences in the first competence area, recognizing hate speech and summarizing information from different sources), but for the majority of the competences (20/27), teachers were quite insecure (CSE of 2-3).

Clearly, and unsurprisingly, this large spread shows that a one-size fits all teacher training approach is not appropriate, as the needs of teachers with low, moderate and strong self-efficacy are very different. When considering teachers with a low self-efficacy, support and guidance is needed in all competence areas except for the first one. Common to all teachers is a need for guidance in programming, licensing (creative commons) and security (protecting digital devices, managing digital traces). Luckily, quite some effort in teacher training initiatives is currently being invested in developing programming competence, which will hopefully strengthen teachers' confidence in this area. For creative commons, on the other hand, it seems that many teachers simply had no idea of what creative commons stands for and therefore rated their self-efficacy low on that particular competence. This is easily remedied by a short introduction to creative commons and how to use it when referring to other people's work as well as when sharing one's own material. Security issues, particularly when it comes to integrity aspects, have most likely not been taught previously, and these are also areas where many struggle as individuals in their everyday lives. This is hence an area, which calls for more focus in teacher training efforts.

The data analysed in our previous study were most likely not representative of the general teacher community, as the responses were collected through social media and emailing lists focusing on teachers currently enrolled in programming courses or those belonging to specific online interest groups related to digital competence and technology. In the current study, the data were collected during teacher training events, but these were voluntary and were marketed with a clear focus on digitalization and digital competence. Nevertheless, the results are much more diverse and appear to be more representative. One can, however, wonder whether the spread would be even larger in a more extensive and generalizable study setting. As there is still a lack of previous research on teachers' self-efficacy in the area of digital competence, there is not a significant body of empirical data, with which to compare our results. Instead, we advance the results presented in this study as a baseline for further studies and more detailed research. For instance, in Sweden, the National Agency for Education (Skolverket) is rolling out online courses on programming, offering professional development conferences throughout the country and giving universities the task to develop and offer courses aimed at teachers. Similarly, there is a need for teacher training departments to revise their curricula in order to prepare pre-service teachers for teaching digital competence. Using the same instrument to follow up on competence levels, makes it easier for both individuals, organisations and policy makers to evaluate the results of given initiatives as well as decide on what to focus on next.

Finally, respondents with a strong CSE level rated themselves very high (7) on the final competence ("I could adapt my ways of working based on new digital tools"). This competence can be seen as one of the most important ones on the list from a life-long learning perspective; in a situation where technology develops and changes at a fast pace, being able to adapt is crucial. Respondents with low self-efficacy, however, also rated themselves low (3) on this particular competence. Previous studies have indicated that teachers perceive knowledge and attitudes as critical precursors to creating a digitally competent school [8]. Training efforts should henceforth not only focus on helping teachers develop their digital knowledge and skills. Attitudes and mindset are likely to be equally important, and deserve more attention and educational investment.

8 CONCLUSIONS

Teacher self efficacy in digital competence and computational concepts is crucial to providing young people with the education they will require in our increasingly technological society. Schools and governments must take the need for continuing education in this area very seriously if we are to meet the challenges identified in this study. The results presented here imply strongly that helping teachers develop their self-efficacy in digital competences is important, as studies show that teachers with a high self-efficacy in the subject they teach are more likely to persist longer, provide a better teaching environment and not burn out as easily [24].

The study also provides some of the underpinnings crucial to addressing future in-service and pre-service teacher training and educational challenges. In particular we have identified some key areas which will require explicit attention. The results presented in this paper can also serve as a baseline for monitoring the development of teachers' self-efficacy over time as well as after particular training efforts. Results from this kind of studies naturally also lend themselves to be compared, thereby providing insight into teachers' self-efficacy in digital competences at a local (school/municipality), national or international level, as well as providing the opportunity to explore the development of instructional capability and capacity over time.

REFERENCES

[1] Albert Bandura. 1977. Self-Efficacy: Toward a Unifying Theory of Behavioral Change. *Psychological Review* 84, 2 (March 1977), 191–215. http://www.eric.ed.gov/ERICWebPortal/detail?accno=EJ161632

[2] Albert Bandura. 1997. *Self-efficacy: The exercise of control.* Macmillan.

[3] Vehbi Celik and Etem Yesilyurt. 2013. Attitudes to technology, perceived computer self-efficacy and computer anxiety as predictors of computer supported education. *Computers & Education* 60, 1 (2013), 148 – 158. DOI:http://dx.doi.org/10.1016/j.compedu.2012.06.008

[4] EU Commission. Digital Competence Framework for Educators (DigCompEdu). https://ec.europa.eu/jrc/sites/jrcsh/files/digcompedu_leaflet_final.pdf. (????). Online, accessed April 22, 2017.

[5] Deborah R. Compeau and Christopher A. Higgins. 1995. Computer Self-Efficacy: Development of a Measure and Initial Test. *MIS Quarterly* 19, 2 (1995), 189–211. http://www.jstor.org/stable/249688

[6] P Eachus and S Cassidy. 1999. Developing the computer self-efficacy (CSE) scale: Investigating the relationship between CSE, gender and experience with computers. *Retrieved April* 24 (1999), 1999.

[7] Mavra Kear. 2000. Concept analysis of self-efficacy. *Graduate research in nursing* 2, 2 (2000), 1–7.

[8] Linda Mannila. 2018. Digitally competent schools: teacher expectations when introducing digital competence in Finnish basic education. *Seminar.net* (June 2018).

[9] Linda Mannila, Valentina Dagiene, Barbara Demo, Natasa Grgurina, Claudio Mirolo, Lennart Rolandsson, and Amber Settle. 2014. Computational Thinking in K-9 Education. In *Proceedings of the Working Group Reports of the 2014 on Innovation & Technology in Computer Science Education Conference (ITiCSE-WGR '14).* ACM, New York, NY, USA, 1–29. DOI:http://dx.doi.org/10.1145/2713609.2713610

[10] Howard Margolis and Patrick P. McCabe. 2004. Self-Efficacy: A Key to Improving the Motivation of Struggling Learners. *The Clearing House* 77, 6 (2004), pp. 241–249. http://www.jstor.org/stable/30190019

[11] William P Moore and Mary E Esselman. 1994. Exploring the Context of Teacher Efficacy: The Role of Achievement and Climate. (1994).

[12] Christine A. Murphy, Delphine Coover, and Steven V. Owen. 1989. Development and Validation of the Computer Self-Efficacy Scale. *Educational and Psychological Measurement* 49, 4 (1989), 893–899. DOI:http://dx.doi.org/10.1177/001316448904900412

[13] Lars-Åke Nordén, Linda Mannila, and Arnold Pears. 2017. Development of a self-efficacy scale for digital competences in schools. In *2017 IEEE Frontiers in Education Conference (FIE).*

[14] Arnold Pears, Valentina Dagiene, and Egle Jasute. 2017. Baltic and Nordic K-12 Teacher Perspectives on Computational Thinking and Computing. In *International Conference on Informatics in Schools: Situation, Evolution, and Perspectives.* Springer, 141–152.

[15] Vennila Ramalingam, Deborah LaBelle, and Susan Wiedenbeck. 2004. Self-efficacy and Mental Models in Learning to Program. *SIGCSE Bull.* 36, 3 (June 2004), 171–175. DOI:http://dx.doi.org/10.1145/1026487.1008042

[16] Vennila Ramalingam and Susan Wiedenbeck. 1998. Development and Validation of Scores on a Computer Programming Self-Efficacy Scale and Group Analyses of Novice Programmer Self-Efficacy. *Journal of Educational Computing Research* 19, 4 (1998), 367–381. DOI:http://dx.doi.org/10.2190/C670-Y3C8-LTJ1-CT3P

[17] John A Ross, Anne Hogaboam-Gray, and Lynne Hannay. 2001. Effects of teacher efficacy on computer skills and computer cognitions of Canadian students in grades K-3. *The Elementary School Journal* 102, 2 (2001), 141–156.

[18] The Royal Society. 2017. After the reboot: computing education in UK schools. (2017).

[19] Erik E.J. Thoonen, Peter J.C. Sleegers, Thea T.D. Peetsma, and Frans J. Oort. 2011. Can teachers motivate students to learn? *Educational Studies* 37, 3 (2011), 345–360. DOI:http://dx.doi.org/10.1080/03055698.2010.507008

[20] Megan Tschannen-Moran and Anita Woolfolk Hoy. 2001. Teacher efficacy: Capturing an elusive construct. *Teaching and teacher education* 17, 7 (2001), 783–805.

[21] Vehbi1 Turel. 2014. TEACHERS' COMPUTER SELF-EFFICACY AND THEIR USE OF EDUCATIONAL TECHNOLOGY. *Turkish Online Journal of Distance Education (TOJDE)* 15, 4 (2014), 130 – 149. http://search.ebscohost.com.ezproxy.its.uu.se/login.aspx?direct=true&db=eue&AN=98889729&site=ehost-live

[22] Ellen L. Usher and Frank Pajares. 2008. Self-Efficacy for Self-Regulated Learning. *Educational and Psychological Measurement* 68, 3 (2008), 443–463. DOI:http://dx.doi.org/10.1177/0013164407308475

[23] YouGov. 2015. TES & Nesta Computing Curriculum. Fieldwork 06/05/2014 – 16/05/2014. (2015).

[24] Marjolein Zee and Helma M. Y. Koomen. 2016. Teacher Self-Efficacy and Its Effects on Classroom Processes, Student Academic Adjustment, and Teacher Well-Being: A Synthesis of 40 Years of Research. *Review of Educational Research* 86, 4 (2016), 981–1015.

[25] Yixin Zhang and Sue Espinoza. 1998. Relationships among computer self-efficacy, attitudes toward computers, and desirability of learning computing skills. *Journal of Research on Computing in Education* 30, 4 (Summer 1998), 420. http://ezproxy.its.uu.se/login?url=http://search.proquest.com.ezproxy.its.uu.se/docview/274681936?accountid=14715 Copyright - Copyright International Society for Technology in Education Summer 1998; Last updated - 2014-05-21.

[26] Barry J. Zimmerman. 2000. Self-Efficacy: An Essential Motive to Learn. *Contemporary Educational Psychology* 25, 1 (2000), 82 – 91. DOI:http://dx.doi.org/10.1006/ceps.1999.1016

[27] Barry J Zimmerman and Albert Bandura. 1995. Self-efficacy and educational development. *Self-efficacy in changing societies* (1995), 202–231.

Professional Learning in the Midst of Teaching Computer Science

Aleata Hubbard
WestEd
Redwood City, California
ahubbar@wested.org

Katie D'Silva
WestEd
Redwood City, California
kdsilva@wested.org

ABSTRACT

The recent groundswell of interest in computer science education across many countries has created a pressing need for computing teachers at the secondary level. To satisfy this demand, some educational systems are drawing from their pool of in-service teachers trained in other disciplines. While these transitioning teachers can learn about computing pedagogy and subject matter at professional learning workshops, daily teaching experiences will also be a source of their learning. We studied a co-teaching program where instructional responsibilities were distributed between teachers and volunteers from the tech industry to explore how specific teaching practices supported teacher learning, with a focus on pedagogical content knowledge (PCK). Through qualitative analysis of questionnaire and interview data gathered from three teachers during one school year, we identified the practices they engaged in and how their learning related to the enactment of those practices. Our results highlight several factors that influenced the ways in which teaching practices provided participants with opportunities to learn PCK: (a) active participation of students and volunteers; (b) teacher's level of content knowledge; (c) interdependent practices; and (d) immediacy of the classroom environment.

CCS CONCEPTS

• **Social and professional topics** → **K-12 education**;

KEYWORDS

Pedagogical content knowledge, high school teachers, teaching practice

ACM Reference Format:
Aleata Hubbard and Katie D'Silva. 2018. Professional Learning in the Midst of Teaching Computer Science. In *ICER '18: 2018 International Computing Education Research Conference, August 13–15, 2018, Espoo, Finland*. ACM, New York, NY, USA, 9 pages. https://doi.org/10.1145/3230977.3230983

1 INTRODUCTION

In the past several years, many countries have started initiatives to expand computer science (CS) education at the primary and secondary level [25]. Across the U.S., where we work, efforts such as CS10K [12] and CS for All [23] are providing more students with access to CS learning opportunities. Some of the largest K-12 districts in the country serving hundreds of thousands of students are implementing computing curricula across their schools [39, 43]. A major requisite to the sustainability of these plans is a sufficient pool of teachers versed in both CS content and pedagogy.

However, there is a shortage of CS teachers at the secondary level in the U.S. One reason for this scarce supply is a limited number of pre-service training programs available to prepare aspiring teachers. Given the paucity of pre-service opportunities, alternative pathways for in-service educators exist through teaching endorsements and accreditation [30]. Yet, manifold pathways make it possible for teachers to enter CS classrooms without adequate preparation. The CS education community has recognized a need to support these transitioning teachers in developing the knowledge and skills needed to effectively teach and increase participation in CS [15].

While professional learning (PL) programs exist for these teachers, many are of insufficient duration and do not focus clearly on teacher knowledge specific to computer science [35] . Furthermore, when participants enter PL experiences with differing backgrounds, amounts of teaching experience, and prior knowledge, it is challenging for teacher educators to create effective learning opportunities [47]. Understanding how in-service teachers incorporate experiences from PL into their practice can (a) provide a realistic portrait of CS teacher knowledge development and (b) inform the design of future, possibly differentiated, PL opportunities. With these goals in mind, we report on our efforts to investigate the teacher learning of educators transitioning into CS through a PL program embedded into their daily teaching.

2 TEACHER KNOWLEDGE AND LEARNING

The craft of teaching draws upon many types of knowledge such as knowledge of subject matter, knowledge of individual students, knowledge of how people learn, and knowledge of curricula [13]. In our work, we focus on pedagogical content knowledge (PCK), a construct introduced by Shulman [45] to characterize the knowledge needed for teaching a particular subject. Shulman originally described PCK as a subset of content knowledge that includes knowledge of student understanding and knowledge of teaching practices to support learning. Familiarity with common errors and evaluating the advantages and disadvantages of representations used for instruction are examples of PCK [5]. This framework has been extremely influential in the study of teacher learning, particularly in mathematics [14] and science [42].

Research on PCK, both within and outside of CS, has produced some consistent findings. First, PCK is subject specific and strongly correlated to content knowledge [8]. In a study of experienced computing teachers learning to teach a new programming paradigm, Liberman et al. [32] explored the connection between PCK and content knowledge. They found teachers entered a state of regressed expertise where they displayed elements of both novice teaching and expert teaching. Second, PCK develops incrementally with a focus first on learners and then later on teaching practices [42]. Buchholz et al. [10] provided anecdotal evidence that pre-service CS teachers progress through stages of complexity in their PCK when developing teaching modules. Similarly, Lapidot's [31] field study with fifteen in-service and pre-service teachers resulted in a model explaining stages of CS teacher learning which progress from a focus on content knowledge, to creating instructional examples, to supporting student understanding, to improving their practice. And third, various personal and contextual factors influence PCK development [2, 40]. Baxter [6] and Griffin, Pirmann, and Gray's [21] case studies comparing experienced CS teachers demonstrated how PCK can vary across teachers with similar levels of expertise and be enacted differently in their classrooms.

Related to PCK is professional learning, or the various activities teachers engage in to improve their knowledge and practice. These activities range from informal chats with colleagues to formal workshops facilitated by teacher educators. Changes in teacher learning take time and vary across individuals [9]. Research points to the value of linking professional learning to authentic practice because it allows for active learning related to the contexts within which teachers work [3, 19]. Some teacher education researchers are beginning to focus less on the components of PCK and more on describing the core practices of teaching that enable educators to apply their knowledge in classrooms [18, 34]. Some of these practices include leading a discussion, assessing student knowledge, presenting ideas, finding examples to make a specific point, connecting a topic to topics taught in prior or future years, appraising content on instructional materials, modifying tasks to be easier or harder, and selecting representations [5, 26]. However, scholars are still undecided about what teaching knowledge is needed for effectively using core practices [4].

In our work, we are studying a PL program that connects to authentic practice through co-teaching with technology professionals. Such collaborations tend to involve joint or distributed effort around planning and teaching [22]. When situated within classrooms, the learning opportunities that these partnerships offer will depend on the contexts within which they occur and on the participating teachers and external partners. Our goal is to understand how such PL embedded within daily teaching can support the learning of transitioning CS teachers, with a focus on PCK. Specifically, we ask: (a) what instructional practices do teachers undertake when planning and enacting their lessons within a co-teaching partnership? and (b) how does teacher learning relate to the implementation of these instructional practices?

3 METHOD
3.1 Study Context and Participants
Our project explores PCK and teacher learning within a multi-year, on-the-job training program that pairs teachers with volunteers from the tech industry to offer CS courses in secondary schools

across the U.S. At the start of the partnership, volunteers lead CS classes while teachers learn course content. Over time, responsibilities shift from volunteers to teachers, with teachers leading their courses independently after two years. The program offers two courses. The semester-long *Introduction to Computer Science Principles* course (Intro) introduces some of the big ideas of computing, discusses the history and future of the field, and teaches students programming with the block language Snap!. Many teachers extended Intro into a year-long course by teaching additional programming languages or curricula the second semester. The year-long *Advanced Placement Computer Science A* course (AP CS A) introduces students to object-oriented programming and the Java programming language. Advanced Placement is a program in the U.S. run by the non-profit College Board that provides college level courses for secondary students. We studied three teachers in the second year of the program: Ms. Robinson, Mr. Miller, and Mr. Perez (all pseudonyms).

Ms. Robinson taught one section of the AP CS A course with four volunteers. At the time of the study, she had 11 years of teaching experience. She also taught geometry and an introductory computing course (not through the PL program). Ms. Robinson's professional experiences prior to teaching involved multiple roles in the tech industry including web designer, quality assurance engineer, and software engineer. However, her tech career occurred 15 years ago. While she remembered some computing concepts, she saw herself as a *"novice teacher in CS field"* who relied on volunteers and experienced students to help her with the course content.

Mr. Miller taught two sections of the Intro course. He taught the first section collaboratively with two volunteers and the second section independently. During the second semester of the course, his team introduced students to HTML and CSS. He had 38 years of teaching experience and he also taught algebra. Mr. Miller had prior programming experience in the 1970s. While he felt confident in his conceptual understanding of computing, he felt his knowledge needed updating.

Mr. Perez taught one section of the Intro course with three volunteers. To extend his course to a full year, he included components of Computer Science Principles (AP CSP), a new computing course offered by the College Board. In the year prior to this study, he taught one section of the AP CS A course. He had two years of teaching experience and he also taught algebra. Mr. Perez felt very comfortable with CS content. In secondary school and college, he took computing courses in BASIC, C++, Java, Racket, Prolog, and Fortran. Mr. Perez had experience tutoring college students in computer science.

Although we present data gathered from three participants, our goal is not to compare the quality or preparedness of the teachers. Instead, we are providing an array of possible ways transitioning teachers might engage in and learn from their instructional practices.

3.2 Data Collection and Analysis
This study spanned an entire school year, beginning in September 2015 and ending in June 2016. Data collection centered around visits, or a set of activities related to an observed classroom lesson. Visits focused on lessons so that participants could draw on their

recent experiences when completing questionnaires and interviews. We conducted five or six visits with each teacher.

Each visit began with a questionnaire teachers completed before the observation. This questionnaire asked ten open-ended items and one close-ended item about teaching knowledge for the upcoming lesson. Most items were drawn from the CoRe [33], a set of prompts to guide groups of teachers in discussing PCK related to a specific topic.

To capture immediate impressions of their teaching, participants were interviewed about their lessons directly after the observation. Probing questions focused on how the lesson supported students, unexpected occurrences, and ideas for revising the lesson. Questions were adapted from protocols used to interview mathematics teachers about the development of their technology PCK [38] . We included three questions focused on the quality of the co-teaching experience, the roles assumed by teachers and volunteers, and the effectiveness of co-teaching in preparing teachers to lead the lesson independently. We also used this interview as an opportunity to clarify any ambiguous or terse comments provided on the pre-lesson questionnaire. Lastly, during half the visits, participants also completed think-aloud interviews where they reviewed either a set of assessment items or a set of student responses to a programming problem (see [24]). While these think-aloud interviews focused primarily on eliciting their PCK for specific computing topics, each teacher made one or two comments related to their teaching practices that are also included in this analysis.

Within two days of the observation, after teachers had time to reflect more on their lessons, they completed a post-lesson questionnaire. The first half of this questionnaire focused on the methods and instructional resources used to prepare and deliver their lesson. Most items were drawn from the Horizon Inside the Classroom Interview Protocol [46] and all items required written responses.

We analyzed interview responses and open-ended questionnaire items to identify instances where participants discussed PCK, content knowledge, instructional practices, or their own growth as a teacher. Our unit of analysis was the entire response provided to a prompt listed on our interview protocol or to a questionnaire item. In dividing the data using this approach, units from interviews might contain multiple questions if the interviewer asked clarifying questions. Our coding scheme, which draws heavily on the work of Shulman [45] and Ball, Thames, and Phelps [5], contains three main categories: CS teaching knowledge (see Table 1), instructional practices (see Table 2), and 'other'. This last category was used to capture instances where teachers either talked about their own development or mentioned ideas outside the other categories.

To conduct an exploratory analysis into the relationship between practices and PCK, we used Ball and Cohen's [3] approach to professional learning as an interpretive guide. Their model highlights how many teaching tasks can support an examination of practice because "in the course of these tasks, teachers may puzzle, weigh alternatives, draw on what they know or can access as resources for judgments and decisions." We examined how different teaching practices discussed by participants allowed for active noticing, interpretation, and working with artifacts of practice.

The second half of the post-lesson questionnaire contained six close-ended items asking teachers to rate the degree to which they and their volunteers contributed to instructional practices related to

Table 1: Teaching Knowledge Coding Scheme

Category	Definition
Student understanding and difficulties	Knowledge of student ideas and misconceptions about CS
Student interest and motivation	Knowledge of student interest and motivation related to CS
Representations and teaching methods	Knowledge of how topics are represented and how topics can be presented to learners
Timing, pacing, sequencing	Knowledge of how topics should be organized to support learners

Table 2: Instructional Practices Coding Scheme

Category	Definition
Planning Lessons	
Find materials	Search for and evaluate instructional materials
Create materials	Create instructional materials
Modify materials	Modify instructional materials created by others
Review materials	Look over existing instructional materials
Practice materials	Complete tasks that will be assigned to students
Organize lesson	Decide on the timing, pacing, sequencing of lessons; Create student groups for team work
Enacting Lessons	
Assist students	Provide help to students
Evaluate learning	Assess students, assign grades, review student progress
Present ideas	Present information through whole class instruction

lesson preparation (i.e., developing lessons, creating assignments), instructional delivery (i.e., delivering lessons, managing the classroom), and evaluation of learning (i.e., assisting students, grading student work). These six practices were drawn from materials created by the PL program to describe the roles of teachers and volunteers. Option choices were: mostly teacher, both volunteers and teacher, mostly volunteer, and no one. We converted these levels into numeric values and averaged engagement in instructional practices over the school year. Since we were most interested in the degree to which teachers engaged in instructional practices, we collapsed the levels of "no one" and "mostly volunteers" to a value of 0, assigned "both volunteers and teachers" a value of 1, and assigned "mostly teacher" a value of 2.

3.2.1 Trustworthiness of Data. Both authors, who were also involved in data collection, coded the interview and open-ended questionnaire data. We went through three steps to establish inter-rater reliability: training, agreement, and reliability. In the training phase, the first author introduced the coding scheme to the second author, providing the second author with examples to illustrate each coding category. In the agreement phase, we reviewed a subset of data files together and discussed how we would code them, resolved discrepancies in our decisions, and made decisions on how to handle similar cases in the future. This form of negotiated agreement is useful when conducting exploratory work and can help to increase reliability [11]. In the reliability phase, we separately coded a subset of the data and compared our coding choices using Krippendorff's alpha reliability measure [28, 29]. Most categories passed Krippendorff's suggested threshold value of .67, one category fell just below the threshold at α = .66 (i.e., knowledge of student interest and motivation), and one category never occurred in the reliability set (i.e., review materials).

Since researchers have cautioned against relying solely on teacher self-report data [41], we compared teachers' self-reported data about the frequency of their instructional practices to observation data gathered by the research team. While the data showed that participants' self-reported data aligned mostly with observation data, there was one discrepancy. Mr. Miller sometimes disagreed with observers on whether he or his volunteers assisted students more in class. We believe Mr. Miller was distinguishing the ways in which he and volunteers were providing support to students (e.g., formal code reviews versus answering individual questions) and that he may have concentrated on a subset of these methods of support when reporting on the distribution of this responsibility.

4 RESULTS

4.1 Instructional Practices Enacted

4.1.1 Distribution of Practices. In the PL program we studied, teams distributed responsibilities across teachers and volunteers. While the PL program offered guidance on the distribution of responsibilities, teams divided their daily teaching tasks differently depending on factors such as teacher readiness and volunteer availability. We first identified the degree to which teachers enacted the six practices highlighted in their PL program materials (see Figures 1-3).

All teachers reported undertaking each of the six practices in their CS classes to some degree. The responsibility of managing the classroom (e.g., taking attendance, making sure students stay on task) fell mostly to the teachers. However, different profiles appeared in our three participants when looking at the other five practices. Ms. Robinson had more opportunities to focus on analyzing student work than on other responsibilities through assisting students in class and grading their work. Mr. Miller had a high level of involvement in multiple responsibilities, but he was noticeably less involved in assisting students and creating assignments. Mr. Perez assumed most of the responsibilities in his class and his volunteers provided support mostly through grading student work.

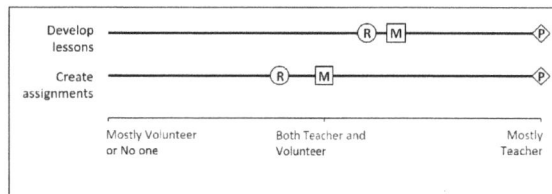

Figure 1: Self-reported distribution of lesson preparation tasks across school year. Letters indicate the first letter of each teachers name.

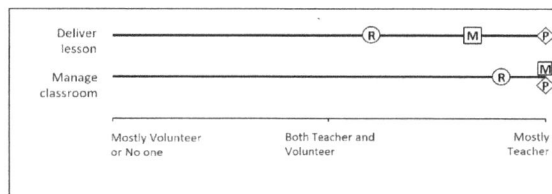

Figure 2: Self-reported distribution of instructional delivery tasks across school year.

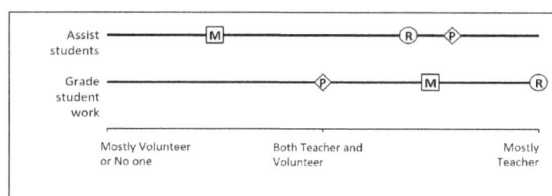

Figure 3: Self-reported distribution of evaluation of learning tasks across school year.

4.1.2 Discussion of Practices. To gain additional insight into the practices participants enacted, we reviewed open-ended questionnaire responses and interviews to identify instances where teachers described instructional practices included in our literature-derived coding scheme. Table 3 shows the number of units in our data set where teachers discussed these practices. For example, Ms. Robinson discussed instructional practices in 28 of her units; 10 units focused on assisting students. Note that units could receive multiple codes, allowing for totals of subcategories to exceed the total of their parent category.

Despite responding to the same questionnaires and interviews, we saw differences in the specific practices each teacher discussed. Ms. Robinson's comments focused more on practices related to enacting her lessons than to practices related to planning lessons. She did, however, discuss one lesson planning practice (i.e., reviewing materials) multiple times. Also, there were two practices she never discussed with us: finding materials and modifying materials. This may be explained by her reliance on volunteers to lead the class and by her teaching team following the PL curriculum closely. As she commented during our first visit to her classroom: *"We are following along the [PL] lesson plan, a guide. So we are using the work - pretty much following it very closely. Sometimes we don't, but most of the time we do."*

Table 3: Number of Units Focused on Instructional Practices

Category	Robinson	Miller	Perez
Planning Lessons	11	23	21
Find materials	0	2	5
Create materials	1	3	6
Modify materials	0	1	3
Review materials	5	6	1
Practice materials	3	2	6
Organize lesson	3	9	8
Enacting Lessons	20	35	11
Assist students	10	9	6
Evaluate learning	7	14	3
Present ideas	4	20	4
Total Units (n)	28	51	29

Similar to Ms. Robinson, Mr. Miller's comments focused more on practices related to enacting lessons than on practices related to planning lessons. He also discussed one lesson planning activity (i.e., organizing lessons) several times. He talked most often about presenting ideas. This may be explained by the setup of his partnership where he co-taught first period and taught independently second period. He sometimes shared with us comparisons of the two lessons or ways he revised his second period lesson based on reactions to the first period lesson. For example, he once said, *"I like that [my volunteer] put in his repeat until [block], because that was a working game - I did it a little differently in second period, I made it a working game."*

Lastly, Mr. Perez' discussion of practices was more evenly distributed across all nine practices. This might be explained by his assuming more of the responsibility in his course than his volunteers, creating the need for him to attend to more of the instructional practices. Based on our first conversation with Mr. Perez, this approach aligned with his goals for the school year:

> So, it being my second year of [the PL program], I have been interpreting that as I should be taking the lead more. And having gone through the training over the summer, I felt like I knew the curriculum a lot better than [the volunteers] did, and so I didn't want to trust my kids to other people.

4.2 Learning through Instructional Practices

In the second phase of our analysis, we reviewed participant data to identify ways in which their instructional practices provided opportunities for teacher learning and factors that influenced these learning opportunities. Since teacher learning is a complex process influenced by personal and contextual factors [2] that might lead to differences in how instructional practices influence the learning process, we present the results for each participant separately.

4.2.1 Ms. Robinson. During this study, Ms. Robinson assumed a mostly supportive role in her course while her volunteers led many of the lessons. As we saw from her questionnaire and interview data, she enacted and talked most about assisting students and

evaluating student learning. It appears these practices supported her own learning by providing multiple artifacts of practice (i.e., student work to the same problems) that allowed her to identify common approaches employed by her students as well as their areas of difficulties. For example, she once discussed how grading a test revealed a common misconception amongst her students of how nested loops execute:

> Well based on the tests that I was correcting yesterday kids were having trouble with for loops. That was the highest commonly missed problem...a nested for loop...In fact, that is one of the things I want to go over with the [volunteers]. It is just understanding that when you start with the first for loop, that is related to the row. (Ms. Robinson, Sept. 25, 2015)

Her ability to enact these practices given her novice level understanding of the course content was supported by reviewing and practicing materials. During these lesson preparation practices, she often reviewed completed solutions from either her volunteers or the PL curriculum. Reviewing completed solutions allowed her to identify salient aspects of the lesson content that guided her assessment of student work. For example, she once described how a completed programming solution helped her decide how to check the methods students wrote to shuffle values:

> I had the solution, so I can compare, like 'Okay, well this is what you are supposed to do.' I mean, I used it as my guide...And I am glad I did look at the code beforehand because I did notice that they had to use math.random and that gives it more of a random mix of shuffle. So if they got at least half of activity three which included the random, I would just move on. (Ms. Robinson, March 28, 2016)

Some of the practices Ms. Robinson discussed did not reveal evidence of how they supported her computing PCK. For example, when discussing how she organized her lessons, she talked about sticking to timelines. Or, when discussing how she presented ideas, Ms. Robinson would often indicate that her presentation lasted longer than expected. In addition to classroom responsibilities, Ms. Robinson was heavily engaged in the expansion of CS education in her region. She acknowledged that attending to advocacy reduced the amount of time she had to focus on learning course content:

> So I am like marketing, advertising, promoting, teaching, and getting people to help because I don't know all of this computer science...And so I am pretty spread thin...I am just trying to get the word out. That is why I don't have that much time to you know even sometimes do the curriculum. But I am taking advantage of the great volunteers that I have, because they can deliver. (Ms. Robinson, December 9, 2015)

While she had little time to learn content, advocacy work seemed to keep Ms. Robinson motivated in her teaching assignment. Other factors, such as motivation, may be as important to developing and sustaining effective teachers as PCK.

4.2.2 Mr. Miller. During this study, Mr. Miller and his volunteers were in a collaborative stage of their co-teaching partnership where all members contributed to the planning and delivery of lessons. His data revealed how combinations of practices provided a cycle of feedback to support his learning. For example, when we visited Mr. Miller in November, his class was working on list traversals. Students had to create a list of names and then create scripts to extract subsets of the list. Mr. Miller described how he first practiced the assignment himself and then, while presenting the lesson, received feedback from a volunteer on improving his script:

> I love the co-teaching because [the volunteer] even pointed out that I had this unnecessary variable in my script. Because I am never sure if I am doing this right. I love it if a programmer can sit down and say 'here is what I would have done instead.' [My solution] worked, so I knew it was somewhat right, but, yeah, there is a better way to do it. (Mr. Miller, November 20, 2015)

Closer to the end of the school year, we visited Mr. Miller during a lesson where the class reviewed a recent quiz on HTML. He described how there was a syntax error in one of the quiz items he created, an error that he only became aware of when grading student responses:

> I took last year's quiz, and it was half on HTML and half on JavaScript. So I just took away all the JavaScript questions and added my own HTML and CSS questions. Thursday night as I was correcting it, I realized I made a mistake in writing the code. I forgot the semi-colon in one place. So I just made it part of the lesson, saying did anybody notice something missing. (Mr. Miller, March 28, 2016)

Grading this quiz also provided Mr. Miller with a bank of student responses from which he identified common errors and habits such as *a lot of people didn't close the opening tag* or *they would use upper case in one place and lower case in another*, all of which helped to build his knowledge of student understanding of HTML and CSS.

There were some ways in which instructional practices did not support Mr. Miller's learning. First, his comments suggest that time and limited student engagement may have constrained his opportunities to learn. For example, he spent less time assisting individual students in class so that he could circulate to more pupils:

> And there are times like that where I am walking through the class, and [the students] will say 'I don't get it, this isn't working.' And I don't always catch [the issue] right away. I feel great when I do, but sometimes it is more complex. I don't have five minutes to stand there and go, 'wait, let's see, let me think out.' So I have to say, 'you should go block by block through it and do the same sort of debugging techniques.' (Mr. Miller, October 2, 2015)

So, assisting students in real time restricted how deeply he could reflect on student work. While this may have limited Mr. Miller's opportunity to learn, it may have enhanced his students' opportunities to learn as they took on more of the debugging work. Also, throughout the school year, Mr. Miller discussed an occasional lack of participation from his students during lectures and how "nobody says anything." When students did not offer answers or

pose questions, Mr. Miller had no feedback to inform his knowledge of student understanding or revisions for his lessons. Lastly, management tasks also presented a barrier for Mr. Miller's learning. Sometimes while he took attendance or passed out prizes provided by the PL program, Mr. Miller relegated more content-focused practices to volunteers:

> I had a little trouble with timing. I was very happy to have the volunteers there because I tried to walk around and let them help students, and then I wanted to deal with the raffle, deal with the warmups, and the one girl who lost her password on the survey. There was another student who asked to use the printer. So all these little interruptions that I try and comply and answer to, it takes away from class time. (Mr. Miller, May 13, 2016)

4.2.3 Mr. Perez. Mr. Perez assumed most of the teaching responsibility in his class so he was involved in all the practices we examined. Much of his activity during the study focused on experimenting with the Computer Science Principles curriculum. He was *"trying riskier strategies, flying blind in an attempt to gather data to inform next year."* Because he was working with a new curriculum, he spent a lot of time finding and modifying materials and then creating a presentation to deliver content or rubrics to students. For example:

> I found sample scripts with bugs through [Beauty and Joy of Computing] and other CS teachers and solved each problem on my own. I also organized these scripts into a presentation that had them in manageable chunks...These resources provided the scripts that guide students' thinking to most effectively practice Boolean operators, script variables, and for loops. (Mr. Perez, October 5, 2015)

Although Mr. Perez felt comfortable with computing, he felt overwhelmed by this cycle of finding, modifying, and creating materials, which left little time for him to reflect on the materials. This was notably apparent in a lesson we observed focused on nesting higher-order functions (i.e., map, keep, combine):

> [I am] feeling like I am still figuring things out, in general. Not making sense of the material, but flying by the seat of my pants in terms of preparing - like, converting it from [Beauty and Joy of Computing] webpage format to working in a high school classroom format. Those things have felt like a little much. (Mr. Perez, October 27, 2015)

Despite this discomfort, and maybe to overcome it, Mr. Perez often practiced the problems he planned to give his students, which supported his initial ideas around organizing lessons. However, it was the enactment of those lessons that gave him feedback on areas where students needed more guidance and on ordering content to better support their learning:

> I would also rethink how I introduce and emphasize nested [higher order functions] so that it is a more deliberate process; I might also want to emphasize composition of functions earlier in the course so that students

are familiar with the idea before applying it to [higher order functions]. (Mr. Perez, October 27, 2015)

Mr. Perez also discussed some of the typical student approaches to tasks in this lesson, such as using *"a bunch of script variables to store intermediate results"* instead of the higher order functions. In addition to student feedback during lessons, he also uncovered this information through assisting students in lab time where he preferred to spend more time with those struggling with content:

> The closer work I was able to do with those struggling students allowed me to get a better idea of the types of ideas students might struggle with, and the types of thinking that would cause them to struggle. This will help me to plan and instruct better this year and in future years. (Mr. Perez, October 27, 2015)

To support this approach, he let his volunteers circulate around to the rest of the students and created a classroom culture where students felt comfortable asking each other for help.

5 DISCUSSION

A teacher's role is multifaceted and involves many responsibilities ranging from subject specific tasks (e.g., preparing instructional materials), general pedagogical activities (e.g., classroom management), and other professional obligations (e.g., coaching extracurricular teams). Teachers are often overwhelmed when confronted with all these responsibilities once they enter the classroom and find it difficult to attend to relevant events [16, 17]. At the same time, experience is a key factor in developing teaching expertise [7]. In our work with transitioning teachers, we have wondered (a) how exactly does this learning from experience happen and (b) can we offer guidance on how transitioning teachers should focus their classroom experiences to better support their development? The co-teaching arrangement we studied provided the opportunity to explore how teaching practices allowed for teacher learning within authentic classroom environments.

We first examined the instructional practices teachers enacted related to specific lessons. Questionnaire and interview data highlighted that teachers were involved in nearly all the practices we examined, but that the distribution of these practices between teachers and volunteers varied across teaching teams. In all cases, co-teaching alleviated some of the workload allowing teachers to focus more on the practices of their choosing. As Mr. Miller once said, *"co-teaching takes much of the pressure to 'do it right' off my shoulders."*

Next we examined how the implementation of these instructional practices related to learning and opportunities for participants to develop their PCK. Enacting these practices allowed teachers to work with authentic artifacts of practice (e.g., student work), evaluate the utility of materials to support student understanding, reflect on how best to present content to students, and apply their content knowledge. While Ms. Robinson, Mr. Miller, and Mr. Perez differed in how they engaged and learned from these practices, we noticed some commonalities across the teachers' experiences.

First, the usefulness of some practices for teacher learning depended on the active participation of students and volunteers. For

example, presenting information during a lecture was helpful when students provided ideas or responded to teachers' questions. Or, creating materials when one was not completely confident with the content was helpful when volunteers highlighted inaccuracies or inefficiencies in the work. In other words, instructional practices became learning moments when teachers and other classroom actors interacted. This finding aligns with sociocultural theories that view teacher learning as "distributed across all participants in professional practice (including, in this case teachers and students) and which relate to both the conceptual and the physical resources available" [27].

Second, content knowledge played a role in the way teachers learned from their practices. For example, Ms. Robinson, who was less comfortable with her course content, benefitted from reviewing completed solutions because they highlighted what she should focus on. In contrast, Mr. Perez, who felt very comfortable with computing, benefitted from completing problems himself because it sparked ideas of how to organize his lessons. Differences mediated by content knowledge were expected because prior research has demonstrated a strong correlation between content knowledge and PCK [8]. Without strong content knowledge, teachers struggle to notice and understand student thinking and to participate in useful discussions with their colleagues [20]. However, we saw evidence that reviewing solutions completed by more knowledgeable others might support PCK development in ways that practicing materials might not afford. Namely, reviewing materials can scaffold teachers' noticing of common or effective approaches. This finding aligns with the literature showing the value of worked examples to support learning [1].

Third, learning often occurred across practices. For example, Mr. Miller created materials for students, but opportunities for his learning occurred when he evaluated student work in response to those materials. Or, in the case of Mr. Perez, he often found materials related to the new Computer Science Principles curriculum to use in his class. But, opportunities for his learning occurred when he began to modify the materials. So, there might be constellations of practices to consider that provide teachers with cohesive experiences where they can notice, interpret, and work with artifacts of practice.

Fourth, enacting practices in real-time did not always allow sufficient time for teacher learning. For example, the need to circulate to all students during lab time made it challenging to spend extended periods with struggling students and learn from their difficulties. Or, the need to create or revise materials to present on a certain date sometimes restricted time to reflect on the best ordering of content to scaffold student learning. This is not entirely unexpected given the cognitive load required to process all the information and activities occurring within a classroom [17]. Furthermore, Ball and Cohen [3], whose ideas we used to analyze data in this study, caution that situating teacher learning in the classroom "confines learning to the rush of minute-to-minute practice" and "interferes with opportunities to learn." Thus, there may be some practices that would support teacher learning better if they happened outside of classroom teaching, at a time where teachers can be more reflective and are not attending to the immediacy of the classroom.

Lastly, not all practices provided opportunities for learning related to PCK, nor should we expect them to. Successful teaching involves more than just content-focused activities. For example, Ms. Robinsons' advocacy work outside the classroom seemed to serve as a motivator for her new role as a CS teacher and a vehicle for connecting with peers. Belonging to a professional community can help teachers overcome the isolation that is common amongst many CS teachers [37]. The data highlighted, however, that reducing some practices might service teacher learning more. For example, aspects of managing the classroom (e.g., distributing materials) could be offloaded to volunteers so that teachers focus on PCK-building practices.

At this point in our work, we have noticed that (a) instructional practices might vary in the opportunities they provide for developing PCK expertise and (b) the usefulness of responsibilities might vary based on a teacher's content knowledge. While still exploratory, these results may have heuristic value for thinking more about the relationship between instructional practices and PCK development. A few limitations in our work are worth noting. Given the semi-structured format of the interviews and the focus on individual lessons, caution should be exercised in interpreting the data. First, the total number of units where teachers discussed instructional practices were few, accounting for less than 25% of each teacher's total units. This study was situated within a larger project focused primarily on PCK, so the majority of participants' units addressed teaching knowledge. Second, study visits focused on individual lessons and not entire units; it is possible that teachers performed other practices outside of the study visits that were not discussed during interviews. Designing more systematic ways of eliciting the ways instructional practices support teaching learning is an obvious next step for this work.

6 CONCLUSION

To expand CS education in primary and secondary schools, many experienced teachers are facing a discipline they themselves have not learned formally. These teachers need to be supported so they develop not only the declarative PCK needed in CS classrooms but also the procedural know-how to use this PCK effectively. This concern, however, is not solely for transitioning teachers. Even experienced CS teachers will need to update their teaching knowledge base to incorporate new material, programming languages, or paradigms into their courses (see [32] for an example). We urge more scholars to focus on the enacted element of PCK so that we can better understand how teachers new to CS or experienced CS educators teaching new topics improve upon their craft through their classroom experiences. Here we end with a few questions to further research in this area.

How can instructional practices be scaffolded to better support teacher learning? We saw earlier that Ms. Robinson benefitted from reviewing materials completed by her volunteers because it drew her attention to salient aspects of the solution. There may be ways in which materials can be designed to encourage noticing of important features. Morrison, Margulieux, Ericson, and Guzdial [36] provide such an example with the use of subgoal labeling of Parsons problems. There may be other ways in which instructional practices can be designed and implemented to support teachers in noticing and reflecting during their work.

How do teachers with no computing background learn from their instructional experiences? Ms. Robinson, Mr. Miller, and Mr. Perez all had prior experience with computer science. In the case of Ms. Robinson and Mr. Miller, this experience dated back several years but it still provided them with familiarity of their course content. Teachers completely new to CS might learn from their instructional practices in different ways than teachers who enter classrooms with some content knowledge.

How do other models of co-teaching support teacher learning? The distribution of instructional responsibilities between teachers and volunteers was influential in providing teachers with learning opportunities. However, the PL program encouraged "one teach, one assist" and "team teaming" [44] models of co-teaching, so we were not able to explore the utility of other co-teaching models. Do other models, such as parallel teaching where each instructor teaches the same material to different groups of students in the same classroom, support PCK development differently? Also, the PL program we studied recruited volunteers from the tech industry. While volunteers brought CS content knowledge to their teaching team, not all volunteers had pedagogical knowledge or experience. Would the supports provided through the co-teaching model differ if volunteers also had computing PCK?

ACKNOWLEDGMENTS

This material is based upon work supported by the National Science Foundation under Grant No.: 1348866. Any opinions, findings, and conclusions or recommendations expressed in this material are those of the authors and do not necessarily reflect the view of the National Science Foundation.

We would like to thank Angela Knotts and Joseph Green for their invaluable support in data collection. We are also grateful to Dr. Yvonne Kao and Dr. Steven Schneider for securing the funding to support this project and for Dr. Kao's feedback on earlier drafts of this paper.

REFERENCES

[1] Robert K. Atkinson, Sharon J. Derry, Alexander Renkl, and Donald Wortham. 2000. Learning from Examples: Instructional Principles from the Worked Examples Research. *Review of Educational Research* 70, 2 (June 2000), 181–214. https://doi.org/10.3102/00346543070002181
[2] Beatrice Avalos. 2011. Teacher Professional Development in Teaching and Teacher Education over ten years. *Teaching and Teacher Education: An International Journal of Research and Studies* 27, 1 (Jan. 2011), 10–20. https://doi.org/10.1016/j.tate.2010.08.007
[3] Deborah Loewenberg Ball and D Cohen. 1999. Developing Practice, Developing Practitioners: Toward a practice-based theory of professional education. *Teaching as the Learning Profession San Francisco: Jossey-Bass* (1999).
[4] Deborah Loewenberg Ball and Francesca M. Forzani. 2009. The Work of Teaching and the Challenge for Teacher Education. *Journal of Teacher Education* 60, 5 (Nov. 2009), 497–511. https://doi.org/10.1177/0022487109348479
[5] Deborah Loewenberg Ball, Mark Hoover Thames, and Geoffrey Phelps. 2008. Content Knowledge for Teaching What Makes It Special? *Journal of Teacher Education* 59, 5 (Nov. 2008), 389–407. https://doi.org/10.1177/0022487108324554
[6] Juliet A. Baxter. 1987. *Teacher Explanations in Computer Programming: A Study of Knowledge Transformation.* Doctoral Dissertation. Stanford University, CA, United States.
[7] David C. Berliner. 2004. Describing the Behavior and Documenting the Accomplishments of Expert Teachers. *Bulletin of Science, Technology & Society* 24, 3 (June 2004), 200–212. https://doi.org/10.1177/0270467604265535
[8] Sigrid Blåmeke and Seån Delaney. 2012. Assessment of teacher knowledge across countries: a review of the state of research. *ZDM Mathematics Education* 44, 3 (July 2012), 223–247. http://search.ebscohost.com/login.aspx?direct=true&db=ehh&AN=76487343&site=ehost-live

[9] Hilda Borko. 2004. Professional Development and Teacher Learning: Mapping the Terrain. *Educational Researcher* 33, 8 (Nov. 2004), 3–15. https://doi.org/10.3102/0013189X033008003 http://media.leidenuniv.nl/legacy/educ-researcher-33-(2004)-3-15—borko—professional-development-and-teacher-learning.pdf.

[10] Malte Buchholz, Mara Saeli, and Carsten Schulte. 2013. PCK and Reflection in Computer Science Teacher Education. In *Proceedings of the 8th Workshop in Primary and Secondary Computing Education (WiPSE '13)*. ACM, New York, NY, USA, 8–16. https://doi.org/10.1145/2532748.2532752

[11] John L. Campbell, Charles Quincy, Jordan Osserman, and Ove K. Pedersen. 2013. Coding In-depth Semistructured Interviews Problems of Unitization and Intercoder Reliability and Agreement. *Sociological Methods & Research* (Aug. 2013), 0049124113500475. https://doi.org/10.1177/0049124113500475

[12] Jan Cuny. 2015. Transforming K-12 Computing Education: AP&Reg; Computer Science Principles. *ACM Inroads* 6, 4 (Nov. 2015), 58–59. https://doi.org/10.1145/2832916

[13] Linda Darling-Hammond. 2008. Teacher learning that supports student learning. *Teaching for intelligence* 2, 1 (2008), 91–100.

[14] Fien Depaepe, Lieven Verschaffel, and Geert Kelchtermans. 2013. Pedagogical content knowledge: A systematic review of the way in which the concept has pervaded mathematics educational research. *Teaching and Teacher Education* 34 (Aug. 2013), 12–25. https://doi.org/10.1016/j.tate.2013.03.001

[15] Barbara Ericson, M. Armoni, J. Gal-Ezer, D. Seehorn, C. Stephenson, and F. Trees. 2008. *Ensuring exemplary teaching in an essential discipline: Addressing the crisis in computer science teacher certification*. Technical Report. The Computer Science Teachers Association, New York.

[16] Sharon Feiman-Nemser. 2003. What New Teachers Need To Learn. *Educational Leadership* 60, 8 (Jan. 2003), 25–29.

[17] David F. Feldon. 2007. Cognitive Load and Classroom Teaching: The Double-Edged Sword of Automaticity. *Educational Psychologist* 42, 3 (2007), 123–137. https://doi.org/10.1080/00461520701416173

[18] Francesca M. Forzani. 2014. Understanding âĂIJCore PracticesâĂİ and âĂIJPractice-BasedâĂİ Teacher Education: Learning From the Past. *Journal of Teacher Education* 65, 4 (Sept. 2014), 357–368. https://doi.org/10.1177/0022487114533800

[19] Michael S. Garet, Andrew C. Porter, Laura Desimone, Beatrice F. Birman, and Kwang Suk Yoon. 2001. What Makes Professional Development Effective? Results From a National Sample of Teachers. *American Educational Research Journal* 38, 4 (Dec. 2001), 915–945. https://doi.org/10.3102/00028312038004915

[20] Lynn T. Goldsmith, Helen M. Doerr, and Catherine C. Lewis. 2014. Mathematics teachersâĂŹ learning: a conceptual framework and synthesis of research. *Journal of Mathematics Teacher Education* 17, 1 (Feb. 2014), 5–36. https://doi.org/10.1007/s10857-013-9245-4

[21] Jean Griffin, Tammy Pirmann, and Brent Gray. 2016. Two Teachers, Two Perspectives on CS Principles. In *Proceedings of the 47th ACM Technical Symposium on Computing Science Education (SIGCSE '16)*. ACM, New York, NY, USA, 461–466. https://doi.org/10.1145/2839509.2844630

[22] Terry Grobe, Susan Curnan, and Alan Melchior. 1990. Synthesis of Existing Knowledge and Practice in the Field of Educational Partnerships. (Dec. 1990).

[23] The White House. 2016. FACT SHEET: President Obama Announces Computer Science For All Initiative [Press Release]. https://www.whitehouse.gov/the-press-office/2016/01/30/fact-sheet-president-obama-announces-computer-science-all-initiative-0

[24] Aleata Hubbard, Yvonne Kao, and Danielle Brown. 2016. Designing Think-Aloud Interviews to Elicit Evidence of Computer Science Pedagogical Content Knowledge. Washington, D.C.

[25] Peter Hubwieser, Michail N. Giannakos, Marc Berges, Torsten Brinda, Ira Diethelm, Johannes Magenheim, Yogendra Pal, Jana Jackova, and Egle Jasute. 2015. A Global Snapshot of Computer Science Education in K-12 Schools. In *Proceedings of the 2015 ITiCSE on Working Group Reports (ITICSE-WGR '15)*. ACM, New York, NY, USA, 65–83. https://doi.org/10.1145/2858796.2858799

[26] Elham Kazemi, Magdalene Lampert, and Hala Ghousseini. 2007. *Conceptualizing and Using Routines of Practice in Mathematics Teaching to Advance Professional Education | Spencer*. Technical Report. Spencer Foundation, Chicago, IL. http://www.spencer.org/conceptualizing-and-using-routines-practice-mathematics-teaching-advance-professional-education.

[27] Peter Kelly. 2006. What is teacher learning? A socioâĂŘcultural perspective. *Oxford Review of Education* 32, 4 (Sept. 2006), 505–519. https://doi.org/10.1080/03054980600884227

[28] Klaus Krippendorff. 2011. Computing Krippendorff's Alpha-Reliability. *Departmental Papers (ASC)* (Jan. 2011). http://repository.upenn.edu/asc_papers/43

[29] Klaus Krippendorff. 2012. *Content Analysis: An Introduction to Its Methodology*. SAGE. Google-Books-ID: s_yqFXnGgjQC.

[30] Karen Lang, Ria Galanos, Joanna Goode, Deborah Seehorn, and Fran Trees. 2013. *Bugs in the System: Computer Science Teacher Certification in the U.S.* Technical Report. Computer Science Teachers Association. http://csta.acm.org/ComputerScienceTeacherCertification/sub/CSTA_BugsInTheSystem.pdf

[31] Tami Lapidot. 2005. *Computer Science Teachers' Learning during their Everyday Work*. Doctoral Dissertation. Technion University, Israel.

[32] Neomi Liberman, Yifat Ben-David Kolikant, and Catriel Beeri. 2012. "Regressed Experts" as a New State in Teachers' Professional Development: Lessons from Computer Science Teachers' Adjustments to Substantial Changes in the Curriculum. *Computer Science Education* 22, 3 (Jan. 2012), 257–283. http://search.ebscohost.com/login.aspx?direct=true&db=eric&AN=EJ980739&site=ehost-live

[33] John Loughran, Pamela Mulhall, and Amanda Berry. 2004. In search of pedagogical content knowledge in science: Developing ways of articulating and documenting professional practice. *Journal of Research in Science Teaching* 41, 4 (April 2004), 370–391. https://doi.org/10.1002/tea.20007

[34] Morva McDonald, Elham Kazemi, and Sarah Schneider Kavanagh. 2013. Core Practices and Pedagogies of Teacher Education: A Call for a Common Language and Collective Activity. *Journal of Teacher Education* 64, 5 (Nov. 2013), 378–386. https://doi.org/10.1177/0022487113493807

[35] Muhsin Menekse. 2015. Computer science teacher professional development in the United States: a review of studies published between 2004 and 2014. *Computer Science Education* 25, 4 (Dec. 2015), 325–350. http://search.ebscohost.com/login.aspx?direct=true&db=ehh&AN=114015739&site=ehost-live

[36] Briana B. Morrison, Lauren E. Margulieux, Barbara Ericson, and Mark Guzdial. 2016. Subgoals Help Students Solve Parsons Problems. In *Proceedings of the 47th ACM Technical Symposium on Computing Science Education (SIGCSE '16)*. ACM, New York, NY, USA, 42–47. https://doi.org/10.1145/2839509.2844617

[37] Lijun Ni and Mark Guzdial. 2012. Who AM I?: Understanding High School Computer Science Teachers' Professional Identity. In *Proceedings of the 43rd ACM Technical Symposium on Computing Science Education (SIGCSE '12)*. ACM, New York, NY, USA, 499–504. https://doi.org/10.1145/2157136.2157283

[38] Margaret Niess, Gogot Suharwoto, K Lee, and Pejmon Sadri. 2006. Guiding inservice mathematics teachers in developing technology pedagogical content knowledge (TPCK). In *Society for Information Technology and Teacher Education Annual Conference*. 20–24.

[39] The City of New York. 2016. Equity and Excellence: Mayor de Blasio Announces Reforms to Raise Achievement Across all Public Schools [Press Release]. http://www1.nyc.gov/office-of-the-mayor/news/618-15/equity-excellence-mayor-de-blasio-reforms-raise-achievement-across-all-public

[40] V. Darleen Opfer and David Pedder. 2011. Conceptualizing Teacher Professional Learning. *Review of Educational Research* 81, 3 (Sept. 2011), 376–407. http://search.ebscohost.com/login.aspx?direct=true&db=eric&AN=EJ936871&site=ehost-live

[41] Justus J. Randolph, G Julnes, E Sutinen, and S Lehman. 2008. A methodological review of computer science education research. *Journal of Information Technology Education* 7 (2008), 135–162. file:///C:/northwestern/compSci_endnote.Data/PDF/randolph_methodologicalreviewofcsedresearch-2730054661/randolph_methodologicalreviewofcsedresearch.pdfinternal-pdf://randolphDissertation-0150228741/randolphDissertation.pdf

[42] Rebecca M. Schneider and Kellie Plasman. 2011. Science Teacher Learning Progressions: A Review of Science Teachers' Pedagogical Content Knowledge Development. *Review of Educational Research* (Oct. 2011), 0034654311423382. https://doi.org/10.3102/0034654311423382

[43] Chicago Public Schools. 2014. CPS Announces First Schools to Implement DistrictâĂŹs Comprehensive K-12 Curriculum [Press Release]. http://cps.edu/News/Press_releases/Pages/PR1_03_19_2014.aspx

[44] Thomas E. Scruggs, Margo A. Mastropieri, and Kimberly A. McDuffie. 2007. Co-Teaching in Inclusive Classrooms: A Metasynthesis of Qualitative Research. *Exceptional Children* 73, 4 (July 2007), 392–416. https://doi.org/10.1177/001440290707300401

[45] Lee Shulman. 1986. Those who understand: Knowledge growth in teaching. *Educational Researcher* 15 (1986), 4–14. 2.

[46] I.R. Weiss, J.D. Pasley, P.S. Smith, E.R. Banilower, and D.J. Heck. 2003. *Looking Inside the Classroom: A Study of K-12 Mathematics and Science Education in the United States*. Technical Report.

[47] Suzanne M. Wilson, Jeffrey J. Rozelle, and Jamie N. Mikeska. 2011. Cacophony or Embarrassment of Riches: Building a System of Support for Quality Teaching. *Journal of Teacher Education* 62, 4 (Sept. 2011), 383–394. http://search.ebscohost.com/login.aspx?direct=true&db=eric&AN=EJ940391&site=ehost-live

Growing Minds - 21st Century Competences and Digitalisation among Finnish Youth?

Kirsti Lonka
University of Helsinki
kirsti.lonka@helsinki.fi

ABSTRACT

Readiness to use digital technologies in meaningful ways is in the focus of national Finnish curricula, implemented in 2016. There is variance in how digitalization is proceeding in education. While many schools are even ahead of their time, there are stills schools that are behind. Because the main strength of the Finnish school system has been equal and free opportunities for all, we do not feel that it is acceptable that the degree of meaningful digitalization varies so much. In my latest book Phenomenal Learning from Finland [5] I discuss this issue from the point of view of developing minds and brains of Finnish youth and look at the situation also from the global perspective.

PISA2015 results showed that Finnish youth, especially girls, were among the best (five) in the world in science, reading and mathematics. The interest in STEM (science, technology, engineering and mathematics) was, however, quite lowamong Finnish youth. We have a problem to attract new generations in STEM. I shall describe some innovations of Finnish science educators. School engagement and life satisfaction are quite good in Finland as compared to other high-achieving OECD countries. Our recent study showed that Helsinki area 6th graders really appreciated their class teachers and the teacher was the main source of their engagement at school [2]. The only aspect where the pupils found that the teacher could not help was supporting their digital engagement at school.

We should bridge the gap that appears to grow between those competences developed at school and those that are required in life after school or outside schools. We should also promote digital engagement and STEM engagement at schools. Not all Finnish youth are smooth in using digital technologies. Less than half of those Finns who were born in 2000 and whom we have followed since they were 6th graders, showed some advanced technological skills. Those young people who were interested in technology, were the least likely to be engaged at school in general and expressed cynical attitudes towards education. Among these were those 25% who were active gamers and those10-15% of youth who created something new by using digital technologies.

Permission to make digital or hard copies of part or all of this work for personal or classroom use is granted without fee provided that copies are not made or distributed for profit or commercial advantage and that copies bear this notice and the full citation on the first page. Copyrights for third-party components of this work must be honored. For all other uses, contact the owner/author(s).
ICER '18, August 13–15, 2018, Espoo, Finland
© 2018 Copyright held by the owner/author(s).
ACM ISBN 978-1-4503-5628-2/18/08. https://doi.org/10.1145/3230977.3230978

In our latest study high school students and university freshmen (including engineering students) were showing quite similar profiles.

The life of an active citizen calls for smooth using of ICT. In modern world, it is almost impossible to do even shopping or banking without being able to use advanced technologies. During the digital era, there is a need for many other broad-based competences that ICT skills, such as multiliteracy as well as socio-emotional and cultural competences. This keynote shall address the intensive reforms, both in research-based teacher education and at school that are going on in Finland. In addition to the new Finnish curricula, the latest developments in education, innovative pedagogical methods, technologies in education and new learning environments are going to be presented.

For more information, see [1, 3, 4, 6]

ACM Reference Format:
Kirsti Lonka. 2018. Growing minds - 21st century competences and digitalisation among Finnish youth?. In ICER '18: 2018 Int.l Computing Education Research Conference, Aug.13–15, 2018, Espoo, Finland. ACM, NY, NY, USA, 2 pages. https://doi.org/10.1145/3230977.3230978

BIO

Professor Kirsti Lonka, PhD, is Professor of Educational Psychology (2005-) at University of Helsinki, Finland. She is also Extraordinary Professor, Optentia Research Focus Area, North-West University, Vanderbiljpark, South Africa (2016-2019)[1] and

Advisory Board Member of Graduate Institute of Digital Learning and Education, National Taiwan University of Science and Technology (NTUST 2015-). She is also Science Rector of Kymenlaakso Summer University. Kirsti is a founding member of Teachers' Academy of University of Helsinki since 2013 and also their first President (2013-2014).

[1]http://news.nwu.ac.za/prof-kirsti-lonka-trailing-digital-nativewithin-educational-context

During 2015 - 2017 she was the Associate Editor of Elsevier journal Learning and Instruction (Impact factor 3.8 in 2017). Professor has worked in many countries on several continents to bring the latest innovations and ideas to Finnish education. She is an international researcher and a popular teacher and keynote speaker who has inspired numerous students, scholars, teachers, and educational leaders globally. Her latest book Phenomenal Learning from Finland appeared in June 2018 by Edita Publishing: phenomenallearning.fi

REFERENCES

[1] K. Hakkarainen, L. Hietajärvi, K. Alho, K. Lonka, and K. Salmela-Aro. 2015. Sociodigital revolution: Digital natives vs. digital immigrants. In International encyclopedia of the social and behavioral sciences (2nd ed.), J. D. Wright (Ed.). Vol. 22. Elsevier, Amsterdam, 918–923.

[2] N. Halonen, L. Hietajärvi, K. Lonka, and K. Salmela-Aro. 2016. Sixth graders' use of technologies in learning, technology attitudes and school well-being. The European Journal of Social & Behavioural Sciences XVIII, 1 (2016), 2307–2324. https://doi.org/10.15405/ejsbs.205

[3] L. Hietajärvi, J. Seppä, and K. Hakkarainen. 2016. Dimensions of adolescents' sociodigital participation. Qwerty - Open and Interdisciplinary Journal of Technology, Culture and Education 11, 12 (2016), 79–98.

[4] L. Hietajärvi, H. Tuominen-Soini, K. Hakkarainen, K. Salmela-Aro, and K. Lonka. 2015. Is student motivation related to socio-digital participation? A personoriented approach. Elsevier Procedia - Social and Behavioral Sciences 171 (2015), 1156–1167.

[5] Kirsti Lonka. 2018. Phenomenal learning from Finland. Edita Publishing.

[6] K. Salmela-Aro, K. Upadyaya, K. Hakkarainen, K. Lonka, and K. Alho. 2017. The dark side of internet use: Two longitudinal studies of excessive internet use, depressive symptoms, school burnout and engagement among Finnish early and late adolescents. Journal of Youth and Adolescence 46, 2 (2017), 343–357. https://doi.org/10.1007/s10964-016-0494-2

Socioeconomic Status and Computer Science Achievement

Spatial Ability as a Mediating Variable in a Novel Model of Understanding

Miranda C. Parker	Amber Solomon	Brianna Pritchett
Georgia Institute of Technology	Georgia Institute of Technology	Georgia Institute of Technology
Atlanta, Georgia	Atlanta, Georgia	Atlanta, Georgia
miranda.parker@gatech.edu	asolomon30@gatech.edu	bpritchett8@gatech.edu
David A. Illingworth	Lauren E. Margulieux	Mark Guzdial
Georgia Institute of Technology	Georgia State University	Georgia Institute of Technology
Atlanta, Georgia	Atlanta, Georgia	Atlanta, Georgia
david.illingworth@gatech.edu	lmargulieux@gsu.edu	guzdial@cc.gatech.edu

ABSTRACT

Socioeconomic status (SES) has a measurable impact on many educational outcomes and likely also influences computer science (CS) achievement. We present a novel model to account for the observed connections between SES and CS achievement. We examined possible mediating variables between SES and CS achievement, including spatial ability and access to computing. We define access as comprised of measurements of prior learning opportunities for computing, perceptions of computer science, and encouragement to pursue computing. The factors (SES, spatial ability, access to computing, and CS achievement) were measured through surveys completed by 163 students in introductory computing courses at a college level. Through the use of exploratory structural equation modeling, we found that these variables do impact each other, though not as we originally hypothesized. For our sample of students, we found spatial ability was a mediating variable for SES and CS achievement, but access to computing was not. Neither model explained all the variance, and our subject pool of US college students had higher than average SES. Our findings suggest that SES does influence success in computer science, but that relationship may not be due to access to computing education opportunities. Rather, SES might be influencing variables such as spatial ability which in turn influence CS performance.

CCS CONCEPTS

• **Social and professional topics** → *Computer science education*;

KEYWORDS

socioeconomic status; spatial ability; access; CS achievement

ACM Reference Format:
Miranda C. Parker, Amber Solomon, Brianna Pritchett, David A. Illingworth, Lauren E. Margulieux, and Mark Guzdial. 2018. Socioeconomic Status and Computer Science Achievement: Spatial Ability as a Mediating Variable in a Novel Model of Understanding. In *ICER '18: 2018 International Computing Education Research Conference, August 13–15, 2018, Espoo, Finland*. ACM, New York, NY, USA, 9 pages. https://doi.org/10.1145/3230977.3230987

1 INTRODUCTION

There is a strong, positive relationship between socioeconomic status (SES) and academic achievement [17, 34, 48]. Students from low-SES households are less likely to attain high scores on achievement tests and grade-point average (GPA) measures, while being from a high-SES household tends to predict academic success. This finding has been replicated in STEM fields [18], and we have evidence that this holds true for computer science achievement as well [24]. Obviously, it is not the mere presence of money that produces the ability to achieve in computer science. SES leads to other benefits, such as living in a neighborhood with less crime and better schools. Those other factors are more likely having an impact on academic achievement rather than just SES.

If we can define how SES impacts CS achievement, we might be able to mitigate the effect by designing interventions that would affect the intermediate variables. Socioeconomic status could affect access to computing hardware, broadband networks, community and family members with positive perceptions of computer science, encouragement to pursue computer science, availability of toys or trips to the museum that develop spatial reasoning skills, or other variables that might give a student a better chance at achieving in computer science [9, 13]. Giving every student enough wealth to boost their SES would likely be impossible. But some of those other intervening variables might be significant and be manipulable with reasonable resources. For example, we might be able to distribute low-cost hardware, if access to computing hardware turned out to be a significant intervening variable.

We wanted to begin to explore the *intervening variables* (also referred to as *mediating variables*) between SES and CS achievement. A better understanding of this could help inform interventions to help level the playing field for all students in CS. Our research question is: *What are the mediating variables X between socioeconomic status and computer science achievement such that socioeconomic status affects X and X affects CS achievement?*

We focus on two possible intervening variables: spatial ability and access to computing. Spatial ability, spatial reasoning, or spatial cognition deals with the locations of objects, their shapes, their relationship to each other, and the manipulation of them [26]. We refer to spatial reasoning as the assessment of spatial ability. Spatial ability is connected to SES [7, 23] and to CS achievement [9]. In this study, access to computing is defined by access to learning opportunities, as well as encouragement to pursue computing, and perceptions of computing. Access to computing is also connected to SES [24] and CS achievement [2, 10]. We chose these variables because of their known connections to SES and CS achievement, but their unknown roles as intervening variables to describe the effect of SES on CS achievement.

We sought to build a novel model for computer science education to account for the observed connections between SES and CS achievement. To do this, we surveyed undergraduate students in their first college computer science course. We administered four surveys to assess SES, spatial ability, prior access to computing, and CS achievement. We created methods to score the surveys and then analyze the relationships between them. We began analyses with Pearson's correlations, which showed significant correlations between each of our four variables. We continued with exploratory structural equation modeling which resulted in a model of spatial ability as an intervening variable between SES and CS achievement, but access to computing was not found to be an intervening variable. We discuss the implications of our findings for the CS Education community.

2 EXISTING LITERATURE

Our work is grounded in the literature of the connections between SES, access to computing, spatial reasoning, and CS achievement. We separate our literature into the two intervening variables we explore: spatial reasoning and access to computing.

2.1 Spatial Reasoning

Our discussion of spatial reasoning in Computer Science stems from a previous report on the connection between these two variables, and the incidental role SES played in the study. Cooper et al. found that students did better on a CS assessment when they offered spatial skills training for 45 minutes for eight of the ten days of a workshop [9]. The other students received additional review time during those 45 minutes. In other words, even with less CS content, students with spatial skills training performed better than students without that spatial skills training and with more time on CS content. Their argument was built on the literature that shows correlations between spatial and programming abilities by attempting to improve spatial abilities in hope of improving programming ability [11, 12, 19, 20, 25, 46].

While SES was not part of the Cooper et al. initial hypotheses, their *post hoc* analysis found an interesting result. They found that spatial skills training helped low-SES students perform at the same level as their high-SES counterparts. The control group had a significant difference in performance between high- and low-SES students.

We build on the Cooper et al. study to understand why these connections occur. Below, we detail prior literature on the connections between SES and spatial reasoning, and spatial reasoning and CS achievement.

2.1.1 SES and Spatial Reasoning. Work in the areas of Developmental and Cognitive Sciences has found a connection between SES differences and disparities in spatial cognition, along with other neurocognitive functions [15, 27]. Furthermore, research has found that spatial reasoning is sensitive to SES differences, moderating the differences in spatial reasoning among gender groups; boys from middle- to high- SES backgrounds outperform girls from similar backgrounds on spatial tasks, but there is little difference in performance among low-SES boys and girls [23]. Other studies have found that SES can affect a student's ability to apply spatial reasoning skills to their academic performance [7]. In Casey et al., spatial skills were found to relate to academic performance in high-SES communities, but not low-SES ones. They found that children in low-income communities were less likely than their affluent peers to benefit, in terms of academic performance, from good spatial skills. This is an extension of work that studies low-SES students with high-level computational skills that are unable to transfer their skills into a mathematics classroom [31, 32].

These results do not give us a clear answer to the question of the role of spatial reasoning and academic performance. Spatial reasoning seems to be playing a role for high-SES students, but not for low-SES students. We suggest that these prior studies are studying students where they are. Perhaps low-SES students take classes that do not tax their spatial reasoning. We can imagine teaching (for example) algebra in ways that make demands on spatial reasoning (e.g., that emphasize the *sides* of an equals sign and the need to *balance* the two sides [1]), or in ways that may not make as many demands (e.g., with a greater focus on mathematical calculation). Because of the differences in classes, we cannot clearly say if the need for spatial reasoning ability is inherent to the demands of these academic disciplines, or if spatial reasoning plays a role only when specific teaching methods are used or only for specific learning outcomes. Our study uses one measure of CS achievement, for students with varying SES backgrounds, in the same introductory classes.

2.1.2 Spatial Reasoning and CS Achievement. Wai et al. have solidified the importance of spatial reasoning in developing expertise in the STEM fields at large [43]. Looking within CS Education, several studies have explored the connection between spatial reasoning and CS achievement [9, 11, 12, 19, 20, 25, 46]. Measuring CS achievement through grades and spatial ability through a visualization task, the correlation is small, but positive [11]. Using the completion time of code comprehension exercises and mental rotation skills, there is a strong correlation [19, 20]. Spatial ability has been found to be a predictor of scores on a Logo program, BASIC exams, and adapted AP CS tests [9, 25, 46]. Other research has found a link between spatial cognition and source code navigation and program comprehension [12].

These studies have measured CS achievement in different ways and defined spatial ability through different measures, which makes it difficult to make a general statement about the relationship. Still, there are consistent positive correlations between spatial reasoning and CS achievement over a variety of measures, definitions, and curricula. These multiple studies showing a positive relationship create a kind of replication of the results across different contexts, strengthening the argument for the relationship between these two variables. In our study, we have a single definition of CS achievement and of spatial ability that we based on our survey instruments, which gives us the opportunity for a clearer statement about the relationship between the two variables.

2.2 Access to Computing

In our study, we hypothesized a path from *socioeconomic status* to *access to computing*, and then *access* to *computer science achievement*. This path was motivated by the existing literature that connected these variables.

We define access to computing across four different dimensions: formal exposure to computing, informal exposure to technology, perceptions of computing, and encouragement to pursue computing. This definition is further explored in Section 3.2.1.

2.2.1 SES and Access. Previous reports have seen that not only are higher-income households more likely to have computers in the home [2], the way in which these computers are used varies by SES. Based on reports from the National Telecommunication and Information Administration [38], SES also impacts the speed of internet connection in the home, number of computers per household, and the quality of those computers. In addition to technical factors, SES can also impact various social factors that relate to access – for instance, having peers [24] and family members [3] who are sophisticated users of technology can impact your own understanding of it, and these can also be affected by SES. Outside of the home, school-level SES can impact how computers are used. For instance, lower-SES teachers often have less technical support for their computers in the classroom [45] so they use them less often. Additionally, because they often can't assume that students will have home access to computers, they spend a large portion of their time teaching basic computer skills and are hesitant to send children home with computer assignments [44]. There are even broader differences in the ways in which access is provided to students in different SES schools – for instance, low-SES schools are more likely to use computers for "remediation of skills" and review, while higher-SES schools are more likely to use computers for creative expression [4].

We know that SES can be a determining variable as to whether students' perceptions of software are more affected by home computer or by in-classroom exposure [30], though how SES was measured in that case is unclear. One study found that SES (measured according to parents' occupation(s)) does not predict computer ownership but does affect attitudes, use, and competencies [40]. We also have evidence that students without prior access, exposure, and opportunities to use technology fall behind in college due to simply not knowing how to use the technological tools that colleges depend on in this digital age [13]. As evidenced above, these studies have operationalized SES differently and cover three different types of technology–software, computer ownership, and college technology use.

2.2.2 Access and CS Achievement. Past literature has also shown a link between home access to computing and achievement, although this research has focused on math and science achievement rather than computer science achievement in particular. For instance, Attewell and Battle [2] find that eighth grade students with

Table 1: Participant demographics

Gender	Race/Ethnicity	Major
71% Female	23% Asian	91% Non-Computing Major
28% Male	5% Black	8% Computing area Major
1% Did not disclose	64% White	<1% Undeclared
	8% Two or more	

home access to computers score an average of 5 points higher on math than those without home computers, even when controlling for various SES predictors. This relationship is found elsewhere as well, with home access to "information and communication technologies" related to math and science achievement in 9th graders in Turkey [10].

3 METHODS

3.1 Student Population

Participants in this study were asked to complete four surveys: (1) *SES survey*, (2) *Access to Computer Science survey*, (3) *Spatial Reasoning Skills survey*, and (4) a *CS Achievement assessment*. These surveys were completed near the end of the participant's first college computing course, which was intentionally placed to prevent a floor-effect on the achievement assessment. Participants were recruited from two universities in the southeastern United States and given three weeks to complete this study for extra credit in their course. Alternatively, students could elect to complete a set of programming problems for the same extra credit. Most of our study population was recruited from an Introduction to Media Computation course, a media-centric computing course designed to interest students that are typically disinterested in traditional computing courses. Six students came from another introductory course designed for computer science majors using the C programming language.

195 responses were recorded to our consent form. However, some participants submitted multiple times or did not complete all the forms. If a student repeated a submission, they were excluded from the final pool if their results were not consistent across submissions. 163 participants met all requirements for inclusion into the study. A summary of participant demographics can be found in Table 1. In addition to those demographics, our participants had a mean SES value of 11.18 on a 14-point scale, with a standard deviation of 1.94.

3.2 Assessment Instruments

Four survey instruments were used in our study to measure each of our variables. We used the validated Family Affluence Scale (FAS III) as our SES survey instrument. This survey consists of five multiple choice questions that reflect "market forces, economic trends, technological advances, as well as cultural, social and geographical norms in consumption across Europe and North America" [16]. We used the Revised Purdue Spatial Visualization Test (Revised PSVT:R) as an indicator of spatial ability. This assessment measures the ability to complete mental rotations, an indication of spatial ability [49]. We developed a survey to measure access to learning computing opportunities. This survey is described in more detail in Section 3.2.1. We measured CS Achievement with an adapted version of the validated psuedocode-based CS1 assessment, SCS1 [29]. We drew 12 questions from the 27 question test, based on their previous difficulty and discrimination values from an item response theory analysis. We chose to maintain the make-up of the exam by including four questions from each question type (definitional, tracing, and code completion) and focused on four content areas (if statements, for loops, while loops, and logical operators). We collected demographic information following the completion of the four surveys to reduce stereotype threat [36].

3.2.1 Access Survey Construction and Quality.
We defined access using four constructs: formal access through school and summer camps; informal access through proximity to internet, technology, and media; perceptions of self and the field; and encouragement to pursue the field. An example of questions in each category can be found in Table 2.

Formal access is defined by access to learning opportunities with a curriculum. We have seen a similar distinction made in computing education research literature when considering the role of curriculum versus exploratory learning opportunities online [22]. Formal access includes traditional education pathways, such as whether students had opportunities to access CS teachers and computing courses in elementary, middle, or high school. We also included in this category outside-of-school learning opportunities with curricula, such as computing clubs or coding camps.

Informal access includes access to technologies that do not have a curriculum, but could be used for exploratory learning. This includes questions on access to the Internet, technology, and media. Questions on access to the Internet included whether they had an internet connection at home, but also what kind of internet access (DSL, dial up, etc.), and whether internet access was limited to a mobile phone. Questions on technology assessed if students had a personal or family computer growing up, where they had access to a computer (at home or a library) and whether they had someone in their household to fix their computer. Questions on media asked if students watched television or movies that were related to programming or computer science, and if they played video games.

Encouragement questions asked if anyone had encouraged the participant to pursue computing and, if so, who. We know from prior work that access can improve perceptions of ability, but perceptions of ability alone do not predict higher self-efficacy or intent to pursue computing without encouragement for females and members of under-represented minority groups [8, 14]. Perceptions of ability alone predicts self-efficacy and intent to persist for white or Asian males [14]. Because access alone is unlikely to be effective for underrepresented groups and women in computing without encouragement, we included encouragement as part of our access construct.

The perceptions portion of the survey included questions on whether students saw themselves represented in computing fields and if they felt they were computer scientists. We also asked questions about what the participants perceived the field to be, if they thought computing would be a viable career to them, and their values and whether computing met those values. We included these all in the perceptions variable, and included them in our hypothesized access construct because we saw the perceptions to be the desirable outcomes of access. As we found in the Principal Component Analysis (Section 4.1), the perceptions variable does not represent the same underlying construct as the other three access components, and thus adds a new dimension to our access survey.

To grade the survey, three coders, including two authors, graded 11% of the questions and 16% of the participants. Each person graded individually. Each question was ranked on a 5-point scale. We performed an inter-rater reliability analysis using Cohen's Kappa to determine consistency among raters. This process was repeated, discussing the questions and codings, until a Cohen's Kappa of 0.7 was achieved. Then one coder graded all the surveys, according to the developed coding scheme, to construct the final access survey score, with accompanying categorical scores.

Since we constructed a survey to assess variables of access to computing, we assessed the reliability of the survey. We found the survey to have a Cronbach's alpha of 0.84, which indicates acceptable reliability [28].

3.3 Procedure
We distributed the study at the end of the semester after students had learned the concepts that were included in the CS achievement assessment. The entire study took place online. After obtaining participants' consent, participants were directed to the next survey. This process of linking surveys continued until all surveys were completed. Participants were directed, in this manner, to complete surveys in the following order: SES, spatial reasoning, access to computing, and CS achievement. We acknowledge that the Revised PSVT:R is supposed to be a timed test; takers are typically only allowed 25 minutes to complete. However, due to technological constraints, we could not make the spatial reasoning assessment timed. For completion of all the surveys and assessments, students received extra credit on one of their homework assignments in their computing course.

3.4 Structural Equation Modeling
In order to determine the relationship between our four constructed variables (SES, access to computing, spatial ability, and CS achievement), structural equation modeling (SEM) was employed. SEM can be thought of as a combination of exploratory factor analysis and multiple regression [41]. This method creates a series of regression equations to represent the hypothesized relationships being studied, and organizes those relations visually to create a clear conceptualization of the theory being explored [6]. SEM allows researchers to explore and test theory regarding how constructs are linked and the directionality of relationships [33]. SEM is the most appropriate method to answer our research question regarding mediating variables between SES and CS achievement.

SEM is confirmatory by nature, because of the emphasis on building models grounded in theory and literature [33]. SEM is not the same as Confirmatory Factor Analysis (CFA) modeling. CFA is a type of SEM, along with path analysis, structural regression models, and latent change models [39]. SEM can be exploratory

Table 2: Participant demographics

Category	Example question	Answer choices
Formal access	Did your school have a computer science teacher in elementary, middle, or high school?	Elementary School, Middle School, High School (Select many)
Informal access	If there was a computer in your family house, who was most likely to fix the computer when something went awry?	Dad, Mom , Brother, Sister, Me, Nobody in my house took care of it, Other (Select many)
Perceptions	Please rate how much you agree or disagree with the following statements: I can picture myself as a computer scientist.	Strongly Agree, Agree, Neutral, Disagree, Strongly Disagree (Select one)
Encouragement	Has anyone offered you personal advice on how to succeed in computing? Select all that apply.	HS Teachers, HS Advisors, College/Univ. Faculty, College/Univ. Advisors, Parents, Friends/Peers, Other (Please explain) (Select many)

when building structural regression models to test or disconfirm proposed theories involving explanatory relationships among various latent variables [39]. We withhold discussion on our individual models until Section 5 due to the importance of these models being considered in comparison with each other, rather than on their own.

There are five steps to build any SEM: model specification, identification, estimation, evaluation, and modifications [39]. Model specification is the step of gathering existing theories to formally state the hypothesized relationships among the variables. Hence, our models are built from the relationships explored in the literature described in Section 2. Model identification involves applying data to the variables in the hypothesized model. This data for our study is described in Section 3.2. Model estimation is using software to determine path coefficients between variables. In our study, we use the EQS software [5] to determine the impact of one variable on another. The scale of impact is described as a path coefficient, which is analogous to β in a regression equation [39]. These numbers are standardized, and typically fall in the range of -1 to 1. Model evaluation is using model fit indexes to determine how well the data fit the model. While there are dozens of fit indexes, we focus on Chi-square difference tests, Root mean square error of approximation (RMSEA), Comparative Fit Index (CFI), and Bayes Information Criterion (BIC). The last step of building a SEM is model modification, which involves adding or removing parameters to improve the fit. One of our models is a modified version of our original model, which lends itself to Chi-square difference tests to compare models. Another one of our models is not a modification of the original model, which necessitates the use of the BIC measure to compare model fit.

A brief history of SEM and a primer for its role in education research and practice can be found in Khine's book on the topic [21].

4 ANALYSIS

4.1 Principal Component Analysis

We used Principal Component Analysis to test whether our measurements of *access*, *spatial reasoning*, and *SES* were reasonable. First, we tested whether all the components of *access* belonged together. Then, we tested whether SES was really part of the same underlying construct as the others.

Formal access, informal access, encouragement, and perceptions were all expected to represent an underlying latent variable: access to computing. To test this expectation, participants' scores on these four components of the access survey were run through a principal component analysis, which tests whether scores on different measurements co-vary and, therefore, represent the same latent variable. The principal component analysis yielded one reliable component, Eigenvalue = 1.47, accounting for 37% of the variance, with an elbow in the scree plot at the second component, Eigenvalue = 0.97 and accounting for 24% of the variance. The loadings onto this variable were acceptable for formal access (0.69), informal access (0.65), and encouragement (0.67), but the loading for perceptions (0.36) was too low to include. Therefore, the latent variable represented by formal access, informal access, and encouragement is likely highly related to access to computing, and perceptions does not reliably represent the *access* variable.

After analyzing these four components in a separate analysis, participants' SES and spatial grade were added to an omnibus principal components analysis to ensure that they did not represent the same latent variable and contributed unique variance to the model. This analysis yielded two reliable components, Eigenvalues = 1.78 and 1.12 and accounting for 30% and 19% of the variance. The third component had an Eigenvalue of 0.93 and accounted for 16% of the variance. The resultant scree plot had no clear elbow, which makes sense given the loadings. The first component had sufficient loadings for formal access (0.59), informal access (0.66), and encouragement (0.56), similar to the previous analysis. The second component had sufficient loadings for spatial grade (0.63) and perceptions (0.52). SES did not load well onto either component (first = 0.49 and second = -0.48). Therefore, SES is likely somewhat related to each component, but independent enough to be its own component, hence the ambiguous third component.

The Principal Components Analysis gave us support for doing our analysis with access, spatial grade, and SES as separate and distinct variables. Although the perceptions variable does not represent the same underlying construct as the other three access components, we kept the variable in our models to represent a different dimension of our access survey.

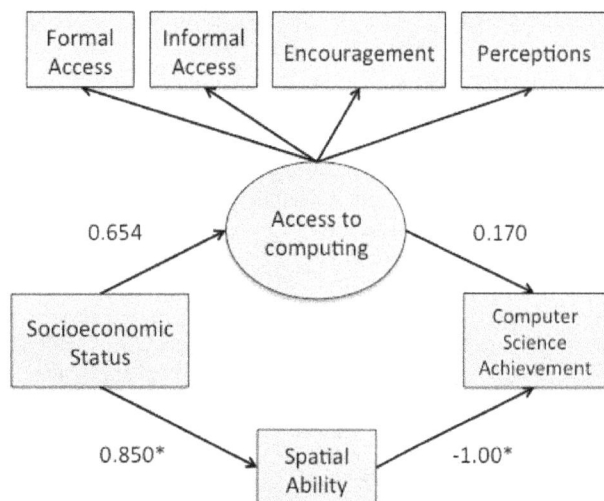

Figure 1: Our Model 1 includes the mediating variables of access to computing and spatial ability such that socioeconomic status affects access and spatial ability and access and spatial ability affects CS achievement.

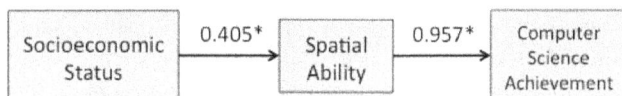

Figure 2: Our Model 2 includes the mediating variables of spatial ability such that socioeconomic status affects spatial ability and spatial ability affects CS achievement.

4.2 Structural Equation Modeling

We present our three models and provide estimation and evaluation statistics for each. As mentioned in Section 3.4, we chose the model fit indexes of Chi-square difference tests, Root mean square error of approximation (RMSEA), and Comparative Fit Index (CFI). When comparing models during an exploratory analysis, the higher CFI value is better and the smaller RMSEA and BIC values are better [33]. A summary of our analysis is presented in Table 3.

4.2.1 Model 1: Access and Spatial Ability. We began by testing the overall fit of our original hypothesized model, as seen in Figure 1. Model 1 stated that SES would have an impact on both access to computing and spatial ability, which in turn would each have an impact on CS achievement. Access to computing was a latent factor which was indirectly measured via scales of formal access, informal access, encouragement, and perceptions, as described in Section 3.2.1. In this model, spatial ability had a strong effect on CS achievement ($\beta = -1$, $p < 0.05$) and SES on spatial ability ($\beta = 0.850$, $p < 0.05$).

4.2.2 Model 2: Spatial Ability. We then tested Model 2, which was a modified version of our Model 1. Model 2, as seen in Figure 2, represented a hypothesis that access to computing did not play a role in affecting CS achievement. Rather, spatial ability is the only

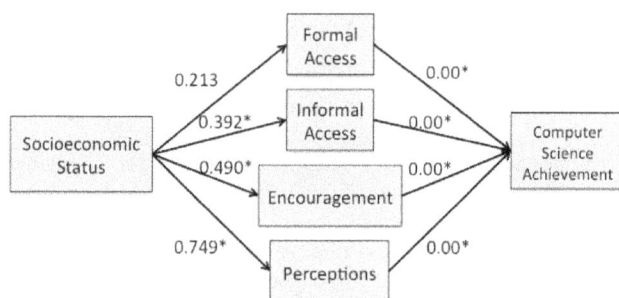

Figure 3: Our Model 3 includes the mediating variables of access to computing such that socioeconomic status affects access and access affects CS achievement.

variable included to mediate the effect of SES on CS achievement. Thus, we removed all variables of access to computing, leaving a simplified model of SES having an impact on spatial ability, which in turn had an impact on CS achievement. This model again found a strong relationship between spatial ability and CS achievement ($\beta = 0.957$, $p < 0.05$) and a relationship between SES and spatial ability ($\beta = 0.405$, $p < 0.05$).

4.2.3 Model 3: Access. We created Model 3 from changing the variables explored in Model 1. Model 3, as seen in Figure 3, isolated access to computing, testing the impact that the components of access would have on CS achievement if spatial ability were not a factor. In contrast to Model 2, we removed the spatial ability variable and allowed for each aspect of access to be a separate, observed variable with a path from SES and to CS achievement. It should be noted that, since we changed the variables within the model, this model is not considered a modification of Model 1. However, this model included a significant relationship between SES and each variable of access, except for formal access. However, we found no relationship between the different variables of access and CS achievement ($\beta = 0$, $p < 0.05$).

5 DISCUSSION

None of our models have statistical measurements that meet individual fit index thresholds for a good model (CFI > 0.95 for acceptance, RMSEA < 0.08) [33]. However, our study and use of SEM is an exploratory one, not confirmatory. Hence, we can compare the models against each other to determine which is the best fit.

5.1 Access and Spatial Ability as Mediating Variables

Model 1 is not as good as Model 2, because of the higher RMSEA and lower CFI. In other words, access and spatial ability are not likely to both be mediating variables. We believed this would be the case, given the evidence in the literature to support each path between SES, access, spatial ability, and computer science achievement. However, the literature support does not necessitate both access and spatial ability being mediating variables, which is mirrored in our model fit index comparisons.

Table 3: A summary of the model variables and fit indexes

Model	Intervening Variable(s)	Standardized Path Coefficient from SES [a]	Standardized Path Coefficient to CS Achievement [a]	χ^2	$\Delta\chi^2$	df	RMSEA [b]	CFI [c]	BIC [d]
1	Access	.654	.170	5712.967	–	21	1.2993	0.006	14386.361
	Spatial ability	.850*	-1.00*						
2	Spatial ability	0.405*	0.957*	5701.378	11.589	28	1.118	0.009	14385.721
3	Formal access	0.213	0.00*	5707.075	5.892	16	1.482	0.006	14452.543
	Informal access	0.392*	0.00*						
	Perceptions	0.749*	0.00*						
	Encouragement	0.490*	0.00*						

[a] * represents significance at the 5% level
[b] RMSEA: Root Mean Square Error of Approximation
[c] CFI: Comparative Fit Index
[d] BIC: Bayes Information Criterion

5.2 Access as a Mediating Variable

Model 3 is not as good as the other models based on CFI and RMSEA values. CFI is lower and the RMSEA is higher in Model 3 than in Model 2 or Model 1. Additionally, because our Model 3 is not nested into Model 1, it is appropriate to compare BIC values between Model 1 and Model 3. The BIC value is larger for Model 3, which again implies that Model 3 is not as good of a model. All of this points to Model 3 not being the best model that we explored. This means that the variables that we used to approximate access (formal access, informal access, perceptions, and encouragement) are not mediating variables between SES and CS achievement, for our sample.

Within the model, SES has a statistically significant impact on the variables that approximate access, except for formal access to CS. However, none of the variables had an impact on CS achievement. It is also interesting to note that the variable with the highest path coefficient with SES is perceptions, which we found in Section 4.1 to be representing a different construct than the other three access variables. We add support to the literature on SES affecting access, which is often assumed rather than shown. However, we encourage further research on the connections between access to computing and CS achievement. Perhaps *when* a child is exposed to computer science is not nearly as important as other factors, and thus the effects are mitigated by an introductory computing course.

5.3 Spatial Ability as a Mediating Variable

Model 2 is the best model among the three tested, implicating spatial ability as a mediating variable between SES and CS achievement. Model 2 has the highest CFI value and the lowest RMSEA value among the models tested. Since this model is nested, we can use a Chi-square difference test to compare Model 2 with Model 3. This test value is insignificant (p>0.05) in our case, which means both models fit equally well and the smaller model (Model 2) can be accepted just as well [47]. Furthermore, each path within the model is significant. SES has a medium effect on spatial ability, and spatial ability has a large effect on CS achievement.

This finding extends the literature on SES, spatial ability, and CS achievement. It means there is a connection between these three

variables, more so than access to computing. Spatial ability is a better mediating variable for SES and CS achievement than access, or in addition to access to computing. We can begin to answer our research question with support that SES affects spatial ability and spatial ability affects CS achievement.

As we mentioned, this model, as is true for the others, did not meet thresholds of individual fit indexes for a "good" model. However, we were not using SEM to confirm a model by fitting it to data. Rather, we were trying to build a novel model for CS education, where there is a lack of theory to account for observed connections between SES and CS achievement. This model can serve as a foundation for continued study to understand how SES affects CS achievement.

6 LIMITATIONS

We identify our study's shortcomings here as we currently see them, in recognition of the need for future research to replicate and extend this work in broader contexts. Our study limitations include a privileged and biased sample, and the use of exploratory rather than confirmatory statistics.

It is important to note that a majority of the students came from an institution with a high average on standardized tests among students, including SAT (1450 out of 1600) and ACT (32 out of 36) scores. Additionally, the median family income is $130,000, which is among the highest among highly selective public colleges. This means that the population that we drew from is skewed towards high-SES and, likely, high-spatial ability participants.

Additionally, all of our participants came from large, public universities in the United States. Our model is thus based on a sample of individuals that are not representative of the whole. We encourage further research into whether our model holds in K-12 settings, private and community colleges, and non-American schools and universities.

Our study was exploratory in nature, rather than confirmatory. While we are not contributing indisputable evidence that spatial ability is a mediating factor between SES and CS achievement, we have compared models and selected the best one to conduct confirmatory analyses with different populations. Our model reduces uncertainty in the community about these variables, and allows for more rigor and systematicity than starting future studies only at the exploratory stage.

7 CONCLUSION

We started this exploration with a hypothesis that socioeconomic status (SES) likely influenced CS achievement through the intervening variable of access. We thought that high-SES students likely had more positive access to computing education before they entered their first CS classes, and that's what led to higher achievement. However, our results do not support that hypothesis.

Instead, we find that spatial ability is a more powerful intervening variable than access. We had prior evidence from Cooper et al. that the impact of SES on CS achievement was mediated by spatial ability [9]. Our study specifically looked at that relationship, and our findings support it. Our results suggest that high-SES students tend to have higher spatial ability, and that higher spatial ability, or the better ability to make use of spatial reasoning, thus predicts greater CS achievement. Students from low-SES backgrounds tend to have lower spatial ability, or are less able to make use of spatial reasoning, which may be inhibiting their success in CS classes.

While surprising, the result is a positive one. Spatial ability can be taught [37]. David Uttal and his colleagues developed an approach to teaching spatial ability that measurably led to improved spatial ability that transfered outside the original testing context and was retained for months later [42]. Sheryl Sorby successfully taught spatial ability to Engineering students, which resulted in better performance in Engineering classes [35]. Spatial ability is an intervening variable that we can manipulate without changing students' SES.

We are not claiming that we have made an exhaustive search for intervening variables. We certainly should explore more. SES, spatial ability, and access do not explain all of CS performance. The more we understand the relationship between SES and CS performance, the more we might be able to mitigate the effects of low-SES background in students.

While we have support for the model explaining SES impact on CS performance with mediation from spatial ability, we are not convinced that this model is complete and exhaustive. Because we gathered data only at the post-secondary school level, we are working from a biased sample. All of the students we studied already made it to post-secondary school. Any low-SES students in our sample already overcame odds to make it to this level. We do not know much about low-SES students who tried CS before the post-secondary level.

There may be different models at play between SES and CS performance at the elementary and secondary school level. In particular, access may play a more critical role in primary or secondary school achievement. Access is likely an important variable in broadening participation in computing, but its impact may not be on CS achievement. For example, a lack of access may lead to higher attrition, so we do not even see the students without access in our sample populations.

Our current model gives us a lever. We now have an explanation for why SES impacts CS performance, and that explanation suggests a possible intervention. That is a useful contribution, both for understanding CS performance and for finding ways to mitigate low-SES conditions.

ACKNOWLEDGMENTS

The authors would like to thank our participants, Rhea Chatterjee, and the members of the Contextualized Support for Learning (CSL) lab at Georgia Tech.

This material is based upon work supported by the National Science Foundation under Grant Nos.: 1432300, 1228352 and the National Science Foundation Graduate Research Fellowship under Grant No.: DGE-1650044. Any opinions, findings, and conclusions or recommendations expressed in this material are those of the authors and do not necessarily reflect the views of the National Science Foundation.

REFERENCES

[1] Abraham Arcavi. 2003. The role of visual representations in the learning of mathematics. *Educational studies in mathematics* 52, 3 (2003), 215–241.
[2] Paul Attewell and Juan Battle. 1999. Home Computers and School Performance. *The Information Society* 15, 1 (1999), 1–10. https://doi.org/10.1080/019722499128628 arXiv:https://doi.org/10.1080/019722499128628
[3] Brigid Barron, Caitlin Kennedy Martin, Lori Takeuchi, and Rachel Fithian. 2009. Parents as learning partners in the development of technological fluency. (2009).
[4] Henry Jay Becker. 2000. Who's wired and who's not: Children's access to and use of computer technology. *The future of children* (2000), 44–75.
[5] Peter M Bentler. 1995. *EQS structural equations program manual.* Multivariate software.
[6] Barbara M Byrne. 1994. *Structural equation modeling with EQS and EQS/Windows: Basic concepts, applications, and programming.* Sage.
[7] Beth M Casey, Eric Dearing, Marina Vasilyeva, Colleen M Ganley, and Michele Tine. 2011. Spatial and numerical predictors of measurement performance: The moderating effects of community income and gender. *Journal of Educational Psychology* 103, 2 (2011), 296.
[8] J McGrath Cohoon and Katharine M Baylor. 2003. Female graduate students and program quality. *IEEE Technology and Society Magazine* 22, 3 (2003), 28–35.
[9] Stephen Cooper, Karen Wang, Maya Israni, and Sheryl Sorby. 2015. Spatial skills training in introductory computing. In *Proceedings of the eleventh annual International Conference on International Computing Education Research.* ACM, 13–20.
[10] Erhan Delen and Okan Bulut. 2011. The relationship between students' exposure to technology and their achievement in science and math. *TOJET: The Turkish Online Journal of Educational Technology* 10, 3 (2011).
[11] Sally Fincher, Bob Baker, Ilona Box, Quintin Cutts, Michael de Raadt, Patricia Haden, John Hamer, Margaret Hamilton, Raymond Lister, and Marian Petre. 2005. Programmed to succeed?: A multi-national, multi-institutional study of introductory programming courses. (2005).
[12] Maryanne Fisher, Anthony Cox, and Lin Zhao. 2006. Using sex differences to link spatial cognition and program comprehension. In *Software Maintenance, 2006. ICSM'06. 22nd IEEE International Conference on.* IEEE, 289–298.
[13] Joanna Goode. 2010. Mind the Gap: The Digital Dimension of College Access. *The Journal of Higher Education* 81, 5 (2010), 583–618. https://doi.org/10.1353/jhe.2010.0005
[14] Mark Guzdial, Barbara Ericson, Tom McKlin, and Shelly Engelman. 2012. A statewide survey on computing education pathways and influences: factors in broadening participation in computing. In *Proceedings of the Ninth Annual International Conference on Computing Education Research (ICER'12).* ACM, New York, NY, 143–150.
[15] Daniel A Hackman and Martha J Farah. 2009. Socioeconomic status and the developing brain. *Trends in cognitive sciences* 13, 2 (2009), 65–73.
[16] Jane E. K. Hartley, Kate Levin, and Candace Currie. 2016. A new version of the HBSC Family Affluence Scale - FAS III: Scottish Qualitative Findings from the International FAS Development Study. *Child Indicators Research* 9, 1 (01 Mar 2016), 233–245. https://doi.org/10.1007/s12187-015-9325-3
[17] John Hattie. 2008. *Visible learning: A synthesis of over 800 meta-analyses relating to achievement.* routledge.
[18] Thomas B Hoffer et al. 1995. Social Background Differences in High School Mathematics and Science Coursetaking and Achievement. Statistics in Brief. (1995).

[19] Sue Jones and Gary Burnett. 2008. Spatial ability and learning to program. *Human Technology: An Interdisciplinary Journal on Humans in ICT Environments* (2008).
[20] Sue Jane Jones and Gary E Burnett. 2007. Spatial skills and navigation of source code. In *ACM SIGCSE Bulletin*, Vol. 39. ACM, 231–235.
[21] Myint Swe Khine. 2013. *Application of structural equation modeling in educational research and practice.* Springer.
[22] Michael J Lee and Andrew J Ko. 2015. Comparing the effectiveness of online learning approaches on CS1 learning outcomes. In *Proceedings of the eleventh annual International Conference on International Computing Education Research.* ACM, 237–246.
[23] Susan C Levine, Marina Vasilyeva, Stella F Lourenco, Nora S Newcombe, and Janellen Huttenlocher. 2005. Socioeconomic status modifies the sex difference in spatial skill. *Psychological science* 16, 11 (2005), 841–845.
[24] Jane Margolis, Rachel Estrella, Joanna Goode, Jennifer Jellison Holme, and Kim Nao. 2010. *Stuck in the shallow end: Education, race, and computing.* MIT Press.
[25] Richard E Mayer, Jennifer L Dyck, and William Vilberg. 1986. Learning to program and learning to think: what's the connection? *Commun. ACM* 29, 7 (1986), 605–610.
[26] Nora S Newcombe. 2010. Picture this: Increasing math and science learning by improving spatial thinking. *American Educator* 34, 2 (2010), 29.
[27] Kimberly G Noble, M Frank Norman, and Martha J Farah. 2005. Neurocognitive correlates of socioeconomic status in kindergarten children. *Developmental science* 8, 1 (2005), 74–87.
[28] Jum C Nunnally and Ira H Bernstein. 1978. Psychometric theory. (1978).
[29] Miranda C Parker, Mark Guzdial, and Shelly Engleman. 2016. Replication, validation, and use of a language independent CS1 knowledge assessment. In *Proceedings of the 2016 ACM conference on international computing education research.* ACM, 93–101.
[30] Nichole Pinkard. 2005. How the Perceived Masculinity and/or Feminity of Software Applications Influences Students' Software Preferences. *Journal of Educational Computing Research* 32, 1 (2005), 57–78.
[31] Geoffrey B Saxe. 2002. Candy selling and math learning. *Teaching and learning: The essential readings* (2002), 86–106.
[32] Geoffrey B Saxe, Venus Dawson, Randy Fall, and Sharon Howard. 1996. Culture and children's mathematical thinking. *The nature of mathematical thinking* (1996), 119–144.
[33] James B Schreiber, Amaury Nora, Frances K Stage, Elizabeth A Barlow, and Jamie King. 2006. Reporting structural equation modeling and confirmatory factor analysis results: A review. *The Journal of educational research* 99, 6 (2006), 323–338.
[34] Selcuk R Sirin. 2005. Socioeconomic status and academic achievement: A meta-analytic review of research. *Review of educational research* 75, 3 (2005), 417–453.
[35] Sheryl A Sorby. 2009. Educational research in developing 3-D spatial skills for engineering students. *International Journal of Science Education* 31, 3 (2009), 459–480.
[36] Claude M Steele and Joshua Aronson. 1995. Stereotype threat and the intellectual test performance of African Americans. *Journal of personality and social psychology* 69, 5 (1995), 797.
[37] Mike Stieff and David Uttal. 2015. How much can spatial training improve STEM achievement? *Educational Psychology Review* 27, 4 (2015), 607–615.
[38] National Telecommunications and Information Administration. 2008. Networked Nation: Broadband in America, 2007. (2008).
[39] Timothy Teo, Liang Ting Tsai, and Chih-Chien Yang. 2013. Applying Structural Equation Modeling (SEM) in Educational Research. In *Application of structural equation modeling in educational research and practice.* Springer, 3–21.
[40] J. Tondeur, I. Sinnaeve, M. van Houtte, and J. van Braak. 2011. ICT as cultural capital: The relationship between socioeconomic status and the computer-use profile of young people. *New Media & Society* 13, 1 (2011), 151–168. https://doi.org/10.1177/1461444810369245
[41] Jodie B Ullman and Peter M Bentler. [n. d.]. *Structural equation modeling.* Wiley Online Library.
[42] David H Uttal, Nathaniel G Meadow, Elizabeth Tipton, Linda L Hand, Alison R Alden, Christopher Warren, and Nora S Newcombe. 2013. The malleability of spatial skills: A meta-analysis of training studies. *Psychological bulletin* 139, 2 (2013), 352.
[43] Jonathan Wai, David Lubinski, and Camilla P Benbow. 2009. Spatial ability for STEM domains: Aligning over 50 years of cumulative psychological knowledge solidifies its importance. *Journal of Educational Psychology* 101, 4 (2009), 817.
[44] Mark Warschauer, David Grant, Gabriel Del Real, and Michele Rousseau. 2004. Promoting academic literacy with technology: Successful laptop programs in K-12 schools. *System* 32, 4 (2004), 525–537.
[45] Mark Warschauer, Michele Knobel, and Leeann Stone. 2004. Technology and equity in schooling: Deconstructing the digital divide. *Educational policy* 18, 4 (2004), 562–588.
[46] Noreen M Webb. 1984. Microcomputer learning in small groups: Cognitive requirements and group processes. *Journal of Educational Psychology* 76, 6 (1984), 1076.
[47] Christina Werner and Karin Schermelleh-Engel. 2010. Deciding between competing models: Chi-square difference tests. *Goethe University. Available online: https://perma. cc/2RTR-8XPZ (accessed on 21 July 2017)* (2010).
[48] Karl R White. 1982. The relation between socioeconomic status and academic achievement. *Psychological bulletin* 91, 3 (1982), 461.
[49] SY Yoon. 2011. Revised Purdue Spatial Visualization Test: Visualization of Rotations (Revised PSVT: R)[Psychometric Instrument]. (2011).

Investigating the Relationship Between Spatial Skills and Computer Science

Jack Parkinson
University of Glasgow
jack.parkinson@glasgow.ac.uk

Quintin Cutts
University of Glasgow
quintin.cutts@glasgow.ac.uk

ABSTRACT

The relationship between spatial skills training and computer science learning is unclear. Reported experiments provide tantalising, though not convincing, evidence that training a programming student's spatial skills may accelerate the development of their programming skills. Given the well-documented challenge of learning to program, such acceleration would be welcomed. Despite the experimental results, no attempt has been made to develop a model of how a linkage between spatial skills and computer science ability might operate, hampering the development of a sound research programme to investigate the issue further. This paper surveys the literature on spatial skills and investigates the various underlying cognitive skills involved. It poses a theoretical model for the relationship between computer science ability and spatial skills, exploring ways in which the cognitive processes involved in each overlap, and hence may influence one another. An experiment shows that spatial skills typically increase as the level of academic achievement in computer science increases. Overall, this work provides a substantial foundation for, and encouragement to develop, a major research programme investigating precisely how spatial skills training influences computer science learning, and hence whether computer science education could be significantly improved.

CCS CONCEPTS

• **Social and professional topics** → **Computing education;**

KEYWORDS

Spatial Skills, academic attainment, theoretical model

ACM Reference Format:
Jack Parkinson and Quintin Cutts. 2018. Investigating the Relationship Between Spatial Skills and Computer Science. In *ICER '18: 2018 International Computing Education Research Conference, August 13–15, 2018, Espoo, Finland.* ACM, New York, NY, USA, 9 pages. https://doi.org/10.1145/3230977.3230990

1 INTRODUCTION

Skills in STEM subjects appear to be related to spatial skills (SS): STEM practitioners are reported to have high SS, relative to others [34]; training in SS can improve abilities in STEM subjects, particularly engineering [24]. There is tantalising evidence of such a relationship in computer science (CS), which, due to the cheap and easily accessible nature of SS training, could lead to higher achievement and lower dropout rates, as with engineering.

Unfortunately, current studies in this area are limited and inconclusive - correlation has been identified [12], but only one study [33] shows that SS training appears to help in computing. Based on this inviting start, further study is warranted.

SS are not easy to define strictly [30], and as such studies contain unclear and contradictory descriptions which are likely to hamper research efforts. Perhaps as a result of this, no studies postulate why the STEM/SS relationship exists to any great extent, and so current work may not be optimally focused. Furthermore, most studies in the field tend to concentrate on a single cohort, typically entry level CS students, without examining effects across experience levels.

Based on these gaps, we present three main additions to the research in the field. First, we summarise what is known about SS, defining core elements of SS and how they can be measured. Second, we propose a model for the relationship between SS and CS, drawing on key cognitive processes which appear to be shared by both fields. Third, we describe an experiment to examine the relationship between SS and CS attainment across a range of CS practitioners, from entry level students to professors.

These deliverables are valuable contributions to our understanding of this area, particularly for laying a stronger foundation for future experiments to examine whether or not, and how best, computing ability can be improved with SS training.

2 RELATED WORK IN SS AND STEM

Spatial skills have been connected with STEM for almost seventy years, since Super and Bachrach examined the skills of mathematicians, engineers and scientists, and found SS to be a factor in all these fields [29]. In a broad study covering the work of dozens of researchers, Super and Bachrach attempted to classify the skills and traits of professionals in science and engineering, reviewing studies on such factors as mathematical ability, verbal ability and several other "special" abilities, including SS. They found that not only are SS prominent in these fields, but that in cases where the relationship was tested, STEM practitioners outperformed non-STEM people in SS tests, even those recognised as being "gifted" in other fields.

Wai *et al.* undertook an investigation of SS pertaining to Project TALENT data [34, 35]. Project TALENT consisted of a series of tests given to over 400,000 high school students in the US in 1960 and subsequent follow up questionnaires up to the 1970s. Of the students who went on to achieve a PhD in a STEM field, most scored highly in the Project TALENT spatial skills tests taken eleven years previously (with 45% being in the top 4% of SS scores). Again, the relationship is not causational; SS are shown only to be correlated to progression in STEM subjects.

The STEM area with most research relating to SS is engineering. Sorby has investigated this relationship for over 20 years, showing that engineering students who receive SS training do better in their engineering courses and have lower dropout rates [24]. In addition to developing a SS training course [26], Sorby has shown positive effects of training SS initially on self-selecting groups of low SS scorers in engineering, and then a similar effect in compulsory courses provided by Michigan Tech [23]. The effect of these studies are significant and well replicated: one can reliably train SS to see an improvement in engineering success.

SS also have relationships with success in other STEM fields. In physics, Kozhevnikov *et al.* discovered that psychology undergraduates with better spatial visualisation skills performed better in, and could explain more clearly, kinematic physics problems [13]. Pallrand and Seeber conducted a separate examination in physics, identifying that not only did students taking a physics course show higher gains in SS compared with students taking liberal arts courses on pre/post tests, an experimental group undertaking additional SS training outperformed the placebo and control groups [16]. This study is like those undertaken by Sorby, showing the effectiveness of a training course which can be taken alongside standard teaching [24]. Crucially, it also shows that SS can be developed while studying a STEM subject, even with no explicit SS training, a point we will return to later.

Carter *et al.* showed that those with higher SS outperformed those with lower SS in a general chemistry course [3]. The same has also been found in organic chemistry, when manipulating and understanding 2D representations of molecular molecules [17].

Tartre identified that spatial orientation ability is applied in certain mathematical problems, and suggested that the ability was specifically related to particular mathematical skills, such as determining the area of irregular shapes and groupings of associated objects [30]. However, Tartre's chosen test for spatial orientation is more typically used as a test of closure speed [8], and one of the selected mathematical problems is very similar to an existing test of spatial relations (shown in figure 4). Another study indicating a connection between spatial visualisation and mathematics was conducted by Fennema and Sherman, who showed that spatial skills are a factor contributing to the gender gap found in mathematics [9].

In addition to these studies, Veurink and Sorby [33] have shown that the training course developed by Sorby and Baartmans [25] (and subsequently developed into a workbook [26]) can be used to potentially improve the results of engineering students undertaking non-engineering modules. Several cohorts of engineering students taking additional modules (in areas such as calculus, physics and chemistry) had their SS measured at the start of the course. Those who failed a SS test were offered a chance to increase their SS on the course, and ultimately those students who took up the offer did better in their respective elective modules than their peers who also failed the test but opted not to take the course [33].

In Veurink and Sorby's paper, another module in which students excelled after SS training was a computing module, specifically introductory programming. Students who initially failed the SS test and opted to take training showed significantly higher GPAs in their computing course than those who failed or marginally passed the test, but did not take additional training. This result is based on 6 cohorts, totaling 74 participants, of self selecting students between 1996 and 2002. This implies a causal relationship from SS to programming, though self efficacy may be a factor in these findings: students self-selected to take the additional training, and it is possible that the students who have a more proactive attitude were both likely to take the course when offered and excel in their elective modules anyway. Additionally, there was no prior measure of computing ability, which could be a confound in the study.

Though not making reference to the study by Veurink and Sorby, Cooper *et al.* attempted to show a similar result [5]. We are surprised that Cooper's study, of which Sorby is a co-author, does not reference this earlier, apparently highly-related, work. Cooper took a selection of summer school students intending to begin a university course in computing, and over a period of two weeks, trained their SS in an experimental group and compared their gains in a standardised computing test. The authors acknowledge some issues with the study, e.g. the questions used to test computing ability may not have been the most effective for the group of students they had. The increase in gains by the experimental group failed to reach significance, except when the six questions from the test with the highest item discrimination only were used in the analysis. Ultimately, the authors clearly state that they are not claiming causation, but a correlation which requires further research.

A similar correlation was displayed earlier by Jones and Burnett [12]. They took a cohort of Masters students who had not previously studied computing, tested their SS and examined their end of year results. They did not see any correlation in the Introduction to Human Factors or the IT Management courses taken by these students, but did see a correlation between the Introduction to Programming course and the Object Oriented Systems course, both of which required a significant amount of programming. This suggests that it is possible that the connection with SS lies not strictly with computing generally, but specifically with programming.

Based on this existing research, we identify two points. First, evidence of a causal relationship between SS and CS is limited, though there is something of interest in the area. Second, no researchers have attempted to explain *why* this relationship exists. In an effort to remedy this, we shall lay groundwork for the existence of such a model. It is our view that a stronger understanding of both SS and how they relate to CS will help researchers to pinpoint the effect of SS training and what gains it may provide in a computing context. Our next step therefore is to chart the SS territory more clearly than we have found elsewhere in the literature.

3 UNDERSTANDING SPATIAL SKILLS

Spatial skills is a broad term lacking a concise definition, and as such making clear, distinct arguments about them can prove difficult. Tartre effectively summarises problems faced in discussing and communicating spatial ability and their impact:

> Attempting to understand and discuss something like spatial orientation skill, which is by definition intuitive and nonverbal, is like trying to grab smoke: The

very act of reaching out to take hold of it disperses it. It could be argued that any attempt to verbalize the processes involved in spatial thinking ceases to be spatial thinking [30].

To reduce ambiguity and overcome issues pertaining to the rift between written descriptions of SS and their practical applications, various tests of specific SS factors are given when they are introduced into discussion. Most of these tests have been extracted from Ekstrom *et al.*'s manual for factor-referenced cognitive tests [8].

Over years of discussion and exploration of this difficult field, Carroll collates a wealth of research into a cohesive model consisting of the following factors [2]:

- Spatial Visualisation
- Spatial Relations
- Closure Speed
- Closure Flexibility
- Perceptual Speed
- Visual Imagery (though Carroll identifies this factor as a theoretical factor, without coming to a clear conclusion on its definition)

Spatial visualisation is the factor that has been most examined in relation to STEM, including CS. McGee identified spatial visualisation prior to Carroll as one's proficiency in being able "to mentally rotate, twist, or invert pictorially presented visual stimuli" [14]. Tartre presents a substructure of two distinct factors contributing to spatial visualisation: mental rotation and mental transformation [31]. Mental transformation involves the manipulation and modification of objects, required for such practical applications as visualising cross sections or intra-part movements. This can be seen in practice in the Mental Cutting Test (MCT) [4] in figure 1. Mental rotation is the ability to perform rotations on mental constructs. Practically this typically translates to the ability to see a physical representation of a structure (a block on a table or an image on a piece of paper) and mentally imagine what this object or shape would look like rotated in a different orientation. Ho and Eastman discovered that 2D and 3D rotations are closely related, supporting Carroll, but also that one capable of performing 2D rotation may not be capable of performing 3D rotation [11]. An example of a test of 2D rotations is displayed in figure 2 [34], and an example of a 3D rotation test can be found in figure 3 [36]

Figure 1: Test of mental transformation, the Mental Cutting Test, consisting of 25 items in 20 minutes - *identify the cross section after the following transformation has occurred (answer: second from right)*

Mental rotation is related to another core factor of SS: spatial relations, which is the ability to understand the arrangement and orientation of objects or patterns within their environment. While this initially appears very similar to mental rotation, spatial relation applications do not strictly require rotation to take place, merely a decent understanding of object orientation. In practice, a test

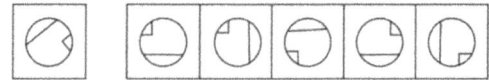

Figure 2: Test of 2D mental rotation, consisting of 24 items and presented as part of a larger test - *which of the following corresponds to the original shape (answer: first from left)*

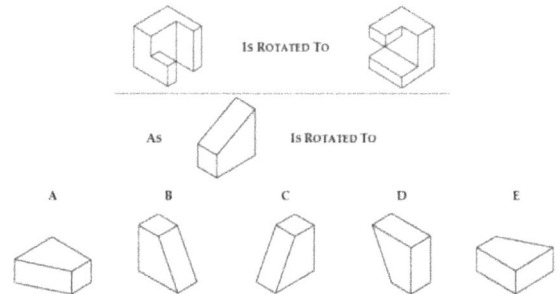

Figure 3: Test of 3D mental rotation, the revised Purdue Spatial Visualisation Test of Rotations (PSVT:R), consisting of 30 items in 20 minutes *(answer: B)*

used to measure spatial relations is the Cube Comparison Test [8], displayed in figure 4 - as can be seen, to find the correct answer, objects do not need to be rotated (which in fact, would be difficult to do with the lack of information of the object); the examinee just needs to be able to relate each face of the cube to its neighbours.

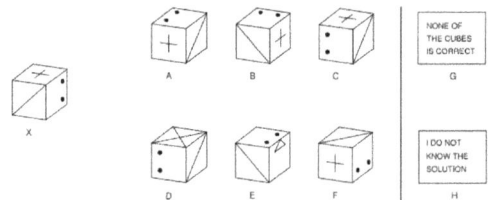

Figure 4: Test of spatial relations, the Cube Comparison Test, consisting of 25 items in 20 minutes - *identify which of the following options corresponds to the original cube (answer: D)*

Three further factors can be defined as follows:

- **Closure Speed:** speed in identifying an *unknown* pattern from an *obscured* environment
- **Closure Flexibility:** speed in identifying a *known* pattern from an *obscured* environment
- **Perceptual Speed:** speed in identifying a *known* pattern from an *unobscured* environment

The easiest way to perceive the application of these these skills is using the tests associated with them. Closure speed is measured by the Gestalt Completion Test [28] (figure 5), which requires the test subject to pick out a representation of an object or image from a highly distorted image (in this example, a flag and hammer head). Closure flexibility can be tested by the Hidden Figures Test [8] (figure 6), in which the test subject is provided with a selection of figures (which are *known*) and a complex pattern, and are required to identify which of the given figures is obscured within the pattern. Perceptual speed is tested by the Identical Pictures Test [8] (figure 7), in which the test subject is presented with a figure and a lineup consisting mostly of figures *similar* to the given figure, with one figure being identical, and must identify the figure from the lineup matching the one provided.

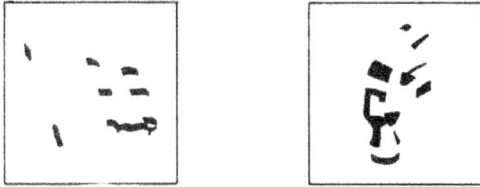

Figure 5: Test of closure speed, the Gestalt Completion Test, consisting of 20 items in 4 minutes *(answers: flag, hammer)*

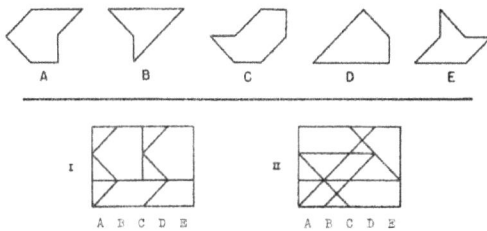

Figure 6: Test of closure flexibility, the Hidden Figures Test, consisting of 32 items in 24 minutes *(answers: A, D)*

Figure 7: Test of perceptual speed, the Identical Pictures Test, consisting of 96 items in 3 minutes *(answer: first from right)*

Carroll also identifies a final first order factor of SS as visual imagery. Visual imagery is a somewhat vague factor in the discussion of SS, and lacks the definition and clarity of other first order factors of SS. Burton and Fogarty attempted to measure this factor, and ultimately decided that the best model they constructed was one which included three second order factors contributing to visual imagery [1]. These are:

- **Quality:** "the ability to generate, maintain, and transform a clear visual image"
- **Self-report:** "ability to generate, control, and/or rotate a visual image"
- **Speed:** "latency measures derived from the experimental tasks" - that is, the tasks which were used to determine the existence of the above two factors

These factors fit into spatial skills beneath the term visual imagery, contributing to the theoretical factor which Carroll identified.

4 MODELING SPATIAL SKILLS AND CS

With an understanding of SS and the factors contributing to them, we can now attempt to show their connection to CS. We note that existing studies relating SS and CS have focused on programming, and we recognise that the underlying skills in programming, such as the development and manipulation of models and the ability to represent these textually and graphically, are core skills across much of CS. Hence we too will focus on aspects of programming.

A fundamental ability in programming is program comprehension. Much research has gone into examining methods and cognitive frameworks involved in program comprehension [20]. One such model, presented by Détienne and Soloway [6], is the model of a mental schema. A schema is a kind of data structure stored in memory which represents some construct: it consists of a plan, which is some generic process or operation as the user understands it, the function the plan carries out, and cues, which are points of reference used to match up a plan with an associated function. In practice, an application of a schema may consist of identifying key variable declarations or structures in code (such as MAX or COUNT, or the beginning of a loop) and matching them with an associated schema (e.g. a find max schema).

The schema model is of significance because operations involved in building and using a schema can be mapped to SS operations. The identification of cues requires that patterns be extracted from obscured environments, not unlike the process required in the application of closure flexibility. These cues are pointers to a model or structure which must be constructed mentally in order to formulate a process. This is similar to several exercises in Sorby's workbook involving the composition of isometric 3D objects from a selection of 2D orthographic views, taking note of specific, useful data points and constructing a more complex structure combining this data.

Another code comprehension framework is the Block Model proposed by Schulte [21]. This involves a process of examining code at four levels, to identify (1) atoms (single words or simple statements in the code), an understanding of which is used to construct (2) blocks ("regions of interest that syntactically or semantically build a unit"), (3) relations (connections involving blocks and atoms such as a *find maximum* code section) and (4) the macro structure (the overall operation of the program). The method of building up from atoms to blocks and relations is similar to Détienne and Soloway's process of schema construction, and likely requires the same cognitive processes, again relating to the application of SS.

Another important aspect of program comprehension is the notional machine, first identified by du Boulay as a combination of knowledge - of the programming language, environment and data - and a mental model [7]. Sorva describes the function of a notional machine as "an idealized abstraction of computer hardware and other aspects of the runtime environment of programs." [27] Sorva closely connects the ability to form notional machines, and therefore appropriately and effectively comprehend programs, with the ability to construct abstract mental models. Experts develop more robust, adaptable mental models than novices, whose mental models tend to be "fragile". Sorva discusses the "runnable" nature of a mental model, based on Norman's work [15], involving the user being able to "envision with the mind's eye how a system works," and directly associates this with working memory and visualisation.

When reviewing spatial skills factors, there are only two which match up with this process of forming a mental model: spatial visualisation (as Sorva briefly suggests) and spatial relations. Closure speed, closure flexibility and perceptual speed are all related to identifying patterns from environments, and visual imagery relates to capturing and recalling images, leaving the two aforementioned factors. An element of spatial relations would be required to construct a mental model, as the user requires an understanding of how various components are linked together (of how they *relate*), but spatial visualisation provides more robust abilities for these tasks. A robust mental model must be subject to development and restructuring as required - the ability to perform these actions mentally is closest to mental transformation (the ability to manipulate or modify a structure mentally) which is part of the spatial visualisation factor. An element of spatial relations may also be included, but typically spatial relations consist of a simple inter-object understanding (see figure 4 for an example) compared with mental rotation, which requires a deeper understanding of the constructs involved (see figure 3). This indicates that when trying to understand more complex constructs in a mental model and what they would look like in a different orientation or situation, spatial relations are likely to work to an extent, but the more complex operations are more likely to require mental rotation (another subset of spatial visualisation).

A difficulty here arises with the definitions of spatial skills factors as given in the literature. From the CS side, considering mental models, we are constructing a mental representation of some operation or process. However, this does not directly relate to a specific factor of spatial skills, forming a neat, clear connection between the two. We identify the closest match as spatial visualisation, where typically the same ability to construct a mental structure is required before then performing some operation on it, such as a rotation or transformation. As such, we theorise that spatial visualisation is very likely to contribute to program comprehension in this regard.

In addition to program comprehension, another core aspect of computing is the procedure of program generation. While generation must be closely related to comprehension, as any generation plan must also involve a process of debugging and review [20], there are elements of program generation not included in comprehension.

Rist observed a method of program generation which he named "focal expansion" [18]. The process of focal expansion involves reviewing a problem and identifying a core function or plan on which to base the implementation. The process which follows involves taking the core plan and building outward, adding and expanding as necessary to facilitate the generation of a program that fully satisfies the problem. Rist links this process to working memory, and associates the ability to track the program generation mentally, from the focal point out to the full solution, with working memory capacity [19]. While this does appear to be the case, it is also possible that visualisation factors into the programmer's ability to track the expansion: to quote Sorva again, "to envision in the mind's eye." Also pertinent to program generation is problem comprehension, the process of identifying a problem from some specification - this process is similar to the schema process of identifying a plan in practice, except that rather than looking for cues in a program they must be extracted from a problem description.

Cues are a recurring concept in both program comprehension and problem comprehension which has briefly been touched on.

This involves the process of identifying potential patterns from a broader environment consisting of more details than the user is currently interested in. There are also factors of SS which, in practical use, are used in performing a very similar task to these operations: closure speed, closure flexibility and perceptual speed. Recall that these processes involve the extraction of patterns (known or unknown) from environments (obscured or unobscured).

The simplest factor is perceptual speed, which is simply identifying a known pattern from an unobscured environment - though rare, this may have an application in cue identification. In code comprehension a case may arise where the user knows the construct they are looking for and the code is laid out in such a way that there is minimal interaction and obscurity between lines (an example of this may be looking for a known variable name in a list of declarations, such as at the top of a file). More likely, the user will be searching for an pattern to match against a record of terms which they feel may have significance based on prior knowledge (such as the start of a loop or declaration of some telling variable). Pictorially, this would be very similar to the test in figure 6, so it is possible that the cognitive process involved in closure flexibility is relevant to this style of program comprehension. And finally we have a case for closure speed, in which an unknown pattern must be derived from an obscured environment. This is akin to an application of the schema model, in which the user searches the code space to identify cues which are not previously known to match them to known schema - at least this would be the case for experts; novices are likely to take a different approach which will involve less searching and pattern matching and more construction.

In this section so far, we have analysed significant aspects of CS and connected them to SS, forming the elements of a model, a diagrammatic representation of which is presented in figure 8.

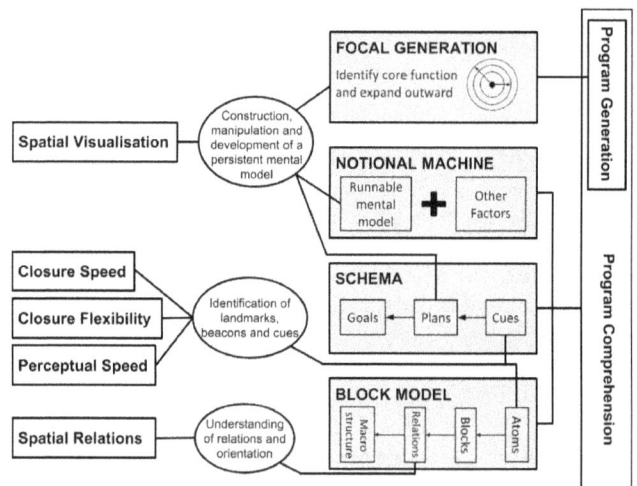

Figure 8: Diagram of the relationships observed between spatial skills and computing science

Bearing this model in mind, we shall now discuss the implications for the development of SS and what this could mean for CS. Sorby notes that the most effective method of training spatial skills is by hand sketching diagrams and drawings [22]. This can be seen in action in her workbook, which poses dozens of short form drawing questions to be completed over a relatively short period of time. We expect that the reason why spatial skills are connected with computing is because *the same* cognitive functions are involved in computing and also in other more obvious applications of spatial ability, such as Sorby's exercises. This view suggests that while SS training could affect one's computing ability positively, as Pallrand observed in physics [16], so too could training in CS develops SS, also as observed by Pallrand for physics.

If this view is correct, why would SS training be of any benefit when the same could be achieved with a standard computing course? We propose that SS training, such as Sorby's workbook, is far more focused and directed than a typical programming course. Whereas in an entry level programming laboratory, students may be expected to write a handful of short programs to achieve given goals over the space of a couple of hours, Sorby's exercises can consist of up to forty sketches to be completed in a similar time frame. Furthermore there are far fewer barriers to advancement: any given drawing could be attempted regardless of the student's experience (a complete novice who has never done any spatial skills training could pick up Sorby's book and attempt the questions), compared with a programming student who must first learn code snippets required for tasks before they can be reused in later tasks. The same skills are being developed, but at a slower rate for programming students who are learning both the CS content and the underlying skills we are interested in here. It is also possible that the students who fall behind in programming are the ones whose SS are not as developed as their peers, and the barriers to their progression are rooted in their inability to construct robust and adaptable mental models (key to programming comprehension and generation).

With this in mind, we suggest that spatial skills themselves do not directly contribute to CS or other STEM domains, but rather than the cognitive functions involved in SS are also involved in STEM domains: such functions as the ability to form, manipulate and develop mental models, identify key points in an environment and understand relations between structures. Based on this theory, we present a simple model for this relationship in figure 9.

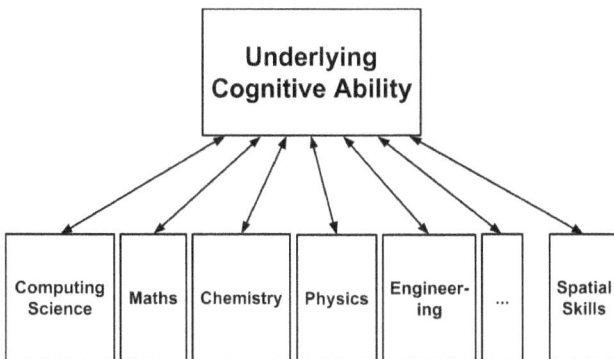

Figure 9: Relationship between cognitive functions behind spatial skills and STEM domains

Notice that the relationships between domains and the underlying cognitive ability are bi-directional. As stated, we believe that these cognitive skills can be developed by pursuing a STEM domain or by training SS, however due to the direct and precise nature of

spatial skills training, this route is likely to produce results more effectively. Moreover, training this ability in one area is likely to have an effect on other areas which make use of the same skills: by training spatial skills, we may see one's ability to write or understand programs improve, or to study physics, chemistry, and so on.

5 SPATIAL SKILLS AND CS ATTAINMENT LEVEL

In previous experiments and studies of SS and CS, it has been typical to examine students either in their first year of study in computing (as an undergraduate degree, a Master's degree or an elective module) or about to start the former. Jones and Burnett's study suggests that those who are better at programming are likely to have better SS, but this is only across a single year.

To better understand the relationship between SS and CS beyond a single year, the SS of students and staff at different levels of attainment in CS at the authors' R1 institution were measured. The study involved two research questions:

- **RQ1:** Do spatial skills vary with academic attainment in CS?
- **RQ2:** Do spatial skills vary with specialisation areas in CS?

For RQ1, given Jones and Burnett's results, it was expected that the higher the attainment and so the "better" the CS skills, the higher the SS will be.

RQ2 draws on Jones and Burnett's finding that SS are not significantly connected to non-programming courses. Each test participant was asked to record their specialised or most favoured area of computing. With this data, it was expected that those involved in heavily programming oriented areas of CS - such as software engineering or systems development - would overall have higher SS than those who were focused on more human based courses, such as HCI or human-centered security.

Furthermore, studies have indicated that gender can affect the SS of participants [9, 32]. In order to account for this potential confound, the gender of each participant was also recorded.

5.1 Method

Five cohorts were selected from which to draw participants:

- First year students, taking a CS0-style course designed for those without programming experience, many of whom are not intending to major in CS
- Honours undergraduate students in their 3rd/4th year majoring in CS, who predominantly take the same courses at the same level
- MSci students, in the fifth year of an undergraduate Masters programme
- PhD students
- Academic staff from the CS department

30 participants were randomly selected from each group and then invited to take the SS test, with the exception of the first years who all took the SS test during a lecture and 30 were randomly selected.

Participants were also required to indicate their specialised or preferred area of research. To reduce the granularity of the data, the participants were arranged according to which of the department's CS primary research areas they fell under, of which there are four. For the purpose of this paper, they are named as follows:

- **HCI:** Human-computer interaction and human factors
- **Data:** machine learning, info retrieval and data science
- **Sys:** systems engineering and networks
- **Th-Alg:** algorithms, computational thinking, formal analysis and mathematical modeling

First year students were not required to indicate a preferred area of computing. Additionally, some participants opted not to provide this information. Table 1 details the breakdown of the participants.

Level	Male	Female	Sys	HCI	Data	Th-Alg	Total
Level 1	19	11					30
H Level	9	4	4	1	3	1	13
MSci	7	2	1	0	4	3	9
PhD	5	5	3	3	1	3	10
Staff	8	2	2	1	1	5	10
Total	43	29	10	5	9	12	72

Table 1: the characteristic breakdown of participants

The test used was the Revised PSVT:R [36]. For all intents and purposes the Revised PSVT:R consists of the same questions as the original PSVT:R by Guay [10], but has been updated to have some graphical errors fixed and the questions arranged in order of difficulty. The test consists of 30 items with a 20 minute time limit.

The test was provided in two separate formats: online and on paper. Online, the test was accessible through the institution's Moodle platform via a quiz with a time limit. On paper, one of the authors was present to ensure that the test was completed within the time limit and that the participants were not looking up answers or conferring. While we cannot absolutely confirm that those who completed the test online did not confer, the timer was not pausable and once the test was begun could not be reset, so in order to cheat participants realistically would have had to have begun the test with the intention of doing so. In addition to the fact that the answers to the PSVT:R are not readily available online, we do not expect that any of the participants would have attempted to invalidate the research deliberately. A more realistic concern is that people who completed the test without supervision may have used scratch paper or some similar aid in completing the questions.

Once the tests were completed, the scores were collated along with level of attainment and demographic data, by which stage no names or other sensitive data was attached to any of the results.

5.2 Analysis of Results

Once the data had been collected, the mean and standard deviation for each group was calculated and are displayed in table 2. After breaking down participants into groups based on attainment level and gender, the SS means of these groups are displayed in table 3.

	Level 1	H Level	MSci	PhD	Staff
Mean	18.97	22.92	24.67	22.00	25.50
SD	6.21	4.59	4.00	6.13	3.60
n	30	13	9	10	10

Table 2: the mean, standard deviation and number of participants for each cohort

To confirm the validity and significance of the experiment, a two way analysis of variance (2-way ANOVA) was conducted. The

	Level 1	H Level	MSci	PhD	Staff	Total
Male	20.42	21.56	24.71	24.60	25.00	22.46
Female	16.46	26.00	24.50	19.40	27.50	20.25
HCI		23.00	-	19.00	27.00	21.40
Data		22.00	24.00	13.00	29.00	22.67
Sys		22.25	20.00	23.00	27.00	22.40
Th-Alg		27.00	25.67	27.00	24.20	25.50
Total	18.97	22.92	24.67	22.00	25.50	21.72

Table 3: the means for each factor being analysed

results of this statistical method are displayed in table 4. Due to the unbalanced nature of the data, sum of squares Type II was used.

Source	DF	SS	MS	F	p
Academic Level	4	429.534	107.383	3.893	0.007
Gender	1	39.507	39.507	1.432	0.236
Academic Level*Gender	4	202.473	50.618	1.835	0.133
Error	62	1710.410	27.587		
Corrected Total	71	2420.444			

Table 4: 2-way ANOVA significance and interaction between factors (in this instance, SS denotes Sum of Squares, MS denotes the Mean Square and DF denotes Degrees of Freedom)

As can be seen here, the main effect of academic level is significant ($p<0.01$). Although the average SS score of male participants was slightly higher, neither this nor the interaction between gender and attainment level were found to be significant.

Once the ANOVA identified that the main effect was significant, the effect size between groups was calculated using Hedges' g, favoured in this case over Cohen's D due to the small sample sizes of some groups. The results of this analysis are displayed in table 5. While recommending caution Cohen suggests that effects of 0.2=small, 0.5=moderate and 0.8=large.

	Level 1	H Level	MSci	PhD	Staff
Level 1	-				
H Level	0.672	-			
MSci	0.963	0.384	-		
PhD	0.480	-0.168	-0.487	-	
Staff	1.124	0.592	0.210	0.667	-

Table 5: the effect size between groups, using Hedges' g

One third of participants completed the test on paper and two thirds completed the test online (with the exclusion of the first year students, who all completed it on paper). In order to check for bias, the average scores two groups were compared. There was a slight bias in favour of the participants who completed the test on paper.

5.3 Discussion

As expected, with the exception of the PhD students, the average SS ability of each cohort increased as academic attainment increased. By examining the effect size between groups, we can see the Honours cohort being better than the level 1 cohort, the MSci cohort were better than them and so on. Although the incremental effect sizes are quite small, they compound to display large differences between cohorts on either ends of the scale.

One theory for the PhD students not fitting this pattern is that their backgrounds are considerably more varied than any of the other cohorts tested. While the first year students will have graduated from differing high school programmes and curricula, all the students tested from the level 1 course specifically chose this course as they had limited programming experience, significantly balancing the background of the cohort. Honours and MSci students will have undertaken different modules, have different preferences and specialisations, but will all be some way along the same course at the same level of assessment. Staff members will also have had a varied background, however it can safely be assumed that they have achieved a relevant PhD and will have several years of experience.

Conversely, PhD students attending the institution in question come from a wide range of first degrees undertaken at universities around the world. Each of these courses will have different focuses, teaching styles and methods of assessment, which may have had an influence on SS development. The test requires some reading at the start, and so there may be language issues. Note also that the deviation in scores for the PhD students is high, and in fact the highest recorded score on the test (a perfect score of 30) was achieved by a PhD student - indicating that rather than the group generally having SS out of sync with their level of advancement, instead, the spread is much broader than in other cohorts.

With the exception of the anomalous PhD students, a clear pattern can be seen in that the average SS of those with higher levels of attainment are higher than those with a lower level of attainment. While this takes us a step closer to understanding the relationship between SS and CS, there are multiple conclusions which can be drawn from this result. One is that as one progresses in computing science, their SS are improved by the exercises and practices they are required to develop, as Pallrand noticed in physics. An alternative theory is that as cohort members progressed, only those with initially higher SS advanced, either because those with lower skills *could not* or *chose not to*. Both options are possible, and a longitudinal study of a cohort progressing through the system would be required to decidedly identify which hypothesis is true, if either.

Concerning the research area of each participant and the mean scores of these groups, the results partially support the study by Jones and Burnett, as the HCI area has the lowest average SS. However, if programming were the primary factor to which SS contributed, it would be expected that the Sys area would have the highest SS, since this is the area most focused on working with programs. The Th-Alg section have the highest average SS, indicating that some other factor in CS is likely to be related to SS.

It must be noted that there are significant differences between the participants involved in this study and those in Jones and Burnett's study. Jones and Burnett's cohort were a relatively known quantity, with participants having different backgrounds but none having done computing, and all being required to take the mentioned courses. The research groups in this institution are far more diverse, with members of staff having differing levels of experience, track records and overlapping interests. Additionally, some participants were not members of a research section and were only able to express their interests. Further, regardless of what research section one is associated with, this does not strictly indicate how much work they do which directly ties into this field. The purpose of collecting this information was to investigate in broad, preliminary terms whether or not this study's matched Jones and Burnett's. We feel that primarily it does, though also indicates that there is more at play than just programming, which supports our model.

Owing to the fact that there was a slight bias in favour of those completing the test on paper vs those completing it online, we should highlight that future experiments of this nature should be conducted using one method only to eliminate this bias. It is an interesting result, however, since we expected that anyone who Âăwas not supervised as they attempted the test would be more likely to have access to scratch paper or some other tools and would therefore score higher. Our suggestion moving forward would be to have everyone complete the test on paper under supervision.

A final thought on the experiment described here was how these results would compare with other subjects, both in STEM and outwith. This was considered, but unfortunately was not feasible with the time and resource constraints of the project. It would be useful to see how closely related the results would be in other STEM fields and particularly to see if non-STEM fields follow the same pattern. However, regardless of what these results may indicate, it is still felt that the somewhat narrower view of this experiment yields valuable insights into the relationship between SS and CS.

6 CONCLUSION

In this paper we have reviewed literature concerning the relationship between SS and STEM, particularly in CS. This literature indicates that a correlation between SS and CS exists, with one study displaying what has been interpreted as a causal effect. Furthermore, we have identified that in one STEM field, SS improve over a period of learning - not as much as if they had received directed SS training, but more than a liberal arts student - which indicates that the relationship is likely to be a biased two-way relationship.

We have also collated and presented a substantial discussion of spatial skills themselves, condensing and summarising a broad field in a format which is easy to grasp for the relatively uninitiated. Based on this, we have presented a model for the relationship between SS and CS. This model is rooted in existing research into cognition in CS, particularly in program comprehension, program generation and problem comprehension. The model indicates that particular factors of SS are likely to have an effect in the reading and identification of key points in code or problems, as well as the mental models constructed in attempting to understand programs and theoretical problems.

Finally, we conducted an experiment to strengthen our understanding of the relationship between SS and CS achievement, showing that in general the average SS of a cohort increases with academic attainment, extending the research undertaken by Jones and Burnett. The experiment also supports our model connecting SS with CS, as the research area with the highest average SS was the section who engage mostly in abstract and theoretical thinking.

Our contribution furthers our understanding of SS and their relation to CS and lays the groundwork for a larger experiment to determine if the relationship is causal. If SS training does benefit computing ability substantially, then it is worth introducing on a large scale, due to its cost-effectiveness, high accessibility and easy implementation.

REFERENCES

[1] Lorelle J Burton and Gerard J Fogarty. 2003. The factor structure of visual imagery and spatial abilities. *Intelligence* 31, 3 (2003), 289–318.

[2] John B Carroll. 1993. *Human cognitive abilities: A survey of factor-analytic studies.* Cambridge University Press.

[3] Carolyn S Carter, Mary A Larussa, and George M Bodner. 1987. A study of two measures of spatial ability as predictors of success in different levels of general chemistry. *Journal of research in science teaching* 24, 7 (1987), 645–657.

[4] CEEB. 1939. CEEB Special Aptitude Test in Spatial Relations, developed by the College Entrance Examination Board, USA. (1939).

[5] Stephen Cooper, Karen Wang, Maya Israni, and Sheryl Sorby. 2015. Spatial skills training in introductory computing. In *Proceedings of the eleventh annual International Conference on International Computing Education Research.* ACM, 13–20.

[6] Françoise Détienne and Elliot Soloway. 1990. An empirically-derived control structure for the process of program understanding. *International Journal of Man-Machine Studies* 33, 3 (1990), 323–342.

[7] Benedict Du Boulay. 1986. Some difficulties of learning to program. *Journal of Educational Computing Research* 2, 1 (1986), 57–73.

[8] Ruth B Ekstrom, Diran Dermen, and Harry Horace Harman. 1976. *Manual for kit of factor-referenced cognitive tests.* Vol. 102. Educational Testing Service Princeton, NJ.

[9] Elizabeth Fennema and Julia Sherman. 1977. Sex-related differences in mathematics achievement, spatial visualization and affective factors. *American educational research journal* 14, 1 (1977), 51–71.

[10] Roland Guay. 1976. *Purdue Spatial Vizualization Test.* Educational testing service.

[11] Chun-Heng Ho, Charles Eastman, and Richard Catrambone. 2006. An investigation of 2D and 3D spatial and mathematical abilities. *Design Studies* 27, 4 (2006), 505–524.

[12] Sue Jones and Gary Burnett. 2008. Spatial ability and learning to program. *Human Technology: An Interdisciplinary Journal on Humans in ICT Environments* (2008).

[13] Maria Kozhevnikov, Michael A Motes, and Mary Hegarty. 2007. Spatial visualization in physics problem solving. *Cognitive Science* 31, 4 (2007), 549–579.

[14] Mark G McGee. 1979. Human spatial abilities: Psychometric studies and environmental, genetic, hormonal, and neurological influences. *Psychological bulletin* 86, 5 (1979), 889.

[15] Donald A Norman. 2014. Some observations on mental models. In *Mental models.* Psychology Press, 15–22.

[16] George J Pallrand and Fred Seeber. 1984. Spatial ability and achievement in introductory physics. *Journal of Research in Science Teaching* 21, 5 (1984), 507–516.

[17] Jeffrey R Pribyl and George M Bodner. 1987. Spatial ability and its role in organic chemistry: A study of four organic courses. *Journal of research in science teaching* 24, 3 (1987), 229–240.

[18] Robert S Rist. 1989. Schema creation in programming. *Cognitive Science* 13, 3 (1989), 389–414.

[19] Robert S Rist. 1995. Program structure and design. *Cognitive Science* 19, 4 (1995), 507–561.

[20] Anthony Robins, Janet Rountree, and Nathan Rountree. 2003. Learning and teaching programming: A review and discussion. *Computer science education* 13, 2 (2003), 137–172.

[21] Carsten Schulte. 2008. Block Model: an educational model of program comprehension as a tool for a scholarly approach to teaching. In *Proceedings of the Fourth international Workshop on Computing Education Research.* ACM, 149–160.

[22] Sheryl A Sorby. 1999. Developing 3-D spatial visualization skills. *Engineering Design Graphics Journal* 63, 2 (1999).

[23] Sheryl A Sorby. 2007. Developing 3D spatial skills for engineering students. *Australasian Journal of Engineering Education* 13, 1 (2007), 1–11.

[24] Sheryl A Sorby. 2009. Educational research in developing 3-D spatial skills for engineering students. *International Journal of Science Education* 31, 3 (2009), 459–480.

[25] Sheryl A Sorby and Beverly J Baartmans. 1996. A Course for the Development of 3-D Spatial Visualization Skills. *Engineering Design Graphics Journal* 60, 1 (1996), 13–20.

[26] Sheryl A Sorby and Anne Francis Wysocki. 2003. *Introduction to 3D Spatial Visualization: an active approach.* Cengage Learning.

[27] Juha Sorva. 2013. Notional machines and introductory programming education. *ACM Transactions on Computing Education (TOCE)* 13, 2 (2013), 8.

[28] Roy Frink Street. 1931. A Gestalt completion test. *Teachers College Contributions to Education* (1931).

[29] Donald E Super and Paul B Bachrach. 1957. Scientific careers and vocational development theory: A review, a critique and some recommendations. (1957).

[30] Lindsay Anne Tartre. 1990. Spatial orientation skill and mathematical problem solving. *Journal for Research in Mathematics Education* (1990), 216–229.

[31] L A Tartre. 1990. Spatial skills, gender and mathematics. In *Mathematics and Gender*, E Fennema and G Leder (Eds.). Teacher's College Press, New York, Chapter 3, 27–59.

[32] David H Uttal, Nathaniel G Meadow, Elizabeth Tipton, Linda L Hand, Alison R Alden, Christopher Warren, and Nora S Newcombe. 2013. The malleability of spatial skills: A meta-analysis of training studies. (2013).

[33] Norma L Veurink and Sheryl A Sorby. 2011. Raising the bar? Longitudinal study to determine which students would most benefit from spatial training. In *American Society for Engineering Education.* American Society for Engineering Education.

[34] Jonathan Wai, David Lubinski, and Camilla P Benbow. 2009. Spatial ability for STEM domains: Aligning over 50 years of cumulative psychological knowledge solidifies its importance. *Journal of Educational Psychology* 101, 4 (2009), 817.

[35] LL Wise, DH McLaughlin, and L Steel. 1979. The Project TALENT data handbook, revised. *Palo Alto, CA: American Institutes for Research* (1979).

[36] So Yoon Yoon. 2011. *Psychometric properties of the revised purdue spatial visualization tests: visualization of rotations (The Revised PSVT: R).* Purdue University.

114

Experiences of Computer Science Transfer Students

Harrison Kwik
The Allen School, DUB Group
University of Washington
Seattle, Washington, USA
kwikh@cs.washington.edu

Benjamin Xie
The Information School, DUB Group
University of Washington
Seattle, Washington, USA
bxie@uw.edu

Andrew J. Ko
The Information School, DUB Group
University of Washington
Seattle, Washington
ajko@uw.edu

ABSTRACT

About half of recent computer and information science graduates attended community college at some point. Prior work on transfer students in general suggests that the transfer process can engage people from underrepresented communities, but can also be academically and socially "shocking". However, we know little about the experiences of transfer students in computer science in particular. We used the Laanan-Transfer Student Questionnaire (L-TSQ) to survey 25 transfer students and 135 native (non-transfer) students and conducted follow-up interviews with 8 transfer students attending a large public 4-year university in a city with significant technology industry presence. We found that while transfer students were more diverse demographically, the support of the university for transfer student orientation tended to mitigate social shocks of transferring. This did not, however, eliminate gaps in academic performance. These findings suggest that there are other non-social factors that influence academic performance that CS programs must support to equitably engage students who transfer.

CCS CONCEPTS

• **Social and professional topics** → **Computing education**; *User characteristics*;

KEYWORDS

transfer students, community college, undergraduate experience, computing education, transfer shock

ACM Reference Format:
Harrison Kwik, Benjamin Xie, and Andrew J. Ko. 2018. Experiences of Computer Science Transfer Students. In *ICER '18: 2018 International Computing Education Research Conference, August 13–15, 2018, Espoo, Finland*. ACM, New York, NY, USA, 9 pages. https://doi.org/10.1145/3230977.3231004

1 INTRODUCTION: TRANSFER INTO CS

Many students do not follow a direct path to a 4-year computer science degree. The National Science Foundation's 2010 National Survey of Recent College Graduates (in the United States) revealed that 52.8% of bachelor's degree recipients in computer and information science attended some form of community college before

graduating. Moreover, students who transferred from community colleges tended to be more diverse racially, ethnically, and socioeconomically than students who only attend 4-year colleges and universities [17]. For example, Hispanic students are over-represented in the public two-year colleges. When students manage to overcome the complex and tangled web of pathways from community colleagues to 4-year colleges [11], they can increase the diversity of CS student populations.

What happens *after* students transfer? Prior work on transfer students in general suggests many possible outcomes. Hills identified that students experienced *transfer shock*, "a severe drop in [academic] performance upon transferring" [9]. A meta-review of 62 subsequent studies on this phenomenon found that many students experienced up to a half grade point drop in GPA, and only some recovered after a year [6].

Later work showed that when experiences are dis-aggregated by academic discipline, significant differences emerged. Cejda found that students in humanities actually experienced *increases* in grade point averages, while students transferring into business, mathematics, and sciences experienced a significant *decrease* in grade point average. [4]. Further research on these discipline-specific findings found that these findings particularly occurred for underrepresented minorities transferring into engineering programs [28], but were not found for students above the age of 24 [20].

While research on engineering transfer students shows persistent evidence of transfer shock, there is some reason to believe that computer science transfer students may experience even more severe challenges. For example, CS has not only severe underrepresentation of women and minority groups [29], but also challenges with offering inclusive learning environments [18]. These factors may further exacerbate transfer shock.

Only a few studies have specifically investigated CS transfer students. One investigated the social experiences of CS transfer students at the University of Central Florida [19]. The study measured relationships between students' self-reported social engagement in school and their graduating GPA, finding that transfer students appear to engage in social and academic experiences less than native students and that students who engaged less tended to have lower GPAs after transferring. A second considered the pathways that community college students take to pursue CS, finding that pathways are diverse, complex, and challenging, and that completion of bachelor's degrees in CS was rare [11]. A companion report found that community college students struggled to prepare for transfer when considering CS transfer pathways, and have limited knowledge of how to apply CS concepts and prepare for careers [16]. Another study reported on a cohort-based transfer program, which allowed students to complete a bachelor's degree in CS in three years [22]. The study found strong transfer and graduation rates, as well as successful employment post-graduation.

These studies, however, have not focused on the specific experiences that transfer students have once they have transferred, leaving gaps in our understanding of factors that may prevent successful graduation. We asked two questions that address these gaps: **1) What are the social and academic experiences of CS transfer students? 2) How do the social and academic experiences of CS transfer students differ from native students?**

To answer these questions, we surveyed transfer and native students, and interviewed transfer students.

2 THEORETICAL FRAMEWORK

We framed this study from the perspectives of Student Involvement Theory, and Social and Cultural Capital, following a similar framing as prior work on transfer students [12, 13, 21].

The first theory is Student Involvement Theory [1], a developmental theory about higher education that attempts to explain how environmental influences impact student development [1]. It defines involvement as *the quantity and quality of physical and psychological energy that the student devotes to the academic experience*. In this model, students have personal characteristics when they enter an institution that interact with the affordances of the institutional environment. An institution's programs, policies, faculty, peers, and educational experiences to which the student is exposed can influence student development, but only to the extent to which students devote physical and psychological energy in learning. In this theory, student involvement is on a continuum of both quantity and quality. This theory states that greater student involvement in college translates to greater development and learning, while also recognizing that students have a finite amount of time and *quality* of involvement is important. The conceptual work of Astin [1] and others suggests that four types of influences need to be considered to understand the relationship between students and their institutional environments: 1) pre-college characteristics relating to student student demographics, 2) organizational or structural characteristics of the institution(s), 3) students' academic experiences, 4) students' nonacademic experiences (e.g. social) [25].

The second part of our theoretical framework related to social and cultural capital. Social capital is "the aggregate of the actual or potential resources which are linked to possession of a durable network of more or less institutionalized relationships of mutual acquaintance and recognition" [3, 27]. It states that investment in social relations can provide an advantage or expected returns [15]. People can benefit from social capital by using it to facilitate information flow, influence others through social ties, validate credentials, and reinforce identity. Transfer students may use social capital to connect with study groups, leverage tutoring resources, and feel included in a CS department's community, all of which may feed back into deeper engagement and learning. Related to social capital is *cultural capital*. For this study, cultural capital refers to how different cultural contexts can impact unequal scholastic achievement [3, 27]. Cultural capital can help explain how internalized values, attitudes, norms, and beliefs that stem from individual and societal cultures can influence stratification that occurs within an educational institution. Prior work has shown that a lack of

related cultural identity or connection can hinder STEM students of color [7, 24] and that adversarial relationships within school culture can limit future work opportunities for graduates [30].

3 METHOD: SURVEY & INTERVIEW

We surveyed and interviewed native and transfer students at the University of Washington, Seattle. We will refer to this university as *UW* throughout the rest of this paper.

3.1 Setting: Large public 4-yr research univ.

UW is a large public 4-year research university in the United States. The campus is located in an urban environment near a large technology hub. During the 2017-2018 school year, 18% (1511 out of 8285) of incoming students were transfer students. Among the incoming transfer student population, 86.7% (1310 out of 1511) of students transferred from a community college in the state. Admittance to UW is moderately competitive, with 40.6% (2307 out of 5683) of the transfer student applicants being admitted. During the 2017-2018 school year, 44.1% of undergraduate students identified as Caucasian, 24.1% as Asian American, 7.4% as Hispanic/Latino, 3.9% as African-American, 1.3% as American Indian/Alaska Native, and 0.9% as Native Hawaiian/Pacific Islander [23].

Admittance into UW does not guarantee admittance to a major unless an applicant applies for and is accepted directly into a department. If a student does not begin their enrollment with a declared major, their major status is denoted as "pre-major." Students may apply for intended major(s) during application periods. Majors at UW are either *open*, *minimum*, *capacity-constrained*, or *mixed*. Open majors can be declared at any time by students in good standing. Minimum majors can be declared at any time by students who have completed a set of prerequisite courses with a minimum GPA. Capacity-constrained majors require that students complete a set of prerequisite courses to be eligible to apply. Applicants to capacity-constrained majors compete for a limited number of spaces. Mixed majors have requirements based on in-major concentration.

For the 2017-18 class, the ten most popular majors were capacity-constrained. This major system is a frequent restriction on students' ability to study desired disciplines and is a commonly cited reason for student frustration. CS, the most popular first-choice major since 2016, admits about one-third of applicants. The majority of CS students are admitted through this process, but most transfer students are admitted through transfer direct admission, and are generally high performing students at their previous institution.

Transfer students who are admitted into the major are encouraged to attend university-wide and department-level orientations. Since the 2016-2017 school year, the CS department offers a short quarter-long *transfer seminar* for incoming transfer students. The seminar provides information about campus and department resources, focused on assisting with transfer student adjustment. Transfer students also commonly meet with academic advisors who assist with course planning and general college preparation.

Regarding the positioning of authors to transfer students, the first author was an undergraduate transfer student majoring in CS at the time of the study. They also helped develop the curriculum of the transfer seminar before beginning the study. Their data was not used in the study. The second author was a native Ph.D. student in a different department than CS, and the third author was an Associate Professor with adjunct appointment to the CS department.

3.2 Survey: adapted from L-TSQ

The goal of our survey was to reach a representative sample of the CS student population at UW. Following our theoretical framework, we adapted our survey instrument from the Laanan's Transfer Student Questionnaire (L-TSQ) (Appendix A of [21], [14]), a survey framed within Student Involvement Theory [1]. The L-TSQ measures transfer students' academic and social adjustment as a function of four stages of perceptions and experiences: 1) background, 2) previous institutions, 3) transfer process, and 4) current university [2, 12, 14]. Within these stages are 18 factors that measure academic and social involvement, perceptions, and details relating to different stages of the transfer process. Because of limited sample size, we relied on the factor analysis of Laanan et al. 2010 to map questions to factors, and factors to stages (Figure 1, Appendix B of [14]).

The *background* stage asked about mother and fathers' education and parental income, and motivations for transferring spanning two factors: *Motivations for transfer* and *Reasons for transfer*. The *previous institution* stage considered experiences with coursework and learning at the transfer student's previous institution. It contained two factors: *Experiences with general courses at previous institution* and *Course learning at previous institution*. The *transfer process* stage had four factors: *Experiences with academic counselors at previous institutions*, *Experiences with faculty at previous institutions*, *Perceptions of the transfer process*, and *Learning and study skills at previous institutions*. The *current university* stage considered six factors relating to perceptions, learning, and experiences at the current university: *General perceptions of the university*, *General perceptions of faculty*, *Satisfaction with the university environment*, *Experiences with faculty at UW*, *Course learning at UW*, and *Stigma as transfer student*. Because this stage relates to both native and transfer students, all respondents responded to these questions.

We also included questions from the L-TSQ about academic adjustment (difficulty of adjustment, experiencing an initial dip in GPA) and social adjustment (difficulty of adjustment, making friends). At the end of the survey, we included three free response prompts that we developed which asked students to discuss factors that contributed to their adjustment, advice that they would give to others, and information that the survey may have not asked about. We asked these questions to capture additional details about student involvement and social and cultural capital.

Because the CS major generally (but not always) admitted students after their 2nd year, and we were interested in students' experiences in the major, our inclusion criteria for participation required that students had been in the major for at least one quarter term and had taken at least one upper-division CS course.

We worked with the CS department's academic advisors to obtain the email addresses of students eligible for the study. This resulted in a list of 930 students. We then sent a recruitment email inviting participants over the age of 18 to complete the survey within the next five weeks. We distributed the survey twice, at the beginning of the fall and winter quarters of the 2017-18 school year. During each distribution period, we sent two additional emails to remind students of the survey. We solicited across two quarters to include

incoming students for the new school year who were not initially contacted in the fall.

Out of the 930 students we contacted, we received 160 survey responses, for a response rate of 17.2%. Of those contacted, 88 were transfer students, with 25 responding, for a response rate of 28.4%.

3.3 Interviews with transfer students

To help interpret the survey data, transfer students who responded to the survey were invited to participate in semi-structured interviews. We conducted interviews with 8 of the 25 students contacted.

We grouped our final interview questions by categories we adapted from the *current university* stage of the L-TSQ survey. We asked about course engagement, engaging with faculty, perceptions of the department culture, and the adjustment process. We conducted interviews remotely and in-person. Prior to the interview, we informed participants of the study objectives and the content of the questions. We also informed participants that they could skip any questions and that the interview would be recorded. Interviews lasted about 30 minutes each, and were audio recorded and later transcribed. We used the factors from the survey to classify responses to the interview; this was straightforward, as we had structured the interview around the factors in the survey. We then compared transfer and native students' responses to *current university*, academic and social adjustment, and free-response questions.

4 RESULTS: STAGES OF TRANSFER EXP.

We organized our results by the four stages of the L-TSQ which considered student involvement and human capital at sequential stages of the transfer process. At each stage, we combined our quantitative and qualitative data.

4.1 Background: older, lower SES

The first stage of the survey was background, which included personal factors about students' lives. Table 1 shows a summary of these factors, comparing native and transfer students.

Only 28% of transfer students came from households with income over $80,000, compared to 68% of native students. Transfer students' parents tended to have less college education, with 44% of transfer students being first generation college students. Native students were twice as likely to have 2 parents with Bachelor's degrees (74%). Nearly all respondents identified as white or Asian, with only 4% of transfer students and 3% of native students identifying as a member of an underrepresented minority group, consistent with the ethnic demographics of the CS department (as reported by academic counselors).

Transfer student were older, with 64% being older than 21, compared to only 9% of native student. Only about half of transfer students lived within walking distance of campus, compared to at least 78% of native students. This age disparity may also explain why 36% of transfer students identified as financially independent, compared to only 5% of native students.

Transfer students' motivations and reasons for attending their new university largely related to job prospects for transferring: 72% agreed that getting a good job was a motivation for transferring to this university whereas only 40% were motivated to transfer because of admission to graduate or professional schools.

Table 1: Demographics of native and transfer students

variable	student type label	transfer (n=25)	native (n=135)
gender identity	male	84%	60%
	female	16%	38%
age group	18-19 years old	16%	30%
	20-21 years old	20%	59%
	22-23 years old	20%	9%
	24-28 years old	20%	0%
	29 years or older	24%	0%
parent's education	first-generation (0 parents w/ BA)	44%	13%
	one parent w/ BA	20%	13%
	two parents w/ BA	36%	73%
parents' household income	less than $20,000	4%	5%
	20,000–39,999	8%	4%
	40,000–59,999	12%	10%
	60,000–79,999	8%	6%
	$80,000 or more	28%	63%
	student is independent	36%	5%
matriculation	transfer from 2 yr	92%	
	transfer from 4 yr	8%	
place of residence	university housing	0%	33%
	non-university housing within walking distance	40%	39%
	non-university housing not walking distance	48%	10%
	with parents or relatives	8%	14%
	fraternity or sorority	4%	4%
ethnicity (some identified as multiethnic)	White (non-hispanic)	60%	41%
	Asian/ Pacific Islander	48%	61%
	African American	4%	0%
	Hispanic or Latinx	0%	2%
	Native American or Alaskan Native	0%	1%
standing at time of survey	1st yr undergrad	0%	1%
	2nd yr undergrad	4%	16%
	3rd yr undergrad	44%	39%
	4th yr undergrad	48%	41%
	5th yr undergrad	0%	1%
	graduated (BA)	4%	1%
	5th yr joint BA/Masters	0%	1%
overall GPA	median	3.61	3.74
	range	2.5-3.9	3.0-4.0

4.2 Previous institutions: felt well-prepared

When describing their activities at previous institutions, transfer students reported high engagement. Of the transfer students, 86% reported often or very often trying to see how different facts and ideas fit together, 84% often or very often considered practical applications of their knowledge. They tended to engage with their peers, with 84% of them often or very often trying to explain materials to friends and 72% often or very often participating in class discussion. About 40% of transfer students reported that the coursework at their previous institution often or very often involved working on a paper or project that integrated ideas from various sources, but 40% reported *never* doing so.

Most transfer students felt their previous institutions' coursework prepared them for being a CS major (76% agree) and for the academic standards at UW (68% agree). They felt that previous coursework developed their critical thinking skills (92% agree) and was intellectually challenging (76% agree), but they were in less agreement about whether coursework required extensive reading and writing (52% agree). When engaging with the course material, transfer students tried to draw connections and interact with peers. These sentiments were reflected in responses: "The quality of the teachers at my previous college for CS were amazing and helpful in getting me where I am today." Those who felt less prepared thought their previous courses were not challenging: "I feel like the courses at my previous college were a bit too easy, making me feel like I'm a little behind from everyone else in my [current] classes."

4.3 Transfer process: resourceful and confident

Transfer students reported overall confidence in their learning and study skills, reflecting the social capital they accrued at their previous institutions. When asked how academic experiences at their previous institutions provided the skills needed for their new university, transfer students were most confident in problem solving skills (76% agree) and writing skills (72% agree) and least confident in reading (56% agree) and research skills (56% agree).

Transfer students were divided about the effectiveness of the academic counselors at their previous institution, with only 48% finding them helpful. Only 32% of students reported meeting with academic counselors regularly, but they often did discuss transferring (76% agree). In contrast, 64% of students also spoke with counselors at their new university, and 80% of students researched various aspects of their new university to get a better understanding of the environment and academic expectations. This data suggests that transfer students consulted with multiple sources to understand the transfer process, although they may have had concerns with the helpfulness of the information they received.

Relationships with faculty at previous institutions were informal and comfortable, with 80% of transfer students often or very often approaching faculty outside of class and 68% often or very often meeting with them informally before or after class. Students tended not to discuss career aspirations (32% did so often or very often), instead speaking about course related topics.

4.4 University experience: a sense of inclusion

Our richest data, and the core focus of this paper, concerned the 4th stage in our framework, *university experience*. We analyzed transfer student interviews to supplement survey data. We discuss the factors that notably impacted student experiences regarding course learning, experiences with faculty members, general perceptions of UW and its CS culture, adjustment process, and college satisfaction. We included quotes from survey and interview responses.

4.4.1 Perceptions of UW Culture. Overwhelmingly, transfer students had positive general perceptions of UW, as they would recommend the university to another transfer student (92% agree) and would have selected the same university had they done their transfer process all over again (84% agree).

Culturally, every interview participant but one believed that students were highly collaborative and social within the department. Five participants described other students in the department as friendly and welcoming, as one participant explained:

> I've never gotten a cold shoulder from somebody or felt like I was bothering them. I think you might have a different reaction if you were in one of the general libraries... but in CS, especially because we have our own labs, it's easier to just turn to somebody next to you and ask them what they're working on.

Participants mentioned a strong culture of working together. One participant suggested that working in a group setting was a universal expectation among students due to difficult coursework.

Academically, interview participants were somewhat split on the competitive culture of the department and how much students cared about their grades. Three participants explicitly described students as "competitive" but had varying impressions of how that impacted them, ranging from "unhealthy" to "motivating". Three participants believed that most students cared a lot about their grades, while two described their peers as not caring. One common explanation for competition within the department was the presence of grading curves, which five participants mentioned, such as in this quote:

> The curves for one just set it up to be competitive. I mean, you feel the curve. It's kind of in a sense everyone against each other when you're graded on a curve.

Interview participants also talked about the competitive major system and its impact on academic culture as well. Multiple participants believed that because most students in the department had to work very hard in their courses to be able to enter the major, focus on grades carried over post-admittance.

4.4.2   College Satisfaction. While 76% of transfer students felt a sense of belonging at the university, only 56% felt that there was a sense of community on campus. They also tended *not* to feel stigmatized by others for being a transfer student, with only 8% perceiving that faculty underestimated them and 16% perceiving that other students underestimated them. Some (20%) agreed that there was a general stigma among students for starting at a community college.

Transfer students tended to be older, live further away from campus than native students, and many were financially independent from their parents, so they may not have spent as much time on campus with other students. This sentiment was echoed by all 4 interview participants who were older than typical native students (≥25 years old). They mentioned their age as a factor that impacted how they interacted with campus life. They found that they were less involved with social events and activities on-campus due to friends outside of the university, distance from younger students, and familial obligations. Despite less social engagement, they still felt as though the department had a friendly and welcoming culture.

Although most interview participant shared positive overall impressions of UW, one participant identified the competitive nature of UW (explained in 4.4.1) as detrimental:

> The competitive nature of UW that is one of the reasons that, as a student who actually wants to learn computer science in a positive way, I would *not* say UW is the best school. (emphasis added)

This interview participant went on to say that the prestige of UW was a source of this negative competitiveness, as students use the reputation as something to "brag about". Two other interview

participants mentioned the reputation of UW, with one finding that it helped enable access to research opportunities:

> UW is this big research school and it's nice to know that you already have an "in" as a student there. You can meet faculty and grad students... It's easier when you have a lot of people around doing a lot of cool things to network and find what you want to do.

Two participants specifically liked that UW was a major research institution. One participant explained:

> I think being at a university where there is a lot of really interesting research going on is pretty cool. I haven't had an opportunity to take advantage of that, but it's definitely something that I intend to do before I graduate. It's cool to know that there are people doing innovative, and cutting-edge work around you.

UW also afforded access to other opportunities, as four participants specifically mentioned the importance of career resources. One participant explained that despite not using the career resources available to them, simply having the opportunity was reassuring and motivating. Another described the significance of finding a job after graduating and the how UW supports that:

> It's great being able to go to a couple of career fairs every year and get experience talking to recruiters. Being able to talk with people you're trying to get a job from, that helps you. The interviewing workshops, stuff like that. The resume workshops. All that extra stuff that is non-course oriented. That stuff is all huge and I think [the CS department] does a great job of that.

Four participants were pleased with the resources available around campus, including study spaces, the department labs, and the university's recreation center.

4.4.3   Course Learning. Transfer students' involvement with courses at the university largely paralleled that at their previous institutions, with the exception of a decrease in participation in class discussion. Similar to what they did at their previous institutions, a majority of transfer students reported often or very often thinking about practical implications of what they were learning (96%), trying to explain materials to friends (88%) and trying to see how different ideas fit together (80%). There was a decrease in the frequency of participation in class discussion, with only 44% reporting that they often or very often participated at the university compared to the 72% that stated that they often or very often participated at their previous institution. Larger class sizes that do not afford discussion may explain this decrease in class participation.

Every interview participant but one described a strong motivation to attend course lectures. The remaining participant explained that they occasionally skipped lectures in favor of watching lecture recordings online. Many students cited difficulty of concepts and inability to learn content using textbooks alone as reasons why lectures were so important to them.

Fewer students attended office hours often. Reasons for infrequent attendance varied, including descriptions of office hours as "for specific questions" or a "last resort," while other students discussed inconvenience and inability due to scheduling.

Most students worked with their peers as a regular part of their study habits, although three of the eight participants mentioned a preference for independent study. One participant that studied alone explained that he initially worked with others when he first entered the major, but stopped once he became accustom to computer science coursework. Those who primarily worked in groups found it to be more helpful, as described by one participant:

> I've found that it's a lot more productive than trying to work it out by yourself. Typically if one person can figure out one part of the problem and another person can figure out another part, it gets done a lot faster and you're more likely to be correct about the answer.

4.4.4 Experiences with Faculty Members. Another difference between transfer students' experiences at their previous institution and UW was with faculty. Transfer students generally felt that faculty at UW were interested in students' development (84% agree), approachable (60% agree) and accessible (64% agree). Despite this, many transfer students reported not often engaging with faculty. Only 44% of transfer students reported often or very often approaching faculty at their current university outside of class, a sharp decrease from the 80% who reported doing so at their previous institution. Only 20% reported often or very often meeting informally before or after class with UW faculty, a decrease from the 68% who reported doing so at their previous institution. This general decrease in reported engagement with faculty may be because students consulted more so with other resources, such as other teaching staff or because of larger class sizes.

This decrease in reported engagement with faculty may not have been problematic, as every interview participant was satisfied with the overall teaching quality of faculty members and their experiences with them. Despite noting larger class sizes and professors seeming busy, participants all described faculty members as accommodating and accessible. One participant explained:

> Access to faculty has been really good here at UW. It was something I was wondering about when I was transferring in because usually classes at community colleges are 30 or 35 people maximum. But then you go to a class here where there might be over 100 people in one lecture hall and there are multiple sections taught by the same professor. So you would think that it would be harder to get in touch with professors, but I haven't found that to be the case at all. Every single one of my professors has had weekly office hours that are usually times that you can get to them.

Faculty members were perceived as high-achieving and intelligent by two participants. This impression of faculty members caused one participant to feel somewhat intimidated, although not enough so to deter interactions. Another participant felt as though the intelligence of faculty members detracted from their teaching:

> Some things [faculty] might think a student understands intuitively, because they understand it intuitively. I feel like they don't always explain... I might not understand intuitively what they're saying.

No participants found that faculty members were so inaccessible or intimidating that they avoided interactions with them, suggesting that transfer students are satisfied with their experiences with faculty despite reporting fewer interactions with them.

4.4.5 Adjustment Process. We identified common factors that interviewees cited when discussing social and academic adjustment.

The most commonly mentioned factor to impact social adjustment among interview participants was friendship, with all 8 participants mentioning friendship as a strong positive influence on their transfer process. Three participants discussed having friends who attended UW before transferring, which eased their transition. One participant found the social adjustment easy:

> I've been living near campus and working on campus for a few years before coming here. I live with a bunch of students. I already have a pretty large friend group outside of school with people who are in other majors. Besides the academics, there wasn't much more of an adjustment to be made. I've been living in this house for a few years and I'm 5 minutes away from campus so I already have my life and it hasn't really changed much besides different academics.

Interview participants noted making new friends after transferring. They found this process relatively easy, although one participant noted challenges with finding a study group:

> Sometimes there are people that are just in their own study group and they don't want other people in their study group. I actually ran across that. I asked someone if I could join their study group and they weren't positive towards that.

While most participants sought out and found friendships, they each had various motivations for making friends and explanations for why friendship was helpful. One participant mentioned that friendship helped ease loneliness and stress; another participant recalled friendship being helpful while he was still at his community college. Most participants described finding friendships within the department, but participants also mentioned meeting others through extracurricular activities, such as clubs and athletics, and communities like campus fraternities and sororities.

Academically, increased difficulty of coursework was a common factor among participants. Some participants felt as though they did not know how large the gap in difficulty between their previous college and UW would be, and all but one participants described a significant increase in challenge upon transferring. Often, this shift in coursework and grading was a primary drawback on adjustment; one participant explained that he ultimately quit his job:

> When I got here the classes were a lot harder and the grading was much more intense. It was almost by a factor of two or something. The difference was big. Big enough that I decided that I needed to stop working, just to focus on school... I think adjusting for me was mostly about stepping up to this intense grading system.

Three participants noted the impact of commuting on their academic adjustment. Commuting made it harder for participants to work with others and access resources such as office hours. Participants cited commute times of up to 1.5 hours. One participant, after describing commuting as taking time away from his family, stated:

> I think one of the things as a transfer student is that being a commuter makes things a little more difficult. The amount of time you have to spend commuting is an added challenge on top of school. I would say that commuting is probably the number one thing there.

Another student noted how commuting impacted collaboration:

> I feel like there is a big culture of people working together to understand material. In some ways, I feel like that's a good thing, and in other ways I feel like that's not really fair to a lot of students. If you work by yourself, you won't understand as much as if you work with other students. If you commute, you can't work with other students.

Two participants mentioned having to adapt to large class sizes. Although neither participant believed that large classes were significantly problematic or could be helped, one participant described how this impacted their relationship with faculty members:

I don't really interact with professors that much outside of class, when I did that a lot in community college. But we had smaller classes and the professor gets to know you inside of class so it's easier to talk to them outside of class. That's not something that necessarily happens at UW for me. So maybe the reason why I'm not going to seek out professors outside of class is because I already feel like I'm a stranger to them when meanwhile at community college I was always having a lot of interactions with professors.

One interview participant, who transferred to UW but did not directly transfer into CS, found that stress caused by the competitive major system impacted his adjustment process. He explained the stress of not immediately gaining admission into the CS major:

Had I been a direct admit, or direct transfer, I would have avoided all this stress from going to UW for a while and not getting in, and having to take engineering "weeder" classes. But it seemed like something too risky for me, because I know how few direct transfers actually get into the department. To me, it seems like the less risky of the two things. I would have avoided a lot of stress, though.

One participant discussed department advisors as having an impact on their academic adjustment, being particularly responsive and positive during times of distress.

4.5 Transfer versus native student experiences

We compared the experiences of transfer and native students both quantitatively and qualitatively.

We used a Wilcoxon rank sum test with continuity correction [26] to determine if there was a significant difference between native and transfer student responses for 6 underlying factors related to university experience and for academic adjustment and social adjustment. We used a Holm correction for the 8 factors we compared to account for Type I error with repeated testing [10]. We found no significant difference between responses to any of the factors relating to university experience or for social adjustment. We found a significant difference in response relating to academic adjustment, $p < 0.001$. We can interpret the test statistic $U = 8511.5$ as *Common Language* (CL) effect size by dividing the test statistic U by the product of the sample sizes of the non-parametric test [5, 8]. We can interpret the test statistic to say there is 68% chance that a random native student response reflects easier academic adjustment than a random transfer student response.

We conducted a post-hoc analysis on the 2 questions that make up the academic adjustment factor. These questions asked students to indicate the extent to which they agreed with the following statements: Q1) Adjusting to the academic standards or expectations at UW has been easy; Q2) I experienced a dip in grades (GPA) during my first semester at UW (question was reverse-coded). For Q1, we again used a Wilcoxon rank sum test and found a significant difference in responses between student types ($p < 0.001$). We interpreted the test statistic $U = 2155.5$ as a CL effect size to say that there is a 69% chance that a random native student more so felt that the adjustment to academic standards at UW was easy when compared to a random transfer student. For Q2, we find a significant difference of $p < 0.0001$. We interpreted the test statistic $U = 2417$ to say that there is a 78% chance that a random transfer student more so felt that they experienced a dip in their GPA the first term at UW when compared to a random native student. We reported on these results in the top half of Table 2.

This perceived difference in academic adjustment led us to compare self-reported cumulative GPAs of transfer and native students to understand if perceptions matched performance. The median self-reported GPA of transfer student respondents (3.60) was less than the median for native students (3.74), and the range of GPAs was wider and lower for transfer students even though there were far more native student respondents (see Table 1). We found a significant difference between reported GPAs of different student types ($p < 0.01$), interpreting $U = 2017.5$ to say that there is a 60% chance that a random native student reported a greater GPA than a random transfer student. This difference may be confounded by the fact that transfer students started later in the undergraduate degree and may have been taking more advanced and difficult courses than native student respondents who were only in their 1st and 2nd years.

Making direct comparisons between GPAs is difficult because there are different grading criteria in different courses. Assuming that students take similar courses in similar years, we compared to GPAs of students by current standing. Because almost all transfer student respondents were the equivalent of 3rd or 4th year undergraduates (92%, see Table 1), we only compared 3rd and 4th year undergraduates. After a Holm correction for repeated tests, we found that there was a significant difference between 3rd year undergraduates ($p < 0.05$). Interpreting $U = 374.5$, we can say that there is a 75% chance that a random "3rd year" transfer student had a lower GPA than a random 3rd year native student (see bottom half of Table 2). Still, GPA is cumulative, so coursework from previous years affected 3rd year native students' GPAs. Although GPAs were difficult to interpret because of varying coursework between student types, we do find a difference in GPAs between student types. Figure 1 shows the difference in distribution between transfer and native students' GPAs by number of quarters in the CS major.

Table 2: Statistical tests on academic adjustment and GPA.
* **denotes** $p < 0.05$, ** **denotes** $p < 0.01$. *** **denotes** $p < 0.001$.

comparison	p-value	U	num. responses transfer	native
factor: academic adjustment	0.00030***	8511.5	48	260
Q1: academic adj. has been easy	0.0016*	2155.5	24	130
Q2: GPA dip 1st term	0.000019***	2417	24	130
reported GPA	0.0016**	2017.5	22	129
reported GPA: 3rd yr	0.013*	374.5	10	50

To further compare transfer and native students, we analyzed free response questions. We found that in nearly all respects, native and transfer students responded with similar sentiments. Both groups cited friendships and study groups as key factors during adjustment and also encouraged other students to seek out peers. Both groups gave advice of working hard and various studying tips. Both groups mentioned using the department advisors as a resource, and cited specific faculty as benefitting their experience.

Two clear sentiments that differed between native and transfer students relate to the transfer seminar and job/internship searches. Transfer students identified the transfer seminar as a factor that contributed to their successful adjustment, mentioning that it helped

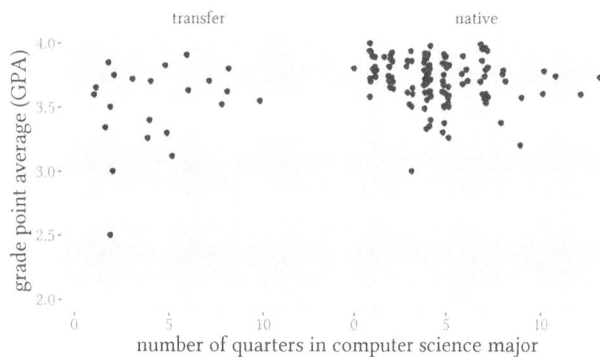

Figure 1: GPAs for native and transfer students by quarters in computer science major. The distributions of GPAs are different, but transfer and native students have different starting points (quarter 0), so direct comparisons are difficult.

them develop friendships and a community early on. Transfer students also discussed career planning and goals at a noticeably higher rate than native students: only three native students (2%) described seeking internships, while six of the 25 transfer students (24%) discussed thinking about internships early and using university resources to prepare for the job search. The importance of job opportunities to transfer students repeatedly appeared in the data.

5 DISCUSSION: FACTORS TO ADJUSTMENT

Our results showed that transfer students at UW were diverse:

- Many were first generation (44%).
- About 2 out of 3 were 21 years or older.
- About 2 out of 3 came from lower socioeconomic backgrounds or were financially independent.
- At least half lived further away from campus.
- Job opportunity was a major factor in their transfer decision.
- They generally felt satisfied with UW, a sense of belonging.
- They felt comfortable interacting with faculty and other students despite mentioning multiple barriers to social engagement (e.g. longer commutes, familial obligations).
- Multiple resources that UW offered (transfer seminar, counselors, career resources) helped their transfer process.

Despite confidence that their previous institutions prepared them well, transfer students still perceived greater difficulty in academic adjustment and had lower GPAs than native students.

There are many ways to interpret these findings. We sampled a self-selected subset of transfer and native students at UW, so this sample may not be representative. Comparing to the demographics of UW's CS department, we found that we ended up with an ethnically proportional sample of respondents, but slightly (+10%) oversampled students who identified as female. We only interviewed 8 (<10% of total) transfer students in UW CS. We also found no significant differences in UW experiences despite a difference in perceived academic adjustment, so the L-TSQ may not have been an appropriate survey instrument to detect differences that might have existed. Due to features unique to UW and its CS department, the generalizability of these results may be limited. Despite potential

questions of respresentativeness, we triangulated across prior work, the L-TSQ, and interviews to identify trends.

Differences in cultural experiences between transfer and native students may be explained by differences in student attributes and preexisting capital. While some transfer students frequently engaged with the UW community, others noted age differences, long commute times, and familial commitments as barriers to engagement. For some, this may not have been an issue, due to short transfer distances and maintained friendships throughout the transfer process that provided preexisting capital. Indeed, most transfer students came from nearby institutions (<1 hr drive from UW, with at least 9 coming from institutions within 20 mins) and were older than native students, so they may have had social and cultural capital outside of the UW community. This may explain why 20% of transfer student respondents reported a feeling of belonging but *not* a feeling of community at UW.

Transfer students overwhelmingly felt that courses from their previous institution prepared them well, but also noted difficulty in academic adjustment. This may suggest that they were not well-informed about the transfer process. Less than half of transfer students found their previous academic advisors helpful and at least 1/3 of transfer students did not speak with UW counselors or visit UW campus before transferring. Many transfer students may have relied on researching information on their own, as 70% reported doing. Future work should further investigate resources to better inform and support the transfer process, such as a cohort-based model from community colleges to 4 year universities [22].

Our data also suggests that UW's CS department buffered students against even worse transfer shock. Transfer students found many of UW's resources helpful to their adjustment, including the transfer seminar, advisors, career resources, orientation, and cultural centers. Some students were reassured by the presence of resources even if they did not use them.

UW resources were not able to support all transfer students, as one transfer student respondent noted: "[the CS department] has done a good job of recruiting women and being inclusive but until [the CS department] does the same for underserved minorities (particularly black and latino students), tech will continue to be plagued with race/ethnic diversity issues and perpetuate the heightened feelings of imposter syndrome that these demographics feel." Interpreted in the lens of cultural capital, this lack of related cultural identity between students and faculty can hinder STEM students of colors, as prior literature has found [7, 24]. So while providing resources and opportunities to support transfer students is important, having a culture that connects with first-generation students and students across broad ranges of ethnicities, ages, socioeconomic statuses, and geographical locations may also support transfer student adjustment.

6 ACKNOWLEDGEMENTS

We have archived materials at:
https://github.com/codeandcognition/archive-2018icer-kwik.

This material is based upon work supported by the National Science Foundation under Grant No. 1703304, 1735123, 1314399, and 12566082.

REFERENCES

[1] Alexander W Astin. 1999. Student Involvement: A Developmental Theory for Higher Education. *Journal of College Student Development* 40, 5 (1999), 13.

[2] Peter Riley Bahr, Christie Toth, Kathryn Thirolf, and Johanna C. Massé. 2013. *A Review and Critique of the Literature on Community College Students' Transition Processes and Outcomes in Four-Year Institutions.* Vol. 28. Springer, Netherlands, 459–511. https://doi.org/10.1007/978-94-007-5836-0_10

[3] Pierre Bourdieu. 1986. *The forms of capital.* Greenwood, Connecticut, 241–258.

[4] Brent D Cejda. 1997. An examination of transfer shock in academic disciplines. *Community College Journal of Research and Practice* 21, 3 (1997), 279–288.

[5] R. N. Conroy. 2012. What hypotheses do âĂIJnonparametricâĂİ two-group tests actually test? *Stata Journal* 12, 2 (2012), 182–190.

[6] Patricia E Diaz. 1992. Effects of transfer on academic performance of community college students at the four-year institution. *Community/Junior College Quarterly of Research and Practice* 16, 3 (1992), 279–291.

[7] Lorelle Espinosa. 2011. Pipelines and Pathways: Women of Color in Undergraduate STEM Majors and the College Experiences That Contribute to Persistence. *Harvard Educational Review* 81, 2 (Jun 2011), 209–241. https://doi.org/10.17763/haer.81.2.92315ww157656k3u

[8] Robert J. Grissom and John J. Kim. 2012. *Effect Sizes for Research: Univariate and Multivariate Applications, Second Edition.* Routledge, London.

[9] John R Hills. 1965. Transfer shock: The academic performance of the junior college transfer. *The Journal of Experimental Education* 33, 3 (1965), 201–215.

[10] Sture Holm. 1979. A Simple Sequentially Rejective Multiple Test Procedure. *Scandinavian Journal of Statistics* 6, 2 (1979), 65âĂŞ70.

[11] Shanna Jaggars, John Fink, and Jeffrey Fletcher. 2016. *A longitudinal analysis of community college pathways to computer science bachelor's degrees.* Technical Report. Google.

[12] Frankie Santos Laanan. 2004. STUDYING TRANSFER STUDENTS: PART I: INSTRUMENT DESIGN AND IMPLICATIONS. *Community College Journal of Research and Practice* 28, 4 (Apr 2004), 331–351. https://doi.org/10.1080/10668920490424050

[13] Frankie Santos Laanan. 2007. Studying Transfer Students: Part II: Dimensions of Transfer Students' Adjustment. *Community College Journal of Research and Practice* 31, 1 (Jan 2007), 37–59. https://doi.org/10.1080/10668920600859947

[14] Frankie Santos Laanan, Soko S. Starobin, and Latrice E. Eggleston. 2010. Adjustment of Community College Students at a Four-Year University: Role and Relevance of Transfer Student Capital for Student Retention. *Journal of College Student Retention: Research, Theory & Practice* 12, 2 (Aug 2010), 175–209. https://doi.org/10.2190/CS.12.2.d

[15] Nan Lin, Karen S. Cook, and Ronald S. Burt. 2001. *Social Capital: Theory and Research.* Transaction Publishers, New Jersey.

[16] Louise Ann Lyon and Jill Denner. 2016. Student perspectives of community college pathways to computer science bachelor's degrees.

[17] Jennifer Ma and Sandy Baum. 2016. *Trends in community colleges: Enrollment, prices, student debt, and completion.* Technical Report. College Board.

[18] Jane Margolis and Allan Fisher. 2003. *Unlocking the clubhouse: Women in computing.* MIT press, Cambridge, MA.

[19] Lisa Massi, Patrice Lancey, Uday Nair, Rachel Straney, Michael Georgiopoulos, and Cynthia Young. 2012. Engineering and computer science community college transfers and native freshmen students: Relationships among participation in extra-curricular and co-curricular activities, connecting to the university campus, and academic success. In *Frontiers in Education Conference (FIE), 2012.* IEEE, IEEE, New York, 1–6.

[20] Jacqueline C McNeil, Matthew W Ohland, and Russell A Long. 2016. Entry pathways, academic performance, and persistence of nontraditional students in engineering by transfer status. In *Frontiers in Education Conference (FIE).* IEEE, IEEE, IEEE, 1–7.

[21] Kristin M. Moser. 2012. *Redefining transfer student success: Transfer capital and the Laanan-transfer students' questionnaire (L-TSQ) revisited.* Ph.D. Dissertation. Iowa State University. https://search.proquest.com/docview/1022973592/abstract/3A54323230EC4F85PQ/1

[22] Sathya Narayanan, Kathryn Cunningham, Sonia Arteaga, William J. Welch, Leslie Maxwell, Zechariah Chawinga, and Bude Su. 2018. Upward Mobility for Underrepresented Students: A Model for a Cohort-Based Bachelor's Degree in Computer Science. In *Proceedings of the 49th ACM Technical Symposium on Computer Science Education (SIGCSE '18).* ACM, New York, NY, USA, 705–710. https://doi.org/10.1145/3159450.3159551

[23] University of Washington Office of Academic Data Management. 2017. Quick Stats of Student Enrollment | UW Student Data. https://studentdata.washington.edu/quick-stats/. "Accessed 6 June 2018".

[24] Maria Ong, Carol Wright, Lorelle Espinosa, and Gary Orfield. 2011. Inside the Double Bind: A Synthesis of Empirical Research on Undergraduate and Graduate Women of Color in Science, Technology, Engineering, and Mathematics. *Harvard Educational Review* 81, 2 (Jun 2011), 172–209. https://doi.org/10.17763/haer.81.2.t022245n7x4752v2

[25] Ernest T. Pascarella, Christopher T. Pierson, Gregory C. Wolniak, and Patrick T. Terenzini. 2004. First-Generation College Students: Additional Evidence on College Experiences and Outcomes. *The Journal of Higher Education* 75, 3 (2004), 249–284. https://doi.org/10.1353/jhe.2004.0016

[26] Judy Robertson and Maurits Kaptein. 2016. *Modern Statistical Methods for HCI.* Springer, New York, NY, USA.

[27] Soko S. Starobin, Dimitra Jackson Smith, and Frankie Santos Laanan. 2016. Deconstructing the Transfer Student Capital: Intersect between Cultural and Social Capital among Female Transfer Students in STEM Fields. *Community College Journal of Research and Practice* 40, 12 (Dec 2016), 1040–1057. https://doi.org/10.1080/10668926.2016.1204964

[28] Margaret D Sullivan, Clemencia Cosentino de Cohen, Michael J Barna, Marisa K Orr, Russell A Long, and Matthew W Ohland. 2012. Understanding engineering transfer students: Demographic characteristics and educational outcomes. In *Frontiers in Education Conference (FIE), 2012.* IEEE, IEEE, New York, NY, USA, 1–6.

[29] Jennifer Wang, Sepehr Hejazi Moghadam, and Juliet Tiffany-Morales. 2017. Social Perceptions in Computer Science and Implications for Diverse Students. In *Proceedings of the 2017 ACM Conference on International Computing Education Research.* ACM, 47–55.

[30] Paul E. Willis. 1977. *Learning to Labor: How Working Class Kids Get Working Class Jobs.* Columbia University Press, New York, NY, USA. Google-Books-ID: 3zmVaLrGIDEC.

Decomposition:
A K-8 Computational Thinking Learning Trajectory

Kathryn M. Rich
Michigan State University
richkat3@msu.edu

T. Andrew Binkowski
University of Chicago
abinkowski@uchicago.edu

Carla Strickland
UChicago STEM Education
castrickland@uchicago.edu

Diana Franklin
UChicago STEM Education
dmfranklin@uchicago.edu

ABSTRACT

As new initiatives in computational thinking and computer science (CS/CT) are being developed and deployed, it is important to identify and understand the key concepts that are essential for student learning. In this study, we present the phases of construction of a learning trajectory (LT) for Decomposition in the context of CS/CT in K-8 education. From an extensive literature review, 63 learning goals representative of decomposition understanding and practices were identified and synthesized into 13 consensus goals. The focus of this paper is how relationships between these consensus goals were identified and used to place the goals into a learning trajectory. We discuss the theories and frameworks that guided the trajectory's construction as well as the methodology and justifications used to draw pathways through the trajectory in each phase. Finally, we discuss potential uses for the trajectory and suggest further explorations for decomposition in CS/CT.

CCS CONCEPTS

• **Social and professional topics** → **Computational thinking**; **K-12 education**; • **Applied computing** → **Education**;

KEYWORDS

Decomposition, Computational thinking, K-8

ACM Reference Format:
Kathryn M. Rich, T. Andrew Binkowski, Carla Strickland, and Diana Franklin. 2018. Decomposition: A K-8 Computational Thinking Learning Trajectory. In *ICER '18: 2018 International Computing Education Research Conference, August 13–15, 2018, Espoo, Finland*. ACM, New York, NY, USA, Article 4, 9 pages. https://doi.org/10.1145/3230977.3230979

1 INTRODUCTION

Decomposition is a fundamental skill in problem solving, as highlighted by the modularity subconcept in the programs and algorithms concept of both the K-12 CS Framework [13] and the CSTA K-12 CS Standards [3]. While these resources provide guidance

ICER '18, August 13–15, 2018, Espoo, Finland
© 2018 Association for Computing Machinery.
ACM ISBN 978-1-4503-5628-2/18/08...$15.00
https://doi.org/10.1145/3230977.3230979

on what students can understand or do at the end of grade bands, learning trajectories seek more detailed information about how such skills could be developed. There are many expected practices of decomposition in CS/CT, for example, breaking a large block of code into functional units [3, 13] or designing a game level-by-level [20, 34]. However, little is known about how these skills might develop incrementally, building from students' everyday experiences.

In this light, we ask the research question, "How can learning goals about decomposition expressed in separate research papers be used to construct a learning trajectory that will be useful to researchers and practitioners?" We present a learning trajectory (LT) for Decomposition and the methodology and approaches for its creation. In particular, we make the following contributions:

- Summarize the explicit and implicit ways that existing research sheds light on students' development of decomposition practices.
- Present an LT for Decomposition, explicating how we used existing research and educational theory across its several stages of development.
- Discuss several ways in which the completed LT might be used by researchers, curriculum developers, and practitioners to advance efforts in K-8 computer science education.

The rest of this paper is organized as follows. We begin by summarizing how decomposition has been studied in CS/CT education literature and presenting the theoretical frames that guided our work. We then present our synthesis of more than 60 independent decomposition-related learning goals articulated by other researchers into a representative set consensus goals. Next, we describe the construction of the Decomposition learning trajectory in four phases guided by different criteria: literature support, constructivist learning theory, computer science teaching pedagogy, and higher-level analysis of dimensions that emerged. Finally, we close with a discussion the various ways we believe the Decomposition trajectory can be used in future research and practice.

2 BACKGROUND

In this section, we review related work on decomposition and on learning trajectories. We also introduce several concepts and frameworks that guided our work.

2.1 Related Work: Decomposition

Standards [3], frameworks [13], and curricula [18] have included decomposition as an important idea, but much of the research on assessing and understanding how students learn CS concepts in K-8 has focused on the use of particular programming concepts such as loops, conditionals, variables, and initialization [14, 17, 37].

A few papers have focused specifically on decomposition. Franklin et al. [15] observed differences in how students decompose the steps to navigate a 2-d grid based on age and math skills, whereas Meerbaum-Salant, Armoni, and Ben-Ari [27] found that patterns students used in Scratch projects (bottom-up development and fine-grained programming) were at odds with accepted decomposition practices. Werner, Denner, and Campe [41] analyzed Scratch games, creating a Game Computational Sophistication measure, which has a relationship to the way students decomposed their games into code. Despite a relative lack of research *focused* on computer science decomposition, our literature search found 31 papers that had embedded learning goals related to decomposition.

The goal of this study is to take that body of work, with both its explicit and implicit treatments of student learning of decomposition, and use the embedded information and a theoretical framework to create a learning trajectory for Decomposition.

2.2 Related Work: Learning Trajectories

Simon [38] described a learning trajectory as "a prediction as to the path by which learning might proceed" (p. 135) via students' engagement in a particular activity. Several computer science education researchers have recently begun developing learning trajectories and progressions for CT-related ideas. Much of this work has used learning analytics or other forms of analysis of students' programming artifacts to detect patterns in student thinking [9, 10, 36, 37, 41]. The resulting LTs tend to address broad tasks and understandings, such as programming [9] and computational thinking as a whole [37]. In prior work, we created trajectories covering more specific components of CT: Sequence, Repetition, and Conditionals [32].

In order to develop LTs for a specific components of CT, including this LT for Decomposition, we took inspiration from work in mathematics education. Since the introduction of the LT construct in 1995, mathematics education researchers have developed and studied LTs for a number of specific mathematics topics, including spatial thinking [6], linear measurement [5], and equipartitioning [11]. When developing our methods for LT construction, we drew, in particular, from the work of Confrey, Maloney, and Corley [11], who developed a set of LTs by first clustering mathematics standards into trajectory clusters, then mapping each cluster onto empirical evidence of student learning drawn from their own research and other literature. We elaborate on how we adapted their process in the Methods section. A more thorough description is in [32].

2.3 Conceptual and Theoretical Background

As will be described futher in the Methods section, our process of creating an LT for Decomposition applied ideas from three theories and frameworks: constructivism, the Use, Modify, Create framework, and dimensions of disciplinary practices. We provide some background on each of these below.

2.3.1 Constructivism. Constructivism is a theory of knowledge that says all information is mediated through a recipient's prior knowledge and thus transformed as it is processed and integrated [1]. That is, learners do not simply receive knowledge, but rather *construct* it. According to constructivism, learning happens when experiences occur that are different than what is expected. These experiences cause disequilibrium that leads to adaptation [38]. Hence, pedagogy based in a constructivist perspective must always strive to take prior knowledge into account and consider how to introduce disequilibrium that results in adaptations to students' current knowledge. We applied constructivist ideas in the creation of our LT by placing the ideas closest to everyday knowledge we expect most students to possess near the start of the trajectory then building toward less familiar ideas. This gradual progression toward less familiar ideas is intended to help teachers and curriculum designers to strategically design activities that introduce manageable levels disequilibrium in students' understanding.

2.3.2 Use, Modify, Create. The Use, Modify, Create pedagogical approach was introduced by Lee et al. [22] as a way to scaffold and build students' ability to apply computing concepts to programming. Students begin by using programs that demonstrate the concept under investigation. Next they modify programs that use the concept in order to exercise their knowledge and explore more fully how the concept works. Finally, they create their own projects that incorporate the core ideas, requiring them to choose when the concept is appropriate and how to apply it. We applied the Use, Modify, Create pedagogical approach to the creation of our LT by placing goals related to using something created through decomposition first, followed by goals focused on the modification such a component, with goals focused on choosing when and how to create such components at the end.

2.3.3 Dimensions of Disciplinary Practices. We consider decomposition to be not only a content topic in computer science, but a disciplinary practice of computer science. As such, our work takes inspiration from work of researchers who have created learning progressions for practices in other disciplines. In Schwarz et al.'s [35] work on scientific modeling and Berland and McNeill's [8] work on scientific argumentation, the learning progressions are described not as a single sequence of levels of understanding, but as a set of dimensions of the practice. The dimensions of a practice are components that are related, but can develop separately. For example, Berland and McNeill's [8] dimensions of argumentation include the *argumentative product* and the *argumentative process*. Based on this prior work in progressions for scientific practices [8, 35], our methods for organizing existing knowledge about decomposition included attention to defining and connecting dimensions of the practice.

3 METHODS

We approached the creation of our Decomposition LT in three steps modeled after the work of Confrey, Maloney, and Corley [11]. First, we reviewed existing literature to identify learning goals. Next, we synthesized these goals to define a set of "stopping points" along our predicted learning path. We call these stopping points *consensus goals*. Third, we used information from the synthesized literature, as well as several conceptual frameworks, to make reasoned predictions about productive pathways students could follow through the consensus goals. Each of these steps is elaborated below.

3.1 Identifying Learning Goals

As a first step in trajectory building, Confrey, Maloney, and Corley [11] grouped a widely accepted set of grade-specific mathematics standards into "trajectory clusters" of related goals. In the absence of a widely accepted, grade-specific set of standards for CS/CT in grades K–8, we began our work by compiling a list of learning goals that had been discussed in extant computer science education literature. We searched the Educational Research Information Center database and the Special Interest Group in Computer Science Education (SIGCSE) and Innovation and Technology in Computer Science Education (ITiCSE) conference proceedings using keywords such as "computational thinking," "computer science domains," and "computer science pedagogy," with the additional signifiers "K–8," "K–5," and "K–12." We reviewed 108 scholarly articles that resulted from this search to identify learning goals (LGs) discussed by the researchers. This review produced 671 LGs. Further details about the review can be found in [31, 32]. Using keyword searches, we organized the LGs into clusters that related to particular CT topics. For the remainder of this paper, we focus on the cluster of LGs related to decomposition, which contained 63 LGs.

3.2 Synthesizing Consensus Goals

Our next step was to synthesize these 63 LGs into a manageable set of goals. The four authors of this paper, two with computer science expertise and two with curriculum development expertise, independently sorted the LGs into collections with common themes. Each of us articulated the themes as *consensus goals* (CGs), or statements intended to capture the consensus idea captured by the LGs in a collection. By comparing and discussing each others' sorts and CGs, we collaboratively came to agreement on a set of CGs that described the ideas captured in the cluster of decomposition LGs. This set of CGs served as the components of the LT to be connected in the next step.

3.3 Connecting Consensus Goals

With a set consensus goals defined, we next turned to defining pathways among the CGs. We defined these pathways by drawing arrows between pairs of CGs. Before describing our four heuristics for drawing arrows, we briefly describe our intended meaning for an arrow.

As noted above, Simon [38] describes a learning trajectory as a prediction about a possible learning pathway. As such, we conceptualize our arrows not as absolute dependencies among CGs, but rather as research- and theory-based predictions about how learning *could* proceed. Our aim is not to definitively prescribe the order or manner in which students learn content. Rather, we aim to apply existing knowledge from literature and existing conceptual frameworks to make reasonable suggestions that can guide curriculum design, teaching, differentiation, and assessment. However, we acknowledge that curricular order is a relationship between teachers, students, and the material. Students may take many different pathways, and even regress on our trajectory, as they develop their understanding [7, 19]. Likewise, teachers may have a different preference based on their understanding of the material.

With this overall aim in mind, we drew arrows between the consensus goals in four steps. First, we returned to the literature base

Table 1: Four LGs synthesized into one Decomposition CG

LG1	"[L]earn that the GUI is composed of different types of components". [29]
LG2	Break existing games into parts according to the types of computational thinking applied. [20]
LG3	"Identify the constituent elements of a system". [40]
LG4	Break "a story down into simple steps" at the appropriate "level of detail." [12]
CG	Systems are made up of smaller parts. (U)

to consider how evidence in the reviewed articles might suggest connections between CGs. This step was modeled after the work of Confrey, Maloney, and Corley [11] who, after organizing mathematics standards into trajectory clusters, mapped their clusters onto existing empirical research. However, because specific research on how student understanding of decomposition progresses is scant, this mapping could only serve as a starting point in articulating our pathways.

To further specify our trajectory, we next applied constructivist ideas to connect CGs into sequences that progressed from ideas we expect to be familiar to students toward less-familiar ideas. Then we applied Lee et al.'s [22] Use, Modify, Create framework to connect CGs. Lastly, we considered the dimensions of the practice of decomposition that were emerging from our work and drew arrows to connect and further define the dimensions. The Results section illustrates the application of each step.

4 RESULTS

We describe our results in five sections that illustrate how the trajectory grew in complexity across its development. First, we describe the 13 consensus goals we synthesized from the pool of learning goals. Next, we describe how we used the limited available evidence from the literature to draw the first arrows connecting the CGs. Finally, we describe how we used three different heuristics based in constructivism, the Use, Modify, Create framework, and practice dimensions, respectively, to further specify connections in the trajectory.

4.1 Consensus Goals

Sixty-three learning goals were used to create 13 consensus goals in the Decomposition trajectory. Detailed discussion of the literature support underlying every CG is beyond the scope of this article. Instead, we provide the full list of supporting LGs for two CGs, choosing examples that illustrate some of the interpretive aspects of our process. After these two examples, we list all 13 CGs in a single table along with one supporting LG for each.

Table 1 shows the four learning goals that were synthesized into the consensus goal, "Systems are made up of smaller parts." Quotation marks around text in the LGs indicate when the text was taken directly from the source articles. The U appearing after the text of the CG in the table indicates that this CG can be addressed with offline, or unplugged, activities.

Table 2: Six LGs synthesized into one Decomposition CG

LG1	Understand "the usefulness of modular code and how abstraction helps with modularity of code". [18]
LG2	"Remix and reuse resources" previously created. [2]
LG3	"Identify common patterns between older and newer problem-solving tasks". [2]
LG4	Use "built in functions". [33]
LG5	Use "built-in functions" when creating a program. [41]
LG6	Use "built-in methods". [30]
CG	Often existing code from other programs can be used to solve parts of a decomposed problem. (P)

The example in Table 1 illustrates the kinds of LGs used to support early goals in the trajectory. Within the CS-education literature, decomposition is typically discussed in terms of breaking apart *problems* or *tasks* into manageable parts [2, 4, 18, 26]. This idea is captured in a different CG in our Decomposition trajectory: "Complex *problems* can be broken into smaller parts." The CG shown in Table 1, "Systems are made up of smaller parts," represents a prerequisite to decomposition of a problem: understanding that many things in the world (not only problems) can be viewed as made up of parts. We chose "systems" as an umbrella term for these many things, from Weintrop et al. [40] (see LG3). As added support for the CG, we include LGs that suggest that students should identify parts within different examples of systems, including a GUI (LG1), a game (LG2), and a story (LG4).

Table 2 shows the six learning goals that were synthesized into the consensus goal, "Often existing code from other programs can be used to solve parts of a decomposed problem." The P appearing after the CG text in the table indicates that this is a programming-specific goal.

This example illustrates the way in which LGs were sometimes considered collectively, rather than individually, to form support for the CG. LG1 and LG2 directly support the CG because they directly address the utility of reusing code across programs. By contrast, LG3–LG6 support the CG collectively. On their own, they do not capture the idea in the CG. Identifying patterns, as noted in LG3, does not necessarily lead to reuse of code, and using a function or method, as in LG4–LG6, does not necessarily imply that the same code is being used for multiple purposes. However, when viewed collectively, LG3–LG6 capture the idea of matching a part of a current problem to a function used previously. This collective interpretation is close to the idea expressed in the CG.

All 13 CGs are shown in the first column in Table 3. The second column contains comments that help to differentiate the CGs from each other. The third column lists one learning goal from the literature we identified as support for the consensus goal. The final column lists the number of LGs that underlie the CG. Comparing the CGs to the example supporting LGs may help readers understand the manner in which we articulated big ideas from collections of specific student actions (the typical form of a learning goal in the literature). CGs that can be addressed through offline, or unplugged, activities are marked with a U in the table and shown in grey in the figures that follow. Programming-specific goals are marked with a P

and shown in white. Further information about the relationships among these CGs is included in the sections that follow, which detail how we connected the CGs into a trajectory.

4.2 Literature-Supported Connections

Figure 1 shows a subset of the decomposition consensus goals, connected with six arrows. In the text below, we describe how we used evidence from the literature to draw these six arrows.

Arrow 1a. In the K-6 CT framework posed by Angeli et al. [2], the act of breaking down a problem is identified as appropriate for students in K-2. By contrast, the act of assembling a solution from parts is identified as appropriate for students in grades 3-4. The authors of the framework therefore advocate a progression from top-down decomposition of a problem to bottom-up assembly of a solution. We used this information to draw an arrow from "Problem decomposition is a useful early step in problem solving." to "Often existing code from other programs can be used to solve parts of a decomposed problem." This arrow represents a transition from generalized, offline problem solving to specifically applying decomposition skills to programming.

Arrow 1b. In a five-day introductory course on parallel programming for fifth graders, Gregg, Tychonievich, Cohoon, and Hazelwood [16] used the pedagogical design of presenting students with sample projects to use as a basis or model for new projects: "Because this course was the first time most of the students had seen any programming language at all, we decided to provide a scaffolding in the form of example programs that they could look at and modify" (p. 54). At the end of the five day course, students enthusiastically presented projects that they had created either from scratch or by significantly modifying an example program. This result suggested the utility of asking students to modify code for particular purposes before using modified code as part of the solution to a broader problem. Thus, we used this information to draw an arrow from "Sometimes it is useful to modify and repurpose existing code." to the capstone goal, "Decomposition and modularization are useful in problem solving." Note that the capstone CG is designated as an unplugged goal to indicated that it is not exclusively about programming. After students have learned how to apply decomposition ideas in a programming context, they can learn to apply those skills to problems that are not exclusively computational in nature.

Arrows 1c and 1d. In her proposed chain of cognitive accomplishments students might go through during programming instruction, Linn [24] described the development of a collection of templates, or "stereotypic patterns of code using more than a single language feature" (p. 16), as an accomplishment that comes before the reuse of those templates. We see the recognition of patterns of code as stereotypic as akin to realizing that parts of code are non-unique. Relatedly, reusing those templates is similar to recognizing that existing code can be used to solve parts of other decomposed problems. Thus, we used this information to draw arrows from "System components are often not unique within or across systems." to "Code is reusable." to "Often existing code from other programs can be used to solve parts of a decomposed problem."

Arrow 1e. Several articles suggested that use of pre-existing functions should precede the creation and use of custom functions.

Table 3: The 13 Decomposition Consensus Goals

Consensus Goal	Comments	Example Supporting LG	No. of LGs
Systems are made up of smaller parts. (U)	See text supporting Table 1.	"Identify the constituent elements of a system". [40]	4
Complex problems can be broken into smaller parts. (U)	This CG identifies *problems* as a kind of system that can be decomposed.	Decompose a problem into "subproblems" that can be solved using computers. [40]	8
Problem decomposition is a useful early step in problem solving. (U)	This CG shifts from the simple fact of problem decomposition to its utility.	Recognize "the need for breaking down problems into smaller manageable tasks". [18]	6
Programs can be decomposed into components. (P)	This CG points out that *programs*, like problems, are systems that can be decomposed.	"[T]rack a program, capturing its various parts, but not the whole entity they form." [27]	5
System components are often not unique within or across systems. (U)	We identified non-uniqueness as a key idea underlying modularity.	Plan "with a sense of available templates in mind" to further reduce the task". [24]	1
Code is reusable. (P)	Reusability is another key idea underlying modularity.	Reuse modular parts of previously developed solutions. [40]	6
Often existing code from other programs can be used to solve parts of a decomposed problem. (P)	See text supporting Table 2.	Understand "the usefulness of modular code and how abstraction helps with modularity of code". [18]	6
Defining general procedures makes code more useful in the future. (P)	This CG calls out *creating* reusable parts as a separate skill from reusing.	"Develop solutions that consist of modular, reusable components". [40]	1
Sometimes it is useful to modify and repurpose existing code. (P)	This CG points out that code need not be reused exactly as given.	"[G]iven pieces of code" "modify for their own" program. [21]	2
A multi-instruction code snippet may serve a single, unified purpose. (P)	The idea of "chunking" code is a key idea underlying procedures.	Read a "function description presented in some language" to "understand what the function does". [28]	3
Code can be written in small parts (called procedures). (P)	This CG identifies procedures as a name for reusable code chunks.	"Code parts of a predesigned program to accomplish specific tasks." [17]	10
Defining procedures allows for easy reuse of code within programs. (P)	This CG connects procedures to reusability.	"[K]now how and when to create a separate method to accomplish a small, recurring task". [25]	10
Decomposition and modularization are useful in problem solving. (U)	This capstone CG ties all ideas in the trajectory together.	"Develop a solution by assembling together collections of smaller parts." [2]	9

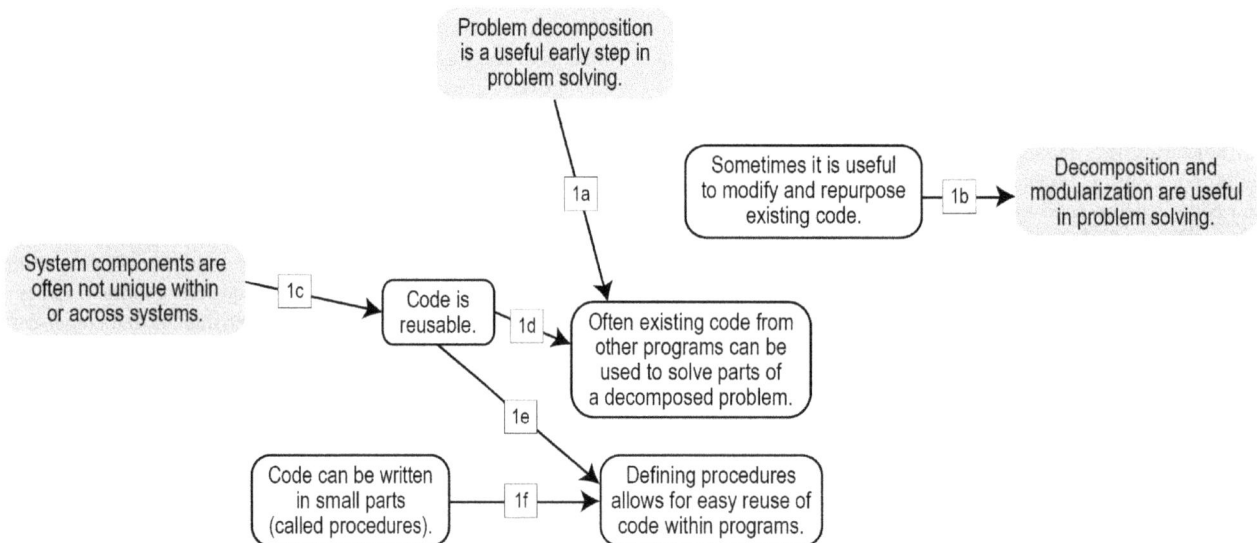

Figure 1: Literature-supported connections among CGs

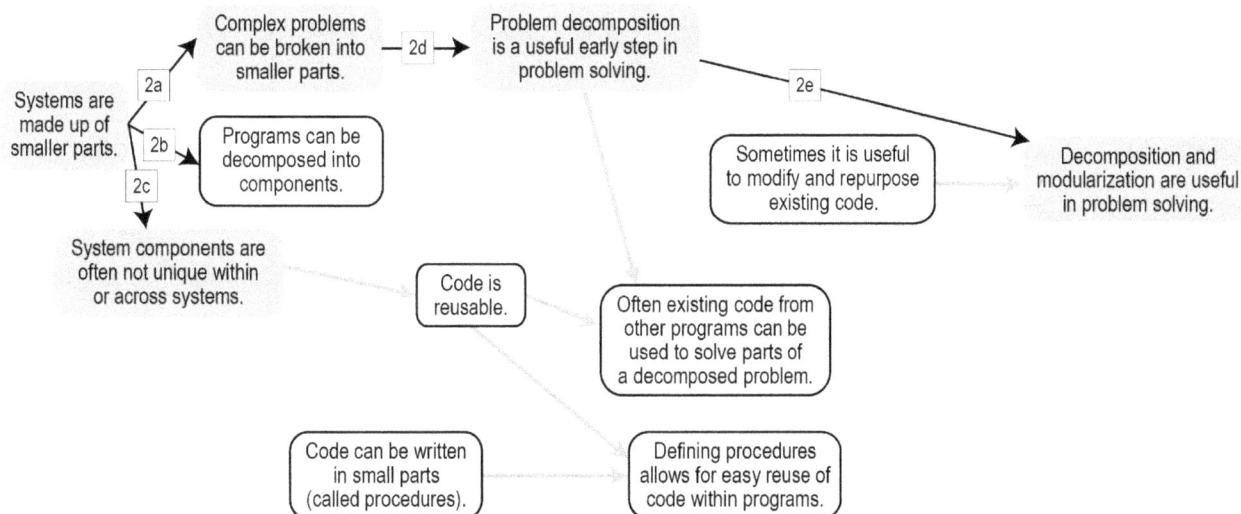

Figure 2: Constructivism-supported connections among CGs

One study found that middle school students spontaneously use built-in functions in Alice more than they created their own functions [33], another study described a pedagogical choice to place use of functions before creation of functions within a curriculum [30], and a third study placed use of functions (versus creation) in a lower level of an expert-developed framework used to analyze programming projects [41]. Using a pre-created function is an illustration that code is reusable, and so we used this evidence to draw an arrow from "Code is reusable." to "Defining procedures allows for easy reuse of code within programs."

Arrow 1f. Lee et al. [23] identified, as a common misconception, lack of understanding of the difference between a function definition (creation) and a function call (use). Students tended to omit the calls. We interpreted this to mean the act of creating a function is different from, and less difficult than, reusing that function within a program. We used this information to draw an arrow from "Code can be written in small parts (called procedures)." to "Defining procedures allows for easy reuse of code within programs."

4.3 Constructivism-Supported Connections

Figure 2 shows three more consensus goals and five additional arrows. These arrows were added based on the constructivist idea that learning should build on existing knowledge. Applying this idea to our particular context, we aimed to place the consensus goals most closely resembling everyday knowledge at the beginning of our trajectory, followed by CT ideas that may apply outside of programming, and then followed by programming-specific ideas.

The consensus goal most closely related to everyday knowledge is, "Systems are made up of smaller parts." As such, we placed this CG at the earliest place in the trajectory. This big idea is a natural stepping off point to three more computational-thinking specific ideas. Arrow 2a shows a progression from breaking *any system* into parts (recall from above that we use the word system to refer to any story, object, or other item that could be broken into parts) to the computational thinking practice of breaking a complex *problem* into

parts. Arrow 2b similarly shows a progression from breaking any system into parts to breaking a *program* into parts. Arrow 2c shows a progression from breaking a system into parts to examining the parts more carefully to note that they are often not unique.

Arrows 2d and 2e are an extension of the progression from breaking down systems to breaking down problems. Once students have begun to focus specifically on problems, a natural next step is to think about *why* breaking down a problem is a useful thing to do (Arrow 2d). At this point students have transitioned from everyday thinking into the computational thinking practice of decomposition. Arrow 2e connects the CG focused on the utility of decomposition to the overall capstone goal of the LT. When students reach this CG, they can coordinate unplugged decomposition ideas with programming-specific ideas about reusability and modularization.

4.4 Connections Based on Use, Modify, Create

Constructivism helped us to position the CGs that can be addressed outside of programming in relation to the initial programming goals. To help us position the programming-specific CGs, we turned to Lee et al.'s [22] Use, Modify, Create framework. Figure 3 shows one additional CG and six additional arrows we placed by applying Use, Modify, Create as a heuristic.

Arrow 3a is an "onramp" to the Use, Modify, Create progression, as it represents a transition from simply understanding that "Programs can be decomposed into components." to realizing that those components are tools that can be *used* in other programs (i.e., "Code is reusable."). Arrow 3b acknowledges that students do not necessarily need to modify those reusable components or create their own components in order to use a decomposition strategy to assemble a solution. It connects the CG that corresponds with the *use* part of the framework directly to the capstone CG ("Decomposition and modularization are useful in problem solving.").

Arrow 3c corresponds to a progression from *use* to *modify*. Arrows 3d–3f bring an aspect of *create* into the trajectory, as they

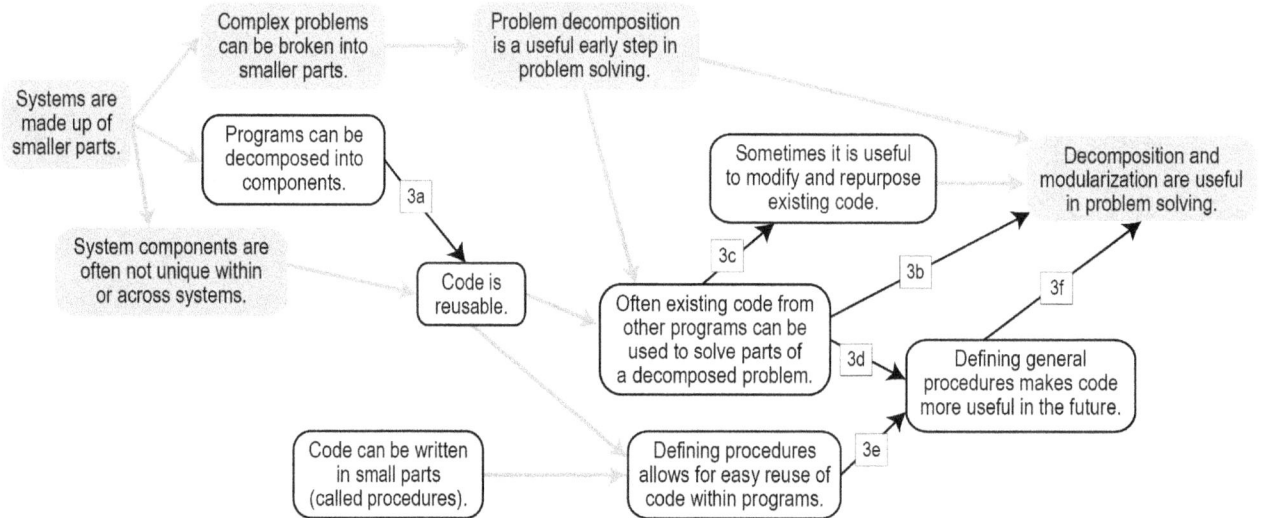

Figure 3: Connections among CGs supported by the Use, Modify, Create framework

connect the creation of procedures with the process of implementing a modularized solution. We did not connect the CG related to modification ("Sometimes it is useful to modify and repurpose existing code.") to the CGs about creating procedures because we did not see the skill of modifying code as directly relating to creating functions. We chose to capture the *modify-to-create* aspect of the framework by showing separate paths to the capstone CG. We would imagine a beginner or intermediate path to the capstone goal to include use of modification, whereas an advanced path to to the capstone goal would include creation.

4.5 Connections Based on Dimensions

After thinking about specific elements about the trajectory as described in the above sections, our final step was to step back and think about the trajectory holistically. Specifically, we looked for dimensions [8, 35] of the practice of decomposition evident within the developing trajectory. Our thinking about dimensions led to the last CG and three more arrows being added to the LT, as shown in Figure 4.

Through discussion we identified two dimensions of decomposition: (1) top-down planning (decomposition of problems) and (2) bottom-up assembly (creation and use of modular code). While this distinction was somewhat useful, the two categories are not easily separable; they intersect and depend on each other. For example, the CG "Programs can be decomposed into components." reflects top-down thinking, yet it provides a foundation for bottom-up assembly. This connection is reflected in Arrow 4a in Figure 4. Students think about how programs can be decomposed into chunks, and that feeds into their exploration of how writing chunks of code is an aspect of creating a modular solution.

A skill related to use and development of code chunks is reflected in the CG, "A multi-instruction code snippet may serve a single, unified purpose." Students must realize that code chunks can have a particular purpose to think about using them within solution. Arrows 4b and 4c show how this idea connects into the LT.

5 DISCUSSION

Here we discuss various potential uses of the Decomposition LT.

5.1 Guiding Future Research

We believe our Decomposition trajectory will serve as a useful frame for guiding future research. Our efforts toward defining connections among consensus goals raised a number of interesting questions. For example, is it necessary, useful, or inconsequential to ask students to discern the purpose of code snippets before writing functions? Is the reusability of code something that needs to be directly addressed before assembly of solutions from parts, or might it make more sense to ask students to assemble solutions from code chunks assumed to be one-time-use? There are many such questions to be answered. We hope our trajectory will inspire many questions as well as studies pursuing answers.

One area of particular interest for us is the relationship between the CT ideas of decomposition and sequence. This Decomposition LT focuses on structural decomposition of problems, with little attention to temporal decomposition. While developing this LT and our LT for Sequence [32], we noted that the act of decomposing a problem into parts was difficult to separate from the act of parsing a task into steps – the latter being a key sequence idea. One way to make sense of the difference is to think of decomposed parts of problems as tasks, which are then decomposed into steps. That is, the difference could be considered one of grain size, with decomposition "parts" being larger and themselves decomposable into sequence "parts." However, our assumed context of K-8 education makes this distinction lose some meaning. When imagining the types of problems we might ask our youngest students to decompose, steps or commands often are the reasonable size of a "part."

Later in the trajectory, when students start to write functions, the aforementioned distinction does make sense. Students write functions using sequence ideas, and the functions form the parts of the larger solution. Thus, our current thinking is that the earliest parts of the Decomposition trajectory may overlap with sequence

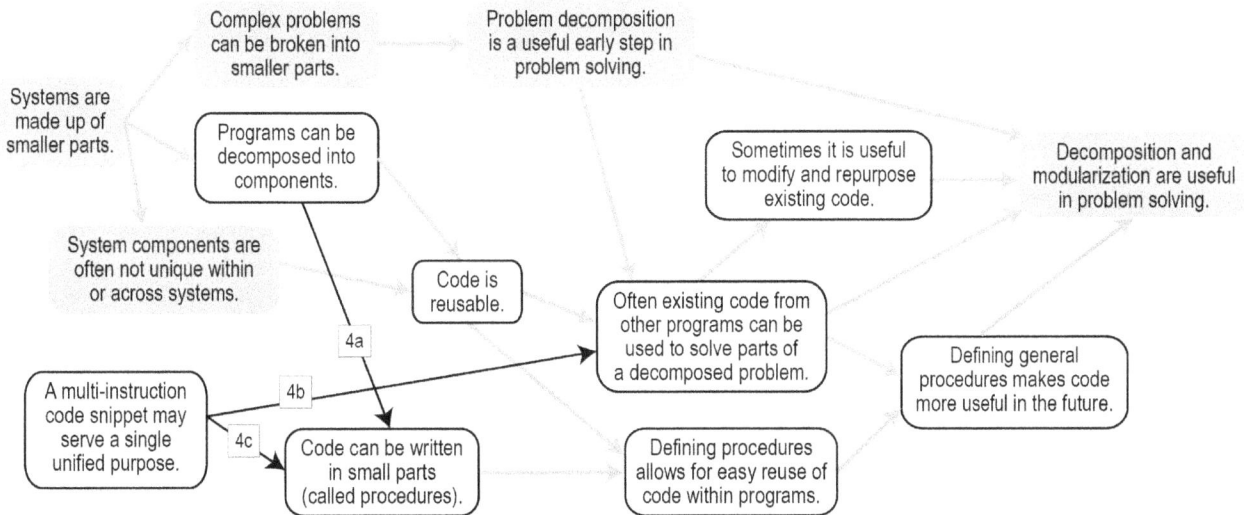

Figure 4: The full Decomposition trajectory, with connections based on dimensions highlighted

ideas in significant ways, but the two topics diverge as problems and solutions become more complex. We think this is an area that would benefit from further research into student thinking.

5.2 Professional Development and Curriculum

In recent years, LTs are being used as crucial components in teacher professional development. Sztajn, Confrey, Wilson, and Edginton [39] posited that "these trajectories can support growth in mathematical knowledge, selection of instructional tasks, interactions with students in classroom contexts, and use of students' responses to further learning" (p. 148). K-8 teachers seeking to integrate CT into mathematics and other subjects may be keen to apply this type of student-centered practice. We hope this Decomposition trajectory would take its place alongside other LTs as elementary teachers plan their curriculum and instruction.

Though not specifically targeted to the teacher audience, the CGs are expressed in appropriate detail to allow teachers to understand how decomposition in CS may manifest in the various elementary grade levels. Also exciting is the potential extension of these decomposition ideas into other subject areas. As discussed in section 4.1, the early CGs use umbrella terms like "systems" for many things in the world. This subset of early (unplugged) goals can easily be applied to ideas in other subject areas like science and art. The potential identification of such points of synergy between CT and other subjects should be a boon to teachers and curriculum developers seeking to integrate CT into existing course materials.

5.3 Formative Assessment and Differentiation

Finally, we think that educators may find our LT useful for formative assessment and differentiation. Although we do not see the LT as outlining definitive paths [7], we do hope that the CGs and the connections between them might serve as a useful lens for teachers in thinking about what aspects of decomposition their students understand, what aspects they do not yet grasp, and productive ways to build on existing knowledge to advance students' understanding.

For example, through questioning and observation, a teacher may discover that her students understand how to build solutions from modular parts, but tend to build all the parts from scratch rather than looking at the potential utility of previously created code. In such a case, our LT might be used as a guide for thinking about how to connect code reusability to the development of modular solutions. In addition, a more formal decomposition measure could be developed by revisiting Werner et al.'s [41] Game Computational Sophistication measure and using it alongside our LT.

6 CONCLUSION

In this paper, we present a learning trajectory for the CT practice of decomposition. The trajectory is the product of an extensive literature review of computational thinking and computer science education research in grades K-8. The literature has been analyzed by a multidisciplinary team to extract learning goals. The learning goals were then synthesized into 13 consensus goals that reflect the overarching ideas expressed by the large collection of learning goals. We describe our approach for drawing connections between goals to indicate logical progressions between CGs. The pathways are rooted in explicit literature references, constructivism ideals, the use-modify-create paradigm, and dimensions of disciplinary practices. This collective approach explores the many possible ways that students can identify and relate to decomposition from previous experiences both in and outside of a computing environment. This trajectory can be used to drive further explorations in the understanding and practice of decomposition for the development of curricular materials, assessment, and professional development.

ACKNOWLEDGMENTS

This material is based on work supported by the National Science Foundation under Award 1542828 and Award 1742466. Any opinions, findings, and conclusions or recommendations expressed are those of the authors and do not necessarily reflect those of the National Science Foundation.

REFERENCES

[1] Edith Ackermann. 2001. Piaget's constructivism, Papert's constructionism: What's the difference? *Future of learning group publication* 5, 3 (2001), 438.

[2] Charoula Angeli, Joke Voogt, Andrew Fluck, Mary Webb, Margaret Cox, Joyce Malyn-Smith, and Jason Zagami. 2016. A K-6 computational thinking curriculum framework: implications for teacher knowledge. *Journal of Educational Technology & Society* 19, 3 (2016), 47.

[3] Computer Science Teachers Association. 2017. CSTA K-12 Computer Science Standards. (2017). Retrieved March 18, 2018 from https://www.csteachers.org/page/standards

[4] Valerie Barr and Chris Stephenson. 2011. Bringing computational thinking to K-12: what is Involved and what is the role of the computer science education community? *ACM Inroads* 2, 1 (2011), 48–54.

[5] Jeffrey E Barrett, Julie Sarama, Douglas H Clements, Craig Cullen, Jenni McCool, Chepina Witkowski-Rumsey, and David Klanderman. 2012. Evaluating and improving a learning trajectory for linear measurement in elementary grades 2 and 3: A longitudinal study. *Mathematical Thinking and Learning* 14, 1 (2012), 28–54.

[6] Michael T Battista. 2007. The development of geometric and spatial thinking. *Second handbook of research on mathematics teaching and learning* 2 (2007), 843–908.

[7] Michael T Battista. 2011. Conceptualizations and issues related to learning progressions, learning trajectories, and levels of sophistication. *The Mathematics Enthusiast* 8, 3 (2011), 507–570.

[8] Leema K Berland and Katherine L McNeill. 2010. A learning progression for scientific argumentation: Understanding student work and designing supportive instructional contexts. *Science Education* 94, 5 (2010), 765–793.

[9] Matthew Berland, Taylor Martin, Tom Benton, Carmen Petrick Smith, and Don Davis. 2013. Using learning analytics to understand the learning pathways of novice programmers. *Journal of the Learning Sciences* 22, 4 (2013), 564–599.

[10] Paulo Blikstein, Marcelo Worsley, Chris Piech, Mehran Sahami, Steven Cooper, and Daphne Koller. 2014. Programming pluralism: Using learning analytics to detect patterns in the learning of computer programming. *Journal of the Learning Sciences* 23, 4 (2014), 561–599.

[11] Jere Confrey, Alan P Maloney, and Andrew K Corley. 2014. Learning trajectories: a framework for connecting standards with curriculum. *ZDM* 46, 5 (2014), 719–733.

[12] Stephen Cooper, Susan H Rodger, Madeleine Schep, RoxAnn H Stalvey, and Wanda Dann. 2015. Growing a k-12 community of practice. In *Proceedings of the 46th ACM Technical Symposium on Computer Science Education*. ACM, 290–295.

[13] K-12 Computer Science Framework. 2016. K-12 Computer Science Framework. (2016). Retrieved March 18, 2018 from https://k12cs.org/

[14] Diana Franklin, Charlotte Hill, Hilary A Dwyer, Alexandria K Hansen, Ashley Iveland, and Danielle B Harlow. 2016. Initialization in scratch: seeking knowledge transfer. In *Proceedings of the 47th ACM Technical Symposium on Computing Science Education*. ACM, 217–222.

[15] Diana Franklin, Gabriela Skifstad, Reiny Rolock, Isha Mehrotra, Valerie Ding, Alexandria Hansen, David Weintrop, and Danielle Harlow. 2017. Using Upper-Elementary Student Performance to Understand Conceptual Sequencing in a Blocks-based Curriculum. In *Proceedings of the 2017 ACM SIGCSE Technical Symposium on Computer Science Education*. ACM, 231–236.

[16] Chris Gregg, Luther Tychonievich, James Cohoon, and Kim Hazelwood. 2012. EcoSim: a language and experience teaching parallel programming in elementary school. In *Proceedings of the 43rd ACM technical symposium on Computer Science Education*. ACM, 51–56.

[17] Shuchi Grover and Satabdi Basu. 2017. Measuring student learning in introductory block-based programming: Examining misconceptions of loops, variables, and boolean logic. In *Proceedings of the 2017 ACM SIGCSE Technical Symposium on Computer Science Education*. ACM, 267–272.

[18] Shuchi Grover, Roy Pea, and Stephen Cooper. 2015. Designing for deeper learning in a blended computer science course for middle school students. *Computer Science Education* 25, 2 (2015), 199–237.

[19] David Hammer and Tiffany-Rose Sikorski. 2015. Implications of complexity for research on learning progressions. *Science Education* 99, 3 (2015), 424–431.

[20] Andri Ioannidou, Vicki Bennett, Alexander Repenning, Kyu Han Koh, and Ashok Basawapatna. 2011. Computational Thinking Patterns. *Paper presented at the Annual Meeting of the American Educational Research Association* (2011).

[21] Yasmin B Kafai and Quinn Burke. 2013. The social turn in K-12 programming: moving from computational thinking to computational participation. In *Proceeding of the 44th ACM technical symposium on computer science education*. ACM, 603–608.

[22] Irene Lee, Fred Martin, Jill Denner, Bob Coulter, Walter Allan, Jeri Erickson, Joyce Malyn-Smith, and Linda Werner. 2011. Computational thinking for youth in practice. *ACM Inroads* 2, 1 (2011), 32–37.

[23] Michael J Lee, Faezeh Bahmani, Irwin Kwan, Jilian LaFerte, Polina Charters, Amber Horvath, Fanny Luor, Jill Cao, Catherine Law, Michael Beswetherick, et al. 2014. Principles of a debugging-first puzzle game for computing education. In *Visual Languages and Human-Centric Computing (VL/HCC), 2014 IEEE Symposium on*. IEEE, 57–64.

[24] Marcia C Linn. 1985. The cognitive consequences of programming instruction in classrooms. *Educational Researcher* 14, 5 (1985), 14–29.

[25] Jiangjiang Liu, Cheng-Hsien Lin, Ethan Philip Hasson, and Zebulun David Barnett. 2011. Introducing computer science to K-12 through a summer computing workshop for teachers. In *Proceedings of the 42nd ACM technical symposium on Computer science education*. ACM, 389–394.

[26] Linda Mannila, Valentina Dagiene, Barbara Demo, Natasa Grgurina, Claudio Mirolo, Lennart Rolandsson, and Amber Settle. 2014. Computational thinking in K-9 education. In *Proceedings of the working group reports of the 2014 on innovation & technology in computer science education conference*. ACM, 1–29.

[27] Orni Meerbaum-Salant, Michal Armoni, and Mordechai Ben-Ari. 2011. Habits of programming in scratch. In *Proceedings of the 16th annual joint conference on Innovation and technology in computer science education*. ACM, 168–172.

[28] Osvaldo L Oliveira, Maria C Nicoletti, and Luis M del Val Cura. 2014. Quantitative correlation between ability to compute and student performance in a primary school. In *Proceedings of the 45th ACM technical symposium on Computer science education*. ACM, 505–510.

[29] Arno Pasternak and Jan Vahrenhold. 2012. Design and evaluation of a braided teaching course in sixth grade computer science education. In *Proceedings of the 43rd ACM technical symposium on Computer Science Education*. ACM, 45–50.

[30] Eileen M Peluso and Gene Sprechini. 2012. The impact of Alice on the Attitudes of High School students Toward Computing. *Journal for Computing Teachers* 7 (2012), 2012.

[31] Kathryn Rich, Carla Strickland, and Diana Franklin. 2017. A Literature Review through the Lens of Computer Science Learning Goals Theorized and Explored in Research. In *Proceedings of the 2017 ACM SIGCSE Technical Symposium on Computer Science Education*. ACM, 495–500.

[32] Kathryn M Rich, Carla Strickland, T Andrew Binkowski, Cheryl Moran, and Diana Franklin. 2017. K-8 Learning Trajectories Derived from Research Literature: Sequence, Repetition, Conditionals. In *Proceedings of the 2017 ACM Conference on International Computing Education Research*. ACM, 182–190.

[33] Susan H Rodger, Jenna Hayes, Gaetjens Lezin, Henry Qin, Deborah Nelson, Ruth Tucker, Mercedes Lopez, Stephen Cooper, Wanda Dann, and Don Slater. 2009. Engaging middle school teachers and students with alice in a diverse set of subjects. In *ACM SIGCSE Bulletin*, Vol. 41. ACM, 271–275.

[34] Emmanuel Schanzer, Kathi Fisler, Shriram Krishnamurthi, and Matthias Felleisen. 2015. Transferring skills at solving word problems from computing to algebra through bootstrap. In *Proceedings of the 46th ACM Technical symposium on computer science education*. ACM, 616–621.

[35] Christina V Schwarz, Brian J Reiser, Elizabeth A Davis, Lisa Kenyon, Andres Achér, David Fortus, Yael Shwartz, Barbara Hug, and Joe Krajcik. 2009. Developing a learning progression for scientific modeling: Making scientific modeling accessible and meaningful for learners. *Journal of Research in Science Teaching* 46, 6 (2009), 632–654.

[36] Linda Seiter. 2015. Using SOLO to classify the programming responses of primary grade students. In *Proceedings of the 46th ACM Technical Symposium on Computer Science Education*. ACM, 540–545.

[37] Linda Seiter and Brendan Foreman. 2013. Modeling the learning progressions of computational thinking of primary grade students. In *Proceedings of the ninth annual international ACM conference on International computing education research*. ACM, 59–66.

[38] Martin A Simon. 1995. Reconstructing mathematics pedagogy from a constructivist perspective. *Journal for research in mathematics education* (1995), 114–145.

[39] Paola Sztajn, Jere Confrey, P Holt Wilson, and Cynthia Edgington. 2012. Learning trajectory based instruction: Toward a theory of teaching. *Educational Researcher* 41, 5 (2012), 147–156.

[40] David Weintrop, Elham Beheshti, Michael Horn, Kai Orton, Kemi Jona, Laura Trouille, and Uri Wilensky. 2016. Defining computational thinking for mathematics and science classrooms. *Journal of Science Education and Technology* 25, 1 (2016), 127–147.

[41] Linda Werner, Jill Denner, and Shannon Campe. 2015. Children programming games: a strategy for measuring computational learning. *ACM Transactions on Computing Education (TOCE)* 14, 4 (2015), 24.

Unravelling the Cognition of Coding in 3-to-6-year Olds

The development of an assessment tool and the relation between coding ability and cognitive compiling of syntax in natural language

Eva Marinus
ARC Centre of Excellence in Cognition and Its Disorders, Department of Cognitive Science, Macquarie University, Sydney, NSW, Australia, eva.marinus@mq.edu.au

Zoe Powell
ARC Centre of Excellence in Cognition and Its Disorders, Department of Cognitive Science, Macquarie University, Sydney, NSW, Australia, zoe.powell@mq.edu.au

Rosalind Thornton
ARC Centre of Excellence in Cognition and Its Disorders, Department of Cognitive Science, Macquarie University, Sydney, NSW, Australia, rosalind.thornton@mq.edu.au

Genevieve McArthur
ARC Centre of Excellence in Cognition and Its Disorders, Department of Cognitive Science, Macquarie University, Sydney, NSW, Australia, genevieve.mcarthur@mq.edu.au

Stephen Crain
ARC Centre of Excellence in Cognition and Its Disorders, Department of Cognitive Science, Macquarie University, Sydney, NSW, Australia, stephen.crain@mq.edu.au

ABSTRACT

There is growing interest in teaching children computer programming ("coding") to prepare them for the demands of our increasingly digital society. However, we do not yet understand what cognitive skills children need in order to learn to code. The aim of our research program is to identify the requisite skills, with the goal of building a cognitive model of coding. The present research used a wooden robot ("Cubetto", www.primotoys.com) to investigate coding ability in young children. Exp. 1 describes the development and evaluation of the assessment instrument, which was tested with 18 3-to-5-year-old children. The instrument ("Coding Development (CODE) Test 3-6") was used in Exp. 2 to investigate the relationship between coding skill and "cognitive compiling" - the ability to formulate mental action plans in natural language. Thirty 5-to-6-year-olds participated in Exp. 2. Using Bayesian statistics, we found evidence that cognitive compiling predicts coding performance above and beyond age and nonverbal intelligence. We evaluate the outcomes and reflect on whether cognitive compiling depends solely on maturation or might be a skill that can be trained, and if so, how this could be done.

CCS CONCEPTS

• Social and professional topics~Student assessment

KEYWORDS

Assessment, programming, coding, natural language ability, cognitive compiling, nonverbal intelligence, children, preschool, kindergarten

ACM Reference format:

Eva Marinus, Zoe Powell, Rosalind Thornton, Genevieve McArthur and Stephen Crain. 2018. Unravelling the cognition of coding in 3-to-6-year olds. In *Proceedings of ACM International Computing Education Research (ICER) conference*, Espoo, Finland, August 2018 (ICER), 9 pages. DOI: 10.1145/3230977.3230984

1 INTRODUCTION

In recent years there has been a growing interest in encouraging and teaching students to learn computer programming ("coding") in order to prepare them for the demands of our increasingly digital society. As a result, there has been an explosion of research in the field of computer science education (e.g., the steady increase in submissions to SIGCSE conferences), and there have been many global and local programming initiatives (e.g., Code.org [4] and Code Club [5]). Countries such as the UK, Estonia and Australia have started to introduce coding and computational thinking into their national K-12 curricula.

In order to optimize the instruction of coding and computational thinking in children, it is critical to understand the cognitive processes underlying these skills. In the curriculum context in particular, we need to know how coding skills and computational thinking develop over time and how they can be assessed [8,7,10,30]. This knowledge will help us to identify and support children who struggle to learn computational thinking and coding (i.e., dyscodia).

A recently commissioned Google survey of the field of pre-college computer science education (CSEd) concluded that CSEd research must become more rigorous and connect more with new and established knowledge in cognitive science, learning sciences and machine learning [1]. These fields of research seemingly have great potential to boost the study of coding and computational thinking, building on the strong foundation that has been established by the field of Computer Science Education over the last decades. The field of Cognitive Science in particular can expand this knowledge via the development of cognitive models of coding and computational thinking using techniques that have produced valid cognitive models in other domains, like reading [6], language, [20], and belief formation [19].

In this research paper, we focus on coding in 3-to-6-year-old children. Our aims were to develop an assessment instrument (Experiment 1), and to determine if there is a relationship between coding ability and cognitive compiling of natural language phrases (Experiment 2). The outcomes of these studies represent early steps towards the ultimate goal of building a valid cognitive model of the acquisition of coding and computational thinking.

2 EXPERIMENT 1: DEVELOPING A CODING ASSESSMENT TOOL FOR 3-6-YEAR OLDS

2.1 Background

The aims of our first experiment were to develop a standardized cognitive assessment of coding for children aged from 3 to 6 years, and to use this assessment to determine if there are individual differences in children's coding skills at this young age (see [3] for a similar approach). We were also interested to find out if these skills improve with development. We developed our assessment tool based on "Cubetto" [24] - a small wooden robot who needs help to find its way on a map. Cubetto is a simplified version of the turtle LOGO programming task developed by Seymour Papert [23] that is suitable for children from 3 to 7 years of age according to its developers [24]. To the best of our knowledge, we are the first research team to develop such an assessment using a tangible robot, and the first to develop an assessment for such a young age group. Previously developed tests typically focus on older children and have used digital environments (e.g., the Computation Thinking test [27], Fairy Assessment in Alice [32], Computational Thinking Patterns in AgentSheets [18], Dr. Scratch [22], Foundations for Advancing Computational Thinking [9], classifying programming responses with SOLO [29]). The only comparable effort with young children that we are aware of was that of Bers [31]. However, she used portfolio and curriculum style-assessments, not a direct measurement of programming in action.

2.2 Methods

2.2.1 Participants. We obtained active consent from the parents of 18 children (11 boys). Before assessment, we also obtained verbal assent from the children. The sample consisted of eight 3-year-olds, eight 4-year-olds and two 5-year-olds. Children ranged from 3 years and 3 months to 5 years and 10 months in age (average age = 4 years and 1 month). Sixteen participants were recruited at a childcare centre on our university campus. The other two children were recruited via an online recruitment website developed at our research centre. All procedures in this study were approved by the Ethics committee at our university (Reference number: 5201600786).

2.2.2 Materials.

2.2.2.1 Coding Development (CODE) Test 3-6 – version 1. The materials for Cubetto are a $1m^2$ grid mat with 6x6 squares, Cubetto (a cube-shaped wooden Robot; see Image 1), and a "remote control" that children control by inserting small wooden blocks into holes (see Image 2). We only used the green (one step forward), yellow (90-degree left turn), and red (90-degree right turn) "instruction blocks" (see Image 2). We developed an assessment protocol that asked children to use these blocks to complete 13 tasks ("items") of increasing difficulty. For every item, children were asked to move Cubetto to a picture on the mat (e.g., the water).

Image 1: Left: Cubetto on the map with pictures. Right: Cubetto with hat and tail, friend, and fruit

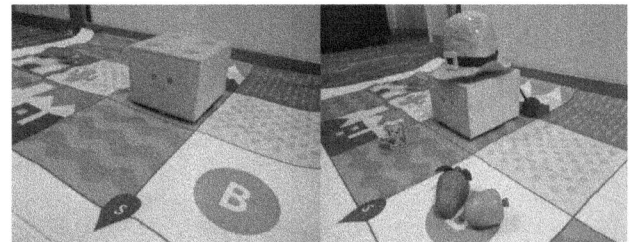

We piloted this initial coding assessment with a 3-year-old and a 5-year-old. This pilot revealed four issues. First, for the 3-year-old child, we needed to improve her understanding of our instructions by facilitating her sense of direction. To this end, we (1) gave Cubetto a hat and tail to make clearer which way he was facing (see Image 1, right side); (2) gave all instructions while the child was sitting behind Cubetto (Note: the child and instructor had to move around the mat with all the materials to ensure that the child kept facing Cubetto's tail); (3) put yellow and red stickers on each child's left and right hand respectively, since many 3-6-year olds do not know left from right [19]. Note: the red and yellow colors corresponded with yellow (left) and red (right) instruction blocks in the remote control.

Second, instead of asking the child to move Cubetto to certain pictures on the map, we introduced the children to a small toy who was Cubetto's friend to make the task seem more dynamic and interactive. Children were asked to join the friend in different activities (e.g., tree climbing) or to 'look at' the friend if the instruction required the child to move Cubetto on a coordinate next to the friend (see Image 1 at the right for a demonstration). We also had some toy fruits at hand that we would ask the children to give to Cubetto, either when we felt they needed a little break or as a smooth way to end the testing session ('reward Cubetto for his hard work') (see also Image 1 at the right).

Third, we adjusted the Cubetto remote control. This control comprises 12 holes for regular instruction plus four holes for a function (see Image 2 on the left). After the fourth hole, the sequence line makes a 180 degree turn, which effectively reverses the direction of the colored blocks. This is very difficult for 3- to 4-year-olds to understand. Thus, we could only use the first four holes to create our items. Fortunately, we were able to generate enough items of increasing difficulty using the first four gaps only. To avoid distractions, we covered all the other gaps (see Image 2 on the right).

Fourth, our younger pilot child struggled to fit the blocks into the holes in the remote control. The delay caused by this led to the child forgetting the instructions for the items. We therefore attached a small transparent handle to each block to make it easier for the child to fit the block in the hole. This had an added benefit of providing the child with an extra cue about which direction the block had to face in order to fit into a hole.

It also became clear that children needed more instructions for each item and needed more than one attempt per item. We revised all the items in the assessment accordingly.

Image 2: Left: Instruction blocks in 'remote control'. Right: with cover and handles on blocks.

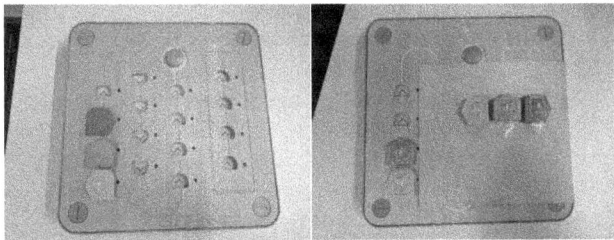

2.2.2.2 Coding Development (CODE) Test 3-6 – final version. The final version of the coding assessment began by familiarising the child with Cubetto and the workings of the remote control. We also assessed if the child could count to four, and whether s/he knew left from right. We assessed each child with the CODE Test 3-6, irrespective of their fail or pass on these assessments.

After the instructions, the child moved on to the test items. The first and easiest item required the child to make Cubetto make one step forward (i.e., insert one green block). The final and hardest item asked the child to make Cubetto collect his friend and bring him to the mountains. This item involved one step forward, turning 180 degrees (i.e., two yellow or red blocks) and another step forward.

There were two types of items: "build" items (10 in total), in which a child was given an empty remote control and asked to create Cubetto's movements from scratch; and "debug" items (3 in total), in which a child was asked to fix Cubetto's existing movements (i.e., debugging). A child had three chances to get each item correct. If their first attempt was correct, then the child was assigned 3 points for that item (Step 1). If a child failed, s/he would be invited to try again. If successful, s/he would earn 2 points for that item (Step 2). If a child failed, s/he was given additional standardized instructions to help the child to solve the item (Step

3). If a child still could not solve the item, s/he was given zero points, and the instructor demonstrated how to do the item correctly (Step 4). This "three-step" approach for each item increased the range of scores from 0-13 to 0-39, allowing for more fine-grained measuring of coding ability. After testing 5 participants, we noticed that they never earned any points after failing on 3 consecutive items. We therefore started using 3 errors in a row as our stopping criterion to reduce the length of the assessment for the child. The final protocol and scoresheet, which include all items and the instructions for the three Steps for both Build and Fix items, can be found on the Open Science Framework (osf.io). See Section 3.2 of Experiment 2 for a link.

2.2.3 Procedure. Sixteen participants were tested at the childcare centre, and two were tested in the language acquisition lab at our university. The sessions in the childcare centre took place in June and July 2017. The other two children were tested in May 2017 and January 2018. The first and second author conducted the testing sessions, which each took between 20 and 40 minutes.

2.3 Outcomes

The raw data of Experiment 1 can be found on the Open Science Framework. See Section 3.2 for the link.

Our first step was to look at the distribution of scores. As can be seen in Figure 1, the scores followed a normal distribution. The average score for our sample was 14.4 with a standard deviation of 7.5. The scoring range was 0-28.

Second, we looked at the relationship between coding ability and age. We found a significant positive correlation, $r = .75$, $p <.001$. Only one child scored at floor (i.e., 0), who was one of the youngest participants (See Figure 2).

Figure 1: CODE Test 3-6 score distribution Experiment 1, 3-5-year olds

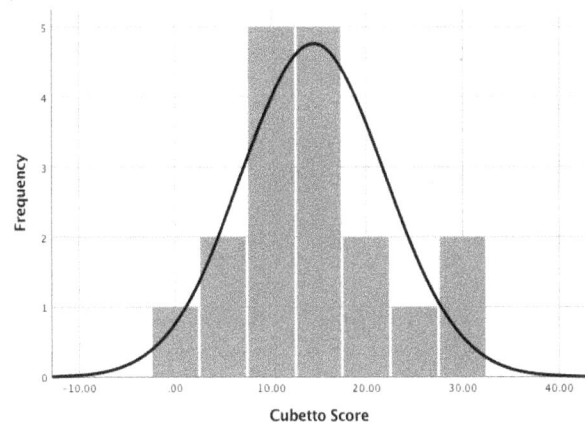

Finally, we examined the scoring patterns of the children across the items and examined whether they benefitted from the three-step approach for each item. As can be seen in Figure 3, accuracy diminished gradually over the items, which suggests that the order of difficulty was appropriate. This was supported by an analysis of the three-step approach for each item (see Figure 3). For example, 10 children needed just one step for Item 1, six needed two steps, and one child needed three steps. In later items (e.g., Item 5), fewer children needed just one step (e.g., five children for Item 5), and more children needed two steps (seven children for Item 5) or three steps (three children for Item 5). Again, this suggests that the order of difficulty was well chosen.

Figure 2: Scatterplot CODE Test 3-6 score and age

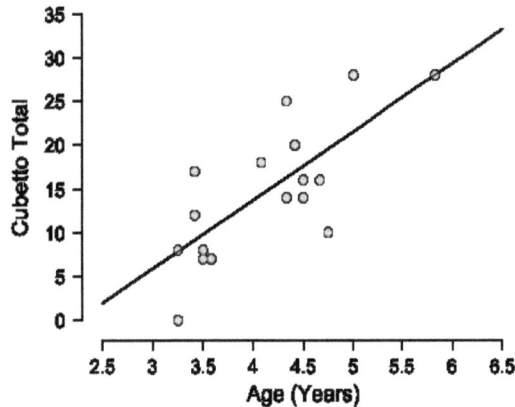

2.4 Discussion

We succeeded in creating a preliminary cognitive assessment for coding ability for 3-5-year olds. The results show a good distribution of skill and no ceiling effects. The scores increased with age, and the three-step procedure for each item worked appropriately. The fact that none of the children - not even the 5-year-olds - scored at ceiling suggested that the assessment instrument would be appropriate for a slightly older population. And it would be appropriate for use in studies that aim to identify the cognitive skills that underpin coding ability in children aged from around three to six. Limitations will be discussed in the General discussion.

Figure 3: Scoring patterns across items and steps, y-axis represents number of children who used a Step

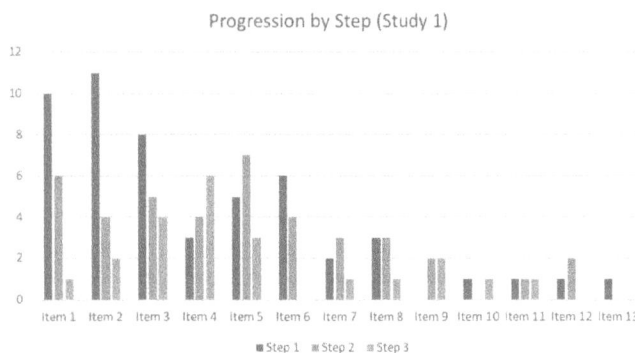

3 EXPERIMENT 2: THE RELATION BETWEEN CODING, AND COGNITIVE COMPILING ABILITY IN 5-6-YEAR OLDS

3.1 Background

To the best of our knowledge, the only studies that have attempted to identify the cognitive processes that underpin the ability to code in children between 3 and 6 years of age have been conducted by Kazakoff and colleagues [17, 16]. These studies targeted sequencing skills as measured by assessing performance on picture sorting. They used an intervention design. Children were measured on sequencing ability before and after a week of programming training involving robots. The results were mixed. The 2012 study reported a larger improvement of sequencing skill by the trained group as compared to the control group, whereas the 2013 study failed to replicate this finding.

One limitation of these pioneering studies is that they did not measure coding ability per se and hence could not investigate the strength of the relationship between coding and sequencing skill. In Experiment 2, the coding assessment that we developed and trialed in Experiment 1 was used to measure the potential relationship between coding ability and cognitive compiling in natural language. With cognitive compiling we refer to the formulation of mental plans to execute actions that are denoted by natural language instructions such as "Point to the third green ball."

We focused on natural language phrases such as "third green ball" for several reasons. First, 5- to 6-year-old children have been found to formulate non-adult action plans in response to instructions that contain such phrases. Despite knowing the meanings of the individuals words "third" and "green" and "ball", children in this age range often fail to point to the third green ball in an array; rather, they point to the third ball in the array, if it is green. Similarly, we found in Experiment 1 that children often used the correct blocks, but in the wrong order. In addition, many of the children, especially the younger ones, preferred to take a sequential approach (i.e., using one block at the time) to bring Cubetto to the target location on the map. We hypothesize that these strategies, or preferences, indicate variability in ability to accurately represent all the different steps in a cognitive action plan. This hypothesis is supported by previous research reporting that children struggle to keep track of events, variables and states that cannot be seen [2, 11]. Programming a robot to make specific moves over a map requires the formation of a specific mental plan involving all the steps and moves in the correct order. The ability to successfully form such plans is the essence of cognitive compiling.

To develop an independent measure of cognitive compiling, we turned to the literature on linguistic skills in young children. In the 1980s, Hamburger and Crain investigated the acquisition of cognitive compiling in natural language [12,13]. Their results showed that young children (ranging in age between 4;4-6;2) are far more able to formulate complex action plans than had been found in previous research [21]. Hamburger and Crain showed that children's successful performance dramatically increased when specific steps were taken to simplify the cognitive load that is required to build an appropriate algorithm or plan for phrases such as "third green ball." In addition to behavioral data, Hamburger and Crain also provided pseudocode 'programs' that visualized the different 'compiling' stages or phases at which a child could make 'errors' in building or executing correct, adult-like plans.

Our aim was to determine if there are individual differences in cognitive compiling in a slightly older sample of children. Although the children in the present study were older than those in the Hamburger and Crain studies, we assumed that some child participants would nevertheless struggle to go through all the steps of cognitive compiling. In addition, instead of relieving the mental load for the children, we chose the most complex task compiling task and offered it without the scaffolding that reduced cognitive load in the Hamburger and Crain studies. We know from previous research that the complexity of a plan significantly increases if elements (e.g., color, shape and number) are combined [12, 13]. Therefore, our task involved asking a child to point to objects presented in arrays that included three elements (position, color and object type) that had multiple operations between each element. For instance, a child was asked to point to the third yellow star that was presented in an array of items. To get this item right, the child has to "compile" third and yellow and star together into a single representation. This involves finding the set of stars, check that they are yellow and then pick the third one of this set (see Image 3).

We used our coding assessment and our cognitive compiling assessment to test three hypotheses. First, based on Experiment 1, we hypothesized that coding ability would be positively correlated with age. Second, based on previous work of Hamburger and Crain, we predicted a positive correlation between cognitive compiling ability and age. Third, we hypothesized that coding performance could be predicted by cognitive compiling despite controlling for both age and non-verbal intelligence. We controlled for the latter since coding could simply depend on general cognitive ability that increases with age and non-verbal intelligence.

3.2 Methods

Prior to conducting this experiment, we preregistered it on the Open Science Framework (OSF). Please see here: osf.io/e3rku. By preregistering we committed to a research plan in advance, before collecting data. This allows for separating hypothesis-generating (exploratory) and hypothesis (confirmatory) research. Making an explicit distinction between the two improves the quality and transparency of research and helps others to build on it. In particular by also making the data and materials available. Therefore, the raw data for Experiments 1 and 2 and the materials for the CODE Test 3-6 and the cognitive compiling test can also be found on the same OSF page.

3.2.1 Participants. The sample consisted of 20 5-year-olds and 10 6-year-old children (16 boys). Children ranged from 5 years and 0 months to 6 years and 10 months in age (average age = 5 years and 8 months). The participants were recruited via an online recruitment website developed at our research centre. The parents of the participants were sent an email including an information letter and a consent form. The lead researcher arranged a time for testing with the parents who gave their written consent. The testing sessions were held on-site at our university. Parents received $15 to cover the costs of travel, and children received their choice of either $10 or a toy of equivalent value in compensation. All procedures in this study were approved by the Ethics committee at our university (Reference number: 5201600786).

3.2.2 Materials.
3.2.2.1 The Coding Development Test 3-6. We used the final version of the CODE Test 3-6.
3.2.2.2 Cognitive compiling task. The cognitive compiling task aimed to determine the child's ability to 'compile' pieces of syntactic information. To do this, we asked the children to point at an object (e.g., 'the second yellow star') in an array presented on a laminated piece of white paper. For all items we made sure that the children were presented with the array of objects before we asked the question. There were 3 pre-test arrays and 16 test arrays.

The pre-test arrays were used to ensure the child could name the colors and shapes used during the testing session, to familiarise the child with the process of counting from left to right and to establish that they knew the meaning of the ordinals 'first', 'second', 'third' and 'last'. Two participants did not successfully complete the pre-test and were thus excluded from the analyses that involved the cognitive compiling task.

Each of the 16 test arrays consisted of 7 objects that could be one of two shapes and one of two colors (e.g., blue squares, blue circles, red squares, and red circles). We created 8 target arrays and 8 filler arrays (i.e., items that will not be analysed). Therefore, the maximum score for this task was 8. The target arrays were designed to distinguish between the adult (from here on, 'correct') answer, and errors that we expected 5-6-year-old children to make.

The most common error we expected was the intersective error. This type of error occurs when the answer focuses foremost on the positioning of the object ('third'), and secondarily on whether the object matches the description (e.g. 'blue square'). So, in the instance of the 'third blue square', the intersective error is the third object from the left in the array and will be selected if the object is a blue square. Each of our target arrays included a valid (i.e., meets the descriptive criteria, in this instance a 'blue square') intersective and correct answer. The other previously identified error was a 'head-set' error, which would occur if the answer is based predominantly on the noun (e.g., find the third square in an array, and select it if it is blue). We also explored the possibility that children may decide on answers based predominantly on the adjective (i.e., the color), in an 'adjective-set' error (e.g., find the third blue object in an array and select it if it is a square). For all of our target arrays, the correct answer could be distinguished from each of these three error types. See Image 3 for examples.

The eight filler arrays had the same format (i.e., 7 objects varying in shape and color). Four of the filler arrays were designed to be easy (e.g., 'the first red star') to make sure that all children felt successful on at least some of the items, and an additional four arrays that were slightly harder, but not informative to what kind of strategy the children were using.

Image 3: Examples of target arrays. I = Intersective, H = Headset, A = Adjective, C = Correct solution.

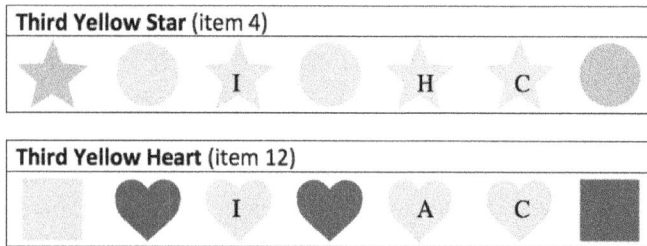

Third Yellow Star (item 4)

Third Yellow Heart (item 12)

3.2.2.3 Nonverbal intelligence task. The Matrices subtest of the Kaufman Brief Intelligence Test (2nd Edition) [15] was used to assess non-verbal intelligence. The Matrices subtest consists of 46 items ordered in increasing difficulty. For each item, a child is presented with picture printed at the top of a page that also illustrates five small pictures at the bottom of the page. One of the small pictures "matches" the picture at the top of the page. Items 1 to 9 present a complete image (e.g. a picture of a shoe, with the correct answer being an image of a foot). From item 10 onwards, the image is missing a part (e.g., a picture of a pattern with a missing section, with the correct answering being the missing section). The Matrices subtest of the KBIT-2 has demonstrated acceptable internal consistency (α = .78 in 4- and 5-year olds, α = .87 in 6-year olds) and acceptable test-retest reliability (adjusted r^2 = .76 over 4 weeks in 4- to 12-year-olds). The administration and discontinuation rules (4 incorrect answers in succession) outlined in the manual were followed. The raw scores were used for further analysis.

3.2.3 Procedure. Testing was carried out by the first two authors and an additional research assistant in the language acquisition lab at our university. The additional research assistant was trained by the first author. In addition to the active consent obtained from the parents, we first briefly explained the nature of the tasks to the children and obtained verbal assent of each child. Following this, the children completed the CODE Test 3-6, which took approximately 25 minutes. With the consent of both parent and child, the administration of the CODE Test 3-6 was filmed for the purposes of scoring and qualitative analysis. They were then given a 5-minute break where they had the opportunity to play with Cubetto. After this, the cognitive compiling task was administered (about 5 minutes), followed by the matrices subtest of the KBIT-2 (about 10 minutes). The entire duration of testing was therefore approximately 45 minutes. The children were tested between mid-December 2017 and early March 2018.

3.3 Outcomes

The raw data for Experiment 2 can be found on the Open Science Framework. See Section 3.2 for the link.

The mean scores of our 30 5- to 6-year-olds was 26.4 on the CODE Test 3-6, with a standard deviation of 7.0. None of the participants scored at floor or at ceiling. The scoring range was from 12 to 38. Two participants failed on the pre-test of the cognitive compiling task. Therefore, all planned analyses that include the cognitive compiling test will have an n=28 instead of 30. The mean score of our sample on the cognitive compiling test was 4.75 with a standard deviation of 3.57. The scoring range was 0-8.

As specified in our preregistration, we used a Bayesian approach to analyse our data. Since we are the first to test correlations between coding ability and cognitive compiling, it was hard to conduct a power analysis to estimate the required sample size. We therefore decided to use Bayesian statistics, which allow for analyzing after collecting data with small sample and analyzing again after increasing the sample size.

All our tests were one-tailed as we had specific predictions about the (positive) direction of correlations between factors. In our dataset, Bayes Factors below 0 indicate evidence for the Null Hypothesis (e.g., there is no positive correlation between CODE Test 3-6 performance and age). Bayes Factors above 0 indicate evidence for the Alternative Hypotheses (e.g., there is a positive correlation between CODE Test 3-6 performance and age). However, Bayes factors between 0 and 3 are typically considered to be equivocal evidence. Bayes factors between 3 and 10 are considered to give some evidence, with BFs above 10 to pose strong evidence and above 30 very strong evidence [28].

Our first hypothesis was that we would replicate the positive relationship between coding ability and age. Indeed, we found a positive correlation, r = .57, with a Bayes factor of 75.6 (n=30). This means we found very strong evidence for a positive correlation between coding ability and age. See Figure 4.

Figure 4: Scatterplot CODE Test 3-6 score and age

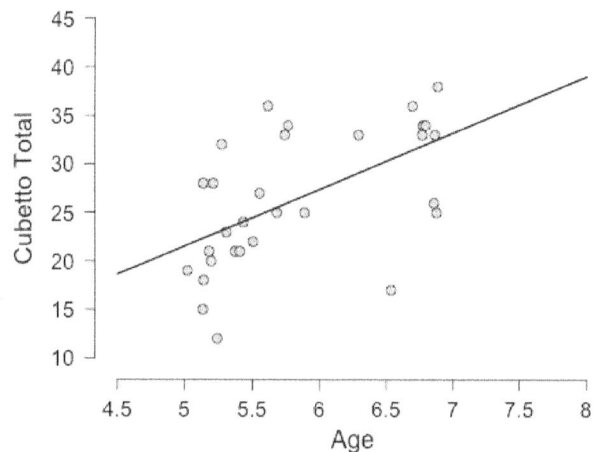

Our second hypothesis was that we would replicate the finding of Hamburger and Crain that demonstrates a positive relation between cognitive compiling skill and age. Indeed, we found a positive correlation between age and cognitive compiling, r = .44, with a Bayes factor of 6.4 (n=28). This means that there is some evidence that the older children tend to use to pick the correct solution, whereas the younger children tend to pick in the intersective solution. See Figure 5.

As can be seen in Figure 5, our cognitive compiling test did not result in a continuous outcome. Instead, the children could be divided into three different categories based on their strategy. First, 12 children obtained a full score. This group clearly mastered the complex compiling strategy needed to properly execute the request. Second, 7 children exclusively picked the 'intersective' solution. As explained above this meant that when asked to point to the second yellow ball, they would focus on the second object in the array and point at this when it was a yellow ball, even if it was not the second yellow ball in the array. Finally, there was a group of 9 children that scored somewhere in between. These children sometimes picked the correct item, but not consistently. Some children made a mix of intersective and correct decisions, others picked a range of different answers.

Figure 5: Scatterplot Cognitive compiling score and age

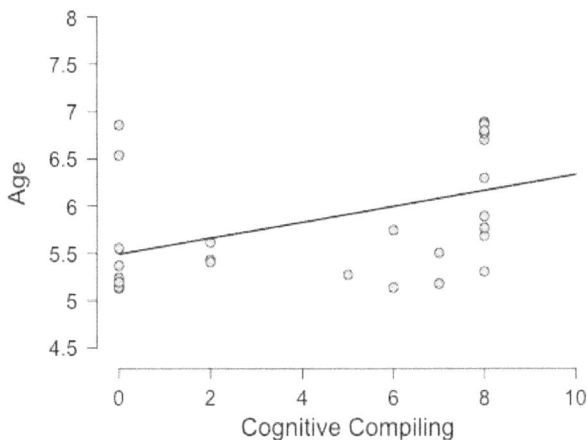

Our third hypothesis was that cognitive compiling would predict coding performance whilst controlling for both age and non-verbal intelligence. As specified in our preregistration, we conducted Bayesian regression analyses and we started by running the regression analysis on the first 20 participants. As we are using a Bayesian approach, the outcome will tell us whether we find more support for our hypothesis that cognitive compiling significantly predicts performance on the CODE Test 3-6 over and beyond nonverbal intelligence and age or that it is more likely that this predictive relationship does not exist. A third option is that more data is needed to judge which possibility gets more support.

We ran our statistical analyses in JASP [14] using the Bayesian Linear Regression option. CODE Test 3-6 score was added as the dependent measure and Age (using one decimal) and Nonverbal intelligence (raw score) were added to the Null model before adding Cognitive compiling as the predictor. The Bayes factor for this model was 1.77. This means that there is about 1.8 times more evidence for a model that also includes cognitive compiling skill than a model that only includes nonverbal intelligence and age as

predictors. Bayes factors between 0 and 3 imply that we either have to collect more data or should develop a more sensitive measure. As specified in our preregistration we added our next 8 participants. The Bayes factor now amounted to 4.7, providing some evidence that cognitive compiling is a meaningful predictor of coding ability, over and beyond age and nonverbal IQ.

4 GENERAL DISCUSSION

In Experiments 1 and 2 we discovered that it is possible to measure coding ability in 3-6 year olds and that coding ability in this age group increases significantly with age. Confirming the predicted positive correlations between nonverbal intelligence and programming ability, and between children's performance on the assessment of cognitive compiling and programming ability provided the requisite initial steps in validating our coding assessment task. Obviously, however, there is a need for further replication and validation [25]. In this context it is important to realise that the field is still working on establishing clear definitions of coding skill and its underlying cognitive skills in (young) children. As a result, further validation will need to go hand in hand with developing more specific definitions of the skills involved.

Our research clearly shows that, with appropriate scaffolding, children as young as 3 years of age can successfully use programming tools like Cubetto. We simplified the task in several ways, most notably by improving children's sense of direction. This was an important simplification for children younger than the age of 5, because they do not typically distinguish right from left [26]. Our results show that coding performance depended on children's ability to correctly compile the multiple components of a program. An interesting question is whether cognitive compiling of multiple programming components is a skill that can be trained or that it is a matter of maturation. If children's abilities are determined by maturation, it may turn out to be necessary to wait until children for children to mature (e.g., around the age of 5) before confronting them with tasks that involve compiling larger movement sequences. Concretely, they could be instructed to work sequentially, with one block at the time, to make Cubetto move over the map.

Another approach would be to train children in the requisite skills that are involved in cognitive compiling. As described in Section 3.1, Hamburger and Crain [12,13] found that the ability of children to formulate the kinds of mental plans that are required in order to execute instructions in natural language (e.g., "Point to the third green ball"), dramatically increased when specific steps were taken to simplify the cognitive load required to build an appropriate algorithm corresponding to such instructions. In their study they discovered two possible ways to facilitate children's compiling of mental action plans. First, they found that children's ability to formulate adult-like plans improved by providing the linguistic instructions first, before revealing the array. This 'phrase before display' manipulation helped children to forestall the premature execution of the piece of the plan that corresponds to the ordinal "third." As a result, the children opted less often for the intersective solution. Second, they found that performance could be improved by asking the children to sort and count sets of objects of the same color or shape. The idea is that pre-handling sets of objects helped the children to become aware that 'second' or 'third' is not necessary tied to a position in an array but could be used to refer to one of the subsets of objects, for example, the green balls.

So what kind of similar strategies could be undertaken to improve cognitive compiling in programming a robot? One way to scaffold children's composition of complex mental action plans could be by encouraging children to verbalize the steps of their plans by thinking out loud. During Experiment 2 we made several observations of 5 and 6-year olds spontaneously verbalising their mental plans before inserting the blocks in the remote control. In parallel to the 'phrase before display' solution by Hamburger and Crain, the trainer could go one step further by taking away the remote control and blocks and ask the children to verbalise the type of actions ('forward', 'turn left', 'turn right') in the correct order before they put the blocks in the remote control. It is less straightforward to identify a similar parallel between the handling strategy for a task with arrays and a programming task with blocks and a remote control. One possibility is that children would benefit from systematic practice with the different types of blocks. For instance, children could be asked to use just one block at the time, pressing the blue button multiple times to reach their goal, before they progressed to putting in multiple blocks in the same program. Future training studies are needed to determine 1) how to effectively train cognitive compiling in children, 2) whether such training also leads to improved coding skills, and 3) whether potential improvements in coding skills hold in the absence of scaffolding strategies.

5 CONCLUSION

We developed a coding ability assessment ("Coding Development Test for children from 3-6 (CODE Test 3-6)") for children from 3 to 6 years of age. The instrument shows a good spread of scores. Performance of the test is positively correlated to age, nonverbal intelligence and cognitive compiling of syntax in natural language. Our second experiment showed that there is evidence that cognitive compiling predicts coding ability in young children over and beyond age and nonverbal intelligence.

ACKNOWLEDGEMENTS

We would like to thank the director, teachers and children from childcare centre Gumnut Cottage at Macquarie University for participating in Experiment 1 and all the children who participated in Experiment 2 and their parents for bringing them to our language acquisition lab. Thank you, Marion Aitchison, for your help with the data collection of Experiment 2. This research was funded by the ARC CCD Cross Program Support Scheme. The first author's salary was paid by funding from the ARC Centre of Excellence for Cognition and its Disorders (CCD) (CE110001021), www.ccd.edu.au.

REFERENCES

[1] Paolo Blikstein. 2018. Pre-College Computer Science Education: A Survey of the Field. Mountain View, CA: Google LLC. https://services.google.com/fh/files/misc/pre-college-computer-science-education-report.pdf

[2] Benedict du Boulay. 1986. Some difficulties of learning to program. *Journal of Educational Computing Research, 2, 1,* 57–73. DOI: 10.2190/3LFX-9RRF-67T8-UVK9

[3] Lucía Gabriela Caguana Anzoátegui, María Isabel Alves Rodriguez Pereira, e Mónica Del Carmen Solís Jarrin, 2017. Cubetto para pre-escolares: programación informática código a código. *Proceedings of the XIX International Symposium on Computers in Education.* 114-118. https://www.eselx.ipl.pt/sites/default/files/media/2017/siie-cied_2017_atas-compressed.pdf

[4] Code.org. 2018. https://code.org

[5] Code Club Australia. 2018. https://codeclubau.org

[6] Max Colthart, Kathleen Rastle, Conrad Perry, Robyn Langdon, and Johannes Ziegler. 2001. DRC: a dual route cascaded model of visual word recognition and reading aloud. *Psychological review 108,* 204-256. DOI: http://10.1037/0033-295X.108.1.204

[7] Katrina Falkner and Rebecca Vivian. 2015. Coding across the curriculum: Resource review. Australian Government: Department of Education and Training. 1-52. https://digital.library.adelaide.edu.au/dspace/bitstream/2440/95629/3/hdl_95629.pdf

[8] Shuchi Grover and Roy Pea. 2013. Computational thinking in K-12: A review of the state of the field. *Educational Researcher, 42,* 1. 38-43. DOI: https://doi.org/10.3102/0013189X12463051

[9] Shuchi Grover, Roy Pea, and Stephen Cooper. 2015. Designing for deeper learning in a blended computer science course for middle school students. *Computer science education, 25, 2,* 199-237. DOI: http://dx.doi.org/10.1080/08993408.2015.1033142

[10] Shuchi Grover and Satabdi Basu. 2017. Measuring student learning in introductory block-based programming: Examining misconceptions of loops, variables, and boolean logic. *Proceedings of the 48th ACM Technical Symposium on Computer Science Education (SIGCSE '17).* Seattle, WA: ACM. DOI: https://10.1145/3017680.3017723

[11] Mark Guzdial. 2015. Learner-centered design of computing education: Research on computing for everyone. *Synthesis Lectures on Human-Centered Informatics, 8, 6,* 1–165. DOI: https://doi.org/10.2200/S00684ED1V01Y201511HCI033

[12] Henry Hamburger and Stephen Crain. 1984. Acquisition of cognitive compiling. *Cognition, 17, 2,* 85-136. DOI:10.1016/0010-0277(84)90015-5

[13] Henry Hamburger and Stephen Crain. 1987. Plans and semantics in human processing of language. *Cognitive Science, 11,* 101-136 DOI: https://doi.org/10.1111/j.1551-6708.1987.tb00864.x

[14] JASP Team. 2018. JASP (Version 0.8.6) [Computer software]

[15] A. S. Kaufman and N. L. Kaufman. 2004. Kaufman Assessment Battery for Children Second Edition. Circle Pines, MN: American Guidance Service

[16] Elizabeth R. Kazakoff, Amanda Sullivan, and Marina Umaschi Bers. 2013. The effect of a classroom-based intensive robotics and programming workshop on sequencing ability in early childhood. *Early Childhood Education Journal 41, 4,* 245-255. DOI: https://doi.org/10.1007/s10643-012-0554-5

[17] Elizabeth R. Kazakoff and Marina Umaschi Bers. 2012. Programming a robotics context in the kindergarten classroom: The impact on sequencing skills. *Journal of Educational Multimedia and Hypermedia, 21, 4.* 371-391 Waynesville, NC USA: Association for the Advancement of Computing in Education (AACE). Retrieved March 26, 2018 from https://www.learntechlib.org/p/39512/

[18] Kyu Han Koh, Ashok Basawapatna, Hilarie Nickerson, and Alexander Repenning. 2014. Real time assessment of computational thinking. *Visual Languages and Human-Centric Computing.* IEEE Symposium, 49-52. DOI: 10.1109/VLHCC.2014.6883021

[19] Robyn Langdon and Max Coltheart. 2000. The cognitive neuropsychology of delusions. *Mind & Language, 15,* 1. 184-218. DOI: https://doi.org/10.1111/1468-0017.00129

[20] Willem Levelt. 1999. Models of word production. *Trends in cognitive science, 3.* 223-232. DOI: https://doi.org/10.1016/S1364-6613(99)01319-4

[21] Edward H. Matthei. 1982. The acquisition of the prenominal modifier sequences. *Cognition, 11,* 301-332. DOI: https://doi.org/10.1016/0010-0277(82)90018-X

[22] Jesús Moreno-León, Gregorio Robles and Marcos Román-González. 2015. Dr. Scratch: Automatic analysis of scratch projects to assess and foster computational thinking. *Revista de Educación a Distancia 46,* 1-23. https://www.researchgate.net/publication/281714025_Dr_Scratch_Automatic_Analysis_of_Scratch_Projects_to_Assess_and_Foster_Computational_Thinking

[23] Seymour Papert. 1980. Mindstorms: Children, computers, and powerful ideas. Basic Books, New York, NY

[24] Primotoys. 2018. https://www.primotoys.com

[25] Miranda C. Parker, Mark Guzdial, and Shelly Engleman. 2016. Replication, Validation, and Use of a Language Independent CS1 Knowledge Assessment. *Proceedings of the 2016 ACM Conference on International Computing Education Research.* 93-101. DOI: 10.1145/2960310.2960316

[26] Robert Rigal. 1994. Right-left orientation: Development of correct use of right and left terms. *Perceptual and Motor Skills 79, 3,* 1259-1278. DOI: 10.2466/pms.1994.79.3.1259

[27] Marcos Román-González, Juan-Carlos Pérez-González, and Carmen Jiménez-Fernández. 2016. Which cognitive abilities underlie computational thinking? Criterion validity of the Computational Thinking Test. *Computers in Human Behavior 72,* 678-691. DOI: 10.1016/j.chb.2016.08.047

[28] Jeffrey N. Rouder, Paul L. Speckman, Dongchu Sun, Richard D. Morey, and Geoffrey Iverson. 2009. Bayesian t tests for accepting and rejecting the null hypothesis. *Psychonomic Bulletin & Review, 16, 2,* 225–237. DOI:10.3758/Pbr.16.2.225

[29] Linda Seiter. 2015. Using SOLO to Classify the Programming Responses of Primary Grade Students. *Proceedings of the 46th ACM Technical Symposium on Computer Science Education (SIGCSE '15).* 540-545. DOI: 10.1145/2676723.2677244

[30] Linda Seiter and Brendan Foreman. 2013. Modeling the Learning Progressions of Computational Thinking of Primary Grade Students. *Proceedings of the 2013 ACM Conference on International Computing Education Research.* 59-66. DOI: 10.1145/2493394.2493403

[31] Marina Umaschi Bers. 2010. The TangibleK Robotics Program: Applied Computational Thinking for Young Children. *Early Childhood Research and Practice, 12,* 2 http://ecrp.uiuc.edu/v12n2/bers.html

[32] Linda Werner, Jill Denner, Shannon Campe, and Damon Chizuru Kawamoto. 2012. The fairy performance assessment: measuring computational thinking in middle school. Proceedings of the 43rd ACM technical symposium on Computer Science Education, ACM Press, New York, NY, 215-220. DOI:10.1145/2157136.2157200

Starting from Scratch: Outcomes of Early Computer Science Learning Experiences and Implications for What Comes Next

David Weintrop
University of Maryland
College Park, MD, USA
weintrop@umd.edu

Alexandria K. Hansen
UC Santa Barbara
Santa Barbara, CA, USA
akhansen@ucsb.edu

Danielle B. Harlow
UC Santa Barbara
Santa Barbara, CA, USA
dharlow@education.ucsb.edu

Diana Franklin
University of Chicago
Chicago, IL, USA
dmfraklin@uchicago.edu

ABSTRACT

Visual block-based programming environments (VBBPEs) such as Scratch and Alice are increasingly being used in introductory computer science lessons across elementary school grades. These environments, and the curricula that accompany them, are designed to be developmentally-appropriate and engaging for younger learners but may introduce challenges for future computer science educators. Using the final projects of 4th, 5th, and 6th grade students who completed an introductory curriculum using a VBBPE, this paper focuses on patterns that show success within the context of VBBPEs but could pose potential challenges for teachers of follow-up computer science instruction. This paper focuses on three specific strategies observed in learners' projects: (1) wait blocks being used to manage program execution, (2) the use of event-based programming strategies to produce parallel outcomes, and (3) the coupling of taught concepts to curricular presentation. For each of these outcomes, we present data on how the course materials supported them, what learners achieved while enacting them, and the implications the strategy poses for future educators. We then discuss possible design and pedagogical responses. The contribution of this work is that it identifies early computer science learning strategies, contextualizes them within developmentally-appropriate environments, and discusses their implications with respect to future pedagogy. This paper advances our understanding of the role of VBBPEs in introductory computing and their place within the larger K-12 computer science trajectory.

CCS CONCEPTS

• Social and professional topics → Professional topics → Computing Education

KEYWORDS

Elementary Computer Science Education; Introductory Computing Curricula; Block-based programming; Learning

ACM Reference format:
D. Weintrop, A. K. Hansen, D. B. Harlow, and D. Franklin. 2018. In Proceedings of the 2018 ACM Conference on International Computing Education Research (ICER '18). ACM, New York, NY, USA, 21-29. DOI: https://doi.org/10.1145/3230977.3230988

1 INTRODUCTION

The call to bring computer science (CS) to all learners has reached a roar as districts, states, and countries around the world are increasingly making CS part of the school experience for learners across the K-12 spectrum. While there exists a diversity of languages, programming environments, and curricula for the oldest K-12 learners, a narrower set of introductory experiences exist for younger students. In elementary school (grades K-8, ages 5-13), CS instruction is largely being taught using visual block-based programming environments (VBBPEs) like Scratch [39] and Alice [9]. Curricula including Creative Computing [6] and the K-8 code.org materials utilize VBBPEs. VBBPEs are popular due to the affordances they provide young learners. Transitioning learners from introductory learning experiences with VBBPEs to more conventional text-based programming environments poses challenges to educators and curriculum designers. The very features of VBBPEs that allow novice learners to be successful may present challenges to future educators, requiring them to more closely consider learners' previous experiences and potentially modify instructional strategies to support learners as they progress.

It is these considerations that we explore in this paper, specifically with the goal of understanding outcomes of using VBBPEs with elementary learners and how this decision should inform subsequent curriculum design and pedagogy. More specifically, we answer the following research questions:

What are examples of strategies that learners develop through introductory experiences with VBBPEs that future educators should be aware of? How and when might these strategies differ from what is taught in subsequent classes where text-based programming languages are used?

To begin to answer these questions, we draw on data from a classroom implementation of a VBBPE and accompanying curriculum. Specifically, we present data on three outcomes of students learning CS with a VBBPE that have potential implications for future instruction: 1) wait blocks being used to manage program execution in two distinct ways, (2) the use of event-based programming strategies to produce parallel outcomes, and (3) the coupling of taught concepts to curricular presentation. For each of these strategies, we present data on how the course materials supported these outcomes, what learners achieved through enacting them, and discuss potential design and pedagogical responses. The goal of this work is to advance our understanding of what learners are able to achieve in a developmentally-appropriate introductory course with a VBBPE and to consider what the implications of these outcomes are for future CS instruction that moves beyond VBBPEs. This paper begins with a review of relevant work before presenting the LaPlaya environment and KELP-CS curriculum. We then present the three strategies and discuss implications of this work.

2 PRIOR WORK

2.1 Visual Block-based Programming Environments

In this paper, we use the term visual block-based programming environment (VBBPE) to capture the set of programming tools that introduce learners to programming through a block-based interface and have a visual execution environment (e.g. sprites on a stage). This type of environment is exemplified by Scratch [39], Alice [9], and Pencil Code [3]. Numerous widely-used introductory environments do not meet this definition of a VBBPE as they only include some of the defining VBBPE features, like MIT App Inventor's [54] use of block-based programming and Greenfoot's use of sprite-like actors [26]. In this section, we discuss three key features of VBBPEs that are pertinent to this study.

The first key component of VBBPEs is the use of a block-based programming interface that leverages a programming-primitive-as-puzzle-piece metaphor to provide visual cues to the user about how and where blocks can be used [4, 30]. Users compose programs in these environments by dragging blocks onto a canvas and snapping them together to form scripts. If two blocks cannot be joined to form a valid syntactic statement, the environment prevents them from snapping together, thus preventing syntax errors but retaining the practice of assembling programs instruction-by-instruction. Along with using block shape to denote use, there are other visual cues to help programmers, including color coding by conceptual use and nesting of blocks to denote scope [30, 47, 53].

A second key characteristic of VBBPEs is the notion of a Sprite – an on-screen, two-dimensional character that follows programming instructions defined by the user. The sprite can be viewed as the modern incarnation of Logo's turtle [36]. In discussing the development and role of the Turtle, Papert invokes Piaget's notion of a mother structure – an intellectual construct from which concepts can be created. In the Turtle, Papert saw the

embodiment of differential geometry in a way that could be anthropomorphized by the learner [35]. While the Sprite can still be used towards these mathematical ends, increasingly it's role is as a computational mother structure, i.e. a means to develop foundational computational ideas. As we will argue in this paper, whereas the path one follows using the turtle as the means to express differential geometry concepts has been mapped [1], it is less clear what path one follows when moving from sprite-driven programming towards more advanced computational ideas that may not be executed visually.

A third central feature of VBBPEs is their support for open-ended and exploratory programming activities. This feature draws directly from the Constructionist design principle of being "discovery rich" [35]. Scratch and other VBBPEs accomplish this by providing an accessible and intuitive set of programming blocks but little in the way of constraints with respect to how they can or should be used. Through designing a platform for open-ended exploratory activities, VBBPEs do not prescribe specific practices, instead supporting an epistemological pluralism [49] that does not favor one specific program approach or one type of project.

2.2 Computer Science in Elementary School

In the last decade, bringing CS to K-8 has become more widespread, facilitated by programming tools designed for young learners [12, 25]. Early work on programming as a means for learning conducted by Papert and colleagues with the Logo language found that programming was accessible to younger learners and could serve as a powerful learning practice [20, 34, 36]. Following these successes, much of the curricular and programming environment design effort has employed Constructionist design principles, foregrounding learning-by-doing and learner-directed activities. This can be seen in growing library of curricula designed for elementary learning, including: Creative Computing [6], Foundations for Advancing Computational Thinking [17], Animal Tlatoque [13], and the KELP-CS curriculum [23]. There are also growing online communities where classroom activities designed for elementary students are curated and shared, like the ScratchEd website and the CS for All Consortium, which includes over 100 organizations that self-identify as content providers for elementary learners. Code.org also offers nine distinct CS courses for students across grades K-8 (ages 5-13), including both conventional computer-based curricula as well as offline activities based on the CS unplugged curriculum [5] and computing activities designed for science classrooms based on Project GUTS [38]. Collectively, these resources capture part of the quickly expanding ecosystem of ways that CS is being introduced into elementary education.

2.3 Research on Learning In VBBPEs

A growing body of research is investigating how block-based programming shapes learners' conceptual understanding of CS concepts and emerging programming strategies. For example, researchers have documented a number of 'habits' of programming learners develop while working in block-based tools, such as an emphasis on bottom-up programming where learners focus on using specific blocks [33]. Other strategies investigated include documenting how learners at different ages design for their audiences [19] and debugging strategies and the requisite knowledge to implement them [28]. Further work has documented programming strategies specific to VBBPEs, looking at how the scaffolds present in the environment support unique patterns of interaction [52]. Likewise, a growing body of research is documenting how novices learn with block-based tools; identifying misconceptions learners may develop in VBBPEs and developmentally-appropriate content for learners [15, 16, 42]. For example, research looking at learners' emerging understanding of the initialization of state and variables in VBBPEs identified four distinct conceptual components of the topic (e.g. when to initialize) and showed how they are differentially manifested in VBBPEs compared to conventional text-based languages [14]. The findings presented herein build on and complement this work by continuing to fill in our understanding of what it means for young learners to develop foundational understandings of computational ideas in VBBPEs. Likewise, our analysis considers if and how ideas and strategies developed in VBBPEs do or do not relate to future instruction and learning in conventional text-based languages.

3 METHODS

The work presented in this paper is part of a larger, design-based research study focusing on the creation of elementary CS classroom materials. We begin this section by presenting the LaPlaya VBBPE and KELP-CS curriculum. We then present details on the participants and study design before concluding the section discussing the data collected and analytic approach used.

3.1 Materials

LaPlaya (Fig. 1) is a VBBPE built on top of the Snap! programming environment [22]. Like Scratch, students program via a drag-and-drop interaction, producing scripts of blocks to control on-screen sprites. LaPlaya is designed to support both guided and open-ended exploration for upper elementary school students (grades 4-6; ages 8-12). To help make programming more accessible to younger learners, LaPlaya includes a number of unique pedagogical scaffolds. For example, when introducing new concepts, students are provided with pre-programmed and locked scripts (Fig. 2a) at the beginning of the new activity. These scripts are visible and accompanied by text descriptions to serve as examples. LaPlaya also includes white, inert scripts (Fig. 2b) that are not executable and serve as templates of how blocks can be used to accomplish a desired outcome.

LaPlaya's blocks were also modified with respect to the original Snap! language in order to remove more advanced mathematical concepts such as percentages, negative numbers, and decimals for our younger students (ages 9-10). In addition, to support learners at varying reading levels, LaPlaya has an audio, read-aloud function so task instructions can be heard. This is particularly important for English language learners. For additional information about LaPlaya and the modifications made to make it more accessible to novice learners, see [21, 23].

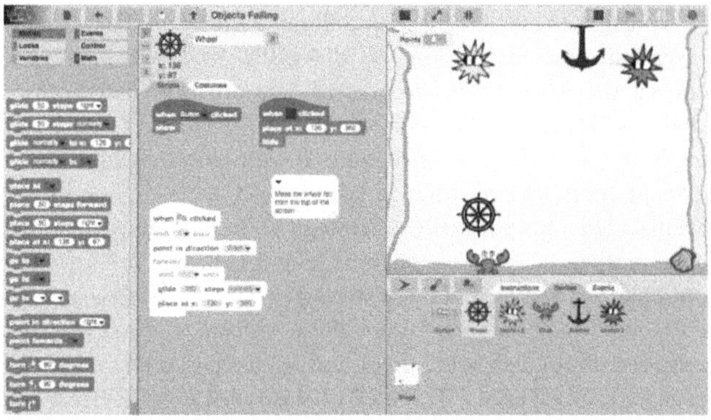

Figure 1. The LaPlaya programming environment.

(a)   (b)

Figure 2. LaPlaya scaffolds: (a) Predefined, locked scripts with textual hints and (b) inert scripts used as templates.

The KELP-CS curriculum was designed for the LaPlaya programming environment with the goal of providing a developmentally-appropriate introduction to foundational CS concepts. KELP-CS consists of a predefined sequence of modules comprised of activities that gradually introduce CS concepts and the associated blocks to students as they progress. KELP-CS includes both these structured tasks with specific conceptual learning objectives as well as an open-ended play area with the module's full set of blocks to keep more advanced learners engaged and provide a space for learner-directed exploration throughout the curriculum. The KELP-CS curriculum has two main types of activities: 1) On-computer assignments and 2) "unplugged" activities completed away from a computer. On-computer activities consisted of small, incremental tasks designed to move students to higher levels of programming sophistication. Unplugged activities were modeled after CS-Unplugged [5] with the goal of connecting computing to students everyday lives. Modules culminate with open-ended projects.

KELP-CS features two main curricular modules, each designed around a different theme: 1) Digital Storytelling and 2) Game Design. Each module is designed to be completed in approximately 15-18 hours of instruction. The modules are meant to be completed sequentially. The first Module (Digital Storytelling) covers the following concepts: Sequencing, Breaking down actions, Events, Initialization, Animating sprites, and Changing scenes. The second module (Game Design) continues with Broadcasting messages, Loops, Conditional logic, and Variables. Both modules culminated with an open-ended programming activity, allowing the learner to employ the concepts learned throughout the unit.

3.2   Participants and Study Design

The data for this paper are drawn from one school located in the Southwestern United States where 4th, 5th, and 6th grade students (ages 9-12) worked through the KELP-CS curriculum over the course of two consecutive school years. In the first year, two classes in each grade, totaling 44 fourth graders, 48 fifth graders and 43 sixth graders, completed the first KELP-CS module (Digital Story Telling). The second year consisted of a single fifth grade class of 18 students who completed the second KELP-CS module (Game Design). This resulted in a total of 135 unique students over the two years. The school where the study was conducted is racially diverse (54% White, 35% Hispanic or Latino, 5% Asian, and 3% Black or African American) with approximately 31% of students coming from economically disadvantaged households and 16% of students schoolwide designated as English-language learners.

Each year, students spent roughly 1 hour per week for 15 weeks working in the KELP-CS curriculum. Each class session was observed by researchers and video recorded for later analysis. Additionally, the LaPlaya VBBPE was modified so as to automatically collect student projects, which serves as the primary data source for the analysis presented in this paper.

3.3   Analytic Approach

The analysis presented in this paper focuses on the 135 summative programs authored by the participants in this study. Our decision to focus on student-authored programs stems from the constructivist learning orientation and the constructionist design philosophy we bring to this work. Constructivist learning theory posits that new knowledge is built through the processes of assimilation and accommodation with learners' existing knowledge. In Constructionist learning environments, that understanding is manifest through the artifacts built by learners, which in this case, are the programs authored [34]. As such, we use these constructed artifacts as a means to gain insight into learners' emerging understanding of CS concepts and look at how concepts are used within the larger program to understand emerging programming strategies.

To analyze this data, each program was statically analyzed using a custom-written script to catalog its contents with respect to type and frequency of blocks used. Next, we undertook a grounded-theory approach [44] with one researcher analyzing each program individually looking for evidence of strategies, patterns, or emerging programming strategies. This initial set of strategies was presented to the larger research team, who further refined the defining characteristics of each strategy and created a qualitative coding manual to describe the usages. The coding manual was then applied to the full set of programs to understand the frequency of each pattern. This approach allows us to situate each pattern within the curriculum as a way to help us understand potential implications with respect to pedagogy and future CS learning.

4   FINDINGS

This section presents three outcomes of learners as expressed in their culminating projects following the completion of modules in KELP-CS. The analysis focuses on emerging learner strategies that

are developmentally-appropriate and productive within the context of the KELP-CS curriculum and have potential implications for how teachers of subsequent classes that use traditional programming languages design instruction. As such, educators should be aware of these strategies and think about how best to productively utilize them to scaffold and support learners as they progress in their CS learning careers. For each strategy, we first present student data demonstrating the strategy in use and documenting its frequency across the participant pool. We then link the strategy to features of KELP-CS or LaPlaya and discuss how the environment productively supports the strategy as well as future challenges that may emerge. We conclude each section discussing ways future educators can respond to it.

It bears repeating that the goal of this work is to identify strategies students develop in VBBPEs that are *different from* those conventionally used in non-VBBPE introductory CS instruction. This is not meant to imply that VBBPEs are inappropriate for introductory computing contexts, instead, we seek to advance our understanding of how best to support learners as they progress along a CS learning trajectory.

4.1   Managing Execution with Wait Blocks

A frequent goal of programs in VBBPE is to coordinate a series of on-screen events such as the speed at which a sprite dances or how and when two sprites interact. Achieving this coordination requires the learner to define specific instructions in their programs. One common way to achieve these behaviors is to manually control the speed of the execution of scripts using the wait block. Seventy-four participants (54.8%) used the wait block at least once in their final projects, while 13 (9.6%) used it more than 10 times. In our analysis, we found this strategy employed in two distinct forms: intra-sprite delays and inter-sprite synchronization, both of which are accomplished using the wait block.

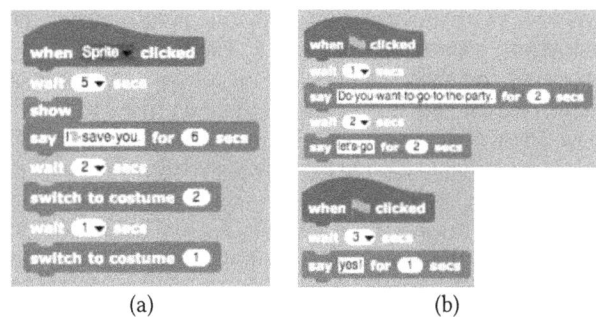

(a)   (b)

Figure 3. Two examples of students using wait block to control the execution of their programs

4.1.1 Intra-script Delays. As part of their final projects, students often wanted to slow down the execution of a script for a single sprite and used the wait block to accomplish this goal. Fig. 3a shows a student project that demonstrates an intra-script delay. In this case, the wait blocks added between the costume change blocks are used for this purpose. The result is that the sprite's appearance changes at the specified rate. This strategy was used as both a storytelling mechanism and a way to animate sprites. Of the 135 projects analyzed, 58 of them (43%) utilized this strategy to control the speed of execution within a script.

4.1.2 Inter-Sprite Synchronization with Wait Blocks. The second use of the wait block to control program execution was to coordinate the timing of actions between sprites. Fig. 3b shows two scripts from a student project that implements a conversation between two sprites. Because the synchronization spans two sprites, the scripts that define this synchronization cannot be viewed on screen at the same time. This means authoring and debugging programs that use this strategy relies heavily on interpreting the outcome of the visual execution environment. Across the full set of participants, 37.8% of final projects included this type of intra-sprite coordination.

4.1.3 Introductory Benefits and Potential Future Challenges. In these two examples, we see how young learners take advantage of the access that VBBPEs give to manipulate how and when scripts are run. Through the use of the wait block, novice programmers were able to create animations and achieve synchronization through parallelization of their programs, both of which are outcomes that would come much later in a conventional, non-VBBPE-based CS instructional sequence. However, these strategies do introduce potential mismatches with future CS instruction. For example, in manipulating execution speed with the wait block, learners both manually control the rate of execution of a program and use that control to slow down the rate of execution. These are reasonable for this context as doing so makes animations clearer and sets the pace of sprite interactions such that the user has time to interpret what is happening on the screen.

However, the characteristic of wanting to control the speed of execution is rarely a goal in early text-based instruction found in K-12 classrooms. High school courses taught in languages like Java, Python, or JavaScript rarely include animations or ask students to control the rate at which things happen, instead, the focus is on non-temporal aspects of programming (like algorithms, sequencing, state, etc.). Further, when time is considered in most introductory text-based programming instruction, the goal is to *speed up* execution time, not slow it down. These strategies suggest to learners that the speed at which computers perform tasks can be easily predicted or controlled.

Additionally, the use of wait blocks to manually and explicitly control timing to achieve parallelization is quite distinct from the parallel programming approaches students might encounter early in text-based programming instruction. This fact can be seen in the design of many VBBPEs directly as many include message passing and broadcasting features to achieve parallel outcomes. Previous work looking at how parallel outcomes are achieved found that students were substantially less likely to use this mechanism than the simpler wait blocks [19]. This finding is replicated by this work as only 16 students used this feature of the VBBPE. Because of the age of the students, the simplicity of wait blocks, and the relative predictability when on a single machine, it is appropriate that students solve problems with wait blocks.

4.1.4 Considerations for Future Educators and Designers. Educators teaching a class comprised of students that recently completed a course using a VBBPE should be aware of the strategies their students may have developed related to the wait block and other temporal blocks, such as say for. Learners may begin to think that speed is a characteristic of the computer that is meant to be programmatically manipulated, alongside aspects like sequential flow and program state. While manually controlling when instructions are evaluated or focusing on speed or timing of a piece of code is an authentic programming strategy, temporal characteristics of programming (such as optimization or parallel computing) usually occur much later in CS instruction. In terms of how this affects educators, the first step is raising awareness of the difference between programming *when* an event occurs versus *how* it occurs. As more students enter second and third computing curricula with prior experience in VBBPEs, teachers may want to include explicit instruction on the temporal dimension of the programs being authored and attend to students' potential desire to pursue solutions that seek to manipulate the speed at which instructions execute as a means to achieve a desired outcome.

Future educators should also be aware of the implication of learners coordinating parallel execution with wait blocks. Using wait block to control the behavior of the program connotes the idea that each object has an internal clock that controls how and when it operates, and that there is a shared universal clock on which they can rely for timing. When learners do eventually encounter synchronization in parallel systems, they will need to be explicitly taught about absolute timing and the assumptions that can and cannot be made based on the technologies and tools being used. This again ties back to the larger theme of deemphasizing *when* commands execute, instead focusing learners' attention on *how* they are used.

4.2 Coordination with Event-based Programming

Visual block-based programming environments often employ an event-based programming approach. In this paradigm, to run a program, you associate a sequence of blocks with an action, be it clicking the green flag (akin to a start button), waiting for an in-program event (like receiving a message), or binding a script to a key press. Events are an intuitive and accessible way to engage novices and younger learners with programming and were very common in student final projects. Students used an average of 13.5 events blocks (*SD* 20.8) per project, with 27 students using more than 20 event blocks, and 6 students defining more than 50 events.

Event-driven programming makes it easy to create interactive programs. It also gives the programmer direct control over how and when behaviors in their programs are run. In addition, it allows a programmer to think and program separately about what should happen at different points in the program, reducing the length of any piece of code. In this way, it helps achieve the low-threshold to programming sought by the designers of VBBPEs and contributes to the engagement and enjoyment of the environment [30].

4.2.1 Introductory Benefits and Potential Future Challenges. The inclusion of a suite of event blocks (such as when key pressed and when sprite clicked) gives the learner a number of intuitive hooks for inserting programmed behavior. This approach is different from many general-purpose programming languages, in which early instruction often focuses on a single main function (often called main) that is called that begins the serial execution of the program. Event-based programming provides a pair of introductory benefits that may turn into potential challenges for future educators.

The first outcome of introducing learners to programming in event-based VBBPEs is tied to the fact that event-based programming environments are inherently parallel. In VBBPEs, multiple sprites can operate in parallel in response to the same event, or a single sprite can perform two tasks in parallel in response to the same event. These parallel programming capabilities are present in the text-based languages that learners may transition to but students are unlikely to encounter these features until later in their CS education paths. Looking across the full set of projects, 106 of the 135 student-created projects utilized concurrency by having multiple scripts linked to the same event.

A second potential outcome from learning to program in event-driven programming is developing habits that are unique to the event-based paradigm and do not have natural analogs in conventional text-based programming languages. For example, students can bind multiple scripts to the same event for the same sprite *even though the events are not intended to execute in parallel.* Fig. 4 depicts an example of this found in a final project showing four of the 12 scripts the student defined for the when left arrow key pressed event of a single sprite. In composing these blocks, the learner directly mapped an event with multiple actions. Conceptually, this both makes sense and is an intuitive approach to achieving a behavior such as making multiple things happen after a single key press. However, this also circumvents the need to define the steps of the program sequentially in a single script. While this is a functional solution, it is not how the same outcome would be achieved in a non-event-based context. A total of 36 final projects included parallel implementations of serial behaviors, which suggests this is a relatively common occurrence and something educators should be made aware of. This distinction is meaningful because if all the commands shown in Fig. 4 were moved into a single script, the numerical values in the wait block would need to change, meaning the shift is not just reorganizing commands, but the underlying logic needs to be modified as well.

4.2.2 Considerations for Future Educators and Designers. The program shown in Fig. 4 is one example of the more general outcome of learners developing programming strategies that

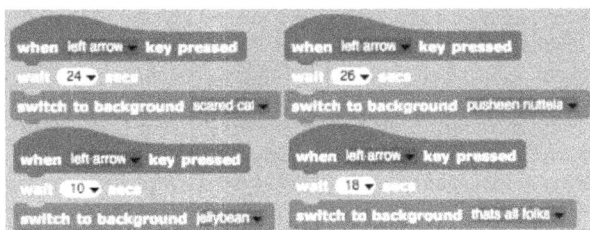

Figure 4. Four of the 12 when left arrow key pressed scripts defined in one students' final project.

leverage features of event-based programming. This is to be expected of novices with little prior experience and shows how they take advantage of affordances present in VBBPEs. This finding suggests that teachers of more advanced courses should

be aware of and prepared to help students move from the parallel thinking supported by events toward the linear, sequential ordering of commands imposed by the languages used in later instruction.

4.3 Coupling Concepts with Specific Contexts

The strategy used to introduce new CS concepts to elementary learners in the KELP-CS curriculum was to situate the concept in a specific context and provide scaffolds to facilitate learners in writing a program to use the concept in a specific way. This strategy serves as the first step in the Use-Modify-Create pedagogical strategy common to introductory computational thinking instruction [27]. KELP-CS had novices first *Use* a new concept, then provided opportunities to incorporate the concept into later programs, either in the same role but different context (*Modify*) or in new ways altogether (*Create*). For example, to introduce learners to conditional logic (the if block), the KELP-CS curriculum helped learners create a maze game, using conditional logic to make sure the player's sprite did not walk through any walls or touch any of the obstacles along the way. In a different game, the if block was used to detect when two sprites touched. In both cases, an if block with a touching block inside it was used to implement collision detection in the game. Fig. 5a shows how these blocks were first introduced to learners through LaPlaya's inert blocks feature. The thing to note about this example is the pattern of nesting the if block inside a forever loop and using the touching block as the test condition of the if block.

To understand the relationship between the way concepts were introduced in the KELP-CS curriculum and how they were used in students' open-ended final project, we developed an analytic coding scheme to situate the use of a concept within the Use-Modify-Create trajectory. In this analytic scheme, concepts can be presented in students' final projects at four levels of sophistication delineated based on their similarity to how the concept was introduced in the curriculum. First, the concept could be absent (as was the case for conditional logic in 6 of the 18 Module 2 projects). Second, the *Use* level of sophistication describes instances where learners use the concept in their final projects in the exact same role as it was used within the lesson. Meaning the use of the forever, if and touching blocks matches the structure shown in Fig. 5a.

The third level of expertise is illustrated by Fig. 5b. In this case, the student applied conditional logic in the same way (i.e. as a mechanism for detecting collisions) and programmed it with the same general structure (an if block nested in a forever block with a touching block as its test condition), but *Modified* its application to integrate other concepts such as a score, sprite placement, timing, and visibility. Two-thirds of the final projects (12 projects) demonstrated the ability to incorporate conditional logic in their programs in a role similar to how it was used in the curriculum. Finally, three students used conditional logic in a different way (beyond a mechanism for detecting collisions), demonstrating a *Create* level of understanding. These data show

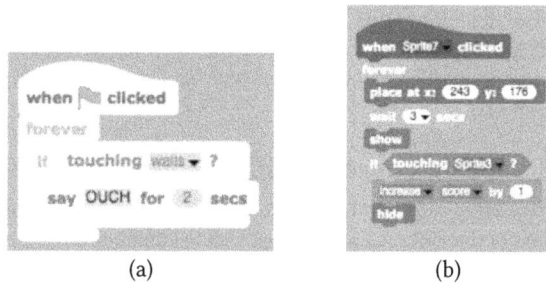

(a)   (b)

Figure 5. (a) The first conditional logic template and (b) an example of how it was incorporated into a final project.

how the Use-Modify-Create progression implemented in KELP-CS is developmentally-appropriate and helped learners at different levels, but also suggests the opportunity for educators to adjust pedagogical strategies to effectively build on these early successes.

4.3.1 Introductory Benefits and Potential Future Challenges. Firstly, it is important to note that in introductory contexts, any application of the concept in a learner-authored program should be viewed as a success. The strategy of students using code exactly as it was taught to them or as it exists in another project can help novices have programming successes early in their exposure to CS content. This form of remixing is a central strategy to computational thinking [7] and a common practice of programmers at all levels of expertise. Likewise, CS educators have argued that it is important to introduce concepts in context to help learners see the relevance and applicability of what is being learned [8, 41]. However, there is also research showing that students are more successful in learning when extraneous material (i.e. context) is absent, arguing the decontextualized presentation is more effective as it decreases the cognitive load associated with the learning task [32, 45]. Based on these seemingly contradictory findings, we came to the same conclusion as Guzdial [18], who concluded: "The only way to achieve decontextualized knowledge is to teach beyond a single context."

As such, in the KELP-CS curriculum, concepts were taught in multiple contexts. In the case of conditional logic in Module 2, that meant using the if block to create different styles of games. The goal in showing these two different applications of conditional logic was to help learners understand the underlying concept and see how it can be used in two distinct ways. However, the results show that it is unclear the degree to which the two contexts helped. In particular, it could have provided two concrete ways of using the concepts as opposed to providing a generalized understanding of the concept of conditional logic.

4.3.2 Considerations for Future Educators and Designers. While the Use-Modify-Create approach was pedagogically productive, our analysis suggests it does pose a potential challenge for future CS educators. By teaching concepts situated in a specific context, there is potential that the concept gets coupled to that particular use (e.g. for building games).

The data presented above, and the characterization of usages within the Use-Modify-Create progression, shows learners using

the concept at all four levels of sophistication. There are two direct implications of this for future educators. First, educators should be aware of how concepts were presented and situated in early lessons so as to be able to present new and complementary uses of concepts. When a concept is presented in a new context, educators should also try and link the new presentation with prior contexts and implement bridging and hugging strategies suggested by research [11, 37].

Second, these data reinforce the fact that full understanding of a concept may require several courses in which concepts are taught in a variety of ways – educators targeting second or third experiences should not consider that "conditionals have already been covered" and assume full understanding. For a subsequent Scratch curriculum, in the case of conditional logic, this may mean using the construct for something other than collision detection or using it outside of a loop. Examples include comparing numerical values as part of a score-keeping mechanism or comparing x or y positions on the screen as to coordinate a dance across multiple sprites. Further, this is especially true when the new context is in a different language, modality, or environment. Doing so will further help students build conceptual bridges between the different forms of programming they will see throughout future CS instruction.

5 DISCUSSION

5.1 Preparing Expert Computer Science Teachers

One of the many challenges faced by districts and schools is recruiting, training, and retaining capable CS teachers. As the demand for CS across K-12 grows, so, too, does the need to bring new teachers into the discipline. One of the goals of this work is to show that when it comes to supporting learners as they progress through the K-12 CS trajectory, teachers should be aware of both previous and future CS courses to best support learners.

This paper documents three specific strategies that teachers charged with moving learners on to the next step in their CS careers should be prepared for. The strategies span curriculum design (defining new contexts to situate content), CS content knowledge (situations where learners focus on temporal aspects of execution), and CS pedagogical content knowledge (how different paradigms affect programming strategies). Collectively, this highlights the challenge that new CS teachers face. We make this point at the same time that one of the prevailing approaches to training new CS teachers is to provide them with a full suite of classroom materials (lessons, environments, assessments, etc.) to make it as easy as possible for them to get up and running quickly in their new discipline. While this is a prudent strategy given the immediate demand, the work presented above gives pause to the view that such an approach is sufficient for training teachers to support learners across the K-12 spectrum. Instead, our hope is this all-in-one approach for teachers serves as only the first step in the career-spanning undertaking of learning how best to support students in learning CS.

5.2 Giving Agency to the Learner

A second discussion point that relates to this work speaks to an emerging trend in the continually shifting landscape of introductory programming. Throughout this paper introductory programming environments have been treated as relatively static entities, i.e. they present a single interface and only support one form of interaction. In the case of VBBPEs, that means block-based programming in a sprite-driven context. This characterization is becoming less-and-less accurate with the emergence of new and more flexible programming environments. For example, dual-programming environments such as Pencil Code [3] and Tiled Grace [24] allow the learner to seamlessly transition back and forth between block-based and text-based modalities. Research is finding that this approach is useful for novice programmers [31, 50].

While the LaPlaya programming environment did provide a scaffolded programming interface that expanded as learners' knowledge and confidence grew in the form of introducing new blocks and categories, this shift was determined by the curriculum rather than the learner. It is easy to imagine what a learner-directed version of this form of scaffolding could look like where the learners themselves are free to decide how and when they want to see more blocks or simplify the programming environment. Scratch offers features similar to this in the form of extensions and Microwrolds [48]. Likewise, it is easy to imagine a curriculum that is designed to give the learner more agency in deciding how and when they progress, a feature that has been implemented by numerous online learning tools. The challenge with this approach is figuring out how to support individual agency while still ensuring shared content coverage across the classroom in order to ensure all learners are suitably prepared for future learning opportunities.

5.3 Choosing the Right Tools and Curricula for Your Classroom

One of the challenges of teaching CS is choosing the right curricula and programming languages and environments for your classroom. This is especially challenging for teachers with little or no prior CS experience. As this work highlights, features of the programming environment and the chosen curriculum both shape leaners emerging understandings of CS concepts and the programming strategies they develop. The challenge of picking the best tools and curricula for the classroom is magnified by the lack of a consensus on sequencing of CS concepts, guidelines for how in depth to cover concepts at different grade levels, and agreement in the community about what programming languages to use for instruction. These are problems that are actively being addressed both in the CS education research community [40, 43] as well as through wide-scale community initiatives to provide guidance to states, standards writers, and curriculum designers [10, 55]. When creating and choosing a curriculum and then deciding what environment (or environments) to accompany it in the classroom, it is important to make sure the two are aligned. At the same time, figuring out when, how or even if it is necessary to transition learners from environments that prioritize accessibility versus computational power and broad applicability, is another line ongoing work [2, 11]. There is also a growing body of research investigating VBBPEs and their affordances and drawbacks for elementary CS classrooms [23] and high school classrooms [51]. As this work progresses, hopefully, clarity will emerge as to how best to match environments with curricula and support teachers in effectively bringing them into their classrooms.

It is also important to note, that throughout this work, we have focused on the goal of conceptual learning of CS concepts. While this is an important goal, it is not always the focus of introductory classrooms, nor should it be. A second goal for introductory CS curricula, and one where VBBPEs have historically excelled, is getting learners excited about the field and changing their perceptions about what CS is and who can be a computer scientist [29, 39]. Getting learners interested, excited, and engaged with CS is potentially more important than conceptual learning, especially for young learners as it can change students views of potential future educational goals [46]. The take away from this discussion is the importance of having clear goals as an educator, and aligning those goals with the tools and curricula you choose. One contribution of this work is providing a deeper understanding of the consequences of this decision, especially if the goal for the course is to prepare students for future computer science learning.

6 CONCLUSION

Whereas computer science was once a subject reserved for the final years of high school and beyond, the subject has a growing presence across the K-12 spectrum. In response to the need for computing education in earlier grades, a growing ecosystem of novice programming environments and curricula has emerged. Increasingly, educators and curriculum designers are turning to VBBPEs to serve as the way novices are introduced to programming. While these environments have excelled in informal spaces, their transition to formal classrooms, and their use to prepare all learners for future CS instruction is not without its challenges. In this work, we sought to identify programming strat4gies novices developed while working in VBBPEs that are distinct from what is typically taught in text-based languages and then consider their implications for educators. In particular, using data from student-authored, open-ended summative projects, we show how novices' uses of the wait block, their coordination of execution through events, and the coupling of concepts to the contexts in which they were first introduced all have potential implications for future instruction. The contribution of this work is to deepen our understanding of the use of VBBPEs in the classroom early in learners' CS careers, especially when the goal is preparation for future CS instruction. In doing so, we shed light on open challenges we face as educators and advance the goal of creating effective, accessible CS learning experiences and bringing CS to all learners.

ACKNOWLEDGMENTS

This work is supported by the National Science Foundation Awards CNS-1240985 and CNS-1738758. We would also like to thank all of the teachers, students, and schools involved in this project.

REFERENCES

[1] Abelson, H. and diSessa, A.A. 1986. *Turtle geometry: The computer as a medium for exploring mathematics*. The MIT Press.
[2] Armoni, M., Meerbaum-Salant, O. and Ben-Ari, M. 2015. From Scratch to "Real" Programming. *ACM Transactions on Computing Education (TOCE)*. 14, 4 (2015), 25:1–15.
[3] Bau, D., Bau, D.A., Dawson, M. and Pickens, C.S. 2015. Pencil Code: Block Code for a Text World. *Proc. of the 14th International Conference on Interaction Design and Children* (New York, NY, USA, 2015), 445–448.

[4] Bau, D., Gray, J., Kelleher, C., Sheldon, J. and Turbak, F. 2017. Learnable programming: blocks and beyond. *Comm. of the ACM.* 60, 6 (2017), 72–80.

[5] Bell, T.C., Witten, I.H. and Fellows, M.R. 1998. *Computer Science Unplugged: Off-line activities and games for all ages.* Citeseer.

[6] Brennan, K. 2013. Learning computing through creating and connecting. *Computer.* 46, 9 (2013), 52–59.

[7] Brennan, K. and Resnick, M. 2012. New frameworks for studying and assessing the development of computational thinking. Paper Presented at the American Education Researchers Association Conference. (Vancouver, Canada, 2012).

[8] Cooper, S. and Cunningham, S. 2010. Teaching computer science in context. *ACM Inroads.* 1, 1 (2010), 5–8.

[9] Cooper, S., Dann, W. and Pausch, R. 2000. Alice: a 3-D tool for introductory programming concepts. *Journal of Computing Sciences in Colleges.* 15, 5 (2000), 107–116.

[10] CSTA Standards Task Force 2016. K–12 Computer Science Standards.

[11] Dann, W., Cosgrove, D., Slater, D., Culyba, D. and Cooper, S. 2012. Mediated transfer: Alice 3 to Java. *Proc. of the 43rd ACM SIGCSE Technical Symposium on Computer Science Education* (2012), 141–146.

[12] Duncan, C., Bell, T. and Tanimoto, S. 2014. Should Your 8-year-old Learn Coding? *Proc. of the 9th Workshop in Primary and Secondary Computing Education* (New York, NY, USA, 2014), 60–69.

[13] Franklin, D., Conrad, P., Aldana, G. and Hough, S. 2011. Animal tlatoque: attracting middle school students to computing through culturally-relevant themes. *Proc. of the 42nd ACM technical symposium on Computer science education* (2011), 453–458.

[14] Franklin, D., Hill, C., Dwyer, H., Hansen, A., Iveland, A. and Harlow, D. 2016. Initialization in Scratch: Seeking Knowledge Transfer. *Proc. of the 47th ACM Technical Symposium on Computing Science Education* (2016), 217–222.

[15] Franklin, D., Skifstad, G., Rolock, R., Mehrotra, I., Ding, V., Hansen, A., Weintrop, D. and Harlow, D. 2017. Using Upper-Elementary Student Performance to Understand Conceptual Sequencing in a Blocks-based Curriculum. *Proc. of the 2017 ACM SIGCSE Technical Symposium on Computer Science Education* (New York, NY, USA, 2017), 231–236.

[16] Grover, S. and Basu, S. 2017. Measuring Student Learning in Introductory Block-Based Programming: Examining Misconceptions of Loops, Variables, and Boolean Logic. *Proc. of the 2017 ACM SIGCSE Technical Symposium on Computer Science Education* (New York, NY, 2017), 267–272.

[17] Grover, S., Pea, R. and Cooper, S. 2015. Designing for deeper learning in a blended computer science course for middle school students. *Computer Science Education.* 25, 2 (Apr. 2015), 199–237.

[18] Guzdial, M. 2010. Does contextualized computing education help? *ACM Inroads.* 1, 4 (2010), 4–6.

[19] Hansen, A., Iveland, A., Carlin, C., Harlow, D. and Franklin, D. 2016. User-Centered Design in Block-Based Programming: Developmental & Pedagogical Considerations for Children. Proc. of the 15th International Conference on Interaction Design and Children (2016), 147–156.

[20] Harel, I. and Papert, S. 1990. Software design as a learning environment. *Interactive Learning Environments.* 1, 1 (1990), 1–32.

[21] Harlow, D., Dwyer, H., Hansen, A., Iveland, A. and Franklin, D. Accepted. Ecological design based research in computer science education: Affordances and effectivities for elementary school students. *Cognition and Instruction.*

[22] Harvey, B. and Mönig, J. 2010. Bringing "no ceiling" to Scratch: Can one language serve kids and computer scientists? *Proc. of Constructionism 2010 Conference* (Paris, France, 2010), 1–10.

[23] Hill, C., Dwyer, H., Martinez, T., Harlow, D. and Franklin, D. 2015. Floors and Flexibility: Designing a programming environment for 4th-6th grade classrooms. *Proc. of the 46th ACM Technical Symposium on Computer Science Education* (2015), 546–551.

[24] Homer, M. and Noble, J. 2014. Combining Tiled and Textual Views of Code. *IEEE Working Conference on Software Visualisation* (BC, CA 2014), 1–10.

[25] Kelleher, C. and Pausch, R. 2005. Lowering the barriers to programming: A taxonomy of programming environments and languages for novice programmers. *ACM Computing Surveys.* 37, 2 (2005), 83–137.

[26] Kölling, M. 2010. The greenfoot programming environment. *ACM Transactions on Computing Education (TOCE).* 10, 4 (2010), 14.

[27] Lee, I., Martin, F., Denner, J., Coulter, B., Allan, W., Erickson, J., Malyn-Smith, J. and Werner, L. 2011. Computational thinking for youth in practice. *ACM Inroads.* 2, 1 (2011), 32–37.

[28] Lewis, C.M. 2012. The Importance of Students' Attention to Program State: A Case Study of Debugging Behavior. *Proc. of the 9th Annual International Conference on International Computing Education Research* (New York, NY, USA, 2012), 127–134.

[29] Maloney, J.H., Peppler, K., Kafai, Y., Resnick, M. and Rusk, N. 2008. Programming by choice: Urban youth learning programming with Scratch. *ACM SIGCSE Bulletin.* 40, 1 (2008), 367–371.

[30] Maloney, J.H., Resnick, M., Rusk, N., Silverman, B. and Eastmond, E. 2010. The Scratch programming language and environment. *ACM Transactions on Computing Education (TOCE).* 10, 4 (2010), 16.

[31] Matsuzawa, Y., Ohata, T., Sugiura, M. and Sakai, S. 2015. Language Migration in non-CS Introductory Programming through Mutual Language Translation Environment. *Proc. of the 46th ACM Technical Symposium on Computer Science Education* (2015), 185–190.

[32] Mayer, R.E. 2002. Multimedia learning. *Psychology of learning and motivation.* 41, (2002), 85–139.

[33] Meerbaum-Salant, O., Armoni, M. and Ben-Ari, M. 2011. Habits of programming in Scratch. *Proc. of the 16th Annual Joint Conference on Innovation and Technology in Computer Science Education* (Darmstadt, Germany, 2011), 168–172.

[34] Papert, S. 1980. *Mindstorms: Children, computers, and powerful ideas.* Basic books.

[35] Papert, S. 1988. The conservation of Piaget: The computer as grist for the constructivist mill. *Constructivism in the computer age.* Lawrence Erlbaum. 3–13.

[36] Papert, S., Watt, D., diSessa, A. and Weir, S. 1979. *Final report of the Brookline Logo Project: Project summary and data analysis (Logo Memo 53).* MIT Logo Group.

[37] Perkins, D.N. and Salomon, G. 1988. Teaching for transfer. *Educational leadership.* 46, 1 (1988), 22–32.

[38] Project GUTS: 2016. *http://www.projectguts.org/.* Accessed: 2017-04-10.

[39] Resnick, M., Silverman, B., Kafai, Y., Maloney, J., Monroy-Hernández, A., Rusk, N., Eastmond, E., Brennan, K., Millner, A., Rosenbaum, E. and Silver, J. 2009. Scratch: Programming for all. *Comm. of the ACM.* 52, 11 (2009), 60.

[40] Rich, K., Strickland, C. and Franklin, D. 2017. A Literature Review through the Lens of Computer Science Learning Goals Theorized and Explored in Research. Proc. of the 2017 ACM SIGCSE Technical Symposium on Computer Science Education (Seattle, Wa., 2017).

[41] Rich, L., Perry, H. and Guzdial, M. 2004. A CS1 course designed to address interests of women. *ACM SIGCSE Bulletin* (2004), 190–194.

[42] Seiter, L. and Foreman, B. 2013. Modeling the Learning Progressions of Computational Thinking of Primary Grade Students. *Proc. of the 9th Annual ACM Conference on International Computing Education Research* (New York, NY, USA, 2013), 59–66.

[43] Stefik, A. and Hanenberg, S. 2014. The Programming Language Wars: Questions and Responsibilities for the Programming Language Community. *Proc. of the 2014 ACM International Symposium on New Ideas, New Paradigms, and Reflections on Programming & Software* (New York, NY, USA, 2014), 283–299.

[44] Strauss, A. and Corbin, J. 1994. Grounded Theory Methodology: An Overview. *Strategies of Qualitative Inquiry.* Sage Publications, Inc. 158–183.

[45] Sweller, J. and Chandler, P. 1994. Why some material is difficult to learn. *Cognition and instruction.* 12, 3 (1994), 185–233.

[46] Tai, R.H., Liu, C.Q., Maltese, A.V. and Fan, X. 2006. Career choice: Enhanced: Planning early for. *Science.* 312, 26 (2006).

[47] Tempel, M. 2013. Blocks Programming. *CSTA Voice.* 9, 1 (2013).

[48] Tsur, M. and Rusk, N. 2018. Scratch Microworlds: Designing Project-Based Introductions to Coding. (2018), 894–899.

[49] Turkle, S. and Papert, S. 1990. Epistemological pluralism: Styles and voices within the computer culture. *SIGNS:: Journal of Women in Culture and Society.* 16, 1 (1990), 128–157.

[50] Weintrop, D. and Holbert, N. 2017. From Blocks to Text and Back: Programming Patterns in a Dual-Modality Environment. *Proc. of the 2017 ACM SIGCSE Technical Symposium on Computer Science Education* (New York, NY, USA, 2017), 633–638.

[51] Weintrop, D. and Wilensky, U. 2017. Comparing Block-Based and Text-Based Programming in High School Computer Science Classrooms. *ACM Transactions on Computing Education (TOCE).* 18, 1 (Oct. 2017), 3.

[52] Weintrop, D. and Wilensky, U. 2018. How block-based, text-based, and hybrid block/text modalities shape novice programming practices. *International Journal of Child-Computer Interaction.* (May 2018).

[53] Weintrop, D. and Wilensky, U. 2015. To Block or Not to Block, That is the Question: Students' Perceptions of Blocks-based Programming. *Proc. of the 14th International Conference on Interaction Design and Children* (New York, NY, USA, 2015), 199–208.

[54] Wolber, D., Abelson, H., Spertus, E. and Looney, L. 2011. *App Inventor: Create Your Own Android Apps.* O'Reilly Media.

[55] 2016. K–12 Computer Science Framework.

Programming Misconceptions for School Students

Alaaeddin Swidan, Felienne Hermans and Marileen Smit
Delft University of Technology
Delft, The Netherlands
{alaaeddin.swidan,f.f.j.hermans,m.i.e.smit}@tudelft.nl

ABSTRACT

Programming misconceptions have been a topic of interest in introductory programming education, with a focus on university level students. Nowadays, programming is increasingly taught to younger children in schools, sometimes as part of the curriculum. In this study we aim at exploring what misconceptions are held by younger, school-age children. To this end we design a multiple-choice questionnaire with Scratch programming exercises. The questions represent a selected set of 11 known misconceptions and relate to basic programming concepts. 145 participants aged 7 to 17 years, with an experience in programming, took part in the study. Our results show the top three common misconceptions are the difficulty of understanding the sequentiality of statements, that a variable holds one value at a time, and the interactivity of a program when user input is required. Holding a misconception is influenced by the mathematical effect of numbers, semantic meaning of identifiers and high expectations of what a computer can do. Other insights from the results show that older children answer more questions correctly, especially for the variable and control concepts. Children who program in Scratch only seem to have difficulties in answering the questions correctly compared to children who program in Scratch and another language. Our findings suggest that work should focus on identifying Scratch-induced misconceptions, and develop intervention methods to counter those misconceptions as early as possible. Finally, for children who start learning programming with Scratch, materials should be more concept-rich and include diverse exercises for each concept.

ACM Reference Format:
Alaaeddin Swidan, Felienne Hermans and Marileen Smit. 2018. Programming Misconceptions for School Students. In *ICER '18: 2018 International Computing Education Research Conference, August 13–15, 2018, Espoo, Finland.* ACM, New York, NY, USA, 9 pages. https://doi.org/10.1145/3230977.3230995

1 INTRODUCTION

It is known from existing research that learning programming is difficult [3, 4, 11]. One source of difficulties is holding programming misconceptions [4, 24], which affects performance in writing or understanding code. A programming misconception is having an incorrect understanding of a programming concept or a set of related concepts, typically affected by prior knowledge from domains other than programming such as mathematics and natural languages [20].

Studying programming misconceptions involves identifying their possible origins in order for both learners and educators to rectify relating concepts. Misconceptions have a harmful effect on the performance of students. The effect starts early [24] and may remain for a long time [17]. They have been found to cause failure in introductory programming courses and, in the long run, even cause students to drop out of programming education [12]. Previous studies focused nevertheless on introductory courses in universities. Nowadays, CS education and programming is increasingly introduced to younger students in primary and secondary schools [2, 10]. Many countries have already integrated programming activities into their school curriculum [9]. Moreover, new programming languages and programming environments are implemented especially for younger children. An example is Scratch[1], a block-based language which is developed by MIT with the aim of teaching children how to program. While CS education is moving down to schools, little is known on whether children develop certain misconceptions at this stage. In this study we aim at exploring the programming misconceptions held by school-age children. We developed a multiple-choice questionnaire containing 11 questions representing a selected set of programming misconceptions known from previous research [21]. In total, 145 children aged between 7 and 17 participated in our study. The participants, who were required to have an experience in programming, additionally provided reasoning for their answers in open-ended texts. From the data collected in this survey, we aim to answer the following research questions:

RQ1 Which programming misconceptions are the most common among Scratch novice programmers?

RQ2 How do children holding those misconceptions explain their answers? How do their explanations differ from the ones of children understanding the concept correctly?

RQ3 How do age and previous programming knowledge affect the holding of a misconception or the correct understanding?

2 BACKGROUND

Research defines a programming misconception as an incorrect understanding of a concept or a set of concepts, which leads to making mistakes in writing or reading programs [20]. Misconceptions can be related to basic, yet fundamental, programming concepts, not only to advanced concepts. Apart from syntactic mistakes, there

[1]https://scratch.mit.edu/

seems an agreement among researchers on particular concepts being difficult for learners. Those language-independent concepts include variables, loops, and conditional statements [4, 7, 11, 13, 17]. An example of a programming misconception: the belief that a variable can hold multiple values, or the belief that a variable's assignment goes the opposite direction [4, 21]. In object-oriented languages, common difficulties are related to the scope and visibility of variables, modularization and decomposition and inheritance [8, 12].

Research focused on understanding where a misconception originates from. A programming misconception does not mean that the learner has a complete lack of knowledge, rather it indicates partial but self-interpreted knowledge which comes from domains other than programming [4]. Some of the known origins include the use of particular analogies in explaining a concept, the ambiguous and double meanings of some of the programming keywords in English as a natural language, and mathematics [4, 15, 19]. Du Boulay [4] introduced what he called the *"notional machine"* as one origin of programming misconceptions. The notional machine refers to the general properties that a student assumes of the machine executing their code. Having an incorrect understanding of the notional machine of a programming language is believed to be the cause of many misconceptions [13, 20]. For example errors were found as a result of what Pea [14] called the *"superbug"* which is the assumption that *"there is a hidden mind somewhere in the programming language that has intelligent, interpretive powers"* [14, p. 32], or *"forgetting about alternative branches because they are too obvious to merit consideration"* [22, p. 6].

Finally, the variety of misconceptions make it difficult for educators to take them fully into account. In this regard, Sorva [21] provides a comprehensive list of programming misconceptions collected from various studies [4, 6, 12, 19, 20]. In this study, we use Sorva's list as the starting point to investigate Scratch misconceptions in school students.

3 SETUP

The goal of our study is to explore the common misconceptions among school-age children in Scratch. To this end, we perform a questionnaire-based study. Participants are given a set of multiple choice questions; each question is a programming exercise in Scratch which tests the holding of a known misconception. Questionnaires have been used to assess the holding of programming misconceptions in previous research [12, 18]. Participants in most cases need to predict the outcome of the script to choose an answer. Figure 2 shows an example question from our study. We provide the full questionnaire (English version) here[2]. In the following sections we describe the study setup in detail.

3.1 Participants

In total 145 children took part in the study. Figure 1 shows the distribution of the participants over the reported age, ranging between 7 and 17 years. Among the participants, 102 (70.3%) are boys, and 51 (29%) are girls; one participant did not specify gender.

[2]http://cli.re/g1zyQM

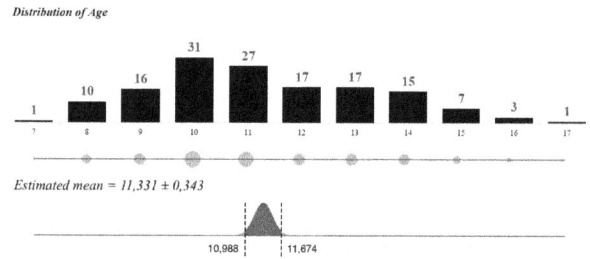

Figure 1: Age distribution of the participants. 70.3% of them are primary school students (12 years old and younger)

3.2 Study environment

We ran this experiment at NEMO science museum [3] in Amsterdam. Children visiting the museum were asked to join an experiment on programming but received no further information on what the experiment would measure. Participants did not get financial compensation for participation, but did receive a certificate for their efforts. The experiment was assigned a 25-minutes window per child and was run in a separate room in the museum that seated 8 children at a time. In total we spent 14 days at the museum, running the experiment for about 5 hours each day. During the experiment each participant had to fill answers to our web-based questionnaire in which the questions were put in static images. The children had access to the machine and the Internet, but we did not observe any participant opened other applications or pages than the questionnaire. The number of participants reported in this study is a subset of the total children who visited our booth, we filtered out participants who did not have programming experiences or who indicated guessing the answers. Asking children in such setup allowed us to study the holding of misconceptions on a sample that is less-dependent on specific teaching methodologies compared to an experiment run in a school.

3.3 Misconceptions selection

Sorva provides a comprehensive list of 162 programming misconceptions known from the literature [21]. We used the list as our starting point to investigate Scratch misconceptions. We followed a two-step approach to achieve that. **First, we selected the most common misconceptions from the list**. A misconception is common if indicated by at least two separate research works. This step reduced the list to 17 programming misconceptions. **Second, since we study Scratch misconceptions, we filtered out the misconceptions that do not fit Scratch as a language.** For example, we eliminated two misconceptions that concern the use of a loop control variable inside the loop's body. In Scratch, loops use a static value and no variable is necessary to iterate through the body. This resulted in 11 misconceptions, shown in Table 1.

3.4 Questions

Before presenting the misconception questions to the participants, we require the participant to answer five close-ended questions in the questionnaire. The answers to those questions indicate the

[3]https://www.nemosciencemuseum.nl/en/

Table 1: Programming misconceptions included in our study from [21].

Code[4]	Description	Prerequisite Concept(s)[5]	Question Description (Pseudo-code)	Misconception Choice(s)
M9	A variable can hold multiple values at a time	Variables	Set [X] to 10; Set [X] to 20; Say [X];	Gobo says 10, 20
M11	Primitive assignment works in opposite direction	Variables	Set [a] to 10; Set [b] to 20; Set [a] to [b];	a=20, b=0 a=20, b=10
M14	A variable is a pairing of a name to a changeable value. It is not stored inside the computer	Variables	We create a variable called message, Where is the variable stored?	Variable is not stored anywhere Variable is only visible on the screen
M15	Primitive assignment stores equations or unresolved expressions	Variables	Set [X] to 1, Set [counter] to [X+1]; Say [counter];	Gobo says X+1
M17	Natural-language semantics of variable names affects which value gets assigned to which variable	Variables	Set [big] to 1; Set [small] to 100; Set [big] to [small];	big=100 small=1 big=100 small=0
M23	Difficulties in understanding the sequentiality of statements	Variables	Set [number1] to 0; Set [number2] to 0; Set [total] to [number1] + [number2]; Set [number1] to 4; Set [number2] to 2; Say [total];	Gobo says 6
M26	A false condition ends program if no else branch exists	IF ELSE	IF touching the color [black] then { Say *"Auw!!"*; }; Say *"I am moving"*;	Gobo does not say anything
M30	Adjacent code executes within loop	Variables & Loops	Set [counter] to 0; Repeat 5 { Change [counter] by 1;}; Say [counter];	Gobo says 1 till 5
M31	Control goes back to start when condition is false	IF ELSE	Say *"I am moving"*; IF touching the color [black] then { Say *"Ouch!!"*; }; Say *"Done!!"*;	Gobo says *"I am moving"*
M33	Loops terminate as soon as condition changes to false	Variables & Loops	Set [number] to 1; Repeat until [number]=3 { Change [number] by 1; Say [number]; };	Gobo says 2
M150	Difficulties understanding the effect of input calls on execution	None	Ask [*"How old are you?"*] and Wait; Say *"Nice! I will move now"*; Move [10] Steps;	Gobo says *"How old are you?"* and immediately Says *"Nice! I will move now"* and Moves 10 steps.

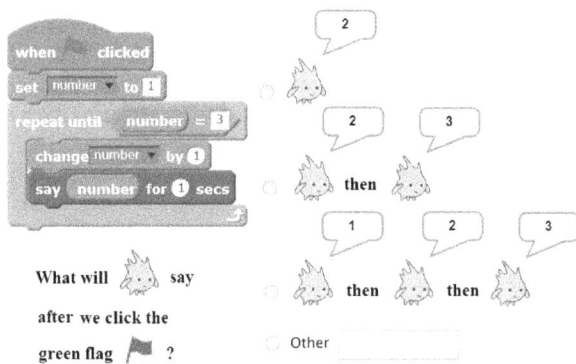

Figure 2: Question and possible answers for M33

participant's familiarity with these programming concepts: variables, IF statements and loops. We use the answers in an automatic branching logic so that we present a set of three to eleven multiple-choice misconception questions (See Table 1) that fit the knowledge of the participant. Each question is designed to elicit one of the

well-known programming misconceptions. For this purpose we use programming problems similar to the ones suggested by Ma [12] for Java students. In our case, we design the question in Scratch both in English and Dutch. Scratch enables programming in one's native language, which eliminates the cognitive load for reading a foreign language for the local children and enables them to focus on the programming challenge [5, 24]. Figure 2 shows an example of one of the questions related to the misconception of a loop terminating as soon as the condition becomes false (M33). We ask the participants to predict the outcome of the program by asking *"What will Gobo say when we click the green flag?"*, where Gobo is one of the characters known in Scratch. The answers are categorized into *Holds_Correct* (Gobo says 2 then 3), *"Holds_Misconception"* (Gobo says 2), and *Other_Wrong* (Gobo says 1 then 2 then 3). An open-ended question follows so that the participant can explain the reasons behind the chosen answer. We used the open-ended text to filter the results. The aim of this filtering is to eliminate answers

---

[4]We add a prefix, M, to the original numbers assigned to the misconception in Sorva's list. This is for the sake of easy referencing in the paper.
[5]This column indicates how we assign questions to participants based on the familiar concepts they report.

for which children admitted that they either guessed the answer or did lack understanding of the question. We note that we initially received 1,306 answers from 178 participants. Due to the filtering process, 545 answers were eliminated. The number of participants included in the study went down to 145 since for some participants their whole answer set was eliminated.

4 RESULTS

This section provides an overview of the answers to the study's research questions based on the questionnaire's data.

4.1 Most common misconceptions

[RQ1] Which programming misconceptions are the most common among Scratch novice programmers?
To answer RQ1, we analyze the answers for each misconception question. Figure 3 presents the percentage of participants who selected the misconception choice per question. The three most common misconceptions are related to different concepts: (i) the sequentiality of executing code (M23), (ii) the variable holding multiple values at a time (M9), and (iii) the human-computer interactivity and its effect on execution (M150). Moreover, we notice that among the least common misconceptions are the misconceptions related control statements: loops and conditions (M31, M33 and M26). In these cases, however, otherwise wrong choices are popular among participants, which indicates the general difficulty to understand those concepts.

4.2 Insights from children explanations

[RQ2] How do children holding those misconceptions explain their answers? How do their explanations differ from the ones of children understanding the concept correctly?

First we quantitatively analyze the open-text provided by participants per their answer category for the top three common misconceptions (see Table 2). To highlight the thinking process of the children both holders of a misconception or the correct concept, we further explore the open-ended answers provided by participants for M14 and M26 in addition to the ones in Table 2. M14 is chosen because two aspects of the misconception are provided in the multiple choices. M26 is chosen because although a choice representing the misconception is not provided separately (See Section 5.4), participants still indicated holding the misconception through their provided open-ended text.

M23: Difficulties in understanding the sequentiality of statements
Participants with the misconception=56.2%, Correct=42.5%, n=73

Misconception: Participants show a focus on the mathematical operation itself, not on the sequence. This is shown in the the top three words as the the words include *"values"* and *"add"*. Additionally, we find explanations such as *"because if you add number 1(4) and number 2 (2) [then] it will say 6"* or simply *"Basic math man"*. Some participants assumed an automatic aspect of the operation: *"when you change values of these variables total value changes also"*, and *"4 + 2 = 6 the computer should calculate that for you"*.

Correct: Participants are able to identify the sequential nature of the code. In the most frequent words we find the word *"before"* which indicates an order. One participant, for example, explains: *"Because total is set to [no.1] + [no.2] so it equals 0. The variables changed after that are irrelevant"*. Another participant suggested a *"fix"* to the code: *"If the block set [total] to [number1]+[number2] was put lower then it would have worked"*.

M9: A variable can hold multiple values at a time/"remembers" old values
Participants with the misconception=42.9%, Correct=42.9%, n=63

Misconception: Most participants referred to the code in the question as their reason without extra highlights. The frequent words used include the words *"first"* and *"numbers"* which shows the attention these participants give to the old value of the variable and both numbers used in the exercise respectively. However, one participant, despite choosing the misconception answer explains: *"I'm not sure, but if two [instances] of the same variable are used with different numbers, if possible, [the result] will give both numbers. Otherwise it would be 20 because that was the last change"*.

Correct: One of the most frequently used words is the word *"variable"*. This might indicate that participants have a basic understanding of what a variable is and thus they use the term more frequently. Moreover, we notice from the explanations of some of the participants referring to the last change made to the variable's value. Examples on this include: *"X= 20 is after X= 10 and the later one will overwrite the earlier one"*. However, one participant shows a full awareness of this aspect of variables: *"variable X is changed to 10, then 20, and a variable can only have one value"*.

M150: Difficulties understanding the effect of input function calls on execution
Participants with the misconception=39.1%, Correct=35.7%, n=115

Misconception: The word *"order"* is the second most frequent mentioned by these participants, highlighting the importance they give to the sequential execution that respects the blocks' order. One participant explains for example: *"This is the order from up to bottom"* and another says: *"because [the answer] is in the correct order"*. Moreover we notice that some participants use the word *"answer"* identifying the question-answer nature of the program. However they still provided the wrong answer because of a variety of wrong assumptions such as that since it is not possible for the participant to fill an answer then the computer will continue. Another assumption is that the question is directed towards the computer, therefore the computer will answer and continue the execution: *"Gobo says i am .. years old and directly says ...[continues the next blocks]"*, and another participant: *"I think that in the game Gobo is asked how old he is, then he ...[continues the next blocks]"*.

Correct: We notice again two forms of reasoning when participants give the correct answer. One has a direct approach and relies on the word *"wait"* being present in the question and in the answer text, stating that the choice comes because *"there is wait"* in both question and answer. The second shows that participants have more precise recognition of the question-answer nature of the program, and hence the need for an answer from the user so that the program can continue. One participant explains: *"if he asks you then you have*

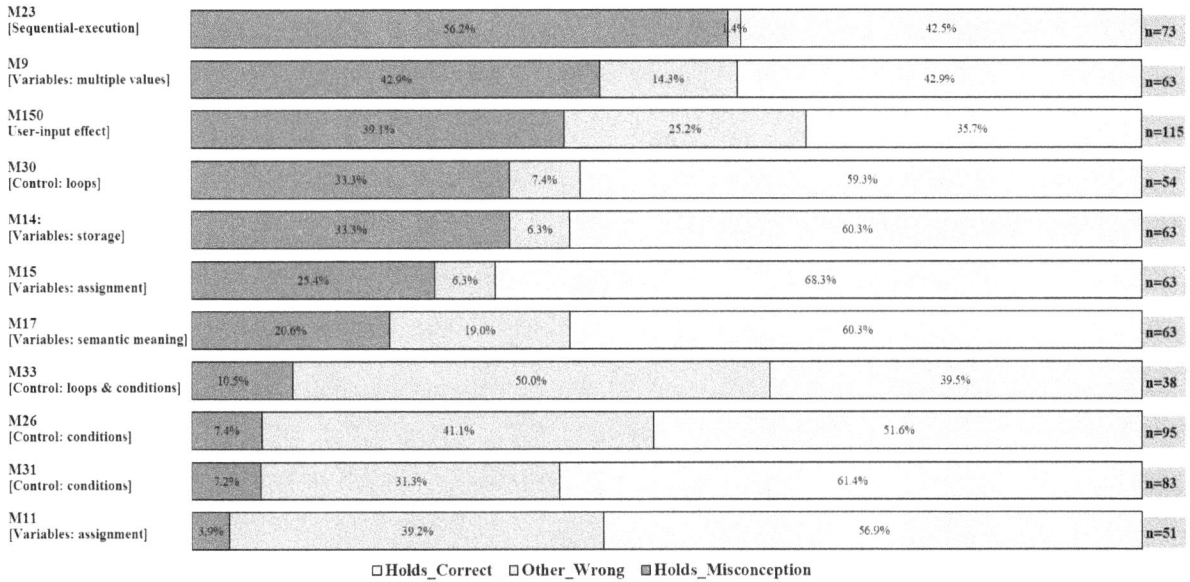

Figure 3: Misconceptions and their answer distribution, ordered from most to less common. M14, M26 in addition to the top 3 misconceptions are further discussed by exploring participants open-ended text.

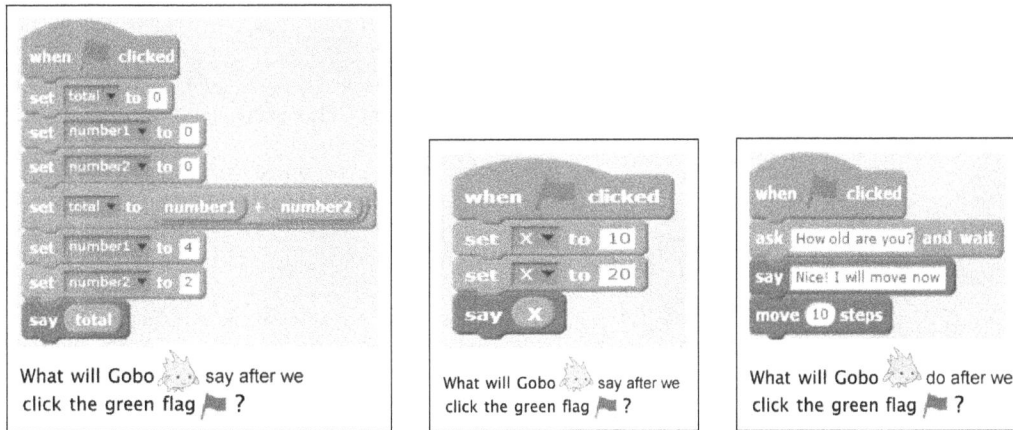

Figure 4: The questions representing M23 (Left), M9 (Middle) and M150 (Right)

Table 2: Most common words in the open-end text provided by children for the top three misconceptions

	M23: sequential-execution			M9: variable's multiple values			M150: user-input effect		
	Rank1	Rank2	Rank3	Rank1	Rank2	Rank3	Rank1	Rank2	Rank3
Holds Correct	before	numbers	values	then	set	variable	wait	answer	until
Holds Misconception	value	then	add	then	first	numbers, makes	answer	order	program
Other Wrong	Not applicable			then	say	picture	what	know	does

to type an answer, then he will respond", and another participant says: "because you have not typed anything".

M14: A variable is (merely) a pairing of a name to a changeable value (with a type). It is not stored inside the computer
Participants with the misconception=33.3%, Correct=60.3%, n=63

Misconception: In total, 33.3% of the participants (n=63) chose a misconception choice (see Figure 3). In a detailed manner, 7.9% of the participants chose the answer indicating that *"the variable is not being stored anywhere"*. Participants who provided their reasons here seem confused by the built-in option provided by Scratch: Cloud variable (stored on server), which was shown as part of the question. Two participants highlighted that their choice came as a result of this option not being ticked, which is the default in Scratch. 25.4% of participants chose the answer that indicates *"the variable is only visible on the screen"*. For these participants, the location at which the storage occurs is important and needs to be sensed. One participant says: *"because you can't see it anywhere else"*, and another one: *"there is nowhere for it to be so it just sits there"*. Another participant, despite choosing the wrong answer, indicates an analytical approach that is one step-away from being correct. The participant is uncertain where a variable should be stored because the program is not run, saying: *"the code will only set to value when run, and as the code is not yet running, the variable is moot"*.

Correct: Participants who answered correctly vary in their reasoning. Some give a concrete reason, for example *"It sits in the RAM memory"*, and *"all computers store data in the hardware, to know what they need to do"*. Others focus on the need to save the whole program for Scratch to *"remember"* it later.

M26: A false condition ends program when no else branch

Participants with the misconception=7.4%, Correct=51.6%, n=95

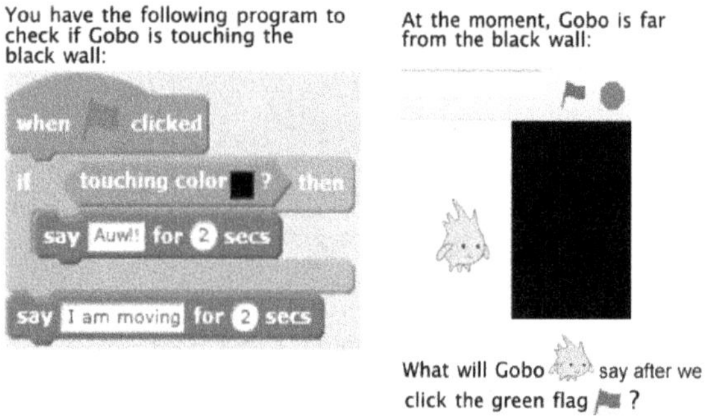

Figure 5: The question representing M26

Misconception: Although we have not provided an answer option to represent the misconception (See Sect. 5.4), some participants (7.4%) show they hold the misconception after analyzing the text they wrote. For those, the code does not execute at all because the condition is `false`. For example, one participant says: *"he [Gobo] does not touch the black, so nothing happens there"*. Another participant finds it illogical to execute the code: *"he [Gobo] is not touching the black so why would he do the commands that only apply to him if he is touching the black"*.

Correct: Participants highlight the false condition as a motive to their answer, from the opposite perspective to the participants with the misconception. The condition being `false` means the program runs, but parts of it are skipped. For example, one participant states: *"he skips the Auw part because he is not standing on the black"*, and another participant agrees: *"Gobo says only I am moving because he does not touch the black wall"*.

4.3 Effect of age and previous programming knowledge

[RQ3] How do age and previous programming knowledge affect the holding of a misconception or the correct understanding?

4.3.1 Age factor.
For the effect of age analysis, we exclude the age points 7 and 17 because only one participant in each of these age categories answered the questionnaire. Results show that a positive correlation exists only between age and holding the correct concept (Spearman's Rank Correlation p-value =0.005). In words, the older the child the more they answer correctly. Additionally, when considering the category of the misconception according to Sorva's original classification (see Table 1), positive correlation is found between age and correctly answer the misconception questions under the *"Variable"* category (Spearman's Rank Correlation p-value=0.015) and *"Control"* category (Spearman's Rank Correlation p-value=0.048).

In the alluvial diagrams (See Figure 6) we observe how age groups contribute to the answers for the top three misconceptions. The contribution is represented by the thickness of the flow from source to destination. The diagrams show that children younger than 12 are more likely to hold a misconception than older children. However, the relation is only significant in holding the correct answer as stated above, and not in holding a misconception.

4.3.2 Previous programming knowledge.
The reported knowledge of programming languages (Figure 7) shows that almost two thirds of the participants programmed before with Scratch, while the remaining third used programming with a variety of other languages such as Lego, Alice, Python or Javascript. Moreover, the participants reported where they learned programming: at school (62%), at home (28%) or other places such as friends, communities or courses (10%). Since we investigate misconceptions in Scratch, we explore how knowing Scratch in particular compares to other programming languages when it comes to holding a programming misconception. The results show the following:

Knowing Scratch and other languages: is found to decrease the tendency to holding a misconception (Pearson Product-Moment correlation, r=-0.077, p-value=0.035) and increase the tendency to holding correct concepts (Pearson Product-Moment correlation, r=0.151, p-value<0.001).

Knowing other languages: is found to increase the tendency to holding a misconception (Pearson Product-Moment correlation, r=0.071, p-value=0.049).

Knowing Scratch only: knowing only Scratch does not correlate with the holding of a misconception. However, results show that it correlates with answering incorrectly under the *"Other_Wrong"* category (Pearson Product-Moment correlation, r=0.081, p-value=0.025).

5 DISCUSSION

5.1 General observations

While some could argue that it is expected that younger children hold such misconceptions, their origins could be different from

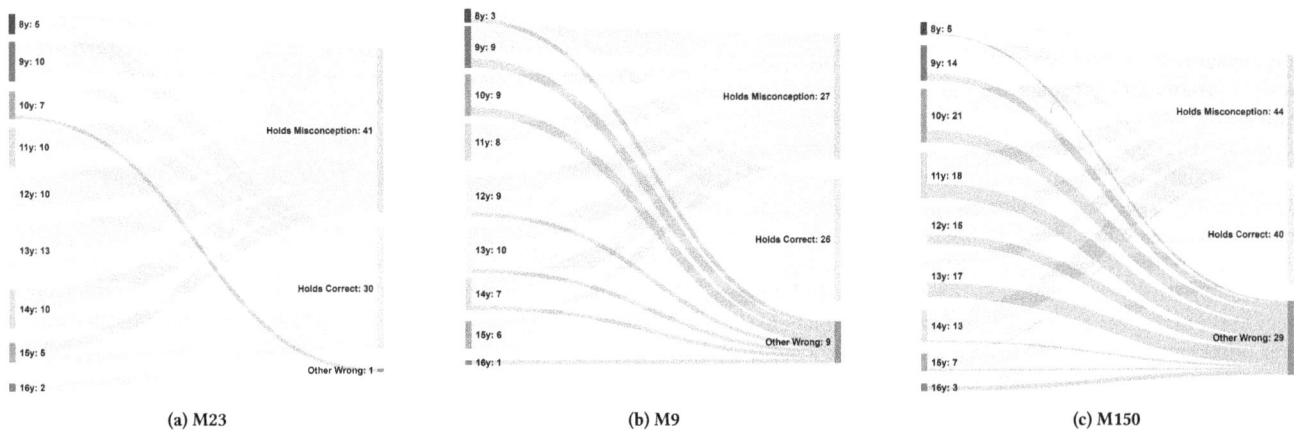

(a) M23   (b) M9   (c) M150

Figure 6: Alluvial diagrams for the top three misconceptions showing the flow of answers from age groups 8y-16y towards the answer categories

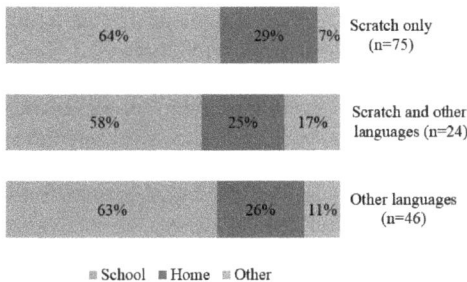

Figure 7: Reported programming languages versus where the child learned them: schools are the primary source of learning programming, while almost one-third of the children indicate home as the learning place for programming.

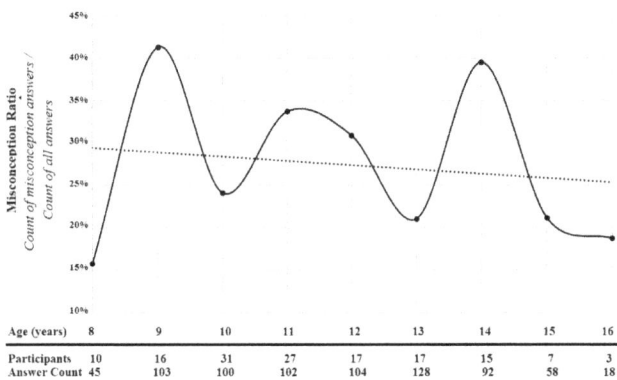

Figure 8: The ratio of misconception answers to the total answers per age (year)

misconceptions in university level students. First, the relation with mathematics seems more pervasive: whenever a question contains numbers, some participants chose to sum the values, even when there is no sum operation in the question (such as M9). The semantic meaning of variables is another recurring aspect that is present in questions other than M17. For example, for misconceptions M33 and M31, since we use the variable name *"counter"*, some participants believe that the program must *"count"* the sequence from one till the end regardless of the loop's condition and the operation inside.

Looking further into the effect of age on misconceptions, we present Figure 8 which shows the misconception ratio for the children per age. The results show that there exists a sudden increase in the holding of a misconception at age=14. The increase is significant compared to the neighboring age groups (13y,15y). Unfortunately, the increase cannot be explained by the currently collected data and need further research.

5.2 Scratch-specific issues

The programming language has its role in eliciting some misconceptions. In previous research this contributed not only to syntactical errors, but also to errors related to the difficulty of understanding the notional machine of this programming language. In our study, we notice that the use of particular blocks in our programming problems caused common and worthy remarks from the participants. First, the *"Say"* block in Scratch caused confusion whenever it was used in the questions. Despite it being a basic and common block, it led to errors when integrated with a variable instead of plain text. Many participants in this case indicated that the program will say the variable's identifier, for example *"X"* or *"total"*, instead of its value. This signifies both a lack of understanding of the variable concept, and the effect of the lingual imperative sense of the verb *"Say"*. A second difficulty we note being related to Scratch is the block used to set a variable to a value: *"Set [variable] to [value]"*. The use of the preposition *"to"* adds ambiguity over the direction of the assignment. Finally, the order of the blocks should be respected because, for some children, the *"visually-attached"* blocks meant that the program will execute in the order from top to bottom even when condition or repeat block exist.

5.3 Reflections on and implications of the results

Misconceptions are considered one area of difficulty in learning how to program. Our results suggest that as we move towards younger children we see more difficulties in answering the questions correctly. This is especially the case for the concepts of variables and control. This result confirms previous research that have shown that children younger than 11 have difficulties understanding those concepts in addition to the concepts of parallelization and procedures [9, 16]. Our results shows, however, some different observations than those in university level students: i) children tend to perform mathematical operations (mostly summations) whenever numbers are present in the exercises, and ii) tend to make assumptions based on their understanding to the semantic names of variables. Consequently, we believe that more diverse exercises should be developed to include operations on strings and booleans, in addition to carefully selecting identifier names in those exercises.

Moreover, our findings suggest that children who indicated programming in Scratch only have difficulties in understanding the concepts correctly and tend to choose other wrong answers. This result highlights two issues. First, educators and researchers are encouraged to identify and realize new misconceptions induced by Scratch as a language. We provided a few observations from our dataset (See Section 5.2), but more research is still needed. Second, our results suggest that younger children start learning programming in Scratch (age positively correlates with the number of programming languages reported in addition to Scratch), and they do it primarily in schools. Those younger *"Scratchers"* seem to have more difficulties to correctly understand the concepts in our study. This result confirms previous research which found Scratch projects to have low percentage of conceptual constructs such as variables, procedures and conditional statements [1, 16, 23]. As a result, we believe that primary education providers are advised to develop more nontrivial and concept-rich materials in Scratch.

Finally, a few participants showed signs of a struggle between contradicting thoughts while reasoning their answers (See Section 4.2). This indicates our belief that holding a misconception is not binary: you either understand the concept or not. On the contrary, it can be a step into grasping the complete concept, and when the confusion is identified it becomes easier to provide the missing piece of information by educators.

5.4 Threats to validity

Like all studies, this paper has some limitations. An external threat to validity comes from the reported experience in programming which the participants provided. In the questionnaire we ask five questions about the previous experience in programming, including questions to identify knowledge of particular concepts. The participants could have still misjudged their own experience and gave false indications. Moreover, a construction threat to validity comes from using multiple choice questions because some children would have guessed the answer despite lacking the knowledge. We eliminated to the minimum those two threats by adding an open-end text following each multiple-choice question, then strictly filtered out any answer for which the participant indicated in the open-end text that they guessed the answer or lacked the understanding of

the question or the knowledge to answer it. An internal threat to validity is the design of the question and possible answers for M26. The answers we provided did not include an answer which reflects the misconception: in this case that the program will do nothing. Despite this design issue, 7.2% of 95 participants who answered this question hold the misconception, which was based on the text they provided using the *"Other"* answer option.

6 CONCLUSIONS

Our paper aims at exploring programming misconceptions held by school-age students. The study is based on a multiple-choice questionnaire with programming exercises in Scratch. 145 children participated in the study, aged between 7 and 17 and have some previous experience in programming. The results show that younger learners in school-age indeed hold misconceptions, which caused them to make errors when tracing a small script in Scratch. The top three common misconceptions span over multiple concepts; M23: the difficulty of understanding the sequentiality of statements, M9: the difficulty of understanding that a variable holds one value at a time, and M150: the difficulty to understand the interactive nature of a program when a user input is required. The origins of these misconceptions vary and include the great influence of numbers and mathematical operations in the mindset of the children, the influence semantic meaning of the variable identifier, and the wrongful expectation of what a computer can do, i.e. misunderstanding the notional machine. When analyzing the age effect we found that older children tend to answer the exercises correctly. Moreover, results show that knowing Scratch in addition to at least one other programming language positively influence choosing a correct answer. While children who reported programming in Scratch only had more tendency to choose other wrong answers. Finally, examples we observed in the experiment signify that holding a misconception is indeed a step towards holding the correct and complete concept. Our findings suggest that educators and school teachers should count for the misconception effect as early as possible. Additionally, we should realize new misconceptions induced by Scratch as a language, due to, among other reasons, the use of visually-attached blocks and the use of special keywords in its block set. Finally, Scratch material and lessons should integrate more concept-rich exercises that highlights areas such as variables and control of execution. This is especially needed for children who start learning programming in Scratch. In future work we have two main directions. First we intend to explore and identify Scratch-specific misconceptions. Second, we aim to study in more depth the effect of learning another programming language on Scratch learners. Finally, we aim at developing and testing teaching materials and methods that have less possibility of inducing misconceptions in children.

ACKNOWLEDGMENT

We would like to thank the team of Science Live program at NEMO and all the staff for their support. We also thank the colleagues and student volunteers who took part in running the experiment at the museum.

REFERENCES

[1] Efthimia Aivaloglou and Felienne Hermans. 2016. How Kids Code and How We Know. *Proceedings of the 2016 ACM Conference on International Computing Education Research - ICER '16* (2016). DOI: http://dx.doi.org/10.1145/2960310.2960325

[2] Erik Barendsen, Nataï£¡a Grgurina, and Jos Tolboom. 2016. A New Informatics Curriculum for Secondary Education in The Netherlands. *Informatics in Schools: Improvement of Informatics Knowledge and Perception* (2016), 105–117. DOI: http://dx.doi.org/10.1007/978-3-319-46747-4_9

[3] A. Berglund and R. Lister. 2010. Introductory Programming and the Didactic Triangle. In *Proceedings of the 12th Australasian Conference on Computing Education*. 35–44. http://dl.acm.org/citation.cfm?id=1862219.1862227

[4] B. Du Boulay. 1986. Some Difficulties of Learning to Program. *Journal of Educational Computing Research* 2, 1 (1986), 57–73. DOI: http://dx.doi.org/10.2190/3LFX-9RRF-67T8-UVK9 arXiv:https://doi.org/10.2190/3LFX-9RRF-67T8-UVK9

[5] S. Dasgupta and B. Hill. 2017. Learning to Code in Localized Programming Languages. *Proceedings of the 4th ACM Conference on Learning @ Scale* (2017). DOI: http://dx.doi.org/10.1145/3051457.3051464

[6] D. Doukakis, M. Grigoriadou, and G Tsaganou. 2007. Understanding the Programming Variable Concept with Animated Interactive Analogies. *Proceedings of the 8th Hellenic European Research on Computer Mathematics & its Applications* (2007).

[7] P. Fung, M. Brayshaw, B. Du Boulay, and M. Elsom-Cook. 1990. Towards a taxonomy of novices' misconceptions of the Prolog interpreter. *Instructional Science* 19, 4-5 (1990), 311–336. DOI: http://dx.doi.org/10.1007/bf00116443

[8] K. Goldman, P. Gross, C. Heeren, G. Herman, L. Kaczmarczyk, M. C. Loui, and C. Zilles. 2008. Identifying important and difficult concepts in introductory computing courses using a delphi process. *ACM SIGCSE Bulletin* 40, 1 (2008), 256. DOI: http://dx.doi.org/10.1145/1352322.1352226

[9] F. Hermans and E. Aivaloglou. 2017. Teaching Software Engineering Principles to K-12 Students: A MOOC on Scratch. In *Proceedings of the 39th International Conference on Software Engineering: Software Engineering and Education Track*. 13–22. DOI: http://dx.doi.org/10.1109/ICSE-SEET.2017.13

[10] Hai Hong, Jennifer Wang, and Sepehr Hejazi Moghadam. 2016. K-12 Computer Science Education Across the U.S. *Informatics in Schools: Improvement of Informatics Knowledge and Perception* (2016), 142–154. DOI: http://dx.doi.org/10.1007/978-3-319-46747-4_12

[11] E. Kurvinen, N. Hellgren, E. Kaila, M. Laakso, and T. Salakoski. 2016. Programming Misconceptions in an Introductory Level Programming Course Exam. *Proceedings of the ACM Conference on Innovation and Technology in Computer Science Education* (2016). DOI: http://dx.doi.org/10.1145/2899415.2899447

[12] L. Ma. 2007. *Investigating and improving novice programmers mental models of programming concepts.* PhD Thesis. University of Strathclyde, UK. http://ethos.bl.uk/OrderDetails.do?uin=uk.bl.ethos.444415

[13] L. Ma, J. Ferguson, M. Roper, and M. Wood. 2011. Investigating and improving the models of programming concepts held by novice programmers. *Computer Science Education* 21, 1 (2011), 57–80. DOI: http://dx.doi.org/10.1080/08993408.2011.554722

[14] Roy D. Pea. 1986. Language-Independent Conceptual ï£¡Bugsï£¡ in Novice Programming. *Journal of Educational Computing Research* 2, 1 (1986), 25–36. DOI: http://dx.doi.org/10.2190/689t-1r2a-x4w4-29j2

[15] R. Putnam, D. Sleeman, J. Baxter, and L. Kuspa. 1986. A Summary of Misconceptions of High School Basic Programmers. *Journal of Educational Computing Research* 2, 4 (1986), 459–472. DOI: http://dx.doi.org/10.2190/fgn9-dj2f-86v8-3fau

[16] Linda Seiter and Brendan Foreman. 2013. Modeling the learning progressions of computational thinking of primary grade students. *Proceedings of the ninth annual international ACM conference on International computing education research - ICER '13* (2013). DOI: http://dx.doi.org/10.1145/2493394.2493403

[17] Simon. 2011. Assignment and sequence. *Proceedings of the 11th International Conference on Computing Education Research* (2011). DOI: http://dx.doi.org/10.1145/2094131.2094134

[18] Simon and S. Snowdon. 2011. Explaining program code. *Proceedings of the 7th International workshop on Computing Education Research* (2011). DOI: http://dx.doi.org/10.1145/2016911.2016931

[19] D. Sleeman, R. Putnam, J. Baxter, and L. Kuspa. 1986. Pascal and High School Students: A Study of Errors. *Journal of Educational Computing Research* 2, 1 (1986), 5–23. DOI: http://dx.doi.org/10.2190/2xpp-ltyh-98nq-bu77

[20] J. Sorva. 2008. The same but different students' understandings of primitive and object variables. *Proceedings of the 8th International Conference on Computing Education Research* (2008). DOI: http://dx.doi.org/10.1145/1595356.1595360

[21] J. Sorva. 2012. Visual program simulation in introductory programming education. PhD Thesis, Aalto University. (2012). http://urn.fi/URN:ISBN:978-952-60-4626-6

[22] Juha Sorva. 2013. Notional machines and introductory programming education. *ACM Transactions on Computing Education* 13, 2 (2013), 1–31. DOI: http://dx.doi.org/10.1145/2483710.2483713

[23] Alaaeddin Swidan, Alexander Serebrenik, and Felienne Hermans. 2017. How do Scratch Programmers Name Variables and Procedures? *2017 IEEE 17th International Working Conference on Source Code Analysis and Manipulation (SCAM)* (2017). DOI: http://dx.doi.org/10.1109/scam.2017.12

[24] D. Teague, M. Corney, A. Ahadi, and R. Lister. 2013. A Qualitative Think Aloud Study of the Early Neo-piagetian Stages of Reasoning in Novice Programmers. In *Proceedings of the 15th Australasian Computing Education Conference*. 87–95. http://dl.acm.org/citation.cfm?id=2667199.2667209

Misconception-Driven Feedback:
Results from an Experimental Study

Luke Gusukuma
Department of Computer Science
Virginia Tech
Blacksburg, Virginia
lukesg08@vt.edu

Austin Cory Bart
Department of Computer Science
Virginia Tech
Blacksburg, Virginia
acbart@vt.edu

Dennis Kafura
Department of Computer Science
Virginia Tech
Blacksburg, Virginia
kafura@cs.vt.edu

Jeremy Ernst
School of Education
Virginia Tech
Blacksburg, Virginia
jvernst@vt.edu

ABSTRACT

The feedback given to novice programmers can be substantially improved by delivering advice focused on learners' cognitive misconceptions contextualized to the instruction. Building on this idea, we present Misconception-Driven Feedback (MDF); MDF uses a cognitive student model and program analysis to detect mistakes and uncover underlying misconceptions. To evaluate the impact of MDF on student learning, we performed a quasi-experimental study of novice programmers that compares conventional run-time and output check feedback against MDF over three semesters. Inferential statistics indicates MDF supports significantly accelerated acquisition of conceptual knowledge and practical programming skills. Additionally, we present descriptive analysis from the study indicating the MDF student model allows for complex analysis of student mistakes and misconceptions that can suggest improvements to the feedback, the instruction, and to specific students.

CCS CONCEPTS

• **Applied computing** → **Education**; Learning management systems; • **Social and professional topics** → **Computational thinking**; **CS1**; **Student assessment**;

KEYWORDS

CS Education; Immediate Feedback; Student Model; Misconception

ACM Reference Format:
Luke Gusukuma, Austin Cory Bart, Dennis Kafura, and Jeremy Ernst. 2018. Misconception-Driven Feedback: Results from an Experimental Study. In *Proceedings of 2018 International Computing Education Research Conference (ICER '18),* Jennifer B. Sartor, Theo D'Hondt, and Wolfgang De Meuter (Eds.). ACM, New York, NY, USA, 9 pages. https://doi.org/10.1145/3230977.3231002

1 INTRODUCTION

Non-computing majors often struggle with introductory programming, because of their limited prior knowledge and low self-efficacy. These students require quality feedback to guide students to correct answers [21, 32], maintain student motivation [28], and become self-regulated learners [22]. While direct feedback from experts is the "gold standard" [5], it has two pragmatic drawbacks. First, the availability of experts is limited, especially in larger classes where the learner-expert ratio is high or in distance-based learning where an expert is remote. Second, expert feedback may be delayed, requiring an arranged time for the expert and learner to interact.

In some cases, feedback opportunities can be determined automatically and presented to the learner immediately, such as the results of unit tests showing how close a learner is to a correct solution. However, this kind of feedback is centered around a model of the problem solution rather than a model of the learner, expecting that simply pointing out a novice's mistakes will help them infer the correct knowledge. Although suitable for advanced learners, such high level of critical thinking may not be available during low level skill acquisition that occurs in the introductory level.

To improve the impact of immediate feedback on learners we present Misconception-Driven Feedback (MDF) based on the idea of a "knowledge component" [1] from cognitive learning theory. In this model, mistakes detected through program analysis provide evidence for a set of misconceptions defined by the instructor. With the misconceptions in mind, feedback messages can be authored by an instructor to target learners' misunderstandings.

We conducted a quasi-experiment comparing students' learning with the help of conventional feedback vs. MDF feedback; the impact was measured by their summative performance on multiple choice quizzes and programming problems. This study controls for the instructors, problems, grading, and learning materials. This paper reports on the experiment and makes these contributions:

(1) A novel feedback approach based on a learner model connecting a learner's mistakes to underlying misconceptions.
(2) Statistical evidence of the positive impact of misconception-driven feedback on student learning and performance.
(3) Descriptive analysis identifying the influence of specific misconceptions on programming mistakes.

2 BACKGROUND

MDF draws on cognitive learning theories, prior work with misconceptions, and general education theories related to feedback. The technology we have created is related to approaches such as Intelligent Tutoring Systems and Hint Generation Systems.

2.1 Cognitive Theory

A fundamental aspect of MDF is the idea of modeling a student's understanding through knowledge components. A knowledge component can be defined as "an acquired unit of cognitive function or structure that can be inferred from performance on a set of related tasks" [19]. Guided by this perspective, we define the related ideas of a (programming) misconception and a (programming) mistake:

- A programming misconception is a unit of cognitive function or structure that can be inferred from a mistake on a programming task.
- A programming mistake is an incorrect configuration of code elements.

We will often elide the word "programming" and write misconception or mistake for simplicity.

2.2 Misconceptions in Programming

There is a body of work on misconceptions that novice programmers encounter. A considerable subset of this work is on discovering existing misconceptions and developing Concept Inventories[7, 15, 20, 27, 29, 31]. The misconception discovery techniques in these works range from interviews [7, 15, 20] and quizzes [7, 27] to analyzing about mistakes in student code [7, 20, 29, 31]. Our work specifically uses misconception discovery methods described in [12]. While there are many techniques for misconception discovery, there is little work on how to use misconceptions in programming assignments, especially with regards to detecting them in student code and delivering appropriate feedback. Some work discusses systems that can detect misconceptions and deliver appropriate feedback such as [30], but do not present a formal model.

2.3 Formative Immediate Feedback

Feedback in various forms and styles is a critical element of virtually all learning theories [32]. Our work focuses on formative feedback: "information communicated to the learner that is intended to modify the learner's thinking or behavior for the purpose of improving learning" [28]. Different approaches to formative feedback include verification, explanation, hints, and worked examples[21]. Feedback presentation can be immediate, meaning without explicit request and/or on-demand (e.g., when a program is executed). Our vision for creating effective formative feedback, which we term misconception-driven feedback, is based on two ideas:

- Feedback should be grounded in an understanding of student misconceptions.
- Feedback should be coupled with instruction.

In this way we can assess and improve feedback in the broader context of teaching and learning.

2.4 Intelligent Tutoring and Hint Generation Systems

Intelligent Tutoring Systems for Programming (ITP) are systems used for learning programming, have pre-scripted programming problems, and adapt based on multiple metrics and an algorithm [10]. These systems have a scaffolded programming learning experience, and are useful for online settings with unsupervised instruction. However, ITPs take much effort to assemble [18] and have different types of constraints from typical Intelligent Tutoring Systems (ITS) [10]. ITPs are typically heavily scripted, difficult to adapt to new contexts, and are meant to be self-contained and divorced from other instruction. In contrast, our intent is to augment conventional classroom instruction with more light-weight feedback.

Hint Generation systems give on-demand, logical next steps for a student to take based on prior students' programs, thus enabling student progress while avoiding instructor involvement (achieving scalability). There are many examples of such systems, typically able to be integrated into existing programming environments [23], [24], [25], and [26]. Although useful tools for helping students, these systems do not aim to help students understand *why* their advice and hints should be followed.

The difficulty and effort of developing intelligent tutoring systems [18], and the weakness of hint generation systems not contextualizing hints with instruction [25], suggests a need for a middle ground for writing and delivering feedback for students. This middle ground is still being explored and is relatively underrepresented. CSF[2] cross references results of unit-tests to identify misconceptions within student mistakes based on prior semester data [13]. Mistake Browser and Mistake Propagator [14] incorporate instructor expertise by having the instructors annotate hints found via typical hint generation techniques like in [26] and [24]. Instructor-supervised feedback systems can provide higher quality feedback than hint generation systems, at a cost lower than intelligent tutoring systems. However, the techniques in [13] and [14] suffer from the typical slow start problem of data-driven approaches.

3 APPROACH

In this section, we elaborate on the role of misconceptions in our learner model, the method for detecting mistakes, and feedback delivery. Key ideas are exemplified in Figure 1 and explained below.

3.1 Learner Model

MDF is centered on a model of breakdowns in the learners' understanding as a set of misconceptions, which can be determined by the instructors through analysis of the curriculum and prior student work. In our case, our curriculum was developed in semesters prior to our experiment. The curriculum was analyzed using selected elements of a formal Instructional Design process; a description of the process used to analyze the instruction can be found in [12].

From the Instructional Design process, anticipated misconceptions and associated mistakes were gathered. A general model of a student was then built from these mistakes and misconceptions. At the core of the model, a mistake is associated with a vector of misconceptions. Mistakes are the "observed performance" of the student. By cross-referencing multiple mistakes, a misconception can be isolated. An example misconception is shown in Figure 1a.

Learner does not know the difference between a count and a sum.

(a) Misconception

```
#presence of:
for x in ___:
    count = count + x
```

(b) Mistake 1 Specification

This problem asks for the number of items in the list not the total of all the values in the list.

(c) MDF Feedback

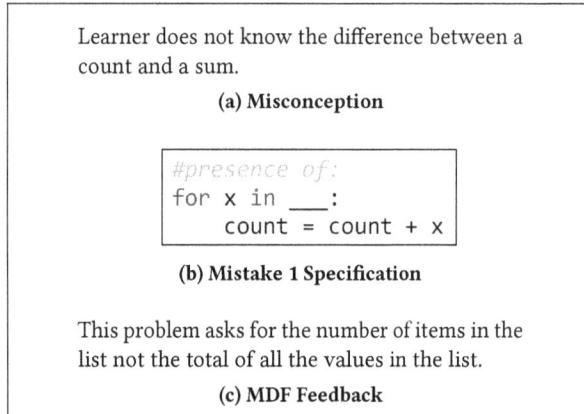

Figure 1: Example of Feedback Specification

3.2 Detecting Mistakes

To provide feedback without human intervention, mistakes can be detected automatically using program analysis, unit tests, runtime violations, and similar tools. In our environment, we use four kinds of mistake detection. First, conventional runtime and syntax errors were detected using the existing execution infrastructure. Second, output checking determined if students met functional correctness. Third, an abstract interpreter checked certain generic mistakes (e.g., def/use errors such as "variables must be defined before they are read"). Fourth, a large set of patterns were prepared which could be matched against students' code. The code pattern matching problem is a variation on the Ordered Tree Inclusion Problem (adapted to ASTs) [17]. Where P is an instructor AST and T is a student AST, we define our Ordered Tree Inclusion variant as follows:

Given labeled partially ordered trees P and T, can P be obtained by deleting nodes from T. Deleting a node u entails removing all edges incident to u and its descendants.

where a partially ordered tree in our context is defined as:

A rooted tree in which the order of the subtrees is significant with the exception of nodes that have commutative properties (e.g. multiplication and addition) whose subtrees do not have side effects.

Experts can write patterns declaratively with corresponding feedback. A total of 88 mistakes were codified into patterns by the instructors. An example mistake pattern is shown in Figure 1b.

3.3 Feedback Delivery

While students worked on programming exercises in BlockPy [3], their code was analyzed to detect mistake patterns. When detected, a relevant feedback message was delivered (either on-demand when the code was executed or while the student was editing code) using BlockPy's built-in feedback mechanisms that are normally used to deliver runtime and output errors. We chose immediate feedback delivery because of its acquisitional efficiency for verbal knowledge and procedural skills [2, 6, 9, 11]. In developing the feedback message, the instructors aimed to explain the misconception found

and the corresponding mistake's location, rather than how the student should fix the mistake. Multiple patterns might be found in the student code; per common practice, we deliver only one feedback message[4]. Figure 1c shows an example of delivered Misconception-Driven Feedback. Feedback delivery did not require modifications to the BlockPy interface.

4 EXPERIMENTAL DESIGN

We hypothesized that Misconception-Driven Feedback would improve student performance on near-transfer tasks, even if MDF was not provided during programming assessments. We also expected that students who received MDF while learning would see gains in their conceptual understanding of the topics. To test these hypotheses, we conducted a quasi-experimental study in an introductory, undergraduate Computational Thinking course for non-majors.

4.1 Class Description

The study was conducted at Virginia Tech, a large public university located in a rural area of the eastern United States. At Virginia Tech, students completing an undergraduate degree in any major must satisfy a set of "general education" requirements by completing designated courses in several broad areas of study. For example, in the area of "quantitative reasoning" students must complete three courses from an approved list of courses in mathematics, computer science, logic, or similar subjects. The computational thinking course in this study is typically used by students in non-STEM majors to satisfy the quantitative reasoning requirement.

The study collected data over three consecutive semesters. The baseline data for the control group was collected in the spring (January-May) term of 2017. Comparative data for the treatment groups was collected in the fall (August-December) term of 2017 and the spring term of 2018. Two sections of the course were taught each semester, each meeting twice a week for 75 minutes. The classroom environment and the sections' weekly schedule remained the same, though the time of day varied. The data was collected under an IRB-approved protocol.

4.2 Demographics

Tables 1 through 3 show demographic information about the students whose data is reported in the study. The enrollment in each semester for each instructor is shown in Table 1. Enrollment in the two treatment semesters was limited by the classroom size.

Semester	S2017	F2017	S2018	Combined
Instructor 1	47 (13%)	61(17%)	66 (19%)	174 (49%)
Instructor 2	47 (13%)	64 (18%)	67 (19%)	180 (51%)
Total	94 (27%)	125 (36%)	133 (38%)	352 (100%)

Table 1: Enrollment Statistics

Table 2 shows the gender and class of students in the study. Students in the study were approximately gender balanced. Also, there were significant numbers of student from each of the four years of study (Freshman through Senior). It is common in general education classes to see this diversity among years, because the class does not serve as a pre-requisite to other courses.

Gender	Class
Female: 172 (49%) Male: 180 (51%)	Freshman: 103 (29%)
	Sophomore: 118 (34%)
	Junior: 74 (21%)
	Senior: 57 (16%)

Table 2: Gender and Class Demographics

Each section in each semester included students from a variety of majors as summarized in Table 3. University Studies and General Engineering are students who have not yet selected a specific major. Building Construction was particularly prevalent because this course is a major requirement. There are 47 other majors that account for the remaining 138 (39%) students. Students self-select to enroll in the class; the instructors have no influence over the students who enroll or in which section.

Major	Population
Building Construction	52 (15%)
Criminology	32 (9%)
Psychology	31 (9%)
University Studies	26 (7%)
Fashion Merchandise and Design	21 (6%)
International Studies	14 (4%)
Statistics	14 (4%)
Political Science	14 (4%)
General Engineering	10 (3%)

Table 3: Major Demographics

4.3 Curriculum and Learning Environment

The curriculum, pedagogy, and technology for the computational thinking course evolved over a period of five (5) semesters and was stable by the start of the study. Details of the curriculum can be found at https://think.cs.vt.edu/ct and in [16]. The major technical topics in the curriculum were data abstraction and algorithms. Throughout the study, the curriculum's resources (readings, assignments, projects, presentation materials, grading scale, etc.) remained fixed with changes limited to correcting typographical mistakes or minor ambiguities. The pedagogy for the course included both active learning and peer learning. Students were organized by the instructors into four person teams that persisted throughout the semester. Groups were formed to maximize diversity of majors and balance gender within each group. Each class day students were engaged in solving problems individually, but encouraged to seek and provide help to others in their group. This group model was used in all semesters of the study. The technology included a learning management system (Canvas), an environment for block-based programming (BlockPy), and a standard Python environment (Spyder). These systems were used throughout the study and no significant changes in functionality were introduced.

The course staff consisted of two instructors, one graduate assistant, and ten undergraduate assistants (UTAs). The UTAs had

completed the course in previous semesters and attended each class. The instructors and GTA were the same throughout the study. The UTAs varied during the study. A staff meeting was held each week to provide guidance and coordination for the UTAs. For the control group the course staff were proactive in providing in-class assistance. In the treatment classes during the period when the feedback intervention was applied the course staff was reactive, only providing assistance when explicitly called upon. Anecdotally, there was a noticeable decline in the support provided by the course staff in the two treatment semesters. The instruction using the block-based language covered a two week period (classes 7-10) with another class (class 12) devoted to a programming project. The topic of list-based iteration was the focus of classes 8-10. One class (class 13) was a transition from blocks to text.

The feedback intervention was focused on the instruction related to iteration (classes 8-10) and a project (class 12). This topic was chosen because it was the first difficult programming concept in the course, was the focus of a lengthy period of instruction, and in prior semesters was known by the instructors to be a time where students struggled, requiring much assistance from the course staff.

4.4 Assessment

The impact of the feedback intervention was measured through one pre-test and two post-tests (administered electronically). The pre-test was administered at the end of the class preceding the start of the iteration unit. The first post-test was administered at the beginning of class 10. This "embedded" post-test came after two classes of instruction and was approximately the mid-point of the instructional unit. The second post-test was administered at the end of the students' work in BlockPy (class 12).

A common element in the pre-test and post-tests was a nine question multiple-choice quiz. The quiz was administered through the learning management system (Canvas). Each question was presented one at a time without the option to return to a previous question. The questions were developed through an instructional design process. A pair of learning objectives were defined for the iteration unit. One learning objective was the ability to write a program using iteration to compute a quantitative measure from a list of data. The other learning objective was to write a program using iteration to produce a visualization from a list of data. Instructional analysis was used to identify the sub-tasks needed to achieve each objective. Multiple performance objectives were created for each task from which the nine multiple choice questions were created. The distractors on each question came from mistakes identified by an analysis of student solutions to iteration problems in the prior semester. Figure 2 shows an example of one of the questions on the pre-test. In this question students were shown a fragment of a block-based program containing a list-based iteration and asked to identify which one of seven alternatives should be placed in the body of the iteration. The figure also shows the most frequently selected distractor (item e) and the correct choice (item g).

The same concepts were tested on the pre-test and post-test quizzes. While the question ordering remained the same, the question wording varied. For example, pre-test question 4 shown in Figure 2 appeared on the first post-test using *distance_sum*, *distance*, and *distance_list* instead of the text shown (the problem changes

When using the iteration shown below to compute the sum of the numbers in the rent_list, which of the following is the correct statement to be in the body of the iteration?

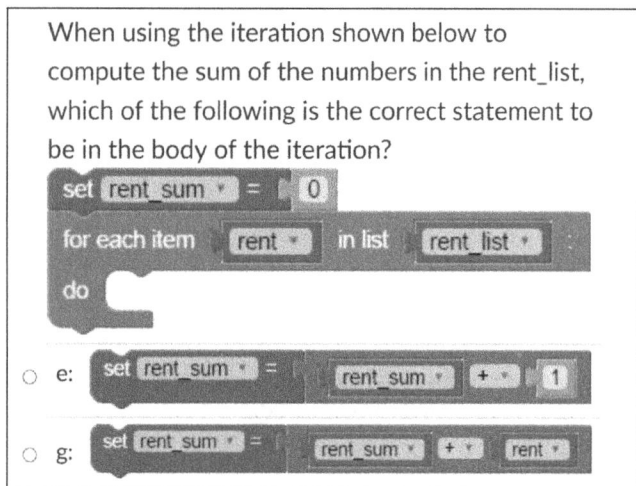

Figure 2: Example Pre-test Question

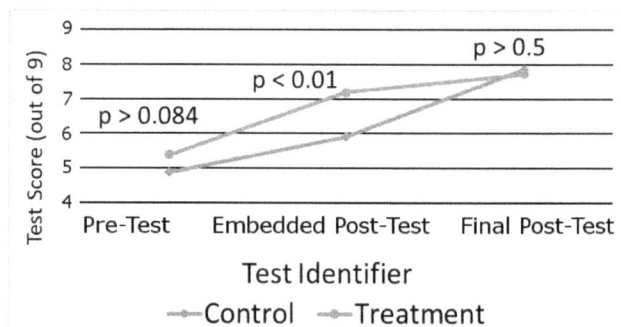

Figure 3: Comparison of Score Over Time Between Control and Treatment

from one about rents to a problem about distances). However, the essential nature of the question remained the same.

In addition to the multiple-choice test, each post-test contained one or two open-ended programming problems. The first post-test contained one programming problem related to the first learning objective (computing a quantitative measure). The material related to the second learning objective (producing a visualization) was not covered until after the first post-test. The second post-test contained two programming problems - each related to one of the learning objectives. The statement of the three programming problems are:

(1) The data block in the BlockPy canvas below provides a list of the number of students taking the 2015 SAT test in each state. Write an algorithm to compute and print the total number of students taking the SAT test in 2015.
(2) The data block in the BlockPy canvas below provides a list of the per capita income of each state. Write an algorithm that computes and prints the number of states with a per capita income greater than 28000 dollars.
(3) The data block in the BlockPy canvas below provides a list of the sale price in US dollars of books sold by Amazon. Write an algorithm that produces a histogram of sale prices in Euros. A dollar amount is converted to a Euro amount by multiplying the dollar amount by 0.94.

The first problem requires an iteration that counts the number of elements in the list. The second problem requires an iteration that counts only some of the elements in the list. The third problem requires an iteration that produces a new list with transformed values; this list is then visualized as a histogram.

It is important to note that during the programming of the open-ended questions, the students were provided limited feedback: only run-time errors were reported (e.g., adding a number to a list or using an uninitialized variable). The feedback was limited to assess the extent that students had internalized the knowledge and ability to write the program without relying on the feedback for guidance. Each question clearly explained that there would be limited feedback and no indication of correct output would be given.

5 RESULTS AND ANALYSIS

In this section, the data from the multiple choice tests and free response (programming) problems are analyzed. Each of the nine questions on the multiple choice test is scored as correct or incorrect. A student's score is the total number of correct answers given. Each free response question is also scored as correct or incorrect. Correct means that the student's program produced the expected output exactly; all other programs are incorrect. A Mann-Whitney U test is used to measure the statistical significance of differences between the performance of students in the treatment group in comparison to the performance of students in the control group. The Mann-Whitney U test is appropriate for this data because the responses are ordinal and we cannot satisfy an assumption of normality.

The tables presented in this section contain four items:

$\overline{x}$: the mean response for the given group
s: the standard deviation from the mean
n: the size of the group
p: the significance
r: the effect size expressed in variance

A p value less than .05 is taken as significant. Modified r for non-parametric effect size is taken as per normal for variance effect size (see [8]). Each table also shows four groups: the control group, the first treatment group (Fall 2017), the second treatment group (Spring 2018), and the two treatment groups combined (All).

5.1 Multiple Choice Tests

First, we compare the pre-test performance of the treatment groups to that of the control group. If the performance of the treatment group is significantly different from that of the control group then the groups are not directly comparable (e.g., students in one group might have a higher level of prior programming experience than students in the other group).

The Pre-test row in Table 4 shows the comparison of the pre-test performance between the groups. There was no significant difference between the control group and the combined treatment groups (All) and no significant difference between the control group and the first treatment group. However, the null hypothesis is not rejected for the second treatment group. Therefore, comparisons to assess the impact of the feedback intervention use the combined (All) treatment group in comparison to the control group.

The impact of the feedback intervention is shown in the two Post-test rows of Table 4. The Embedded Post-test data shows that there is a significant difference between the control group's mean performance ($\overline{x} = 5.9067$) and the treatment group's mean performance ($\overline{x} = 7.1878$). On average, the combined treatment group performed better by the equivalent of one full question on the test. Statistically, this difference is a large effect size. Recall that the embedded post-test occurs midway through the instruction. However, the Final Post-test row in Table 4 shows that there is no significant difference between the treatment and control groups. The mean response data ($\overline{x}$) is also shown in Figure 3.

Finally, considering each column in Table 4 separately, the gain in student learning within each group can be seen. The mean response in all treatment groups shows similar improvement.

Assessment	Control ($\overline{x}$,n)	Treatment ($\overline{x}$,n,p,r)		
	S2017	F2017	S2018	All
Pre-test	$\overline{x} = 4.8806$ $s = 2.1499$ $n = 67$	$\overline{x} = 5.1982$ $s\ 1.9485$ $n = 111$ $p = 0.2970$ $r = 0.0783$	$\overline{x} = 5.5536$ $s = 2.0961$ $n = 112$ $p = 0.0396$ $r = 0.1539$	$\overline{x} = 5.3767$ $s = 2.0272$ $n = 223$ $p = 0.0845$ $r = 0.1013$
Embedded Post-test	$\overline{x} = 5.9067$ $s = 1.2646$ $n = 75$	$\overline{x} = 7.1500$ $s = 1.6291$ $n = 100$ $p < 0.0001$ $r = 0.4148$	$\overline{x} = 7.2212$ $s = 1.5853$ $n = 113$ $p < 0.0001$ $r = 0.4171$	$\overline{x} = 7.1878$ $s = 1.6026$ $n = 213$ $p < 0.0001$ $r = 0.3717$
Final Post-Test	$\overline{x} = 7.8611$ $s = 1.3972$ $n = 72$	$\overline{x} = 7.7300$ $s = 1.5561$ $n = 100$ $p = 0.6443$ $r = 0.0353$	$\overline{x} = 7.7232$ $s = 1.4900$ $n = 112$ $p = 0.4852$ $r = 0.0516$	$\overline{x} = 7.7264$ $s = 1.5179$ $n = 212$ $p = 0.5121$ $r = 0.0390$

Table 4: Student performance on multiple choice assessment

5.2 Free Response Tests

The free response tests consisted of individual programming problems as described in Section 4. The Embedded Post-test had one programming problem and the Final Post-test had two programming problems. As described in Section 4.4 the students were told that they would receive limited feedback on these problems. The results of the free response tests are shown in Table 5 and Table 6.

Table 5 shows the analysis of all three programming problems grouped together (row 1) and the two Final Post-test programming problems grouped together (row 2). Overall, there was a significant difference between the control and the combined treatment groups (All), with a small effect size. This suggests that MDF supports their acquisition of programming skills. On average, 32% of the control group completed all three problems correctly versus 41% of the treatment group. A similar result occurs when considering only the two Final Post-test questions. In this case 38% of the control group completed the two programming problems correctly compared to 48% in the combined treatment groups.

Table 6 shows the analysis for each of the three problems separately. Although similar differences and effect sizes between the

treatment and control groups are reported in Table 6 as in Table 5, the sample size is not large enough to claim statistical significance. It can be noted that the effect size is consistent despite the increasing complexity of the problems. The last Post-test problem requires list construction, list appending, and plotting that are not part of the other problems. However, the same difference between control and treatment is seen for this problem as for the others.

5.3 Discussion

The data in Table 4 and summarized in Figure 3 indicates that there is an accelerated level of learning in the treatment over the control group at the point of the embedded post-test, but that by the end of the instruction the control group has closed the gap with the treatment groups. Two interpretations of this data are possible. One interpretation is that additional practice (classwork and homework problems) and additional interaction with the course staff (in class and during office hours) can compensate over time for the lack of more effective feedback. Even with this interpretation the potential demotivating impact on students of more failed attempts and the need for more staff interaction should be kept in mind. Anecdotally, there was a highly noticeable decline in the need for interaction with the course staff during the two treatment semesters. A second interpretation is that the quality of the feedback in the first part of the instruction is better than that during the later part of the instruction. Our analysis of student solutions for the later part of the instruction should be revisited in this light. If the feedback can be improved, it is possible that the performance gap might persist.

On the programming tasks, the feedback intervention helped to improve the level of success by about 10%. We believe that with refinement, this degree of improvement can be increased.

Another impact of the feedback intervention can only be reported anecdotally. In the case of the control group the course staff played a proactive role in probing students' progress and offering help. This included undergraduate teaching assistants who were paired with fixed groups of students in a ratio of approximately 16:1. In contrast, during both interventions the course staff played a reactive role, only providing assistance when explicitly asked for by a student. The course instructors noted a dramatic drop in the level of help required of the course staff. This is especially significant in the light of the students' increased performance on the post-tests.

Another observation is that while the treatment group performed equivalently on conceptual questions (multiple choice test) compared to the control group by the end of the intervention, the treatment group performed better on the free response questions. It is positive that the feedback intervention did support a higher level of students' programming ability. However, this improvement in programming ability did not seem to be associated with an improvement on the multiple-choice test. One interpretation is that the feedback intervention occurred in the context of free-response questions similar to the questions on the post-tests. Thus, the effect of the improved feedback transferred better to a similar, constructive task, but not to the recall and analysis tasks of the multiple-choice test. However, this explanation is not completely satisfactory because the embedded post-test seemed to indicate that there was a positive impact on the multiple-choice tests earlier. Another interpretation is that after being given the same multiple choice test three different times (albeit, contextualized differently) the students may have "learned" how to answer the questions. Additional analysis will be needed to resolve this question.

Problems	Control ($\overline{x}$,n)	Treatment ($\overline{x}$,n,p,r)		
	S2017	F2017	S2018	All
All Post-Test Free Response	$\overline{x}$ = 0.3227 s = 0.2781 n = 94	$\overline{x}$ = 0.3920 s = 0.3115 n = 125 p = 0.0919 r = 0.1140	$\overline{x}$ = 0.4987 s = 0.3585 n = 133 p = 0.0001 r = 0.2549	$\overline{x}$ = 0.4137 s = 0.3078 n = 258 p = 0.0127 r = 0.1330
Final Post-Test Free Response	$\overline{x}$ = 0.3855 s = 0.3648 n = 83	$\overline{x}$ = 0.4858 s = 0.3544 n = 106 p = 0.0498 r = 0.1428	$\overline{x}$ = 0.4835 s = 0.3707 n = 121 p = 0.0622 r = 0.1307	$\overline{x}$ = 0.4845 s = 0.3636 n = 227 p = 0.0316 r = 0.1224

Table 5: Cumulative Student Performance on Post-Test Programming problems

Problems	Control ($\overline{x}$,n)	Treatment ($\overline{x}$,n,p,r)		
	S2017	F2017	S2018	All
Embedded Post-Test Free Response	$\overline{x}$ = 0.3253 s = 0.4948 n = 83	$\overline{x}$ = 0.4259 s = 0.3976 n = 108 p = 0.1576 r = 0.1024	$\overline{x}$ = 0.4463 s = 0.3873 n = 121 p = 0.0838 r = 0.1212	$\overline{x}$ = 0.4367 s = 0.3914 n = 229 p = 0.0774 r = 0.1000
Final Post-Test Free Response 1	$\overline{x}$ = 0.3780 s = 0.4934 n = 82	$\overline{x}$ = 0.4571 s = 0.5013 n = 105 p = 0.2792 r = 0.0792	$\overline{x}$ = 0.4793 s = 0.5019 n = 121 p = 0.1550 r = 0.0999	$\overline{x}$ = 0.4709 s = 0.5010 n = 226 p = 0.1565 r = 0.0808
Final Post-Test Free Response 2	$\overline{x}$ = 0.4125 s = 0.5006 n = 80	$\overline{x}$ = 0.5294 s = 0.5016 n = 102 p = 0.1185 r = 0.1158	$\overline{x}$ = 0.5268 s = 0.5010 n = 112 p = 0.1194 r = 0.1125	$\overline{x}$ = 0.5280 s = 0.5001 n = 214 p = 0.0785 r = 0.1027

Table 6: Student Performance on Individual Post-Test Programming Problems

5.4 Mistake Driven Analysis

The previous sections have established that Misconception-Driven Feedback supports acquisition of student programming skills and conceptual knowledge. This section focuses on the particular role that misconceptions play in deeply analyzing student programming problems. Recall from Section 3.1, that a mistake is a vector of misconceptions. By cross-referencing mistake vectors we mean identifying the misconceptions common to the cross-referenced mistakes. Through cross-referencing we can isolate misconceptions. To highlight the power of this approach, we present some examples below. Specifically, we divide the discussion into three parts. The first part demonstrates how MDF can be used to more

deeply analyze mistakes. The second part demonstrates how new misconceptions can be discovered by using MDF. The third part demonstrates how MDF can be used to understand and reason about the impact of the feedback on students.

To illustrate this approach, we analyze mistakes made by students that were identified in the second free response problem:

> The data block in the BlockPy canvas below provides a list of the per capita income of each state. Write an algorithm that computes and prints the number of states with a per capita income greater than 28000 dollars.

This problem asks a student to count (the number of states) and filter (include only a portion of the data) using iteration.

5.4.1 Deeper Analysis. One mistake we observe in this problem is the absence of the pattern seen in Figure 4. This pattern indicates

```
#absence of:
for _item_ in _list_:
    count = count + 1
```

Figure 4: Mistake Example 2

that a student is missing the statement to count the items in the list. In the treatment group, 43.81% exhibited this mistake, while 57.32% of the control group exhibited this mistake. While this is an improvement over the control group, MDF can facilitate a deeper analysis. Mistake 2 is indicative of multiple possible misconceptions, including but not limited to:

- The student does not understand the difference between summing and counting.
- The student does not understand the difference between an accumulator (count) vs. the iteration variable (item).
- The student does not understand that the iteration variable (item) takes on each value of the list (list).

In the treatment group, 99 of 226 treatment solutions made mistake 2. To more deeply analyze this mistake, we also detect the co-occurence of another mistake: the presence of the code pattern shown in Figure 1b. By cross-referencing these two mistakes, we increase the evidence that the student has the misconception of not understanding the difference between summing and counting. However, this pairing of mistakes accounts for only 20 of the 99 occurrences of mistake 2, suggesting that the remaining 79 occurrences have to be one of the other misconceptions associated with mistake 2. By cross-referencing with other mistakes we might be able to isolate the frequency of the other two misconceptions.

5.4.2 Discovering New Misconceptions. Cross-referencing mistakes can also reveal new misconceptions. For example, in the above problem, 61 students had mistake 2 plus another anticipated mistake: a missing print statement. An inspection of the programs of these 61 students showed that 51 of them incorrectly used an append statement. This pairing of mistakes, made by a substantial number of students, indicates the existence of an unexpected misconception: confusing creating a list of items with counting the number of these items. Although recognizable in retrospect, this misconception only emerged through the MDF analysis.

5.4.3 Understanding Anomalies. Finally, MDF can be used to diagnose anomalous results in student data. Consider mistake 3 shown in Figure 5, the absence of a necessary conditional check. The control group exhibited this mistake in 1.22%(1) of its population whereas the treatment condition exhibited mistake 3 in 12.83%(29) of its population. While overall performance of the treatment group was better than the control group with respect to the free response in general, this particular mistake contradicts the general result. Cross-referencing mistakes allows us a deeper understanding and suggests why the feedback had a negative impact on this mistake.

```
#presence of equivalent expression
if x > 28000:
    pass
```

Figure 5: Mistake Example 3

These three cases cross-reference mistake 3 with other mistakes:

Case 1 : income >= 28000 or income <= 28000 or income < 28000

- condition wrong and no other feedback

Case 2 : income > "28000" or income >= "28000"

- condition wrong, output wrong, and incompatible types

Case 3 : income > 2800 or income >= 2800

- condition wrong, and output wrong

The feedback associated with this mistake is "In this problem you should be finding XXX above/below XXX units", where XXX, above/below, and units are contextualized with specific problems).

Case 2 is interesting because students in the treatment group did not receive feedback about incompatible types (the runtime feedback the control received by default), because this message was superseded by the feedback associated with mistake 3. This case accounts for 38%(11) of the occurrences of mistake 3 in the treatment group. This particular error indicates an issue with students' awareness of operations on data types. This particular misconception coincides with results from our post-tests, as discussed in [12]. This suggests a failure of our feedback, contradicting our goal of grounding feedback in misconceptions. Our failure lay in choosing to provide feedback about the mistake (pointing to the incorrect comparison) rather than the underlying misconception (confusing the types of numbers vs. strings). Case 3, rather than being a misconception, is likely a typo or careless reading by the students. Case 3 captures 41%(12) of the occurrences of mistake 3. Of the 12 in Case 3, 11 were "income > 2800." This means of the 29 occurrences of mistake 3, only 7 of these were issues with conditionals. Correcting for these, misconceptions with conditionals parallels performance in the control group (1.22% vs 3.1%). These nuances demonstrate how MDF allows more critical analysis of free response data.

6 THREATS TO VALIDITY AND LIMITATIONS

While the results presented in this work are promising, there are several threats to validity. First, in the pretest for the control group,

one of the class sections for the control had technical difficulties and took the quiz outside class. However, a Mann-Whitney U test between the two sections in the control showed no significant differences in pretest results. Second, feedback creation, misconception identification, and analysis were all done by the same researchers. Despite our efforts to be guided by the analysis of data and the principles of instructional design, it is possible that the perspectives of the team were too similar, allowing alternate explanations to be overlooked. Third, UTAs were instructed to be more passive in the treatment group as opposed to the active assistance they provided in the control group. This change may have required students to be more self-reliant in their learning even in the absence of the MDF feedback. However, one of our aims is to reduce UTA workload.

There are limitations in this work. First, our population was a specific demographic of non-technical majors. It is unknown how MDF would affect CS majors. Second, we only targeted a specific unit of instruction (collection-based iteration). Future work includes targeting different units of instruction. For both limitations, the specific misconceptions and feedback may change with different populations or topics. However, we do believe that the method itself would prove equally useful in other contexts.

7 CONCLUSIONS

In this paper we presented and assessed misconception-driven feedback (MDF). Informed by cognitive learning theory, the learner model underlying MDF focuses on the mental misconceptions that learners reveal by their observed mistakes. The philosophy of MDF is that immediate formative feedback about an observed mistake should address the underlying misconception. We evaluated MDF using both quantitative and descriptive analysis of a three semester quasi-experimental study. Quantitatively, there was a statistically significant, 10% increase in performance on open-ended programming problems and an acceleration in performance on a multiple-choice quiz. This improvement occurred despite the removal of MDF during the assessment and the deliberate reduction of proactive assistance from the course staff during the instruction. The cross-referencing of mistakes allowed us to reason about the underlying misconceptions in more precise way than would otherwise be possible. This analysis also revealed new misconceptions, allowing additional feedback to be created. The analysis enables instructors to have deeper insight into their learners and identify instructional improvement that will address persistent misconceptions.

In a broader context, MDF provides a novel and practical connection between learning and instruction about programming. Misconceptions result from cognitive breakdowns in learning. Mistakes, the manifestation of the breakdown in practice, point to areas of insufficient instruction or where the instruction should be reconsidered. This connection between the theory of learning and the pragmatics of instructional design offers not only an opportunity for more effective feedback but also the possibility of more coherent and integrated learning environments.

ACKNOWLEDGMENTS

This work is supported in part by National Science Foundation grants DUE 1624320, DUE 1444094, and DGE 0822220.

REFERENCES

[1] John R Anderson, Daniel Bothell, Michael D Byrne, Scott Douglass, Christian Lebiere, and Yulin Qin. 2004. An integrated theory of the mind. *Psychological review* 111, 4 (2004), 1036.

[2] John R Anderson, Frederick G Conrad, and Albert T Corbett. 1989. Skill acquisition and the LISP tutor. *Cognitive Science* 13, 4 (1989), 467–505.

[3] Austin Cory Bart, Javier Tibau, Eli Tilevich, Clifford A Shaffer, and Dennis Kafura. 2017. BlockPy: An Open Access Data-Science Environment for Introductory Programmers. *Computer* 50, 5 (2017), 18–26.

[4] Brett A Becker. 2015. *An exploration of the effects of enhanced compiler error messages for computer programming novices*. Master's thesis. Dublin Institute of Technology.

[5] Benjamin S Bloom. 1984. The 2 sigma problem: The search for methods of group instruction as effective as one-to-one tutoring. *Educational researcher* 13, 6 (1984), 4–16.

[6] Gary M Brosvic and Beth D Cohen. 1988. The horizontal-vertical illusion and knowledge of results. *Perceptual and motor skills* 67, 2 (1988), 463–469.

[7] Ricardo Caceffo, Steve Wolfman, Kellogg S. Booth, and Rodolfo Azevedo. 2016. Developing a computer science concept inventory for introductory programming. In *Proceedings of the 47th ACM Technical Symposium on Computer Science Education*. ACM, 364–369.

[8] Jacob Cohen. 1988. Statistical power analysis for the behavioral sciences. 2nd.

[9] Albert T Corbett and John R Anderson. 2001. Locus of feedback control in computer-based tutoring: Impact on learning rate, achievement and attitudes. In *Proceedings of the SIGCHI conference on Human factors in computing systems*. ACM, 245–252.

[10] Tyne Crow, Andrew Luxton-Reilly, and Burkhard Wuensche. 2018. Intelligent tutoring systems for programming education: a systematic review. In *Proceedings of the 20th Australasian Computing Education Conference*. ACM, 53–62.

[11] Roberta E Dihoff, Gary M Brosvic, and Michael L Epstein. 2003. The role of feedback during academic testing: The delay retention effect revisited. *The Psychological Record* 53, 4 (2003), 533–548.

[12] Luke Gusukuma, Austin Cory Bart, Dennis Kafura, Jeremy Ernst, and Katherine Cennamo. 2018. Instructional Design+ Knowledge Components: A Systematic Method for Refining Instruction. In *Proceedings of the 49th ACM Technical Symposium on Computer Science Education*. ACM, 338–343.

[13] Georgiana Haldeman, Andrew Tjang, Monica Babeş-Vroman, Stephen Bartos, Jay Shah, Danielle Yucht, and Thu D Nguyen. 2018. Providing Meaningful Feedback for Autograding of Programming Assignments. In *Proceedings of the 49th ACM Technical Symposium on Computer Science Education*. ACM, 278–283.

[14] Andrew Head, Elena Glassman, Gustavo Soares, Ryo Suzuki, Lucas Figueredo, Loris D'Antoni, and Björn Hartmann. 2017. Writing Reusable Code Feedback at Scale with Mixed-Initiative Program Synthesis. In *Proceedings of the Fourth (2017) ACM Conference on Learning@ Scale*. ACM, 89–98.

[15] Lisa Kaczmarczyk, Elizabeth Petrick, J Philip East, and Geoffrey L Herman. 2010. Identifying student misconceptions of programming. In *Proceedings of the 41st ACM technical symposium on Computer science education*. ACM, 107–111.

[16] Dennis Kafura, Austin Cory Bart, and Bushra Chowdhury. 2015. Design and Preliminary Results From a Computational Thinking Course. In *Proceedings of the 2015 ACM Conference on Innovation and Technology in Computer Science Education (ITiCSE '15)*. ACM, 63–68.

[17] Donald E Knuth. 1969. The art of computer programming. Vol. 1: Fundamental algorithms. Second printing.

[18] Kenneth R Koedinger, Vincent Aleven, Neil Heffernan, Bruce McLaren, and Matthew Hockenberry. 2004. Opening the door to non-programmers: Authoring intelligent tutor behavior by demonstration. In *International Conference on Intelligent Tutoring Systems*. Springer, 162–174.

[19] Kenneth R Koedinger, Albert T Corbett, and Charles Perfetti. 2012. The Knowledge-Learning-Instruction framework: Bridging the science-practice chasm to enhance robust student learning. *Cognitive science* 36, 5 (2012), 757–798.

[20] Einari Kurvinen, Niko Hellgren, Erkki Kaila, Mikko-Jussi Laakso, and Tapio Salakoski. 2016. Programming misconceptions in an introductory level programming course exam. In *Proceedings of the 2016 ACM Conference on Innovation and Technology in Computer Science Education*. ACM, 308–313.

[21] Nguyen-Thinh Le. 2016. A classification of adaptive feedback in educational systems for programming. *Systems* 4, 2 (2016), 22.

[22] David J Nicol and Debra Macfarlane-Dick. 2006. Formative assessment and self-regulated learning: A model and seven principles of good feedback practice. *Studies in higher education* 31, 2 (2006), 199–218.

[23] Chris Piech, Jonathan Huang, Andy Nguyen, Mike Phulsuksombati, Mehran Sahami, and Leonidas Guibas. 2015. Learning program embeddings to propagate feedback on student code. *arXiv preprint arXiv:1505.05969* (2015).

[24] Thomas W Price, Yihuan Dong, and Tiffany Barnes. 2016. Generating Data-driven Hints for Open-ended Programming.. In *EDM*. 191–198.

[25] Thomas W Price, Yihuan Dong, and Dragan Lipovac. 2017. iSnap: Towards Intelligent Tutoring in Novice Programming Environments. In *Proceedings of the 2017 ACM SIGCSE Technical Symposium on Computer Science Education*. ACM, 483–488.

[26] Kelly Rivers and Kenneth R Koedinger. 2017. Data-driven hint generation in vast solution spaces: a self-improving python programming tutor. *International Journal of Artificial Intelligence in Education* 27, 1 (2017), 37–64.

[27] Takayuki Sekiya and Kazunori Yamaguchi. 2013. Tracing quiz set to identify novices' programming misconceptions. In *Proceedings of the 13th Koli Calling International Conference on Computing Education Research*. ACM, 87–95.

[28] Valerie J Shute. 2008. Focus on formative feedback. *Review of educational research* 78, 1 (2008), 153–189.

[29] Teemu Sirkiä and Juha Sorva. 2012. Exploring programming misconceptions: an analysis of student mistakes in visual program simulation exercises. In *Proceedings of the 12th Koli Calling International Conference on Computing Education Research*. ACM, 19–28.

[30] Juha Sorva and Teemu Sirkiä. 2011. Context-sensitive guidance in the UUhistle program visualization system. In *Proceedings of the 6th Program Visualization Workshop (PVWâĂŹ11)*. 77–85.

[31] JC Spohrer and Elliot Soloway. 1986. Alternatives to construct-based programming misconceptions. In *Acm sigchi bulletin*, Vol. 17. ACM, 183–191.

[32] Marieke Thurlings, Marjan Vermeulen, Theo Bastiaens, and Sjef Stijnen. 2013. Understanding feedback: A learning theory perspective. *Educational Research Review* 9 (2013), 1–15.

Identifying Student Difficulties with Basic Data Structures

Daniel Zingaro
University of Toronto Mississauga
daniel.zingaro@utoronto.ca

Cynthia Taylor
Oberlin College
ctaylor@oberlin.edu

Leo Porter
University of California, San Diego
leporter@eng.ucsd.edu

Michael Clancy
University of California, Berkeley

Cynthia Lee
Stanford University

Soohyun Nam Liao
University of California, San Diego

Kevin C. Webb
Swarthmore College

ABSTRACT

To be effective instructors and CS education researchers, we must identify and understand student difficulties surrounding core computing topics. This study examines student difficulties with the basic data structures commonly found in CS2 courses. Initial exploration of student thinking began with think-aloud interviews with students. These interviews centered on open-ended questions that were iteratively improved upon based on analysis of interview transcripts. The revised open-ended questions were then posed to 249 students during an end-of-term final exam study session. Using the explanations and justifications included by students, responses to the questions were coded and summarized. This work characterizes the difficulties revealed by student responses, and provides details of their prevalence among the examined student population.

CCS CONCEPTS

• **Social and professional topics** → **Computing Education**;

KEYWORDS

CS2, data structures, difficulties

ACM Reference Format:
Daniel Zingaro, Cynthia Taylor, Leo Porter, Michael Clancy, Cynthia Lee, Soohyun Nam Liao, and Kevin C. Webb. 2018. Identifying Student Difficulties with Basic Data Structures. In *ICER '18: 2018 International Computing Education Research Conference, August 13–15, 2018, Espoo, Finland.* ACM, New York, NY, USA, 9 pages. https://doi.org/10.1145/3230977.3231005

1 INTRODUCTION

It is important for instructors to be aware of common student difficulties and errors related to the content domain being learned [20]. For example, a recent study of middle school physical science teachers and students found that teacher familiarity with student wrong answers was positively correlated with student learning gains [18].

Prior research has discussed both student misconceptions and student difficulties [4, 16]. A student **conception** describes a belief, theory or explanation previously developed to explain some behavior observed in the world [1]. When these beliefs are in conflict with accepted scientific theories, they become **misconceptions** [1]. A **difficulty** refers to an observable error committed by students [4]. The present paper focuses on student difficulties, which through additional study and corroboration may illuminate upstream misconceptions.

There are many studies that examine student difficulties and misconceptions in CS1 [17, 22]. In contrast, the relevant literature for data structures is in its infancy; for example, linked lists have received very little attention [10].

This work aims to further our understanding of student difficulties regarding Basic Data Structures, including ArrayLists, singly- and doubly-linked lists, and binary search trees. We began by recruiting students to participate in think-aloud interviews about Basic Data Structures problems. The interview results informed our authoring of a series of questions aimed to elicit student difficulties. To gather a larger data set, we then presented the questions to 249 students during a final exam study session. The students responded with an answer and a justification for that answer, which we coded to identify common difficulties. We explore these difficulties here.

2 BACKGROUND

There is a vast literature around student difficulties in introductory programming (CS1). That work has led to the discovery of surprising student misconceptions and has informed concept inventory development [5]. For example, researchers have found that students infer unwarranted relationships between variables, and believe that memory is reserved for uninstantiated objects [5]. Even fundamental concepts typically taught at the start of CS1, such as primitive/object variables, value/reference assignment, and parameter passing, are associated with considerable variation in student understanding [7, 8, 21]. Several comprehensive literature reviews demonstrate the extent to which researchers over the years have studied CS1 misconceptions and difficulties [17, 22]. In fact, one such literature review calls for the community to move away from identifying additional misconceptions for CS1 and to instead begin working to foster changes in CS1 in response to those that have already been identified [15].

Recent work highlights two core components of typical CS2 courses: Recursion and Basic Data Structures [14]. A large number of difficulties and misconceptions associated with recursion have been documented [4, 9]. By comparison, there are fewer reports of difficulties for introductory data structures topics. Tenenberg and Murphy tested students on data structures as part of a project on student self-assessment, and found that students performed best on questions about stack, queue and tree interfaces, and worst on questions concerning the runtime efficiency of different searches [24]. Some have studied student misconceptions of heaps, including the ways that heaps can be represented or constructed [13, 19]. Particularly relevant to the present study is work by Karpierz and Wolfman [6], who used interviews and exam/project analysis to identify student misconceptions of binary search trees (BSTs) and hash tables. The discovered BST misconceptions are: (1) a separate search through the tree is required to ensure that the element is not already in the tree before inserting it, (2) all keys in the tree must be inspected before inserting a new key, and (3) a BST is balanced by default. Interestingly, some have found that students conflate binary search trees and heaps [2, 13], while others have not replicated this [6].

For several reasons, we argue for the continued study of student difficulties with introductory data structures. First, echoing arguments from other researchers [25], student difficulties serve as sources of pedagogical content knowledge (PCK), helping instructors anticipate likely struggles and how to guide student understanding in the context of those struggles. Second, introductory data structures are a core component of many CS2 courses, and CS2 itself often serves as the entrypoint to a CS major [14]. Finally, difficulties with some data structures (e.g., linked lists, trees) are studied in only a small number of papers [10, 11]. That is, while the community has been urged to stop itemizing CS1 difficulties [15], there is much that we do not know about post-CS1 difficulties.

3 METHODOLOGY

We began by developing open-ended questions designed to cover a set of learning goals and topics found to be important to the teaching of Basic Data Structures [14]. In order to ensure that these questions highlight a range of student understanding, we conducted interviews in which students were asked to think aloud while solving these problems. Through the course of these interviews, we frequently modified and adapted the questions to better reflect and surface student difficulties.

A total of 65 interviews were conducted at three different North American schools: one private and two public research-intensive universities. Students were recruited for participation from each institution at the end of the course that taught Basic Data Structures. Participation was approved by the Human Subjects Board for each institution, and students were compensated for their time with gift cards.

After completing and analyzing our student interviews, we presented the open-ended questions to students at a public, research-intensive university as part of a final exam study session for a Java-based CS2 course. We describe the test as "open-ended", even though some questions included multiple choice options, because every question asked students to provide written justifications for their answers. The justifications often provided insight into difficulties, sometimes even when students selected correct answers.

Question 1

The Node and LinkedList class defined above implement a singly-linked list with head and tail references. Head refers to the first node of the list, and tail refers to the last node of the list.

Given below is a method in the LinkedList class to add an element to the end of the list.

```
DEFINE addEnd(n)
    IF tail == nil THEN
        head = tail = new ListNode(n)
    ELSE
        //MISSING CODE
    END IF
ENDDEF
```

Supply the missing code:

Two hundred forty-nine students gave consent for their responses to be used in this research project. We coded the responses for each question using an open coding technique in which categories were developed from common patterns in student answers. Each question was coded by one member of the research team.

4 STUDENT DIFFICULTIES

In this section, we present our questions, characterize the students' answers, and highlight common difficulties. To avoid distractions that may stem from the low-level details of any particular programming language, we developed our questions using pseudocode. Our pseudocode is modeled after that of [12], with a few small additions to better support data structures (e.g., a nil value).

4.1 Adding to the Tail of a Linked List

We designed Question 1 to test students' ability to implement linked list methods. A correct answer to this question is the following:

```
tail.next = new ListNode(n)
tail = tail.next
```

In our open-ended test, 67% of students answered this question correctly. We identify three common errors, with each coded separately (as such, percentages may add to greater than 100%): 16% of students failed to update the tail pointer, 12% failed to correctly attach the new node, and 10% unnecessarily looped through the list to find the tail.

4.1.1 Failure to Update the Tail Pointer. A representative example of a student response that included this mistake appears below. In this response, the student correctly creates a new node and connects that new node to the end of the list, but then fails to set the tail to point to the new end of the list.

```
ListNode end = new ListNode(n)
tail.next = end
```

For this error and the next, it is difficult to discern whether the mistake reflects a misconception (e.g., students do not believe they are responsible for maintaining the invariant that the tail points to the last element in this list), or whether they simply forgot to update the pointer.

4.1.2 Failure to Attach the New Node. For this error, students fail to add the new element to the end of the list. An example of a student response expressing this mistake appears below:

```
tail = new ListNode(n,nil)
```

In this response, the student assumes that there exists a constructor that takes both the element and the next node as parameters. While this is not consistent with the provided sample code, we did not mark this as incorrect. However, they fail to correctly set the old tail to point to the new tail.

We note that this error was slightly more common in conjunction with the "unnecessary loop" mistake that we discuss next. Similar to the prior mistake, we are unclear as to whether the students fundamentally misunderstood the need to correctly point the second-to-last element to the last element or instead that they made a careless mistake.

4.1.3 Unnecessary Loop to Find the Tail. A representative example of a student response demonstrating this inefficiency appears below:

```
ListNode newNode = new ListNode(n)
ListNode curr = head

WHILE curr.next != tail DO
    curr = curr.next
ENDWHILE

curr.next = newNode
tail = newNode
```

This difficulty is of interest as it embodies both **using and not using** the tail pointer. Students do understand that the tail pointer is present, and that it points to the last node: in 23 of the 25 cases where the student uses a loop, they also use the tail pointer somewhere in their code. In the sample response above, the student uses the tail pointer to find the node just before the end of the list in the while-loop, and updates the tail pointer to point at the new last node (unfortunately discarding the old last node). Other student responses correctly loop to the last node and then properly update the tail. None of these students, however, makes the leap to use the tail pointer to avoid the costly iteration through the loop. They may have simply memorized that looping through the list is always how the last node in a singly-linked list is accessed. This indicates that instructors may want to encourage students to thoroughly consider the impact of modifications to a data structure.

4.2 Fast Access to an Index

Question 2 was designed to test students' ability to choose an appropriate data structure when implementing a program. The correct answer to this problem is *d*, an ArrayList, since an ArrayList allows $O(1)$ access time to a specific position in the list, while either

---

Question 2

Suppose that your program is initialized with a set of numbers that is each added to a list. The user is then permitted to query for the number at a given position (index) in the list, and can make as many queries as they wish.

Which List data structure implementation would provide the best performance for the initialization and the user queries? You may assume that the number of user queries is many times more than the number of elements in the list.

a. a singly-linked list

b. a sorted doubly-linked list

c. an unsorted doubly-linked list

d. an ArrayList

Briefly explain your reasoning:

---

a singly- or doubly-linked list will take time $O(N)$ to access an element based on its position in the list.

Seventy-five percent of students correctly chose option *d*, and 165 of the 188 students who answered correctly discussed fast access by index in their justification.

4.2.1 Binary Search on the Sorted Doubly-Linked List. Ten percent of students incorrectly chose *b*, the sorted doubly-linked list. Of the 26 students who chose this answer, five specifically discussed using binary search on a doubly-linked list, despite the impossibility of accessing the list by index. It may be that these students have some fundamental misconceptions about either the requirements of binary search or how elements are accessed in a linked list.

4.2.2 Binary Search on an ArrayList. Five percent of students correctly selected the ArrayList, but then justified it by saying that an ArrayList is searchable in $O(logN)$ time with binary search. These students are likely missing that search is not necessary to solve this problem, perhaps due to typical comparisons of data structures that focus on search time.

4.2.3 Searching from Both Ends of a Doubly-Linked List. Four percent of students claimed that a doubly-linked list would be faster to search because one could search from either end, depending on where the index was closest. For example, "The doubly link[sic] list will allow you to determine the start of the search. If the index is on the right half of the list, then you would want to start at the tail & move backwards." This justification was used for selecting both the sorted and unsorted doubly-linked list.

Regardless of whether the list is sorted or unsorted, searching from both ends will not give any sort of performance optimization. Students using this justification with a doubly-linked list appear to believe they can somehow search from both directions in parallel, or can instantly figure out from which end to start the search.

Suppose that we wanted to insert the numbers 1 to 15 into a binary search tree. In what order should we insert the elements so that the tree is as balanced as possible?

4.3 Inserting into a BST

Question 3 probes students' ability to reason about the shape of a binary search tree (BST). In particular, students are expected to choose an insertion order for a range of numbers such that it ultimately produces a desirable BST structure: a fully balanced tree. Overall, 44% of students provided at least one correct insertion order. An additional 10% described a correct procedure to generate the order without specifying a sequence of integers, and another 5% drew a fully balanced tree containing all the values without indicating how such a tree might be constructed.

4.3.1 Starting in the Middle, Alternating Outwards. A common and interesting difficulty surfaced in which 6% of the students applied the correct logic to identify the root node, but then abandoned that logic for subsequent nodes under the root. That is, they identified that 8 should be the root of the tree, which produced two equally-sized trees below the root, but then generated a long chain of nodes for each of the root's subtrees. After inserting 8, these students provided sequences that alternated inserting values that were one larger or smaller than what was inserted previously. For example,

8, 7, 9, 6, 10, 5, 11, 4, 12, 3, 13, 2, 14, 1, 15.

Our interpretation of this result is that some students believe that only the root needs to contain an equal number of children on the left and right for the tree to be considered balanced. They do not consider applying the same criterion recursively, despite properties of BSTs often being defined recursively.

4.3.2 Starting at the Wrong Root (7). Another 6% of the student responses make the mistake of starting with 7 to be the root rather than 8. This error indicates that some students have difficulty choosing the root of the tree, particularly when the maximum element (15) is not evenly divisible by 2. We saw similar misunderstandings during our think-aloud interview phase. In those interviews, when students made the initial choice of 7 as the root, they repeatedly struggled to balance the tree rather than reevaluate their choice of root.

4.3.3 Randomness. Four percent of the responses asserted that, to be balanced, the values must be inserted in random order. This response suggests that some students may equate "random order" with "good order", despite a random order not being guaranteed to produce a balanced tree.

4.3.4 Min- or Max-Heap. Prior to collecting our student responses, we expected that some students might respond to Question 3 with answers that conflate binary search trees with heaps, as shown by Danielsiek et al [2]. Like Karpierz and Wolfman [6], we found that very few student responses—only 1%—seemed to exhibit this confusion.

Consider a binary search tree containing N values whose root is presently the median value in the tree. Suppose that N more values are added to the collection using the standard tree insertion algorithm, with all N larger than the largest value currently stored. Which of the following is true? (There may be more than one correct answer.)

a. The root still has a median value in the tree.

b. There are more values in the right subtree of the updated tree than in the left subtree.

c. Adding the Nth new value to the collection can take time proportional to log N.

d. Adding the Nth new value to the collection can take time proportional to N.

e. Adding the Nth new value to the collection can take time proportional to N^2.

Briefly explain your reasoning:

4.4 BST Changes After Insertions

Question 4 was designed to test students' ability to predict the behavior of an algorithm that operates on a data structure.

The correct answer to this problem is *b*, *c*, and *d*. Option *a* is no longer true, since the root will stay the same but the median value of the tree will change as all the added values are larger than the largest value currently in the tree. Option *b* is true, since all of the new values will be added to the right subtree. Option *c* will be true if the new values have been added in an order that makes the right subtree a balanced tree. Option *d* will be true if the new values have been added in an order that makes the right subtree unbalanced. Option *e* cannot be true, since there are fewer than N^2 values in the tree. Only 12% of students answered this question correctly.

4.4.1 Adding Cannot Take O(N) Time. Forty-five percent of students did not select *d*, indicating they did not think the time to insert could be $O(N)$. This may be an example of the "default balanced" misconception identified by Karpierz and Wolfman [6], in which students assume that BSTs will automatically have a balanced shape. The large number of students who failed to select this answer indicates that instructors should emphasize the worst-case results of insertion into a BST.

4.4.2 Adding Cannot Take O(logN) Time. Twenty-nine percent of students did not select *c*, indicating they did not think the time to insert could be $O(logN)$, with the majority of these students indicating they had interpreted the question to mean that every inserted value was larger than every previously inserted value, rather than just being larger than the original values in the tree. (The question has since been clarified.)

Question 5

Consider the design of a new data structure we will call a *generalized array*. A *generalized array* is like a list, except that its subscript values may be any collection of integers and not just a contiguous range of integers. For example, one might set up a *generalized array* named vals to have three subscripts—say, -5, 42, and -7001—and then to assign to or access vals[-5], vals[42], and vals[-7001]. An attempt to access the *generalized array* using any other subscript values would be illegal.

An implementation of a *generalized array* should allow fast access to its elements for large subscript sets. You have control over how you create the data structure (e.g., which data structure, insertion order of elements, etc.) Which of the following data structures best satisfy this requirement? **(There may be more than one correct answer.)** Assume that the set of subscript values is defined before the program is executed and does not change during the program run.

a. an ArrayList of subscript/value pairs, ordered by subscript

b. an ArrayList of subscript/value pairs, ordered by value

c. a linked list of subscript/value pairs, ordered by subscript

d. a linked list of subscript/value pairs, ordered by value

e. a binary search tree of subscript/value pairs, ordered by subscript

f. a binary search tree of subscript/value pairs, ordered by value

Briefly explain your reasoning:

4.4.3 The Root Remains the Median. Twenty-one percent of students chose *a*, indicating that they thought the root would stay the median. Of the 53 students that selected *a*, 32 of these students explicitly offered the fact that the root would stay the same as a justification for their answer. (Of the remaining 21 students, only two offered an alternate justification for their answer, with the rest not explaining their answer in any way.) This indicates that students have internalized the idea that once in a BST, a node will stay in the same position unless nodes are removed; however, they have memorized this idea to the extent that it did not occur to them that while the root value will not change, the median value will.

4.5 Generalized Array

We designed Question 5 to assess students' ability to choose an appropriate implementation of a data structure. The correct answer is both *a* and *e*, since the design should optimize for quick access by

subscript, and does not need to optimize for insertion or deletion time. Both a sorted ArrayList and a BST ordered by subscript will enable finding a subscript in time $O(logN)$, since binary search can be used on the sorted ArrayList and elements can be inserted appropriately into the BST to make it balanced. Only 22% of students answered this question correctly.

4.5.1 Binary Search Tree is Always Fastest. The most popular answer to this question, chosen by 24% of students, was *e*, a binary search tree ordered by subscript. Student answers specifically mentioned the quick time to find an element in a BST; e.g., "A BST allows for the fastest search time complexity of the three, at $O(logN)$." However, these answers overlook the fact that an ArrayList can also be searched in $O(logN)$ time using binary search. This error may be caused by instructors focusing on the ability to quickly find an element in a BST, while not emphasizing the same ability for sorted ArrayLists.

4.5.2 Accessing by Negative Index. Twelve percent answered only option *a*. Of the 30 students who answered this way, 19 of them justified their answer by saying that an ArrayList would offer direct or fast access to an index. This suggests that they believe that accessing an ArrayList with a negative index would be possible. This may partially have been prompted by our using array style references in the problem description; we have since rewritten this problem to avoid that array-like syntax. However, even with this problem phrasing, these students believing that vals[-5] is a valid way to access an ArrayList is troubling, and may point to a misconception about valid ArrayList indices.

4.5.3 Ignoring Performance. Twelve percent of students' answers included either of the linked list responses (*c* or *d*), with the most popular of these answers being *a*, *c*, and *e* (answered by 4% of students). The justifications for these answers generally did not mention performance, and focused on the fact that an implementation **could** be built using any of the data structures. (A sample student answer is "All three data structures should work as long as they arrange the elements by subscript meaning that if the subscript can't be found in all three of the structures, it wouldn't exist in general and you can't access its value unless you know the subscript.") As we discuss in Section 4.6.1, this indicates that instructors may wish to enhance their coverage of performance tradeoffs.

4.6 Implementing Undo

We designed Question 6 to test students' ability to correctly use existing data structures when implementing program functionality. The correct answer to this problem is *d*, to add and remove from the head, as this will maintain a LIFO ordering and both of these operations can be performed in constant time.

Seventy-two percent of the students correctly chose *d* for this problem, and of these, 60% mentioned the LIFO property in their explanation of their answer. Seven percent chose *a* or *b*, choices that do not provide a LIFO property.

4.6.1 Ignoring Performance. Thirteen percent of students chose both *c* and *d*, and an additional 4% chose only *c*. (Four percent did not answer the question.) The relatively large percentage of

Question 6

Imagine you are implementing "undo" functionality in a program: you want to save the user's actions with the ability to undo them in reverse order. For example, if a user performs operations a, b, and then c, activating your undo function would undo first c, then b, then a. **With the goal of providing the best performance for your undo operation, which of the following data structures would you use to store the user's actions? Check all that apply.**

For each of the following choices, assume the Singly-linked List implementation has a reference only to its head (but not its tail).

a. A singly-linked List that adds to tail and removes from head.

b. A singly-linked List that adds to head and removes from tail.

c. A singly-linked List that adds to tail and removes from tail.

d. A singly-linked List that adds to head and removes from head.

Briefly explain your reasoning:

Question 7

What shape is a binary search tree that contains the keys 1, 2, 3, 4, 5, 6, and 7? (Keys were not necessarily inserted in that order.)

a. Exactly this shape:

```
        7
       6
      5
     4
    3
   2
  1
```

b. Exactly this shape:

```
      4
   2     6
  1 3   5 7
```

c. Exactly this shape:

```
1
  2
    3
      4
        5
          6
            7
```

d. There is not enough information to tell.

Briefly explain your reasoning:

students who chose *c*, either in addition to *d* or instead of it, indicates that students may not well understand the performance differences between the two, or may have not explicitly considered performance in their answers. Of the 180 correct answers, 138 of them mentioned time complexity as a justification for their answer. Only one student who selected *c* as an answer mentioned time complexity, and they appeared to erroneously believe that *c* and *d* would take the same amount of time.

Instructors may want to spend more time discussing performance and time complexity when covering how to choose an existing data structure for use in a larger program. That is, while multiple data structures may each be "correct", implementation choices should also depend on performance considerations given the methods that will be frequently called.

4.7 Shape of a BST

Question 7 was adapted from Karpierz and Wolfman [6] to test students' ability to predict how inserting into a binary search tree would change its shape. In the Karpierz and Wolfman question, there was an additional distractor answer:

This shape with either 1 or 7 at the root and other keys arranged appropriately:

```
    *
  *   *
 * * * *
```

We eliminated this distractor as it did not occur in our open-ended interviews for the question. In the pilot of the Karpierz and Wolfman concept inventory, students perform poorly on this question, with 42.3% answering correctly. In contrast, our students performed very well on this question, with 87% correctly choosing *d*.

4.7.1 Default Balanced. Karpierz and Wolfman [6] identify a "default balanced" misconception, where students assume that binary search trees will automatically be balanced. Thirty-six percent of their students demonstrate this misconception by selecting either *b* or their other balanced distractor answer. Only 6% (15) of our students chose *b*. Twelve of these students mentioned the tree being balanced in their answer, suggesting that the default balanced misconception is present in our students, but to a lesser extent. It may be that this misconception is population-dependent, or depends in some way on sequencing or coverage of related course content. Another possible explanation is that there is a priming effect of Question 3, as that question asks in what order elements should be inserted to form a balanced BST.

At the end of a course on Basic Data Structures, students should be able to:

(1) Analyze runtime efficiency of algorithms related to data structure design.
(2) Select appropriate abstract data types for use in a given application.
(3) Compare data structure tradeoffs to select the appropriate implementation for an abstract data type.
(4) Design and modify data structures capable of insertion, deletion, search, and related operations.
(5) Trace through and predict the behavior of algorithms (including code) designed to implement data structure operations.
(6) Identify and remedy flaws in a data structure implementation that may cause its behavior to differ from the intended design.

Figure 1: Course-Level Learning Goals for Basic Data Structures [14]

4.7.2 Root Decides Shape. Among students who correctly chose *d* for the answer, 7 students (2% of total answers) provided explanations specifying that one would have to know the value of the root node, rather than the insertion order. This implies that some students believe the final shape of the tree is entirely dependent on the root, and that the insertion order of the other elements does not matter. Instructors may want to specify that all nodes, not just the root, affect the shape of the final tree.

5 DISCUSSION

In this section we discuss the implications and limitations of our work.

5.1 Question Relevance to Learning Goals

Recent work by Porter et al. [14] identified six course-level learning goals for Basic Data Structures. These goals were reached through a lengthy consensus process involving multiple experts at a variety of institution types, and can be found in Figure 1. We mapped our questions to those learning goals, and found that our questions address four of the six goals. As our questions are aligned to well-accepted goals for a core component of CS2, we hope that the questions will be of use to instructors seeking to provide formative feedback to their students.

A summary of our questions, student difficulties, and applicable learning goals appears in Table 1. Although our questions address the majority of the learning goals for Basic Data Structures, we believe based on ongoing interviews that we have uncovered only a small subset of relevant student difficulties. Further work, using a variety of additional questions and students, is warranted.

5.2 Overmemorization

Many of the difficulties that we identified could be interpreted as students trying to memorize facts about data structures, rather than

engaging core data structure concepts. For example, students may memorize that they should use a loop to find the last node in a singly-linked list, and so they do this even when there is a pointer to the tail node. They may have memorized that the root of a BST will never change, and so they claim the root will stay the median value, even though the median changes. They may have memorized that BSTs are used to quickly find an element, and so they overlook that the same performance can be achieved using binary search on an ArrayList.

Overall, this points to the need to augment how data structures are taught. It seems that some students can excel in data structures simply by memorizing a set of facts about each data structure covered. Rather than focusing on recall, instructors should focus on how students can use the facts about a given data structure to predict data structure behavior and evaluate tradeoffs between data structures.

5.3 Incorporating Student Difficulties

Awareness of common student difficulties is an important component of pedagogical content knowledge. We hope that the collection of difficulties identified during our interviews can both confirm and supplement such knowledge that faculty who teach CS2 may have acquired over time through their student interactions. This knowledge has immediate application to the classrooms of all CS2 instructors, because it suggests the need for targeted interventions, of whatever sort are customary for that instructor and class, to address these areas of potential gaps in student mastery. For example, an instructor who uses Peer Instruction in lectures could add a clicker question to target each difficulty. An instructor who uses an online platform for small coding exercises could similarly select or write more-targeted exercises. Durable and broadly-used curricular materials, such as textbooks and video-based online courses, could also be updated to better target these difficulties.

5.4 Threats to Validity

Interview and test subjects were drawn from classes at highly selective, research-focused schools. Although all students enrolled in CS2 at those schools were encouraged to participate, this student population may differ from CS2 students in other programs and types of institutions. Additionally, students who self-select to participate in interviews about CS2 or consent to have their work used in research projects may not reflect the general CS2 population.

To account for this, at-scale validation of future drafts will include a broader range of institutions. This will likely not contribute to further discovery of difficulties, a purpose served by the interviews and open-ended test, but will allow calibration on question difficulty and validation that the identified difficulties are shared by the new student populations.

Because this work was the first time these questions were administered to a large group, there are instances where ambiguous wording in the question led to confusion for students. We discussed these issues earlier in the text where they are relevant. Though we saw no evidence of language-related confusion, our choice to use a pseudocode language could cause students to incorrectly answer a question that they might otherwise have answered correctly had it been presented in their preferred programming language.

Table 1: Summary of Questions, Difficulties, and Applicable Learning Goals

Question	Goal	Data structure	Question Description	Difficulties
1	4	LL	Add to tail	Failing to update tail
				Failing to attach new node
				Unnecessarily looping to find tail
2	3	Many	Fast index access	Binary-searching doubly-linked list
				Searching instead of indexing
				Searching from both ends of a DLL
3	5	BST	Insertion order to balance BST	Starting in the middle, alternating outward
				Starting at the wrong root
				Inserting in random order
4	5	BST	Impact of BST insertions	Adding cannot take $O(N)$ time
				Adding cannot take $O(\log N)$ time
				Root remaining the median
5	3	Many	Generalized array	Binary search trees are always fastest
				Indexing by negative indices
				Ignoring performance
6	2	LL	Data Structure for undo	Ignoring performance
7	5	BST	Shape of a BST	Default balanced [6]
				Root determining shape

5.5 Future Work

This work is part of a long-term research project with the goal to create and validate a programming language-independent concept inventory (CI) for the Basic Data Structures component of CS2. A CI is a standardized test instrument designed to determine whether students correctly grasp core concepts of a topic area [23]. A reliable, valid CI can catalyze research and improvements in pedagogical practice for a subject by providing a common point of reference for measurements of student outcomes. Without an available CI, researchers are forced to cull questions from various sources and independently verify the effectiveness of the test that they construct [24].

Two early steps in the CI development process are the identification of student difficulties and the creation of an open-ended test [23]. Future work involves the creation of a test containing questions in multiple-choice format; validating these questions through additional rounds of interviews; and administering the questions to several large classes for the purposes of statistical analysis.

6 CONCLUSION

In this work, we explore student difficulties about Basic Data Structures, adding to the limited but growing work in this area. In particular, our work explores similar difficulties to those of Karpierz and Wolfman [6], Danielsiek et al [2], and Paul and Vahrenhold [13]. We offer a look at related, and in some cases the same, material, but with a different student population, and discover both similar and different student difficulties.

We hope that these difficulties provide instructors new insight into problems students may have when learning data structures. However, we caution against assuming that these are the only difficulties that students may have. Student difficulties may vary based on student population and the way course content is covered, both in Basic Data Structures and in courses they have previously

taken, as the contrast between some of our results and the results of previous work with different student populations shows [2, 6, 13]. Our future work includes extending our measurement of these difficulties to a much broader student population across a variety of institutions and instructors.

This work represents a first step towards quantifying student difficulties about Basic Data Structures. Some instructors may feel that some of these difficulties are obvious (or perhaps outlandish, depending on what they have observed of their own students) and dispute the need for formal work in this area. However, rigorous steps towards eliciting and measuring student difficulties allow instructors to focus their limited time and resources to where students are most likely to struggle. It is known that instructors often fail to anticipate student difficulties or understand the misconceptions that lead students to generate incorrect and "confusing" interpretations of concepts [3]. We urge further exploration of Basic Data Structures difficulties so as to facilitate more productive discussion and learning of this critical material among our students.

ACKNOWLEDGMENTS

The authors gratefully acknowledge the contributions of the following collaborators: Meghan Allen, Owen Astrachan, Darci Burdge, Stephanie Chasteen, Maureen Doyle, John Glick, Paul Hilfinger, Kate Sanders, Paramsothy Thananjeyan, and Steve Wolfman. This work was supported in part by NSF award 1505001.

REFERENCES

[1] J. Confrey. Chapter 1: A review of the research on student conceptions in mathematics, science, and programming. *Review of research in education*, 16(1):3–56, 1990.
[2] H. Danielsiek, W. Paul, and J. Vahrenhold. Detecting and understanding students' misconceptions related to algorithms and data structures. In *Proceedings of the 43rd ACM Technical Symposium on Computer Science Education*, pages 21–26, 2012.

[3] M. Guzdial. Learner-centered design of computing education: Research on computing for everyone. *Synthesis Lectures on Human-Centered Informatics*, 8(6):1–165, 2015.

[4] S. Hamouda, S. H. Edwards, H. G. Elmongui, J. V. Ernst, and C. A. Shaffer. A basic recursion concept inventory. *Computer Science Education*, 27(2):121–148, 2017.

[5] L. C. Kaczmarczyk, E. R. Petrick, J. P. East, and G. L. Herman. Identifying student misconceptions of programming. In *Proceedings of the 41st ACM Technical Symposium on Computer Science Education*, pages 107–111, 2010.

[6] K. Karpierz and S. A. Wolfman. Misconceptions and concept inventory questions for binary search trees and hash tables. In *Proceedings of the 45th ACM Technical Symposium on Computer Science Education*, pages 109–114, 2014.

[7] L. Ma, J. Ferguson, M. Roper, and M. Wood. Investigating and improving the models of programming concepts held by novice programmers. *Computer Science Education*, 21(1):57–80, 2011.

[8] S. Madison and J. Gifford. Modular programming. *Journal of Research on Technology in Education*, 34(3):217–229, 2002.

[9] R. McCauley, S. Grissom, S. Fitzgerald, and L. Murphy. Teaching and learning recursive programming: a review of the research literature. *Computer Science Education*, 25(1):37–66, 2015.

[10] R. McCauley, B. Hanks, S. Fitzgerald, and L. Murphy. Recursion vs. iteration: An empirical study of comprehension revisited. In *Proceedings of the 46th ACM Technical Symposium on Computer Science Education*, pages 350–355, 2015.

[11] L. Murphy, S. Fitzgerald, S. Grissom, and R. McCauley. Bug infestation!: A goal-plan analysis of CS2 students' recursive binary tree solutions. In *Proceedings of the 46th ACM Technical Symposium on Computer Science Education*, pages 482–487, 2015.

[12] M. C. Parker, M. Guzdial, and S. Engleman. Replication, validation, and use of a language independent CS1 knowledge assessment. In *Proceedings of the 2016 ACM conference on International Computing Education Research*, 2016.

[13] W. Paul and J. Vahrenhold. Hunting high and low: Instruments to detect misconceptions related to algorithms and data structures. In *Proceedings of the 44th ACM Technical Symposium on Computer Science Education*, pages 29–34, 2013.

[14] L. Porter, D. Zingaro, C. Lee, C. Taylor, K. C. Webb, and M. Clancy. Developing course-level learning goals for basic data structures in CS2. In *Proceedings of the 49th ACM technical symposium on Computer Science Education*, pages 858–863, 2018.

[15] Y. Qian and J. Lehman. Students' misconceptions and other difficulties in introductory programming: A literature review. *Transactions on Computing Education*, 18(1):1:1–1:24, 2017.

[16] N. Ragonis and M. Ben-Ari. A long-term investigation of the comprehension of OOP concepts by novices. *Computer Science Education*, 15(3):203–221, 2005.

[17] A. Robins, J. Rountree, and N. Rountree. Learning and teaching programming: A review and discussion. *Computer Science Education*, 13(2):137–172, 2003.

[18] P. M. Sadler, G. Sonnert, H. P. Coyle, N. Cook-Smith, and J. L. Miller. The influence of teachers' knowledge on student learning in middle school physical science classrooms. *American Educational Research Journal*, 50(5):1020–1049, 2013.

[19] O. Seppälä, L. Malmi, and A. Korhonen. Observations on student misconceptions—a case study of the Build-Heap Algorithm. *Computer Science Education*, 16(3):241–255, 2006.

[20] L. S. Shulman. Those who understand: Knowledge growth in teaching. *Educational researcher*, 15(2):4–14, 1986.

[21] J. Sorva. The same but different: Students' understandings of primitive and object variables. In *Proceedings of the 8th Koli Calling International Conference on Computing Education Research*, pages 5–15, 2008.

[22] J. Sorva. Notional machines and introductory programming education. *Transactions on Computing Education*, 13(2), 2013.

[23] C. Taylor, D. Zingaro, L. Porter, K. C. Webb, C. B. Lee, and M. Clancy. Computer science concept inventories: past and future. *Computer Science Education*, 24(4):253–276, 2014.

[24] J. Tenenberg and L. Murphy. Knowing what I know: An investigation of undergraduate knowledge and self-knowledge of data structures. *Computer Science Education*, 15(4):297–315, 2005.

[25] S. Zehra, A. Ramanathan, L. Zhang, and D. Zingaro. Student misconceptions of dynamic programming. In *Proceedings of the 49th ACM technical symposium on Computer Science Education*, pages 556–561, 2018.

Automated Plagiarism Detection for Computer Programming Exercises Based on Patterns of Resubmission

Narjes Tahaei
University of California, Merced
Electrical Engineering & Computer Science
ntahaei@ucmerced.edu

David C. Noelle
University of California, Merced
Electrical Engineering & Computer Science
dnoelle@ucmerced.edu

ABSTRACT

Plagiarism detection for computer programming exercises is a difficult problem. A traditional strategy has been to compare the submissions from all of the students in a class, searching for similarities between submissions suggestive of copying. Automated tools exist that compare submissions in order to help with this search. Increasingly, however, instructors have allowed students to submit multiple solutions, receiving formative feedback between submissions, with feedback often generated by automated assessment systems. Allowing multiple submissions allows for a fundamentally new way to detect plagiarism. Specifically, students may struggle with an exercise until frustration leads them to submit work that is not their own. We present a method for detecting plagiarism from the sequence of submissions made by an individual student. We have explored a variety of measures of program change over submissions, and we have found a set of features that can be transformed, using logistic regression, into a score capturing the likelihood of plagiarism. We have applied this method to data from four exercises from an undergraduate programming class. We show that our automatically generated scores are strongly correlated with the assessments of plagiarism made by an expert instructor. Thus, the scores can act as a powerful tool for searching for cases of academic dishonesty.

CCS CONCEPTS

• **Social and professional topics** → **Computer science education**; • **Applied computing** → **Computer-assisted instruction**;

KEYWORDS

Computer Programming Instruction; Plagiarism Detection; Automated Assessment System; Submission Pattern

ACM Reference Format:
Narjes Tahaei and David C. Noelle. 2018. Automated Plagiarism Detection for Computer Programming Exercises Based on Patterns of Resubmission. In *ICER '18: 2018 International Computing Education Research Conference, August 13–15, 2018, Espoo, Finland*. ACM, New York, NY, USA, 9 pages. https://doi.org/10.1145/3230977.3231006

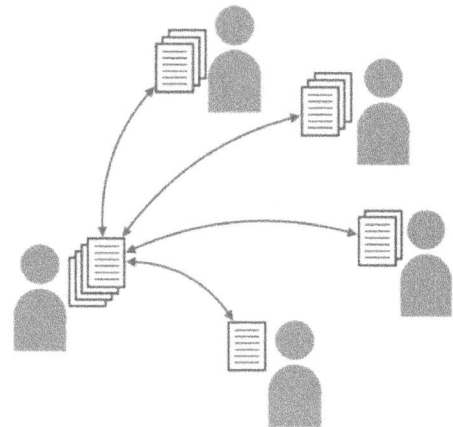

Figure 1: A depiction of the traditional approach to plagiarism detection, comparing a student's submission to the programs submitted by others.

1 INTRODUCTION

Educational experiences intended to instill computer programming skills regularly require students to complete programming exercises. These typically involve presenting students with a functional specification, and sometimes further supporting information, and the students are expected to generate the source code for a program that performs as directed. The frequent use of programming exercises likely reflects a sense that mastering computer programming requires extensive hands-on practice. Unfortunately, students often avoid such practice and opt, instead, to submit plagiarized solutions as their own. Plagiarism on computer programming exercises not only hinders the equitable evaluation of student knowledge and skill development, but also results in a kind of failure to deliver educational experiences that are important for student learning. For these reasons, instructors regularly pursue methods to discourage plagiarism, including reducing the motivation to plagiarize by penalizing students who submit exercise solutions that are found to be plagiarized.

Plagiarism in the context of computer programming exercises is a serious and growing problem. There is data to suggest that a full 30% of plagiarism cases in undergraduate academic settings involve computer program source code [12]. Studies indicate that the rate of plagiarism among students has increased within last two decades due to reduced access to teachers and easier access to information on the Internet [3, 4]. Large class sizes and limited instructional resources may introduce too large of a labor burden to

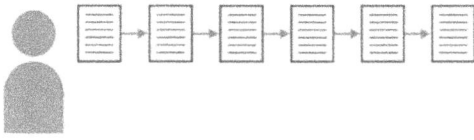

Figure 2: A depiction of the proposed approach to plagiarism detection, comparing consecutive submissions by each individual student and checking for patterns of resubmission indicative of plagiarism.

reliably detect cases of plagiarism, and regular failures of detection may contribute to student decisions to plagiarize. The tendency to plagiarize examinations and assignments in online learning environments is even greater than in traditional class settings [3]. As the number of students and the number of exercises increases, the tedious task of manually identifying plagiarized program submissions becomes increasingly prohibitive in terms of labor cost. Thus, there is a great demand for methods to assist instructors in the detection of plagiarism in programming exercises.

Automating the detection of plagiarism is difficult, however [4]. Unlike natural languages, computer progamming languages make use of a highly rigid syntax, are often insensitive to whitespace, allow for variation in instruction sequencing, and treat identifier names as arbitrary [6]. These properties make it possible for functionally identical programs to exhibit very different surface features and appearances. Thus, while the plagiarism of passages in natural language might be automated, with some success, by detecting patterns of identical word sequences, such superficial comparisons are often not adequate to detect plagiarized programs.

Despite the difficulty of the problem, considerable research has been done on methods to automatically detect plagiarized code. In general, all such methods can be categorized into *attribute-counting* or *structure-based* approaches [9]. Attribute-counting methods measure the similarity between a submitted program and a potentially plagiarized source program by comparing numerical program features that generally vary across independent solutions. For example, these methods might count the number of unique or distinct operators/operands or the total usage of all operators/operands in each program. Structure-based methods consider the overall structures of the programs in order to assess similarity. In general, the structured-based approach has been shown to be more effective than the counting of attributes [9].

It is worthy of note that all of these approaches depend on measuring the similarity between a student's submission and a potentially plagiarized source. There are automated systems that score pairs of programs in a set, identifying suspicious cases of similarity. It is common to compare all pairs of submissions from the students in a given course, working under the assumption that, in cases of academic dishonesty, students will copy solutions from other students. As online resources increase, this assumption becomes more difficult to justify. It is becoming increasingly difficult to assemble a good collection of candidate sources of plagiarism in order to make use of similarity-based approaches.

This paper presents and evaluates a novel approach to computer program plagiarism detection that does not depend on measuring the similarity between one student's solution and a set of potential sources. Our approach is inspired by the use of automated assessment systems to provide formative feedback to students as they work on an exercise, allowing each student to repeatedly submit solutions, hopefully improving each successive submission guided by the provided feedback. In the simplest case, the automated assessment system executes a student submission on a set of test cases and provides the student with feedback based on their program's performance on those test cases. The student is then given an opportunity to use the provided feedback to modify their submission, and this process of repeated submission can continue until all test cases are passed. Of course, simple "correct/incorrect" feedback has drawbacks [15]. More sophisticated automated assessment systems provide more pedagogically rich formative feedback, but these systems also allow students to generate a sequence of submissions with the hope that each consecutive submission is an improvement on the last, eventually leading to a correct solution [16]. Our approach to plagiarism detection focuses on an automated analysis of each individual student's sequence of submissions when using such a system, avoiding the need to compare a student's solution to potentially plagiarized sources.

Anecdotally, students sometimes begin addressing a programming exercise with earnest effort, but they later become frustrated by the difficulty of the exercise or anxious about a rapidly approaching deadline. At that point, they may decide to plagiarize another source, submitting a program that may differ substantially from their early submissions. With this intuition in mind, our approach involves comparing consecutive submissions for a given exercise from an individual student, collecting a sequence of pairwise similarities across the sequence of program submissions. We hypothesize that there are features of the submission sequence that are indicative of plagiarism, and these can be used to automatically estimate the probability of plagiarism for a given student.

The fundamental difference between our approach and more traditional approaches is illustrated in Figure 1 and Figure 2. As depicted in Figure 1, plagiarism detection typically involves comparing a student's submission to the submissions of others. In our approach, characterized by Figure 2, plagiarism is assessed based only on the sequence of submissions made by the student of interest for a given exercise. Thus, our approach does not require any knowledge of potential sources of plagiarized code.

In the remainder of this paper, we suggest a data driven method for determining the relationship between features of a student's submission sequence and the probability of plagiarism. We then evaluate that method against data collected from actual students enrolled in an undergraduate computer programming class at a research university. While the scores assigned to students by our automated approach do not perfectly separate plagiarized submissions from original submissions, we demonstrate a surprisingly strong correlation between these scores and actual cases of plagiarism. Thus, our method shows much promise as a guide to instructors, highlighting the submissions that are most likely to be cases of plagiarism, allowing the instructor to focus investigative efforts only on these most likely cases.

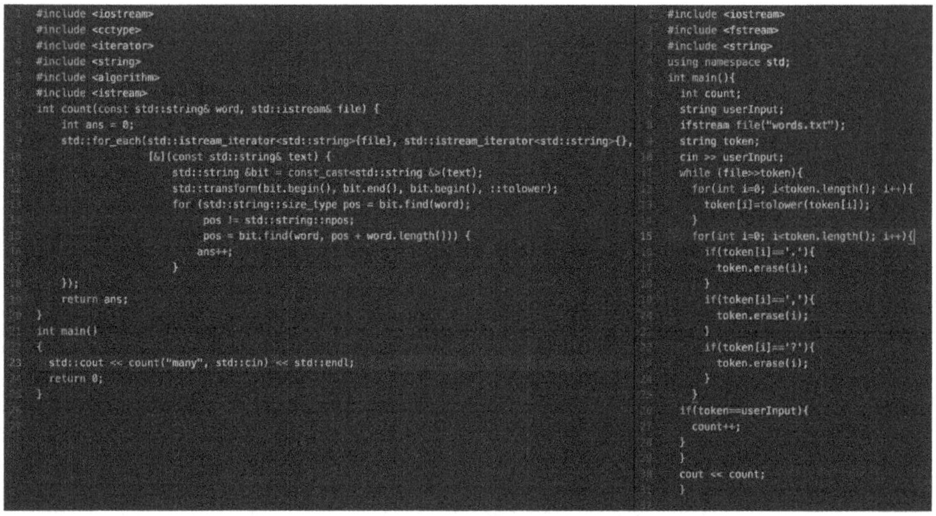

Figure 3: Example of Two Consecutive Submissions

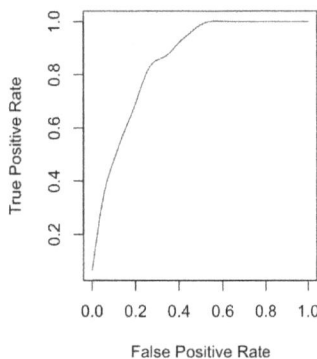

Figure 4: ROC Curve Relating True Positive Rate (TPR) to False Positive Rate (FPR) Using Number of Submissions and Maximum Difference as Predictors

2 RELATED WORK

In this section, we review some of the previously published efforts to automate plagiarism detection for computer programming exercises. We focus on approaches that have either informed our work or substantially contrast with it.

MOSS [2] is a widespread tool for automatic plagiarism detection for computer programming assignments. MOSS largely makes use of a structure-based approach, measuring the similarity between programs based on the functional structure of the code [2]. The system is also capable of highlighting code fragments that are particularly similar between two programs. Typically, MOSS is used to compare the final exercise submissions for every pair of students in a set, producing scores of pairwise similarity. This system is particularly useful when plagiarism involves several students sharing a common solution, perhaps making only superficial changes between student submissions.

Early plagiarism detection tools for computer programs used attribute counting methods [9]. Ottenstein applied basic software science measures in the context of detecting plagiarism in Fortran modules [18]. The programs were categorized into different levels of plagiarism based on their styles, with style captured by counting features like the number of unique operators, the number of unique operands, the total number of occurrences of operators, and the total number of occurrences of operands.

Arabyarmohamady and colleagues have also proposed a method for characterizing a student's style of programming [4]. Style information is collected by attribute counting and is stored in a "profile" for each student. Comparing styles can be used for plagiarism detection. The output of this approach is much like that provided by MOSS, providing pairwise similarities between programs.

Brixtel and colleagues introduced a plagiarism detection approach based on clone detection techniques [8]. This approach is not constrained by the properties of the programming language being used.

AC is an open source plagiarism detection software system [13]. It uses three different metrics to compare pairs of programs: compression similarity distance, token counting similarity distance, and variance similarity distance. These metrics are aggregated to rate the similarity between two programs. AC also includes visualization tools that make it useful not only for plagiarism detection but also for inspecting individual student submissions.

Methods for automatically rating the similarity of natural language documents have also been explored in the context of program source code. For example, a token co-occurrence statistical approach using Latent Semantic Analysis (LSA) [10] has been used to identify reusable code fragments across source code files using multiple programming languages [11]. While the aim of this work was to find reusable code, the similarity ratings that are produced are appropriate for detecting computer program plagiarism. A similar tool, SoCo-C3G, has been used to find similar code fragments in large code bases. It has been applied to Google Code Jam and programs on Coursera [12].

Once again, note that all of these methods focus on rating similarity between two programs in order to detect plagiarism. The approach proposed here does not have that requirement.

3 METHOD

3.1 Submission Sequence Features

Our central conjecture is that the submission sequence for an individual student on an individual exercise contains information that is relevant for determining if that student plagiarized that exercise by the time of the final submission in the sequence. In order to demonstrate this, we need to identify relevant features of submission sequences, select a subset of them that are useful, and produce a function that maps from the values of these useful features to an estimate of the probability of plagiarism. Thus, the first step involves exploring potential features of submission sequences.

The literature on student behavior when writing computer programs provides some clues to potentially relevant features. There are studies in which student learning is assessed by monitoring various aspects of their behavior. Patterns in student programming behavior have been identified. For example, it has been proposed that programming patterns can be used to classify students as either *tinkerers* or *planners* [7]. Students who are planners change their code, over time, in a systematic fashion, in order to solve the given problem. In contrast, students who are tinkerers prefer a non-goal-oriented style, more broadly exploring the space of possible programs until a solution is found. Tinkerers do not necessarily end up understanding all of the aspects of their solution program or how those aspects lead to correct performance [5]. Blikstein and colleagues have provided some evidence that, if the state of a student's program is recorded at regular intervals as it is being written, the frequency and size of changes are indicative of this difference in programming style. Specifically, small and frequent code changes were associated with tinkering, whereas larger and less frequent code changes were associated with planning [7].

With this research in mind, we imagined that many students who become frustrated while trying to complete an exercise and finally opt to plagiarize might start by making small and frequent changes from one submission to the next, suggesting a potential lack of understanding, and then make a large change by discarding their code and replacing it with code from some other source. Thus, we saw some measure of program change, from one submission to the next, as potentially important. We also considered the possibility that a large number of submissions in a submission sequence might indicate problems of understanding, with the student using the automated assessment system to evaluate small and uninformed program modifications.

While the number of submissions in a submission sequence is readily available, some metric is needed to measure program change from one submission to the next.

3.2 Submission Difference

For our initial explorations, we sought a measure of program change that was simple, unambiguous, and fairly easy to understand. Inspired by the UNIX diff utility, we focused on comparing two consecutive program submissions as plain text files, identifying

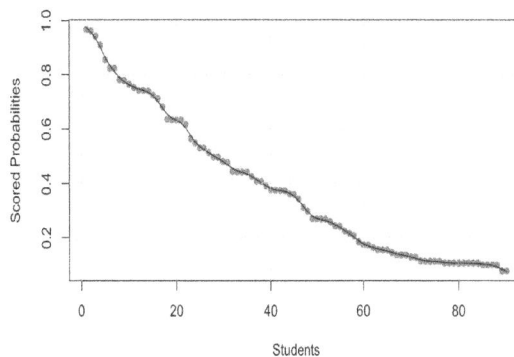

Figure 5: Probability Scores for All Test Students

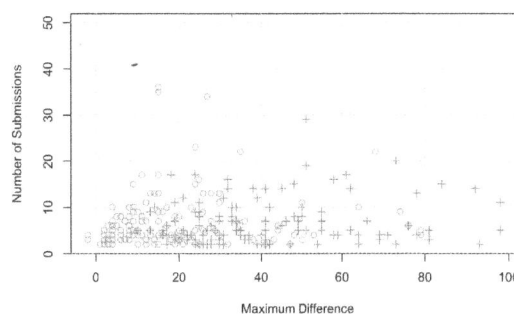

Figure 6: Scatterplot Over the Two Dimensional Feature Space Composed of Maximum Difference and Number of Submissions (Plagiarism Cases as Red Crosses)

common subsequences of text lines in the files and measuring program change in terms of the minimum number of lines that need to be added and deleted in order to transform one program file into the other. This measure is similar to the Levenshtein distance [17]. Historically, the UNIX diff utility was mostly used to identify changes between two versions of the same file. Since the files in a submission sequence can be seen as different versions of the same program, this simple measure seemed natural. The calculation of this *submission difference* was performed as described below.

Given two program files to compare, each file was first preprocessed to focus on contentful text lines. All program comments were removed from the files.[1] Also, blank lines were removed. After this preprocessing, the minimum number of line additions and deletions needed to transform one file into the other was computed using a common diff algorithm [14]. This was taken as the *submission difference* between two consecutive submissions.

---

[1] We recognize that inline comments might be useful for detecting plagiarism, but we opted to focus on functional aspects of the programs. Anecdotally, we have often seen students modify comments in order to disguise plagiarism.

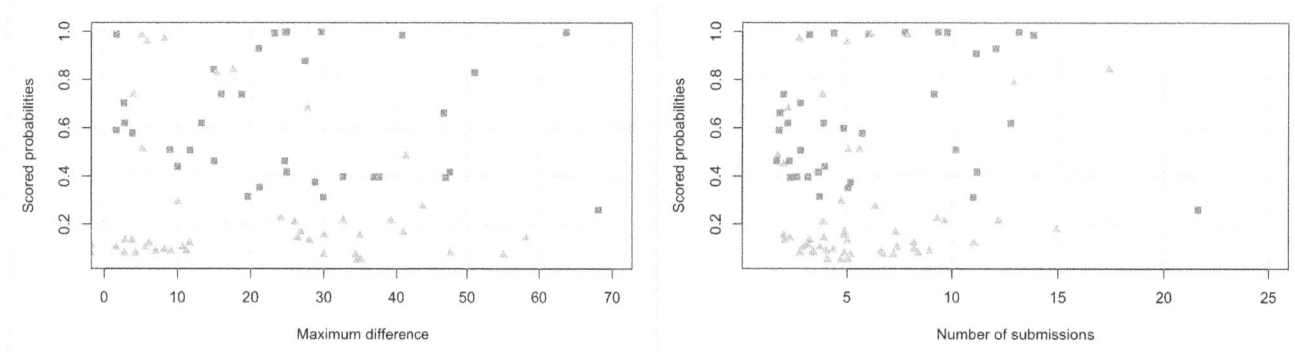

Figure 7: Scatterplots of Probability Score as a Function of Maximum Difference (Left) and of Number of Submissions(Right).

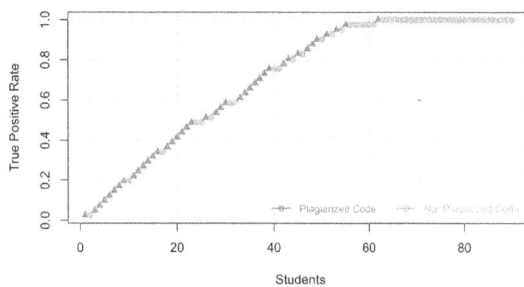

Figure 8: True Positive Rate Over Sorted Test Students

3.3 Difference Vector

For a submission sequence containing n submissions, a vector of dimensionality $n - 1$ can be assembled from the submission differences of each pair of consecutive submissions, starting with the difference between the first and second submissions. Along with the number of submissions in the submission sequence, we took this *diff-vector* as a characterization of the given submission sequence.

3.4 Considered Features

We considered using a variety of descriptive statistics of a submission sequence. Specifically, we examined:

- *Number of Submissions*: The number of program files that were submitted for the exercise.
- *Average Difference*: The average of all elements of the *diff-vector*.
- *Maximum Difference*: The maximum value of the elements in *diff-vector* .
- *Minimum Difference*: The minimum value of the elements in *diff-vector*.
- *Last Difference*: The value of the last element in *diff-vector*.

We investigated using each of these features in isolation to detect plagiarism, and we also investigated every pair of features. We also tried using all five features, together. Given one or more of these features, a method was needed to transform their values into a probability of plagiarism. We opted to determine the nature of this transformation in a data-driven manner.

3.5 Plagiarism Probability

As described in Section 4, we collected submission sequences from undergraduate students enrolled in a computer programming course who worked on exercises for that course. An instructional expert familiar with the course curriculum examined all of the programs in the submission sequences and labeled all of the clear cases of plagiarism as such. Note that this human expert had access to all of the submissions and could compare submissions between students in order to identify the cases of plagiarism. While it is likely that this expert made some errors in this labeling process, we took the labels as "ground truth", separating the plagiarism cases from the honest cases. (We could think of no more reliable standard, given our data.) We divided the labeled submission sequences into a "training set" and a disjoint "testing set". The method used to construct these sets is discussed in Section 4.

For each examined subset of the five submission sequence features, we performed a logistic regression, identifying logistic sigmoid parameters that maximized plagiarism classification accuracy over the training set items. These parameters were then used to calculate a plagiarism probability score for each submission sequence:

$$score = \frac{1}{1 + e^{-(\vec{w} \cdot \vec{x} + \beta)}}$$

...where e is the base of the natural logarithm, the feature values of the submission sequence form $\vec{x}$, and the $\vec{w}$ and β parameters were selected to optimize accuracy on the training set items. This is a standard approach to automated classification, producing a score that can be interpreted as a probability [1].

In order to assess the utility of the various subsets of the five features, we calculated the probability of plagiarism scores for the submission sequences in the testing set of submission sequences. These probabilities were then compared to the ground truth labels of the testing set items, and the subset of the five submission sequence features that exhibited the greatest accuracy on the testing set items was discovered. This feature set was taken to be the most informative for detecting plagiarism, and the logistic sigmoid parameters for that feature set were used to produce plagiarism probability scores for any considered submission sequence.

In this way, we used labeled data to produce a mathematical transformation from *diff-vector* representations of submission sequences to plagiarism scores between zero and one.

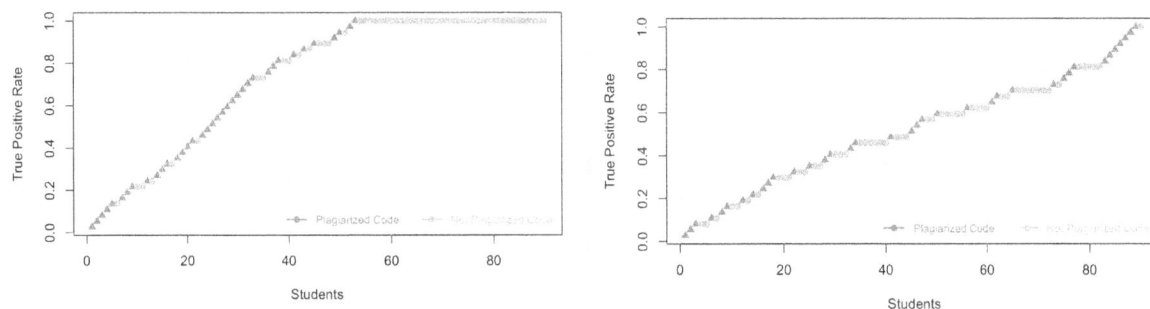

Figure 9: True Positive Rates for Single Feature Scores: Maximum Difference (Left) & Number of Submissions (Right)

3.6 Plagiarism Score Quality

Given our labeled data, the plagiarism probability scores could be evaluated in the same manner that many data-driven classifiers are assessed [1]. For a given threshold value, a submission sequence could be categorized as plagiarized if and only if its score was above the threshold. Given our ground truth labels, we could then measure the *true positive rate* (TPR), which is the fraction of truly plagiarized cases detected, and the *false positive rate* (FPR), which is the fraction of the honest cases incorrectly categorized as plagiarism cases. These values are inherently in opposition. A low threshold will tend to increase TPR but will also raise the undesireable FPR. A high threshold will reduce false positives but will also lower the hit rate. One common way to assess this trade-off is to plot TPR versus FPR for a variety of threshold values. This is called an ROC curve. An example ROC curve, using the combination of the *Maximum Difference* and *Number of Submissions* features on the data described in Section 4 is shown in Figure 4.

It is not clear, however, that this standard method for evaluating classifiers is the best method, here. In the case of plagiarism detection, there is an asymmetry between categorizing a submission sequence as plagiarized and categorizing one as honest. In many situations, an instructor would manually inspect cases automatically categorized as plagiarism before actually accusing a student of academic dishonesty. In this way, the instructor protects against false positives. In evaluating the automatically generated plagiarism probability scores, this fact should be taken into account.

We imagine the scores being used in a particular way. We imagine the instructor carefully examining some set of submissions with the highest plagiarism scores. We assume that the instructor, through this careful examination, will be able to identify the true plagiarism cases among those in the examined set. Given this use of the scores, the question of interest involves the fraction of all plagiarism cases detected for a given number of examined submissions. This is a plagiarism "hit rate" or "true positive rate" *for the set of submissions with the highest scores of a specified size.* If the instructor opts to examine a larger number of submissions, then more plagiarism cases will likely be discovered, but this will happen at the cost of additional labor. Thus, the best plagiarism scoring function is one that assigns higher scores to all of the true plagiarism cases than to any of the honest cases. For such a function, any

additional labor on the part of the instructor increases the detection of plagiarism cases, until all such cases are detected.

In order to visualize this assessment for a given set of submissions, we sort the submissions from highest scoring (most likely to be plagiarism cases) to the lowest scoring. For each submission, we plot the "true positive rate" if that submission is examined by the instructor along with all submissions having higher scores. In such a plot, a good plagiarism scoring function will have the "true positive rate" rise quickly as more submissions are examined, when they are examined in the order of decreasing score. Plots of this kind appear in the following section.

4 RESULTS

4.1 Data

In order to evaluate our approach, we applied it to a collection of computer programming exercise submissions collected from an actual undergraduate course at a research university. The course provided an introduction to object-oriented programming using C++, and it was offered in 2016. Students were expected to complete about eight C++ programming exercises every week. They were allowed to repeatedly submit solutions to an online automated assessment system, up until a final deadline. With each submission, the automated assessment system provided detailed formative feedback, and it would indicate if the student's submission passed all tests for correctness. There were 95 exercises completed by 73 students, producing a total of 14,345 submissions to the system. The number of submissions from each student varied between 0 and about 70. To assess our proposed method for plagiarism detection, we made use of the recorded submissions for four arbitrarily selected programming assignments, with each assignment potentially containing multiple exercises.

The exercises involved simple file processing and string manipulation tasks. For example, in one exercise, students were asked to write a program that opens a text file and counts the number of appearances of a specified word in the file. To illustrate this, two consecutive submissions for one student are shown in Figure 3. The large difference between these two consecutive submissions (36 lines) makes the case suspicious.

4.2 Aggregate Analysis

Our initial analysis makes use of the data from all four of the selected programming assignments. From these data, all submission sequences containing only a single submission were removed, as they contained no submission difference information. (This limitation of our approach is discussed in Section 5.) This left 297 submission sequences. A careful examination of these by an expert instructor identified a full 122 of them as cases of plagiarism. Of the sample of 297 submission sequences, approximately 70% (207) of them were randomly sampled (without replacement) to form a training set (88 plagiarized). The remainder (90) formed a testing set (34 plagiarized). Logistic regression using the training set was applied to various combinations of submission sequence features. The set of features that resulted in the greatest accuracy on the testing set was the combination of *Maximum Difference* and *Number of Submissions*. The distribution of submission sequences over this two dimensional feature space is shown in Figure 6. Note how the non-plagiarism cases are clustered around low values for both of the features, as well as how predictive *Maximum Difference* is. We examined the ability of these two features, transformed into a probability score using the fit logistic sigmoid, to detect plagiarism in the testing set submission sequences.

The 90 testing set students were sorted by score, in decreasing order. Figure 5 shows the distribution of assigned scores. This plot shows that the students with the lowest scores (on the right) all had similar low scores, while the scores for the higher scoring students descended almost linearly across the probability range. There is no abrupt change in scores, suggesting that the logistic regression process did not find a sharp distinction between the plagiarism and the honest cases. Plots of scores as a function of each of the two selected features are shown in Figure 7. Note that most cases with high *Maximum Difference* are plagiarism cases, and there is a dense cluster of non-plagiarism cases with low *Number of Submissions*.

As discussed in Section 3.6, the most important desired property of the probability score involves plagiarism cases having higher scores than non-plagiarism cases. Figure 8 shows that this property is present. If students are examined by score, from highest to lowest (left to right in Figure 8), very few honest cases are encountered until after most all plagiarism cases are seen. The "true positive rate" almost reaches 1.0 before most non-plagiarism cases are considered. Using our scoring method could allow for the discovery of about 82% of the actual plagiarism cases by examining the work of only 40% of the students. Recall that a full 38% of these test cases were plagiarism cases.

This analysis was repeated using only the *Maximum Difference* feature alone and only the *Number of Submissions* feature alone (Figure 9). Notice that *Maximum Difference* is a much better guide to detecting plagiarism than *Number of Submissions*. Also note that *Maximum Difference* performs almost as well as the two features combined. Simply sorting students in decreasing order of *Maximum Difference*, requiring no logistic regression parameter estimation, produces results almost as good as those shown in Figure 8.

The quality of the dual-feature probability scores can also be captured by plotting the "false positive rate" — the fraction of examined cases that are not plagiarized — for a growing subset of the

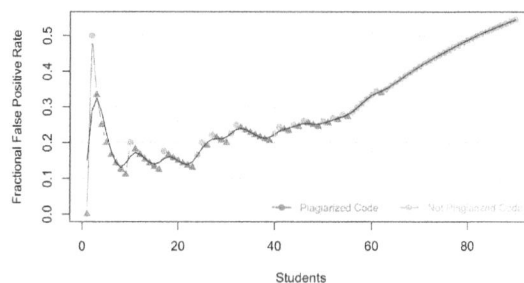

Figure 10: Fractional False Positive Rate Over Sorted Students

students, starting with the highest scoring students and adding students to the subset in descending order of score. This is shown in Figure 10. Note that the false positive rate stays well below 25% until most of the plagiarism cases are examined. In other words, if an instructor were to inspect cases in decreasing order of probability score, more than 3 out of 4 inspected cases would actually be plagiarized, up until the majority of the plagiarism cases were found.

These analyses show that submission sequences can provide very useful information for detecting plagiarism.

4.3 Individual Assignment Analysis

In the previous analysis, data from four assignments were mixed. It would be worthwhile to see if logistic regression parameters calculated for one set of assignments generalized to other assignments. In order to examine this, we subsampled 170 of the previous set of 297 submission sequences, discarding some of the data from one of the assignments which contained many more submission sequences than the others. For Assignment 1, there were 63 submission sequences, with 28 plagiarized. For Assignment 2, there were 48 submission sequences, with 17 plagiarized. For Assignment 3, there were 14 submission sequences, with 7 plagiarized. For Assignment 4, there were 34 submission sequences, with 5 plagiarized. We performed four separate logistic regressions, each using aggregated data from three of the assignments as a training set and using data from the fourth assignment as a testing set. In this way, we could investigate generalization across assignments.

The results of these four analyses are shown in Figure 11. Testing sets involving Assignment 1 and Assignment 2 are shown on the left, and testing sets involving Assignment 3 and Assignment 4 are shown on the right. These figures show that plagiarism cases generally receive higher probability scores than honest cases, even when those scores are generated using logistic regression parameters tuned by data from other assignments. This is evidence that our method generalizes across programming assignments.

4.4 Comparison to MOSS

Since MOSS is a popular tool for detecting plagiarism on computer programming exercises, we attempted to perform a direct comparison between our approach and MOSS. We subsampled 49 students from the Assignment 1 data, all of whom made at least two submissions. We also collected MOSS scores using the Assignment 1 final

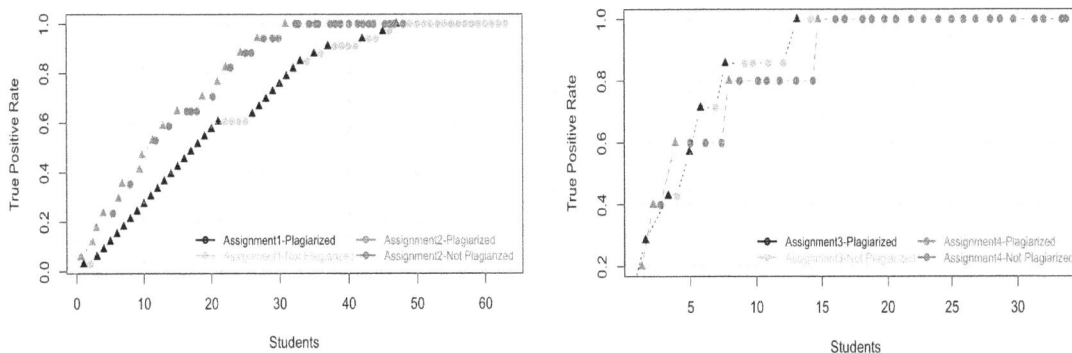

Figure 11: True Positive Rates Separately Plotted for Four Different Assignments. (Triangle Marks are Plagiarized, and Circle Marks are Not.)

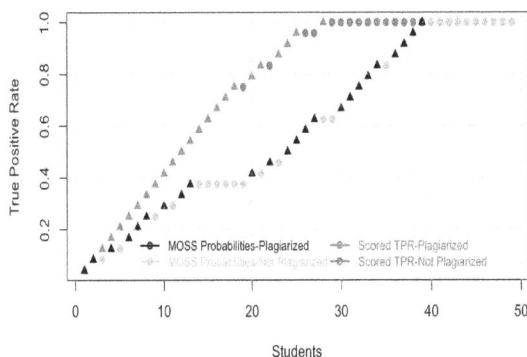

Figure 12: Comparing True Positive Rates: MOSS vs. Probability Scores. (Triangle Marks are Plagiarized, and Circle Marks are Not.)

submissions from all of the students. If we sort the 49 students in order of decreasing MOSS score and plot the "true positive rate", as done previously, much poorer performance is exhibited than if the 49 students are sorted in order of decreasing probability score (calculated from training set data from the other three assignments). This is shown in Figure 12. MOSS gives high scores to many more honest cases and low scores to many more plagiarism cases in comparison to our approach. These results suggest that resubmission patterns of an individual student may be more predictive of plagiarism than similarity measures of final program submissions across students in a class.

5 DISCUSSION

No known plagiarism detection mechanism for computer programming exercises is sufficiently robust to be completely trusted with academic dishonesty decisions. Some human investigation is always necessary to establish wrongdoing. Given the typically high labor demands placed on instructors, automated systems that provide reliable guidance toward likely plagiarism cases would be quite valuable. We have provided evidence that such guidance can be found in the resubmission patterns of individual students.

The traditional approach of using similarity metrics to compare the submissions of students in a class is becoming increasingly problematic. In introductory computer programming courses, exercise solutions may be so simple that independently generated solutions still exhibit high similarity, introducing risks of false alarms. Assuming that plagiarized sources are the submissions of other students is becoming less justified, as students increasingly find online support for plagiarism. Our approach offers an escape from these limitations by focusing on the resubmission patterns of individual students.

One major weakness of our method, however, is that it is inapplicable to students who make only a single submission for an exercise. In such a case, there is no resubmission history to analyze. Single submissions may arise from students who carefully test their programs before submitting them, and they may arise from students who opt to avoid ever attempting to complete an exercise on their own. There is no clear reason to interpret a single submission in one way or the other. Future work will need to address this weakness, perhaps by combining our method with other approaches.

Finally, it is reasonable to worry that students who discover the metrics being used to detect plagiarism may modify their behavior to escape detection based on those metrics. This is certainly a weakness of our proposed method, but it seems likely that this same weakness arises in most any automated system for plagiarism detection. If the detector is well understood, a clever malcontent might always find a way to circumvent its effectiveness. While plagiarism detection may always involve a kind of arms race, it is an important problem that cannot be ignored, and, as this paper shows, there are innovative methods that have yet to be thoroughly explored.

ACKNOWLEDGMENTS

The authors thank Dr. Angelo Kyrilov for providing the online automated assessment system data. Thanks are also given to the participating students.

REFERENCES

[1] Alan Agresti. 2013. *Categorical Data Analysis*. Wiley, New York.
[2] Alex Aiken. 2004. MOSS: A System for Detecting Software Plagiarism. *http://www. cs. berkeley. edu/~ aiken/moss. html* (2004).
[3] Gökhan Akçapınar. 2015. How Automated Feedback through Text Mining Changes Plagiaristic Behavior in Online Assignments. *Computers & Education* 87 (2015), 123–130.
[4] S. Arabyarmohamady, H. Moradi, and M. Asadpour. 2012. A Coding Style-Based Plagiarism Detection. In *Interactive Mobile and Computer Aided Learning (IMCL), 2012 International Conference on*. IEEE, 180–186.
[5] Matthew Berland, Taylor Martin, Tom Benton, Carmen Petrick Smith, and Don Davis. 2013. Using learning analytics to understand the learning pathways of novice programmers. *Journal of the Learning Sciences* 22, 4 (2013), 564–599.
[6] Bradley Beth. 2014. A Comparison of Similarity Techniques for Detecting Source Code Plagiarism. (2014).
[7] Paulo Blikstein, Marcelo Worsley, Chris Piech, Mehran Sahami, Steven Cooper, and Daphne Koller. 2014. Programming Pluralism: Using Learning Analytics to Detect Patterns in the Learning of Computer Programming. *Journal of the Learning Sciences* 23, 4 (2014), 561–599.
[8] Romain Brixtel, Mathieu Fontaine, Boris Lesner, Cyril Bazin, and Romain Robbes. 2010. Language-Independent Clone Detection Applied to Plagiarism Detection. In *Source Code Analysis and Manipulation (SCAM), 2010 10th IEEE Working Conference on*. IEEE, 77–86.
[9] Paul Clough. 2000. Plagiarism in Natural and Programming Languages: An Overview of Current Tools and Technologies. (2000).

[10] Scott Deerwester, Susan T. Dumais, George W. Furnas, Thomas K. Landauer, and Richard Harshman. 1990. Indexing by Latent Semantic Analysis. *Journal of the American Society for Information Science* 41, 6 (1990), 391–407.
[11] Enrique Flores, Alberto Barrón-Cedeño, Lidia Moreno, and Paolo Rosso. 2015. Cross-Language Source Code Re-Use Detection Using Latent Semantic Analysis. *J. UCS* 21, 13 (2015), 1708–1725.
[12] Enrique Flores, Alberto Barrón-Cedeño, Lidia Moreno, and Paolo Rosso. 2015. Uncovering Source Code Reuse in Large-Scale Academic Environments. *Computer Applications in Engineering Education* 23, 3 (2015), 383–390.
[13] Manuel Freire and M. Cebrian. 2008. Design of the AC Academic Plagiarism Detection System. *Technical report, Tech. rep., Escuela Politecnica Superior, Universidad Autonoma de Madrid* (2008).
[14] James W. Hunt and M. Douglas McIlroy. 1976. *An Algorithm for Differential File Comparison*. Technical Report 41. Bell Laboratories. Computing Science Technical Report.
[15] Angelo Kyrilov and David C. Noelle. 2015. Binary Instant Feedback on Programming Exercises can Reduce Student Engagement and Promote Cheating. In *Proceedings of the 15th Koli Calling Conference on Computing Education Research*. ACM, 122–126.
[16] Angelo Kyrilov and David C. Noelle. 2016. Do Students Need Detailed Feedback on Programming Exercises and Can Automated Assessment Systems Provide It? *Journal of Computing Sciences in Colleges* 31, 4 (2016).
[17] Vladimir I. Levenshtein. 1966. Binary Codes Capable of Correcting Deletions, Insertions, and Reversals. *Soviet Physics Doklady* 10, 8 (1966), 707–710.
[18] Karl J Ottenstein. 1976. An algorithmic approach to the detection and prevention of plagiarism. *ACM Sigcse Bulletin* 8, 4 (1976), 30–41.

Objects Count so Count Objects!

Ewan Tempero
The University of Auckland
Auckland, New Zealand
e.tempero@auckland.ac.nz

Paul Denny
The University of Auckland
Auckland, New Zealand
paul@cs.auckland.ac.nz

Andrew Luxton-Reilly
The University of Auckland
Auckland, New Zealand
a.luxton-reilly@auckland.ac.nz

Paul Ralph
The University of Auckland
Auckland, New Zealand
paul@paulralph.name

ABSTRACT

One means to determine whether a student understands the fundamentals of good object-oriented design is to assess designs the student has created. However, providing reliable assessment of designs efficiently is difficult due to the many viable designs that are possible and the high level of expertise required. Consequently, design assessment tends to be limited to identifying the most basic of design problems. We propose a technique—"object counts"—that involves counting the objects created at runtime. This is more efficient than manual grading because the data is gathered automatically and more reliable than using rubrics because it is based on objective data. The data is relevant because it captures the fundamental property of an object-oriented program—the creation of objects—and so provides good insight into the student's design decisions. This provides support for both summative and formative feedback. We demonstrate the technique on two corpora containing submissions for a typical first assignment of an introductory course on object-oriented design.

ACM Reference Format:
Ewan Tempero, Paul Denny, Andrew Luxton-Reilly, and Paul Ralph. 2018. Objects Count so Count Objects!. In *ICER '18: 2018 International Computing Education Research Conference, August 13–15, 2018, Espoo, Finland.* ACM, New York, NY, USA, 9 pages. https://doi.org/10.1145/3230977.3230985

1 INTRODUCTION

Assessing a student's object-oriented design is difficult. In part, this is because even small designs require a significant amount of time to understand. For example, Sanders and Thomas [17], in presenting guidelines for educators grading object-oriented programs, observe:

> "We realise that frequently when grading we are so rushed for time that we look at superficials: does it compile, does it fulfil the test cases, are there some comments?"

They found that working programs sometimes included subtle errors that suggest serious misconceptions and that it took a great deal of time ("spending hours reading and re-reading each program") to identify these errors.

Assessment is difficult because we have little in the way of objective criteria to use. Christensen [8] observes that many teachers provide feedback to students such as *"Your design is not really object-oriented"*, but judging a design as either object-oriented or not is: *"a complex interplay between exact science, experience and craftsmanship, and personal taste".* In this paper we present a means to improve our ability to provide reliable, efficient and consistent assessment of object-oriented designs. It is conceptually simple, yet surprisingly powerful. The technique is based on counting the objects created at runtime.

For example, consider an assignment for a simple payroll system that takes a file containing employee records and calculates income and taxes. We might expect a design to have an Employee class. If we ran the program on a file with 100 employee records we would expect to see 100 Employee objects. If we did see 100 objects, we would have some assurance as to what this class is for. If we saw a different number (e.g. one) it would raise questions as to what the Employee class is really representing. So knowing the object count can give some insight into a design. The question is whether this generalises. Our research goal is therefore: *to determine whether counting objects is useful for evaluating object-oriented designs in a software engineering education context.*

The rest of the paper is organised as follows. In the next section, we will present a more detailed motivating example of the problem we want to address. Section 3 then discusses background material and related work. In Section 4, we discuss the counting objects approach in more detail. We then present results from applying the technique to the submissions for two assignments requiring development of a small program (Section 6). We discuss the results in Section 7 and present our conclusions in Section 8.

2 MOTIVATION

Our aims are to improve the efficiency of assessing the quality of object-oriented designs of students' programs , and to improve the quality of both formative and summative ("marking") assessments.

As an example of the kind of assignment we are concerned with, consider the need for a program that will take two arguments from

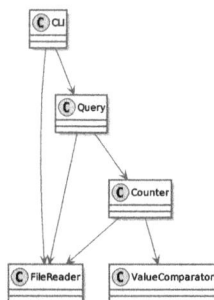

Figure 1: Simplified class diagram for design 1078 for the dependency analysis assignment. "C" means class and arrows indicate "uses" relationships.

the command line: a dataset and a query. The program has to apply the query to the dataset and output the results to standard output. The dataset consists of a set of records, one per row. Each record describes a "dependency" from a source "module" to a target "module". A dependency can have various properties, and different queries may apply only to dependencies that have those properties. An example of a query is to report, for each unique module, how many dependencies it is the source for (DepCount). Another example is, for each unique module, how many unique modules does it have a dependency with (FanOut). The specific details of the assignment are available on the project website [20].

This assignment is an example of the standard assignment set for the introductory course on object-oriented design at The University of Auckland for many years. It can be completely implemented in only a few hundred lines of Java code, however, part of the assessment criteria given to the students is that their solutions must demonstrate their understanding of object-oriented design.

The difficulty we have faced with assessing this assignment is exactly that raised by Christensen. We see designs that to us are "not object-oriented", but providing feedback is difficult. Students who do not understand the object-oriented paradigm can neither produce object-oriented designs nor understand our criticism of their designs. We want to be able to provide concrete and specific feedback. We also want to be able to gather the data necessary to provide the feedback in less time than it would take to manually review all of the code.

Consider Figure 1, which shows a simplified UML class diagram for a design for the above assignment. This design, D1078, has several classes that interact with each other and so might be considered acceptable. However, further analysis raises some questions. The Counter class is not an obvious abstraction for the problem being solved, and in fact it essentially has all of the functionality, being larger (444 lines) than the other classes combined (273 lines in total). Further, the Query class, which does seem like a reasonable abstraction based on its name, does not in fact represent a query, but rather determines what query is required and invokes the appropriate method from the Counter class. These observations can be determined fairly easily from brief inspections of the source code.

What is not so easy is assessing designs such as D1022 (Figure 2) and D1053 (Figure 3). These designs and D1078 have the same functionality (determined using automated tests). These designs look better than D1078. There are more classes, and the class names correspond to reasonable abstractions for the problem being solved. They both use inheritance, with D1053 having an interface and D1022 having an interface and classes extending one another. The designs are obviously different from each other, but it is not clear how these differences might translate into different marks—it is not even obvious how to rank the two. It would seem reasonable to give both of these designs full marks.

However, assessing a submission based on just a (very much simplified) UML class diagram is problematic. Often a diagram is not available or lacks important details. There is a concern that the diagram may contain errors, or have a misleading presentation. We need to identify the main design decisions that have been made in each case. Traditionally, this is done by examining the source code and piecing together the overall design. As noted in the introduction, Sanders and Thomas observed that this requires significant time and experience.

The subjective nature of design quality means we cannot expect a fully-automatic procedure; nevertheless, having objective data that helps us more efficiently and effectively identify the main design decisions would be of great value. The question is, what data should we use? This paper explores whether object counts are useful.

3 BACKGROUND AND RELATED WORK

3.1 Object-oriented design

To assess object-oriented designs we must be clear as to what criteria we are assessing against. There have been many discussions as to what "object-oriented" means, but they generally discuss what this means in terms of *programming language features* not *designs*. For example, Kay, who arguably has the best claim to having invented the term, states "I invented the term object-oriented, and I can tell you that C++ wasn't what I had in mind" [13], clearly referring to the design of the language. Stroustrup's discussion also applies to the language [19].

However, most commentators on object-oriented programming (including Kay and Stroustrup) are aware of the distinction between the language used to express the design of a program and the behaviour of the program as it executes. This view is commonly presented in textbooks. For example, Budd [5] comments "Working in an object-oriented language [...] is neither a necessary or sufficient condition for doing object-oriented programming. [...] the most important aspect of OOP is the creation of a universe of largely autonomous interacting agents." That is, the result of executing an object-oriented program is the *creation of objects that send messages to each other*.

3.2 Teaching Object-Oriented Design

How we assess design depends on what we teach about design. There is surprisingly little in textbooks for object-oriented programming on how to develop an object-oriented design, perhaps an indication of the difficulty of knowing what to teach. Cross reviewed studies of design cognition from an interdisciplinary and domain-independent view, and observed "Designers appear to be 'ill-behaved' problem solvers, in that they do not spend much time

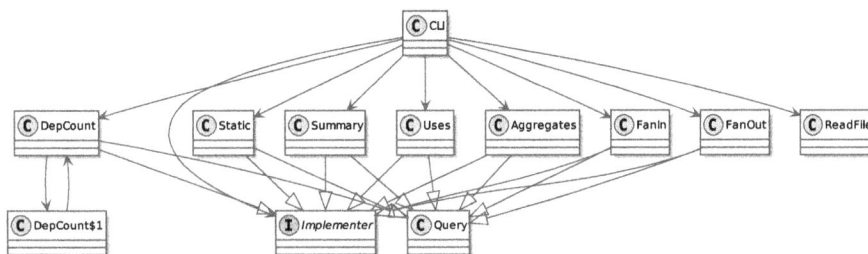

Figure 2: Simplified class diagram for design1022 from the CA corpus. "C" means class, "I" interface, open arrow heads indicate inheritance, and other arrows indicate "uses" relationships.

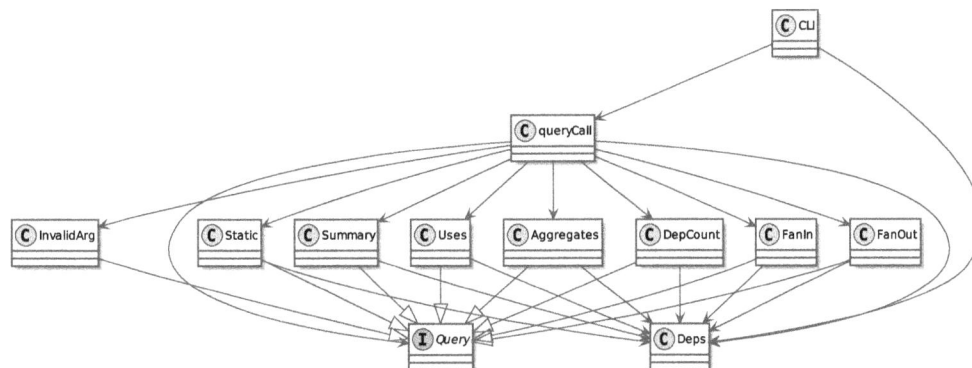

Figure 3: Simplified class diagram for design1053 from CA corpus. "C" means class, "I" means interface, open arrow heads indicate inheritance, and other arrows indicate "uses" relationships.

and attention on defining the problem." [9] He concluded "In design education we must therefore be very wary about importing models of behavior from other fields." Model curricula provide little help. Ralph examined model curricula from both the Association for Computing Machinery and the Association for Information Systems and concluded "[both model curricula] insufficiently cover how to generate design candidates." [16]

Textbooks mostly focus on what the different language features are and how to use them to create classes, but say little on how to decide which classes to create (e.g. [10, 23]). Of those that do discuss design, the most common technique presented seems to be the "noun/verb" method. For example, Barnes and Kölling [2, p.394] say "Classes in a system roughly correspond to **nouns** in the system's description. Methods correspond to **verbs**" (emphasis theirs).

Budd [5] advocates responsibility-driven design [22]. This approach first identifies the responsibilities, grouping them into roles, and then identifying the objects that should play those roles.

Beck and Cunningham introduced the Class-Responsibility-Collaborator (CRC) card technique for teaching object-oriented design [3]. Both Budd, and Barnes and Kölling, use this technique.

Christensen [8] identified three perspectives used in textbooks to define what an "object" is: the language perspective, which emphasises how the language constructs are used to describe objects; the model centric perspective, where objects are part of the wider context (the model); and the responsibility centric perspective, focusing on roles and responsibilities. He demonstrated how different perspectives lead to different designs, indicating how choice of

perspective in teaching impacts the kinds of designs students will produce.

3.3 Assessing Object-Oriented Design

Although several studies have investigated assessment of program quality (e.g. [18]), they have typically focused on code syntax and structure, such as Documentation, Presentation, Algorithms (comprising Flow and Expressions) and Structure (comprised of decomposition and modularization), rather than the design of an object-oriented program.

Armstrong reviews research that characterises the fundamental ideas of object-oriented programming, and categorises object-oriented concepts into Structural elements (Abstraction, Class, Encapsulation, Inheritance, Objects) and Behavioural elements (Message Passing, Methods, Polymorphism) [1]. Sanders and Thomas developed a checklist for designing and grading object-oriented programs based on Armstrong's list of object-oriented concepts. Their checklist for "indications that a student understands basic OO concepts" has 23 items. One item is "Multiple instances of same class," however they do not suggest counting the number of instances created.

Studies of student understanding of object-oriented concepts found several misconceptions: they do not have a clear understanding of the difference between classes and instances [11, 12]; they have difficulty modelling the real world as objects, sometimes produce solutions that look like a procedural programming design rather than an object-oriented design, and separate the data from the code that acts on that data [15]. In other words, they are not modelling the objects as entities that have both data and behaviour.

In an evaluation of the object-oriented examples used in textbooks, Borstler et al. [4] identify five object-oriented qualities that are intended to capture accepted guidelines of object-oriented design. They found that the textbook examples typically had reasonable abstractions that plausibly modelled the problem domain, but few examples explicitly supported the idea that object-oriented programs were a collection of collaborating objects.

Turner et al. [21] asked students to engage in code review of object-oriented programs (in Java) developed by their peers. They provided a rubric focusing on six dimensions (Style, Functionality, Decomposition, Encapsulation, Abstraction, and Testing Completeness) to the students. The study identified several misconceptions relating to the nature of object-oriented design which were grouped into categories of Decomposition, Encapsulation and Abstraction. Problems falling into both Decomposition and Abstraction relate to the design of the classes and how they were used to model the problem domain.

The difficulty with checklists or rubrics is that they typically have a number of items that need to be checked, which can be time-consuming to apply. Often items are subjective, cannot be treated in isolation, and assessing their interaction can require considerable expertise.

3.4 Software Metrics

When seeking an objective means on which to base assessment, it would seem reasonable to consider software metrics. There is little available describing experience with the use of such metrics, and even less on using them to assess design. For example, Cardell-Oliver described use of metrics for summative and formative assessment, and also as a diagnostic tool to identify students' learning styles [6]. However, she did not address assessment of design.

Many software metrics have been proposed, including the so-called "CK metric suite" proposed by Chidamber and Kemerer [7], and many more based on the CK metrics. The difficulty with using such metrics is that they are only applied to a single class. For example, the CBO metric from the CK metric suite is intended to measure coupling for a class. To use this to assess a design requires gathering measurements for each class in the design and then interpreting those individual measurements. The interpretation seems as difficult as understanding the design by reading the code. The CK metric suite has six metrics. A design with 10 classes would thus yield 60 measurements to be interpreted, making interpretation even more difficult.

Another issue is that measurements from most metrics are meant to be interpreted as "larger means lower quality." Typically thresholds are provided with the interpretation that measurements that exceed the thresholds indicate a poor design. However, most student assignments are quite small. Since the measurements often depend on program size, the corresponding measurements are often very low and so do not exceed the thresholds.

4 ASSESSING OBJECT-ORIENTED DESIGNS

4.1 Counting Objects

Our goal is to improve our ability to provide good quality summative and formative assessment. This requires efficiently identifying the important design decisions. One means for improving efficiency is to have a procedure for automatically gathering relevant data about a design. As noted in Section 3, existing software metrics apply only to individual classes and the measurements require careful interpretation by experienced software designers. We need data that reflects the whole design, has a clear interpretation, and indicates the decisions that it encompasses.

We start from first principles. As noted previously, any object-oriented design should result in an executing system consisting of objects sending messages to each other. It follows that the objects that get created must reflect important design decisions that have been made. The basis of our assessment procedure can be simply stated as:

> **Count the number of objects created for each class during execution.**

This data, which we will colloquially refer to as "object counts", captures an important class of design decisions. The objects, and their interaction, must provide the prescribed functionality. The choice of objects must indicate how the designer has chosen to distribute the functionality in the design, in particular the roles the objects are meant to play in providing the functionality.

To count objects, the program must be executed and so inputs must be supplied. Like testing, the inputs used should provide reasonable coverage of the program. Unlike testing, we do not need to cover all possibilities; we are only concerned with inputs that cover all the cases where objects are created. Our experience is that a small number of inputs is sufficient for the kinds of assignments we address. The object counts are recorded for each input.

The object counts for the design are then compared with what might be reasonably expected in the problem domain. What might be reasonably expected is domain dependent, and so this requires that the instructor have a good understanding of it. Even within a given domain, there may be more than one interpretation of a reasonable number of objects. The instructor must interpret the object count with respect to such possibilities. This interpretation then forms the basis for developing the final summative or formative feedback. We illustrate the proposed approach below and provide more detail in Section 6.

Our assessment procedure has the following benefits:

- The data can be acquired automatically and quickly.
- The data indicates an important class of design decisions, decisions we argue are central to what it means to be "object-oriented."
- The interpretation of the data is made with respect to the problem being solved.
- The data can be used to justify feedback given to students.

4.2 Illustration

We illustrate our procedure with the examples from Section 2.

First, we must decide on the inputs. The analysis program takes two inputs, the dataset and the query. The variation in the inputs comes from the contents of the dataset and the choice of query. We created a dataset that has records that together represent all the variation we might expect for the data. This means we can use the same dataset for all executions. We then execute the implementation of the design seven times, once for each query with that dataset.

Table 1 shows the object counts for D1078. The table shows the counts for the different inputs in columns corresponding to the different queries. The left-most column shows the name of the classes for which objects are created. For brevity, package names have been omitted. We also omit classes for which no objects are created. For example CLI has only a single static method, the entry point method `main`, and so has no objects created (see Figure 1). As the data shows, for D1078 at most one object from each class is ever created.

Compare the object counts of D1078 to those of D1053 (Table 2). For this design, 95 objects are created for each input. To interpret this number, the assessor needs to be aware of the nature of the input. In particular, the dataset used has 93 rows (recall that each row represents a dependency). From this alone we can hypothesise that the Deps class represents an individual dependency rather than a collection, as indicated by the (plural) name, since there are always 93 instances of it created. If this is the case, then "Deps" is perhaps not the best choice of name. From the classes for which a single object is created for each input, we might also hypothesise which of the classes are responsible for which query. While this may have been guessed at from their names, the object counts provide evidence to support that guess.

Another point to note from the data is that several classes in Figure 3 have no object counts, such as `NameChecker`, `SharedActions`, `LineProcessor`, and `CLI`. There are two possible explanations. One is that these classes only have static methods (as was the case for CLI in D1078). The other is that they are involved in an inheritance relationship with other classes—more on this in Section 5.1.

Table 3 shows the object counts for D1022. This data reveals a significant difference between this design and D1053. This design does not have a representation for a dependency. As with D1053 we can hypothesise the relationship between some classes and the query but given there is no more than one object created per class for any execution the decomposition appears more procedural than object-oriented. An argument can be made that D1022's decomposition based on objects is better than for D1078.

We have made a number of observations about these designs without having to inspect any code. We have learned much about the similarities and differences between the designs, and indications for the key design decisions made in each case, based solely on knowing the number of objects created from each class. We know of no other software metric that can easily provide this kind of insight.

That said, assessors may still need to inspect some of the code. The names of the classes play a role in the interpretation, but they could be inappropriately-named. There are some aspects of the design that are not visible from just counting objects. For example, abstract classes and interfaces are never instantiated and so would not be represented in the data.

The assessment for each design still has to be determined. How this is done depends on the assessment criteria for the assignment, and the learning outcomes for the course. For example, if the criteria is only to demonstrate a basic understanding of how to distribute functionality across classes, then all three designs may be given the same mark. If the criteria is to demonstrate how to create objects that play a recognisable role in the problem domain, then the designs would be ranked (lowest) D1078, D1022, D1053 (highest). These decisions can be justified directly from the object count data in terms of what it means to be an object-oriented program.

Perhaps of more value is how object counts can help provide formative feedback. The student who produced D1078 appears to be struggling with the general idea of how to create a set of objects that collaborate to provide functionality. For D1022, the student seems to understand the basics but also missed a good opportunity by not representing dependencies. For D1053, the student might benefit from giving more thought to the names of classes.

5 METHODOLOGY

Our goal is to investigate whether object counts are useful for assessing students' designs. We address this with three specific research questions, as discussed below.

For any measurement to be useful for assessment, it needs variation. Student assignments for courses introducing object-oriented programming are typically small, on the order of a few hundred lines of code. They are often tightly constrained. It is therefore possible that there can be little variation in the choice of designs, and so little variation in the number of objects that might be created. Our first research question is therefore:

RQ1 Is there significant variation of object counts for student designs?

Furthermore, for object counts to be useful, differences in object counts should reflect differences in designs. Conversely, similar designs should have similar object counts. Our second and third research questions are therefore:

RQ2 Do significantly different object counts typically indicate significantly different design decisions?

RQ3 Do similar object counts typically indicate similar design decisions?

To investigate our research questions we need to be able to count objects. This requires a measurement instrument and something to measure. For this first study, we consider designs implemented in the Java Programming Language. The remainder of this section describes how we make the measurements and what we measure.

5.1 Counting objects

The obvious starting point to counting objects is to count the number of times a constructor is executed. However this has some problems. One problem is that there are many constructors executed in a Java program that were not written by the developer. If the design uses classes from the standard library, or any third-party libraries, then constructors for those classes will be executed. As we want to assess the design *as determined by the student*, then such classes should not be assessed, and so their objects should not be counted.

Use of inheritance in a design complicates the analysis. If a class `Child` inherits from class `Parent`, then when a constructor for

Table 1: Objects per class for design1078

Class	Query							Total
	Aggregates	DepCount	FanIn	FanOut	Static	Summary	Uses	
Counter	1	1	1	1	1	1	1	7
FileReader	1	1	1	1	1	1	1	7
Query	1	1	1	1	1	1	1	7
ValueComparator	0	1	0	0	0	0	0	1
Total	3	4	3	3	3	3	3	

Table 2: Objects per class for design1053

Class	Query							Total
	Aggregates	DepCount	FanIn	FanOut	Static	Summary	Uses	Total
Aggregates	1	0	0	0	0	0	0	1
DepCount	0	1	0	0	0	0	0	1
Deps	93	93	93	93	93	93	93	651
FanIn	0	0	1	0	0	0	0	1
FanOut	0	0	0	1	0	0	0	1
Static	0	0	0	0	1	0	0	1
Summary	0	0	0	0	0	1	0	1
Uses	0	0	0	0	0	0	1	1
queryCall	1	1	1	1	1	1	1	7
Total	95	95	95	95	95	95	95	

Table 3: Objects per class for design1022

Class	Query							Total
	Aggregates	DepCount	FanIn	FanOut	Static	Summary	Uses	Total
Aggregates	1	0	0	0	0	0	0	1
DepCount	0	1	0	0	0	0	0	1
DepCount$1	0	1	0	0	0	0	0	1
FanIn	0	0	1	0	0	0	0	1
FanOut	0	0	0	1	0	0	0	1
ReadFile	1	1	1	1	1	1	1	7
Static	0	0	0	0	1	0	0	1
Summary	0	0	0	0	0	1	0	1
Uses	0	0	0	0	0	0	1	1
Total	2	3	2	2	2	2	2	

Child executes it must also execute a constructor from Parent. So, while only one object is created, two constructors are called. Thus just counting constructor calls can result in an incorrect measurement. Instead, constructor calls of ancestor classes should not be counted.

Another consideration that must be taken into account is that in Java, all classes must have a constructor, and if the developer does not provide one, then the compiler will do so, the so-called *default* constructor. Objects from such classes will be created, but the constructor only appears in the compiled code (bytecode) and not the source code.

Java has the enum type. The way enums are implemented means that when a program starts, all possible objects from the enum type are created. If a design has an enum with many values, the number of objects created for the enum can be larger than all objects from the other classes, obscuring the roles played by the other classes. As enums are meant to represent simple constants, we have decided not to count such objects.

The data presented in this paper was gathered with a tool developed using AspectJ [14]. This is used to instrument the code to record when constructors are called. This allows the tool to capture every call and execution to constructors. It then post-processes the results to remove unwanted data (e.g. standard library constructor calls) and to correctly count objects created in the context of inheritance, as discussed above. The tool uses so-called post-compile time or binary weaving in AspectJ, meaning it is the bytecode of the classes that are instrumented, to deal with the issue of default constructors. The tool is provided on the project website [20].

5.2 Corpora

Two corpora, each consisting of multiple designs for a small system, are used in this study. They come from an assignment in two offerings of an undergraduate course in software engineering at The University of Auckland. The course introduces object-oriented design principles, and the assignment is the first in which students try to apply the principles. The stated main criteria for these assignments is that the submitted designs demonstrate that the student understands the principles of object-oriented programming.

One corpus, CA, has 86 submissions for the dependency analysis assignment described in section 2 (D1078, D1022, and D1053 are members). Of these, 14 did not pass all of the automated tests,

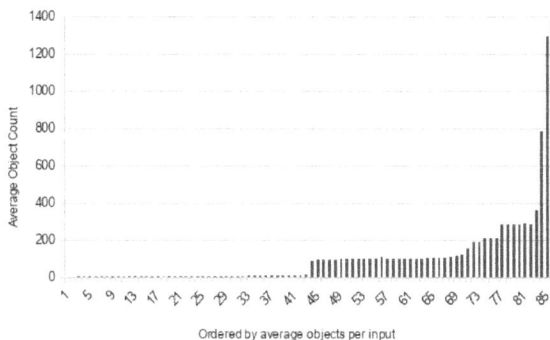

Figure 4: Average objects created by CA designs per input in order of average objects. (One outlier omitted)

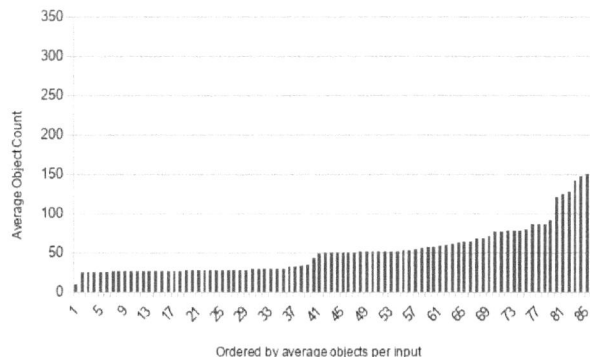

Figure 5: Average objects created by CB designs per input in order of average objects.

but in all but 4 cases the faults were assessed as minor (all are included). The object count data for CA was gathered by executing each submission seven times, once for each different query, on the same dataset that had 93 lines of data, that is, 93 dependencies.

The second corpus, CB, also has 86 submissions for an assignment that took two arguments: a file containing timesheet information and a command describing how to process the timesheets. The object count data for CB was gathered by executing each submission four times, once for each processing command, on the same dataset that had 24 lines of data, that is, 24 timesheets. The majority of the submissions satisfied the correctness requirements.

These corpora are available from the project website [20].

6 STUDY RESULTS

Figure 4 shows the results for the CA corpus. The values shown are the average object counts over the seven executions for a single design. The designs are ordered by average object count. The variation between executions is typically very small, so the average counts are representative of the design behaviours. The range for the chart is 0–1,292. The designs fall into 4 main groups. The first group (G1, 43 designs) has a range of 0–15, the second (G2, 24) 86–102, the third (G3, 6) 188–208, and the fourth (G4, 6) 280–284. Not shown is an outlier (D1009), with an average of 17,847, because it would make the chart unreadable.

Figure 5 shows the results for the CB corpus, again showing average number of objects per input. Three main groups are evident, with averages of 24–34 (38), 48–56 (20), and 76–78 (6), although the groupings are less clear-cut than for CA.

Regarding RQ1, whether there is variation in the number of objects created by student designs, the answer is clearly yes.

To answer RQ2 and RQ3, further discussion of the problem domain is needed. Due to space constraints we will focus on CA. There are many choices a student could make, but two possible choices are: explicitly represent a dependency (with a class) or not, and explicitly represent a module or not. This gives four design options: no representation for either dependency or module (D1), representing dependency but not module (D2), representing module but not dependency (D3), or representing both (D4). Translating this into expectations for object counts, D1 would give zero objects per dependency, D2 gives one object, D3 two objects, and D4 three objects.

This means, for a dataset with 93 dependencies, for design option D2 we would expect a minimum of 93 objects for each query, we would expect 186 for D3, and 279 for D4. For D1, the number of objects would be independent of the size of the dataset (but may depend on the query). If the rest of the required functionality is provided by just a few objects (e.g. 2–10), then the expected number of objects for the four design options matches the groups G1, G2, G3, and G4 identified above in the data. This indicates that design choices are reflected in the object counts, answering RQ2.

Most designs show some variation across inputs so there are not many with exactly the same total object counts. Three that do are D1053, D1065 and D1084, with a total object count of 665, corresponding to exactly 95 objects for each input. From the analysis above, we hypothesise that these all chose design option D2.

All are similar in nature (see Table 2 for D1053). All have a class that represents a dependency (called Dependency in both D1065 and D1085). All have classes providing the functionality for the individual queries (the relevant classes are often named after the query), and all are similar in what they do. One point of difference is that D1065 and D1084 provide the required output in a shared parent class (named Query) whereas D1053 implements an interface (also Query) and each implementation provides its own output. So while the designs are similar, there is some variation. This indicates that designs with the same object count are not identical, but are generally similar (RQ3).

The above analysis could have been done without the object counts; however, it would have taken careful analysis of the source code. The object counts make it obvious, for example, that Deps in D1053, despite the plural, likely plays the same role as the classes named Dependency in the other designs. This is immediately obvious as there are 93 objects created from each class for all inputs. Having established this hypothesis, it can be quickly confirmed by scanning the source code.

Another advantage of object counts is that it highlights designs that have unusual characteristics. For example, the design with the largest number of objects (1,292) in Figure 4 is D1050. In six of the seven inputs the class FileLine has 930 objects created. The name suggests (confirmed by inspecting the code) that the class is intended to represent one line of data. There is no obvious explanation for why so many objects would be needed, suggesting there may be a problem with the design. In fact it is a consequence of a complicated interaction between three classes (one an abstract superclass) that suggests confusion on the part of the student as to which class has the responsibility for reading the file.

Not shown in Figure 4 is D1009, which averages nearly 18,000 objects per input. The class that contributes most of these objects is Dependency (more than 17,000 for all inputs). Examining the source code for where Dependency objects were being created revealed that the only place was in the Dependency class itself—an extremely questionable design!

Neither of these designs were noticed as having such unusual characteristics when they were originally graded (using traditional grading processes based on rubrics), and even when the code was scrutinised for this paper it was not evident that they would behave so strangely. Without the object count data to point the way, we would not have been able to properly assess them, illustrating the usefulness of counting objects.

7 DISCUSSION

Our contribution is that determining how many instances of each class is created—counting objects—provides useful information for assessing a design. We base this on the view that an object-oriented program must create objects. The objects that get created are concrete indications of the decisions the student has made regarding how responsibilities have been assigned to which roles, which is necessary to understanding the design. It is like assessing a house by looking at the house, rather than trying to assess it from the blueprints. The objects that are created are the reification of the design.

The tool we have developed is a prototype, with no thought to performance, yet it is able to gather the data for a corpus in a matter of seconds. We have applied the technique to other corpora, and a larger design (JUnit), and encountered no performance issues.

We are not suggesting that "more objects means more object-oriented"! As D1050 and D1009 from CA indicate, "too many" objects can be a sign of a poorly-conceived design. The object counts must be interpreted in the context of the problem being solved. In the case of CA, we interpret the object counts knowing there are 93 lines of data. This allows us to, based just on the object counts, hypothesise what design decisions have been made (e.g. D1–D4).

Nor are we suggesting that assessment should be done solely on the basis of object counts. It is still the case that the source code should be examined. The difference is that instead of trying to understand what design decisions have been made, we instead inspect the code to confirm a hypothesis about the design based on the object counts. For example, D1014 of CA typically has 95 objects per input, suggesting it uses the D2 design option. However the class with 93 objects is Module. We might hypothesise that this is a poorly-named class and examine it to confirm this hypothesis. In fact, we find a mix of module, dependency, and query elements, providing a good source of information for providing formative feedback to the student.

What the object counts do is provide guidance as to what to look for in a design, such as the Module class for D1014, the FileLine class for D1050, or the Dependency class for D1009. Manually inspecting the source code may or may not reveal these design problems. In particular, D1050 looks reasonable if the use of FileLine is not closely examined.

Counting objects provides more useful information about a design than just statically considering the abstractions represented in the design. An inappropriate choice of name can mislead as to what abstraction a class represents, whereas the object count can convey more clearly what is intended (e.g. Deps for D1053). Furthermore, a design can have abstractions that have no objects created. For example, D1053 has an interface Query. Focusing just on those classes that create objects simplifies the assessment task.

A consequence of the decisions described in Section 5.1 is that superclasses do not get counted. This may seem problematic if we regard inheritance as the defining characteristic of object-oriented programming. However, a program that creates few objects despite extensive inheritance may indicate a lack of understanding of object-oriented design. We advise assessing use of inheritance separately from, and after, inspecting object counts. For example, D1022 from CA has 10 classes and an interface. However, it creates only two objects for six of the inputs, and three for the seventh. The interface in fact adds no value to the design, which overall is more procedural than object-oriented.

We define an object-oriented program as one that when executing has objects sending messages to each other; however, we focus on the objects, not the messages. While there may be value in considering the messages, and we originally planned to do so, what we have found is that there is considerable value in just looking at the object counts. Small experiments we have done suggest interpreting message data is quite difficult, and so for now we are concentrating on just the objects.

A limitation of object counts is that it requires an executable solution. In our case, we require that submissions be executable, in part because we use automatic marking to assess correctness. However, in courses on object-oriented design with no requirement to produce code, object counts may be of little help.

The assignments we have presented here are very similar in nature, raising the question as to how generalisable object counts may be. However, we have applied object counts to two other designs of similar size to CA and CB (one a board game, the other the server side of an interactive application) from 4 different student cohorts, and found the data to be as effective as our discussion here indicates. The measurements show similar degrees of variation as seen in CB and CA, and have shown similar value for understanding the designs.

8 CONCLUSIONS

We have presented how object counts can be used to assess object-oriented designs. The assessment is based on objective data, meaning it is reliable. The data is gathered automatically, and so can be done efficiently. A particular benefit is that characteristics of designs indicated by the object counts are indicative of the design decisions made, and so provide an objective basis on which to give feedback to students. We believe object counts can be used for more than just student assessment, and we plan to explore their use in other contexts in the future.

REFERENCES

[1] Deborah J. Armstrong. 2006. The Quarks of Object-oriented Development. *Commun. ACM* 49, 2 (Feb. 2006), 123–128. https://doi.org/10.1145/1113034.1113040

[2] David J. Barnes and Michael Kölling. 2006. *Objects First with Java: A Practical Introduction Using BlueJ* (3rd ed.). Prentice Hall.

[3] Kent Beck and Ward Cunningham. 1989. A Laboratory for Teaching Object-Oriented Thinking. In *Proc. of OOPSLA-89: ACM Conference on Object-Oriented Programming Sy stems Languages and Applications.* 1–6.

[4] Jürgen Börstler, Marie Nordström, and James H. Paterson. 2011. On the Quality of Examples in Introductory Java Textbooks. *Trans. Comput. Educ.* 11, 1, Article 3 (Feb. 2011), 21 pages. https://doi.org/10.1145/1921607.1921610

[5] Timothy A. Budd. 2001. *An Introduction to Object-Oriented Programming* (3rd ed.). Addison-Wesley Longman Publishing Co., Inc., Boston, MA, USA.

[6] Rachel Cardell-Oliver. 2011. How Can Software Metrics Help Novice Programmers?. In *Proceedings of the Thirteenth Australasian Computing Education Conference - Volume 114 (ACE '11).* Australian Computer Society, Inc., Darlinghurst, Australia, Australia, 55–62. http://dl.acm.org/citation.cfm?id=2459936.2459943

[7] S. Chidamber and C. Kemerer. 1994. A metrics suite for object oriented design. *IEEE Transactions on Software Engineering* 20, 6 (1994), 476–493.

[8] Henrik Baerbak Christensen. 2005. Implications of Perspective in Teaching Objects First and Object Design. In *Proceedings of the 10th Annual SIGCSE Conference on Innovation and Technology in Computer Science Education (ITiCSE '05).* ACM, New York, NY, USA, 94–98. https://doi.org/10.1145/1067445.1067474

[9] Nigel Cross. 2001. Design cognition: results from protocol and other empirical studies of design activity. In *Design knowing and learning: cognition in design education,* W. Eastman, C.; Newstatter and M. McCracken (Eds.). Elsevier, Chapter 5, 79–103.

[10] Paul J. Deitel and Harvey Deitel. 2015. *Java How To Program (late objects)* (10 ed.). Pearson.

[11] Anna Eckerdal and Michael Thuné. 2005. Novice Java Programmers' Conceptions of "Object" and "Class", and Variation Theory. In *Proceedings of the 10th Annual SIGCSE Conference on Innovation and Technology in Computer Science Education (ITiCSE '05).* ACM, New York, NY, USA, 89–93. https://doi.org/10.1145/1067445.1067473

[12] Simon Holland, Robert Griffiths, and Mark Woodman. 1997. Avoiding Object Misconceptions. In *Proceedings of the Twenty-eighth SIGCSE Technical Symposium on Computer Science Education (SIGCSE '97).* ACM, New York, NY, USA,

131–134. https://doi.org/10.1145/268084.268132

[13] Alan Kay. 1997. The computer revolution hasn't happened yet. Keynote at OOPSLA. http://files.squeak.org/Media/AlanKay or https://www.youtube.com/watch?v=oKg1hTOQXoY, timecode 10m 34s.

[14] Gregor Kiczales, Erik Hilsdale, Jim Hugunin, Mik Kersten, Jeffrey Palm, and William G. Griswold. 2001. An Overview of AspectJ. In *Proceedings of the 15th European Conference on Object-Oriented Programming.* 327–353. http://dl.acm.org/citation.cfm?id=646158.680006

[15] Rachel Or-Bach and Ilana Lavy. 2004. Cognitive Activities of Abstraction in Object Orientation: An Empirical Study. *SIGCSE Bull.* 36, 2 (June 2004), 82–86. https://doi.org/10.1145/1024338.1024378

[16] Paul Ralph. 2012. Improving coverage of design in information systems education. In *International Conference on Information Systems.* AIS, Orlando, FL, USA.

[17] Kate Sanders and Lynda Thomas. 2007. Checklists for Grading Object-oriented CS1 Programs: Concepts and Misconceptions. In *Proceedings of the 12th Annual SIGCSE Conference on Innovation and Technology in Computer Science Education (ITiCSE '07).* ACM, New York, NY, USA, 166–170. https://doi.org/10.1145/1268784.1268834

[18] Martijn Stegeman, Erik Barendsen, and Sjaak Smetsers. 2014. Towards an Empirically Validated Model for Assessment of Code Quality. In *Proceedings of the 14th Koli Calling International Conference on Computing Education Research (Koli Calling '14).* ACM, New York, NY, USA, 99–108. https://doi.org/10.1145/2674683.2674702

[19] Bjarne Stroustrup. 1988. What Is Object-Oriented Programming? *IEEE Softw.* 5, 3 (May 1988), 10–20. https://doi.org/10.1109/52.2020

[20] Ewan Tempero, Paul Denny, Andrew Luxton-Reilly, and Paul Ralph. 2018. "Objects count so count objects!" Project Website. http://qualitas.cs.auckland.ac.nz/data/icer2018.

[21] Scott A. Turner, Ricardo Quintana-Castillo, Manuel A. Pérez-Quiñones, and Stephen H. Edwards. 2008. Misunderstandings About Object-oriented Design: Experiences Using Code Reviews. In *Proceedings of the 39th SIGCSE Technical Symposium on Computer Science Education (SIGCSE '08).* ACM, New York, NY, USA, 97–101. https://doi.org/10.1145/1352135.1352169

[22] Rebecca Wirfs-Brock, Brian Wilkerson, and Lauren Wiener. 1990. *Designing Object Oriented Software.* Prentice Hall.

[23] C. Thomas Wu. 2008. *A comprehensive introduction to object-oriented programming with Java.* McGraw-Hill.

Blackbox, Five Years On: An Evaluation of a Large-scale Programming Data Collection Project

Neil C. C. Brown
King's College London
London, UK
neil.c.c.brown@kcl.ac.uk

Amjad Altadmri
King's College London
London, UK
amjad.altadmri@kcl.ac.uk

Sue Sentance
King's College London
London, UK
sue.sentance@kcl.ac.uk

Michael Kölling
King's College London
London, UK
michael.kolling@kcl.ac.uk

ABSTRACT

The Blackbox project has been collecting programming activity data from users of BlueJ (a novice-targeted Java development environment) for nearly five years. The resulting dataset of more than two terabytes of data has been made available to interested researchers from the outset. In this paper, we assess the impact of the Blackbox project: we perform a mapping study to assess eighteen publications which have made use of the Blackbox data, and we report on the advantages and difficulties experienced by researchers working with this data, collected via a survey. We find that Blackbox has enabled pieces of research which otherwise would not have been possible, but there remain technical challenges in the analysis. Some of these – but not all – relate to the scale of the data. We provide suggestions for the future use of Blackbox, and reflections on the role of such data collection projects in programming research.

CCS CONCEPTS

• **Social and professional topics** → **Computing education**; •
General and reference → *Empirical studies*; Evaluation;

KEYWORDS

Blackbox; Shared Data; Mapping Study

ACM Reference Format:
Neil C. C. Brown, Amjad Altadmri, Sue Sentance, and Michael Kölling. 2018. Blackbox, Five Years On: An Evaluation of a Large-scale Programming Data Collection Project. In *ICER '18: 2018 International Computing Education Research Conference, August 13–15, 2018, Espoo, Finland*. ACM, New York, NY, USA, 9 pages. https://doi.org/10.1145/3230977.3230991

1 INTRODUCTION

Researching programming education can be difficult. A researcher may have several interesting research questions, but finding or generating sufficient data can be a challenge. Many studies are published based on limited data (quantitative or qualitative) gathered from a single cohort, often with only a few dozen participants. Statistical analyses of such a dataset, as well as generalised conclusions, are necessarily of limited reliability and value – both because of the

small sample size, and because the data is from a single-institution, often a single teacher (who may be the researcher themselves).

It seems advantageous to have a central large shared data pool which researchers could access. This idea led to the creation of the Blackbox project. Blackbox [9, 34] is a data collection project, designed and implemented by the creators of the BlueJ IDE, an educational Java development environment. Blackbox collects activity data from BlueJ users, including source code, edit sequences, testing and execution interactions, and compilation results.

Participation in the Blackbox data collection is voluntary, via an explicit opt-in choice of each user. Approximately 40% of BlueJ users choose to participate. Since BlueJ has several million users (who are typically novice programmers) per year, Blackbox has a large repository of novice programmer interaction data, which can form the basis of various research studies. Blackbox currently contains records of over 30 million programming sessions, including 300 million compilation events.

Blackbox was intended, from its conception, as a shared data repository that would be made available to various research groups for the investigation of many different research questions. It was hoped that the project could enable, maybe even stimulate, research that would otherwise be difficult or impossible to conduct.

This goal implicitly poses opportunities and difficulties. Making the data available to other interested researchers can increase the value of the data collection, thus better justifying asking users to participate and the effort in collecting and storing it. However, collecting observational data without a specific experiment carries multiple risks. The activity data is devoid of demographic and contextual data: we do not know who is programming, any details about them, or what their aim is. Additionally, the trade-offs of granularity and complexity of data collection and storage formats had to be designed based only on tentative predictions of future research questions and researchers' needs. It was possible that the data collected would not be useful to anyone.

Thus at the outset of the project there were several open questions about the project's success. Would it be possible to collect a meaningful amount of data? Would a single dataset in a fixed data format be useful to multiple different and diverse researchers and studies? Would other researchers be interested in working with an observational dataset when they had no opportunity to influence the details of the collected data or apply an intervention? Could a data access format be provided that makes it sufficiently easy, at the same time as sufficiently flexible, to be accessed with available technical expertise in research groups? Blackbox has now collected data for almost five years, and the repository has been available for researcher access for the whole duration. This is sufficient time to now conduct an investigation into the answers to these questions.

In this paper, we present a retrospective of the Blackbox project to date. Our contributions include:

- Quantitative results of the data collection. This includes the counts and size of the collected data, as well as some logistic details of operating a large-scale collection project, including server load and storage (Section 2).
- A mapping study of the literature published using Blackbox data. This helps us examine the use of the data by multiple research groups and provides a lens through which to assess the project's impact (Section 3).
- A survey of the researchers who used Blackbox or similar datasets, to examine the successes and difficulties of using such data for programming education research (Section 4).

The results presented here illustrate some of the possible scope and limitations of using Blackbox, and will be of use to other researchers contemplating working with this data in future. This paper also provides a useful examination of the more general role of large-scale datasets within computing education.

1.1 Related Work

The most closely related pieces of work are the studies based on the Blackbox data, which are covered in the mapping study in section 3. There exist several other similar datasets of novice programming data, such as code.org's Hour of Code dataset [5] and CloudCoder [32]. Ihantola et al. [16] and Hundhausen et al. [15] present useful overviews of these kinds of dataset. We are, however, not aware of a detailed retrospective evaluation of the usefulness and impact of a single dataset as presented in this paper.

2 BLACKBOX DETAILS

The first time a new user starts BlueJ, a novice Java IDE often used in programming instruction at school or introductory university level, they are asked whether they want to opt-in to the Blackbox data collection. Out of approximately 2.2 million unique users per year, roughly 40% do so. If a user has opted in, the Blackbox infrastructure collects activity details, including:

- The full source code of the user's project. For anonymisation purposes, the header comment of each class is removed.
- Edit actions at the source line level. Each time the cursor leaves a line, or the user compiles, the edit step is recorded.
- Compilation events, including success or failure, and any associated error information (source position and message).
- Use of BlueJ's testing tools, interactive method invocations, and various other IDE features.

Data collection began in June 2013. As of April 2018, the Blackbox database consumes 2.31 terabytes of disk space. It contains records of 32.1 million sessions from 2.58 million users, and 306 million compilation events. The server has received 2.36 billion separate activity items. (All items given to 3 s.f.)

2.1 Practical details

The data is collected into a MySQL database on a single machine. Typical processor load on the collection server (a machine purchased in 2013, see Brown et al. [9] for specifications) is estimated at less than one core, and up to 2–4 cores during peak times.

The database is live-mirrored to a second machine which is used for analysis purposes. The decision to separate the recording machine from the analysis machine has worked well. The analysis machine is used sparsely, but when it is used, is often used to maximum capacity. Separating data collection and analysis across two machines provides a guaranteed prevention of the analysis interfering with the data collection.

Data collection has been almost continuous since 2013, with only a small number of interruptions. Only three recording outages lasted longer than a few minutes:

(1) The initial data collection was not multi-threaded, and some data was lost due to server requests timing out during busy periods before this was fixed.
(2) The domain registration was accidentally allowed to lapse, and for a day or two some data was not recorded.
(3) The only major change to the schema to date was performed in August 2017, involving recording down-time of 6 days. Unlike the others, this outage was pre-planned and Blackbox researchers were notified in advance.

2.2 Original data estimates

The original Blackbox proposal [34] included an upper limit estimate of the expected data volume, based on user numbers at the time and the maximum 100% opt-in rate, which was used to decide the required specification of the server hardware. It stated:

> "At current usage levels... this will lead to a maximum of around 27,000 users per day, performing on average 3 sessions per day, and generating about 100 events per session over an average period of 90 days. This would mean overall a maximum case of 8 million events per day, or just under 100 events per second, and a total of 3 terabytes of data per year."

We can now compare these initial estimates (adjusted to the actual opt-in rate of 40%) to actual observed data volumes. Blackbox presently sees 5,000 to 20,000 users per day, performing an average of 2-2.5 sessions per day, with around 80 events per session. The average so far in 2018 is 2 million events per day, and the total data size is now 2.3 terabytes. This means that most of the estimates were quite accurate, even though they were made before any data was recorded. The main discrepancy is that the overall database size is smaller than estimated, probably due to the compression afforded by storing only diffs for edits.

2.3 Project administration

To gain access to the data, a lead-researcher has to be identified who is a permanent member of staff of an established research institution. This lead-researcher can then request access for other researchers, who may be students. All access requests require the lead-researcher to provide a short description of the research aims, and to sign an ethics declaration and code of conduct, which includes assurances to maintain the confidentiality of the data. Researchers are given a copy of the 60 page Blackbox handbook.

The Blackbox analysis machine has accounts for around 130 users. At a rough estimate of an average of three users per research group, this means a little over 40 research groups have likely signed up for access.

As Blackbox administrators, we offer the following observation: our contact with users interested in the dataset has typically consisted of talking to academics about the initial data access, followed by correspondence with students about intricacies of the actual data access and analysis. In several cases, the queries we received from students indicated a weak understanding of SQL database queries and incomplete programming knowledge.

3   BLACKBOX USAGE: A MAPPING STUDY

Blackbox has been running for almost five years. Although research publication has an inherent lead-time, this seems long enough to investigate the studies which have resulted from the Blackbox data so far. Therefore we conducted a small mapping study. A mapping study, such as the one performed by Kaijanaho [19], examines the research that has been carried out in an area, with a focus on which topics have been investigated. Unlike a systematic review, a mapping study does not try to synthesise the results of the research. In planning the study, we followed the guidelines by Petersen et al. [27] for conducting mapping studies in software engineering.

3.1   Design

3.1.1   Scoping. In this study, we were interested in any papers that had directly analysed Blackbox data (primary studies), or had used any results of primary studies in a detailed further analysis (secondary studies). This narrow focus meant that the studies (which shared the same data source) could be summarised coherently – we deliberately chose not to consider studies performed on similar datasets to Blackbox, which would have been a much wider analysis.

3.1.2   Search Strategy. We conducted our search with the assumption that all published Blackbox studies will cite at least one of the original Blackbox papers. Thus we conducted a snowball search (as per Wohlin [36]), beginning with two early publications on Blackbox [9, 34], and one of the better-known results papers by the administrators of the Blackbox dataset [3]. We first looked for all citing papers of these initial three in both the ACM digital library and Google Scholar (de-duplicating by hand). Then, any papers found to be Blackbox primary or secondary studies had their citations examined, repeating until we found no more Blackbox primary or secondary studies in the references. As a sanity check, before conducting the snowball search we wrote down any Blackbox papers we knew *a priori*, and we made sure that they were in the returned results.

3.1.3   Classification. We did not decide classifications ahead of time. Instead, each relevant paper was examined by two of the authors, who independently constructed categorisations for the full set of papers. These keywords were then compared and merged into a single set of categorisations through discussion, and papers were re-categorised using this single categorisation. A narrative summary was then produced.

3.1.4   Pre-registration. The protocol described above was pre-registered on 21st February 2018 at https://osf.io/y2amu/ before conducting the search.

3.2   Search Outcome

The search was carried out on the 21st to 23rd of February 2018. The pre-registered protocol was followed with minor adjustments for two unanticipated situations. Google Translate was used to examine non-English papers (a situation not anticipated in the original protocol). We also discovered one paper via Google Scholar which at the time was an accepted pre-print; we included this as a search result. In total, 304 citation links were assessed, which resulted in 135 unique papers being examined. Including 2 of our original 3 seed papers[1], 16 publications were found that that were primary Blackbox studies [2–4, 7–9, 11, 18, 20, 22, 24–26, 28–30]. No secondary studies were found.

All papers that were known to us before beginning the search were found in the search, except McCall and Kölling [23]. This paper is indexed by Google Scholar and did cite Brown et al. [9] but it seemed that a technical issue with IEEE's citation extraction meant that this citation was not automatically processed (and the paper did not cite any other Blackbox papers, so was not found otherwise by our snowball search). We manually added this paper to the results.

In hindsight, our search protocol was over-elaborate: every primary Blackbox study would have been found by simply looking through the Google Scholar citations for Brown et al. [9] (except for that paper itself).

We made one further unplanned alteration to the search. The original search took place before the papers from SIGCSE 2018 were indexed on the ACM digital library and Google Scholar. Conscious that there may be relevant papers published at SIGCSE 2018, we re-checked the direct citations of the Brown et al. [9] paper on the ACM digital library and Google Scholar on 5th March 2018, which yielded one further publication by Becker et al. [6], for a final total of 18 publications (16 original, 1 manual correction, 1 extra) [2–4, 6–9, 11, 18, 20, 22–26, 28–30].

3.3   Analysis Outcome

Two of the authors acted as coders. They independently created a tagging scheme for the full set of 18 publications, and then jointly agreed a single tagging scheme. They then independently tagged all 18 publications using the new scheme. This resulted in 89% agreement (of all tag-paper pairings), 5% where one or both researchers felt more clarification was needed on tag definitions, and 6% disagreement. A final discussion achieved 100% agreement.

Most papers described work which had been carried out, while some papers (in particular, Kurtiker and Wagh [22], Mirza et al. [24, 25]) described work which was planned. We tagged all work by topic regardless of whether it had or had not been carried out (in the spirit of a mapping study – which looks at topics, rather than results). In our results section, however, we note the planned versus carried-out distinction.

3.4   Results

Of the 18 papers examined, three were published in 2014, four in 2015, three in 2016, five in 2017, and three in 2018 (up to early

---

[1]Utting et al. [34] was a seed paper for the search but featured no Blackbox analysis, therefore is not eligible for consideration as a result of the search.

March). Seven of the papers had one or more of the Blackbox administrators as authors[2], and the remaining papers could be separated into nine disjoint author clusters (thus ten in all).

3.4.1 Topics. The most popular topic was examining errors in code, with 13 of the 18 papers [2–4, 6–9, 18, 22, 23, 26, 28, 29] investigating some aspect of programming errors. Five of these papers relied solely on using the content of the Java compiler's error messages (which are known to change between versions, making the analysis fragile), while eight [2–4, 7, 8, 23, 26, 29] made use of a custom error classification system that was partially or totally independent of the compiler. Six papers split the errors into higher level categories (e.g. syntax vs semantic), ten investigated error frequencies, six analysed time-to-fix. Two papers looked at the content of error messages, and two investigated suggesting possible fixes for errors. Four papers examined code style issues and two were concerned with plagiarism detection.

In total, thirteen papers performed a manual or automatic analysis of Java source code, while the others were based on non-source data, such as numbers of compile errors, numbers of edits, etc. Only Santos et al. [29] made any use of machine learning techniques to analyse the data.

Not all data collected in Blackbox saw much use. Only de Souza et al. [11] made use of the JUnit test-related data subset. Kurtiker and Wagh [22] planned to make use of local participant tagging to add demographic data, but to date only Ahadi et al. [2] have actually done so. Jadud and Dorn [18] used the location to analyse country differences, and two other papers [6, 26] have made use of country locations to constrain analysis sets. Several other parts of the data (e.g. dynamic invocations, exceptions) have not yet been used in any published work.

3.4.2 Research Methodologies. Ten papers applied a pre-existing theory to analysing the dataset. Three of them used the data to construct a model which could be used in future work (and a further paper planned to do so). Many of the papers performed exploratory data analysis without a particular theory, and/or reported results without using them to construct an explicit model.

Two papers described replications of previous work[3]: Jadud and Dorn [18] used the dataset to replicate earlier work on Jadud's error quotient, and Ahadi et al. [2] replicated earlier Blackbox work by Brown and Altadmri [8] in a local context.

4 BLACKBOX USAGE: RESEARCHER SURVEY

The published papers on Blackbox reveal some interesting information about topics of interest, but they cannot capture two aspects in particular. One is the detailed experience of researchers in using the data (was it easy or hard, what were the challenges, etc.) and the other is the possible experience of researchers who were perhaps interested, but did not use the data for a completed published study. To try to study these two cases, we conducted an online survey of programming researchers.

4.1 Design

4.1.1 Motivation. We had three informal primary hypotheses which we wanted to investigate:

- Sharing the Blackbox data is useful to researchers, due to the large data size and the convenience of not needing to collect your own data.
- Complex SQL databases are too difficult for many computing education researchers and their students to work with effectively.
- Many researchers have interesting questions, but frequently computing education researchers lack the analysis techniques to be able to map high-level research goals to actual analysis strategies of source code.

We were also generally interested in opinions and experiences surrounding the use of Blackbox (or similar datasets) even if they did not relate directly to these three themes.

4.1.2 Survey Design. The online survey had two main branches. A key question early in the survey was:

What is your relationship to Blackbox?
(1) I have signed up for access and have used the data for research.
(2) I have signed up for access, but have not really used it.
(3) I have heard of it before now, but I have not signed up for access.
(4) I have not heard of it before now.

If the respondent answered with one of the top two options (a "Blackbox user"), they were asked a set of questions about their actual or planned use of Blackbox, in order to capture the experience of users who used or planned to use the data. If one of the bottom two answers were chosen (a "Blackbox non-user"), they were asked questions about their use of, and opinions on, similar datasets, in order to capture the experience with other datasets for potential comparison. These open-ended text questions were primarily designed as prompts to help explore one of our three themes. The study followed appropriate ethical procedures and was approved by the King's College London ethics committee.

4.1.3 Pre-registration/Materials. The study was pre-registered on 14th February 2018, prior to the beginning of data collection, at https://osf.io/z48v7/ which includes the full survey in the Files section.

4.1.4 Outcome. Data collection was carried out from 14th February to 2nd March 2018 inclusive. The survey was advertised on the Blackroom (a Blackbox users' forum), the mailing list for a relevant Dagstuhl seminar, the csed-research mailing list, on Twitter by several of the authors, and by directly emailing all listed authors on the original 17 papers we found (see section 3.2) who did not work for King's College London (the authors' own institution). We received 21 complete responses to the survey: 13 responses were from Blackbox users, and 8 were from non-users.

4.1.5 Threats to validity. One threat to the survey's validity is that we may not have a representative sample of the Blackbox users and non-users. Researchers may have been more likely to return the survey if they used the data, and we may not have captured non-users who could have used it but did not. However, it is difficult to see how this threat to validity can be avoided.

---

[2]To clarify: authorship is not a condition of dataset use, so this means the administrators were actively acting as researchers in this work.
[3]Several papers presented tables of compiler error frequencies and compared them to previous such results in other work, but we did not class this alone as a replication.

Another threat to validity is that the survey was advertised and analysed by the authors, several of whom act as Blackbox administrators. Although the survey was anonymous, the answers about the respondent's own research potentially allowed identification. Participants were specifically assured that their responses would be treated professionally and that any decision to respond (or not) or response content would not influence any future treatment by the Blackbox administrators. However, it is possible that some participants may have altered their content of their responses to be less negative about the project.

4.1.6 Analysis. The responses were analysed by two of the authors performing an iterative process of open coding for thematic analysis: first, they made a pass through the whole dataset and formed an individual set of tags for the responses. Then they agreed on a canonical set of tags, and made another pass to tag the data using this set of tags. Inter-rater reliability was assessed using Cohen's Kappa. This was found to be low (less than 0.75) so an additional pass was made after discussing and clarifying the definition of the tags. This second pass resulted in a median Kappa of 0.735, and another pass was not conducted – the union of the two researchers' tagged items was used for each tag, and since these results were primarily used as a basis for a higher level manual summary, we considered this level of agreement to be sufficient.

4.2 Results

4.2.1 Demographics. Participants were asked about their research area (free text response): 12 mentioned computing education, 7 mentioned software engineering. They were asked for their role: 11 were permanent academic staff, 8 were postgraduate students, none were postdocs. They were asked for their relation to Blackbox: 9 were users who had signed-up and used the data, 4 said they had signed up but not really used the data, 6 had heard of the project but not signed up, and 2 had not heard of it before.

We asked each respondent for the role of the person responsible for directly analysing the data. Of the 13 responses from those who had signed up, 3 mentioned academic staff, 4 mentioned undergraduate students, 7 mentioned postgraduate students and 1 mentioned research assistants. The numbers do not add up as some responses mentioned multiple groups, and there could be double-counting if both a PhD student and their supervisor filled in the form (which we cannot know as the survey was anonymous). However, this does indicate that the majority of analysis was performed by students.

4.2.2 Ranking Exercises. The results of all ranking exercises given here use the mean rank, specified to one decimal place.

Blackbox users were asked to perform two ranking exercises. The first involved ranking Blackbox's features in importance to the respondent's work (rank 1 being most important, 7 least important):

Feature	Mean rank
Large size of data set	2.8
Access to source code	2.8
Ability to see edits over time for each user	2.9
Compiler error data	3.8
Other IDE usage data	4.9
Ability to geographically partition users	5.0
Ability to tag users for local experiments	5.8

The next question asked for rankings of Blackbox's features in terms of how problematic they were (rank 1 being most problematic, rank 7 least problematic):

Feature	Mean rank
Lack of information on what tasks users are accomplishing (lack of specific assignments)	2.5
The need to write your own software to pull information from the database	3.3
The need to write your own analysis of Java source code	3.7
Short-lived duration of many users in the dataset	4.1
Lack of demographic information on individual users	4.2
Data is Java-only; no other programming languages	4.8
Data is BlueJ-only; no other Java IDEs/editors	5.5

Blackbox non-users were asked to perform one ranking exercise: to rank Blackbox's features by what would have made the data more suitable (rank 1 being most important, rank 8 least important):

Feature	Mean rank
Adding more programming languages besides Java	3.0
Information on the user's current assignment/task	3.1
Adding demographic information	3.9
Adding more editors/IDEs besides BlueJ	4.0
More long-term tracking of users	4.4
Better support for tools to analyse source code data	5.7
More advertising (I was unaware of Blackbox)	5.9
Better support for tools to access/filter the data	6.0

4.2.3 Text Responses. One theme of interest was how important the Blackbox data was to each respondent's research. Five respondents said that Blackbox was essential to their research: "The research was only made possible by having Blackbox available", "I was only going to go after this question because of the existence of Blackbox", "Without Blackbox much of this work would not be possible. I would have had to alter everything." Five other respondents mentioned that the scale of the data was a major advantage: "[The] worldwide availability of such facility Blackbox data collection project made our research more fascinating and interesting", "Some things we concluded from mining the Blackbox data we would hesitate to conclude using [our own data]."

The Blackbox dataset is an SQL database with many different tables. Eight respondents mentioned having difficulty understanding the structure of the database: "There's such rich data that understanding the table structure can take a while", "We spent a long time trying to figure out to get what we wanted", "it was difficult to link so many tables". Five respondents explicitly stated that more examples or tutorials would be useful.

Four respondents expressed a desire to be able to export the data to a single CSV file. Four respondents also stated that they would like to be able to download the data locally to their own machine for analysis.

Three respondents independently stated that all they wanted was a temporal succession of source code snapshots with compiler errors, without the rest of the data that Blackbox provides, suggesting that this is a particularly common use-case. One respondent had a particular use case (omitted here to guarantee respondent anonymity) which Blackbox satisfied, stating "if anything like that was overlooked it would be problematic".

The most common desire for additional data in Blackbox was for information about the task the student was working on and/or their progress towards a correct answer, with eight respondents making mention of this: "[I would like] information on the task that the student is trying to achieve, including information on the correctness of the solution".

Respondents reported a wide variety of topics. We choose not to report specific individual items here (as, especially combined with the mapping study, this could identify who responded), but common higher-level themes were analysis of students' behaviour either with respect to success (four respondents) or to details like emotional state (two respondents). Two respondents mentioned plagiarism detection. Two others used the data as a code repository for testing error detection or correction tools. Programming errors were a very common item, mentioned by nine respondents.

Three respondents mentioned doing some analysis by hand. Where they mentioned programming languages that they used or would like to use for analysis, the main languages mentioned were Python (four respondents) and R (three respondents).

5 DISCUSSION

For further discussion, we now synthesise the results of the mapping study and the user survey.

5.1 Impact

Our mapping study found eighteen publications that used the Blackbox data. This figure is perhaps unrepresentative of the impact of Blackbox, as several of the publications featured Blackbox administrators as authors. However, excluding the Blackbox administrators, a total of nine disjoint sets of researchers used the data, which we believe is sufficient to show that the dataset has had a reasonably wide impact: we are not aware of another computing education dataset with such wide usage.

5.2 Topics and outputs

Our survey and mapping study confirmed that the study of programming errors remains the most popular topic to investigate with Blackbox. An initial flurry of papers looked at compiler message frequency. This is a somewhat shallow analysis technique, both in the sense that it requires little processing and also that compiler error messages can change with different Java releases and between different compilers, rendering the results quite fragile.

Overall, however, topics that have been investigated are not restricted to programming errors, and it seems that the dataset is versatile. Several of the publications and survey responses made mention of using the database solely as a repository of program code without mention of education.

5.3 Data capture

One of the central challenges of the Blackbox project was that the data capture is designed independently of any individual experiment or analysis. The intention of the original design was to capture data that would support a wide variety of experiments. Therefore it is to be expected that several researchers in our survey found the data to have more information than they individually needed. However, it is clear from the survey that there is one especially common use case: the need to obtain a series of temporally ordered source code snapshots plus compile errors. This data is present in the Blackbox dataset, but perhaps more could be done to make this view of the data easier to access for new researchers. For any individual researcher, more is not better – but the set of researchers overall would be smaller if not all data was recorded. As one respondent said, "One advantage... is the detail of the data. If anything like [the unique feature they needed] was overlooked it would be problematic."

There remain several features of the Blackbox data which have seen little exploration. Blackbox includes some run-time behaviour such as exceptions and invocation results, which have not yet been used in any published work. The testing framework aspects have only been used by one publication [11] while the version control recording has also not been used. The general pattern is that IDE-agnostic, code-centric features such as source code and compilation errors have been the focus of much analysis, while the more IDE-related and workflow features (code invocations, testing, version control) have received little attention.

One of the major drawbacks of the Blackbox dataset is that the recording of programming activity is not explicitly linked to any information on what the programmer is trying to achieve, or any measure of their progress. This is inherent in the design: we record users of the BlueJ tool, and they could be using the tool for any purpose. This drawback was confirmed as an issue by existing Blackbox users in our survey, and was ranked the second most important drawback by non-users. A further issue is the lack of demographic information in Blackbox, although this was mentioned less by existing users, and ranked lower by non-users. Blackbox includes a mechanism that allows researchers to establish unique ID numbers, which could then be used to collect and link contextual and demographic data about individual users. However, only one paper [2] has used this mechanism.

Another additional mechanism is that BlueJ extensions can be implemented to record extra data (to a separate server controlled by the individual researcher) that can be tallied against Blackbox users. This mechanism has not yet been used by any researchers. It seems that in general, the convenience of the large-scale pre-existing dataset outweighs any additional gain from implementing extra tools or gathering additional information from a local study.

The highest-ranked drawback for Blackbox by non-users was that the data is Java-only, suggesting that the single language aspect (again, inherent in using BlueJ as the data source) may prevent several researchers making use of the data. One researcher responding to the survey mentioned that they ended up using Java in their work because they wanted the scale of Blackbox: "We actually had to switch languages that we supported to use Blackbox data. We used [other programming languages] to begin with and Blackbox was all Java."

5.4 Scale

The scale of Blackbox is reflected in our results as both an advantage and disadvantage. Survey respondents mentioned scale as an important aspect that helped to better generalise their results (and was ranked as the joint most important feature in a ranking exercise), and several papers used the scale of the data as a way to "sell" their paper. However, it was also mentioned by survey respondents as causing difficulties with the analysis, leading to long-running or more complex analysis. Several uses of the country-identification feature of Blackbox in published papers felt to us like a way to simply subset the data to a more manageable size.

In some senses, for unfiltered analysis, Blackbox is now as large as it needs to be. One of the authors of this paper recently ran some analysis on the data, which took a long time to run on the full data-set: approximately 120 [wall clock] hours usage of all 12 cores on the analysis machine. For parallelisation, it was randomly sliced into a hundred sub-tasks. Each sub-task produced results that were almost exactly equal to each other (due to the law of large numbers), leading to the obvious question: if one percent of the data produces a statistically reliable sample of the full dataset, is there any need to analyse the full dataset? It should be noted that this point quickly disappears if the data is filtered: for example, only one or two percent of Blackbox users make use of BlueJ's version control support, and separately only a few percent use unit tests. Therefore, if one wanted to analyse the intersection of two such features, the dataset of interest can be much smaller than the full dataset.

5.5 Privacy

One faster way to analyse the full dataset would be to use big data tools, such as a map-reduce framework. These tools tend to introduce a tension between the faster analysis available in the cloud, versus controlling access to the data [13, 33]. It is impossible to completely anonymise source code without almost destroying it. There are examples in the Blackbox dataset of users using people's names for classes, variables, in string literals and so on. Unless every token in the data is replaced with a generic example (which would remove useful context, not to mention the technical challenges of also anonymising compiler and run-time errors and so on), it is inevitable that some of the data is not truly anonymous. For this reason, access to the data is restricted, and requests both for an anonymous subset (which we believe to be impossible without human examination) and to take copies of the data for analysis elsewhere have been refused: all primary analysis should take place on the analysis machine. Thus at present, the data access policy prevents the use of big data analysis in an external cloud or use in public data challenges such as the annual Mining Software Repositories data challenge.

5.6 Tools and techniques

A number of researchers developed software tools for themselves to aid in their analysis of the data. Theoretically, some of these tools might be shared between researchers, and the Blackbox team provides a forum to facilitate this sharing of tools and information. No-one in the survey, however, made mention of re-using tools besides those provided by the Blackbox administrators. In the published papers, some researchers re-used their own tools from previous studies, but apart from one replication [2] where tools were re-used, there was no tool sharing between researchers. The forum for the Blackbox community (the "Blackroom") receives very low traffic. This may be because there are few long-term users of the Blackbox dataset: apart from the Blackbox administrators, only

two research groups have issued multiple publications using the Blackbox data. Given that each researcher seems to conduct only an isolated piece of research with the data, there is little opportunity to build cohesive sets of tools that are shared and maintained.

With machine learning being a popular area of interest with many researchers at the moment, and tools like Google's TensorFlow [1] and techniques such as deep learning gaining in popularity, it was interesting that none of the survey respondents mentioned machine learning, and only one paper [29] actually used machine learning on the data. This may be because machine learning is difficult to directly apply to program code (which has a complex and exact intra-relational structure), or because the researchers who are using the data do not have a machine learning background with the required knowledge and skills.

Anecdotal observations of the Blackbox administrators were backed up by the survey, suggesting that most of the people doing analysis on Blackbox data are undergraduate and postgraduate students. The difficulties in analysing Blackbox thus appear at "both ends": the dataset itself is a complex relational database of large size, and those who are trying to analyse it sometimes fall short of being fully competent and practised programmers.

5.7 Methodologies

Many of the Blackbox papers lacked a formal theory as the basis for their investigation, and most did not construct any kind of model from the data that could be used for future work. Many of the papers were largely exploratory in nature, analysing and reporting on the dataset without an explicit connection to wider theory. This may simply be symptomatic of being "early days" in analysing these kinds of dataset: given a new data source it is perhaps to be expected that the early work is exploratory. It may mirror a wider pattern in computing education literature, where papers have been criticised for being largely experience-centric rather than theory-driven (see Valentine [35] for the original critique, and Guzdial [14] for a rebuttal). Alternatively, it may be a sign of "looking for your keys under the street lamp": the easily available large-scale dataset may encourage researchers to build their work around the data, rather than approach the data with an existing theory.

Blackbox functions as a global dataset, but can also be used as a data collection platform for local studies by adding an identifying tag for a local population. So far, only one study [2] has made use of this possibility, and respondents ranked it as the least important feature. It is interesting that respondents generally disliked the lack of contextual and demographic information about users in the dataset, but did not seem to contemplate performing local data collection using Blackbox, which would allow them to collect such data for participants. It seems that the scale and prior availability of the data is the most important feature, and worth trading-off against the lack of context.

In our mapping study, we found two replication papers [2, 18]. Two out of eighteen papers is not a high proportion, but given that Kaijanaho [19] previously found only three replications in an analysis of forty *years* of research, it can be viewed as a promising amount.

6 CONCLUSIONS

The Blackbox dataset provided the basis of eighteen publications by ten research groups in its first five years. Some researchers who used it stated that their research could not have been carried out without Blackbox, several more said it would have been difficult to find other data, and some stated that they could not otherwise have had access to this scale of data. Thus we believe the project can be viewed as a success and a positive asset in computing education and software engineering research. It is also a vindication of the original decision to make the Blackbox open to other researchers: had its use been constrained only to the Blackbox creators, some of this research would not have been possible. Two of the Blackbox papers have been replications, which is encouraging in light of the so-called replication crisis in Psychology and other fields [10].

Researchers have found that analysis with Blackbox can be challenging. Some of these challenges are inherent: the scale of the data means that manual analysis is of limited utility, and that analysis software and database queries may need optimisation to be practical. The way that the data is collected from BlueJ users means that contextual data (such as demographic data and especially data about the user's current task) is not available, which hampers some analyses. Some of the challenges relate to trade-offs in the data: Blackbox records a wide variety of data to support multiple different use cases, but this in turn makes each individual researcher's use of the data more complicated. Finally, other challenges may be solvable by improving the analysis tools or tutorials available, especially to support common use cases such as analysis of sequences of code snapshots punctuated by compiler error data.

We believe that large data collection projects and datasets have a useful place in programming research. Blackbox demonstrates that it is possible to create a dataset decoupled from a specific purpose, and for it to provide the basis of differing studies by multiple research groups. Careful sharing of this data has enabled more research to proceed and achieve more generalisable results than otherwise would have been possible. There is, however, a careful trade-off to be made between, on the one hand, richer detail and higher granularity in the data, which may notionally enable more types of research, versus, on the other hand, a simpler data schema which makes the data easier to work with. More data may be better, but more detail not necessarily so. Additionally, there remain concerns about the "gravitational pull" of such datasets. Researchers view the easy availability of large-scale data as a positive, but there may be an opportunity cost of not investigating important questions which can only be answered with different, perhaps smaller datasets.

An interesting question is whether large-scale data only produces a quantitative shift in research results. Computing education does not really have a central model of the programming process (the plan-composition model is perhaps the most comprehensive attempt [12, 31]) or many reliable metrics (Jadud's error quotient [17] being one of the few). Thus, the way that analyses conducted on Blackbox tend to focus on concrete observables such as compiler errors, rather than the complete programming process, is completely in line with previous research. There are no signs that having larger scale data will by itself produce a qualitative shift in the types of analysis performed on student code.

For better or for worse, analysis of large-scale data like Blackbox must be done using a program. This adds the side benefits of specificity and rigour: a program is an unambiguous and reproducible way of conducting analysis. However, it also excludes the possibility of rich, nuanced qualitative analyses. The work of McCall and Kölling [23] indicated that human categorisation of errors, which does not scale, was a more promising route than simpler automatic classification – although the work did use a subset of the Blackbox data as part of its source data. This would seem to be a good model for the use of large-scale data in computing education research: not as a panacea, but as part of the classic observe-hypothesise-experiment cycle, where large-scale datasets can aid in parts of the observe and experiment phases, sometimes in tandem with additional small-scale local observations or analyses.

6.1 Future work

There are some aspects of the Blackbox dataset which have yet to be explored. This may simply be data that is of no use to anyone, but we believe that there are interesting studies which could still be conducted. For example, information on which exceptions students encounter may be interesting to explore, as would be the interplay between code execution and code editing, or test frequency and correctness. Several studies we found consider student behaviour after receiving a compiler error, but not after receiving a runtime output. We also believe that there may be interesting uses of the data involving the local data collection mechanism, which allows the addition of demographic data. Our survey, however, suggests that most researchers to date do not consider this to be a feature of particular interest.

The Blackbox project has collected nearly five years of data. BlueJ has so far maintained its popularity, and the Blackbox server is still running; there is no obvious reason why the project cannot continue for another five years. Recently, in August 2017, the first major changes were made to the database schema since the project's inception. These were necessary to accommodate the changes introduced in the release of BlueJ 4: support for recording Stride [21] data was added, as well as changes reflecting BlueJ's move to continuous background error checking. Blackbox remains available for interested researchers who wish to access the data.

ACKNOWLEDGMENTS

We are grateful to Philip Stevens and particularly to Ian Utting for their work on starting and administering the Blackbox project. We thank Amelia McNamara for making us aware of the Centre for Open Science's pre-registration facility.

REFERENCES

[1] Martín Abadi, Paul Barham, Jianmin Chen, Zhifeng Chen, Andy Davis, Jeffrey Dean, Matthieu Devin, Sanjay Ghemawat, Geoffrey Irving, Michael Isard, Manjunath Kudlur, Josh Levenberg, Rajat Monga, Sherry Moore, Derek G. Murray, Benoit Steiner, Paul Tucker, Vijay Vasudevan, Pete Warden, Martin Wicke, Yuan Yu, and Xiaoqiang Zheng. 2016. TensorFlow: A System for Large-scale Machine Learning. In *Proceedings of the 12th USENIX Conference on Operating Systems Design and Implementation (OSDI'16)*. USENIX Association, Berkeley, CA, USA, 265–283.
[2] Alireza Ahadi, Raymond Lister, Shahil Lal, and Arto Hellas. 2018. Learning Programming, Syntax Errors and Institution-specific Factors. In *Proceedings of the 20th Australasian Computing Education Conference (ACE '18)*. ACM, New York, NY, USA, 90–96. https://doi.org/10.1145/3160489.3160490

[3] Amjad Altadmri and Neil C. C. Brown. 2015. 37 Million Compilations: Investigating Novice Programming Mistakes in Large-Scale Student Data. In *Proceedings of the 46th ACM Technical Symposium on Computer Science Education (SIGCSE '15)*. ACM, New York, NY, USA, 522–527. https://doi.org/10.1145/2676723.2677258

[4] Amjad Altadmri, Michael Kölling, and Neil C. C. Brown. 2016. The Cost of Syntax and How to Avoid It: Text versus Frame-Based Editing. In *2016 IEEE 40th Annual Computer Software and Applications Conference (COMPSAC)*, Vol. 1. 748–753. https://doi.org/10.1109/COMPSAC.2016.204

[5] Ashok Basawapatna and Alexander Repenning. 2017. Employing Retention of Flow to Improve Online Tutorials. In *Proceedings of the 2017 ACM SIGCSE Technical Symposium on Computer Science Education (SIGCSE '17)*. ACM, New York, NY, USA, 63–68. https://doi.org/10.1145/3017680.3017799

[6] Brett A. Becker, Cormac Murray, Tianyi Tao, Changheng Song, Robert McCartney, and Kate Sanders. 2018. Fix the First, Ignore the Rest: Dealing with Multiple Compiler Error Messages. In *Proceedings of the 49th ACM Technical Symposium on Computer Science Education (SIGCSE '18)*. ACM, New York, NY, USA, 634–639. https://doi.org/10.1145/3159450.3159453

[7] Neil C. C. Brown and Amjad Altadmri. 2014. Investigating Novice Programming Mistakes: Educator Beliefs vs. Student Data. In *Proceedings of the Tenth Annual Conference on International Computing Education Research (ICER '14)*. ACM, New York, NY, USA, 43–50. https://doi.org/10.1145/2632320.2632343

[8] Neil C. C. Brown and Amjad Altadmri. 2017. Novice Java Programming Mistakes: Large-Scale Data vs. Educator Beliefs. *Trans. Comput. Educ.* 17, 2, Article 7 (May 2017), 21 pages. https://doi.org/10.1145/2994154

[9] Neil C. C. Brown, Michael Kölling, Davin McCall, and Ian Utting. 2014. Blackbox: A Large Scale Repository of Novice Programmers' Activity. In *Proceedings of the 45th ACM Technical Symposium on Computer Science Education (SIGCSE '14)*. ACM, New York, NY, USA, 223–228. https://doi.org/10.1145/2538862.2538924

[10] Open Science Collaboration. 2015. Estimating the reproducibility of psychological science. *Science* 349, 6251 (2015). https://doi.org/10.1126/science.aac4716 arXiv:http://science.sciencemag.org/content/349/6251/aac4716.full.pdf

[11] Draylson Micael de Souza, Michael Kölling, and Ellen Francine Barbosa. 2017. Most common fixes students use to improve the correctness of their programs. In *2017 IEEE Frontiers in Education Conference (FIE)*. 1–9. https://doi.org/10.1109/FIE.2017.8190524

[12] Kathi Fisler, Shriram Krishnamurthi, and Janet Siegmund. 2016. Modernizing Plan-Composition Studies. In *Proceedings of the 47th ACM Technical Symposium on Computing Science Education (SIGCSE '16)*. ACM, New York, NY, USA, 211–216. https://doi.org/10.1145/2839509.2844556

[13] Andreas Grillenberger and Ralf Romeike. 2014. Big Data – Challenges for Computer Science Education. In *Informatics in Schools. Teaching and Learning Perspectives*, Yasemin Gülbahar and Erinç Karataş (Eds.). Springer International Publishing, Cham, 29–40. https://doi.org/10.1007/978-3-319-09958-3_4

[14] Mark Guzdial. 2013. Exploring Hypotheses About Media Computation. In *Proceedings of the Ninth Annual International ACM Conference on International Computing Education Research (ICER '13)*. ACM, New York, NY, USA, 19–26. https://doi.org/10.1145/2493394.2493397

[15] C. D. Hundhausen, D. M. Olivares, and A. S. Carter. 2017. IDE-Based Learning Analytics for Computing Education: A Process Model, Critical Review, and Research Agenda. *ACM Trans. Comput. Educ.* 17, 3, Article 11 (Aug. 2017), 26 pages. https://doi.org/10.1145/3105759

[16] Petri Ihantola, Arto Vihavainen, Alireza Ahadi, Matthew Butler, Jürgen Börstler, Stephen H. Edwards, Essi Isohanni, Ari Korhonen, Andrew Petersen, Kelly Rivers, Miguel Ángel Rubio, Judy Sheard, Bronius Skupas, Jaime Spacco, Claudia Szabo, and Daniel Toll. 2015. Educational Data Mining and Learning Analytics in Programming: Literature Review and Case Studies. In *Proceedings of the 2015 ITiCSE on Working Group Reports (ITiCSE-WGR '15)*. ACM, New York, NY, USA, 41–63. https://doi.org/10.1145/2858796.2858798

[17] Matthew C. Jadud. 2006. Methods and Tools for Exploring Novice Compilation Behaviour. In *Proceedings of the Second International Workshop on Computing Education Research (ICER '06)*. ACM, New York, NY, USA, 73–84. https://doi.org/10.1145/1151588.1151600

[18] Matthew C. Jadud and Brian Dorn. 2015. Aggregate Compilation Behavior: Findings and Implications from 27,698 Users. In *Proceedings of the Eleventh Annual International Conference on International Computing Education Research (ICER '15)*. ACM, New York, NY, USA, 131–139. https://doi.org/10.1145/2787622.2787718

[19] Antti-Juhani Kaijanaho. 2014. The extent of empirical evidence that could inform evidence-based design of programming languages: A systematic mapping study. *Jyväskylä licentiate theses in computing; 1795-9713; 18.* (2014).

[20] Hieke Keuning, Bastiaan Heeren, and Johan Jeuring. 2017. Code Quality Issues in Student Programs. In *Proceedings of the 2017 ACM Conference on Innovation and Technology in Computer Science Education (ITiCSE '17)*. ACM, New York, NY, USA, 110–115. https://doi.org/10.1145/3059009.3059061

[21] Michael Kölling, Neil Brown, and Amjad Altadmri. 2017. Frame-Based Editing. *Journal of Visual Languages and Sentient Systems* 3 (July 2017), 40–67. http://doi.org/10.18293/VLSS2017-012

[22] Prathmi Kurtiker and Ramrao Wagh. 2016. Understanding and analyzing students frustration level during programming. In *Proceedings of the 24th International Conference on Computers in Education*. Asia-Pacific Society for Computers in Education, 7–9.

[23] Davin McCall and Michael Kölling. 2014. Meaningful categorisation of novice programmer errors. In *2014 IEEE Frontiers in Education Conference (FIE) Proceedings*. 1–8. https://doi.org/10.1109/FIE.2014.7044420

[24] Olfat M. Mirza, Mike Joy, and Georgina Cosma. 2017. Style Analysis for Source Code Plagiarism Detection – An Analysis of a Dataset of Student Coursework. In *2017 IEEE 17th International Conference on Advanced Learning Technologies (ICALT)*. 296–297. https://doi.org/10.1109/ICALT.2017.117

[25] Olfat M. Mirza, Mike Joy, and Georgina Cosma. 2017. Suitability of BlackBox dataset for style analysis in detection of source code plagiarism. In *2017 Seventh International Conference on Innovative Computing Technology (INTECH)*. 90–94. https://doi.org/10.1109/INTECH.2017.8102424

[26] Cormac Murray. 2016. *A Comparative Study of Java Compiler Error Profiles Using the Blackbox Dataset*. Master's thesis. University College Dublin.

[27] Kai Petersen, Sairam Vakkalanka, and Ludwik Kuzniarz. 2015. Guidelines for conducting systematic mapping studies in software engineering: An update. *Information and Software Technology* 64 (2015), 1 – 18. https://doi.org/10.1016/j.infsof.2015.03.007

[28] David Pritchard. 2015. Frequency Distribution of Error Messages. In *Proceedings of the 6th Workshop on Evaluation and Usability of Programming Languages and Tools (PLATEAU 2015)*. ACM, New York, NY, USA, 1–8. https://doi.org/10.1145/2846680.2846681

[29] Eddie Antonio Santos, Joshua Charles Campbell, Dhvani Patel, Abram Hindle, and José Nelson Amaral. 2018. Syntax and Sensibility: Using language models to detect and correct syntax errors. In *25th IEEE International Conference on Software Analysis, Evolution, and Reengineering (SANER 2018)*, Vol. 29. 1–5.

[30] Stewart D. Smith, Nicholas Zemljic, and Andrew Petersen. 2015. Modern Goto: Novice Programmer Usage of Non-standard Control Flow. In *Proceedings of the 15th Koli Calling Conference on Computing Education Research (Koli Calling '15)*. ACM, New York, NY, USA, 171–172. https://doi.org/10.1145/2828959.2828980

[31] Elliot Soloway. 1986. Learning to Program = Learning to Construct Mechanisms and Explanations. *Commun. ACM* 29, 9 (Sept. 1986), 850–858. https://doi.org/10.1145/6592.6594

[32] Jaime Spacco, Paul Denny, Brad Richards, David Babcock, David Hovemeyer, James Moscola, and Robert Duvall. 2015. Analyzing Student Work Patterns Using Programming Exercise Data. In *Proceedings of the 46th ACM Technical Symposium on Computer Science Education (SIGCSE '15)*. ACM, New York, NY, USA, 18–23. https://doi.org/10.1145/2676723.2677297

[33] Bhavani Thuraisingham. 2015. Big Data Security and Privacy. In *Proceedings of the 5th ACM Conference on Data and Application Security and Privacy (CODASPY '15)*. ACM, New York, NY, USA, 279–280. https://doi.org/10.1145/2699026.2699136

[34] Ian Utting, Neil Brown, Michael Kölling, Davin McCall, and Philip Stevens. 2012. Web-scale Data Gathering with BlueJ. In *Proceedings of the Ninth Annual International Conference on International Computing Education Research (ICER '12)*. ACM, New York, NY, USA, 1–4. https://doi.org/10.1145/2361276.2361278

[35] David W. Valentine. 2004. CS Educational Research: A Meta-analysis of SIGCSE Technical Symposium Proceedings. In *Proceedings of the 35th SIGCSE Technical Symposium on Computer Science Education (SIGCSE '04)*. ACM, New York, NY, USA, 255–259. https://doi.org/10.1145/971300.971391

[36] Claes Wohlin. 2014. Guidelines for Snowballing in Systematic Literature Studies and a Replication in Software Engineering. In *Proceedings of the 18th International Conference on Evaluation and Assessment in Software Engineering (EASE '14)*. ACM, New York, NY, USA, Article 38, 10 pages. https://doi.org/10.1145/2601248.2601268

Using Social Cognitive Career Theory to Understand Why Students Choose to Study Computer Science

Amnah Alshahrani[*†], Isla Ross[*], Murray I Wood[*]

[*]Department of Computer and Information Sciences, University of Strathclyde, Glasgow, UK

[†]Princess Nourah bint Abdulrahman University, Saudi Arabia

{amnah.alshahrani | isla.ross | murray.wood}@strath.ac.uk

ABSTRACT

The aim of this research is to use Social Cognitive Career Theory (SCCT) to identify and understand reasons why students choose to study Computer Science (CS) at university. SCCT focuses on students' prior experience, social support, self-efficacy and outcome expectation. The research is partly motivated by the desire to increase female participation rates in CS, particularly in the UK. Policymakers can use the factors that both females and males identify as influencing their choice of studying CS to enhance the experiences of all students prior to coming to university, but female students in particular. The study uses a semi-structured interview with 17 mixed gender subjects currently studying CS at three Scottish universities. The findings are that social support from family, teachers, friends and mentors is a particularly important factor in choosing to study CS, especially for female subjects. The career paths offered by a CS degree is another major factor, not just the potential jobs, but also the general value of a CS education and the potential to make useful contributions to society. School education appeared to have limited influence, though exposure to problem solving, programming, online self-learning and internships are positive influences. The stereotypical view of CS students as 'geeks' is outdated and unhelpful – it is more appropriate to see them as 'analytical' or 'over-achievers'. Subjects make many suggestions for improving the CS education provided at school, especially to make it more attractive to females, including: make it compulsory, teach it earlier, include more programming and problem solving, and increase the visibility of female exemplars and role models.

CCS CONCEPTS

• Social and professional topics → Computer science education

KEYWORDS

Social Cognitive Career Theory; Gender; Computer Science; Education; Careers; Students.

ICER '18, August 13–15, 2018, Espoo, Finland
© 2018 Association for Computing Machinery.
ACM ISBN 978-1-4503-5628-2/18/08...$15.00
https://doi.org/10.1145/3230977.3230994

ACM Reference Format:
A. Alshahrani, I. Ross, and M. Wood. 2018. Using Social Cognitive Career Theory to Understand Why Students Choose to Study Computer Science. In *Proceedings of ACM ICER conference, Espoo, Finland, August 2018 (ICER '18)*, 10 pages. https://doi.org/10.1145/3230977.3230994

1 INTRODUCTION

The gender gap amongst students choosing to study certain subjects at university has received considerable attention in recent years. In Western countries, Computer Science (CS) in particular has a gap that challenges governments, industry and education. For example, Pappas et al. [45] highlight the potential shortage in Europe: "*The European Commission predicted that by 2020, in Europe, there will be a shortage of more than 800,000 professionals in the field of Computer Science*". As a result of this huge increase in demand in technology fields, female representation in CS is now a key factor for the economic and labour market [7]. However, in countries such as Scotland, females make up only 16% of students studying CS at university [27]. Recently, there have been significant efforts from scholars and researchers to investigate this issue, to understand the factors that cause it, and to determine how it might be addressed.

This study contributes to that effort by using Social Cognitive Career Theory (SCCT) [37] to try to identify and understand the reasons that influence students to choose to study CS at university, particularly female students. Through understanding those reasons, it may be possible to change pre-university experiences to increase the likelihood of females choosing to study CS. The contribution of this study is to help policymakers design guidance to tackle the gender gap in CS.

SCCT is a framework for understanding how personal, cognitive and contextual factors influence career and/or academic choices. Its academic / career choice model consists of four components - prior experience, social support, self-efficacy and outcome expectation. This study used SCCT as a theoretical foundation from which to construct a semi-structured interview. Seventeen subjects (11 female, 5 male, 1 gender-neutral) participated, all of whom are currently studying CS at one of three Scottish universities. A qualitative, content analysis of the individual interview transcripts was then performed using NVivo [1].

The findings include the importance of social support from family, teachers, friends and mentors when choosing to study CS, particularly for females. Career paths offered by a CS degree is another factor – not just the range of jobs available, but also the general value of a CS education and the potential to contribute to society. The stereotypical views of CS students as 'geeks' are still prevalent but are seen as outdated by students themselves. The impact of current (pre-university) school education appears to be of limited significance but exposure to problem solving, programming, online self-learning and internships are important positive influences.

These findings have the potential to help schools, universities and other policymakers shape pre-university CS experiences into something more appealing. The results can be used to help present a more positive view of a CS education to schoolchildren, their families and their teachers. The results also contain numerous suggestions from subjects as to how this might be done, especially to make CS more attractive to females: make it compulsory, teach it earlier, incorporate more programming and problem solving, and increase the visibility of female exemplars and role models.

The next section includes a brief summary of previous research exploring factors that influence the choice to study CS. There is also a review of previous work that has used SCCT to understand academic choices. Section 3 presents a description of the qualitative study design. Section 4 is a brief description of the data analysis procedure. Section 5 presents a detailed description of the interview results. Section 6 presents the findings based on the results and relates them to prior research. The paper concludes with discussion of threats to validity in Section 7 and a summary of the findings, their implications and potential further work in Section 8.

2 RELATED WORK

2.1 Factors Influencing the Choice to Study Computer Science

A number of studies have discussed the factors that appear to make female students reluctant to study CS at university [7, 9, 35]. Moreover, scholars and researchers have explored why females are under-represented in Computer Science [35, 62]. Others have investigated the factors that influence students' intention to pursue a CS major [12, 17, 36].

Some of the studies exploring the factors behind female under-representation in CS found that cultural factors influence choices made by students. Varma [60] investigated the factors behind the under-representation of females in CS and computer engineering at some higher education institutions in USA. In her study, "*gendered socialization*" (more support for boys) and "*technology anxiety*" were identified as key factors. In the UK, Sinclair and Kalvala [55] found that gender stereotypes (computer science for boys) and cultural expectations (parents' discouragement) were the significant factors that could influence the decisions of females not to study CS. Cohoon and Aspray [15] also argued that social and cultural factors affect gender participation in computing fields, not biological gender differences. In the Netherlands, Rommes et al. [49] found that teenagers seemed to be influenced by 'prototype' impressions of professions where the image of CS was male, 'nerdy' and unattractive. Wong [64] found that even among the digitally skilled, the view of a computer person as clever but antisocial still prevails, which can be unattractive to youths, particularly girls, with few aspiring to be a computer person.

However, there appears to be a lack of studies that use a theoretical basis to investigate these factors. Cohoon and Aspray [15] suggest that the use of a theory could help to evaluate and transform information that is gathered in to knowledge and then to predict the results of any associated action.

2.2 Social Cognitive Career Theory (SCCT)

Social Cognitive Career Theory (SCCT) [37] is derived from Social Cognitive Theory (SCT) which focused on the interaction between person, environment and behaviour [5]. The SCCT framework focusses on personal, cognitive and contextual factors for career/academic choices. It has three models: the interest model, choice model and performance model. Lent et al. [37] argued that "*… our model may help explain the academic paths that people select*". A review of empirical research based on SCCT by Sheu and Bordon [53] found that "*The majority of studies tested hypotheses of the interest/choice and satisfaction models among adolescents and college students in Asian and European countries*". Beyer [7] also suggested that "*Social psychological variables are excellent candidates for factors to be studied because they have been shown to influence career choices*".

There are a number of other models of motivation such as the Expectancy Value Model (EVM) [20] that could have been used as the basis of this research. SCCT was chosen because prior work has shown that its constructs can help identify the factors that influence career/academic choice [53]. Based on the previous studies, this study has adopted four factors from SCCT to help identify and understand reasons why students choose to study CS at university: These are: prior experience, social support, self-efficacy and outcome expectation. These factors are explained, and their choice justified, in the following sections.

2.3 Prior Experience

Prior experience refers to exposure to the subject prior to making the choice to study at university. In this case, it includes computer exposure and usage, computing subjects studied at school and programming-related activities. Taylor and Mounfield [56] found that there was a significant relationship between female success in CS at college and prior experience in computing. Beyer [7] also found that prior experience is a significant factor influencing female participation in computing courses. Similarly, He and Freeman [28]) conclude "*Results suggest that females feel less confident with computers because they have learned less and practiced less*" (this could also be categorized as 'self-efficacy' – see later). Cohoon and Aspray [15] argue that computer experience either formal, such as computer courses at school, or informal, such as computer games, provide students with initial impressions and information about computing. Schulte and Knobelsdorf [51] observed that the nature of prior computing experience can shape attitudes and foster commitment from some while deterring others from pursuing CS. Denner et al. [18] suggest that three widely held beliefs - support from others, motivation, and prior experience - play a vital role in the intention of females to pursue CS. Brown et al. [10] found that concentrating on students in early ages at schools helped to promote interest in CS.

2.4 Social Support

Social support refers to the surrounding environment, such as family, peers and teachers. A recent Google report emphasised the need for parents, students and educators to be made more aware of the benefits of CS education [26]. Numerous studies have identified the significance of social support as an influence on females to choose to study CS [19, 57, 61, 63]. Mishkin et al. [43] found that female students making an engineering career choice are influenced by social support more than male students. Some studies indicate the importance of role models for female students [4, 8, 60]. According to Alvarado and Judson [3] introducing female students to female role models in CS could encourage them to pursue a computing degree. On the other hand, Heinze and Hu [30] argue that support from family and friends is not a powerful influence on the choice of students to pursue careers in IT. Social support and role models were not considered top factors for CS students in studies in Kuwait [21], Armenia [24] or Serbia [42].

2.5 Self-efficacy

According to Social Cognitive Theory (SCT), people perform tasks based on their capabilities and beliefs [5]. The main component of SCT is self-efficacy, defined by Bandura [5] as *"... people's judgments of their capabilities to produce designated levels of performance"*. Self-efficacy has been examined in numerous studies [7, 14, 29, 30, 63]. Self-efficacy for female students in computing is influenced by both prior experience and knowledge of computers [28]. In Taiwan, Fan and Li [23] found that female CS students felt more confident in their ability than male students because of prior computing experience. Heinze and Hu [30] and Beyer [7] suggest that self-efficacy, interest and knowledge of computers all make females less likely than males to study CS. Similarly, a Google report [25] suggests that females are less confident in their skills and therefore less likely to study CS. Often the confidence and self-efficacy of females towards STEM subjects are less than of males, even though females perform just as well as males [2]. Lehman, Sax, and Zimmerman [36] found that female students rated themselves lower than male students in terms of CS ability. Most people are attracted to, and pursue, tasks and fields in which they are confident.

2.6 Outcome Expectation

Outcome expectation refers to the desired result of an action or behaviour. Lent et al. [38] suggest that there are a number of theories which suggest that outcome expectation can play a key role in motivating behaviour. Advisers should be aware of negative expectations, because some of these expectations are often misguided, or illogical, and may influence students' choices [54]. In Kuwait, El-Bahey and Zeid [21] found that the most important factor influencing a decision to study CS to be career and future considerations. A Google investigation [25] into factors that influence young women to pursue degrees in CS found that the *"...perception of Computer Science as a career with diverse applications and a broad potential for positive societal impact"* was a top factor. Similarly, a later Google report [26], found that *"... most students and parents in the U.S. have a positive image of computer science work"*. Thus, the perceptions of parents regarding CS may also encourage females to study CS degrees (see also section 2.4 Social Support).

3 STUDY DESIGN

3.1 Research Aim and Question

The aim of this study is to investigate the factors that motivate students to choose to study CS at university. The study is the first phase of a larger study that will also include a wide-scale questionnaire-based survey constructed from the findings reported here. The aim is addressed by the following research question: *What influence do students' prior experience, social support, self-efficacy and outcome expectation have in the choice to study a computer science degree at university?*

3.2 Design of the Interview

The instrument used in this study was a semi-structured interview. In a semi-structured interview, questions are pre-planned, but the researcher can change the question order or ask additional questions to explore related topics, depending on how the conversation evolves [48].

The interview was constructed using Social Cognitive Career Theory as a foundation [37]. Interview questions were constructed for each of the four SCCT components using a range of prior research that had also used this theory as a foundation [13, 16, 34, 46, 52, 59, 66]. As a result, 32 questions were identified, 10 exploring prior experience, 5 on social support, 6 on outcome expectation, 3 on self-efficacy, and 8 questions on related topics. The study was given university ethics approval in September 2017[1].

The prior experience questions explored: favourite subject at school; when subjects first used a computer and for what purpose; aspects of CS studied at school; what aspects were enjoyable or not; class environment for males and females; any programming experience; view on the importance of studying CS at school; how school experience influences the choice to study CS at university.

The social support questions explored: sources of encouragement to study CS; influential figures that may have inspired the choice to study CS; the role of parents, teachers counsellors and school in the choice; differences between male and female in terms of support.

The outcome expectation questions explored: expectations prior to studying CS; expectations now; career expectations; expectations after graduation; the influence of expectations on the choice to study CS; whether CS-related careers are attractive to females.

The self-efficacy questions explored: perceived ability to study CS; programming and problem solving skills; thoughts on the importance of programming and problem solving skills.

Other questions explored: CS student characteristics; society perceptions; what can be done to attract more females into CS; when it was decided to study CS; why chose to study CS; biggest influence in choice.

Subjects were asked their name, nationality, gender and to describe the type of school that they attended prior to university. Subjects were also told that interviews would be recorded and that all data would be anonymised - their names would never be recorded with their data. Throughout this paper subjects are referred to by their subject number and gender e.g. P16(F) represents subject number 16 who is female.

3.3 Pilot Study

At the start of the research, the interview questions and process were tested in a small pilot study with two subjects. This was to ensure that the interview process ran smoothly, to check that none of the questions appeared to cause difficulty and to get an idea of the time taken to complete an interview. No major issues were

---

[1] The final set of survey questions is openly available at: http://dx.doi.org/10.15129/7c80a42a-9b70-4d60-a28f-42f75b45e783

encountered in this pilot. The estimated interview time of 30 minutes came from this stage. As there were no major issues, the data from these subjects are included in the final results.

3.4 Subjects

Seventeen subjects participated in the interviews, 11 female (F), 5 male (M) and 1 gender-neutral (Mx). The students were all at varying stages of a Computer Science (or CS-related) undergraduate degree at one of three Scottish universities – Strathclyde (3M, 6F, 1Mx), Stirling (1M, 2F) and Edinburgh (1M, 3F). In order to obtain insights from CS students at different stages of their degree, subjects from all years of undergraduate study were interviewed.

The subjects had a range of backgrounds prior to university, both in terms of type of education and the country of education. Although all the interviews took place at Scottish universities, seven of the subjects were educated at schools outside of Scotland (2 England, 2 Spain, 1 Italy, 1 Latvia, 1 India). Furthermore, the type of schools varied – the majority of subjects were educated at state schools but five were educated at fee-paying schools. One subject attended a female-only school.

Subjects were obtained by sending an email to student mailing lists, it requested participation and told them the purpose of the interview. The email stated that the researchers were particularly keen to interview female subjects. Subjects were told that the interview would last approximately 30 minutes, that it had ethics approval and that their names would not be associated with their interview responses. Subject were all given a £5 shopping voucher as compensation for their time.

4 DATA ANALYSIS

A content analysis approach was using in this study to analyse the data. Content analysis is "… the intellectual process of categorizing qualitative textual data into clusters of similar entities, or conceptual categories, to identify consistent patterns and relationships between variables or themes" [32]. According to Elo and Kyngäs [22] content analysis has three stages: preparing the data, organizing the data into categories and subcategories, and reporting the findings.

The data preparation stage consisted of transcribing the recorded interviews. The transcription of one interview generated about 10 pages of data. Categorisation of data was done using NVivo [1]. Transcripts were read carefully within NVivo and content categorized according to its relevance to SCCT constructs. As well as the categories included in SCCT, two further were identified – 'Perceptions' and 'Suggestions' – which were used for potentially interesting content that did not appear to belong in the SCCT categories. 'Perceptions' related to subjects' perceptions of students who study CS and also their perceptions of society's view of such students. 'Suggestions' captured suggestions made by subjects for schools and universities to improve the uptake of CS degrees, particularly by females. The content in these two additional categories was gathered partly in response to the 'other' questions, beyond SCCT, mentioned in section 3.2.

5 RESULTS

In this section, the main results are reported under the four SCCT categories: prior experience, social support, self-efficacy, outcome expectation; together with additional categories: perceptions and

suggestions. This section reports the data – mostly using counts and example quotations. It is acknowledged that stating the numbers of respondents in qualitative studies such as this is potentially controversial [41]. In the following, the number of subjects making a point is often stated, the intention being to make statements such as 'some' or 'most' more precise [6]. There is no attempt to interpret the significance of the stated numbers.

5.1 Prior Experience

The prior experience category includes formal and informal learning, computing class environment and any internships fulfilled before university. Twelve of the subjects stated that they had studied a computing subject at school. However, there was considerable differences in the computing curricula studied. Two subjects only studied computing at school when they moved from abroad to Scotland in their last year of school.

Three subjects stated that they gained programming experience while at school, P5(F) said: "I had a good teacher who did a lot of extra projects with us, and we got to do a lot of programming, we learned Python as a part of the course in school". Another subject, P13(F), reported a similarly positive school experience: "I had a really good experience when I took Computer Science in my high school. … And all of that encouraged me to take up Computer Science in my university".

Others reported that their computing experience was limited to information technology and the use of applications. P7(F) said: "We just did Microsoft programs, no coding or anything like that, it would just be IT". Similarly, P15(F): "It was mainly just learning what the internet is and internet safety. We didn't really do much actual computing until I came to university".

Three subjects experienced no computing at school. P13(F) said: "I didn't actually take it at school, I thought it was a bit useless to be honest". P17(M) said that they chose to study CS at university despite not studying any at school: "I don't think it would had made much difference for me personally, because I was already interested and knew a fair bit".

Seven of the subjects gained their computing experience outside of school, often using online courses or teaching themselves. P6(M) said: "Outside I used Code Academy to learn Python". In addition, two of the subjects did a computing internship while at school, and then they decided to study CS. P1(F) said: "I went to a company and did a four week internship where I did some computer science stuff in a real working environment. That's when I decided to choose it".

A few subjects commented on the compulsory nature of their school class and its impact on the gender mix. P16(F) said: "It was fine. It was a mandatory class, so it wasn't really male-dominated …". On the other hand, P6(M) stated: "… in Advanced Higher there was only eight of us, all boys".

5.2 Social Support

The social support theme includes encouragement from others, which might influence the student's choice to pursue CS, such as family, peers, teachers and mentors.

Nine of the subjects talked about how their family encouraged them to choose CS. For example, P12(F) said: "My parents were always supportive when I was talking about it. They didn't have to suggest it because I was the first person to come up with it, but they were very happy and excited about the choice." P5(F) said: "When I mentioned it to my parents, they obviously thought yeah, that's *really good, you're talented at that*". P8(F) said: "*My dad didn't want me to do Maths and he suggested Computer Science*". Some subjects mentioned their cousins or uncles, for example, P13(F) said: "*My cousin who kind of influenced me in my early years*".

Eight of the subjects stated that they had been influenced by school teachers to pursue CS. For example, P12(F) said: "*I think, in my case, the fact that the teacher had made it sound very interesting and important, it made it a really clear choice for me to go and study Computer Science.*" Some of the subjects said that their computing teachers were their favourite teacher at school. For instance, P1(F): "*I actually really enjoyed the teacher I was with. He was just a really fun teacher to have*". P8(F) mentioned that her Maths teachers suggested the CS degree to her: "*I did ask my Maths teachers in high school that I wanted to do something related to Maths, but not Maths, and not any engineering, and they suggested Computer Science*".

Other sources of social support were friends and internship mentors. P14(M) said that: "*One of my dad's friends, I went to talk to before the university, because he actually works in ... Computer Engineering.*" P17(M) mentioned his friends: "*I have quite a few friends who study and work in computer-related subjects. They told me about what they were learning, so I want to do that*". P1(F) identified the encouragement of a mentor: "*... only through the internship. I was given a mentor who ... really encouraged me to do Computing*".

5.3 Outcome Expectation

The expectation category includes career options, desire to gain knowledge of CS, and to help society. These three expectations were gathered mainly using responses to the questions: What do you expect from studying computer science? What do you expect to do after graduation?

Sixteen of the subjects identified the career options associated with a CS degree. P10(F) said that a CS degree: "*... will help you get a job quick*", while P14(M) mentioned job-variety and salary: "*... there are quite a lot of good, well-paid jobs that are available*". Some of the subjects mentioned the potential to set up your own business, P5(F) said: "*... you can be self-employed, do your own apps, and make your own things*".

Seven of the subjects identified the general value of CS knowledge across a range of subject areas and skills. P11(F) said: "*I think it just gives you very useful skills that really put you ahead in life*".

Six subjects identified helping society as an outcome expectation. P13(F) said: " *...maybe doing* [CS] *benefits society, and maybe discovering something or making something really good which would be beneficial for everyone*".

Eleven of the subjects indicated that they chose to study CS rather than their favourite subject at school due to the perceived career opportunities. This was explored explicitly with the questions on favourite subject at school, and, if it wasn't CS, why they chose to study CS instead. For example, P3(M) said: "*I didn't see a clear career path with history*". Also, P5(F) said: "*There's plenty of jobs available in it. I'm quite lucky that I enjoy Computing rather than Art, because Art is a lot harder to get a job in at the end*".

Interestingly, nine of the subjects indicated that they planned to continue to postgraduate study after completing their first degree in a CS-related subject.

5.4 Self-Efficacy

The self-efficacy category includes subjects' opinion of their abilities, skills, verbal persuasion and emotions [5].

Twelve of the subjects said that they had a good background in computing and mathematics, and indicated a confidence in their ability and skills to study CS. P13(F) said: "*Before university, I could do programming in C++. I could do a bit of SQL, and Mathematics was one of my main subjects in high school, I could do a lot of problem solving as well, so I am quite confident actually in my ability*". P12(F) stated that: "*I had very little of a Computing background, but I really enjoyed Maths, I did a few Maths competitions, which are purely based on problem solving. I feel more confident about the Computing part*". P14(M) said: "*I had a Maths background, which was quite useful coming into this, I'm gaining confidence in myself as I go along*".

Five female subjects expressed a lack of confidence. Some were in terms of their perceived mathematical ability. P1(F) said: "*The only downside for me is just the maths*". P16(F) said: "*My confidence in my maths ability kind of hinders me*". Another two expressed more general concerns. P2(F) said: "*I'm not confident, I'm struggling. It's not easy, I wouldn't say I have skills, I'm on my way to gaining skills*". Another who came from abroad P8(F) said: "*I didn't have it at school. And most people who live here had it at school and it was a normal subject. So I'm not very confident in my ability.*"

Another of the self-efficacy aspects is verbal persuasion. This is the support and motivations provided by individuals or institutions. P6(M) stated that they had a self-encouragement: "*I think when I started doing programming for real, it was essentially oh wait, I'm actually okay at this. I would quite like to do stuff like this for my career*". P17(M) said: "*You see the results that you're getting and that either encourages you or discourages you. And because I've got good results, it's encouraging me*". Other subjects identified support from others, such as the university. Another P9(Mx) mentioned parents: "*My parents always told me I was good at it*". P5(F) mentioned other people: "*I didn't really realise it was a strength how much I was enjoying it until other people actually said you're really good at this...*".

Also related to self-efficacy is the positive or negative emotions expressed by a subject based on their feelings and experiences from studying CS. Subjects expressed a wide range of emotions including: 'good', 'great', 'challenge', 'happy', and 'stressed'.

P2(F) mentioned: "*My experience in high school, it made me scared of Computer Science*". P8(F) said: "*It makes me feel different, because I'm a woman doing Computer Science, ... But it also makes me feel interesting, in a way, since again I'm a woman but I enjoy the subject*". When discussing her feelings, P1(F) said: "*I was feeling a bit stressed. And I was angry because I was like "am I not good enough to do this course"? It's kind of I feel stressed, and then someone explains and then I feel better*". P11(F) identified a range of emotions: "*... sometimes empowered, sometimes it's a struggle for me. I think it's a hard degree. When you compare it to other degrees. But at the same time, I'm quite happy because it gives me so many possibilities. So in that sense I feel very lucky*".

Three of the subjects associated challenge with the study of a CS degree, often in a positive sense. For example, P13(F) said: "*... sometimes I'm tired. But I'm never frustrated, I'm never sad that I'm doing it because it makes me feel happy. So I feel challenged, I take the challenge positively*". Another P5(F) said: "*Challenged, a lot of* the time ... And that does make me motivated to do more and do better". Three of the subjects related their enjoyment in creating and building new things to their study of CS. P4(M) said "My passion was driven by the love of creation". P5(F) said: "I really enjoyed doing the programming, and building my own things".

A number of subjects suggested that it was important to have certain passions and skills such as problem solving when choosing to study CS. P10(F) said: "I think if you're good at problem solving then you would like CS or Maths, because they're strongly connected. If you like programming you should consider CS". P5(F) said "I think some people are put off by the sound of problem solving, because they think of Maths and kind of difficult things". However, other subjects argued that some skills are not essential before studying CS. P5(F) reported "A lot of people are put off by a lack of programming knowledge, and I think if they understood that you just need to start with an ability to learn and understand things, then you can really do quite well in a way".

5.5 Perceptions

The perceptions category is not part of the SCCT model. This category was introduced as a result of subjects' responses to questions such as: How are CS students perceived by society in general? What do other people think are the characteristics of CS students? Do you think a CS major is a male dominated major? This category is potentially important since perceptions about students who study CS may influence the choice to study the subject.

There were a range of positive and negative words used by the subjects about the characteristics of CS students, such as 'smart', 'shy' and 'nerd'. Nine of the subjects suggested characteristics associated with being non-social. P13(F) described CS students as "People who don't really go out and talk much, and just stay inside their houses or their labs and stare at their computer screens and aren't really sociable". P2(F) stated: "... socially not very adept". Six of the subjects used the words "nerd" or "shy", while the word "geek" was used by three of the subjects.

Three of the subjects mentioned that CS students are mostly male. P1(F) said that "I think most people would automatically think it has to be a man. Even though there are girls". Other characteristics included "... playing lots of video games" P11(F), "... eating unhealthy things" P17(M), and "... if you have long hair and you are male, you are probably into computing" P4(M).

On the contrary, a few subjects associated quite positive characteristics with CS students. For example, P2(F) said: "I just see them as very smart and sort of like wealthy people", and P16(F) described them as: "... very analytical", and "... over-achievers".

The perceptions of family and society were also identified. P11(F) talked about families who have a negative attitude toward CS "In my case, my parents maybe wanted me to be more maths, and be a teacher, or study maybe Biology ... Computer Science was never something that was mentioned". P12(F) said: "Lots of parents see Computer Science as a very boring job ... I have lots of my friends (girls) whose parents would never let them do Computing Science because they think it's a very guy job".

Some of the subjects mentioned other STEM fields of study. P15(F) said: "I guess Computer Science is sometimes lumped in with Physics, which is mostly male-dominated", P17(M) stated: "I think that's the way all over the world. It's called STEM subjects. Historically and now male-dominated even though it has been slowly attracting more women".

Some subjects suggested that females were more likely to be encouraged to study business subjects. P10(F) said: "Most girls I think do business". P1(F) stated: "In my school, I don't know why, but a lot of girls were encouraged to do admin, which is much easier than Computing".

A number of female subjects thought that many females do not choose to pursue CS because it is a male-dominated subject. P2(F) said: "Maybe it's not very attractive for women who do not want to be among guys". P11(F) also mentioned: "One thing that would discourage me from studying CS would be thinking that I would be surrounded mostly by males ... as a young girl, that would be very discouraging".

Some of the subjects mentioned societal bias or stereotypes associated with females studying CS. For example, P17(M) stated: "There are stereotypes regarding Computing, that it's a man's subject and women should not do it, even though Ada Lovelace was the first programmer ever ... So personally I don't have any biases or preferences, as long as you're good at the subject". Also, P2(F) said: "More guys study it. I think because guys are more encouraged to do it. ... And girls are like go and design some clothes or go and learn how to do make-up. Or psychology that's for you". P5(F) pointed out: "I'm happy to say that in my class it's roughly half split, and we're all as equally knowledgeable as each other, and there's no real bias in that regard. But I think in wider society as a whole, especially in kind of the old guard of Computer Science there's still a bit of a stereotype and a bias".

Finally, P7(F) mentioned the role of the media saying: "I think just media and marketing, just having a very even spread and just not discriminating over gender whatsoever. Which is a bit tricky, because obviously in a male dominated field, there are just going to be more men to take photos of".

5.6 Suggestions

A final category that emerged from the data was suggestions by subjects about how to attract more female students to study CS at university. These include suggestions for both schools and for universities themselves.

The suggestions for schools included thoughts on how to prepare students to study CS and how to make them think about CS as a potential degree to study. Five subjects suggested that the computing subject taught at school needs to become more practical. P10(F) said: "I think they need to make it more practical, have more coding, rather than a textbook which tells you the file size, or a picture".

Six subjects said that computing at school should be seen as more important, even making it compulsory. P15(F) mentioned: "I would probably say, encourage people to take it at Standard Grade at least. Because for us, it wasn't compulsory ... I didn't realise the importance of computers".

Five subjects said that there should be more visits, talks and events about CS. P2(F) stated: "Send girls who are doing Computer Science. Inspiring girls. I'm going to say the same about female Computer Science teachers, because that worked very well for me".

P4(M) suggested more exposure at an early age might help address gender imbalance: "I think that making computing more accessible to students of a young age, could be one way, since it would prevent early age judgement from different sexes to other sexes".

The final sub-category consisted of suggestions for universities to attract more females to study CS. Nine subjects suggested more visits and talks from females working in CS to the schools, especially potential role models. P8(F) explained her experience as: "*Some people from the university came to my school to give talks about CS. They were telling people what their project was for the last year and showing them how they built it. And I thought it was quite interesting, and other people as well thought that it's something they would like to do*". Also, P15(F), said: "*I suppose there could be more female role models in CS ... because most people you see who you generally associate with being good at CS are male*".

Finally, six subjects mentioned more promotion and advertising of CS as a degree. P16(F) stated: "*... I don't really think Computer Science is really well pushed. I think they tend to push the more popular subjects ...*". Also P6(M) suggested: "*Perhaps having special female-specific events, like having a women-only open day ...*".

6 DISCUSSION AND IMPLICATIONS

This section aims to draw out the main findings from the above results, together with their implications, and to relate them to prior work.

6.1 Prior Experience

The findings show that most of the subjects studied a computing subject at school but the role and influence of computing at school seems complicated. The computing curricula seems focused mainly on computer usage and applications, and does not appear to be a significant factor in the decision of subjects to pursue a CS degree. A few subjects did identify good experiences, focusing on programming and problem solving, aided by good teachers. Many subjects had influential experiences outside of school via online self-learning and two subjects were influenced by their internships.

These findings are similar to those of Varma [59] and Buzzetto-More et al. [11] who found only a small percentage of CS and engineering students believed that their high school computing courses prepared them for a CS degree. Some of these subjects mentioned that their informal learning influenced them to pursue the CS degree. Nugent et al. [44] also found that a youth summer robotics camp helped influence students to choose to study CS.

Two female subjects changed their choice of degree to CS after experiencing introductory programming classes in their original degree. Four of the subjects chose to pursue a CS degree despite not studying CS at school. Numerous subjects expressed an interest in mathematics and problem solving at school and saw a CS degree as a way to further this interest. In their study of students in India, Hewner and Mishra [31] also found an association between an interest in mathematics and choosing to study CS.

6.2 Social Support

The findings highlight the important role that social support played for the subjects – the support of family, teachers, friends and mentors. This was particularly true for female subjects. This finding is consistent with the work of Teague [57] who found that the primary factor for females choosing computing was the encouragement they received. It is also supported by previous studies that found the support of parents and family members to be important [19, 40, 58]. Some of the subjects in this study stated that their parents and teachers observed their enjoyment of computing and therefore encouraged their pursuit of a CS career.

The finding here that some female subjects were encouraged by their teachers differs from the findings of Varma [59] who found that teachers rarely encouraged female students to choose a CS degree – in contrast to male students who were encouraged. Similarly, Kahle and Schmidt [33] concluded that: "*It appears that most women are not encouraged by others to pursue a computer science career*". Beyer and Haller [8] highlighted the importance of female computing teachers to influence female students to pursue CS, but in this study, there did not appear to be a clear influence of teacher gender on student choice.

6.3 Outcome Expectation

Another finding was the importance of career path for almost all the subjects. However, career path was not just concerned with the prospective job, but the value of a CS education for general careers and also the potential to help society using CS-related knowledge and skills. The potential career path seemed to attract many subjects whose favourite subjects were different from computing at school.

The issues raised in this study only partially fit with Bandura's [5] three categories of outcome expectation: physical (e.g. money), social approval (e.g. social position) and self-satisfaction outcomes. Career options may be partially influenced by money but also job satisfaction. Helping society is closely related to societal approval, though altruistic individuals are not necessarily driven by approval. Gaining knowledge of CS might be motivated by future financial or societal rewards. Margolis and Fisher [40] found that many females chose a CS degree because of the potential to apply their skills and knowledge in related fields to the benefit of society.

The majority of subjects mentioned the availability and variety of CS-related jobs, as well as the pay. This finding is similar to those of Hewner and Mishra [31] and Yasuhara [65]. Some subjects said that they chose to study CS rather than their favourite subjects at school, such as art or history, due to the associated career paths. Some subjects mentioned that they were drawn to the practical side of CS, as opposed to a theoretical science. Teague [57] previously found that female students were attracted to CS by the practical side of computing.

6.4 Self-efficacy

Self-efficacy is concerned with individuals' judgement of their abilities and potential. Most of the subjects expressed confidence in their ability to study CS - some of this confidence may stem from their background and experience in maths and computing. However, some of the females subjects did express a lack of confidence in their maths and/or CS ability, in keeping with the prior findings from Google [25]. Related to this, many subjects said that skills in maths, computing and problem solving helped build confidence. Again, social support seemed to play an important role helping to build self-confidence.

Overall, the study found a variety of attitudes towards CS, but the positive attitudes outweigh the negative - this is likely to be a reflection of the fact that all the subjects had chosen to study CS.

6.5 Perceptions

Perceptions was added as a category because there were many interesting points made by subjects that fell outside the original SCCT categories. Perceptions captures subjects' own views of students who study CS and their views on how society in general views them. In keeping with prior work [39, 47, 49, 50, 64], most of the characteristics identified by subjects were rather negative – describing the traditional stereotypical view of CS students as 'geeks' or 'nerds'. However, often a subject would then say that the characteristic did not apply to them self or their colleagues " *... but I don't really follow any of those stereotypes*". Another female subject said: "*I would just say they're normal people like me do Computer Science*". Subjects identified CS students as 'smart' or 'over-achievers'. Some subjects blamed society for these stereotypical perceptions of CS students.

Therefore, an important finding is that subjects recognise that society may still have quite a negative view of the typical CS student, which could potentially be off-putting for females in particular. However, it is important that the subjects themselves do not seem to have that negative viewpoint, generally seeing themselves and their colleagues as 'normal'.

6.6 Suggestions

There were numerous suggestions to help promote CS as a subject at schools, particularly to females, such as: provide early exposure before children start to form a view that it is a male-dominated subject; make it compulsory so both genders take it; make computing at school more practical (programming and problem solving); encourage female visitors to school to promote CS; improve marketing to females; and, emphasise female role models.

Other findings that could encourage increased female participation included: the importance of social support for females; emphasising the potential career paths, especially the value to society; challenging the traditional stereotypes; and, helping to improve self-confidence of females.

7 THREATS TO VALIDITY

There are a number of threats to the validity of this study. Perhaps the most significant is the threat posed by the choice of subjects. Firstly, they all currently study CS so the study does not collect the views of non-CS students. In this study the intention was to gather insights into the reasons why students chose to study CS. Future work could extend the work to investigate why students who might choose to study CS decide not to. The small numbers in the study are a major limitation on the generalisability of the results, as is the fact that the students are all from three Scottish universities. The intention is to broaden the survey with a more widespread, follow-up questionnaire study. Also, the subjects in this study self-selected themselves and may therefore have particular biases and opinions that they were keen to express, quite possibly views that are not representative of typical CS students.

The use of SCCT as a theoretical model on which to base the research is also a threat. Other models such as EVM [20] could be equally valid theoretical bases for the research. SCCT helped identify a wide range of questions on topics that might not otherwise have been explored e.g. on social support and career paths. There were also a number of more general questions at the end of the interview that were intended to identify any additional influences. The fact that later interviews rarely introduced factors not already mentioned in earlier interviews provides some reassurance that the most important factors were discussed.

Finally, an important threat is the approach taken to analysis, which is open to research bias and interpretation. To address this concern the paper documents the data content analysis used and aims to record a traceable route from results, to findings, to conclusions. To try to ensure reliability of transcription the first author checked all transcripts against the original audio recordings. The second and third authors checked the transcripts and the resultant codes to try to ensure consistency in the categorisation process.

8 CONCLUSIONS

This research has used Social Cognitive Career Theory to identify the factors that influence a student to choose to study Computer Science at university. The main findings include that social support was important to subjects, including encouragement from family and teachers, particularly for females. The career paths offered by a CS degree was also a major factor, not just the potential jobs, but also the general value of a CS education and the potential to make useful contributions to society. The stereotypical view of CS students as 'geeks' is still prevalent but is seen as outdated by students themselves. School education appeared to have limited influence on students' decision to study CS, though exposure to problem solving, programming, online self-learning and internships appeared to be important positive influences.

These findings have the potential to help schools and universities make a CS degree more appealing to students, especially to female students. Students and their families should be encouraged to see benefits of an education in CS, especially the breadth of opportunities it offers. More can be done to promote a much more positive view of CS and the students who study it. Much can be done, still, to improve the experiences that students have of CS during their school years. Subjects made numerous suggestions to make CS more attractive to females including: making it compulsory, teaching it earlier, making it more 'practical' involving programming and problem solving, and increasing the visibility of female exemplars and role models.

SCCT was found to be a useful theoretical model on which to base this research study, particularly to help identify the interview topics and questions. As a result, subjects appeared to provide a comprehensive insight into the factors that influenced their choice to study CS. The interview seemed to cover the majority of the factors that subjects considered important - by the end of the interviews it was rare for subjects to identify factors that had not already been discussed. The use of SCCT has led to novel findings on the potential importance of social support and outcome expectancy (career paths) as well as interesting insights into the role of prior experience and self-efficacy.

This study is the first of two phases of research. Future work will use these results to construct an online survey to explore these findings quantitatively with a larger subject base. The same topics are to be investigated with students from a different country and culture. Finally, it would be interesting to broaden the study to include students still at pre-university school and to students who considered the choice of a CS degree at university but instead chose to study a different degree subject.

ACKNOWLEDGMENTS

Amnah Alshahrani acknowledges the funding that she has received from Princess Nourah bint Abdulrahman University. The authors would also like to thank Neil Heatley from Edinburgh University and Carron Shankland from the University of Stirling for helping to identify subjects for the study. The authors are also extremely grateful to the 17 subjects who agreed to participate in this study.

REFERENCES

[1] *NVivo, version 10.* 2014, QSR International.

[2] *Research Briefing looking at gender balance in STEM subjects at School.* September 2015, Scotland Education: http://www.educationscotland.gov.uk/Images/GenderBalanceBriefing_tcm4-869326.pdf.

[3] Alvarado, C. and E. Judson, *Using targeted conferences to recruit women into computer science.* Communications of the ACM, 2014. **57**(3): p. 70-77.

[4] Amelink, C.T. and E.G. Creamer, *Gender differences in elements of the undergraduate experience that influence satisfaction with the engineering major and the intent to pursue engineering as a career.* Journal of Engineering Education, 2010. **99**(1): p. 81-92.

[5] Bandura, A., *Social foundations of thought and action: A social cognitive theory.* 1986: Prentice-Hall, Inc.

[6] Becker, H.S., *Field work evidence.* Sociological work: Method and substance, 1970.

[7] Beyer, S., *Why are women underrepresented in Computer Science? Gender differences in stereotypes, self-efficacy, values, and interests and predictors of future CS course-taking and grades.* Computer Science Education, 2014. **24**(2-3): p. 153-192.

[8] Beyer, S. and S. Haller, *Gender Differences and Intragender Differences in Computer Science Students: are Female CS Majors More Similar to Male CS Majors or Female Nonmajors?* Journal of Women and Minorities in Science and Engineering, 2006. **12**(4).

[9] Bock, S., et al., *Women and minorities in computer science majors: results on barriers from interviews and a survey.* Issues in Information Systems, 2013. **14**(1): p. 143-152.

[10] Brown, N.C.C., et al. *Bringing computer science back into schools: lessons from the UK.* in *Proceeding of the 44th ACM technical symposium on Computer science education.* 2013. ACM.

[11] Buzzetto-More, N.A., O. Ukoha, and N. Rustagi, *Unlocking the barriers to women and minorities in computer science and information systems studies: Results from a multi-methodolical study conducted at two minority serving institutions.* Journal of Information Technology Education: Research, 2010. **9**: p. 115-131.

[12] Chachashvili-Bolotin, S., M. Milner-Bolotin, and S. Lissitsa, *Examination of factors predicting secondary students' interest in tertiary STEM education.* International Journal of Science Education, 2016. **38**(3): p. 366-390.

[13] Chao, S.-H., *Exploring the gender inequity in tertiary computer science courses: influential factors in females' choices in Australia and Taiwan.* 2013, Monash University. Faculty of Education.

[14] Cheryan, S., et al., *Why are some STEM fields more gender balanced than others?* Psychological Bulletin, 2017. **143**(1): p. 1.

[15] Cohoon, J. and W. Aspray, *A critical review of the research on women's participation in postsecondary computing education.* 2006: Mit Press.

[16] De Lara, E. and L.Y. Liu, *Identification, and the Crucial Role of Key Factors that Affect Women's Interest in Computer Science-A Qualitative Study of Women From Sweden, Mexico and India,* in *Department of Computer Science and Engineering.* 2016, University of Gothenburg

[17] Denner, J., et al., *Community College Men and Women: A Test of Three Widely Held Beliefs About Who Pursues Computer Science.* Community College Review,SAGE 2014. **42**(4): p. 342-362.

[18] Denner, J., L. Werner, and L. O'Connor, *Women in Community College: Factors Related to Intentions to Pursue Computer Science.* NASPA Journal About Women in Higher Education, 2015. **8**(2): p. 156-171.

[19] DuBow, W., J. Weidler-Lewis, and A. Kaminsky. *Multiple factors converge to influence women's persistence in computing: A qualitative analysis of persisters and nonpersisters.* in *Research on Equity and Sustained Participation in Engineering, Computing, and Technology (RESPECT), 2016.* 2016. IEEE.

[20] Eccles, J., et al., *& Midgley, C.(1983). Expectancies, values and academic behaviors.* Achievement and achievement motivation: p. 75-146.

[21] El-Bahey, R. and A. Zeid. *Women in computing A case study about Kuwait.* in *2013 IEEE Frontiers in Education Conference (FIE).* 2013. IEEE.

[22] Elo, S. and H. Kyngäs, *The qualitative content analysis process.* Journal of advanced nursing, 2008. **62**(1): p. 107-115.

[23] Fan, T.-S. and Y.-C. Li, *Gender issues and computers: college computer science education in Taiwan.* Computers & Education, 2005. **44**(3): p. 285-300.

[24] Gharibyan, H. and S. Gunsaulus, *Gender gap in computer science does not exist in one former soviet republic: results of a study.* ACM SIGCSE Bulletin, 2006. **38**(3): p. 222-226.

[25] Google, *Women Who Choose Computer Science _ What Really Matters The Critical Role of Encouragement and Exposure.* 2014.

[26] Google. *Images of Computer Science: Perceptions Among Students, Parents and Educators in the U.S.* 2015; Available from: https://services.google.com/fh/files/misc/images-of-computer-science-report.pdf.

[27] Graham, H., et al., *Women in ICT and Digital Technologies: An investigation of the barriers to women entering, staying, and progressing in the sector, and actions to ameliorate this - Executive Summary.* 2016: Edinburgh: Skills Development Scotland.

[28] He, J. and L.A. Freeman, *Are men more technology-oriented than women? The role of gender on the development of general computer self-efficacy of college students.* Journal of Information Systems Education, 2010. **21**(2): p. 203.

[29] He, J. and L.A. Freeman, *Understanding the formation of general computer self-efficacy.* Communications of the Association for Information Systems, 2010. **26**(1): p. 12.

[30] Heinze, N. and Q. Hu, *Why college undergraduates choose IT: a multi-theoretical perspective.* European Journal of Information Systems, 2009. **18**(5): p. 462-475.

[31] Hewner, M. and S. Mishra. *When Everyone Knows CS is the Best Major: Decisions about CS in an Indian context.* in *Proceedings of the 2016 ACM Conference on International Computing Education Research.* 2016. ACM.

[32] Julien, H., *Content analysis.* The SAGE encyclopedia of qualitative research methods, 2008. **2**: p. 120-122.

[33] Kahle, J. and G. Schmidt, *Reasons women pursue a computer science career: perspectives of women from a mid-sized institution.* Journal of Computing Sciences in Colleges, 2004. **19**(4): p. 78-89.

[34] Lang, C., *Factors that shape student decision-making related to Information Technology study and career choices: a gendered analysis,* in *Centre for the Study of Higher Education.* 2007, University of Melbourne.

[35] Laosethakul, K. and T. Leingpibul, *Why females do not choose computing? A lesson learned from China.* Multicultural Education & Technology Journal, 2010. **4**(3): p. 173-187.

[36] Lehman, K.J., L.J. Sax, and H.B. Zimmerman, *Women planning to major in computer science: Who are they and what makes them unique?* Computer Science Education, 2017. **26**(4): p. 277-298.

[37] Lent, R.W., S.D. Brown, and G. Hackett, *Toward a unifying social cognitive theory of career and academic interest, choice, and performance.* Journal of vocational behavior, 1994. **45**(1): p. 79-122.

[38] Lent, R.W., et al., *Social cognitive career theory,* in *Career choice and development.* 2002. p. 255-311.

[39] Lewis, C.M., R.E. Anderson, and K. Yasuhara. *I Don't Code All Day: Fitting in Computer Science When the Stereotypes Don't Fit.* in *Proceedings of the 2016 ACM Conference on International Computing Education Research.* 2016. ACM.

[40] Margolis, J. and A. Fisher, *Unlocking the clubhouse: Women in computing.* 2003: MIT press.

[41] Maxwell, J.A., *Using numbers in qualitative research.* Qualitative inquiry, 2010. **16**(6): p. 475-482.

[42] Mirjana, I., et al., *A Note on Performance and Satisfaction of Female Students Studying Computer Science.* Innovation in Teaching and Learning in Information and Computer Sciences, 2010. **9**(1): p. 32-41.

[43] Mishkin, H., et al., *Career Choice of Undergraduate Engineering Students.* Procedia-Social and Behavioral Sciences, 2016. **228**: p. 222-228.

[44] Nugent, G., et al., *A model of factors contributing to STEM learning and career orientation.* International Journal of Science Education, 2015. **37**(7): p. 1067-1088.

[45] Pappas, I.O., et al. *Gender Differences in Computer Science Education: Lessons Learnt from an Empirical Study at NTNU.* in *NIK.* 2016.

[46] Patterson Hazley, M., *Successful female students in undergraduate Computer Science and Computer Engineering: Motivation, self-regulation, and qualitative characteristics.* 2016, University of Nebraska-Lincoln, College of Education and Human Sciences.

[47] Powell, R.M. *Improving the persistence of first-year undergraduate women in computer science.* in *ACM SIGCSE Bulletin.* 2008. ACM.

[48] Robson, C., *Real world research.* 2nd. Edition. Blackwell Publishing. Malden, 2002.

[49] Rommes, E., et al., *'I'm not Interested in Computers': Gender-based occupational choices of adolescents.* Information, Community and Society, 2007. **10**(3): p. 299-319.

[50] Sáinz, M. and M. López-Sáez, *Gender differences in computer attitudes and the choice of technology-related occupations in a sample of secondary students in Spain.* Computers & Education, 2010. **54**(2): p. 578-587.

[51] Schulte, C. and M. Knobelsdorf. *Attitudes towards computer science-computing experiences as a starting point and barrier to computer science.* in *Proceedings of the third international workshop on Computing education research.* 2007. ACM.

[52] Shah, P., *Cultural influences and new programs affecting women in Technology.* 2011.

[53] Sheu, H.-B. and J.J. Bordon, *SCCT research in the international context: Empirical evidence, future directions, and practical implications.* Journal of Career Assessment, SAGE, 2017.

[54] Shoffner, M.F., et al., *A qualitative exploration of the STEM career-related outcome expectations of young adolescents.* Journal of Career Development, 2015. **42**(2): p. 102-116.

[55] Sinclair, J. and S. Kalvala, *Exploring societal factors affecting the experience and engagement of first year female computer science undergraduates.* 2015: p. 107-116.

[56] Taylor, H.G. and L.C. Mounfield, *Exploration of the relationship between prior computing experience and gender on success in college computer science.* Journal of educational computing research, 1994. **11**(4): p. 291-306.

[57] Teague, J., *Women in computing: What brings them to it, what keeps them in it?* ACM SIGCSE Bulletin, 2002. **34**(2): p. 147-158.

[58] Tillberg, H.K. and J.M. Cohoon, *Attaching women to the CS major.* Frontiers: a journal of women studies, 2005. **26**(1): p. 126-140.

[59] Varma, R., *Exposure, Training, and Environment: Women's Participation in Computing Education in the United States and India.* Journal of Women and Minorities in Science and Engineering, 2009. **15**(3).

[60] Varma, R., *Why so few women enroll in computing? Gender and ethnic differences in students' perception.* Computer Science Education, 2010. **20**(4): p. 301-316.

[61] Wang, J., et al., *Gender Differences in Factors Influencing Pursuit of Computer Science and Related Fields.* 2015: p. 117-122.

[62] Whitecraft, M.A. and W.M. Williams, *Why aren't more women in computer science.* Making software: What really works, and why we believe it, 2010: p. 221-238.

[63] Wilson, B.C., *A Study of Factors Promoting Success in Computer Science Including Gender Differences.* Computer Science Education, 2010. **12**(1-2): p. 141-164.

[64] Wong, B., *'I'm good, but not that good': digitally-skilled young people's identity in computing.* Computer Science Education, 2016. **26**(4): p. 299-317.

[65] Yasuhara, K. *Choosing computer science: Women at the start of the undergraduate pipeline.* in *Proceedings of the American Society for Engineering Education Annual Conference.* 2005.

[66] Zeldin, A.L., S.L. Britner, and F. Pajares, *A comparative study of the self-efficacy beliefs of successful men and women in mathematics, science, and technology careers.* Journal of Research in Science Teaching, 2008. **45**(9): p. 1036-1058.

How Mother and Father Support Affect Youths' Interest in Computer Science

Jody Clarke-Midura
Utah State University
2830 Old Main Hill
Logan, Utah 43017-6221
jody.clarke@usu.edu

Frederick J. Poole
Utah State University
2830 Old Main Hill2
Logan, Utah 43017-6221
frederick.poole@usu.edu

Katarina Pantic
Utah State University
2830 Old Main Hill
Logan, Utah 43017-6221
katarina.pantic@aggiemail.usu.edu

Chongning Sun
Utah State University
2830 Old Main Hill2
Logan, Utah 43017-6221
vincent.sun@aggiemail.usu.edu

Vicki Allan
Utah State University
4205 Old Main Hill2
Logan, Utah 43017-6221
vicki.allan@usu.edu

ABSTRACT

Parental support is a predictor of children's career interest and aspirations. However, mother and father support affects youth career choices differently. To understand how perceived mothers' and fathers' support affect career interest in computer science (CS), we developed two path models using both mother and father support gains to predict youths' interest in CS. We hypothesized that perceived father's and mother's support would relate to youths' interest in CS via youths' perception of CS utility value as a mediator. We found that both mother and father support leads to interest in CS. However, father support was found to affect CS interest via the mediator utility-value beliefs. To provide explanations for these differences we used student interview data to explore how participants in our study perceived parental support.

CCS CONCEPTS

• **Applied computing** → **Education**; *Computer-assisted instruction*;

KEYWORDS

Father support, mother support, computer science, career interest, middle school

ACM Reference format:
Jody Clarke-Midura, Frederick J. Poole, Katarina Pantic, Chongning Sun, and Vicki Allan. 2018. How Mother and Father Support Affect Youths' Interest in Computer Science. In *Proceedings of 2018 International Computing Education Research Conference, Espoo, Finland, August 13–15, 2018 (ICER '18),* 8 pages.
https://doi.org/10.1145/3230977.3231003

1 INTRODUCTION

Parental support has consistently been found to be a predictor of career interest and aspirations for youth [22, 32, 33, 38]. However, simply investigating parental support as an umbrella construct for both mother's and father's support is problematic because individual parental contributions and their effects are not taken into account. Previous research has found that the effectiveness of parental support on academic behavior depends on the gender of both parent and child [1, 12, 33]. While there is research that shows that mothers and fathers influence career choices differently, there is a dearth of research on how their support affects youth interest in computer science (CS). This is relevant because increasing workforce demands in CS industries have highlighted the need for more research on how to best recruit future computer scientists, particularly female computer scientists, who are currently underrepresented in the field [2, 4, 30]. The purpose of this study was to explore both direct and indirect pathways linking perceived mother and father support to interest in CS, and to investigate any potential differences in these pathways.

According to Eccles' [10, 40] expectancy-value theory, academic behaviors, such as performance, perseverance, and choice are directly affected by expectancy and task-value beliefs. In this model, expectancy beliefs refer to one's beliefs about how well they will do in a task, while task-value beliefs refer to the degree in which a) one perceives the task as enjoyable (intrinsic interest), b) the task affirms one's personal values (attainment value), c) one perceives the task as useful (utility value), and d) the cost of engaging in the activity [10, 11]. Both expectancy and task-value beliefs are said to be influenced by several environmental factors, such as, societal and cultural values, family demographics, and support from teachers, peers, and parents among others. However, of interest in this study is how perceived parental support affects perceptions of CS utility value, and subsequently CS interest. We argue that the relationship between parental support and utility value is particularly important because, as Harackiewicz et al. [19] state, it may be easier for parents to influence perceived utility value than it would be to influence other parts of the task value construct. In other words, by simply having a conversation about the value of CS and the future opportunities afforded by a CS degree, parents may be able to improve their child's perception of CS utility value. Changing one's perception of intrinsic interest, attainment value, or self-efficacy, on the other hand, may be much more complex.

For the past three years, we have been investigating the effects of one-week, summer App camps on middle school-aged youths' interest in CS. One of the unique aspects of our camp is that campers are given an android device to build their Apps on and are encouraged to take their phones home to show their app designs to their family members. Through exchanges with campers and parents, we came to understand that the phones may have been acting as a mediator between campers and their parents for conversations about CS as a useful skill and as a career. Such insights sparked an interest in the effect of perceived parental support on campers' perceptions of CS utility value and conversely, on CS interest. However, given prior research on the unique experiences and support that mothers and fathers provide their children with [11], we argue that it is important to investigate these effects for both mother and father independently. In the following section, we will first situate this study in the current literature by reviewing studies that have investigated the effect of CS interventions on middle school participants' interest in CS. In addition, we will review past studies that have examined not only the effects of parental support on career interest, but also how mothers and fathers uniquely influence their child's career choices.

2 BACKGROUND LITERATURE

2.1 Middle School Youth and Computer Science

Middle school is the developmental level when youth start to make decisions about careers [9, 13, 20]. Consequently, research has shifted toward a focus on how to engage middle school students in CS by using programming environments that are more user-friendly and have the potential to lower the cognitive threshold for novice programmers, such as Scratch [16, 34], Alice [23, 24] and other similar programs. Overall, studies repeatedly found that environments like the ones mentioned above are effective in the acquisition of basic programming skills and concepts [25, 26, 34]. As an example, Meerbaum-Salant, Armoni, and Ben-Ari [28], in their investigation of the effectiveness of Scratch, found that while Scratch was not equally effective for all CS concepts, the program did help middle schoolers learn most of the targeted CS concepts.

Although research has demonstrated the effectiveness of a variety of strategies for increasing middle school-aged youths' understanding of CS concepts, the findings on increasing interest and attitudes towards CS have been mixed. There is some evidence to show that storytelling environments raised the interest of female middle schoolers in CS [23, 24]. In our own research, we found that mentor relatability of near-peer mentors significantly predicted both self-efficacy and interest gains of middle school campers [7]. Other studies, however, provide different results. Mouza et al. [29], for example, investigated both the effectiveness of an after-school CS program using Scratch taught by undergraduate CS majors and the impact of the program on student affect towards CS. The researchers found that while middle schoolers gained knowledge related to CS concepts, there were no significant gains in their feelings and attitudes towards CS. The authors did acknowledge, however, that this was probably because the participants all volunteered to attend the program and thus already held favorable perceptions of CS. Huang et al. [21] attempted to use Plushbots to motivate and increase positive attitudes in middle school students towards CS. Unfortunately, the researchers did not find any growth in student interest or attitudes towards CS. Similarly, while studying a 7-week CS introductory course designed for middle schoolers, Grover, Pea and Cooper [18] did not find a change in student affect towards CS. However, it should be noted that they did report significant gains in participants' knowledge of CS concepts.

One strategy for increasing youth interest in CS may be to elicit parental involvement. Harackiewicz et al. [19] conducted a 15-month intervention in which educational brochures about the importance of mathematics and science in everyday life as well as how to relate such information to children were sent home to parents. They found that children whose parents received the brochures were more likely to take advanced STEM courses in high school. Furthermore, they conducted a path analysis which illustrated that their intervention was associated with an increase in parental STEM utility value beliefs, which was then associated with an increase in student STEM utility value beliefs. They also found that their intervention was associated with more conversations between parents and their children about STEM related careers. The number of conversations reported were associated with student perception of STEM utility value beliefs. These findings suggest that parents play a role in broadening and increasing youth participation in CS related activities. Few studies have looked at how CS interventions affect the relationship between parent and child, particularly the perceptions a child has of parental support when they started to show an interest in CS. Understanding this dynamic is important because, as the following literature will illustrate, perceived parental support and involvement predict youth career choices and interests.

2.2 Parental Support and Career Interest

Several studies in STEM related subjects have investigated the impact of parental support on student career interest and learning experiences [22, 32, 33, 38]. Not only was parental encouragement in math and science found to significantly influence student learning experiences [15], it has also been reported that parental support increased career decidedness and career self-efficacy, which subsequently increased persistence in the area of study [36]. According to Turner and Lapan [38], parent support accounted for as much as 29-43% of the total unique variance in vocational self-efficacy of middle school adolescents. Alliman-Brisset, Turner, and Skovholt [1] further found that the primary predictor of girls' self-efficacy was their parents' emotional support, while for boys it was their career-related modeling. In terms of CS, Denner [9] found that parental support was significantly associated with higher utility value beliefs which was significantly associated with an increase in computing interest. However, it should be noted that such studies have generally examined parental support as one construct combining both mother and father measures. This is problematic given that mother and father support may be perceived and/or manifested differently. The following section reviews literature concerning differences between mother and father support.

2.3 Differences in mother support and father support

Research on the different effects of mother and father support in relation to career aspirations have also been somewhat conflicting. Some studies, for example, seem to suggest that fathers are more important for influencing interest in technical careers and mothers are more important for more social-oriented careers. Gates [17] found that women who studied engineering reported their fathers as influencing their decision (20.1%) more than women who studied education (11.0%). However, the percentage of participants who reported their mothers as influential in their career decision making process was similar for both women who studied engineering (19.4%) and those who studied education (18.1%). Simpson [37] concluded that mothers' influence significantly affected the pursuit of public service degrees, whereas fathers' influence affected the pursuit of a technical degree.

However, other studies reported that mothers are more important regardless of career choice. Otto [31], for example, found that youth went to their mothers more often than their fathers for career advice. Similarly, Bahar and Adiguzel [3] found that mothers were more influential than fathers in developing career aspiration in youth. This may be due to the fact that mothers were also found to be more intensely involved and in a more concrete manner when it comes to career-related plans, as found by Palos and Drobot [33]. Given the importance of parental support for youth interest development and the potential different effects found between mother and father support on youth interest, we set out to understand how perceived parental support influenced camper gains in perceived CS utility value and interest in CS. In the following section, we provide a description of the app camps in which the data was collected. In addition, we highlight key areas that we believe may have had an impact on parents' involvement in the campers' CS interest, and also the campers' perception of parental support.

3 APP CAMPS

During the summer of 2016, we ran three camps on learning how to program using MIT App Inventor for middle school aged youth. Each camp ran for five days, three hours per day (15 hours total). During this time, campers designed and programmed 9 apps. For a full description of the camp and programming activities please see [6]. Campers worked at their own computer and were provided with an android device to use and take home during the camp. Support in these camps was primarily provided by high schoolers who served as near-peer mentors. Keeping the literature in mind, we designed certain activities we thought would have an impact on the campers and their perceptions of parental support. These activities and design choices include the following:

- We let campers take their android device home each night to share designs with family members, or continue working on their apps, which most campers did.
- We showed videos that provided information about what it was like working in the CS industry.
- The Dean of the College of Engineering and CS, who was female, came in and spoke to the campers about the benefits of working in CS and being able to solve world problems.

We believed that by allowing campers to take home their devices, both camper interest in CS and parental interest in their child's apps would become more salient. In other words, by having an artifact (the android device) to illustrate what was accomplished in the camp, the campers and parents have a starting point for conversing about CS as an interest and potentially as a career. Artifacts, both material and conceptual, have long been known to regulate human interactions in addition to mediating human psychological processes [8]. In addition, we believed that by providing more information about CS opportunities via videos and the Dean talk, we would again provide talking points for the campers to engage in with their parents. Considering these ideas, we make three hypotheses about the effect of our camp in the next section.

4 HYPOTHESES

This study was interested in exploring the relationship between parental support, CS utility-value perceptions, and interest in CS for further learning or as a career. With these goals in mind, we formulated the following hypotheses:

Hypothesis 1: We will find significant changes in campers' perception of parental support, interest in CS, and CS utility-value beliefs.

Hypothesis 2: A positive association will be found between increases in perceptions of parental support, gains in interest in CS, and gains in CS utility-value beliefs.

Hypothesis 3: Perceived mother and father support will both manifest itself and influence campers' interest in CS differently.

5 METHODS

5.1 Participants

All the participants in this sample volunteered to attend our camp and came from a rural area in the Intermountain West of the United States. We advertized our camp at local schools and through organizations focused on youth (e.g. 4-H). Our sample consisted of ninety-two youth (46 males and 46 females) aged nine through thirteen (M= 11.6).

5.2 Data Collection Procedures

Data for this study came from two sources: surveys and interviews. Campers completed a survey on their interest and affect towards CS and programming prior to the camp on the first day (pre-) and then again on the last day of camp (post-). Surveys were administered online via Qualtrics survey software. A description of survey design is provided below in the Measures section. In addition to surveys, nineteen campers (4 males, 15 females) across the three camps were randomly selected to be interviewed on the first and last day of camp. Due to limited time and resources, we were not able to interview all the campers. Interview protocols focused on interest, self-efficacy, perceived support, and camp experience. All interviews were audio recorded and transcribed verbatim.

5.3 Measures

The survey (aka Affect Survey) was adapted from several established STEM (science, technology, engineering, and mathematics) affect self-report scales, including Fennema-Sherman Mathematics

Attitude Scale [14], Carrico and Tendhar [5] engineering career choice survey, Vekiri et al. [39] ICT attitude survey, Denner [9] technical curiosity scale, and McLachlan ICT Survey [27]. All items were modified to focus on computer science. The items measured perceived father and mother support in computing, general technical curiosity, goals in seeking a computer science related college degree, self-efficacy and interest in computing, value beliefs toward computing, and outcome expectations for working in a CS related field. All questions were measured on six-point Likert scales (1 = Entirely Disagree, 6 = Entirely Agree). This study was primarily interested in the effect of parental support on interest and as a result only four of the constructs were used for data analysis. Finally, in addition to affect questions, the pre-survey also asked background information such as age, father's highest degree, and mother's highest degree.

5.4 Constructs of Interest

For this paper, there were four constructs of interest: interest in CS, value beliefs, perceived mother/father support and mother/father highest education. The term interest refers to what an individual likes and dislikes, as associated with specific tasks, activities, or objects [5]. Utility-value refers to campers' beliefs about the current and future usefulness of the task [39]. Finally, perception of parental support refers to campers' perception of their mothers or fathers' interest, encouragement, and confidence in their CS ability. It also includes the campers' perception of their mother's or fathers' example as an individual interest in, confidence of, and awareness of the importance of computing [14].

6 RESULTS

Our first hypothesis states that the camp would cause an increase in camper perceptions of father and mother support, interest in CS, and CS utility-value beliefs. We made this hypothesis based on two camp designs. First, in our camp we encouraged campers to take their android devices home and continue to work on their apps. Second, we provided situations for campers to learn about CS opportunities. We believed that both of these strategies would increase either parental involvement in the campers' interest and/or camper perceptions of parental support.

6.1 Wilcoxon Signed-rank Test

Many of the campers reported high scores on all of our constructs of interest in the pre-survey (see table 1). This not only presented a ceiling effect problem, but also resulted in skewed data. Therefore, we used a nonparametric test, the Wilcoxon signed-rank test to determine if there were significant differences in our constructs of interest from pre- to post-intervention.

As Table 1 shows, we only found a significant gain in the perception of mother support and CS interest after the camp. Given that our campers started with a median of 5.40 on utility-value beliefs and 5.00 on father support, it is not surprising that we did not find significant gains for these constructs. The boxplots in Figure 1 illustrate that although there may not have been a significant growth in parental support, there was enough variance to warrant further exploration. Our next hypothesis investigates the effect of these changes in perception of parental support on interest in CS.

	Pre			Post			Wilcoxon Test (Z)
	Med	SD	α	Med	SD	α	
Interest	5.00	0.96	0.88	5.20	1.01	0.93	2.51**
Value Beliefs	5.40	0.88	0.84	5.20	0.91	0.89	0.88
Father Support	5.00	0.98	0.86	5.00	0.90	0.79	1.42
Mother Support	5.00	0.95	0.82	5.20	0.87	0.85	2.98**

Table 1: Wilcoxon-Signed Rank Test

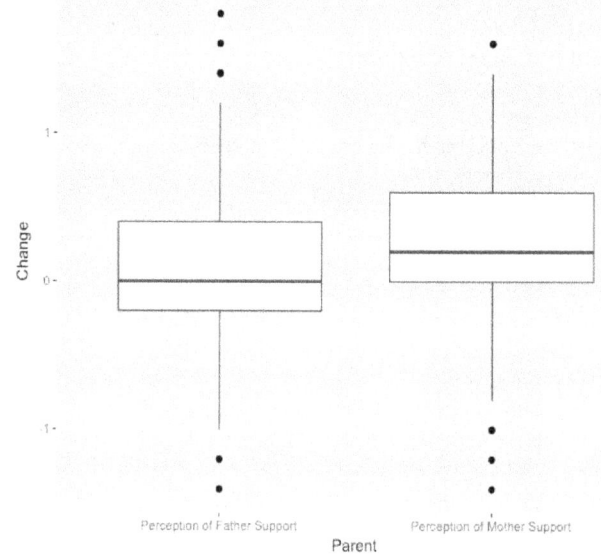

Figure 1: Perception of Father and Mother Support Change.
Note: Boxplots illustrate distribution of change scores. All change scores are on a 1-6 scale and were calculated by subtracting the pre-scores from the post-scores.

Previous literature has found that father and mother support are positively associated with career interest development [32, 38]. However it should be noted that some studies have found that the influence of mother and father support on career interest affects sons and daughters differently [.e.g. 1], especially when the type of career is considered (e.g. social, technical) [.e.g. 37]. Given these findings, we hypothesized that gains in parental support would also be associated with gains in CS interest. To explore our second hypothesis, we first conducted a correlation analysis with our constructs of interest. Figure 2 shows that all constructs were significantly correlated. Please note that for this analysis we used gain scores as our dependent variables because we were interested in exploring what factors predicted these changes.

Next, we conducted a step-wise multiple linear regression analyses in R [35]. To ensure that there were no violations of assumptions of normality, linearity, multicollinearity, and homoscedasticity, preliminary analyses were conducted. In the first step, gender of the camper was added to control for gender differences. In step two, utility-value beliefs, which has been shown to be a strong predictor

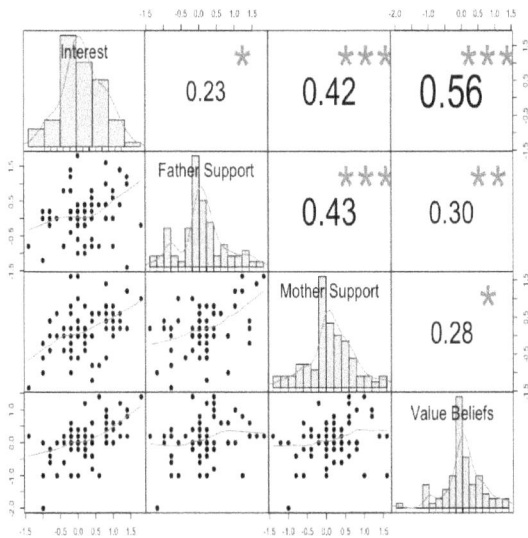

Figure 2: Correlation Matrix with Bivariate Scatter Plots
Note: Variables presented in this figure are gain scores.

Interest Gain Model

	Dependent variable:		
	Interest Gain		
	(1)	(2)	(3)
Gender (Male)	-0.000	0.102	0.131
	(-0.295, 0.295)	(-0.144, 0.348)	(-0.106, 0.368)
Utility Value Gain		0.646^{***}	0.564^{***}
		(0.432, 0.859)	(0.349, 0.779)
Mother Support Gain			0.337^{**}
			(0.117, 0.558)
Father Support Gain			-0.035
			(-0.240, 0.171)
Constant	0.211	0.109	0.048
	(0.002, 0.419)	(-0.067, 0.284)	(-0.126, 0.221)
Model Fit (ChiSq)		.000***	.010*
Observations	76	76	76
R^2	0.000	0.325	0.406
Adjusted R^2	-0.014	0.306	0.372
Residual Std. Error	0.656 (df = 74)	0.543 (df = 73)	0.516 (df = 71)
F Statistic	0.000 (df = 1; 74)	17.558^{***} (df = 2; 73)	12.124^{***} (df = 4; 71)
Note:			$^*p<0.05;\ ^{**}p<0.01;\ ^{***}p<0.001$

Figure 3: Multiple Regression Output

Outcome	Determinant	Unstd.	SE	p	std.
Mother Support	Utility Gain	.303	.118	0.10*	.290
Utility Gain	Interest	.498	.092	.000*	.484
Mother Education	Utility Gain	.049	.055	.364	.096
Mother Support	Interest	.309	.096	.000*	.484

Table 2: Path Analysis Output: Mother Support Model

of career interest was added. Then, in step three both mother and father support were added to the model. Finally, we ran an ANOVA to determine if the added variables in each step significantly increased the amount of variance explained by the model. As can be seen in Figure 3, both Model 2 and Model 3 explained more variance than the previous models. The final model with both mother and father support explains more variance in CS Interest gain than the second model with just gender and utility-value beliefs ($\chi^2(2)$= 2.58, p = .01) and is significant ($F(4,71)$ = 12.12, $p<$ .001), with an R^2 of .372. In other words, the addition of the mother and father support variables accounted for approximately 7.2% more variance than was accounted for by Model 2. However, it should be noted that in this final model, father support was not significant. This will be discussed further when looking at our third hypothesis. For mother support gain, which was significant, a one-unit increase in gains in perception of mother support on a 6-point scale is associated with a .337 increase in CS interest. In other words, as campers' perceptions of mother support increases so does their interest in CS.

Although father support was not significant in our third model (see figure 3), research suggests that it is. Furthermore, given our third hypothesis that mother and father support will be perceived differently and thus have unique impacts on interest, we decided to use a path analysis to further explore the potential mediating effect of utility value for father and mother support on CS interest.

6.2 Path Analyses

To investigate our third hypothesis, we created two path models with mother and father support. Only those participants who completed pre- and post-surveys were included in the analysis. No univariate or multivariate outliers were detected. The univariate and multivariate linearity assumption was tested and satisfied. Gain

scores from pre- to post-surveys were again used for this data analysis. In this path analysis, we examined the mediating effect of utility value for both mother and father support gains. These path analyses were conducted using maximum likelihood estimation (MLE) and were conducted in R [35].

6.2.1 Father Support Model. Results of the path analysis for the father support model with all participants included found that the model fit the data well according to multiple indices of fit: χ^2 (1) = 0.016, p = .899, RMSEA = .000, SRMR= .003, CFI = 1.00, TLI = 1.13. Each of the individual paths were significant and in the hypothesized direction with the exception of the path between father support and CS interest, p = .533 and father's highest education and utility value, p=.174.

6.2.2 Mother Support Model. Results of the path analysis for mother support with all participants found that the model fit the data well according to multiple indices of fit: χ^2 (1) = 0.931, p = .335, RMSEA = .000, SRMR = .022, CFI = 1.00, TLI = 1.00. Each of the individual paths were significant and in the hypothesized direction with the exception of the path between mother's highest education and utility value gain, p = .364.

The path analyses showed a difference between mother and father support in that mother support had both a direct and indirect effect on gains in CS interest, whereas gains in father support only

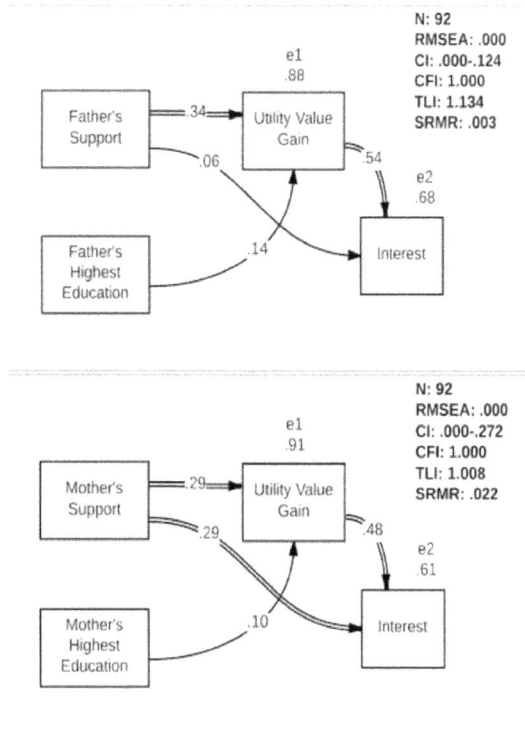

Figure 4: Mother and Father Support Gain Models
Note: All variables, with the exception of highest education, are gain scores. Double lines indicate significant relationships.

Outcome	Determinant	Unstd.	SE	p	std.
Father Support	Utility Gain	.326	.107	0.002*	.341
Utility Gain	Interest	.561	.098	.000*	.545
Father Education	Utility Gain	.069	.051	.174	.141
Father Support	Interest	.059	.095	.533	.060

Table 3: Path Analysis Output: Father Support Model

had an indirect effect via utility value on gains in CS Interest. In other words, gains in camper perception of father support were shown to be significantly associated with gains in utility-value beliefs, which was subsequently associated with gains in CS interest. However, gains in perceived mother support are significantly associated with gains in both utility-value beliefs and CS interest directly. To further understand why this difference exists, we looked to the interview data concerning camper relationships with their parents.

6.3 Interview Data

Our third hypothesis stated that parental support would both be perceived differently by campers and, subsequently, affect camper interest in CS differently. In our path analyses, we found that gains in mother support had a direct influence on gains in camper CS interest whereas gains in father support had an indirect effect on

CS interest gains via gains in utility-value beliefs. We conducted a thematic analysis of nineteen interviews with campers from the three camps to explore how and if camper perceptions of parental support might provide insight into how mother and father support was manifested. Furthermore, we were interested to see if such differences in manifestations could explain the differences found in our path analyses. The thematic analysis revealed four themes from the data: parent as an instructor, parent as a model, emotional/administrative support, and co-learning.

6.3.1 Parent as Instructor. Of the 19 participants interviewed, five campers noted examples of their fathers providing support in the form of instruction, whereas no campers reported such examples of their mothers. In these examples, campers typically reported that their father taught them a programming language or showed them how to build a website or a game. When asked to describe what made her father a computer scientist, a young female participant said, "he makes a lot of websites for his job…and he's pretty…smart…he taught me how to program stuff." This camper went on to explain how her father had helped her make a gummy bear themed website. Four other participants reported that their fathers taught them a programming language such as: Java, Scratch and HTML.

6.3.2 Parent as Model. Of the 19 participants interviewed, six campers noted examples of their fathers providing support in the form of modeling, whereas no campers reported their mothers as a model. In these examples, campers usually reported watching or being aware of their fathers' work involving CS. For example, one female camper noted that when her father programs "he seems like he's having a fun time doing it, so I thought it would be a fun thing to do." Another camper explained how her father influenced her interest in CS by saying, "just like watching him do all that stuff it really interested me because I mean, it requires like, like memory and stuff, and like, you type a lot of stuff if you want to do coding by hand." Other participants simply stated that they see their father programming "all the time" or that they went to their father's work place and "just saw what they did and I thought it was cool." Finally, one participant also noted that she could see herself going into the CS industry, when asked why she said, "my dad is a computer scientist and I know how much it pays."

6.3.3 Emotional and Administrative Support. In terms of emotional and administrative support, ten of the 19 participants reported examples of their mothers providing emotional/administrative support, whereas only four participants reported such support from their fathers. Examples of emotional and administrative support included expressing an interest in the child's interest, driving the child to and from camps, and encouraging the child to learn more. For example, one female camper noted, "my mom mostly gets me involved with the things that can help me learn more." This camper went on to confirm that her mother signed her up for our camp. When asked how her family has shown interest in what she's doing, another camper said, "my mom took me here and every time I come back to the car, she's like what did you do today? I just hand her the phone and I'm like, Go crazy! and she's like Oh yea, this is, this is fun." Similarly, four other campers noted that their mothers asked to see what they did each day after the camp. A few campers also noted that their fathers provided emotional support in the form of showing interest. One female camper said, "my dad kind of encouraged me to learn a little bit more about computers because I'm the most electronic one in the family." Three other campers noted that their father thought their apps were cool.

6.3.4 Parent as a Co-Learner. In the parent as a co-learner theme, two participants noted that their mother acted as a co-learner, whereas no campers reported their fathers in such roles. Parent as a co-learner refers to instances where the parent learns with their child. For example, when one female camper was asked how her mother influenced her perception of computer science she said:

> well my mom she came with me to the university thing, and she was doing really good at the robot thing, then I tried at it and I didn't do too well and that just made me want to do better so that I could be as good as her.

Another camper, when commenting on his past programming experience, recalled learning Scratch with his mother, "like my mom, me and my mom did like, there's like a notebook that you look at and it teaches you stuff…like scratch stuff."

Findings from the interviews seem to suggest that campers saw their mothers as more active participants in their interests. More mothers were reported as encouraging involvement in the CS activities, as facilitating the logistics of such activities, as showing interest in camper achievements, and in some cases as participating in the learning. On the other hand, many campers reported father support as a model. In other words, many campers simply noted how observing their fathers working in the CS industry or having fun with CS-related activities motivated them to learn more. When campers did report father involvement, it was in the role of an instructor. This may explain why fathers only had an indirect effect on CS interest via camper utility-value beliefs. In other words, by seeing their fathers use CS in everyday life, and by receiving hands-on instruction in computing, these campers may be more likely to see the value in CS than other campers. We will further expand on these findings in the following section.

7 DISCUSSION

In this study, we set out to explore the relationship between perceived parental support and youth interest in CS. Specifically, we were interested in investigating how gains in perception of mother and father support affected gains in CS utility-value beliefs and interest. To that end, we hypothesized that mother and father support would affect camper perceptions of CS differently. We found that gains in mother support was significantly associated with gains in both CS utility-value beliefs and interest. Interview data suggest that this may have been due to mothers' active involvement in developing their child's interest by showing their interest in their child's work, encouraging their child to participate in CS activities, and providing logistical support, which is consistent with findings from the Palos and Drobot [33] study. For gains in father support, we found a significant association with gains in CS utility-value beliefs but not in interest. However, gains in utility-value beliefs were significantly associated with gains in CS interest which means that gains in father support had an indirect effect on CS interest but was mediated by gains in CS utility-value beliefs. Interview data

suggest that fathers may have had a direct influence on utility-value beliefs due to camper perceptions of father support and influence. Several campers reported being aware of their fathers working on CS related projects or working in a CS career, which may explain the indirect connection between these two constructs. In addition, some of the campers noted that their father had taught them aspects of a programming language. This may have contributed to utility-value beliefs as it provided an opportunity for campers to see what is possible with CS skills.

This project and our hypotheses were originally inspired by our beliefs that our camps were promoting parental involvement in our campers CS interest. Some earlier research concluded that parental involvement can be effective in fostering children's career planning if the parents are supported by a structured program [32]. To provide structure for the children as well as their parents, we not only provided our campers with information regarding potential CS careers, but we also allowed the campers to take their android devices home, and we encouraged campers to share their projects with their family members. We believed and hoped that these camp design choices would foster conversations between parents about the child's interest in CS, and subsequently, would lead to increased perceptions of parental support. These findings suggest that camps designed to broaden participation in CS should find ways to integrate parental involvement into the curriculum.

8 CONCLUSION, LIMITATIONS, AND FUTURE RESEARCH

Although past research has found positive results for increasing middle schoolers' knowledge of CS concepts, there have been several studies that have reported mixed results in regard to student interest and affect towards CS. This study not only found a significant increase in middle schooler interest in CS, but also identified both mother and father support gains as significant predictors of gains in CS interest. Albeit, gains in father support only had a significant indirect effect on gains in CS interest. Furthermore, by looking at the interview data, we identified potential reasons for these relationships as well as some approaches for involving parents in their child's interest. These findings are encouraging given the current call for recruiting diverse groups of youth into CS fields. However, more research must continue to investigate other approaches for involving parents in the recruitment process. Furthermore, it is important to confirm that such approaches are in fact eliciting the hypothesized effects. Finally, it is also necessary to compare how parental support strategies affect children of different genders, which we hope to focus on in our future research on this project.

There were a few limitations that must be acknowledged for this study. First, we hypothesized that gains in mother and father support were a result of our campers returning home with an android device. However, we were unable to collect data from parents to confirm if this was a factor. Secondly, our sample sizes were not ideal for conducting path analyses, and thus, we were forced to create reduced models. It may have been that a more complicated model could better represent the relationship between parental support and CS interest. However given our sample size we were unable to test this. We plan to combine our current data with future data to further test some of these findings.

ACKNOWLEDGEMENTS

This work was supported by a grant (#1614849) from the National Science Foundation. Any opinions, findings, and conclusions or recommendations expressed in this paper are those of the authors and do not necessarily reflect the views of the National Science Foundation or Utah State University.

REFERENCES

[1] Annette E. Alliman-Brissett, Sherri L. Turner, and Thomas M. Skovholt. 2004. Parent support and African American adolescents' career self-efficacy. *Professional School Counseling* 7, 3 (2004), 124–133.

[2] Catherine Ashcraft, Elizabeth Eger, and Michelle Friend. 2012. *Girls in IT: the facts*. Technical Report. Boulder, CO.

[3] Abdulkadir Bahar and Tufan Adiguzel. 2016. Analysis of Factors Influencing Interest in STEM Career : Comparison between American and Turkish High School ... Analysis of Factors Influencing Interest in STEM Career : Comparison between American and Turkish High School Students with High Ability. *Journal of STEM Education* 17, 3 (2016), 64–69.

[4] Bureau of Labor Statistics. 2015. *Household Data*. Technical Report. 1–10 pages. http://www.bls.gov/Cps/Cpsaat11.Pdf

[5] Cheryl Carrico and Chosang Tendhar. 2012. The Use of the Social Cognitive Career Theory to Predict Engineering Students' Motivation in the Produced Program. In *ASEE Annual Conference and Exposition, Conference Proceedings, 119th ASEE Annual Conference and Exposition*.

[6] Jody Clarke-Midura, Frederick Poole, Katarina Pantic, and Vicki Allan. 2017. Playing Mentor: A New Strategy for Recruiting Young Women into Computer Science. *Journal of Women and Minorities in Science and Engineering* 23, 3 (2017).

[7] Jody Clarke-Midura, Frederick Poole, Katarina Pantic, Megan Hamilton, Chongning Sun, and Vicki Allan. 2018. How Near Peer Mentoring Affects Middle School Mentees. In *Proceedings of the 49th ACM Technical Symposium on Computer Science Education*. Baltimore, Maryland, USA, 664–669.

[8] Michael Cole. 1998. *Cultural psychology: A once and future discipline*. Harvard University Press.

[9] Jill Denner. 2011. What Predicts Middle School Girls' Interest in Computing? *International Journal of Gender Science and Technology* 3, 1 (2011), 53–59.

[10] Jacquelynne Eccles. 2009. Who am I and what am I going to do with my life? Personal and collective identities as motivators of action. *Educational Psychologist* 44, 2 (2009), 78–89.

[11] Jacquelynne S Eccles. 1994. Understanding women's educational and occupational choices: Applying the Eccles et al. Model of Achievement-Related Choices. *Psychology of Women Quarterly* 18 (1994), 585–609.

[12] Jacquelynne S. Eccles. 2015. Gendered Socialization of STEM Interests in the Family. *International Journal of Gender, Science and Technology* 7, 2 (2015), 116–132.

[13] Jacquelynne S Eccles and Rena D Harold. 1993. Parent-school involvement during the early adolescent years. *Teachers College Record* 94, 3 (1993), 568–587. https://doi.org/0161-4681-93/9403/568$1.25/0 arXiv:NIHMS150003

[14] Elizabeth Fennema and Julia A. Sherman. 2017. Mathematics Attitudes Scales : Instruments Designed to Measure Attitudes toward the Learning of Mathematics by Females and Males Author (s): Elizabeth Fennema and Julia A . Sherman Source : Journal for Research in Mathematics Education ,. *Journal for Research in Mathematics Education* 7, 5 (2017), 324–326.

[15] Tamara R. Ferry, Nadya A. Fouad, and Philip L. Smith. 2000. The Role of Family Context in a Social Cognitive Model for Career-Related Choice Behavior: A Math and Science Perspective. *Journal of Vocational Behavior* 57, 3 (2000), 348–364. https://doi.org/10.1006/jvbe.1999.1743

[16] Deborah Fields, Lisa Quirke, Tori Horton, Jason Maughan, Xavier Velasquez, Janell Amely, and Katarina Pantic. 2016. Working toward equity in a constructionist Scratch camp: Lessons learned in applying a studio design model. In *Constructionism in Action*, Arnan Sipitakiat and Nalin Tutiyaphuengprasert (Eds.). Bangkok, Thailand, 291–298.

[17] Janet L. Gates. 2002. *Women's career influences in traditional and nontraditional fields*. Technical Report.

[18] Shuchi Grover, Roy Pea, and Stephen Cooper. 2015. Designing for deeper learning in a blended computer science course for middle school students. *Computer Science Education* 25, 2 (2015), 199–237. https://doi.org/10.1080/08993408.2015.1033142

[19] Judith M. Harackiewicz, Christopher S. Rozek, Chris S. Hulleman, and Janet S. Hyde. 2012. Helping Parents to Motivate Adolescents in Mathematics and Science: An Experimental Test of a Utility-Value Intervention. *Psychological Science* 23, 8 (2012), 899–906. https://doi.org/10.1177/0956797611435530

[20] Nancy E. Hill and Ming Te Wang. 2015. From middle school to college: Developing aspirations, promoting engagement, and indirect pathways from parenting to post high school enrollment. *Developmental Psychology* 51, 2 (2015), 224–235.

https://doi.org/10.1037/a0038367

[21] Yingdan Huang, Jane Meyers, Wendy Dubow, Zhen Wu, and Michael Eisenberg. 2013. Ubiquitous and Mobile Learning in the Digital Age. In *Ubiquitous and Mobile Learning in the Digital Age*, Demetrios G. Sampson, Pedro Isaias, Dirk Ifenthaler, and Michael Spector (Eds.). Springer-Verlag New York, New York, NY, 215–226. https://doi.org/10.1007/978-1-4614-3329-3

[22] Kathleen M. Jodl, Alice Michael, Oksana Malanchuk, Jacquelynne S. Eccles, and Arnold Sameroff. 2001. Parents' Roles in Shaping Early Adolescents' Occupational Aspirations. *Child Development* 72, 4 (2001), 1247–1266. https://doi.org/10.1111/1467-8624.00345

[23] Ciltlin Kelleher and Randy Pausch. 2007. Using storytelling to motivate programming. *COMMUNICATIONS OF THE ACM* 50, 7 (2007), 59–64.

[24] Jordana Kerr, Mary Chou, Reilly Ellis, and Caitlin Kelleher. 2013. Setting the scene: Scaffolding stories to benefit middle school students learning to program. In *2013 IEEE Symposium on Visual Languages and Human Centric Computing*. 95–98. https://doi.org/10.1109/VLHCC.2013.6645250

[25] D Midian Kurland and Roy D Pea. 1985. Children's mental models of recursive LOGO programs. *Journal of Educational Computing Research* 1, 2 (1985), 235–243.

[26] John Maloney, Kylie Peppler, Yasmin B. Kafai, Mitchel Resnick, and Natalie Rusk. 2008. Programming by choice: urban youth learning programming with scratch. In *Proceedings of the 39th SIGCSE technical symposium on Computer science education*. Portland, OR, USA, 367–371. https://doi.org/10.1145/1352135.1352260

[27] Christine McLachlan, Annemieke Craig, and Jo Coldwell. 2010. Student perceptions of ICT: A gendered analysis. In *Proceedings of the Twelfth Australasian Conference on Computing Education*, Vol. 103. Brisbane, Australia, 127–136.

[28] Orni Meerbaum-Salant, Michal Armoni, and Mordechai (Moti) Ben-Ari. 2013. Learning computer science concepts with Scratch. *Computer Science Education* 23, 3 (2013), 239–264. https://doi.org/10.1080/08993408.2013.832022

[29] Chrystalla Mouza, Alison Marzocchi, Yi Cheng Pan, and Lori Pollock. 2016. Development, implementation, and outcomes of an equitable computer science after-school program: Findings from middle-school students. *Journal of Research on Technology in Education* 48, 2 (2016), 84–104. https://doi.org/10.1080/15391523.2016.1146561

[30] National Science Foundation. 2017. *Women, minorities, and persons with disabilities in science and engineering: 2017 Report*. Technical Report. 1–21 pages. https://doi.org/SpecialReportNSF17-310

[31] Luther B Otto. 2000. Youth Perspectives on Parental Career Influence. *Journal of Career Development* 27, 2 (2000), 111–118.

[32] Sylvia Palmer and Larry Cochran. 1988. Parents as Agents of Career Development. *Journal of Counseling Psychology* 35, 1 (1988), 71–76. https://doi.org/10.1037/0022-0167.35.1.71

[33] Ramona Palos and Loredana Drobot. 2010. The impact of family influence on the career choice of adolescents. *Procedia - Social and Behavioral Sciences* 2, 2 (2010), 3407–3411. https://doi.org/10.1016/j.sbspro.2010.03.524

[34] Katarina Pantic, Deborah A. Fields, and Lisa Quirke. 2016. Studying situated learning in a constructionist programming camp. In *Proceedings of the The 15th International Conference on Interaction Design and Children*. Manchester, UK, 428–439. https://doi.org/10.1145/2930674.2930725

[35] R Core Team. 2016. *R: A Language and Environment for Statistical Computing*. R Foundation for Statistical Computing, Vienna, Austria. https://www.R-project.org/

[36] Simon Lloyd D. Restubog, Afryll R. Florentino, and Patrick Raymund James M. Garcia. 2010. The mediating roles of career self-efficacy and career decidedness in the relationship between contextual support and persistence. *Journal of Vocational Behavior* 77, 2 (2010), 186–195. https://doi.org/10.1016/j.jvb.2010.06.005

[37] Jacqueline C. Simpson. 2003. Mom matters: Maternal influence on the choice of academic major. *Sex Roles* 48, 9-10 (2003), 447–460. https://doi.org/10.1023/A:1023530612699

[38] Sherri Turner and Richard T. Lapan. 2002. Career self-efficacy and perceptions of parent support in adolescent career development. (2002), 44–55 pages. https://doi.org/10.1002/j.2161-0045.2002.tb00591.x

[39] Ioanna Vekiri and Anna Chronaki. 2008. Gender issues in technology use: Perceived social support, computer self-efficacy and value beliefs, and computer use beyond school. *Computers and Education* 51, 3 (2008), 1392–1404. https://doi.org/10.1016/j.compedu.2008.01.003

[40] Allan Wigfield and Jacquelynne S Eccles. 2000. Expectancy–value theory of achievement motivation. *Contemporary educational psychology* 25, 1 (2000), 68–81.

"I told you this last time, right?": Re-visiting narratives of STEM education

Sebastian Dziallas
School of Computing
University of Kent
Canterbury, CT2 7NF, United Kingdom
sd485@kent.ac.uk

Sally Fincher
School of Computing
University of Kent
Canterbury, CT2 7NF, United Kingdom
S.A.Fincher@kent.ac.uk

ABSTRACT

The stories we tell ourselves and others – both as individuals and as a community – reflect how we make sense of our lives. Our work using narrative methods has explored how university graduates make sense of their learning experiences and how these fit within their wider learning trajectories. In this paper, we discuss work we conducted with a group of a dozen students who, when first interviewed, were in the second half of their undergraduate education at Olin College of Engineering. All twelve participants were re-interviewed four years later, after they had graduated, using the same narrative protocol that asked them to describe their learning 'life' as if it was a book, and to identify and describe individual chapters of their experience.

The pairs of interviews were analysed with respect to their form and their content. In regard to form, a classification of these repeated stories is derived. Thematic analysis of the content examines a) how students come to study and practice computing and b) the continuing, and changing influence of a university education over time, as students construct an individual sense of coherence.

CCS CONCEPTS

• **Social and professional topics~Computer science education**

KEYWORDS

narrative methods, qualitative research, longitudinal work

ACM Reference format:
Sebastian Dziallas and Sally Fincher. 2018. "I told you this last time, right?": Re-visiting narratives of STEM education. In *Proceedings of 2018 International Computing Education Research Conference (ICER '18). ACM, New York, NY, USA, 9 pages.* https://doi.org/10.1145/3230977.3230989

1 INTRODUCTION

The work we present in this paper was inspired by the concept of *rephotography*, a practice of photographers who capture a picture of a place from the same vantage point, sometimes as much as 100 years apart [5, 14]. The pictures (also called "doubles") are then presented side-by-side, or super-imposed, to expose the passage of time. As Paul Berger writes: "By holding one factor constant – the place, person, or event – these doubles direct our attention toward the time that separates them." [4]

We are similarly interested in changes that occur over time, in students' wider reflections of their learning trajectories and specifically how they incorporate their experience of higher education within that. While photographs are the medium that expose changes in the context of rephotography, we use narratives in our work, as they are an effective way of exploring how students and graduates make sense of their learning experiences [9, 28]. As Mishler observes, "research participants are the historians of their own lives. They tell and retell their stories in variant ways and, thereby, continually revise their identities." [23]

There are few existing longitudinal studies that rely on narratives and, according to McAdams, in 2011 there were "no long-term efforts to trace continuity and change in narrative identity over decades of adult development." [17] Work with college students in the realm of narrative studies has mostly focussed on quantitatively examining the continuity of a variety of themes (such as agency and communion) across repeated elicitations [8, 20]. There are also a few CompEd studies that have examined students' identity development (e.g. [13], [33]), but they generally do not rely on narrative methods. For instance, Peters conducted a phenomenographic study using written reflections with students in two programmes over the course of three years [27]; McCartney and Sanders used semi-structured interviews a longitudinal study with American computing students [21].

In this paper, we are not concerned with "whole" identity – with the sum of what makes up a person – but with participants' "learning life", and with how the stories they tell about their learning experiences change over time. We present two separate parts: The first concentrates on form and identifies the ways in which stories our participants tell about their learning experiences have (or have not) changed. The second focusses on content and explores graduates' reflections of their acquisition and use of disciplinary knowledge within and beyond their undergraduate education.

2 METHODOLOGY

We obtained ethical approval from the Research Ethics Advisory Group of the Faculty of Sciences at the University of Kent and conducted initial interviews with twelve students from Olin College of Engineering who were (with one exception) in the second half of their college education in the summer of 2013. There were seven women and five men among the participants. All participants volunteered by responding to an email solicitation sent to all students entering the third or fourth year of their Olin education; there was no deliberate selection policy (e.g. to obtain a stratified sample or the like). Four years later, the same interviewer re-interviewed all twelve participants (who had by then graduated) using the same prompt. This is an unusually high retention rate for work of this kind.

We use an approach developed by Dan McAdams. He argues that we, as individuals, construct an internal *life story*, which is part of our identity, to make sense of our lives [19]. He elicits these in a structured *life story interview* [18]. We use a modified version of the life story prompt, to focus on participants' learning experiences.

> *I'd like you to think about your learning career, your learning 'life', as if it were a book. Each part of your learning composes a chapter in the book. Certainly the book is unfinished at this point: still, it probably contains a few interesting and well-defined chapters. Please divide your learning 'life' into its major chapters and briefly describe each chapter. You may have as many or as few as you like, but I'd suggest at least 2 or 3 and at most 7 or 8. Think of this as a general table of contents for your book. Please give each chapter a name and describe its overall contents.*

As part of the prompt, participants identified "chapters" in their learning lives. Life-story chapters elicited in this way have "identifiable beginnings and endings" [32] and, according to Steiner et al., "represent relatively stable autobiographical periods governed by overarching themes and goals" [31]. In titling their chapters, some participants simply name locations of their education, such as schools (and, later on, employers), whereas others use more interpretive names. For us, these chapters are a form of *self-signification*, in that participants – rather than us, as researchers – indicate personal significance in the name they choose [29]. In this, they sometimes reveal aspects of an experience that would not otherwise be apparent [9].

In some cases, interviewees did not explicitly name a chapter (for the first interviews, the interviewer was less experienced and did not always press participants to identify chapter titles). However, we can identify segments based on their descriptions, as the beginning and end points of each segment remain clear, even without a title. Where we have named a chapter, this is represented in curly brackets.

At the end of the interview, we then asked participants:

> *Looking back over your learning career, can you discern a common theme or a central message?*

In both series of interviews, the prompt was sent to participants a week in advance, and some used this time to make explicit preparation. We purposely did not revisit the original interviews before the second intervention (and indicated this to the participants, if asked) as we did not want to be primed to expect specific events, or anticipate sequences, nor be tempted to prompt for them. The first interviews lasted between 10 and 40 minutes, while some of the second interviews were more detailed and lasted between 20 and 60 minutes. The interviews were professionally transcribed and we use pseudonyms throughout this paper. Where we have changed details to preserve participants' identity, this is represented in square brackets. In the sections below, we identify quotes with the participants' name and the year of the interview. Identity is preserved across years and between accounts (so "Jane" is always "Jane" whether talking herself or being referred to by someone else).

3 OLIN CONTEXT

We conducted this work with students from Olin College of Engineering, an undergraduate institution in the United States which was founded in 1997 with an explicit mission to transform engineering education [12].

Olin is a highly selective institution with an acceptance rate of around 10% in recent years and uses a two-step admissions process. In addition to the typical college application that involves essays, grades, and letters of recommendation, applicants are selected to visit campus for a mandatory "Candidates' Weekend". As part of this, they meet current students, faculty, and staff. They participate in a design-build challenge designed by current students and take part in individual and group interviews [10]. The purpose of Candidates' Weekend is not to evaluate candidates' technical abilities, but to expose them to the campus community and to assess their cultural fit with the institution. Each year, around 200 candidates are invited and approximately 60% are offered admission.

The college has a total undergraduate population of 350 students and, unusually for an engineering school, is equally gender balanced. All students are required to live on campus and to subscribe to an all-inclusive meal plan; they have access to all buildings and classrooms at all times of the day. Olin does not have academic departments and offers no tenure; faculty are instead hired on renewable, five-year contracts.

Olin offers ABET-accredited degrees in electrical and computer engineering, mechanical engineering, and general engineering. For this latter degree, students can design their own concentration or choose from a number of predefined concentrations, such as computing, design, bioengineering, or robotics. There is significant flexibility surrounding the major declaration: While students are expected to initially declare a major in their sophomore year, they are able to change their degree as late as in their senior year (provided they can fulfil the necessary course requirements).

The curriculum emphasises small, project-based classes and incorporates principles of active learning and interdisciplinary activities [30]. Many courses are taught in studio environments, sometimes by several faculty members as part of a teaching team. Olin aims to introduce real-world engineering activities and team-based learning from early in the curriculum.

All incoming students take four courses in their first term, which are designed to provide immediate hands-on engineering experience. User-centred design also features prominently in the curriculum: "Our curriculum is based on the idea that engineering starts with people – understanding who we're designing for, what they value, and where opportunities to create value exist – and ends with people – appreciating the social context of our work and making a positive difference in the world." [26] *User-Oriented Collaborative Design* is a required course that all students take together in their sophomore year. The curriculum ultimately culminates in a year-long capstone project – either a design project with the goal to address poverty in communities around the world, or one offered and sponsored by a company.

4 ON REPEAT

"Probably most stories are potentially repeatable but not necessarily repeated." [24] We interviewed our participants in 2013 and in 2017 and our first reading of the data was to look at the difference between the interviews. As with re-photographs, we expected to recognize much as the past events would not be different, the participants would still have attended the same schools and been taught by the same teachers. And some within our cohort told recognisably similar stories on both occasions. We call these *stable stories*.

Others, however, followed different patterns. A second pattern we called *compression stories*. As human beings, as we move through time, more recent events are closer, the details are sharper, and they may take greater prominence. Telling a story, then, "… is about a distortion of time, prolonging a few precious moments, skimming a month at a time, entire years, intimating the ending in the beginning, blithely shifting scenes and times and sequences in order to further the plot." [16] We had some in the cohort that displayed this type of difference.

A third pattern we termed *landmark stories*. As time progresses, events that happened a long time ago remain very familiar, and may act as anchors for a particular meaning, or serve a narrative necessity "of course it happened like that". Some participants had such fixed elements in their twin narratives. More difficult to account, are *different stories*: narratives that are so wildly dissimilar that, without external knowledge, one would not know they were from the same person at all. Finally, a valuable – if frustrating – product of the method are *omitted stories*, things told in one interview but not the other.

4.1 Stable Stories

For some participants, the way they narrated their learning life remained recognisably similar across the two interviews. The chapters they identified straightforwardly match the specific schools they attended, with additions for the companies they worked at since graduating. This is particularly apparent three accounts of Michelle Young, Kathryn Benz, and Peter Webb, where the chapters they identified remained consistent across both interviews.

For instance, the chapters Peter identified in 2013 were "{home schooled}", "{high school}", "{[large public research university]}", and "{Olin}". In 2017, he named them "Home Alone", "High School", "My Year at [large public research university]", and "Olin". Kathryn's sequence is superficially dissimilar as she did not name chapters in her initial interview, and has 3 additional chapters in 2017. However, her chapters refer to the same periods of time, with the same beginning and ending markers.

4.2 Compression Stories

In our original interviews, participants spoke a lot about their formative learning experiences and high school careers, but little about their experience at Olin. We guessed that this might be because high school was still prominent in their learning lives. In 2017, then, we expected that their undergraduate studies would take that place and that they would recall those years in detail, with less emphasis on prior experience. And for some that was true.

> Obviously, I guess the thickest chapter here would be moving to Olin and that experience there. (George Andrews, 2017)

Susana Clinton, articulated in 2017 how she remembered little of her earlier learning experiences.

> I feel like a lot of my learning career has lumped together now. I feel like I would have defined it based on areas of interest, or school years, before. Now, it's like *before Olin* and *during Olin*, and *after Olin*. … Man, everything before Olin is kind of a blur all together. (Susana Clinton, 2017)

We saw similar themes in the chapter titles of several other participants. For Natalie Lee, her learning experiences at school were originally three individual chapters. Now, she gathers them under a single umbrella called "school learning". And Jesse Walker, who previously formed four separate chapters, "{elementary school}", "{fifth and sixth grade}", "{seventh and eighth grade}", and "{high school}" subsequently identifies this time with in just a single chapter entitled "Buying In".

4.3 Landmark Stories

For other participants, while the larger structure of their stories evolved, some episodes did not change. This may not seem unusual, but it was surprisingly rare. Across all the interviews, we encountered only four of these "doubles" and they share similar features: they are often described in the same language, the episodes stand out of the timeline (no matter whether it is expanded or compressed around them) like landmarks, and they have a significance to the participant greater than the content of the event would suggest to us as observers. We report on three here.

> Basically it was down to one test, and the way [my state] grades is if you are 89.5 or higher, that is an A. Oh my gosh, I rocked those 89.5s like nobody's business. I just remember that day, that I had a B and I needed to get the A, I literally had an 89.57, and I got my A. (Natalie Lee, 2013)

> In [my state] ... an A is an 89.5 and I lived the 89.55, 89.57, 89.6. If you were to look at my grades, most of them were that. It was not a good situation. Trying to get just enough to get by. (Natalie Lee, 2017)

This episode is clearly an important one for Natalie and is stabilised by her using the same language. But it is not necessarily told in the same way in both accounts. In 2013, she describes this in the context of being offered the chance to take a special calculus class in her senior year if she meets the grade requirements and her claim of "rocking" the A grades sounds very positive: it is an achievement. In 2017, Natalie tags the recollection by saying that "It was not a good situation" and now seems disapproving of her former self.

Another example is in the stories of Evelyn Finn and her dislike of a particular teacher.

> The sad part was, the teacher that I didn't like in fourth grade moved up with us to fifth grade. (Evelyn Finn, 2013)

This experience is clearly meaningful for Evelyn in relation to her learning but she says no more about it. In 2017, she relates the same instance:

> It was actually really funny in my elementary school, I had a teacher in my fourth-grade year that I didn't really like. We did a lot of quiet work sheets in her class or watching videos and I was just not into it. Then she moved up to fifth grade when I moved up to fifth grade. I was just like, "Oh." (Evelyn Finn, 2017)

There is more nuance and detail in this telling. The teacher's style – relying on "quiet work sheets" – does not seem to work for Evelyn, who is clearly a well-performing and self-motivated student. Indeed, she says that she "felt like I was learning key words a lot. ... I was just like, 'What is this? Why am I doing this?'" She indicates both disappointment in this way of learning, and her resignation to it, with the inclusion of the final "Oh".

Another participant, Samuel Cline, talks extensively in his first interview about a planetary space exploration programme he attended while he was in high school.

> ... the biggest moment ... was a [planetary space exploration programme] I participated in ... doing some real (to the extent young high school students could do) real scientific experiments that actually had worth. ... I was doing actual experiments and they weren't just things like little experiments with M&Ms

or something, that anyone who knew anything about the basic concepts knew exactly what the experiment was going to do at the end. (Samuel Cline, 2013)

This is clearly a significant experience for Samuel, he describes it as the "biggest moment" and, later, as "a pretty big transition in the way that I viewed my own learning". In 2017, Samuel talks less extensively about the program, but the force it had for him remains clear:

> It was one of the first times in a science class that going into a lab I couldn't guess the outcome before it, because it was actually doing something that I didn't know the answer to. Not, "Here's a boxed lab that we went over the material last week, and now you're getting to see it,".... (Samuel Cline, 2017)

The common element across the two tellings of his learning life remains his exposure to authentic scientific practice and the powerful effect it had on him.

These stories were not more vivid than those others told, but these episodes act as anchors for meaning that is persistent across interviews. This is not something that would have been evident in a single elicitation, the strength of the meaning is only revealed (to us) through repetition.

4.4 Different Stories

The accounts of some participants had so few points of similarity that, if presented without identification, it would be hard to say they were stories of the same person. And it is not only in the overall structure of the account that there is divergence, but in the individual incidents also. For example, in 2013, Jesse Walker describes his transition from school to college in this way:

> In high school we had a very traditional learning environment. The teachers were all old and wise but they helped me out. They gave me some advice, told me Olin might be a good place since I didn't seem to like the traditional stuff. Then I got into Olin. I don't know how. (2013)

In this account, there is a feature which is part of a common theme across almost all the interviews: school is a "traditional learning environment" and Olin is not. Aside from that, the rest of the incident is personal. Olin is suggested because his teachers know he does not like "traditional" learning, they are "old and wise", and from this formulation we adduce "kindly"; there is no sense of malice, no sense that these teachers are not acting in his interests. Actually getting into Olin seems to be a process of almost magical transfer "I don't know how".

In 2017, the same incident is recounted differently.

> I was advised that because I'm talented, or because I got good grades in the maths and sciences, that engineering school is a good place. Also, that seeking the best ranked school that I could possibly fit into is, obviously, what I want to be doing because I want to be maximising my earning potential, my learning potential. So, I was like, okay, cool, I'll do that.

I knew [Olin] was going to be a little bit unexpected and a bit like veering from some sort of upward and outward path. But, at the same time, it was the best ranked engineering school I got into. Which is exactly what I was aiming for. (2017)

Here, the quality of the advice is different. His advisers now are impersonal and they treat him impersonally. Their generic advice is proffered on the basis of "good grades in the maths and sciences" and that "obviously" the purpose of going to college is to get a job that will make a lot of money. From these axioms it follows that engineering is a good subject choice and a high-ranked university desirable: the same advice could apply to anyone. And maybe it wasn't appropriate to Jesse. This time, the process of getting into Olin is a very deliberate act. Olin was the highest-ranked university (of the high-rank universities that he applied to) that accepted him: "which is exactly what I was aiming for".

Our prompt encourages not only a narrative recounting (i.e. a sequenced, often chronological, report) but also a storied one. By asking participants to recount their learning life "as if it were a book" we are making available constructs such as plot and narrator. Even though we elicit our stories from the protagonist, they are in a privileged position as narrators, and that privilege comes from knowledge: a narrator knows the ending. As Mattingly observes, a narrator "is able to select the relevant events and reveal their causal relations because he knows how events unfolded to bring about the particular ending which, narratively speaking, gives meaning to those events. ... The story's structure exists because the narrator knows where to start, knows what to include and exclude, knows how to weight and evaluate and connect the events he recounts, all because he knows where he will stop." [16] In contrast to fictional stories, the ending in a life story is usually the present time. And the narrators – our interviewees – make sense of their experience from their present point of view.

It would be easy to cast Jesse Walker's 2013 and 2017 accounts as simply inconsistent. But between the two tellings of this story, the ending has changed: the student has graduated and Olin is now an episode, not present, lived experience. Jesse is now in employment and looking to an unknown future. In re-telling his story, the new ending has changed both the interpretation of, and the accounting of, his transition into Olin; an inconsistent account does not imply an incoherent account.

4.5 Omitted Stories

For all participants there were elements that appeared in only one narrative. Omissions took various forms. Some were very personal details (illness, family deaths or thoughts of suicide); others were vivid, apparently important, scenes of learning that we heard only once. An example of this is in the account of Kathryn Benz, who, in 2013, does not mention computer science or programming at all. However, in the re-interview, she talks repeatedly about computer science, and describes several early experiences of computing at school. This sort of omission may be a result of the changed viewpoint of the narrator. At the time of the first interview Kathryn may not have been considering a

career in Computing, however by 2017 she had entered a computer science PhD programme. Given this new situation, previously unreported details of her past have become salient and, as narrative researchers term it, "tellable" [15].

Although frustrating to us as researchers, these silences are not intended to deceive. For example, when in 2017 a participant freshly revealed "I'd heard about Olin through my brother ... my brother was recruited by Olin and didn't end up going" they tagged it with "I told you this last time, right?"

5 COMMON THEMES

"Predominantly, narratives of personal experience focus on past events, i.e. they are about "what happened". However, such narratives link the past to the present and future life worlds ... The telling of past events is intricately linked to tellers' and listeners' concerns about their present and their future lives." [25] For all our participants, the space between the interviews was one of personal change, at the minimum, out of undergraduate education, for some of them much more, starting jobs or changing countries.

Our research focus is a) *computing education at university* and b) *the place and value of university education in students' lives*, and we undertook thematic analysis, looking for those elements in the interviews, to investigate both of these. For the first question we looked only at the six people interviewed who were computing students or subsequently pursued a career in computing (this is reported in section 5.1). For the second question we included all the interviews (reported in 5.2 and 5.3).

5.1 Acquisition and use of disciplinary knowledge

The computing curriculum at Olin is deliberately small [7]. This is in part due to pressures that are similar to those at liberal arts institutions – a small number of computing faculty and a larger number of general requirements than at technical institutes [7]. A concentration in computing at Olin requires students to take *Software Design* (an introductory programming course using Python), *Discrete Math*, *Foundations of Computer Science* (a higher-level course that combines aspects from traditional algorithms, programming languages, and compilers courses), and *Software Systems* (which draws on materials on operating systems and networks, among other topics). This is complemented by at least two other elective courses of the student's choosing.

5.1.1 Coming to know CS. Our participants came to computing in different ways. In their origin stories (that is, the backstory of their exposure to computing), we see well-known influences for taking a technical degree, such as knowing someone who is associated with computing. This matches other researchers' findings: in engineering education, the *Academic Pathways Study* showed that several motivational factors influence students' decision to pursue a technical degree, including mentor and parental influences [2]. Ching and Vigdor identify these "catalyst people" and, in their study, found them only out-of-school, not in teachers or formal advisors [6]. Our data confirmed this: this sort of engagement was not found in the educational environment.

> I was raised by an electrical engineer who was very hands-on. He was one of the first computer engineers, so he very much believed in getting your hands dirty. (Leon Clay, 2013)

> Yes, so when I was in fifth grade, we had a family friend who went to [a local university], and she studied computer engineering. At that age, she was my favourite person, she got me a shirt [from the local university], I was super excited! So, in our yearbook I wrote, "When I grow up I want to be a computer engineer." And I had no idea what that meant. (Irene Luna, 2017)

It may be that this prevalence of personal contact as a motivator to study computing is generational. As computing becomes a more common subject in schools students may find their way to the subject through charismatic and engaging teachers, as already happens in other disciplinary contexts.

> ... we had a really fantastic maths teacher named [name], who I had for Tenth Grade and Twelfth Grade. He was actually a British rocket scientist who couldn't get a job because of clearance issues. You can't work for NASA. So, he ended up teaching high school maths and he tied it into physics, and all of us wanted us to be engineers – everyone in his class. (Kathryn Benz, 2017)

Kathryn had mixed experiences early on, particularly in computing classes at school, and found her way back into computing when another Olin student became a mentor for her.

> How I learn to like CS, I think was a very interesting path, ... not really liking it in Ninth Grade ... and not really liking it, Tenth Grade or Twelfth Grade. Then, coming to Olin and not really wanting to be a computer scientist. Thinking I was going to be a mechanical engineer. It was really [another Olin student] dragging me to hackathons and then starting to do projects with me. He'd be like, "Do you want to be on my team?" That got me into computer science. (Kathryn Benz, 2017)

In terms of student attitudes and pathways into computing, a number of researchers have examined how the computing experiences a student has prior to applying to study computer science influence their time at university. Schulte and Knobelsdorf explore the influence of *biographical effects* on students' attitudes towards computing [28]. They note that prior experiences, such as programming courses in high school, may serve as a starting point or as a barrier for students, as we have seen in Kathryn's story.

5.1.2 Learning computing. Some, although not all, of our participants learned computing in the classroom. Other participants did not consider that computing was learned through the formal curriculum at all.

> [At Olin] ... I did software-y things, but my internships were with the government, instead of being with

industry, and they were around, sort of, more machine learning and data science stuff. ... I think most people at Olin who knew software engineering got that stuff more through internships, and my internships weren't in that space. (Michelle Young, 2017)

And indeed, Michelle's impression is borne out in the experience of another participant, one of his most important learning experiences came through an internship.

> So after my sophomore year, I got my first internship at a company called [name]. I was answering emails. I was going into people's websites and figuring out what was wrong, what was going on, what errors were they seeing and stuff. I would not do it again, but it was probably one of the most valuable experiences I've ever had, because you get to see how exactly people are reacting to your product. (Peter Webb, 2017)

We also learned about participants' transition from college to work. Begel and Simon, who explore new software developers' experiences at Microsoft, saw them undergo a transition from novice to expert when they enter university, and again as they start their first job [3]. We saw a similar phenomenon in our interviews:

> In the same way that going from high school to college was a very fundamental contextual change, going from school to career was also a fundamental contextual change. ... Certainly, the first six months were overwhelming just as a new adult and all of the things that go along with life and moving into a city. (George Andrews, 2017)

Begel and Simon also identified a lack of social and teamwork skills, as well as the negotiation of what the new employees in their study feel they can ask their colleagues. They write: "Asking questions, however, reveals to your co-workers and managers that you are not knowledgeable, an exposure that most new developers felt might cause their manager to reevaluate why they were hired in the first place." [3] This, however, does not appear to be a universal issue, as we see Michelle's retelling.

> Like, sometimes, it's a little embarrassing to be like, "So guys, tell me more about what you mean when you say the word 'code review'. What is that word, exactly?" You know, you only have to ask those questions once. There are a lot of context clues around. People are super-willing to forgive 21-year-olds for not knowing anything. So, it didn't take that long and it wasn't that hard to pick that stuff up. (Michelle Young, 2017)

5.2 Re-positioning university education: "Olin as inevitable"

Looking at both sets of interviews, we saw a shift in how participants positioned their experience at Olin. In the first narratives, Olin is often represented as an achievement, a sort of capstone to their learning life.

I think for the majority of my time in public school, I felt like I was learning in spite of my classes, maybe. Like I learned things for a test and I would take the test; it would be fine and I would forget them. ... But I feel like Olin gets what the right thing to teach is. Like the idea that it's about skills and about developing your ability to adapt. Sort of figuring out how to do things and what to do, not necessarily learning facts. Like the fact that they get that makes the classes really awesome. (Michelle Young, 2013)

In the second narratives, the Olin experience has been re-positioned. It is now subsumed into a single sequence and a theme of "Olin as inevitable", or, rather, as a continuation of previous experience, emerges.

> when I think about Olin... when I was reflecting on thoughts about learning, I think that really college was just like... I called it 'Solidification'. ... so I had already thought that there are lots of ways to learn, and these are all valuable. ... [Olin] just did a great job of saying, "Yes, these are all valid [ways]." (Ashley Hayes, 2017)

> ... I wonder how much Olin had an effect on me, or [whether] these things already were in place. I think we tend to look back on Olin and think that Olin had a huge dramatic impact on us. I do think it did. It's interesting to me that when I think about stories that affect my learning, ... I had already known that's how I want to learn, and Olin just happened to be a case study in that. (Kathryn Benz, 2017)

Here, Ashley and Kathryn similarly reflect on the position of their Olin education in their learning lives, and these reflections may be more than individual. As Olin overtly positions itself as providing a different kind of engineering education, this identification may be a *master narrative* that they have previously adopted as students [22]. As Andrews writes: "One of the key functions of master narratives is that they offer people a way of identifying what is assumed to be a normative experience. In this way, such storylines serve as a blueprint for all stories; they become the vehicle through which we comprehend not only the stories of others, but crucially of ourselves as well." [1]

Kathryn makes this point particularly explicit. Throughout her time at school, she participated in a creative problem-solving team competition, which she identifies as "one of the reasons I wanted to go to Olin."

> I already knew that [the creative problem-solving team competition] was how I wanted to learn and how I learned best. Then, Olin happened to be four years of that. So, it provided me with a methodology and a way to do that, but it didn't fundamentally change how I thought about learning. (Kathryn Benz, 2017)

Samuel Cline similarly expresses a sense that he was looking for – and that Olin offered – a different kind of education, perhaps as a result of the planetary space exploration programme he took part in.

And I think it kind of works nicely with the experiences from high school. By the end of high school, I was pretty clear that I wanted something different. ... Olin kind of offered that, in terms of having a very different education style and obviously having a lot of self-directed learning. (Samuel Cline, 2017)

For these graduates, Olin is now a continuation of the ways of learning that they had previously been exposed to. However, it does not diminish the effect of the education. Rather, it exposes a refashioning of what it means to be a graduate. These students are now "products" of Olin, which is an externally visible and tradable attribute, and are incorporating that as they make sense of their continued learning

This may be the result of an evolution in the narrator's stance. As Mattingly says, narratives "are ordered around an ending and it is the ending which has a fundamental role in shaping the meaning of the narrated events" [16].

One of the central elements of the life story are several forms of coherence [11]. Habermas and Bluck identify four kinds of coherence in their work: causal coherence, temporal coherence, thematic coherence, and the cultural concept of biography (which reflects the ways in which people in different cultures tell life stories) [11]. The repositioning we identify provides causal coherence across these stories of participants' learning lives, as they are told now, several years after graduation: now "of course" they ended up at Olin. The participants are then telling their stories in a way that exposes their continuing ways of making sense of their experience.

5.3 Beyond university education: always be learning

None of the participants talked about their university education as preparation for work; and some of them were quite explicit:

> I probably can't point to anything [from Olin] that's like, "Yes, this experience definitely helped me last Wednesday, when I needed to do X, Y, or Z," or helped me get the job I have now, or anything like that. (Samuel Cline, 2017)

> I just think it's funny, like I'm not remembering specific courses or teachers or anything, when I'm talking about education. (Peter Webb, 2017)

However, even though these graduates do not articulate the point at which they learned something (or learned how to do something) there is a notable strand of professionalism in how they approach their working lives. For example, Peter Webb, talks about his current role in a small software company.

> I've had to write a lot of emails explaining to people, 'Don't write code like this, because it'll cause these sorts of bugs.' I've also had to do unit tests and just general testing and stuff. They are smart people: I won't deny that. But there's some common-sense stuff. Like one of my co-workers ... none of his code is commented. There are well over 100 files. ... I was like, "*Seriously*?" (Peter Webb, 2017)

Peter's reaction to this situation is not that of a novice. He knows what good practice is, and works with colleagues to move the company towards that.

This attitude of professionalism is not confined to technical skills. Susana Clinton started her career at a major software company in a project management role.

> So I also feel like I've probably gotten better at convincing people. Holding people accountable. Presenting my ideas clearly. Distilling information down for somebody who has no context of my area, which is both my leadership team and also new partners. So, it's a different kind of learning now. (Susana Clinton, 2017)

In fact, the clearest theme that emerged from the second interviews was that of continued learning, and this had several aspects. Firstly, there was the translation of learning from education to work:

> I think in college you think that after college you're done learning. (Ashley Hayes, 2017)

> As a student you call it learning but as an employee you call it professional growth. (George Andrews, 2017)

But secondly, learning had importance to them for their own well-being and sense of self, especially in its absence:

> It certainly feels like I am learning more, and I'm doing things that are new and that are difficult, but it also still doesn't feel like I'm getting as much from it as I would like to. (Samuel Cline, 2017)

> I am bored at work, like every day. So I spend a lot of time sitting here being like, "What can I do next that's going to get me to the next place?" ... I'm feeling like if I just sit here and do this work every day I'm going to go backwards, I'm going to forget everything. (Irene Luna, 2017)

Perhaps because they had always identified themselves (and been identified by their education) as learners, learning for its own sake was often praised.

> I do really love diving into things and making things or tinkering with things. I think I get frustrated by that because I don't feel as free to dive and tinker ... at work you can't really be like, "I'm doing this because it's a good learning opportunity." (Evelyn Finn, 2017)

It was also striking that several participants single out metacognitive skills for special mention. Both Evelyn and George particularly associated reflective skills with their education.

> I really love the type of reflection you do at Olin where, at the end of something, you say, "Okay, what did we like about this? What can we change?" (Evelyn Finn, 2017)

> That's where I think things like Olin have been so valuable because you are constantly thinking about, "What have I learned from this situation?" and how to do things differently. It's surprising how many people *don't* look at experiences and situations in that regard.

They just look at it as it happened. They want to move on and get to something that will hopefully be better. (George Andrews, 2017)

Perhaps because metacognition as a disposition is non-specific, their recollections here contrast starkly with the quotes at the start of this section, where participants did not make, indeed felt unable to make, an explicit link between their college education and the work they were now engaged in. And we find an echo of that earlier, in George's recollection of the value of what he learned in high school.

> Public speaking certainly didn't have any content to learn. It's even questionable whether that really helped me with any college admissions or things that were important at the time. But the skills and mentality that I learned from those events have lasted me longer than AP Physics did. (George Andrews, 2017)

6 CONTRIBUTION & LIMITATIONS

This work is limited in its situation in non-traditional, elite education. However, we believe that the re-positioning of these students' undergraduate education in the wider context of their learning trajectories is applicable to graduates of more than a single institution. Re-interview as method, as in re-photography "... involves the presentation of sequential image pairs, in which the second modifies and expands our understanding of the first" [4]. Just as photographs of the "same" scene taken years apart expose different changes, our re-told narratives show events that stay the same, stories that are virtually identical, and experiences that have become differently important.

In this paper we have examined both the method of re-interviewing and what it can reveal. In terms of method we have described a preliminary classification for twice-told stories. In terms of analysis we have seen how university education is differently valued by students when they are in undergraduate study and when they are past it. For the students in this study, the content of their course was ultimately unimportant, to the point that they find it hard to recall concrete details of material or teachers (this may be because they were extremely able students on entry to university, and confident of their ability to learn, essentially, whatever they wanted to). What they do take away is lodged in their attitude to learning and associated metacognitive skills "... If you were to take Eighth Grade me and dot me in the world, I would be okay. But I probably wouldn't be as prepared to continue learning and motivate myself as I felt after Olin."

Other students, students from other institutions, will not show the same quality of difference. However, the method used in this paper exposes the distinctive, and lasting, characteristics of a degree programme. As academics, we rarely see students after graduation, and then not systematically: this permits a longer view.

ACKNOWLEDGEMENTS

We would very much like to thank the anonymous reviewers. Their pointers to additional literature and suggestions for emphasis in reporting have helped us make this a stronger paper.

REFERENCES

[1] Andrews, M. 2004. Counter-narratives and the power to oppose. Considering Counter-Narratives: Narrating, resisting, making sense. M. Bamberg and M. Andrews, eds. John Benjamins Publishing. 1–6.

[2] Atman, C.J., Sheppard, S.D., Turns, J., Adams, R.S., Fleming, L.N., Stevens, R., Streveler, R.A., Smith, K.A., Miller, R.L., Leifer, L.J., Yasuhara, K. and Lund, D. 2010. Enabling Engineering Student Success: The Final Report for the Center for the Advancement of Engineering Education. Center for the Advancement of Engineering Education.

[3] Begel, A. and Simon, B. 2008. Novice Software Developers, All over Again. Proceedings of the Fourth International Workshop on Computing Education Research (New York, NY, USA, 2008), 3–14.

[4] Berger, P. 1984. Doubling: This Then That. Second View: The Rephotographic Survey Project. M. Klett, ed. University of New Mexico Press. 45–52.

[5] Brand, S. 1994. How Buildings Learn: What Happens After They're Built. Viking Adult.

[6] Ching, C. and Vigdor, L. 2005. Technobiographies: Perspectives from Education and the Arts. (May 2005).

[7] Downey, A.B. and Stein, L.A. 2006. Designing a small-footprint curriculum in computer science. Frontiers in Education Conference, 36th Annual (Oct. 2006), 21–26.

[8] Dunlop, W.L., Guo, J. and McAdams, D.P. 2016. The Autobiographical Author Through Time: Examining the Degree of Stability and Change in Redemptive and Contaminated Personal Narratives. Social Psychological and Personality Science. 7, 5 (Jul. 2016), 428–436. DOI:https://doi.org/10.1177/1948550616644654.

[9] Dziallas, S. and Fincher, S. 2016. Aspects of Graduateness in Computing Students' Narratives. Proceedings of the 2016 ACM Conference on International Computing Education Research (New York, NY, USA, 2016), 181–190.

[10] Frey, D.D., Horton, A. and Somerville, M. 2002. Breaking the ice with prospective students: a team-based design activity to introduce active learning. Frontiers in Education, 2002. FIE 2002. 32nd Annual (2002), T1A-1-T1A-6 vol.1.

[11] Habermas, T. and Bluck, S. 2000. Getting a life: The emergence of the life story in adolescence. Psychological Bulletin. 126, 5 (2000), 748–769. DOI:https://doi.org/10.1037/0033-2909.126.5.748.

[12] Kerns, S.E., Miller, R.K. and Kerns, D.V. 2005. Designing from a Blank Slate: The Development of the Initial Olin College Curriculum. Educating the Engineer of 2020: Adapting Engineering Education to the New Century. National Academies Press. 98–113.

[13] Kinnunen, P., Butler, M., Morgan, M., Nylen, A., Peters, A.-K., Sinclair, J., Kalvala, S. and Pesonen, E. 2018. Understanding initial undergraduate expectations and identity in computing studies. European Journal of Engineering Education. 43, 2 (Mar. 2018), 201–218. DOI:https://doi.org/10.1080/03043797.2016.1146233.

[14] Klett, M. 1984. Second View: The Rephotographic Survey Project. University of New Mexico Press.

[15] Labov, W. 1972. Language in the Inner City: Studies in the Black English Vernacular. University of Pennsylvania Press.

[16] Mattingly, C. 1998. Healing Dramas and Clinical Plots: The Narrative Structure of Experience. Cambridge University Press.

[17] McAdams, D.P. 2011. Narrative Identity. Handbook of Identity Theory and Research. Springer, New York, NY. 99–115.

[18] McAdams, D.P. 2008. The Life Story Interview. The Foley Center for the Study of Lives, Northwestern University.

[19] McAdams, D.P. 1995. What Do We Know When We Know a Person? Journal of Personality. 63, 3 (Sep. 1995), 365–396. DOI:https://doi.org/10.1111/j.1467-6494.1995.tb00500.x.

[20] McAdams, D.P., Bauer, J.J., Sakaeda, A.R., Anyidoho, N.A., Machado, M.A., Magrino-Failla, K., White, K.W. and Pals, J.L. 2006. Continuity and Change in the Life Story: A Longitudinal Study of Autobiographical Memories in Emerging Adulthood. Journal of Personality. 74, 5 (Oct. 2006), 1371–1400. DOI:https://doi.org/10.1111/j.1467-6494.2006.00412.x.

[21] McCartney, R. and Sanders, K. 2015. School/Work: Development of Computing Students' Professional Identity at University. Proceedings of the Eleventh Annual International Conference on International Computing Education Research (New York, NY, USA, 2015), 151–159.

[22] McLean, K.C. and Syed, M. 2015. Personal, Master, and Alternative Narratives: An Integrative Framework for Understanding Identity Development in Context. Human Development. 58, 6 (2015), 318–349. DOI:https://doi.org/10.1159/000445817.

[23] Mishler, E.G. 2004. Historians of the Self: Restorying Lives, Revising Identities. Research in Human Development. 1, 1–2 (Mar. 2004), 101–121. DOI:https://doi.org/10.1080/15427609.2004.9683331.

[24] Norrick, N.R. 1997. Twice-Told Tales: Collaborative Narration of Familiar Stories. Language in Society. 26, 2 (1997), 199–220.

[25] Ochs, E. and Capps, L. 1996. Narrating the self. Annual Review of Anthropology. 25, 1 (Oct. 1996), 19–43. DOI:https://doi.org/10.1146/annurev.anthro.25.1.19.

[26] Olin College Course Catalog 2017-18: 2017. http://olin.smartcatalogiq.com/en/2017-18/Catalog. Accessed: 2018-03-21.

[27] Peters, A.-K. 2017. Learning Computing at University: Participation and Identity.

[28] Schulte, C. and Knobelsdorf, M. 2007. Attitudes Towards Computer Science-computing Experiences As a Starting Point and Barrier to Computer Science. Proceedings of the Third International Workshop on Computing Education Research (New York, NY, USA, 2007), 27–38.

[29] Snowden, D. 2011. Naturalizing Sensemaking. Informed by Knowledge: Expert Performance in Complex Situations. K.L. Mosier and U.M. Fischer, eds. Psychology Press. 223–234.

[30] Somerville, M. et al. 2005. The Olin curriculum: thinking toward the future. IEEE Transactions on Education. 48, 1 (Feb. 2005), 198–205. DOI:https://doi.org/10.1109/TE.2004.842905.

[31] Steiner, K.L., Thomsen, D.K. and Pillemer, D.B. 2017. Life Story Chapters, Specific Memories, and Conceptions of the Self. Applied Cognitive Psychology. 31, 5 (Sep. 2017), 478–487. DOI:https://doi.org/10.1002/acp.3343.

[32] Thomsen, D.K., Steiner, K.L. and Pillemer, D.B. 2016. Life Story Chapters: Past and Future, You and Me. Journal of Applied Research in Memory and Cognition. 5, 2 (Jun. 2016), 143–149. DOI:https://doi.org/10.1016/j.jarmac.2016.03.003.

[33] Zander, C., Boustedt, J., McCartney, R., Moström, J.E., Sanders, K. and Thomas, L. 2009. Student Transformations: Are They Computer Scientists Yet? Proceedings of the Fifth International Workshop on Computing Education Research Workshop (New York, NY, USA, 2009), 129–140.

TA Marking Parties: Worth the Price of Pizza?

Evaluating TA Confidence and Efficacy in Group vs. Individual Marking Scenarios

Brian Harrington
Department of Computer and
Mathematical Sciences
University of Toronto Scarborough
brian.harrington@utsc.utoronto.ca

Marzieh Ahmadzadeh
Department of Computer and
Mathematical Sciences
University of Toronto Scarborough
marzieh.ahmadzadeh@utoronto.ca

Nick Cheng
Department of Computer and
Mathematical Sciences
University of Toronto Scarborough
nick@utsc.utoronto.ca

Eric Heqi Wang
Department of Computer and
Mathematical Sciences
University of Toronto Scarborough
ericheqi.wang@utoronto.ca

Vladimir Efimov
Department of Computer and
Mathematical Sciences
University of Toronto Scarborough
vladimir.efimov@mail.utoronto.ca

ABSTRACT

Student teaching assistants marking examinations is a reality for many undergraduate computer science courses, and with the explosion in enrolments in CS programs, and the increase in class sizes, it is becoming ever more common. Many institutions employ a "marking party" model in which instructors and TAs gather together to mark exams collectively. This system is naturally more logistically difficult than simply dividing up the papers and allowing TAs to mark in their own time. However the reasoning is that the group nature of the marking party makes it easier for markers to ask for clarification and second opinions on tricky cases, and results in better, more consistent marking.

In this work we evaluate the marking party model by performing an experiment in which TAs are randomly assigned to either a marking party or solo marking when grading the final exam of a CS1 course. However, in addition to the student papers, each TA receives "fake" papers, constructed to lead to marking errors if TAs are not attentive or do not carefully follow the assigned marking rubric. We also evaluate the time that each method of marking takes, as well as survey the TAs as to their personal opinions on the two marking methods.

Our results show that the marking party not only allows TAs to mark faster, but produces more consistent marking, with fewer errors, and better intra and inter-marker reliability. There is clear evidence that organizing marking parties is likely worth the effort (and cost of providing lunch), as the benefits to students are significant, and the overhead of the logistics may be less than that of fixing marking errors and dealing with re-mark requests. And as an added bonus, the TAs seem to enjoy it.

CCS CONCEPTS

• **Social and professional topics** → **Computing education**; **Computer science education**; **CS1**;

KEYWORDS

Assessment, CS1, Grading, Teaching Assistants, Evaluation

ACM Reference Format:
Brian Harrington, Marzieh Ahmadzadeh, Nick Cheng, Eric Heqi Wang, and Vladimir Efimov. 2018. TA Marking Parties: Worth the Price of Pizza?: Evaluating TA Confidence and Efficacy in Group vs. Individual Marking Scenarios. In *ICER '18: 2018 International Computing Education Research Conference, August 13–15, 2018, Espoo, Finland.* ACM, New York, NY, USA, 9 pages. https://doi.org/10.1145/3230977.3230997

Brian Harrington, Marzieh Ahmadzadeh, Nick Cheng, Eric Heqi Wang, and Vladimir Efimov

1 INTRODUCTION

With growing enrolment in computer science programs worldwide, it is becoming increasingly necessary at many institutions to rely on larger and larger numbers of teaching assistants to mark assignments and examinations, particularly in larger introductory courses. There are many advantages to having a large number of TAs on a teaching team including enhanced flexibility and coverage of possible hours of help for students. However, one major disadvantage is the increased effort required to manage logistics. In the University of Toronto Scarborough's Department of Computer and Mathematical Sciences, we regularly hold "marking parties" in which the entire teaching team for a course meet in a single room to mark exams, usually handing out stacks of papers at random, and having students mark questions in teams, moving on to the next question once they have finished marking all exams. As the number of TAs has increased, it has become increasingly difficult to find times when they are all free for a large enough timespan to mark an entire test or examination. As a department, we have attempted to persist with this model despite the logistical headache, on the basis that these marking parties resulted in a higher quality of marking with more consistency between markers and improved accountability resulting in fewer errors. However, as the number of students, and therefore TAs, has increased, many colleagues have moved to a more traditional "solo" marking system, where TAs mark exams on their own time at home or in a shared workspace.

The assumption, that marking parties are better for the students than simply giving TAs access to the exams and allowing them to mark on their own time, seems intuitive. But one could argue that perhaps the marking parties are actually causing the TAs to be less focused, chatting with their friends and colleagues, and being distracted or uncomfortable in a large full room. And it may be possible that the added overhead of the marking parties is slowing down the marking process, resulting in more hours for the TAs. Furthermore, we have received occasional complaints from TAs that the system was unfair, as some questions were easier to mark than others, and no one was paying attention to how many papers each TA had marked. So some markers would work diligently, while others would chat with their friends or take more frequent breaks. It is also possible that the marking setup has no effect on the quality or efficiency of the marking, and thus instructors should feel free to choose whichever version they find most convenient.

In this paper, we detail an experiment in which we set out to discover whether there is in fact any reality to these assumptions about marking parties. Our primary research questions are:

- Do marking parties result in better inter-marker consistency than solo marking?
- Do marking parties result in better intra-marker consistency than solo marking?
- Do marking parties complete marking in more or less time than solo marking?
- Do TAs prefer marking parties over solo marking?

For the purposes of this study, we define a marking party as: A gathering of teaching assistants at a predetermined time and place to mark an examination, with the ability for the TAs to easily and continually communicate during the marking process. We define solo marking as: A system whereby TAs can mark papers at a time and in an environment of their own choosing, with access to ask for clarification only in an asynchronous manner such as e-mail (without the presumption of immediate and continuous feedback).

While marking the final examination of our CS1 course, we split our TA team into 2 groups: a "marking party" group and a "solo marking" group and randomly assigned 10 TAs to each group. Each TA was randomly assigned the same number of exam papers to mark, and given the same rubric. Unbeknownst to the TAs, they each received 2 additional exam papers in their pile which were not written by students in the course, but which were instead created by the experimenters, containing subtle errors that would be easy to overlook, or questions that could easily be given an inaccurate mark if the marking rubric was not followed carefully. After all papers were marked, the TAs were asked to self-report the total time it had taken them to mark all exams, and to fill in a short survey asking questions about their personal opinions on the marking setup.

Our results were surprisingly clear given the small sample size. Not only did the TAs prefer the marking party, and felt it was better for both them and the students, the marking party group took less time to complete their tasks than the solo marking group. Most interesting of all was the analysis of our 'fake' exams. We found that the marking party group made fewer errors and were, on average, closer to the expected mark than their solo marking counterparts.

2 BACKGROUND

Although a reasonable amount has been published documenting the effectiveness of TA training [2, 5, 6, 12], and a wealth of research has been done on qualitative analysis of marking [7], research focusing on consistency of TA's marking has been much more sparse.

Shannon et al. studied the correlation of TA training and students' perceived effectiveness of the TA by providing a questionnaire to the TAs asking if they had prior teaching experience [8].

Wiley and colleagues, studied student and TA perception of grading before and after group discussion, and found that both groups felt that they've been marked more fairly and received better quality feedback when the TAs had first discussed the marking as a group [9]. Further research also showed that group discussions improved both consistency of marks (as measured by difference in average mark between tasks), and confidence of the markers [10, 11].

Huang et al. developed a profile for a marker over many courses, and found that assigning markers to different groups based on attributes of their profiles resulted in a small decrease in marking errors [3].

One study focusing on the inter-marker consistency is similar to the solo-marking portion of the experiment detailed in this study. A group of 5 TAs was assigned the same paper to grade with no communication or discussion, and the experimenters found that the standard deviation was worryingly high [4].

3 METHODOLOGY

Exam Design

CSCA08: Introduction to Computer Science I is a CS1 course offered at University of Toronto for students planning on pursuing a major or specialist degree in computer science. In the Fall term of 2017 564 students wrote the final examination. 20 teaching assistants (TAs) were assigned to the course, all of whom were senior undergraduate CS students or graduate students in the department. All TAs taught weekly tutorial sections and supervised labs, and also underwent training in both course content and teacher training that included advice and guidance on marking [2]. All TAs marked 5 weekly quizzes and 3 programming assignments throughout the term as well as 2 term tests prior to the final exam and had participated in at least one 'marking party' and one 'solo marking' session prior to the commencement of this study.

The exam consisted of 4 questions[1] worth a total of 54 marks. The questions were:

- **ADT (10 marks)**: Students were provided with code to implement a standard Queue abstract data type, and asked to explain why the given code failed to provide good quality abstraction, and then to fix the code to avoid abstraction leaks.
- **Tracing (10 marks)**: Students were given code (focusing on understanding of OOP in Python) and asked to reproduce the output of the code.

---

[1]There was actually also a 'Question 0' which was worth 1 mark, and awarded for correctly filling out identification information on the cover sheet, but this question was ignored for the purpose of this study

- **Mangler (14 marks)**: Students were provided code that had been mangled by the "Code Mangler" [1], and asked to re-create the original code.
- **UML (20 marks)**: Students were provided with user requirements as a simple text dialogue, and asked to draw a UML class diagram for a proposed system.

A copy of the exam as well as the raw marking data can be found at http://uoft.me/markingparties.

Experimental Setup

The 20 TAs were randomly assigned to either the marking party group or the solo marking group. The solo marking group was told that they could pick up their exams for marking from a secured drawer with a combination lock at any time during a 4 day period. They could mark the exams in the TA office or take them to one of the study rooms in the building, but the exams could not leave the campus. Once the exams were marked, they were to enter the marks into a database and return their papers to the drawer. The marking party group was given a time and place to meet (after finding a time that was amicable to all the TAs involved), and all marking would be done over the course of a single day.

Members of both groups were each provided with a stack of 28-29 exam papers, and a marking scheme with instructions on how to mark each question. They were provided with identical instructions for how to mark, including the line: *"If you are unsure about anything, please ask for clarification rather than guessing.".* Since the course instructors were part of the experiment, in order to avoid undue bias, the TAs in the marking party were told that they had urgent business to attend to elsewhere and so would not be present during the marking party as is the normal custom. But one instructor would check in periodically during the party, and was available via e-mail to markers in both groups.

In addition to the regular student exam papers, each marker received 2 'fake' exams (one placed 2 tests from the top of their pile and one placed 2 tests from the bottom). These fake exams, were hand written and assigned a fake name and credentials [2], and created according to a specific rubric. The rubric was designed to ensure that all fake tests should receive the same mark and make the same errors, but still allowed for enough variation in answers so as not to appear suspiciously similar. The rules for creating fake tests are given in Figure 2[3]. The corresponding marking scheme given to TAs is shown in Figure 1.

40 total exams were hand written by the authors using the rules shown in Figure 2. Independent analysis by two experienced TAs not associated with the study confirmed that a marker carefully following the marking scheme and instructions should have awarded these exams a final score of 34/54. These exams were then randomly assigned to the TAs, with each TA receiving two fake exams to mark.

Once all tests had been marked and collated, the markers were asked to complete a short survey asking them to report the total time they had taken to complete all exams, not including breaks or preparation, as well as a series of questions about the marking setup. The marking party and solo marking arrangements were defined and explained (no mention was made at this point of the fake tests, only the logistics of the two testing setups were included), and the markers were asked a series of questions including:

- Which marking setup would you have personally preferred?
- Which marking setup is faster?
- Which marking setup is more fair from a marker's perspective?
- Which marking setup is more fair from a student's perspective?
- Which marking setup should we use in future?

Markers were also given a freeform text section in which they were told they could explain or expand upon any of their answers.

Research Ethics

As this project involved not only the use of student exam information, but also the willful deception of teaching assistants, and the addition of extra work on the part of the TAs, ethical considerations were important in our experimental design.

There was an additional concern that, should the results show a systematic bias towards students marked by one of the marking groups, an adjustment would need to be made in the final exam marks.

For the handling of student data, normal protocols at the University of Toronto were followed. Students in the course had opted into an experimental consent form at the beginning of the term in which they consented to their exam grades being used in an aggregate fashion, properly anonymized, for pedagogical and educational studies.

In order to gain the consent of the teaching assistants, they were told they would be participating in a study on marking effectiveness. They consented to self-report their own marking time and to participate in a post-study survey a priori. They also consented to a potentially increased marking load, not to exceed 5% of their regular exam marking duties (this also fell well within their contractual time allocation for the course). They were not provided with the details of the purpose of the study, as this would have possibly biased their performance.

Upon completion of the study, all parties were informed of the purpose of the study, and the resulting data was made available to both the students and the TAs.

A post hoc analysis of the "real" student exams found that the bias towards leniency in the solo marking group was still present, but was not statistically significant. A secondary marking check was conducted for elements of the marking scheme found to be regularly mis-marked, but no global adjustment was made. It appears that the mistakes made by the students were generally not nuanced enough to be falling through the gaps in the marking scheme at the same rate as our targeted fake exams.

4 RESULTS

The experiment ran as expected for the most part. No markers showed any signs of suspecting that the fake submissions weren't genuine or appeared to have treated them any differently than the

---

[2]In an earlier experiment, we attempted to use photocopied examinations, but this immediately raised suspicions among the markers, we also found that it was important to match the name to the writing style, as one subject mentioned 'there's no way this is female hand-writing'

[3]Some of the rules have been paraphrased slightly from what was given to the TAs in order to provide details that would have been clear to the markers in context.

Q1:

- 1 mark for mentioning private variables, 1 mark for correcting (adding underscores)
- 1 mark for explanation of why private variables are important, 1 mark for example
- 1 mark for explanation of why private variables are important, 1 mark for example
- 1 mark for mentioning abstraction, one mark for explaining what it means
- 2 marks for creating error classes
- 2 marks for correctly raising errors
- 1 mark for modifying docstring

Q2:

- 1 mark off for every deviation from solution (maximum of 1 mark for formatting)
- block deviations should count as a single deviation. e.g., if all A's output comes before B, that's only 1 mark off
- repeated errors should only be penalized once. e.g., if they swapped X with Y, don't penalize repeated instances of Y where there should be X.

Q3:

- Docstring
  - 1 for type contract
  - 1 for examples
  - 2 for description (1 for clear/concise, 1 for having all necessary info)
  - Watch out of examples/description copied directly from handout
- Internal Commenting
  - 2 marks for nested loops
  - 1 mark for explaining if structure
  - 2 marks for explaining looping structure
- Code
  - 1 mark off for each deviation from solution
  - Block deviations count as a single deviation

Q4:

- Classes
  - 1 mark off for each missing class
  - Do not take marks off for extra classes if they are reasonable
- Relationships
  - 1 mark off for each missing/incorrect relationship
- Formatting
  - 1 mark off for missing/non sensible relationship names
  - 1 mark off for missing/incorrect cardinalities
  - 1 mark off for missing/incorrect inheritance arrows
  - 1 mark off for missing privacy
  - 1 mark off for missing type contracts
- Methods
  - 1 mark off for each missing/incorrect method
  - Max 1 mark off for missing initialization methods
  - Don't take marks off for extra methods if they are reasonable
  - Do take off marks if method appears in child class when it should only be in parent

Figure 1: Marking Scheme Provided to TAs

rest of their papers. There were several requests for clarification from both the marking party and the solo markers, and in all cases e-mails clarifying points were sent to all members of both groups. None of the questions seemed to be specific to any of the fake papers from our study.

One issue that did arise was that three of the markers in the solo marking group decided to mark during the same time as the marking party was being held, and decided to join the marking party. Since the original pretence offered to the TAs for why some were marking solo while others were in the marking party was logistic in nature (since many of the TAs are friends outside of school, the information was bound to leak out, so we simply told those in the marking party that the others weren't there due to scheduling conflicts), there was no good reason to exclude them.

Q1:
- Add underscores to the variables and say that the code "breaks the ADT" or "violates the abstraction" or some combination of the two, but do not explain how or why
- Include an error class, but don't give Error as the parent class instead of Exception
- When raising the exception, don't include an error message

Q2:
- Replace every A with either a B or a C in the 3rd line of the output
- Move the parent section of the last line to the end so it appears after the grandparent output

Q3:
- Copy the description from the handout *almost* exactly, just piecing together the words we gave them, but in a way that is very clearly not "your own words"
- Have your comments repeat exactly what each line of code is doing without providing any additional context or information
- Un-indent the second for-loop so that it could be mistaken for not being inside the outer loop

Q4:
- Have type contracts in most of your methods, but skip 2-3
- Include at least one class from a word that is in the handout, but shouldn't really be a class (e.g., hospital, needle)
- Put the cardinalities backwards on the relationships
- Don't include any initialization methods

Figure 2: Rules for Creating Fake Exams

Table 1: Self Reported Time to Grade 40 Exams

	Party	Solo
Avg. Reported Time	7 hr 30 min	8 hr 45 min
Max. Reported Time	8 hr 30 min	10 hr
Min. Reported Time	7 hr	5 hr

This means that rather than having 10 TAs in the marking party group and 10 in the solo marking group, we ended up with 13 in the marking party group and 7 in the solo marking group. The potential problems this may have caused for our data collection and our analysis are further discussed in section 5.

Time Taken

The markers did not strictly monitor their time, but they were asked to self-report how long the entire marking process took in 15 minute increments, excluding breaks or distractions. This is obviously not a rigorous result, but post study discussion indicates that the TAs felt confident that their answers were accurate to within a window of between 15 to 30 minutes. Furthermore, it may be argued that the actual time taken to mark exams is less important than the perceived time from the graders' perspective, if the goal is to analyze marking setups in terms of preferences and TA morale.

The average reported time to mark all 30 exams (28 real and 2 fake) for the solo marking group was **8 hours 45 minutes**, the time reported for the marking party group was **7 hours 30 minutes**. The times reported for the marking party were much more consistent, with all reports being between 7 hours and 8 hours 30 minutes, while the times for the solo marking group ranged from 5 hours 30 minutes to 10 hours. The details are summarized in Table 1.

While it is difficult to verify the veracity of this data, as it was not rigorously measured, and students may have motivations to over/under report the time taken for grading, it is interesting to note that the average time in the solo marking group was over an hour longer than the marking party. This runs counter to our initial hypothesis that the added distractions of group marking would slow down the process, making the marking party group take longer to complete their tasks.

TA Surveys

In the survey administered at the end of the study, it was clear that the students believed that the marking party setup was superior in almost every respect. There was very clear personal preference for marking parties, as well as a belief that it was faster and more fair from the student perspective. The only question that did not show a clear preference for the marking party was *"Which marking setup is more fair from a markers perspective?"*. In post study discussion, it was clear that this question was interpreted as ambiguous by the markers. Some of them were unclear as to whether we were asking about the "traditional" marking party where students just worked on arbitrary stacks of papers and no one kept track of who marked which papers, or the style of marking party we were using in the experiment, where each TA had a set number of papers to mark. Many of the TAs also expressed uncertainty as to what exactly was meant by "fair" in this context. The results of the survey can be found in Table 2.

In the freeform text section of the survey, many of the markers discussed the difference between this style of marking party and the traditional style. With several commenting to the effect that while this style is more fair (with each marker being responsible for the same number of papers), the traditional style allowed them

Table 2: Marker Answer Counts for the Prompt: *"Which marking setup..."*

	Marking Party	Solo Marking	Don't Know/No Opinion
would you have personally preferred?	17	2	1
is faster?	13	5	2
is more fair from a marker's perspective?	5	7	8
is more fair from a student's perspective?	20	0	0
should we use in future?	20	0	0

- *"Once we get a good feel for the questions, it's more efficient to do it solo without distraction, but staying in a group ensures that any last quirks in the questions can be sorted out with a full consensus."*
- *"Being able to mark on own time allows for more flexibility. Being in a marking party allows for quicker consensus on how questions are marked."*
- *"If this were a course I had TAed many times, I might prefer to mark on my own, but I think the marking party is really good for first timers so we can be sure that we're doing things the right way"*

Figure 3: Selected Comments from Marker Feedback

to focus on a smaller number of questions for a larger number of papers, which was generally interpreted to be faster and require less effort overall. Selected comments can be found in Figure 3.

Inter-Grader Consistency and Examination Errors

In order to analyze whether the marking setup has an effect on the quality of the marks received, we first looked at the total marks given by each grader, to see which marking setup would result in our fake students receiving grades that deviated from what they should have received had the marking scheme been strictly followed.

The question error was defined as the absolute value difference between the grade given on each question, and the expected grade provided by the experienced TAs carefully following the marking scheme. Each question error was then summed for each test, and for each marker, their two errors were then added to produce a total error for each participant.

Some of the total errors are alarmingly large [4]. However, it is important to remember that the fake papers were designed specifically to contain as many borderline, ambiguous, or easy to miss errors as possible, and that the total error is a sum of the absolute errors, so in practice many of these would cancel out (as we will later see). The total error for all graders is given in Table 3.

It is immediately obvious that the total errors in the solo marking group are consistently higher than those in the party group, with an average error 5.8 marks higher. A boxplot of the two distributions is shown in Figure 4.

Due to the low sample size, we first ensured that both groups passed the Shapiro-Wilk test for normality ($W_{solo} = 0.86\ p_{solo} = 0.16$, $W_{party} = 0.96\ p_{party} = 0.7$), and an F-test for homogeneity

---

[4]Author's Note: We have set a personal wager on how long it will be before the first student of ours tries to use this paper to justify an increase to their exam grade

Table 3: Total Examination Errors (Sum of absolute errors on all questions)

Grader	Test 1 Error	Test 2 Error	Total Error
Solo1	4	10	14
Solo2	12	10	22
Solo3	11	10	21
Solo4	5	13	18
Solo5	8	3	11
Solo6	7	5	12
Solo7	11	11	22
		AVG:	17.14
Party1	8	9	17
Party2	5	3	8
Party3	4	8	12
Party4	3	4	7
Party5	2	2	4
Party6	6	5	11
Party7	5	6	11
Party8	5	11	16
Party9	3	6	9
Party10	3	6	9
Party11	8	8	16
Party12	6	6	12
Party13	5	10	15
		AVG:	11.30

of population variance ($F = 1.48$, $df_{num} = 6$, $df_{denom} = 12$, $p = 0.53$).

The total error distribution in the two groups was shown to be statistically significant by both a t-test with pooled variance ($t = 2.95$, $df = 18$, $p = 0.0087$), and a Wilcoxon rank sum test with continuity correction ($W = 75$, $p = 0.021$). From this data, it is clear that the marking party was statistically less likely to produce examination errors than the solo marking group.

Analyzing Intra-Grader Consistency

In addition to evaluating the inter-grader reliability and average error of the marking setups, we also wanted to evaluate the effect on the marking within an individual marker's papers. It was for this reason that each marker received two fake papers, one near the top of their pile and one near the bottom. The assumption was that the markers would evaluate each paper in the order they were presented in the bundle. However direct observation as well as self reporting in post study discussion revealed a slight flaw in that assumption. Generally the markers completed marking all of the

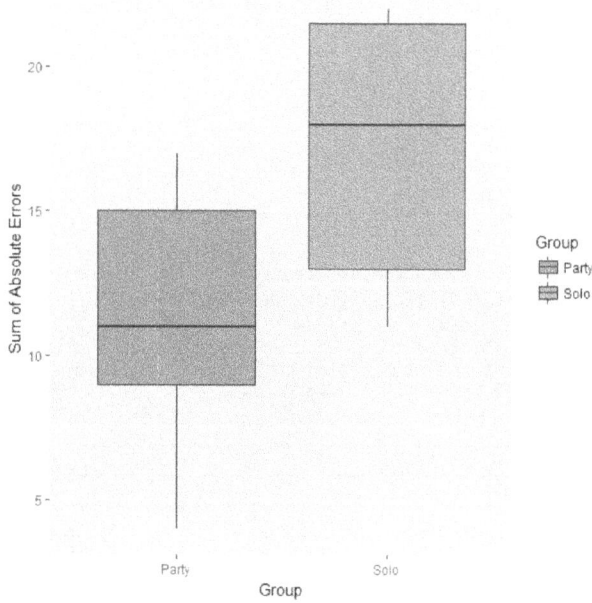

Figure 4: Total Examination Errors vs Marking Group

first question before moving on to the second, and as each paper was removed from the top of the pile and marked, it would be transferred to a second pile. Some of the markers would keep the papers oriented the same way and some would turn them over. Thus when marking the second question, some markers would be marking the papers in the same order, and some would mark in the opposite order. For this reason, the actual order of the fake papers within the pile did not produce any significant results. However, the fact that they were well separated within the piles seemed to have the desired effect in that none of the markers wound up marking two of the same 'fake' questions in quick succession.

Our exam error evaluation only took into account the absolute error of the final mark and ignored the direction. However, it is possible that markers in one group were either consistently over or under-marking, while markers in the other group were being less consistent. For this reason, we analyzed the mark range of each marker.

For this study, we define the mark range as the difference in mark assigned to a question on the two papers evaluated by a single marker. If a marker is consistently awarding marks above the expected average or consistently below, they will have a high error, but a low range. If a marker is awarding some marks above the expected average and some marks below, they may have a lower error, but will have a higher range. The mark range for all markers is given in Table 4.

Once again, the average range for the solo group was found to be higher than the party group. Though in this case, the party group appears to have a larger variance. A box-plot for the two distributions is given in Figure 5.

We attempted to discover whether the difference in total mark ranges was statistically significant for the two groups. Due to the small sample size, we again ensured that the distributions passed

Table 4: Mark Ranges
(Difference in marks awarded on separate tests)

Grader	Q1	Q2	Q3	Q4	Total
Solo1	4	1	2	1	8
Solo2	2	2	0	2	6
Solo3	1	0	8	0	9
Solo4	3	4	2	1	10
Solo5	1	5	0	1	7
Solo6	2	0	6	4	12
Solo7	4	2	1	1	8
				AVG:	8.57
Party1	1	2	2	0	5
Party2	0	0	3	3	6
Party3	1	1	6	4	12
Party4	2	0	3	2	7
Party5	1	0	1	2	4
Party6	1	0	3	3	7
Party7	1	0	0	0	1
Party8	2	9	0	3	14
Party9	1	2	1	5	9
Party10	0	0	2	1	3
Party11	2	2	0	0	4
Party12	0	0	1	1	2
Party13	2	0	6	1	9
				AVG:	6.38

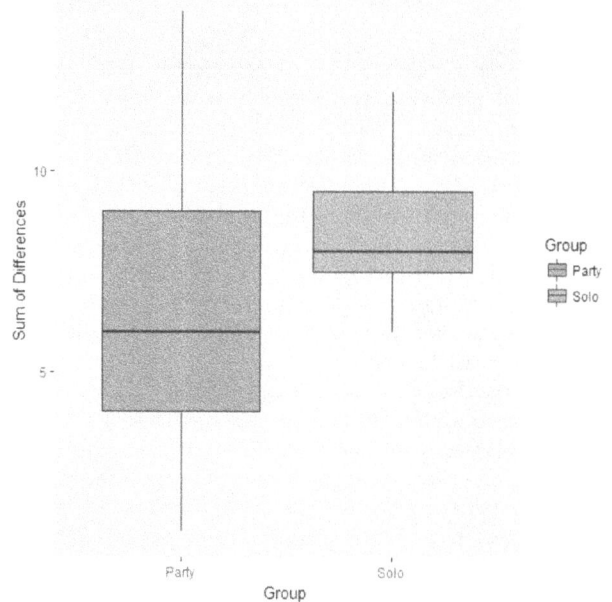

Figure 5: Total Mark Ranges vs Marking Group

Table 5: Question Error (Deviation From Expected Question Mark)

	Solo Marking			Marking Party		
	Min Error	Max Error	Average Error	Min Error	Max Error	Average Error
ADT	0/10	7/10	2.21/10	0/10	4/10	0.93/10
Tracing	0/10	5/10	2.43/10	0/10	5/10	1.31/10
Mangler	1/14	5/14	3.21/14	0/14	5/14	2.31/14
UML	0/20	4/20	2.00/20	0/20	4/20	1.96/20

both the Shapiro-Wilk test for normality ($W_{solo} = 0.97$ $p_{solo} = 0.88$, $W_{party} = 0.96$ $p_{party} = 0.73$), and an F-test for homogeneity of population variance ($F = 0.27, df_{num} = 6, df_{denom} = 12, p = 0.12$). However, in this case it was not possible to establish statistical significance of the difference between the two populations by either a t-test with pooled variance ($t = 1.40, df = 18, p = 0.18$), or a Wilcoxon rank sum test with continuity correction ($W = 65, p = 0.13$).

While it does appear that the marking party group may have been generally more internally consistent, due to the higher average, the small sample size and high variance, it is not possible to say that the effect was statistically significant.

Question Analysis

Examination error and mark range both look at the papers overall. However it is possible that the differences between the groups came from individual questions rather than being a consistent and persistent problem. For this reason we also evaluated individual questions. The minimum, maximum and average error for each question by each marking group can be found in Table 5.

Once again, we find that the marking party has lower average per-question errors on all questions except for the one on UML. A two-way ANOVA failed to show any statistically significant results, which is not surprising given the very small sample sizes. However, it is clear from these results that the differences found in the previous tests were not isolated to a single question or a specific error, but rather appear to be systematic across multiple elements of the marking scheme.

5 THREATS TO VALIDITY & FUTURE WORK

This study was as rigorous and as authentic as possible under the circumstances. However, there are several possible threats to validity. The marking party in the study was slightly different from our traditional group marking in that the TAs were not allowed to 'trade' marking in a 'I'll mark your question A if you mark my question B manner', and the solo markers were not allowed to take the papers out of the building. This means that our findings may not generalize to more traditional marking setups where group marking is less regulated, and individual graders are allowed to work from home with all the comforts and distractions that may imply.

The fact that some of the markers assigned to the solo marking setup decided to attend the marking party could be a contaminating factor in some of our analysis. As it is possible that either the imbalance of the group sizes led to difficulties in the statistical analysis, or that there is something about the personalities of the markers

who chose to attend even though they were not assigned to the marking party could be introducing bias, as the participants were no longer randomly assigned to groups. The data does not seem to show any obvious difference between these three participants and others in the experimental group, but this could simply be due to data sparsity.

Since we had to hand-create each fake paper, minor variations in answers could have accounted for noise in the data. Something as simple as different handwriting could impact some of the more subtle points of marking. Unfortunately, simply photocopying the results led to immediate detection in our pre-study, and even having identical answers with different handwriting led to graders becoming suspicious of possible plagiarism. This threat to validity is also a barrier to replication, as our team spent approximately 25-30 hours hand-crafting the fake papers. Future work will look into ways that this study could be replicated without the need for manual creation of so many papers. If possible, this could allow us to replicate the study across various types of exams, groups of TAs, and levels of details in the marking scheme.

Another avenue for future pursuit is to analyze marker's behaviours over time. Do TAs eventually get better at collaborating in marking parties and enhance the differences from the solo markers? Or do the solo marking TAs eventually get better at avoiding distraction, and therefore reduce the difference between the setups? To evaluate this we would need to assign TAs to a particular marking setup, and have them continue with that setup throughout the year in order to track the change in the various effects.

6 CONCLUSION

In this paper we set out to evaluate marking parties and compare them to solo marking on four metrics. We were able to provide a convincing qualitative analysis that TAs preferred marking parties, and at least perceived them as being more time efficient. Our experimental results showed a possibility that marking parties resulted in better intra-marker consistency, however the data was not conclusive. We were able to show clear, statistically significant evidence that the marking parties resulted in better inter-marker consistency, with fewer errors.

This study was performed on a single group of TAs, for a single course. It is not obvious that the results will generalize to other institutions which may have different marking requirements and TA cultures. However, we feel that this study does provide valuable evidence to support our initial supposition that the benefits of marking parties, are worth the extra setup time, logistical effort, and strain on the departmental pizza budget.

REFERENCES

[1] Nick Cheng and Brian Harrington. 2017. The Code Mangler: Evaluating Coding Ability Without Writing Any Code. In *Proceedings of the 2017 ACM SIGCSE Technical Symposium on Computer Science Education (SIGCSE '17)*. ACM, New York, NY, USA, 123–128. https://doi.org/10.1145/3017680.3017704

[2] Francisco J. Estrada and Anya Tafliovich. 2017. Bridging the Gap Between Desired and Actual Qualifications of Teaching Assistants: An Experience Report. In *Proceedings of the 2017 ACM Conference on Innovation and Technology in Computer Science Education (ITiCSE '17)*. ACM, New York, NY, USA, 134–139. https://doi.org/10.1145/3059009.3059023

[3] Zhuhan Jiang1and Jiansheng Huang. 2017. Improving Fairness On Students'overall Marks Via Dynamic Reselection Of Assessors. *International Journal on Integrating Technology in Education (IJITE)* 6, 3 (June 2017).

[4] E. A. Jackson. 1988. Marking Reliability in B.Sc. Engineering Examinations. *European Journal of Engineering Education* 13, 4 (1988), 487–494.

[5] Sasha Nikolic, Peter James Vial, Montserrat Ros, David Stirling, and Christian Ritz. 2015. Improving the laboratory learning experience: a process to train and manage teaching assistants. *IEEE Transactions on Education* 58, 2 (2015), 130–139.

[6] Chris Park. 2004. The graduate teaching assistant (GTA): Lessons from North American experience. *Teaching in Higher Education* 9, 3 (2004), 349–361.

[7] D Royce Sadler. 2010. Beyond feedback: Developing student capability in complex appraisal. *Assessment & Evaluation in Higher Education* 35, 5 (2010), 535–550.

[8] David Shannon, Darla Twale, and Mathew S. Moore. 1998. TA Teaching Effectiveness: The Impact of Training and Teaching Experience. *The Journal of Higher Education* 69 (07 1998), 440–466.

[9] Keith Willey and AP Gardner. 2010. Improving the standard and consistency of multi-tutor grading in large classes. In *ATN Assessment Conference*. Institute for Interactive Media and Learning, University of Technology Sydney, Sydney.

[10] Keith Willey and Anne Gardner. 2010. Perceived differences in tutor grading in large classes: Fact or fiction?. In *Frontiers in Education Conference (FIE), 2010 IEEE*. IEEE, S2G–1.

[11] Keith Willey and AP Gardner. 2011. Building a community of practice to improve inter marker standardisation and consistency. In *SEFI 2011 Annual Conference: Global Engineering Recognition, Sustainability, Mobility*. Instituto Superior de Engenharia de Lisboa.

[12] Stacy L Young and Amy M Bippus. 2008. Assessment of graduate teaching assistant (GTA) training: A case study of a training program and its impact on GTAs. *Communication Teacher* 22, 4 (2008), 116–129.

Exploring how Students Perform in a Theory of Computation Course Using Final Exam and Homework Assignments Data

Christiane Frede
Universität Hamburg
Department of Informatics
Vogt-Kölln-Straße 30
22527 Hamburg, Germany
frede@informatik.uni-hamburg.de

Maria Knobelsdorf
Universität Wien
Department of Computer Science
Währinger Straße 29
1090 Wien, Austria
maria.knobelsdorf@univie.ac.at

ABSTRACT

Computer Science (CS) students continue to struggle in Theory of Computation (ToC) courses and empirical research continues to be required that is investigating this situation. In order to gain a differentiated picture and to learn more about potential challenges that CS students face when studying ToC, we used an exploratory data analysis to examine student performance in an undergraduate ToC course. In particular, we used final exam results and homework assignment scores to explore our research field and to develop hypotheses about it comparable to qualitative approaches. Our results indicate that despite their finale grade all students were particularly challenged by formal proof assignments covering ToC concepts. These results bolster the evidence of a need for pedagogical approaches in ToC that address all students and are particularly focused on teaching them formal proof techniques within this domain.

KEYWORDS

Computer science education; theory of computation; exploratory data analysis; formal languages and automata theory; regression analysis; student performance

ACM Reference format:

G. Gubbiotti, P. Malagò, S. Fin, S. Tacchi, L. Giovannini, D. Bisero, M. Madami, and G. Carlotti. 1997. SIG Proceedings Paper in word Format. In *Proceedings of ACM Woodstock conference, El Paso, Texas USA, July 1997 (WOODSTOCK'97)*, 4 pages. https://doi.org/10.1145/123 4

1 INTRODUCTION

Computer Science (CS) undergraduate students are required to take at least one Theory of Computation (ToC) course within

ICER '18, August 13–15, 2018, Espoo, Finland
© 2018 Association for Computing Machinery.
ACM ISBN 978-1-4503-5628-2/18/08...$15.00
https://doi.org/10.1145/3230977.3230996

their study program (e.g. [17], p. 55-60, [30], p.13, p. 21-23). These courses and their corresponding introductory literature cover topics like regular languages, grammars, logic, automata theory, as well as algorithms, data structures and complexity (cf. [8][16][27]). From anecdotal evidence, it is known that a high number of students fail to pass final exams, and only a minority of students manage to perform very well. Because A-students usually also do well during the entire Theory course, it is tempting to assume that they have gained an overall strong understanding of ToC, while students scoring low have not. Such conclusion from one final exam result is not necessarily an effective indicator, though, as it sums up an entire spectrum of domain-specific competences of ToC. Also, the extent to which high or low scores reflect students' overall high or low performance has not yet been sufficiently taken into account in research studies about ToC.

Questioning potential reasons why students fail, anecdotal evidence offers narratives that often consist of one or more of the following arguments: Students do not invest enough time, do not attend regularly lectures and exercise sessions, are not motivated, interested, or simply not smart enough to cope with ToC (cf.[6][23]). Pedagogical approaches have been introduced that build on some of these assumptions aiming to improve students' low performance in ToC courses (e.g. [9][13][14][18][25][32][33]). Another line of research in this field has been tools and environments which were suggested as part of the course's pedagogy (e.g.[3][7][10][12][15][24]). All of these approaches and tools have been developed with the assumption that students' difficulties with ToC are mainly caused by students' lack of interest and motivation as well as their inabilities to understand the concepts and theorems involved due to the abstract and formal nature of ToC. Unfortunately, none of these assumptions has been empirically validated in advance in order to inform pedagogical considerations by detailed insights about the nature of students' difficulties.

Recently, single case studies have been offered, e.g., [19][22], which provide insights into students' potential issues with ToC (like specific difficulties with mastering mathematical language and creating formal proofs in corresponding assignments of ToC). But these studies usually focus on only few students and one specific ToC concept. As ToC covers a broad field of concepts and domain-specific competencies, the question remains as to what is mainly challenging the majority of students: Specific ToC concepts or required domain-specific competencies relevant to all ToC chapters?

In order to gain a more differentiated and comprehensive picture of what is particularly challenging for students in a ToC course, we conducted a study investigating student performance. For this, we used submitted homework assignment scores and final exam results from an introductory ToC course attended by over 500 students during the winter term 2016/2017 at Technische Universität Berlin in Germany.

Using an explorative data analysis approach, we provide insights into student performance and develop hypotheses grounded in our data. The paper is structured as follows: We start by giving an overview of previous research (Section 2). We continue by explaining the research method and the course that is situated behind our data (Section 3). Then, we present and discuss our results as well as resulting hypotheses about this research field (Section 4). Finally, we end with a conclusion about our work (Section 5).

2 RELATED WORK

Existing approaches to improving undergraduate education of ToC in majority rely on assumptions build from individually gathered students feedbacks and teachers' belief about students' difficulties with ToC rather than on empirically validated research (cf.[6][15][24][25]). There are few studies investigating students' actual difficulties with specific assignments, but these studies have been limited to specific ToC topics of corresponding courses (e.g., NP-completeness [19], regular and context-free languages [23]). In a case study, Knobelsdorf and Frede (2016) observed students solving a proof by reduction; their results showed that students actually seemed interested in ToC topics and understood the ToC concept of NP-completeness, but they were challenged with mastering mathematical language and creating formal proofs related to this concept [19]. However, due to the nature of a single case study we cannot exclude or assume with reasonable certainty that students had also further issues with proof techniques related to other ToC concepts. Though, other case studies indicate a certain pattern. For example, Armoni (2009) conducted a document analysis of students' solutions to algorithm assignments focusing on reduction proofs [1]. Armoni's results show that students "do not seem to treat reduction as a general problem-solving strategy applicable in many domains for solving different kinds of problems" (p. 20). Pillay (2010) analyzed three tests and weekly tutorials from thirteen students to identify learning difficulties they seemed to experience. She concludes in her study that the students' main difficulty was a general inability to problem solving [23]. Nevertheless, the outline of Pillay's study was also limited by only covering automata, regular and context-free languages and only thirteen participants. A broader analysis about what ToC concepts students have difficulties with during a course about algorithms, data structures and complexity was conducted by Enström (2014). She used mainly an automated assessment system and included surveys, oral feedback, and student grades to measure student performance [11]. She also concludes that

students displayed problems with proof assignments and that complexity proofs seemed to be particularly difficult.

Except for [11], all above mentioned studies focus their investigations on one or only a few selected topics from an entire range of ToC topics covered in their specific ToC course. Therefore, the question remains open as to how the investigated students performed on all assignments covered during a ToC course. The existing research and results are, therefore, not sufficient in offering a detailed and differentiated overall picture as to which ToC topics, concepts, or related competencies challenge students most and if there are differences among students with different final grades. Building on this current state of research, we want to ask the following questions:

- **RQ1:** What kind of assignments usually covered during an ordinary, undergraduate introductory ToC course are causing students most difficulties? Are these in majority formal proof assignments, and are they related to specific topics?

- **RQ2:** Are there differences among low and high performing students, especially regarding these potentially different assignment types?

3 RESEARCH DESIGN

In this section we introduce our research design. After presenting the research method, the course setup is illustrated as well as what kind of data we have been using.

3.1 Research Method

For our research design, we chose to work with Exploratory Data Analysis (EDA), which was influenced by Tukey [28][29]. Comparable to qualitative approaches like grounded theory, this method advocates using numerical data in order to explore a specific field of research or observed phenomenon if there are no hypotheses, available models, or broad insights available. Tukey describes EDA as "numerical detective work" [28] summarizing several different and not final ways to explore available data. Typically, when starting to explore quantitative data, the used data is usually an easily available sample to support the answering of open questions instead of hypothesis testing. In contrast to limiting the analysis of data to that which would be necessary to analyze a hypothesis, EDA techniques are used to provide a clear picture of the whole data set as complete as possible [2].

One possible way to begin with EDA is summarizing the data, picking out more important features to clarify the general data structure, and getting ideas for further analysis steps (cf. [5][21]). Therefore, summary statistics can be calculated for the whole data as well as subgroups (e.g. mean, deviation). Moreover, data plotting is a valuable way to give an overview of the data and to make interesting anomalies directly visible. Commonly used diagrams are histograms, boxplot diagrams and scatterplot diagrams depending on the data and open questions. This combination of different kinds of exploration techniques can be used to build theories and hypotheses by a detailed overview of the research topics and can enable further kinds of analyses.

Therefore, EDA supports creating an overview of a broad research field such as ours and may be appropriate for getting closer to it.

Because of its exploratory nature, there is no explicit theoretical background framing our research field and research questions. As the very beginning of this research focus, there are purely statistical terms without restrictions. This shall keep open the possibility of gathering all anomalies and observations occurring. For the statistical analysis of our study, we used the software SPSS. According to EDA, we started with summarizing our different data sets to get an overview of the data structure and to help us identify interesting patterns and deviations. We visualized these with the help of different kinds of diagrams and tables. In addition, we used open coding techniques [20] for assignment categorization in order to obtain an overview of the content-related distribution of our data. To find correlating values in our data, we used regression analysis and the Pearson correlation coefficient (cf. [4], p. 341 et seq.). Building on our findings, we formulated hypotheses related to our research focus.

3.2 Course Setup

As data, we chose to use non-reactively gathered data from an actual class because we wanted to investigate student performance as it usually occurs in a typical, undergraduate ToC course without using a particular intervention. We felt, there is not yet enough knowledge gained about students' overall difficulties with ToC to create a well-controlled experiment. Also, well established instruments to precisely measure domain-specific competences in this field are missing. Therefore, we decided to work with the same kind of student data that instructors see every semester and to see if we could gain new insights from these data first. For this, we chose to use a large data set of student performance in their homework assignments and final exam from an introductory ToC course. Students' homework assignments provide formative information about their performance during the course, while the final exam results are of summative nature. We used data available from a course that was offered during the 2016/2017 winter term at Technische Universität Berlin in Germany and was attended by 571 CS undergraduate students.

The chosen course introduced formal languages and automata (FLAT) and covered mappings, words, grammars as well as minimization of automata and closure properties. In addition, the first half of the course also included mathematical topics like sets, propositional logic, predicate logic and functions. For a detailed list of all topics, please see Table 3. The course was mandatory for all CS undergraduate students and was a course usually taken in their first year of studies. Within the undergraduate CS program, an introductory mathematics course was offered during the same term covering topics from analysis and linear algebra, which CS students were also required to attend as well.

The FLAT course consisted of a weekly lecture (90 minutes) presenting relevant course topics, central concepts, algorithms and their proofs and illustrating them with examples using slides and live annotation in a lecture hall. Additionally, there were tutorial sessions (90 minutes) where a teaching assistant solved practice assignments with the help of about 30 students visible for everyone on a blackboard. Attending lecture and tutorial sessions was not mandatory. Sample solutions for the presented assignments were given to the students at the end of every week. Usually, there were a lot more assignments (and corresponding sample solutions) available than the number that could be discussed in the tutorial sessions. Hence, the teaching assistants focused on covering every topic and discussed a variety of topics and assignment types. Furthermore, the students could submit four sets of homework assignments during the entire course with each set containing a different number of assignments and 31 assignments in total. For these submissions, students were required to work in small study groups from two to four and to submit their solutions as a group.

Additionally, students were provided with teaching videos about some of the course's topics and a formulary. Individual consultation was offered every week by teaching assistants.

During the entire course, students had to collect so-called portfolio points which summed up to their final grade (with 100 as the maximum amount of portfolio points). Portfolio points could be gained by submitting altogether four sets of homework assignments distributed over the semester. Every set of homework made up to 5 portfolio points in sum, adding up to 20 portfolio points in total for all homework assignments. Additional 30 portfolio points could be gained by an online multiple choice test in the middle of the course covering the mathematical basics from the first half of the course. The final exam at the end of the course covered only the Theory topics from the second half of the course, and made another 50 portfolio points. Students would pass the course if they reached at least 50 portfolio points altogether.

3.3 Data Sources

At the beginning of the course, 571 students submitted their first set of homework, while the fourth and last set of homework was submitted by 497 students, indicating an overall dropout of 74 students. Students did not submit every assignment within one set of homework, but we still considered their data in our analysis as long as they submitted every set of homework. This was necessary because only a minority of students submitted all assignments from all four sets of homework. We do not have reliable insights why students did not work on all assignments. Possible reasons could be, for example, that students did not understand an assignment or know what to do to solve it, or lacked time, interest, or motivation to work on it.

Independent from the homework submissions, 419 students attended the final exam at the end of the course. Among these, eight students attended the repeat exam four weeks later and another eight attended just the latter. In sum, the course suffered from a dropout rate of 25%. Among the 427 students attending one of the exams, around 295 (69%) passed it with more than 49% of possible exam points. Regarding their portfolio points, 339 students passed the entire course, which sums up to 59% of the originally 571 students starting the course.

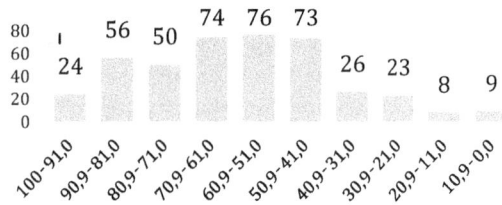

Figure 1: Distribution of points from the final exam: The x-axis illustrates the points, the y-axis the number of students

Grade	Points	Students
A	100 – 81	80
B	80 – 70	67
C	69 – 59	88
D	58 – 50	61
F	< 50	123

Table 1: Required points in the final exam, corresponding grades, and amount of students receiving them

The numbers from winter term 2016/2017 correspond to former performances in this particular ToC course at Technische Universität Berlin. Despite the lack of empirical evidence, failure rates in introductory ToC courses in undergraduate CS programs in Germany tend to be very high (50% and more are not unusual). Therefore, these numbers seemed to reflect a typical student performance.

This is supported by the fact that no student selection procedure is undertaken at Technische Universität Berlin, so this course represented a typical CS undergraduate student population as it can be found at many German universities.

Furthermore, the specifics of the portfolio collection are not relevant for our analysis as we considered homework and exam performance. Both are typical elements of ToC courses used in CS undergraduate programs at German universities. Talking to ToC instructors in other European as well as Anglo-Saxon countries, there is anecdotal evidence that weekly homework assignments and final exams are classical pedagogical elements in their corresponding ToC undergraduate courses and that they also suffer from quite considerable dropout and student failure rates. Therefore, this chosen course and related student data represent, to our best knowledge, a typical outcome of student performance in an introductory, undergraduate ToC course.

4 RESULTS AND DISCUSSION

Presenting our results, we start by discussing students' final exam scores, namely grade distribution and performance on each assignment. Furthermore, we also discuss each assignment's topic and how this might be related to students' performances. We continue this kind of evaluation with students' performances in their homework assignments. This is followed by a regression analysis correlating the final exam grades with homework assignments. In the end, we conclude by developing hypotheses based on our results and provide suggestions for possible future work. As this is an exploratory data analysis, we decided to present one step of analysis at a time and discuss it immediately afterwards before continuing with the next step.

G A	A	B	C	D	F
E1	91%	86%	78%	74%	43%
E2	95%	90%	82%	79%	44%
E3	95%	89%	81%	78%	44%
E4	74%	52%	29%	16%	5%
E5	89%	64%	43%	27%	10%
E6	76%	54%	41%	32%	14%

Table 2: Percentage of achieved points for each exam assignment differentiated by grading groups

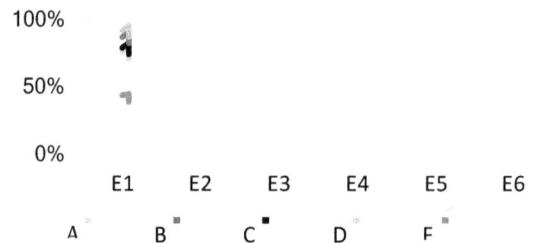

Figure 2: Performance in the final exam assignments

4.1 Final Exam Results

We started our analysis by investigating students' final exam results in more detail. Figure 1 shows the distribution of points which 419 students gained in the final exam. The exam results display, more or less, a bell curve indicating that the difficulty of the final exam seemed to be appropriate according to the student population of the course. Table 1 shows the general grading system used for this part of student performance. From this, we can see that 296 students (70%) of all students attending the exam received a grade higher than F (i.e. got more than 50% of the points). It also shows that 80 students (20%) scored an A, while the majority of students, that is around 50%, reached an average grade between B-D.

There are different narratives regarding how to interpret students' performance displayed in Table 1 and Figure 1. It is not uncommon to explain high scores as well as high failure rates with so-called "good" and "bad" student categories. From that point of view, it is acknowledged that some students are simply very smart and hardworking, while others do not master an understanding of ToC and either do not work hard enough to score better or lack have what is intellectually required to be a top student in ToC. With regard to our research questions, we started questioning this black-and-white picture and wondered whether high or low scoring students can actually be related to an overall strong of proof performance. For this, we were questioning whether there are certain assignments that cause all students to gain far less or far more points than other assignments, therefore preventing preventing all students to gain more points (i.e., a better grade or even to pass the course). To understand whether there are certain assignments with a high difficulty for most of the students, we looked into their actual performance of each of the six final exam assignments. To get an overview of the student performance, we divided all students in groups depending on their grade and compared how many points every grading group reached per assignment.

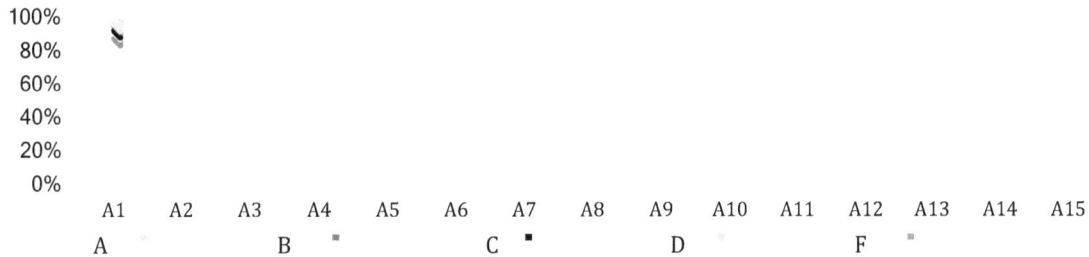

Figure 3: Performance in the homework assignments A1 - A15

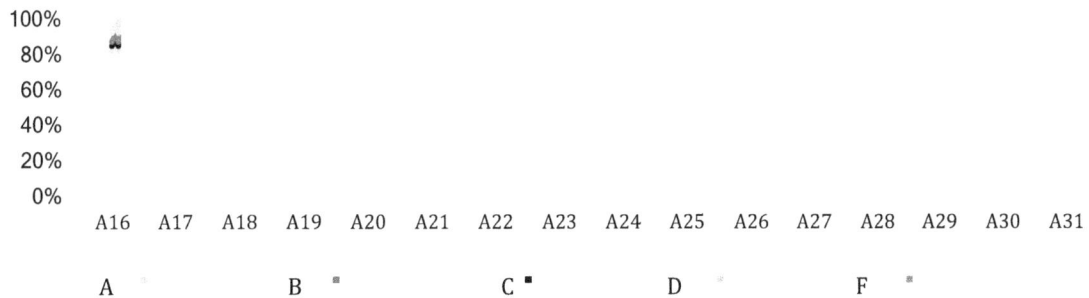

Figure 4: Performance in the homework assignments A16 - A31

Because every assignment had a different number of points, we normalized the percentages by assigning the full score of the points as 100% and calculated the average of the reached points for a certain assignment per grading group. Table 2 shows the values per group (G) and assignment number (A) where E1 to E6 corresponds to the six exam assignments.

At a first glance, there is nothing extraordinary about the data in Table 2. Group A performed best in every assignment confirming their "good student" status, group B and C had average scores, while the performances of group D and F related to "bad" or "not smart" students. A remarkable observation is that when comparing groups and assignments together, we find a point drop in assignments E4, E5, and E6 for every single grade group. The drop is the strongest with assignment E4. If we visualize these numbers as a line chart, we can see immediately this pattern (see Figure 2). While this drop in points is around 10-30% for group A and B, the gap is around 40-60% for group C and D and around 30% for group F. Thus, there is a noticeable point drop for each of the five grading groups. At this point, it seems questionable to argue that students achieving an A or B were smarter or better coping with ToC than the remaining student groups as, despite their overall performance group, they all seem to have trouble with the same kind of assignments.

With regard to our first research question, we started wondering what is different about E4, E5, and E6 in comparison to the other assignments, and what might cause all students to perform worse on these. For this part of our analysis, we will first summarize each assignment's topic and required activity:

- **E1:** Regular languages, required to specify a non-deterministic automaton (NFA) for a given language, a grammar for a given language and to derive words from a given grammar.
- **E2:** Automata, required to construct a NFA from a given deterministic automaton (DFA).

- **E3:** Minimization of a DFA, required to decide if a state is not reachable, applying the table-filling-algorithm to minimize a DFA, specifying equivalence classes that revealed from the previous table, visualizing the minimized DFA.
- **E4:** regular languages, required to prove that a language is not regular by using the Pumping lemma ([16], p.55-58), specifying all equivalence classes of the Myhill-Nerode relation regarding a given language.
- **E5:** context free languages, required to specify a type-2 grammar and to construct a pushdown automaton (PDA).
- **E6:** context free languages, required to give derivations from a given PDA and to prove that a given language is not regular only by using decidability properties.

If we examine what is different within the assignments E4, E5, and E6 in comparison to the first three assignments, we find that E4 and E6 require students to create a formal proof, among other subtasks. On the other hand, E1, E2, and E3 require students to specify and construct automata and grammars by applying specific algorithms. E4, the assignment with the highest point drop, is also the assignment requiring students to perform the most formal proof by using the Pumping lemma. Hence, the data indicates that all students had issues with this task, no matter if they scored an A, B, C, D or F on the final exam. Concluding, this first analysis step supports the results from other single case studies that students seem to have particular problems with proof assignments from ToC (see section 2).

4.2 Homework Assignments

Building on our insights from the previous analysis, we were wondering whether students were also challenged by formal proof assignments already during homework tasks. Because of this question, we took a closer look at their performance on the homework assignments. We performed the same point distribution analysis each of the 31 homework assignments, as we did for the exam assignments before (see previous subsection).

Because of space reasons, we have included only the corresponding line charts that visualize how each grade group scored in their entire homework spectrum (see Figure 3 and Figure 4). Again, we can discover the pattern that group A scored highest for each assignment, B and C were the second this time the difference between the groups is less remarkable than it was in the exam results. Instead, we also find assignments with a strong point drop, and this holds again for every grading group. The most noticeable point drops for the first half of the homework assignments can be found for assignments A2, A5, A6, A7, A8, A10 and A15 with point drops from 15-50% compared to the remaining assignments (Figure 3). Figure 4 shows almost the same distribution for the remaining assignments A16-A31, but the gap between grading group A and the other groups seem to increase. Nevertheless, the grading groups show performance drops in the same assignments again. Noticeable point drops can be found in assignments A20, A21, A24, and A29 with drops from 10-40% to the usual performance.

To gain more insight into those homework assignments with strongest point drops and to find commonalities and differences, we summarize briefly what each of these particular assignments was about:

- **A2:** The topic were sets, required to prove or disprove specific properties.
- **A5:** Propositional logic, required to prove or disprove specific variable assignments.
- **A6:** Predicate logic, required to prove a given statement for two predicates.
- **A7:** Predicate logic, required to specify the first step of a contradiction.
- **A8:** Sets, required a mathematical induction over a checksum of a set of numbers.
- **A10:** Relations and functions, required to develop a proof about orders.
- **A15:** Equivalence classes, required to prove that two variables from set S are equivalent if S is a representative system from the equivalence relation R on a set X.
- **A20:** Words and languages, required a proof by induction about a given alphabet and words.
- **A21:** Grammars, required to specify deductions for words and languages.
- **A24:** Regular languages, required to develop a proof with the Pumping Lemma.
- **A29:** Regular languages, required to specify all equivalence classes of the Myhill-Nerode relation regarding a language A.

If we compare these eleven assignments, we can detect that all but three assignments (A7, A21, A29) needed the students to create proofs. Apart from that, most assignments differed regarding their topic and expected kind of proof. Interestingly,

Assignment	Topic	Assignment type
A1	Sets	Calculating
A3	Propositional Logic	Proving
A4	Propositional Logic	Proving
A9	Relations / orders	Specifying
A11	Functions / mappings	Specifying
A12	Functions / mappings	Proving
A13	Relations / orders	Specifying
A14	Relations / orders	Specifying
A16	Functions / mappings	Specifying
A17	Words / languages	Specifying
A18	Words / languages	Specifying
A19	Words / languages	Specifying
A22	Grammars, Chomsky hierarchy	Specifying
A23	Grammars, Chomsky hierarchy	Specifying
A25	Automata	Specifying
A26	Automata	Constructing
A27	Minimization of automata	Specifying
A28	Minimization of automata	Constructing
A30	Regular languages	Specifying
A31	Minimization of automata	Specifying

Table 3: Categorization of homework assignments without noticeable point drop

A24 was a proof that expected students to use the Pumping lemma like the exam assignment E4 (see subsection 4.1), which students scored worst on during their final exam. However, this very striking performance drop cannot be observed for A24 although the performance is comparatively low. The other part exam assignment E4 covered was about the Myhill-Nerode characteristic. The corresponding homework assignment was A29. Here, the students performed between 30-76%. of points providing, in sum, slightly lower values than A24. In sum, eight out of eleven homework assignments with a noticeable point drop required the students to develop a proof. In particular, the Pumping lemma and Myhill-Nerode tasks seemed to challenge students in their homework as well as in their later final exam.

Beyond these above discussed point drops, we also questioned what the remaining assignments without high point drops had in common and what might explain students' higher scores with these. Due to space reasons, we summarize the remaining assignments shortly in Table 3.

Following the question, we checked all assignments topics and assigned them to their superordinate topic drawn from the course formulary. Additionally, we used a summarizing technique based on qualitative content analysis [20] to categorize the assignments to assignment types. Here, we derived the following categories: *proving* (assignments required to develop a proof), *specifying* (assignments required to specify, e.g., derivations, languages, relations, or grammars from a corresponding given element), *constructing* (assignments required to construct an automaton from a given language and vice versa), *calculating* (e.g. sets) as most abstract summary of possible tasks.

From Table 3 we can see that most assignments without point drop require *specifying* activities while only one assignment requires *calculating* and two *constructing* activities. Additionally, there are still three proof assignments without point drop (A3, A4, A12) and we were wondering if there are patterns that explain why these three assignments do not suffer from a point drop as those proof assignments with a noticeable point drop. For that matter we analyzed these three assignments regarding the nature of proof required.

Assignments A3 and A4 had very schematic instructions for the development of a proof (e.g., specific usage of truth tables and equivalence transformations from propositional logic). A12 covered an assignment to prove cardinality with the usage of a bijection. This is the only proof within the thematic block "functions and mappings" but otherwise there was no striking abnormality we could detect in the corresponding kind of proof. Nevertheless, we found eleven assignments with noticeable performance drops and eight of these assignments required formal proofing. Furthermore, we could not detect a specific topic or only one kind of proof in the noticeable assignments. Two of three assignments with a higher performance had very schematic and less formal instructions for the development of a proof. Summarizing the described analysis step in this subsection, we conclude that low performance in proof assignments of the final exam was in majority also found in homework assignments.

4.3 Comparing Final Exam Results with Homework Assignments

After identifying an overall low performance in proof assignments of both final exam and homework, we were wondering if these two were related to each other and whether students performing high or low in the final exam, performed similarly high or low in the homework assignments. In other words, we were interested in answering the question, if the homework assignments, especially those with a significant point drop, could predict students' final exam results. For this, we correlated the final exam results with every single homework assignment score using only parts of our data, and we will explain this necessity next. As described in section 3.2, students were allowed to submit their homework in groups (by two to four people) and it is not unlikely that students could submit a very good homework that they might not be able to create on their own due to the overall group performance. For this, we used only data where all members of one group performed comparably in the final exam (i.e., same or one grade difference). Students that did not participate in the final exam were omitted, but their group members still remained in the data set used here. We assume that it is unlikely that a student that has done all the work with the homework would not participate in the final exam. After data cleansing, we were left with performance information about 247 students. We also would like to emphasize that not all 247 students submitted a solution for every homework assignment, and, therefore, the number for every

submitted assignment differs between 247 and 119. These numbers were considered for data analysis while missing submissions were ignored.

	r	p	n
A1	.367 **	.000	246
A2	.209 **	.001	246
A3	.031	.628	246
A4	.133 *	.039	243
A5	.390 **	.000	240
A6	.247 **	.002	160
A7	.256 **	.001	156
A8	.278 **	.001	140
A9	.239 **	.001	184
A10	.253 **	.003	132
A11	.337 **	.000	239
A12	.306 **	.000	185
A13	.091	.205	197
A14	.266 **	.000	196
A15	.349 **	.000	119
A16	.275 **	.000	198
A17	.114	.084	232
A18	.318 **	.000	143
A19	.242 **	.000	232
A20	.390 **	.000	127
A21	.294 **	.000	231
A22	.398 **	.000	170
A23	.337 **	.000	229
A24	.269 **	.002	126
A25	.289 **	.000	232
A26	.119	.072	231
A27	.427 **	.000	139
A28	.344 **	.000	166
A29	.290 **	.001	139
A30	.436 **	.000	130
A31	.164 *	.042	154

Table 4: Regression analysis for final exam and homework assignments: r = Pearson correlation coefficient, p = significance (** = significant correlation < .010; * = significant correlation < .050), n = number of students who submitted their homework

We decided to work with the incomplete data set because we did not know anything about the students' reasons and, therefore, had no valid argument not to do it. We simply assumed that either lack of time, understanding, motivation, or any other plausible reason caused students to omit certain assignments. Due to the overall high number of submissions for each assignment, we still considered this analysis step reasonable enough to create valuable insights.

Table 4 shows the results of the regression analysis. Specifically, it shows for all considered students the correlation between total points reached in the final exam and each homework assignment. Due to the distribution of the mathematical and theoretical topics within the course (see Section 3.2), the assignments A1 to A16 were about the mathematical half of the course, and A17 to A31 were about the ToC topics from the second half. As a first result from the numbers in Table 4, we can see that there is no high correlation for any homework assignment (because r < .500). This value shows that there is a statistically significant connection between the final exam grade and the corresponding homework assignment and the probability that this is a random connection is less than 1%. This means that it is not possible to predict the final exam results from one specific homework assignment and a low performance in the homework assignments does not necessarily lead to a low performance in the final exam. From this, we can conclude that homework assignments served their formative purpose and left room for students to practice ToC related tasks without influence on their final exam grade.

4.4 Developing Hypotheses

In this section, we will summarize our results and discuss them by answering our research questions (see also Section 2).

- **RQ1:** What kind of assignments usually covered during an ordinary, undergraduate introductory ToC course are causing students most difficulties? Are these in majority formal proof assignments, and are they related to specific topics?
- **RQ2:** Are there differences among low and high performing students, especially regarding these potentially different assignment types?

Building on these questions, we summarize our findings and build hypotheses grounded in our results.

Outcome 1: Our analysis indicates that there are specific assignments causing all students difficulties independent from their final exam grade. In more detail, we detected three assignments in the final exam that showed a significantly lower performance, of which two assignments were about proving (Section 4.1.). From eleven proof assignments in the homework, eight had a low performance as well (Section 4.2). Furthermore, we could not recognize that the noticeable assignments are related to specific topics. From that, we found the lowest scores for all students occurring in assignments that required formal proofs. This answer to our first research questions leads to the following hypothesis:

Hypothesis 1: Formal proof assignments, independent from their ToC topic, are the most challenging assignments for all students in ToC introductory courses, and performance decreases with the increasing level of formalization.

Outcome 2: We did not find a performance difference among the different grading groups and assignments types. Independent from their final exam grade, all students performed high and low in the same assignments. However, comparing to group A to D, students reaching an F in the final exam reached a score less than 50% for the first three exam assignments. Therefore, even without a point drop for the noticeable assignments E 4 to E6, group F would have not passed the final exam. This overall observation leads to the following hypothesis:

Hypothesis 2: Independent from their final exam grade, all students have noticeable lower scores in the same final exam and homework assignments.

Referring to the related work of our analysis and the single case studies discussed in Section 2, our results and hypotheses support the observation that students have particular problems with proof assignments increasing with the level of formalization and also independent from their overall performance.

5 CONCLUSION

In this paper, we have used exploratory data analysis to get an overview of student performance in a Theory of Computation (ToC) course. By summarizing the data and using tables and diagrams, we revealed patterns and anomalies in students' final exam and homework assignments scores. One particular finding is that all students, independent from their final exam grade, showed a low performance in exam and homework assignments which required formal proof techniques. In addition, this performance drop seemed to correspond to the assignments' required level of the formalization. From our evaluation, we hypothesize that students' issues with ToC are mainly due to a lack of formal proof techniques supporting comparable results from previous single case studies. In sum, our large data set, the view of the data from multiple perspectives, and the hypotheses grounded in data contribute important insights for future ToC pedagogies that should rather focus on stronger practicing of formal proofing techniques within the field of ToC.

Even though our results might seem like an obvious finding, we would like to emphasize that, so far, suggested pedagogical approaches and tools for ToC assume students are lacking motivation and interest. No pedagogical approaches can be found that support CS undergraduates especially with mastering proof techniques within the field of ToC, and no evidence has been provided that students' problems in ToC are those with formal proving. Furthermore, this issue is not limited to students performing low in the final exam but including students from grading group A as well.

To identify if there are specific assignment groups instead of single assignment predicting the final exam grade, we will continue our research with further correlation analyses. In order to strengthen the reliability of our results, we see a necessity of repeating the entire analysis with data from the same course but from another cohort (e.g., one year later). For future work, additional studies will be required to test our hypotheses with reactively gathered data and valid measuring instruments securing further the validity of our initial results. Qualitative observations and findings from mathematics education research will also be used in future studies to gain deeper insights into the specific difficulties students have with ToC proof assignments.

ACKNOWLEDGMENTS

We would like to thank Prof. Uwe Nestmann and his research group "Models and Theory of Distributed Systems" at Technische Universität Berlin (Germany) for supporting our research study.

REFERENCES

[1]   M. Armoni. 2009. Reduction in CS: A (mostly) quantitative analysis of reductive solutions to algorithmic problems. *Journal on Educational Resources in Computing (JERIC)* 8.4: 11.

[2]   J.T. Behrens and C.-H. Yu. 2003. Exploratory Data Analysis. *Handbook of Psychology. One:2:* 33–64.

[3]   D. Berque, D. Johnson, and L. Jovanovic. 2001. Teaching theory of computation using pen-based computers and an electronic whiteboard. *ACM SIGCSE Bulletin,* 33, 3, 169- 172.

[4]   A. Bryman. 2015. Social Research Methods. Oxford university press.

[5]   C. Chatfield. 1986. Exploratory data analysis. *European journal of operational research* 23.1: 5-13.

[6]   S. Chesñevar, M. González, and A. Maguitman, A. 2004. Didactic strategies for promoting significant learning in formal languages and automata theory. *In Proceedings of the 9th annual SIGCSE conference on Innovation and technology in computer science education. ACM:* 7-11.

[7]   D, Chudá. 2007. Visualization in Education of Theoretical Computer Science. *In Proceedings of the 2007 international conference on Computer systems and technologies. CompSysTech '07.* 84.

[8]   T. H. Cormen, C.E. Leiserson, R.L. Rivest and C. Stein. 2009. Introduction to Algorithms. MIT press.

[9]   P. Crescenzi, E. Enström, and V. Kann. 2013. From theory to practice: NP-completeness for every CS student. *In Proceedings of the 18th ACM conference on Innovation and technology in computer science education. ITiCSE '13. ACM:* 16-21.

[10]   V. Devedzic, J. Debenham, and D. Popvic. 2000. Teaching Formal Languages by an Intelligent Tutoring System. *Educational Technology and Society 3,* 2, ISSN 1436-4522.

[11]   E. Enström. 2014. On difficult topics in theoretical computer science education. Diss. *KTH Royal Institute of Technology.*

[12]   C. García-Osorio, I. Mediavilla-Sáiz, J Jimeno-Visitación, and N. García-Pedrajas. 2008. Teaching push-down automata and turing machines. *ACM SIGCSE Bulletin,* 40, 3.

[13]   H. Habiballa, T. Kmet. 2004. Theoretical branches in teaching computer science. *International Journal of Mathematical Education in Science and Technology.* 35, 6: 829-841.

[14]   W. Hämäläinen. 2004. Problem-based learning of theoretical computer science. In *Proceedings of the 34th ASEE/IEEE Frontiers in Education Conference.* S1H/1 -S1H/6 Vol. 3.

[15]   M. Hielscher, C. Wagenknecht. 2006. AtoCC: learning environment for teaching theory of automata and formal languages. *In Proceedings of the 11th annual SIGCSE conference on Innovation and technology in computer science education. ITICSE '06. ACM,* 306-306.

[16]   J. E. Hopcroft. 1979. Introduction to Automata Theory, Languages, and Computation, Addison-Wesley Publishing Company.

[17]   IEEE Computer Society and ACM: 2013. Computer Science Curricula. DOI: 10.1145/2534860

[18]   L. Korte, S. Anderson, H. Pain and J. Good. 2007 Learning by game-building: a novel approach to theoretical computer science education. *ITiCSE '07 Proceedings of the 12th annual SIGCSE conference on Innovation and technology in computer science education,* pages 53–57.

[19]   M. Knobelsdorf, C. Frede. 2016. Analyzing Student Practices in Theory of Computation in Light of Distributed Cognition Theory. *In Proceedings of the 2016 ACM Conference on International Computing Education Research (ICER '16).* ACM, New York, NY, USA, 73-81.

[20]   P. Mayring. 2000. Qualitative Content Analysis. *Forum: Qualitative Social Research [Online Journal],* 1, 2, Art. 20.

[21]   S. Morgenthaler. 2009. Exploratory data analysis. *Wiley Interdisciplinary Reviews: Computational Statistics 1.1:* 33-44.

[22]   M. Parker and C. Lewis. 2014. What makes big-O analysis difficult: understanding how students understand runtime analysis. *Journal of Computing Sciences in Colleges 29.4.* 164-174.

[23]   N. Pillay. 2010. Learning difficulties experienced by students in a course on formal languages and automata theory. *SIGCSE Bulletin 41.4:* 48-52.

[24]   S. H. Rodger, B. Bressler, T. Finley and S. Reading. 2006. Turning automata theory into a hands-on course. *In Proceedings of the 37th SIGCSE technical symposium on Computer science education. SIGCSE '06. ACM.* 379-383.

[25]   A. Schäfer, J. Holz, T. Leonhardt, U. Schröder, P. Brauner and Martina Ziefle. 2013. From boring to scoring - a collaborative serious game for learning and practicing mathematical logic for computer science education. *Computer Science Education 23:* 87-111.

[26]   S. Sigman. 2007. Engaging students in formal language theory and theory of computation. *ACM SIGCSE Bulletin. Vol. 39. No. 1. ACM.*

[27]   M. Sipser. 2012. Introduction to the Theory of Computation. Cengage Learning.

[28]   J. W. Tukey. 1977. Exploratory data analysis. Vol. 2

[29]   J. W. Tukey, F. Mosteller and D.C. Hoaglin. 2000. Understanding robust and exploratory data analysis. *Wiley Classics Library ed New York.*

[30]   O. Zukunft. 2016. Empfehlungen für Bachelor- und Masterprogramme im Studienfach Informatik an Hochschulen. Bonn. *Gesellschaft für Informatik e.V.*

[31]   R. Verma. 2005. A visual and interactive automata theory course emphasizing breadth of automata. In *Proceedings of the 10th Annual SIGCSE Conference on innovation and Technology in Computer Science Education. ITiCSE '05.* ACM, 325-329.

[32]   M. Wermelinger, A. Dias. 2005. A prolog toolkit for formal languages and automata, *ACM SIGCSE Bulletin.* 37, 3

[33]   Z. Zingaro. 2008. Another approach for resisting student resistance to formal methods, *ACM SIGCSE Bulletin,* 40, 4.

Applying a Gesture Taxonomy to Introductory Computing Concepts

Amber Solomon
School of Interactive Computing
Georgia Institute of Technology
Atlanta, GA
asolomon30@gatech.edu

Mark Guzdial
School of Interactive Computing
Georgia Institute of Technology
Atlanta, GA
guzdial@cc.gatech.edu

Betsy DiSalvo
School of Interactive Computing
Georgia Institute of Technology
Atlanta, GA
bdisalvo@cc.gatech.edu

Ben Rydal Shapiro
The Space Learning and Mobility Lab
Vanderbilt University
Nashville, TN
ben@benrydal.com

ABSTRACT

Gestures, or spontaneous hand movements produced when talking, are an untapped resource for understanding student knowledge in computing education. This paper develops a conceptual framework to support future studies of learning and teaching that incorporate gesture studies in programming contexts. In particular, this paper introduces how gesture has been used to study teaching and learning in another discipline, mathematics; critically reviews and interprets what concepts and methods may be most relevant to programming contexts; and also discusses what unique challenges programming contexts present to studies of gesture (e.g. differences in abstract versus concrete). We ground our understandings of gesture by using an observational study where we observed novice students learning to program. This paper concludes by suggesting potential avenues for future research in computing education that incorporate analyses of gesture in studies of teaching and learning.

CCS CONCEPTS

• **Social and professional topics** → **Computing education**;

KEYWORDS

gesture, taxonomy, abstract, concrete

ACM Reference Format:
Amber Solomon, Mark Guzdial, Betsy DiSalvo, and Ben Rydal Shapiro. 2018. Applying a Gesture Taxonomy to Introductory Computing Concepts. In *ICER '18: 2018 International Computing Education Research Conference, August 13–15, 2018, Espoo, Finland.* ACM, New York, NY, USA, 8 pages. https://doi.org/10.1145/3230977.3231001

1 INTRODUCTION

Gestures, or spontaneous hand movements produced when talking, constitute a pervasive element of human communication and reflect human cognition [38]. While we often think of gestures that are used for emphases (e.g., head nods for the affirmative or head shakes for negative statements), they can also be visible, external representations of what people are thinking [3].

Gestures are an integral part of communication about concepts in the classroom. Teachers routinely gesture along with their speech. Gestures may play an important role in communicating knowledge to learners [4]. Students routinely gesture as they talk about the concepts they are learning. In a number of other academic disciplines, gestures have been identified as important aspects of understanding learning and improving learning.

For example, gestures produced during instruction and teacher-student interaction shed light on the mechanisms involved in learning from instruction [4]. Additionally, gestures externalize aspects of speakers' knowledge, helping learners manage the "working memory demands of mathematical thinking and explanation" [1]. In mathematics, understanding how gestures are used helps understand performance, instruction, assessment, and learning. Alibali et al. suggest that the study of gesture in mathematics helps explain why certain types of problems are more difficult than others, identify assessment methods that accurately gauge knowledge, design more effective learning environments, select appropriate methods for instruction, and understand why learners have greater success with some instructional methods than with others [4].

Moreover, in learning sciences literature we find a number of analyses of people's interaction and conversation which include gesture [41, 42]. Some work uses gesture studies to provide insights to internal sense making [11], while other work seeks to incorporate multi-scalar analyses of gesture and movement to inform the production of social learning contexts and the design of learning experiences [43]. However, in computing education research there are few instances where the gestures of teachers or students are considered in analysis, but it is a promising direction for future work. Computing education might be able to draw on gesture research to provide similar insights to explain student behavior and provide insights into design of interventions.

In this paper, we develop a conceptual framework to support future studies of learning and teaching that incorporate gesture studies in programming contexts. In particular, this paper introduces how gesture has been used to study teaching and learning, with a particular focus on one discipline (mathematics); critically reviews and interprets what concepts may be most relevant to programming contexts; and discusses what unique challenges programming contexts present to studies of gesture. We ground our explanation of the possible role of gestures by introducing examples from an observational study where we observed novice students learning to program. This paper concludes by suggesting potential avenues for future research in computing education that incorporate analyses of gesture in studies of teaching and learning.

Our contributions are from the lens of a scholarship of integration, where we consider how well the current gestures and learning literature integrates with issues in learning in computing. We offer an initial gesture taxonomy for computing education and suggest a research agenda to incorporate analyses of gesture in computing education.

2 LITERATURE ON GESTURES RELEVANT TO COMPUTING EDUCATION

Gesture has been studied to understand its role in teaching and learning in several domains (e.g., mathematics, physics) with a research lens informed by embodied cognition, learning sciences, and educational psychology. In this paper we focus on the study of gestures from a learning sciences and educational psychology perspective with an emphasis on disciplinary education research in mathematics. We limit our focus first, because mathematics offers the tightest connection to computing and second, because the literature on the use of gestures in learning is expansive, and thus our limited focus helps set boundaries for this initial exploration of gesture research to computing education.

2.1 Gestures Defined

While there is a common perception of gestures, within the learning literature characteristics of gestures have been described to establish a shared understanding. Gestures are defined as visible, external representations of what people are thinking [18]. They are spontaneous hand movements produced when talking [17]. Yet, while gestures are hand movements, not all hand movements are gestures [38]. Gestures can be distinguished from other hand movements by four characteristics [20, 21, 38]:

(1) Gestures begin from a position of rest, move away from this position, and then return to rest.
(2) Gestures have a peak structure, also referred to as the stroke, which is generally recognized as a moment of accented movement to denote the function of meaning of a movement.
(3) The stroke phase is preceded by a preparation phase and succeeded by a recovery phase in which the hand and arm move back to their rest position. Consequently, gestures have a clear beginning and ending.
(4) Gestures are often symmetrical.

2.2 Gesture Can Reveal What a Learner Knows

Gestures have been found to be beneficial for instruction and understanding student knowledge. Gestures produced while students explain their reasoning provides unique insight into their thought processes [31]. For example, Novak and Goldin-Meadow describe a child who believes that the amount of water changes when it is poured from a tall, thin container into a short, fat container which indicates the child does not understand the concept of conservation of liquid quantity [31]. The child justified their belief by saying, "this one is taller than this one," while making a C-shaped gesture to indicate the narrow width of the tall container, followed by a wider C-shaped gesture to indicate the larger width of the short container. The child is highlighting one dimension of the containers in speech (height), but his hands make it clear that he is beginning to think about a second dimension (width). Their gesture is conveying different information than their words. When someone produces different information in gesture than in speech, it reveals that they know more than they say. The information a learner conveys uniquely in gesture is often implicit knowledge, not yet accessible to explicit understanding [2].

2.3 Gesture Production Can Support Learning

Gesture may provide an avenue through which learners can consider new ideas. Broaders et al. found that children told to gesture added novel strategies to their repertoires that were found only in gesture [5]. These children were also more likely to profit from instruction in math. After the lesson (when they were no longer gesturing), the children were able to solve math problems on a paper-and-pencil test that they could not solve before the lesson.

2.4 Seeing Gesture Can Support Learning

A number of studies have identified that students are more likely to profit from instruction when a teacher gestures [7, 34, 48]. Ping et al. found that children who received instruction with gesture improved more than children who did not [35]. This might be because of gesture's ability to ground the abstract language of the lesson to the concrete physical environment and gesture's ability to convey ideas through "its representational form" [35, 48]. Physical environment refers to the setting for the interaction, the interlocutors, the focal tasks, and the representations, tools, technological resources, and social dimensions [4].

2.5 The Connection Between Gesture and Learning

Previous research suggests gesture promotes learning by engaging motor systems and encouraging students to link abstract concepts. Gesture enhances spoken communication. Ping found that the effects of gesture on learning stem from its capacity to engage the motor system [36]. Gesturing thus supports learning because it is a type of action. Yet, a gesture is a representational action and not an action on objects, which is typically intended to carry out specific functions. This difference is responsible for gesture's unique effects on learning. Action on objects leads to shallow learning since it tends to lead people to think that their learned actions are relevant only to those objects [26]. This may hinder generalization by focusing learners on details that get in the way of transfer. In contrast, gesture, which occurs apart objects, provides a "physical distance," which facilitates abstraction and generalization to new contexts yet still engages motor systems. This distinction is what improves learning [32]. Gesture leads to deeper and more flexible learning.

3 GESTURE TAXONOMY

Taxonomies of gesture classify gesture based on certain functions or models of gesture production [15, 16, 37]. McNeill's taxonomy is widely used in gesture studies on educational issues and is considered applicable to gestures "in any type of discourse or any content area" [4, 38]. For our analysis, we will use McNeill's taxonomy as a framework.

McNeill's taxonomy outlines four types of gesture: (1) deictic, or pointing gestures that indicate objects or locations, (2) iconic, which are gestures that depict semantic content directly via the shape or motion trajectory of the hand(s), (3) metaphoric, which depict semantic content via metaphor, and (4) beat, which are motorically simple, rhythmic gestures that do not express semantic content but that instead align with the prosody of speech [27]. Using mathematics as a domain, we will explore each of these types of gestures in more depth.

3.1 Gesture Types in Mathematics

Using McNeil's taxonomy, Alibali et al. present a gesture taxonomy for mathematics [4]. In their taxonomy of deictic, iconic, metaphoric, and beat gesture types, they make the following claims: (1) Deictic gestures reflect the grounding of cognition in the physical environment, (2) iconic gestures manifest mental simulations of action and perception, and (3) metaphoric gestures reflect conceptual metaphors, and (4) beat gestures have no meaning.

3.1.1 Deictic Gestures Reflect the Grounding of Cognition in the Physical Environment. Deictic gestures, or pointing gestures, "physically link speech and associated mental processes to the physical environment" [27]. Speakers use deictic gestures to index physically present objects or inscriptions and to evoke non-present objects or inscriptions [19, 29].

Alibali et al. describe an example of deictic gestures used in a mathematics class [4]. An elementary school student explained his solution to the problem 6 + 3 + 4 = ? + 4: "6 plus 3 is 9, plus 4 is 13, plus . . . 13 plus 4 is 17," and he pointed to each of the numbers in the problem. He used his left hand to point to the left-side of the equation (6 + 3 + 4), and his right hand to point to the right-side of the equation (? + 4) and to his solution. This showed his awareness of equations having two sides.

This example illustrates how students and teachers use deictic gestures to index the referents of their speech when talking about mathematical ideas and illustrates the speaker's grounding of mathematical ideas in the physical environment. Deictic gestures affect listeners' comprehension of the speech that accompanies them, "particularly when that speech is ambiguous or complex relative to the listeners' skills" [25, 45]. Pointing is uninterpretable without the environmental ground to give it meaning [1]. Deictic gestures "anchor" the information expressed in the verbal channel in the material world [50], and thus reflect the grounding of cognition in the physical environment [4]. Grounding here refers to mapping an abstraction with its concrete referent, like an object [22].

Figure 1: An iconic gesture that simulates action on a mathematical object: changing the slope of a line [4].

Grounding of this sort may support the transfer of knowledge to new situations.

3.1.2 Iconic Gestures Manifest Mental Simulations of Action and Perception. Iconic, or representational, gestures represent concrete ideas and are used to convey information about the size, shape, or orientation of the object of discourse [47]. They draw their "communicative strength" from being perceptually similar to the phenomenon that is being talked about [27]. Iconic gestures are therefore said to have a transparent relationship to the idea they convey, particularly within a narrative event in which they depict concrete objects and events [27]. Whereas speech and gesture develop out of the same psychological structure, iconic gestures, because of their similarity relation, require less transformation. Speakers produce iconic gestures to convey semantic information [38]. They reflect the content of the semantic model more faithfully. It is therefore possible to catch a glimpse of students' understanding of a given concept in the gestures they adopt even when having difficulty articulating their understanding [8].

In mathematics, an example of an iconic gesture is when a teacher gestures to simulate the action of something, like altering the slope of a line (see Figure 1). This type of gesture helps to link related mathematical ideas during instruction.

Iconic gestures reveal simulated perceptions and simulated actions. The slope is not actually moving on the graph, but the student may mentally simulate the motion in concert with the teacher's gesture. In talk about mathematics, such gestures often reveal perceptual characteristics of inscriptions [4].

Chu and Kita examined the types of gestures people make when explaining their strategies for a mental rotation task [6]. People initially used gestures that mimed the act of rotating the object. Over the course of the session, however, people began to use more abstract gestures. They concluded this shift in gesture reflected "an internalization of the action strategy," which had transitioned from concrete to abstract.

3.1.3 Metaphoric Gestures Reflect Conceptual Metaphors. Metaphoric gestures are similar to iconic gestures, however they represent an abstract, and not concrete, idea [47]. Both iconic and metaphoric gestures are commonly used to depict phenomena and concepts that are hard to describe in words [24].

This type of gesture frequently appears in discussions on abstract content, particularly in areas like mathematics and physics [1, 39]. Alibali et al. describe metaphorical gestures used in a mathematics class [4]:

> For example, a mathematician holding steady one hand while she moves the other hand towards it until the two palms touch as she discusses the concept of 'approaching the limit' is using a metaphorical gesture, as is a student modeling a mathematics speed problem by the use of his hands.

Metaphoric gestures "structure understanding and perceptions of the world, and they are manifested in a range of expressions in everyday language" [38]. They often are manifestations of one's conceptual metaphors [27]. Lakoff and Johnson state that conceptual metaphors derive from image schemas regarding space, moving, forces, and other aspects of human experience [23].

3.1.4 Beat Gestures Have No Meaning. Beat gestures are the simplest type of gesture: "a simple kinetic realization of the underlying pulse" [46]. They are outward-focused movements timed to important content words [38]. McNeil suggests beat gestures "do not present a discernible meaning even when the visual channel is available" [27]. They do not depict specific math content and do not convey semantic information [4, 27].

3.2 A Gesture Taxonomy in Computing Education

While the previous work outlined above describes how gesture has been influential on understanding learning and teaching in mathematics there has been little or no focused work on describing how exploring gesture can help us understand computing education and learning. In the following sections we present an observational study of novices learning to program followed by an analysis of the type of gestures produced by teacher and students' interactions. Our aim in doing so is to make an initial exploration of gestures in computing education research and to set the stage for future studies.

Computing is characterized by the notional machine that cannot be perceived directly through the senses. Concrete and abstract have different conceptualizations in computing versus other abstract domains like mathematics. Mathematics typically has many lived experiences that one can draw upon to reason and understand. For instance, a gesture of a slope of a line can still be used through experiencing a slope of walking on a hill. However, in computing, concepts often do not have real-world, concrete counterparts. If one were to theoretically gesture a loop, what it represents in concrete is unknown. There is potentially a difference between pointing in computing versus in mathematics, and there may be gestures that have the same meaning and serve the same function. In the next sections, we ground the discussion of gestures in computing education and connect it the previous taxonomies through examples seen in a classroom observation study. We conclude with a discussion of the gaps in our knowledge about gesture in computing education.

4 AN EXPLORATORY OBSERVATIONAL STUDY

We recently conducted an exploratory observational study of novice students learning to program in a classroom. The goal of this study was to gain an initial understanding of the type of gestures students and teachers produce in computing classrooms to help in building a taxonomy of computing gestures that could be used to facilitate learning.

During the Spring of 2017, the first author spent 90 minutes teaching an introductory high school programming course once a week for 12-weeks. The curriculum for these 12-weeks included content on variables, if and if-else statements, while statements, and conditional statements. Class was in an alternative high-school which serves students who had challenges in traditional academic learning environments. There were eight students: six males and two females, seven Black students and one Hispanic student. Students had varying level of math skills and were taking either Algebra 1 or Geometry. None had experience with Calculus.

Each class period, students worked on different Scratch projects, ranging from music video creation to creating a game based on a social justice issue. We often had students work in groups of two or three and present their work for peer student critiques.

We taught them variables in a lecture. Students individually completed a worksheet about variable manipulation and declaration and then the class discussed the answer to each question on the worksheet. We taught conditionals, if-statements, and loops by having students convert their favorite lyrics to code. The students wrote the "code" on a white board and had to explain it to the class. We would also write "code" on a white board and would have students explain it.

At the end of the 12-weeks, we conducted 15-minute structured interviews with each student where we had them tell us the output of eight pieces of code. Each piece of code covered different computing topics (variables, if-statements, and while loops). We had students explain their responses since explanations tend to be a rich source of gesture data.

The first author took observation notes at the end of each class period. Observation notes were taken using a two-column approach, with observations in one column and corresponding reflections added after the session in another column. When students were observed making gestures, we wrote a description of a gesture and its accompanying speech. The observation and gesture notes were analyzed to identify types of gestures, how they might map to existing taxonomies of gestures, and the student knowledge they might convey.

In the Fall of 2017 we worked with the same students, conducting a 4-day programming workshop. This gave us an opportunity to observe certain gestures and ask for further explanations based upon questions from our first pass at analysis.

We are not presenting a study that tests a hypothesis or evaluates an intervention. Our data cannot be independently verified, and at best, we can say our analysis is a plausible interpretation. However, for an initial study, this level of observation and reporting is reasonable to provide foundational work in this under-researched space. We are noting what gestures we saw and connecting them to existing taxonomies. With more precise methodology and data collection (e.g., videotaping interactions), future studies could produce data that could be more rigorously analyzed.

5 THE TYPES OF GESTURE IN A COMPUTING CLASSROOM

In this section, we present the different types of gestures we observed in the computing classroom that comprised our study. We then describe how these gestures were used during instruction within this context and also what these gestures potentially revealed about student knowledge.

5.1 Deictic

As described previously, deictic gestures, or pointing gestures, point to establish the location of an object [27]. In mathematics, these gestures reflect the grounding of cognition in the physical environment [4].

In our study, deictic gestures may also reflect the grounding of cognition and may help uncover students' understanding of code execution. Computing teachers often face the challenging task of helping their students see connections between different ideas, events, or lessons. When explaining concepts to students, we would gesture by pointing to the lines of code we were referring. These gestures seemed to help guide students' attention to those inscriptions; for example, we indicated that a variable was being manipulated in different spaces, causing the value of that variable to change by pointing to each line of code.

In mathematics, pointing to these inscriptions while providing explanations helped link the teacher's verbal stream to its referents and ground the cognition. This may also be the case in computing. Grounding makes information conveyed verbally more accessible to students, thus fostering students' learning of content and scaffolding students' understanding [30]. In computing, these deictic gestures seem to help show process: what the code is doing (or at least what the person thinks it is doing) during execution. Thus, when teachers use deictic gestures, it may help scaffold students understanding of the way code executes.

Students also used deictic gestures. During interviews, some students gestured while they tried to understand the control flow (see Figure 3). Most students that did not gesture while trying to figure out the code were not able to correctly predict the output. These gestures may help students trace code, helping students reason about answers. These types of gesture may serve as a problem-solving function, helping to bring about strategies for reasoning. Examining student's gestures while they problem solve, may help reveal misconceptions and how well they understand code execution.

Square brackets indicate the words that accompany each gesture. Gestures are numbered below the bracketed corresponding speech and described in detail below the speech transcript.
Teacher: So, tell me what you think the output is
Student: Well, it will [check if this is the case] and since

1

it's not, it won't do this and [will go straight here]. I

2

think the cat will say "yes."

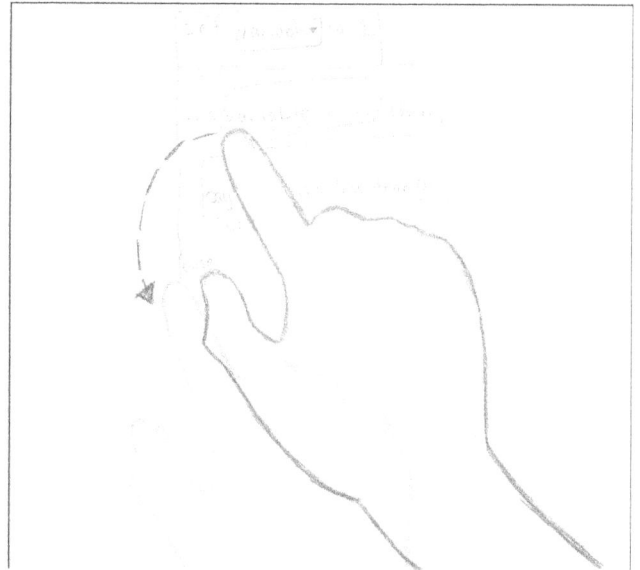

Figure 2: A student using deictic gestures while they trace a program's control flow.

1. Right index finger points to first line of the if-statement
2. Right index finger then points to the line after the conditional statement

5.2 Iconic

As we previously discussed, iconic gestures represent concrete ideas and are used to convey information about the size, shape, or orientation of the object of discourse [47]. In mathematics, iconic gestures manifest mental simulations of action and perception [4].

In computing, iconic gestures also seem to manifest simulations of action and perception and can help to understand the different conceptual models that students are forming. In mathematics, these gestures are produced when someone thinks and speaks about mathematical ideas. Alibali et al. suggest these gestures may be intentionally produced to facilitate thinking about such ideas or to communicate such ideas [4]. In computing, these gestures seemed to help facilitate communication and simulate actions.

Students would often have to present their work to the class. Before presentations, we would give a brief lecture on how to talk about code, telling them not to say what each line was doing, but to just generally say "my code does this, and I used this if statement, for example, to do it." During presentations students often used iconic gestures to help them talk about their code.

Student 1: My code rotates the cat a certain number of times depending on where it is. My code first figures out where the cat is and depending on the location, [it keeps going until...]

1

Student 2: My code rotates the cat a certain number of times depending on where it is. To do this, [I have this variable, then I have an if statement that says if the cat is here...]

2

1. Made circular gestures with both hands to show understanding of repetition.
2. Used right index finger to point to each line.

In that example, we noticed students who did not use iconic gestures, and who instead used deictic gestures, talked about their code at a low, code-focused level. Chu and Kita describe the shift from pointing gestures to iconic gestures shows a change in an internalization of action strategy, which had become less tied to concrete actions and thus more abstract [6]. Students' gestures might match how abstracted their knowledge is. Understanding how gestures transform over time, could have implications for formative assessment.

5.3 Metaphoric

Metaphoric gestures, as illustrated earlier, are similar to iconic gestures; however, they represent an abstract, and not concrete, idea [38]. In mathematics, metaphoric gestures reflect conceptual metaphors that underlie mathematical concepts [4, 33].

In computing metaphoric gestures might help communicate abstract concepts and might uncover misconceptions a student has about a concept that could be difficult to understand or even notice through other means.

Computing instructors have the challenge of helping novice students build strategies and mental models. Like in mathematics classrooms, computing teachers often use various teaching methods to do this, including using metaphors to teach abstract concepts [10]. Metaphors provide a strategy for understanding, by mapping abstract concepts to familiar, real-world concepts [40].

We often used metaphoric gestures when describing concepts to our students. During the lecture on variables, we described it as "some type of object that holds something." We used a gesture forming our hand into a cup, suggesting the metaphor of a variable as a cup, capable of holding something.

One feature about metaphors is they have limitations: "A feature of many metaphors is that when their mappings are pushed beyond their user's intended limits, they eventually break down" [40]. The metaphors used to describe computing concepts might lead to misconceptions about computing concepts. There have been catalogs of misconceptions students have about computer behavior and basic programming constructs [44]. One of the examples of a misconception alludes to the conceptual metaphor students use to understand the concept: "students commonly consider classes to be containers for objects" [44]. Teachers use of metaphoric gesture might communicate unintended misconceptions to students.

Teacher to the class: Does anybody know what a variable is?
Student: Uhhh, I guess something that changes.
T: Well, yeah that's what variable means, and I guess that relates, but what about a variable in programming?
Class: blank stares
T: A variable is some [type of object that holds something].
1
It's like a container. If there's some value or data you want

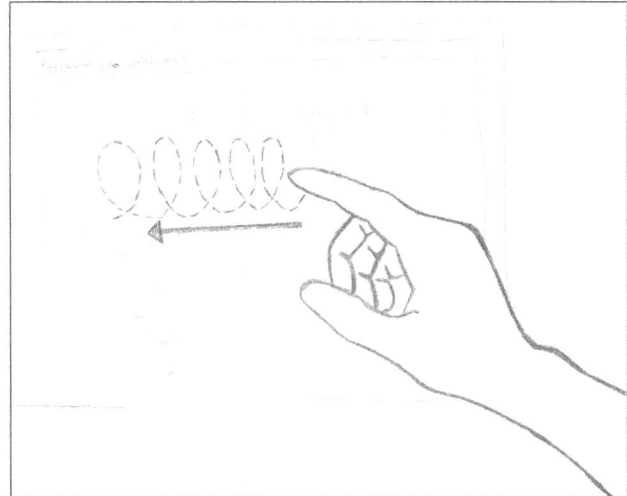

Figure 3: A student using a metaphoric gesture while they described a loop.

to store or keep for later, you put it in a variable.

1. Right hand forms a cup, while left hand goes inside the "cup."

Students also used metaphoric gestures when describing their code. A student was having trouble building a game. We noticed the student was using a loop and asked the student to explain that code segment (see Figure 3). They described a loop as "a loop," similar to a roller coaster loop.

It is helpful for instructors to know the misconceptions of students in order to provide appropriate help. Metaphoric gestures may reveal the underlying conceptual metaphors students have which can reveal uncovered misconceptions. This may also help reveal where their misconceptions come from if they have a conceptual metaphor that does not map well to the computing term.

In the example (Figure 3), although their definition of loop seems correct, the students metaphorical gesture potentially reveals a misconception they have about loops. Thinking of a loop as a roller coaster loop is correct in that both types of loops have a start and end point. The student, however, might not completely understand a loop conceptually. Their gesture moving backwards (or from right to left) could suggest a misconception of state changes.

Teacher: Wait, tell me about this. What is this doing?
Student: Oh that's for if they still have lives they can keep playing the game. [It's a loop, so it's like a loop, it repeats].
1

1. Right index finger moves in several loop-de-loops, going from right to left.

5.4 Beat

As discussed previously, beat gestures are the simplest type of gestures - a simple "kinetic realization of the underlying pulse" [47]. Beat gestures do not depict specific content but are just gestures timed to important content words. Beat gestures are talked about in mathematics, but do not convey semantic content and thus have no meaning.

We did not see beat gestures in our observations. However, we can *imagine* what a beat gesture might mean in computing education.

In computing, beat gestures could be used to represent iterative process across a sequence of data. Novice computing students have difficulties understanding memory-related concepts because they are abstract [13, 14, 28]. Teachers could use these gestures as a visualization for showing data or memory in some space. A teacher might produce beat gestures when they talk about iterating through an array or other collection. While the teacher talks about iterating through each index, the teacher may "point" to each index in space. The pace of the gesture may indicate the iteration where a function or body of the loop is being applied to each element of the data.

6 DISCUSSION

We were challenged to fit into McNeil's taxonomy the gestures that computing teachers and students produced in our study. There were obvious instances where the taxonomy fit. For instance, when people were pointing to text, the gesture was obviously deictic. Many of these gestures could technically fit into different types. The mapping of McNeil's taxonomy is not one to one with computing.

We see two particular challenges to developing a gesture framework for computing education. First, deictic gestures ground cognition by connecting thought to real world objects. While a deictic gesture does direct attention and "place (cognition) in the real world," it is hard to say what grounding means when pointing in computing. In math, if a teacher points to a 3, students have multiple sense of the number "3" to use in grounding to the real world, e.g., any set with three elements, the numeral 3, the word "three," a picture of three things, and so on. Wilensky has argued that abstraction to concreteness is a spectrum, and concreteness reflects the number of ways in which someone can reference the concept [49]. In computing, if a teacher points to a variable or a line of code, there is no physical or real-world counterpart to help that make sense. If the point of deictic gesture is to connect the abstract to the concrete, we in computing have very little concrete to reference. There are lines of code on the screen, and there are behaviors in the world.

Second, what we categorized as a beat gesture could also be a deictic gesture. If we are pointing to data (even a spatial, gestural sense of data), we are technically pointing to *something* in a location. There are gestures that appear in computing education that do not fit cleanly into the taxonomy.

We suggest that the complexity arises because we in computing are referencing both process and data. The deictic gestures that we observed seemed to more often refer to process. The producer of the gesture most often was describing the way code flows or executes. Beat gesture may be more commonly used to reference data elements, but at a pace that represents process.

We were similarly challenged to distinguish between metaphoric gesture and other gesture types like iconic and beat. We had to loosen our definition of concrete versus abstract. Instead, we focused on what information was being conveyed. There is a duality

of computing because computer programs can be characterized by their physical implementations on physical devices (i.e., there is a physical device that is running the program) and their conceptual implementations in programmers' minds which does not necessarily know or care where the physical device is located [9]. Programmers' create conceptual implementations metaphors, e.g., like imagining a "server farm" or "cloud" where the program is being executed. Many of the gestures produced while explaining concepts, could in fact be metaphoric gestures. But the metaphors may not lend themselves to mapping to gestures, e.g, the challenge of pointing at "the cloud."

By including gesture in our analysis of computing education, we believe that we add a new perspective to our research, and we may be able to expand the roles that gestures play. Computing is different than other disciplines because of how we play with concrete and abstract, with process and data. Gestures are important to cognition, so they can help us gain new insights into cognition and learning. But the role of gesture may be different in computing than in mathematics (or other STEM disciplines), which gives us a unique lens on gesture. The study of gesture in computing education gives us an opportunity to advance our own knowledge and that of the learning sciences, too.

7 CONCLUSION

In this paper, we are starting to explore gesture in computing education. Our goal is to identify connections to relevant literature on gesture, raise important questions for computing education, and generate interesting hypotheses for future testing. From our analysis, we saw gesture potentially used as a problem-solving strategy, as a way to communicate one's understanding, and a way to communicate abstract concepts. Devlin suggests computing is about constructing, manipulating, and reasoning about abstractions [12]. Studying gesture in computing could help us understand how students reason about abstract ideas and help us understand the different strategies students use to make sense of computing. By studying gesture, we might develop better ways of presenting and communicating knowledge to novices and better understand how novices are communicating their misconceptions and understandings to teachers. Likewise, the study of gesture could lead to new instructional practices that lead to more effective learning.

REFERENCES

[1] Martha W Alibali. 2005. Gesture in spatial cognition: Expressing, communicating, and thinking about spatial information. *Spatial cognition and computation* 5, 4 (2005), 307–331.
[2] Martha W Alibali and Susan GoldinMeadow. 1993. Gesture-speech mismatch and mechanisms of learning: What the hands reveal about a child's state of mind. *Cognitive psychology* 25, 4 (1993), 468–523.
[3] Martha W Alibali, Sotaro Kita, and Amanda J Young. 2000. Gesture and the process of speech production: We think, therefore we gesture. *Language and cognitive processes* 15, 6 (2000), 593–613.
[4] Martha W Alibali and Mitchell J Nathan. 2012. Embodiment in mathematics teaching and learning: Evidence from learners' and teachers' gestures. *Journal of the learning sciences* 21, 2 (2012), 247–286.
[5] Sara C Broaders, Susan Wagner Cook, Zachary Mitchell, and Susan Goldin-Meadow. 2007. Making children gesture brings out implicit knowledge and leads to learning. *Journal of Experimental Psychology: General* 136, 4 (2007), 539.
[6] Mingyuan Chu and Sotaro Kita. 2011. The nature of gestures' beneficial role in spatial problem solving. *Journal of Experimental Psychology: General* 140, 1 (2011), 102.

[7] Ruth Breckinridge Church, Saba Ayman-Nolley, and Shahrzad Mahootian. 2004. The role of gesture in bilingual education: Does gesture enhance learning? *International Journal of Bilingual Education and Bilingualism* 7, 4 (2004), 303–319.

[8] R Breckinridge Church and Susan Goldin-Meadow. 1986. The mismatch between gesture and speech as an index of transitional knowledge. *Cognition* 23, 1 (1986), 43–71.

[9] Timothy Colburn and Gary Shute. 2017. Type and metaphor for computer programmers. *Techné: Research in Philosophy and Technology* (2017).

[10] Timothy R Colburn and Gary M Shute. 2008. Metaphor in computer science. *Journal of Applied Logic* 6, 4 (2008), 526–533.

[11] Elaine M Crowder. 1996. Gestures at work in sense-making science talk. *The Journal of the Learning Sciences* 5, 3 (1996), 173–208.

[12] Keith Devlin. 2003. Require. *Commun. ACM* 46, 9 (2003), 37.

[13] Benedict Du Boulay. 1986. Some difficulties of learning to program. *Journal of Educational Computing Research* 2, 1 (1986), 57–73.

[14] Alireza Ebrahimi. 1994. Novice programmer errors: Language constructs and plan composition. *International Journal of Human-Computer Studies* 41, 4 (1994), 457–480.

[15] David Efron and Stuyvesant van Veen. 1972. *Gesture, race and culture.*

[16] Paul Ekman and Wallace V Friesen. 1969. The repertoire of nonverbal behavior: Categories, origins, usage, and coding. *semiotica* 1, 1 (1969), 49–98.

[17] Susan Goldin-Meadow. 2009. How gesture promotes learning throughout childhood. *Child development perspectives* 3, 2 (2009), 106–111.

[18] Susan Goldin-Meadow, Susan C Levine, Elena Zinchenko, Terina KuangYi Yip, Naureen Hemani, and Laiah Factor. 2012. Doing gesture promotes learning a mental transformation task better than seeing gesture. *Developmental science* 15, 6 (2012), 876–884.

[19] Susan Goldin-Meadow, Carolyn Mylander, and Cynthia Butcher. 1995. The resilience of combinatorial structure at the word level: Morphology in self-styled gesture systems. *Cognition* 56, 3 (1995), 195–262.

[20] Adam Kendon. 1980. Gesticulation and speech: Two aspects of the process of utterance. *The relationship of verbal and nonverbal communication* 25, 1980 (1980), 207–227.

[21] Adam Kendon. 1984. Did gesture have the happiness to escape the curse at the confusion of Babel. *Nonverbal behavior: Perspectives, applications, intercultural insights* (1984), 75–114.

[22] Kenneth R Koedinger, Martha W Alibali, and Mitchell J Nathan. 2008. Trade-Offs between grounded and abstract representations: Evidence from algebra problem Solving. *Cognitive Science* 32, 2 (2008), 366–397.

[23] G Lakoff and Mark Johnson. 1985. M.(1980). Metaphors We Live By. *ChicagoLondon: University of ChicagoPress* (1985).

[24] Jay L Lemke. 1999. Typological and topological meaning in diagnostic discourse. *Discourse Processes* 27, 2 (1999), 173–185.

[25] Nicole M McNeil, Martha W Alibali, and Julia L Evans. 2000. The role of gesture in children's comprehension of spoken language: Now they need it, now they don't. *Journal of Nonverbal Behavior* 24, 2 (2000), 131–150.

[26] Nicole M McNeil and David H Uttal. 2009. Rethinking the use of concrete materials in learning: Perspectives from development and education. *Child development perspectives* 3, 3 (2009), 137–139.

[27] David McNeill. 1992. *Hand and mind: What gestures reveal about thought.* University of Chicago press.

[28] Iain Milne and Glenn Rowe. 2002. Difficulties in learning and teaching programmingâĂŤviews of students and tutors. *Education and Information technologies* 7, 1 (2002), 55–66.

[29] Marolyn Morford and Susan Goldin-Meadow. 1992. Comprehension and production of gesture in combination with speech in one-word speakers. *Journal of child language* 19, 3 (1992), 559–580.

[30] Mitchell J Nathan. 2008. An embodied cognition perspective on symbols, gesture, and grounding instruction. *Symbols and embodiment: Debates on meaning and cognition* 18 (2008), 375–396.

[31] Miriam Novack and Susan Goldin-Meadow. 2015. Learning from gesture: how our hands change our minds. *Educational psychology review* 27, 3 (2015), 405–412.

[32] Miriam A Novack, Eliza L Congdon, Naureen Hemani-Lopez, and Susan Goldin-Meadow. 2014. From action to abstraction: Using the hands to learn math. *Psychological Science* 25, 4 (2014), 903–910.

[33] Rafael Núñez. 2006. Do real numbers really move? Language, thought, and gesture: The embodied cognitive foundations of mathematics. In *18 unconventional essays on the nature of mathematics.* Springer, 160–181.

[34] Michelle Perry, Denise Berch, and Jenny Singleton. 1995. Constructing shared understanding: The role of nonverbal input in learning contexts. *J. Contemp. Legal Issues* 6 (1995), 213.

[35] Raedy M Ping and Susan Goldin-Meadow. 2008. Hands in the air: Using ungrounded iconic gestures to teach children conservation of quantity. *Developmental psychology* 44, 5 (2008), 1277.

[36] Raedy M Ping, Susan Goldin-Meadow, and Sian L Beilock. 2014. Understanding gesture: Is the listenerâĂŹs motor system involved? *Journal of Experimental Psychology: General* 143, 1 (2014), 195.

[37] Bernard Rimé and Loris Schiaratura. 1991. Gesture and speech. (1991).

[38] Wolff-Michael Roth. 2001. Gestures: Their role in teaching and learning. *Review of educational research* 71, 3 (2001), 365–392.

[39] Wolff-Michael Roth and Manuela Welzel. 2001. From activity to gestures and scientific language. *Journal of research in science teaching* 38, 1 (2001), 103–136.

[40] Joseph P Sanford, Aaron Tietz, Saad Farooq, Samuel Guyer, and R Benjamin Shapiro. 2014. Metaphors we teach by. In *Proceedings of the 45th ACM technical symposium on Computer science education.* ACM, 585–590.

[41] Paul Seedhouse. 2005. Conversation analysis and language learning. *Language teaching* 38, 4 (2005), 165–187.

[42] Mi-Suk Seo and Irene Koshik. 2010. A conversation analytic study of gestures that engender repair in ESL conversational tutoring. *Journal of Pragmatics* 42, 8 (2010), 2219–2239.

[43] Ben Rydal Shapiro and Rogers Hall. 2017. *Making Engagement Visible: The Use of Mondrian Transcripts in a Museum.* Philadelphia, PA: International Society of the Learning Sciences.

[44] Teemu Sirkiä and Juha Sorva. 2012. Exploring programming misconceptions: an analysis of student mistakes in visual program simulation exercises. In *Proceedings of the 12th Koli Calling International Conference on Computing Education Research.* ACM, 19–28.

[45] Laura A Thompson and Dominic W Massaro. 1986. Evaluation and integration of speech and pointing gestures during referential understanding. *Journal of experimental child psychology* 42, 1 (1986), 144–168.

[46] Kevin Tuite. 1993. The production of gesture. *Semiotica* 93, 1-2 (1993), 83–106.

[47] Fereydoon Vafaei. 2013. Taxonomy of gestures in human computer interaction. (2013).

[48] Laura Valenzeno, Martha W Alibali, and Roberta Klatzky. 2003. Teachers' gestures facilitate students' learning: A lesson in symmetry. *Contemporary Educational Psychology* 28, 2 (2003), 187–204.

[49] Uri Wilensky. 1991. Abstract meditations on the concrete and concrete implications for mathematics education. In *Constructionism*, Idit Harel and Seymour Papert (Eds.). Ablex, Norwood, NJ, 193–203.

[50] Robert F Williams. 2008. Gesture as a conceptual mapping tool. *Metaphor and Gesture [Gesture Studies 3]* (2008), 55–92.

Emotions Experienced by First-Year Engineering Students During Programming Tasks

Zahra Atiq
School of Engineering
Education Purdue University
USA
satiq@purdue.edu

ABSTRACT

Learning programming is hard for novices and may induce both positive and negative emotions. This dissertation research employs a novel multi-modal research design in an attempt to understand emotions that novices experience while learning programming in an introductory undergraduate programming course. I want to participate in the doctoral consortium to get feedback on my research, specifically on how to improve my data analysis strategy and to make sense of the data.

CCS CONCEPTS

• Social and professional topic → Computer science education; *CS1*

KEYWORDS

Emotions, Computer programming, Multi-modal data

ACM Reference format:

Z. Atiq. 2018. Emotions Experienced by First-Year Engineering Students During Programming. In *Proceedings of International Computing Education Research, Espoo Finland, August 2018 (ICER'2018)*, 2 pages. https://doi.org/10.1145/3230977.3231014

1 PROGRAM CONTEXT

I am a fourth-year doctoral candidate at the School of Engineering Education at Purdue University. As a doctoral student, I have performed research in both engineering and CS education. For my dissertation research I am conducting a qualitative investigation of the emotions experienced by first-year Engineering (FYE) students while working on programming problems. I have completed data collection, and have to analyze the data, write, and defend my dissertation. Although, this research is being conducted in the context of engineering, it is easily transferrable to CS, because every CS undergraduate program offers introductory programming courses.

2 CONTEXT AND MOTIVATION

Novice students have difficulty learning programming; it requires practice and perseverance [1]. Hence, students may experience different emotions that may either promote or hinder their performance and learning [2]. Specifically, negative emotions like continued frustration may lead students to not only give up on a programming task but also to drop out of engineering/computing altogether [3]. Although emotions are crucial for learning, little is known about how emotions affect novices in an introductory programming course.

While studying and teaching CS for more than fifteen years, I have encountered scores of peers and students who have experienced anxiety in learning programming. As a consequence, they have performed inadequately, or have avoided programming altogether. I have always been curious about these attitudes and through my dissertation research, I found an opportunity to investigate students' emotions in the context of programming.

3 BACKGROUND AND RELATED WORK

Few prior research studies have examined emotions in the context of programming courses. The most notable study was a qualitative investigation by Kinnunen and Simon of the students' experiences in introductory programming courses [4]. This study connected students' positive and negative experiences with programming to their self-efficacy beliefs. Building on this work, Lishinski quantitatively investigated the connection of emotions with learning outcomes and self-efficacy beliefs in a programming course [5]. In addition to using just one source of data, this study lacked an established theoretical framework and validated instruments.

Bosch et al. collected students' facial expressions and screen capture data as they worked on programming problems. After completing the programming session, students themselves labeled their emotions in a retrospective affect judgment session [6]. The students' labels were then quantitatively analyzed using different statistical techniques. Although this study went a step further than the previous two studies in collecting data concurrently and retrospectively, a major limitation of the study was the bias in students' self-reported data. To reduce the effect of this bias, more sources of data are needed for triangulation purposes.

None of these previous studies accounted for the multi-componential (affective, cognitive, physiological, expressive, and motivational) nature of emotions, which evolve rapidly. In order to investigate a complicated phenomenon like emotions, researchers have suggested the use of multi-modal data [6], [7]. This dissertation research will address the shortcomings of previous research by using many sources of data (mentioned in the data collection section), to understand the emotions of students as they work on programming problems.

4 STATEMENT OF THESIS PROBLEM

The purpose of this study is to identify the different emotions that FYE students experience while they work on programming tasks. Specifically, I ask the following research questions: 1) What emotions do FYE students experience while working on a programming task, and how these emotions change as a result? 2) What reasons do students describe for experiencing different emotions? and 3) What self-regulation strategies do students use to cope with these emotions?

5 METHODS

Sample: During the Spring 2018 semester, I recruited 18 participants from ENGR 132 (Transforming Ideas to Innovation II), a two-credit course introducing programming in MATLAB to FYE students at Purdue University. I considered only domestic students who were novice programmers and were not taking another programming course along with ENGR 132.

Data Collection: To understand the complicated nature of emotions, I have collected quantitative and qualitative data, both concurrently and retrospectively. This variety of data promotes the trustworthiness of the study [8]. Each participant took part in two sessions: a programming session and a retrospective think-aloud interview. During the *programming session*, the participant worked on four programming problems of varying difficulty for 30 minutes. In this session different types of data were collected: facial expressions, electrodermal activity, eye-gaze data, responses to the Achievement Emotions Questionnaire, and screen capture. At the end of the programming session, a post-task interview was conducted to ask follow-up questions. This interview was audio recorded. The participants were called back 3 – 5 days after the programming session for a *retrospective think-aloud interview*. During this interview, which was audio recorded, they viewed a video of their programming session (screen capture, eye gaze, and facial expressions). After every two minutes of viewing, the video was paused, and they were asked questions about what emotions they thought they were experiencing during that segment, why, and what strategies they adopted to cope with the emotions experienced.

Proposed Data Analysis: My first goal is to qualitatively analyze the interview transcripts. For this analysis, I am using the control-value theory of achievement emotions [7] to design a codebook to code the data. This codebook will evolve by adding new codes as I analyze the data. My second goal is to use other sources of data for triangulation with the interview data. For instance, the electrodermal activity data will be analyzed and matched up with interview excerpts to provide insights about emotions that the students thought they experienced and the physiological changes in their body. Finally, for inter-coder reliability, I will ask a fellow researcher to code four transcripts.

6 DISSERTATION STATUS

I have successfully defended my dissertation proposal, conducted two pilot studies to refine my data collection and analysis methods, and successfully collected the data. My dissertation proposal comprises working drafts of the first three chapters of my dissertation. During the final year of my doctoral studies, 2018-19, I plan to analyze the collected data, write, and defend my dissertation. I would like to use the expertise of researchers at the doctoral consortium to refine my data analysis strategy, to make sense of the data I have collected, and to discuss possible future directions for my research.

7 EXPECTED CONTRIBUTIONS

This dissertation project contributes to research in engineering and computing education in multiple ways. First, I am employing a novel research design by combining multi-modal data. Second, I am using control-value theory in the context of programming. This theory has not yet been used extensively in the context of programming. A better understanding of student emotions, why they experience those emotions, and how they cope with the emotions will enable educators to design curriculum, pedagogy, and interventions (e.g., affect sensitive learning environments) that may foster positive emotions and mitigate the effects of negative emotions.

ACKNOWLEDGMENTS

I would like to thank my co-adviser, Dr. Michael Loui, Dale and Suzi Gallagher Professor in Engineering Education at Purdue University, for providing financial support for this dissertation. I would also like to thank the Bilsland dissertation fellowship for supporting the last year of my dissertation research.

REFERENCES

[1] C. Rogerson, and E. Scott. 2010. The Fear Factor: How it Affects Students Learning to Program in a Tertiary Environment. *J. Inf. Technol. Edu Res.*, vol. 9, no. 1, 147–171.

[2] M. Zeidner. 2014. Anxiety in education. In *International handbook of emotions in education*. Routelage, 265–288.

[3] S. Secules, A. Gupta, A. Elby, and C. Turpen. 2018. Zooming out from the Struggling Individual Student: An Account of the Cultural Construction of Engineering Ability in an Undergraduate Programming Class. *J. Eng. Educ.*, vol. 107, no. 1, 56–86.

[4] P. Kinnunen, and B. Simon. 2012. My Program is ok – am I? Computing Freshmen's Experiences of doing Programming Assignments. *Comput. Sci. Educ.*, vol. 22, no. 1, 1–28.

[5] A. Lishinski. 2016. Cognitive, Affective, and Dispositional Components of Learning Programming. In *Proceedings of International Computing Education Research*, 261–262.

[6] N. Bosch, and S. D'Mello. 2015. The affective experiences of novice programmers. *Int. J. Artif. Intell. Educ.*, 1–26.

[7] R. Pekrun, and R. P. Perry. 2014. Control-value theory of achievement

L. Linnenbrink-Garcia (Eds.). Routelage, 120–141.

[8] S. Afzal, and P. Robinson. 2015. Emotion data collection and its implications for affective computing. In *The Oxford handbook of affective computing*, R. A. Calvo, S. K. D'Mello, J. Gratch, and A. Kappas (Eds.).

Towards a Theory of HtDP-based Program-Design Learning

Francisco Enrique Vicente G. Castro
Department of Computer Science
Worcester Polytechnic Institute
Worcester, Massachusetts, USA
fgcastro@cs.wpi.edu

ABSTRACT

Program-design is an essential skill students in introductory computing courses must learn, but which continues to be difficult for students. Many introductory curricula focuses on low-level constructs, even when students are expected to gain higher-level problem-solving and program-design skills. *How to Design Programs* (HTDP) is a curriculum that teaches a multi-step approach to program-design, promoting multiple, interrelated program-design skills. My research explores how novice programmers use HTDP-based techniques to design programs, the design-related skills students learn and use, the factors that drive their design decisions, and how these weave into a conceptual framework of HTDP-based program-design.

KEYWORDS

Program-design; CS1; novice programmers; qualitative research

1 PROGRAM CONTEXT

I am a fourth year PhD candidate in the Computer Science program at WPI; my program includes learning sciences courses to inform my research. I have defended my dissertation proposal in the early-Spring of 2018. My early research explores the planning behavior of CS1 students. I have built on this work through think-alouds and interviews with a new cohort of early-CS university students from which I have developed a SOLO-based framework of program-design-related skills and narratives of how students use the HTDP process to design programs. I will begin the next iteration of my studies in the upcoming school year.

2 CONTEXT AND MOTIVATION

Learning program-design remains a nontrivial goal for novice programmers in CS1 [2, 5, 12], requiring students to make various design choices: from lower-level concerns of choosing relevant programming language constructs to higher-level concerns of identifying and clustering subtasks into code blocks. Plan-composition is noted as a major difficulty among novices [12] yet most introductory programming courses focus heavily on teaching low-level programming constructs even when students are also expected to develop higher-level programming and problem-solving strategies, often through trial-and-error [5].

How to Design Programs [6] is an introductory computing curriculum that teaches a multi-step process of program-design. It

ICER '18, August 13–15, 2018, Espoo, Finland
© 2018 Copyright held by the owner/author(s).
ACM ISBN 978-1-4503-5628-2/18/08.
https://doi.org/10.1145/3230977.3231020

has been adopted in higher-education institutions and some K-12 programs, yet the program-design skills it fosters and how students learn with HTDP remains largely unexplored in CSEd research. My work explores how novice programmers use the HTDP process to design programs, looking at the relationships around their use of program-design-related skills and techniques, and the contributing factors that drive their programming. Understanding how program-design-related skills and techniques are used, and the affordances and limitations around these provides valuable insight for designers of CS curricula and pedagogy.

3 BACKGROUND & RELATED WORK

More recent investigation into students' program-design skills have mostly looked at code outputs of students who are learning in different curricula [11] or after interventions that teach design strategies [5, 10]. These have showed varied results and often focused on *code-level techniques* (e.g. merging code). Others captured students' *mastery* of specific programming-related skills by assessing student output using taxonomies of skill progressions [8, 9].

On the other hand, HTDP [6] teaches students to work through a progression of steps when designing programs. Some of these steps include writing concrete examples of data, writing test cases for proposed functions, and writing code skeletons (*templates*) that fully traverse the input type. From this perspective, program-design isn't just a single strategy of merging relevant code blocks [9] or the application of recurring patterns [10], but also involves strategies such as using tests to model program behavior or designing programs based on data types instead of simply selecting language constructs. This multi-step process promotes the learning and use of techniques and multiple interrelated skills for program-design. This research aims to develop a more nuanced understanding of how students design programs using HTDP-based design techniques and skills and the factors that drive their design decisions.

4 STATEMENT OF THESIS/PROBLEM

The *How to Design Programs* curriculum teaches learners program-design through the development of a set of multiple, interrelated component skills [3]. We want to develop a conceptual framework of how novice programmers use HTDP to design programs. Interesting sub-questions include:

(1) What skills do HTDP-trained students display when they use HTDP to design programs? How might variations in the ways that students perform these skills look like?

(2) What affordances, difficulties, or limitations of the HTDP process can be observed from accounts of students' use of HTDP?

(3) How might differences in programming problem context influence students' use of HTDP? (e.g. solving problems for which students have seen applicable solution-structures vs. no prior knowledge on applicable solution-structures)

(4) What other factors seem to influence students' (a) use of program-design-related skills and/or (b) use of HTDP-based design techniques and what relationships among these do we observe?

5 RESEARCH GOALS & METHODS

I approach my research questions with the following methods:

• **Conduct interviews and think-alouds with students.** I will conduct studies with students in HTDP-based CS1 courses that involve (1) giving the students programming problems to solve from scratch while thinking-out loud and (2) interviewing students about their approaches towards solving programming problems. These provide opportunities to engage with students and capture students' narratives about how they're using HTDP to design programs. The interviews will focus on the skills students are using (sub-question 1), accounts of their use of HTDP-based techniques (sub-questions 2, 3), and other factors and relationships that may influence their skill/technique-use and overall design practice (sub-question 4).

• **Develop a framework of program-design skills and narratives of students' use of HtDP.** We will code the think-aloud and interview data to identify relevant program-design skills. To date, we have developed a SOLO-based [1] framework that details the skills students use in their program-design practice, as well as the variations in the way each skill is applied. We will also code for accounts of how students use the techniques promoted by HTDP, with a particular focus on their use of the HTDP template design pattern. On top of these, we will also identify other underlying factors that may influence students' use of these program-design related skills and techniques. These analyses will enable us to gain an understanding of the skills that HTDP fosters, a sense of how to measure them, and a sense of the extent to which these skills and techniques can be applied – the affordances they offer, the difficulties that arise in their use, and their observed limitations.

• **Validate the conceptual frameworks of HtDP-use.** Developing the HTDP-based conceptual framework of novice program-design raises the subgoal of validating this framework to determine whether it accurately describes how novices use HTDP to design programs. We approach this validation in two ways: (1) we will replicate our studies and analyses across student cohorts from (1 to 2) other institutions that use an HTDP-based CS1 curriculum and (2) we will have other HTDP-expert instructors replicate our analyses on a subset of our data. The first approach allows us to generalize our findings across different HTDP student cohorts and account for differences in learning contexts (e.g. instructors, programming problems used in courses, etc.). The second allows us to check whether our framework captures similar nuances and relationships observed by other experienced HTDP instructors.

6 DISSERTATION STATUS

I have completed an exploratory study [2] of student programming behavior as they worked on novel problems. Findings show that students were unable to adapt their design processes to solve complex problems, tinkering on-the-fly rather than planning ahead. In a follow-up study [4], where we asked students to both produce and evaluate multiple structurally different solutions for a set of programming problems, students raised interesting factors that drove their design choices in evaluations of their own work. This led us to expand our work: I conducted think-alouds and interviews

with students at multiple points during the course of their CS1 and through to CS2 to identify skills and influencing factors in students' design decisions and explore how these interact with their use of HTDP-based design techniques. Our analysis of the CS1 data resulted in the development of a SOLO-based framework [3] of the program-design-related skills and the variations in ways students perform these skills, as well as the development of narratives of students' use of HTDP-based design techniques to solve multi-task programming problems [7]. Going forward, I will validate and refine this framework by analyzing similar data from HTDP-trained students in 1 to 2 other institutions, as well as have other HTDP instructors replicate our analyses on a subset of our data.

7 EXPECTED CONTRIBUTIONS

My dissertation contributes to the development of CS education pedagogy. Understanding the meaningful distinctions in the variations of novices' skill-performance enables educators to assess instructional material to concretely identify content that support the development of particular design-related skills. Furthermore, understanding these skills and how students use design techniques enables us to capture the cognitive nuances that support the use of these skills and techniques. Second, it provides evidence towards the efficacy of an alternative method for program-design for novices. Understanding the affordances and accounts of how students use the HTDP-techniques in practice provides evidence towards the effectiveness and limitations of the techniques. In particular, the template design pattern in HTDP departs from traditional, implementation-focused patterns by drawing on data types instead of mappings between problem types and stereotype-patterns. This provides a useful alternative program-structuring method for novices who may not have experience or schema for certain problems, but can draw on data types to retrieve viable schemas.

REFERENCES

[1] J. B. Biggs and K. Collis. 1982. *Evaluating the Quality of Learning: the SOLO taxonomy*. Academic Press, New York.

[2] Francisco Enrique Vicente Castro and Kathi Fisler. 2016. On the Interplay Between Bottom-Up and Datatype-Driven Program Design. In *Proceedings of the 47th ACM Technical Symposium on Computing Science Education*. ACM, 205–210.

[3] Francisco Enrique Vicente Castro and Kathi Fisler. 2017. Designing a Multi-faceted SOLO Taxonomy to Track Program Design Skills Through an Entire Course *(Koli Calling '17)*. ACM, New York, NY, USA, 10–19.

[4] Francisco Enrique Vicente Castro, Shriram Krishnamurthi, and Kathi Fisler. 2017. The Impact of a Single Lecture on Program Plans in First-year CS *(Koli Calling '17)*. ACM, New York, NY, USA, 118–122.

[5] Michael de Raadt, Richard Watson, and Mark Toleman. 2009. Teaching and Assessing Programming Strategies Explicitly. In *Proceedings of the Eleventh Australasian Conference on Computing Education*. Darlinghurst, Australia, Australia.

[6] Matthias Felleisen, Robert Bruce Findler, Matthew Flatt, and Shriram Krishnamurthi. 2001. *How to Design Programs*. MIT Press. http://www.htdp.org/

[7] Kathi Fisler and Francisco Enrique Vicente Castro. 2017. Sometimes, Rainfall Accumulates: Talk-Alouds with Novice Functional Programmers *(ICER '17)*. ACM, New York, NY, USA, 12–20.

[8] David Ginat and Eti Menashe. 2015. SOLO Taxonomy for Assessing Novices' Algorithmic Design *(SIGCSE '15)*. ACM, New York, NY, USA, 452–457.

[9] Cruz Izu, Amali Weerasinghe, and Cheryl Pope. 2016. A Study of Code Design Skills in Novice Programmers Using the SOLO Taxonomy *(ICER '16)*. ACM, 251–259.

[10] Orna Muller, David Ginat, and Bruria Haberman. 2007. Pattern- oriented Instruction and Its Influence on Problem Decomposition and Solution Construction *(ITiCSE '07)*. ACM, New York, NY, USA, 151–155.

[11] Otto Seppälä, Petri Ihantola, Essi Isohanni, Juha Sorva, and Arto Vihavainen. 2015. Do We Know How Difficult the Rainfall Problem is? *(Koli Calling '15)*. ACM, 87–96.

[12] E. Soloway. 1986. Learning to Program = Learning to Construct Mechanisms and Explanations. *Commun. ACM* 29, 9 (Sept. 1986), 850–858.

Towards an Instructional Design of Complex Learning in Introductory Programming Courses

Rodrigo Duran
Aalto University
Aalto, Finland, 00076
rodrigo.duran@aalto.fi

ABSTRACT

To provide effective learning strategies to complex content, educational psychology produced frameworks that holistically integrate skills at a controlled pace achieved by sequencing tasks by its complexity. However, to apply such frameworks to introductory programming courses, there is a dearth of established methodologies for assessing how difficult such tasks are from the student's cognitive perspective. My goals are twofold: in order to design an instructional intervention that applies and adapt frameworks aimed to complex learning, I first establish and empirically validate a model to evaluate the complexity of programs from a cognitive perspective, providing metrics to quantify different aspects of program's complexity. I want to explore how to refine and expand this model analysis, what kind of evidence can be extracted from its empirical validation and how to impact instructional design with the results of my work.

CCS CONCEPTS

• **Social and professional topics** → **Computer science education**; *Model curricula*; Student assessment;

KEYWORDS

Model of Hierarchical Complexity; Cognitive Load Theory; Program Cognitive Complexity; Complexity; Plan-Composition Strategies

ACM Reference Format:
Rodrigo Duran. 2018. Towards an Instructional Design of Complex Learning in Introductory Programming Courses. In *ICER '18: 2018 International Computing Education Research Conference, August 13–15, 2018, Espoo, Finland.* ACM, New York, NY, USA, 2 pages. https://doi.org/10.1145/3230977.3231007

1 PROGRAM CONTEXT

I am in my 3rd year of doctoral studies in Computer Science Education (CSE) at Aalto University under the supervision of Prof. Lauri Malmi. I recently first-authored one paper outlining the theoretical framework of my thesis [4]. As I intend to defend my dissertation in 2020, I am working towards publishing papers on my model's empirical validation and evaluation of my pedagogical intervention.

2 CONTEXT AND MOTIVATION

To develop successful learning interventions, instructional designers must consider student's learning trajectory. Ideally, tasks should not overwhelm students but at the same time challenge them, as proposed by Vygotsky's Zone of Proximal Development. To assist teachers in designing instruction to complex content, research in educational psychology has produced frameworks such as the 4C/ID [11]. At the core of this framework is the required skill to sequence tasks based on its complexity, therefore promoting effective schema construction and automation. However, there is a gap in research since current methods described by Computing Education Research (CER) do not formally define or provide enough detail in how each program's components impact program's complexity from a cognitive perspective. How to compare program's complexity to another? What makes a program complex?

3 BACKGROUND & RELATED WORK

While Bloom's and SOLO taxonomies were extensively used by CER to classify activities [5, 6], this work aims to complement such approaches by characterizing the *content* of an activity, not the activity itself or the connectedness of its outputs. Whether discussing how programming structures can have different complexities ("Is an assignment statement easier to read and understand than a print statement?" [9]), or building learning trajectories to CSE [8], understanding the complexity of programs by evaluating its structures is a significant part of the analytical work.

The Cognitive Load Theory (CLT) [1] aims to improve the instructional design by investigating how learning is constrained by a limited working memory (WM) where a small number of schemas, chunks of related elements, are processed. Element interactivity (EI) determines the degree of interconnectedness between elements in the WM, which is the main component of Intrinsic Load (IL), the amount of simultaneously necessary elements required for learning, characterizing complexity in CLT. As experience grows, we construct hierarchies of increasingly complex higher-level schemas that encompass many low-lever schemas, which in turn decreases IL by reducing the number of active elements in the WM. Soloway [10] introduced a plans (schema) and goals tree in the programming context representing abstractions of strategies to solve a problem that students later realize by composing a program with code.

The Model of Hierarchical Complexity (MHC) [3] is a Neo-Piagetian framework applied to analyze the complexity of tasks. It defines stages of development based on a hierarchy of actions organized by coordinating rules. The axioms of MHC establishes that a more complex action coordinates in a non-arbitrary way at least two lower-level actions, thus defining complexity as a recursion over constituent elements of a task.

4 STATEMENT OF THE THESIS/PROBLEM

My work aims to inform the instructional design of a complex subject (programming) to novices (introductory courses) adapting theoretical frameworks from educational psychology specifically intended for complex tasks. To be able to achieve my overall goal, first I aim to develop and validate a model of cognitive complexity that enables an a priori fine-grained analysis of programs. This model extends the previous analysis of plans by providing metrics to evaluate different facets of complexity, including the trajectory of schema (plan) acquisition, and an evaluation of how plans interacting using different code composition strategies impact complexity.

5 RESEARCH GOALS & METHODS

Conceptualize a model to evaluate computer programs from a cognitive perspective: The Cognitive Complexity of Computer Programs (CCCP) framework is a theoretical model for reasoning about the complexity of computer programs and generating metrics that summarize aspects of complexity [4]. The CCCP analyzes the schema construction applying the MHC axioms to create a hierarchical representation of the plans in a program, defining the *plan depth metric*. The *plan interactivity metric*, an adaptation of CLT's element interactivity, estimates which plans need to be kept in the WM simultaneously while the programmer mentally manipulates the (higher-level) plans of the program using a given code composition strategy.

Validate the framework with empirical results: I will collect data from CS1 and K12 students to evaluate their program comprehension using tracing and code completion exams with different levels of complexity. The data consists of performance measurements, subjective ratings of clarity and difficulty[7] and identifiable concepts to evaluate the program. A pre-test will be administered to select subjects with no previous knowledge, and a post-test will summarize a rank of program complexity. The exams will be administered along with the regular coursework in order to ensure that they are measuring schema construction for each content. Performance outcomes will be analyzed by an extended Rasch model [2] to rank the exam items. I will investigate a correlation between the predicted complexity of programs with student's performance and triangulate it with existing methods [7] using quantitative and qualitative data.

Create a pedagogical intervention for CS1 informed by an instruction design aimed at complex learning: My goal is to adapt the 4C/ID framework to create a pedagogical intervention designing learning tasks and performance assessments. I will sequence learning tasks to create tasks classes (same knowledge content, varying complexity), design supportive information, mental models representations, part-task practices and cognitive rules. I will also perform analysis of cognitive strategies and pre-requisite knowledge aimed at introductory programming courses.

6 DISSERTATION STATUS

I have conceptualized the first iteration of the CCCP model using a series of case studies of short programs as a proof of concept to present the plan depth and plan interactivity metrics. To validate this model I will pilot the first data collection with a smaller cohort (N=200) of CS1 students, refine the model and the data collection

instrument to later collect data in a larger cohort (N=600) of CS1 students from the same university. I expect that this data can validate the model and provide me enough insight and evidence to design the final pedagogical intervention.

Since my model is not yet supported by empirical evidence, at the doctoral consortium I would like to discuss its limitations and possible refinements to improve it. I hope to receive feedback on my empirical validation plan and discuss how to make it more reliable, what kind of additional data could be collected and how to present concrete evidence of the model validation. Since the model and data analysis itself is a necessary step to design a pedagogical intervention aimed to teach a complex subject (programming), I hope to receive feedback on future applications of such intervention, how to evaluate it and future extensions of the model.

7 EXPECTED CONTRIBUTIONS

This research will improve the conceptualization and evaluation of program's cognitive complexity providing a more detailed analysis based on the content of programs and the cognitive effort demanded to comprehend them. The final result of my work, a pedagogical intervention aimed for complex learning of programming may influence practitioners, teachers, and examiners. My model can influence stakeholders in several CER areas, such as: assessment, creating learning trajectories to CS1 courses, personalized exams, design of "more learnable" programming languages based on the complexity of its structures, plan-composition strategies and its impact on learning and performance, and theoretical impacts of interventions that deal with complexity of programs.

REFERENCES

[1] Hwan-Hee Choi, Jeroen JG Van Merriënboer, and Fred Paas. 2014. Effects of the physical environment on cognitive load and learning: towards a new model of cognitive load. *Educational Psychology Review* 26, 2 (2014), 225–244.

[2] Michael Lamport Commons, Eric Andrew Goodheart, Alexander Pekker, Theo Linda Dawson, Karen Draney, and Kathryn Marie Adams. 2008. Using Rasch scaled stage scores to validate orders of hierarchical complexity of balance beam task sequences. *Journal of Applied Measurement* 9, 2 (2008), 182.

[3] Michael Lamport Commons, Edward James Trudeau, Sharon Anne Stein, Francis Asbury Richards, and Sharon R Krause. 1998. Hierarchical complexity of tasks shows the existence of developmental stages. *Developmental Review* 18, 3 (1998), 237–278.

[4] Rodrigo Duran, Juha Sorva, and Sofia Leite. In review. Towards an analysis of program complexity from a cognitive perspective. *In review* (In review).

[5] Cruz Izu, Amali Weerasinghe, and Cheryl Pope. 2016. A study of code design skills in novice programmers using the SOLO taxonomy. In *Proceedings of the 2016 ACM Conference on International Computing Education Research*. ACM, 251–259.

[6] Susana Masapanta-Carrión and J. Ángel Velázquez-Iturbide. 2018. A systematic review of the use of Bloom's Taxonomy in computer science education. In *Proceedings of the 49h ACM Technical Symposium on Computer Science Education (SIGCSE '18)*. ACM, 441–446.

[7] Briana B Morrison, Brian Dorn, and Mark Guzdial. 2014. Measuring cognitive load in introductory CS: adaptation of an instrument. In *Proceedings of the tenth annual conference on International computing education research*. ACM, 131–138.

[8] Kathryn M. Rich, Carla Strickland, T. Andrew Binkowski, Cheryl Moran, and Diana Franklin. 2017. K-8 Learning Trajectories Derived from Research Literature: Sequence, Repetition, Conditionals. In *Proceedings of the 2017 ACM Conference on International Computing Education Research (ICER '17)*. ACM, New York, NY, USA, 182–190. https://doi.org/10.1145/3105726.3106166

[9] Simon, Mike Lopez, Ken Sutton, and Tony Clear. 2009. Surely we must learn to read before we learn to write!. In *Conferences in Research and Practice in Information Technology Series (ACE '09)*, Margaret Hamilton and Tony Clear (Eds.), Vol. 95. Australian Computer Society, 165–170.

[10] Elliot Soloway. 1986. Learning to program = Learning to construct mechanisms and explanations. *Commun. ACM* 29, 9 (1986), 850–858.

[11] Jeroen JG Van Merriënboer and Paul A Kirschner. 2017. *Ten steps to complex learning: A systematic approach to four-component instructional design*. Routledge.

A Study on the Assessment of Introductory Computational Thinking via Scratch Programming in Primary Schools

Janne Fagerlund
Department of Teacher Education
University of Jyväskylä, Finland
janne.fagerlund@jyu.fi

ABSTRACT

Computational thinking (CT), a transversal intellectual foundation integral to computer science, is making its way into compulsory comprehensive education worldwide. Students are expected to attain skills and knowledge in such interdisciplinary CT principles as Algorithmic thinking, Data representation, and Debugging. Problem-solving by designing and manipulating interactive media with Scratch, a graphical programming tool, is popular especially at the primary school level. However, there has been confusion regarding how introductory CT can be operationalized for educational practice. Teachers and students need research-based knowledge for setting appropriate learning goals in addition to instruments for formative assessment that potentially improve the quality of learning. This study contributes to these issues by developing the assessment for learning of CT via Scratch in primary school settings. A review on prior studies involving the assessment of CT-related computational ideas in Scratch has led to the conceptualization of a revised assessment framework. Next steps in the study are analyzing fourth grade students' ($N=58$) Scratch projects and exploring complementary methods for analyzing CT in video recordings of the students' programming processes.

KEYWORDS

Computational thinking; graphical programming; Scratch; assessment; primary school; education

ACM Reference Format:
Janne Fagerlund. 2018. A Study on the Assessment of Introductory Computational Thinking via Scratch Programming in Primary Schools. In *ICER '18: 2018 International Computing Education Research Conference, August 13–15, 2018, Espoo, Finland.* ACM, New York, NY, USA, 3 pages. https://doi.org/10.1145/3230977.3231013

1 PROGRAM CONTEXT

This doctoral thesis is carried out in the Doctoral Programme in Education in the Doctoral School in Education and Psychology at the University of Jyväskylä, Finland. The major subject is Education, and the targeted degree is Doctor of Philosophy (Education). The thesis is an article-based doctoral dissertation, which comprises

three articles that will be published in scientific, international, peer-reviewed journals or edited books.

2 CONTEXT AND MOTIVATION

The computer revolution has resulted in the disciplinary ways of computer science to become ubiquitous in the world. Compulsory comprehensive education is attempting to follow these societal changes by defining curricula that foster CT, a broad intellectual capability, which is expected to support solving a wide range of computational problems in various professional and everyday contexts [6]. Finland is among the front-runners by providing all primary school students with the opportunity to learn the basics of computer programming as per guidelines of the new national primary school core curriculum that came into effect in 2016.

In practice, the curricular reform sets new requirements in terms of, for example, learning material design and the assessment for learning of CT via age-appropriate programming activities. However, the lack of established theoretical models and the scarcity of prior empirical evidence of learning from authentic school environments makes research-based and well-grounded pedagogical decision-making troublesome [5]. There is an urgent pragmatic need to clarify CT contents for the design of learning situations as well as discover appropriate assessment methods that are potentially beneficial for learning in school settings.

3 BACKGROUND RELATED WORK

The key contents in CT have varied across previous literature [5]. A widely recognized line of discourse underlines that its conceptual and practical components comprise interdisciplinary capabilities or competence areas instead of context-specific knowledge in, for example, computer programming. The International Society for Technology in Education (ISTE) and the American Computer Science Teachers Association (CSTA) developed a categorization [1] for transversal CT concepts and capabilities, such as Abstraction and Problem decomposition, for primary and secondary education. Other similar categorizations that define various interdisciplinary CT components and their core characteristics have also surfaced.

Scratch is a free block-based programming environment, which allows the manipulation of interactive media, such as games and animations, with a commitment to the constructionist principles of learning [3]. Among others, students' Scratch projects and their programming processes are complementary entry points in assessing CT in a holistic way [4]. The pedagogical purpose of assessment is to support the process of learning. Especially formative assessment, which establishes "where the learner is going", "where the learner is right now", and "how to get there", is potentially beneficial for supporting learning [2]. As programming is a demonstration of

CT and an activity during which students can receive supports for their learning processes [5], authentic programming activities are potentially fruitful platforms for formative assessment in this context.

4 STATEMENT OF THESIS/PROBLEM

The goal of this thesis is to develop the premises of a pedagogically meaningful instrumental system for typifying and assessing introductory CT in Scratch at the primary school level. This goal is addressed in the following ways. Firstly, prior frameworks and instruments for assessing CT-related ideas in Scratch are reviewed for their theoretical and operational capabilities, limitations, and opportunities for formative assessment. Secondly, revised frameworks for assessing CT in students' Scratch projects and their programming processes are designed. These frameworks are designed to conjoin parts to a holistic assessment system that is potentially helpful for improving the quality of learning. The frameworks are used with samples of data comprising students' authentic Scratch projects and video recordings of their programming processes to provide empirical evidence for primary students' CT capabilities.

5 RESEARCH GOALS METHODS

This study employs a literature review and an empirical case study. In the first phase (2017-18), the literature review is conducted for prior peer-reviewed studies concerning the assessment of introductory computational contents in Scratch. The contents are categorized according to the descriptive characteristics assigned for interdisciplinary CT components in seminal background literature (e.g., [1]). Preliminary results suggest that a myriad of computational content that relates in many ways to CT is scattered across multiple prior studies. The review will produce a synthesis comprising fundamental conceptual and practical ideas in CT, their respective operational introductory contents in Scratch, and indications towards assessing said ideas and contents.

The second phase (2018-19) involves the development of a revised framework, the "CT Alphabets" (CT-ABCS), for contextually typifying and assessing the CT indicated by students' Scratch projects. The framework is applied in practice with a sample of data to empirically investigate students' CT capabilities. The participants were fourth grade students (N=58) who attended an introductory Scratch programming course (twelve 45-minute lessons in total). All Scratch projects that the students programmed as groups and returned during the course (339 projects in total) were stored for analysis. The analysis of CT indicated by the projects is currently in progress.

Additionally, eight student groups (1-3 students per group) were video recorded while they programmed their final project assignments: interactive Scratch games or stories (approximately 560 minutes of video in total). The third phase (2019-20) is set to involve an in-depth examination regarding how the analysis of programming processes complements the analysis of Scratch projects.

6 DISSERTATION STATUS

The thesis document has been outlined and drafted. The document comprises an introduction, a theoretical background, a methods section, a summary of results from the three articles in addition to

conclusions drawn from the study. The three articles correspond with the three data analysis phases described above. The report of the literature review (phase 1) will shortly be submitted for peer review in a scientific journal.

The development and the application of the CT-ABCS framework has been initiated based on the preliminary results received in the literature review. Currently, the main pursuits are adjusting the conceptual and operational premises of the framework and seeking further content validation for it. The next larger step in the study is exploring prospects for analyzing the students' programming processes alongside their projects.

7 EXPECTED CONTRIBUTIONS

Pragmatically, the thesis is expected to contribute pedagogically meaningful instruments and their conceptual premises for typifying and assessing introductory CT in primary school students' Scratch projects and programming processes. However, considering the advised time for completing the thesis, further testing and validation for the frameworks could be necessary after the case studies. Moreover, a pedagogically convenient instrumentalization of the frameworks (e.g., automatization into a digital learning-support system) for educational practice could be a next step.

The attained empirical evidence regarding fourth grade students' CT capabilities in Scratch is expected to provide valuable knowledge for pedagogical decision-making, such as the appropriate setting of CT-related learning objectives and assessment criteria in addition to indications towards courseware and learning material design.

Moreover, the development process of the assessment system and the developed conceptual notions regarding assessment could possibly be analytically generalized into other learning contexts concerning CT and programming as well (e.g., robotics, digital game-play, text-based programming).

REFERENCES

[1] Valerie Barr and Chris Stephenson. 2011. Bringing computational thinking to K-12: What is involved and what is the role of the computer science education community? *ACM Inroads* 2, 1 (March 2011), 48–54. https://doi.org/10.1145/1929887.1929905
[2] Paul Black and Dylan Wiliam. 2009. Developing the theory of formative assessment. *Educational Assessment, Evaluation and Accountability* 21, 1 (February 2009), 5–31. https://doi.org/10.1007/s11092-008-9068-5
[3] Karen Brennan and Mitchel Resnick. 2012. *New frameworks for studying and assessing the development of computational thinking.* Paper presented at the meeting of AERA 2012, Vancouver, CB, Canada. Retrieved June 7, 2018 from https://web.media.mit.edu/~kbrennan/files/Brennan_Resnick_AERA2012_CT.pdf
[4] Shuchi Grover, Marie Bienkowski, Satabdi Basu, Michael Eagle, Nicholas Diana, and John Stamper. 2017. A Framework For Hypothesis-Driven Approaches To Support Data-Driven Learning Analytics In Measuring Computational Thinking In Block-Based Programming. In *Proceedings of the Seventh International Learning Analytics Knowledge Conference.* ACM, New York, NY, 530–531. https://doi.org/10.1145/3027385.3029440
[5] Sze Yee Lye and Joyce Hwee Ling Koh. 2014. Review on teaching and learning of computational thinking through programming: What is next for K-12? *Computers in Human Behavior* 41 (September 2014), 51–61. https://doi.org/10.1016/j.chb.2014.09.012
[6] Matti Tedre and Peter Denning. 2016. The Long Quest for Computational Thinking. In *Proceedings of the 16th Koli Calling International Conference on Computing Education Research.* ACM, New York, NY, 120–129. https://doi.org/10.1145/2999541.2999542

A Misconception Driven Student Model to Author Feedback

Luke Gusukuma
Computer Science
Virginia Tech
Blacksburg, Virginia
lukesg08@vt.edu

ABSTRACT

Getting novice programmers over initial misconceptions is difficult because learning programming is difficult. Practice is one of the best ways for novices to learn. However, in the absence of feedback contextualized to instruction and focused on misconceptions, misconceptions become a difficult hurdle. To improve feedback, I present the Misconception-Driven Student Model (MDSM). MDSM is a cognitive model that lends itself to a framework to scalably deliver Misconception-Driven Feedback (MDF). I show MDF's impact through a quasi-experimental study that indicates that MDF significantly supports programming skill development. I plan on verifying these results by running another experimental study.

CCS CONCEPTS

• **Applied computing** → **Education**; Learning management systems; • **Social and professional topics** → **Computational thinking**; **CS1**; **Student assessment**;

KEYWORDS

CS Education; Immediate Feedback; Student Model; Misconception

ACM Reference format:
Luke Gusukuma. 2018. A Misconception Driven Student Model to Author Feedback. In *Proceedings of 2018 International Computing Education Research Conference, Espoo, Finland, August 13–15, 2018 (ICER '18)*, 2 pages.
https://doi.org/10.1145/3230977.3231015

1 PROGRAM CONTEXT

I am a computer science PhD student. My current research project started in Fall of 2016. I am analyzing a cognitive model I have developed, the Misconception Driven Student Model (MDSM). I have run one of two planned quasi-experimental studies to analyze the impact of MDSM on student learning. My work includes two published papers on MDSM and the experimental study's results. I plan on publishing additional results from the firs experiment and data from the second experiment.

2 CONTEXT AND MOTIVATION

Programming is difficult to learn; increasing programming experience is one of the most effective ways to learn programming[9].

To increase the efficiency of knowledge acquisition, students need frequent practice with plentiful immediate feedback, grounded in instruction [8]. However, delivering well-designed feedback for numerous programming problems to build that experience can be a time-consuming task.

3 BACKGROUND & RELATED WORK

Creating immediate feedback for programming problems has two popular approaches: hint generation and unit testing (e.g. [7] and [3]). Hint generation suggests code edits to students while unit tests deliver feedback regarding program output. Both approaches require little instructor effort, but frequently fail to give feedback about program solutions [4] and contextualize feedback to instruction [3, 7]. While intelligent tutoring systems address this issue, they require significant extra effort and expertise[5]. In contrast, my approach intimately involves the instructor and mitigates instructor burden through technology and several reuse strategies by leveraging what current hint generation and unit testing techniques currently lack, a well articulated model to contextualize immediate feedback to instruction for several programming problems.

4 STATEMENT OF THESIS/PROBLEM

To contextualize automated feedback to instruction, I propose the following thesis: *authoring feedback using a cognitive student model supports student learning of programming*. This thesis requires confronting a number of challenges:

(1) What is an appropriate cognitive student model?
(2) How can this model be used practically by instructors to author feedback contextualized to their instruction?
(3) How can the impact of the feedback on learning be measured?

5 RESEARCH GOALS & METHODS

The cognitive model I propose is the Misconception-Driven Student Model (MDSM). MDSM models student knowledge by mapping observed programming mistakes to sets of inferred misconceptions; this model enables detection of misconceptions, linking of feedback to instruction, immediate generation of feedback, and finer grained evaluation of students and feedback. While applicable to the learning of programming by all novice learners, I explore the impact of MDSM on non-computing majors.

MDSM builds on the idea of knowledge components, "an acquired unit of cognitive function or structure that can be inferred from performance on a set of related tasks."[6]. Framing misconceptions as undesirable knowledge components and mistakes as student performance, I define two interrelated ideas, a (programming) misconception and a (programming) mistake, as follows:

- A programming misconception is a unit of cognitive function or structure that can be inferred from a mistake on a programming task.
- A programming mistake is an incorrect configuration of code elements.

The model is defined as follows: a programming mistake maps to an associated (inferred) set of programming misconceptions. This model's major implication is that automatically detecting programming mistakes inherently implicates the underlying misconceptions. This model relies on having a set of discovered misconceptions that we can map to a set of mistakes. This model and the challenges posed in section 4 leads to four research questions:

5.1 Research Question 1

What is an appropriate cognitive student model on which to base feedback for students learning to program? My tentative answer to this question is MDSM. This model may need to be refined as the research proceeds and new insights and evidence are gained.

5.2 Research Question 2

How can we discover misconceptions? Usage of MDSM, necessitates misconception discovery. As misconceptions are inferred from mistakes, experts (e.g. instructors) must discover these mistakes. Mistake discovery techniques are described in [1]; they include observing code, machine learning, and personal experience.

5.3 Research Question 3

How can we detect misconceptions in student code and deliver instructor-authored immediate feedback based on misconceptions? My proposal for authoring of contextualized feedback is a specification language for authoring mistakes' automatic detection and feedback delivery. I have outlined this specification in [2]. I refer to instructor-authored feedback contextualized in misconceptions as Misconception-Driven Feedback (MDF). The implementation of the specification involves implementing a modified tree-inclusion algorithm for ASTs and abstract interpretation.

5.4 Research Question 4

How does feedback grounded in instruction impact student learning? I plan on measuring the impact of MDF through experimental studies using multiple choice tests, programing problems, surveys, and log data. I use multiple choice tests to measure students' recall and understanding. I use programming problems to identify deficiencies in students' practical skills by viewing distributions of misconceptions detected by MDF. I use surveys to measure the students' perceptions of MDF on their learning.

6 DISSERTATION STATUS

I have used MDSM to develop an instructional design process (Instructional Design + Knowledge Components a.k.a. ID + KC)[1] and MDF. ID + KC is a misconception discovery-centric Instructional Design process used to develop an instructional unit on iteration that was deployed in classrooms.

I completed program analysis software implementation of MDF and deployed it to collect treatment data regarding the impact of MDF. This experiment was run on 290 students over one control semester and two treatment semesters; instructors, course content, number of TAs, etc. were controlled to isolate the MDF's effect. Summarily, the experiment's results suggests that MDF supports development of programming skills to a significant degree with an average score increase of 10%. These results help to answer research questions 3 and 4 and have been submitted for review.

The continuation of this research includes reviewing more log data, and applying the MDSM and MDF to a different programming context. None of my dissertation has been written yet. This is pending on first completing my research proposal document and an estimated dissertation completion date of Fall of 2019.

7 EXPECTED CONTRIBUTIONS

My expected contributions are as follows:

(1) The Misconception Driven Student Model, a cognitive model suitable for formulating immediate feedback
(2) Two Quasi-experimental studies analyzing the impact of Misconception Driven Feedback, a product of the MDSM
(3) A software implementation of program analysis techniques to detect mistakes and deliver Misconception Driven Feedback.

I anticipate the results of the second experiment will also provide evidence that MDF supports student learning.

ACKNOWLEDGMENTS

This work is supported in part by National Science Foundation grants DUE 1624320, DUE 1444094, and DGE 0822220.

REFERENCES

[1] Luke Gusukuma, Austin Cory Bart, Dennis Kafura, Jeremy Ernst, and Katherine Cennamo. 2018. Instructional Design+ Knowledge Components: A Systematic Method for Refining Instruction. In *Proceedings of the 49th ACM Technical Symposium on Computer Science Education*. ACM, 338–343.
[2] Luke Gusukuma, Dennis Kafura, and Austin Cory Bart. 2017. Authoring feedback for novice programmers in a block-based language. In *Blocks and Beyond Workshop (B&B), 2017 IEEE*. IEEE, 37–40.
[3] Georgiana Haldeman, Andrew Tjang, Monica Babeş-Vroman, Stephen Bartos, Jay Shah, Danielle Yucht, and Thu D Nguyen. 2018. Providing Meaningful Feedback for Autograding of Programming Assignments. In *Proceedings of the 49th ACM Technical Symposium on Computer Science Education*. ACM, 278–283.
[4] Hieke Keuning, Johan Jeuring, and Bastiaan Heeren. 2016. Towards a systematic review of automated feedback generation for programming exercises. In *Proceedings of the 2016 ACM Conference on Innovation and Technology in Computer Science Education*. ACM, 41–46.
[5] Kenneth R Koedinger, Vincent Aleven, Neil Heffernan, Bruce McLaren, and Matthew Hockenberry. 2004. Opening the door to non-programmers: Authoring intelligent tutor behavior by demonstration. In *International Conference on Intelligent Tutoring Systems*. Springer, 162–174.
[6] Kenneth R Koedinger, Albert T Corbett, and Charles Perfetti. 2012. The Knowledge-Learning-Instruction framework: Bridging the science-practice chasm to enhance robust student learning. *Cognitive science* 36, 5 (2012), 757–798.
[7] Thomas W Price, Yihuan Dong, and Dragan Lipovac. 2017. iSnap: Towards Intelligent Tutoring in Novice Programming Environments. In *Proceedings of the 2017 ACM SIGCSE Technical Symposium on Computer Science Education*. ACM, 483–488.
[8] Marieke Thurlings, Marjan Vermeulen, Theo Bastiaens, and Sjef Stijnen. 2013. Understanding feedback: A learning theory perspective. *Educational Research Review* 9 (2013), 1–15.
[9] Chris Wilcox and Albert Lionelle. 2018. Quantifying the Benefits of Prior Programming Experience in an Introductory Computer Science Course. In *Proceedings of the 49th ACM Technical Symposium on Computer Science Education*. ACM, 80–85.

Practical Thinking while Programming

A Deweyan Approach to Knowledge in Computer Science

Kristina von Hausswolff
Department of Information Technology
Uppsala University
Box 337, SE-751 05 Uppsala, Sweden
kristina.von.hausswolff@it.uu.se

ABSTRACT

Digital competencies are important in today's schools. This can mean practical programming skills as well as more conceptual thinking tool developed within the discipline of computer science. Central to my research interests is the specific situation when students encounter programming for the first time. The complex dependencies between practice and theory in the computer lab are analyzed from a pragmatic perspective. My focus is on *actions* and the situational *thinking* while *doing* programming, that is, 'practical thinking'. This situation is being researched both in naturalistic and controlled settings. A pair-programming setting highlights both the interaction with the programming language, the software, and with the Computer Science tradition. One preliminary finding is the importance of resources directed to the problem at hand, including the importance of timing—which could be framed in terms of the Deweyan concept of inquiry.

CCS CONCEPTS

Social and professional topics → Computing education

Keywords

Pragmatism, hands-on, novice programming

ACM Reference Format:

Kristina von Hausswolff. 2018. Practical Thinking while Programming A Deweyan Approach to Knowledge in Computer Science. In ICER '18: 2018 International Computing Education Research Conference, August 13–15, 2018, Espoo, Finland. ACM, New York, NY, USA, 2 pages. https://doi.org/10.1145/3230977.3231025

1. CONTEXT AND MOTIVATION

As a PhD student in Computer Science with specialization in Computer Science Education Research at Uppsala University, I am about 1.5 years in to a four-year PhD program. The research is in the domain of novice programming at the university and upper secondary levels. Students are learning to program as part of their formal education and more programming is included in in the curriculum for Swedish upper secondary school in 2018 following a decision by the Swedish Government. This demands for more research within the area of teaching and learning programming, with a special emphasis on novices.

My research is closing in on a specific situation but at the same time broadening the perspective of that situation: students

(16-25 years old) who are introduced to text-based programming in a formalized teaching situation. They work with structured tasks in a pair programming setting, where one student writes (hands-on) and both discuss. Pair programming setting is common in novice programming and in my case enables insight into the problem-solving process through the pair discussions. Although the studied situations are unique—a specific content, a specific language, a particular teacher—the situation is normal in the sense that similar situations are common at university and upper secondary school. Embedded in this is the Computer Science tradition and its history, values, and knowledge content, which I have chosen to focus on.

2. BACKGROUND & RELATED WORK

The embrace of the practice in education is not a new phenomenon. The pragmatic thinker and educationalist John Dewey argues practical *action* as a necessary part of acquiring knowledge, in his action and communication theory [1]. Dewey specifically directs focus to the importance of habits when thinking: "The concrete fact behind the current separation of body and mind, practice and theory, actualities and ideals, is precisely this separation of habit and thought. Thought which does not exist within ordinary habits of action lacks means of execution." [2, p. 17]. This connection between habit and thinking underpins my concept of practical thinking, building upon by the Deweyan rejection of the dichotomies above. The complex and intertwining dependencies between practice and theory in the computer lab is further examined by Eckerdal [4].

With a pragmatic perspective, my focus is on actions and the situational thinking while doing programming. This *thinking-while* is what I call 'practical thinking'. The basis for my knowledge analysis is the *transaction* in Dewey's theory [3]. The transaction is "the point of contact" between an environment and organism. The reality exists, but is only perceived as a function of the transaction. Transactions create experiences, and knowledge becomes a form of experience with which we approach the world. The organism tries to establish a balance with the environment and develops patterns of possible actions, *habits*. "The very operation of learning sets limit to itself, and makes subsequent learning more difficult. But this holds only of a habit in isolation, a non-communicating habit. Communication not only increases the number and variety of habits, but tends to link them subtly together, and eventually to subject habit-forming in a particular case to the habit of recognizing that new modes of association will exact a new use of it." [3, p. 280]. Dewey denotes this process of acquiring knowledge of the world, i.e. learning, *inquiry* [1, p. 58].

Students' talk and actions can be analyzed by the method pragmatic epistemology analysis (PEA) [9], grounded in pragmatism. This analysis takes place according to the continuity principle, meaning that there is a history for both the student being taught and in the subject itself. The student uses their previous knowledge and experiences in the meeting with a new subject. But continuity also means that there is a purpose with the learning situation in which the individual and the subject will meet and new developments take place. Dewey also says that not all experience is meaningful learning—only experiences that enable many new experiences in the future.

3. STATEMENT OF THESIS/PROBLEM
In understanding practice, the roles of interaction and tradition play a part as well as understanding the 'situationness' of the learning environment including the curriculum and the teachers' didactical choices in creating the situation. My initial focus was on how hands-on comes into play [5]. Hands-on experience of programming is an integrated part of learning the subject, and the role of student engagement, motivation, and the interaction between students are all factors that play a part in the whole of the learning experience. An interesting question to study empirically would then be: How can the experiences of the students while programming be related to knowledge traditions in computer science? This question is examined further in [6].

4. RESEARCH GOALS & METHODS
My research is part of a broader research project with several research questions further described in [5]. One research question that is central to my research is: How do students experience the practical learning to program? This includes hands-on experience and its impact on their practical knowledge and conceptual understanding. This also involves what roles different parts of that experience play in gaining skills and knowledge, as described by the CS community's standards [8]. Different factors of interest are (reported) motivation; engagement in the task; stress in the learning situation; brain activities; and long-time memory—alongside the measured learning outcomes. The goal is to be able to sketch a model of hands-on learning in a pair programming setting with correlations of important factors.

The theoretical standpoint, the Deweyan action and communication theory is coupled with a mixed methodology in answering the research question. This entails two studies. Study one is a controlled study with students with no prior programming experience. Study two is an authentic classroom study at the university level. In study one a pair programming setting is used and one in the pair writes all the time, they never switch as is the common way pair programming is used in education. Data of both quantitative and qualitative character is collected and analyzed within the framework.

In study two a qualitative education research approach will then later be used to further investigate factors important to learning programming, this time in several authentic classroom situations. We will follow two or more groups of students taking an introductory programming course at a Swedish university throughout. The 'practical thinking' will be observed in action as well as described in interviews. In line with the mixed methods research approach, a wide range of data will be collected to support triangulation and to obtain a rich holistic picture. My research uses video recordings of the pair programming sessions, both when students first are introduced to programming and also when they are a couple of weeks in to their course. Interactions with the code/software environment, and interactions of the student pair are recorded simultaneously. The data collected also includes structured observation of the lab situation, interviews in connection to the labs, and analyzing the teaching materials. The plan is then to analyze the collected data using methods connected to pragmatic theory, notably PEA [9].

5. DISSERTATION STATUS
Two pre-studies have been conducted during the first 1.5 years of my PhD. The pre-study for Study one is aimed at constructing a valid assessment tool that is context-specific to the controlled three-hour teaching setting mentioned above [7]. The pre-study for Study two examines methods of studying students' experiences in an authentic classroom setting related to hands-on and pair programming. The main finding here is the importance of resources directed to the problem at hand, including the importance of timing—which could be framed in terms of the Deweyan concept of inquiry. The interaction within a student pair also played a part in who gets to program hands-on. Study one is currently about to come to an end, meaning data analysis and processing during fall 2018. At the same time, the second study will be finalized. I am also aiming at publishing a theoretical paper expanding on pragmatism as a philosophical foundation within CSE.

6. EXPECTED CONTRIBUTIONS
One expected contribution is connecting the learning outcomes in programming to the practical experience in the lab situation, and building a model for how and why different factors as hands-on come in to play. This could give knowledge important to the classroom situation and to curriculum design. Furthermore, to develop and frame the practical hands-on experience in a pragmatic setting could be beneficial to didactics in other subjects like science where the practical lab work is an essential part of the subject.

7. ACKNOWLEDGMENTS
The Swedish Research Council under grant 2015- 01920 supported this work.

8. REFERENCES
[1] Biesta, G., Burbules, N. 2003. *Pragmatism and educational research*. Lanham, MD: Rowman & Littlefield.

[2] Dewey, J. 1922/2002. *Human Nature and Conduct: An Introduction to Social Psychology*. Great Books in Philosophy. Prometheus Books: New York.

[3] Dewey, J. 1925/1995. *Experience and Nature*. Dover, New York.

[4] Eckerdal, A. 2015. Relating theory and practice in laboratory work: A variation theoretical study. *Studies in Higher Education*, vol. 40(5), pp. 867–880.

[5] von Hausswolff, K. 2017. Hands-on in Computer Programming Education. In *Proceedings of the 2017 ACM Conference on International Computing Education Research (ICER '17)*. ACM, New York, NY, USA, 279-280

[6] von Hausswolff, K. 2017. Practical thinking in programming education. In *Proceedings of the 17th Koli Calling International Conference on Computing Education Research* (Koli Calling '17). ACM, New York, NY, USA, 203-204.

[7] von Hausswolff, K. In press. Measuring Programming Knowledge in a Research Context. In *Proceedings of the 48th ASEE/IEEE Frontiers in Education Conference*

[8] Joint Task Force on Computing Curricula, Association for Computing Machinery (ACM) and IEEE Computer Society. 2013. Computer Science Curricula 2013: Curriculum Guidelines for Undergraduate Degree Programs in Computer Science. ACM, New York, NY, USA.

[9] Wickman, P.-O. 2013. *Aesthetic Experience in Science Education: Learning and Meaning-making as Situated Talk and Action*. Routledge, New York and London.

Data Mining and Machine Learning in Education with Focus in Undergraduate CS Student Success

William Gregory Johnson
Department of Computer Science
Georgia State University
Atlanta, GA 30303 USA
wjohnson6@student.gsu.edu

ABSTRACT

Computer science (CS) enrollments are at an all-time high, [1] and successful undergraduate CS graduations are indisputably important. With a student population of approximately 51,000, Georgia State University is a USA based state university which is diverse and forms a rich big data footprint as students navigate pathways to graduation. Quoted in a July 2017 article from HigherEd.com, "Georgia State's extensive predictive analytics efforts are leading to better grades and student retention – and more minorities graduating from STEM programs." This doctoral project builds upon current data mining and modeling, machine learning applications, and learning analytics for predicting student success that is beyond retention. Gaining knowledge of CS student learning, developing better alerting models for success, and discovering behavioral indicators from learning analytics reporting is the goal of this research. Using this knowledge as evidence based data for improving the CS student experience will aid in performance improvements and increase pathways to graduation. My supporting research project is building CS student datasets to represent the student as directed graphical models, investigating their relationships using machine learning frameworks, and complex mathematical computations (tensors or gradient boosting) along with graph data mining techniques.

CCS CONCEPTS

• **Social and professional topics** → **Computer science education**;

KEYWORDS

STEM student retention; graduation pathways; educational data mining; graph data mining

ACM Reference Format:
William Gregory Johnson. 2018. Data Mining and Machine Learning in Education with Focus in Undergraduate CS Student Success. In *Proceedings of 2018 International Computing Educational Research Conference (ICER '18)*. ACM, New York, NY, USA, 2 pages. https://doi.org/10.1145/3230977.3231012

1 PROGRAM CONTEXT

CS education is the center focus of my career. After a Bachelor's in CS and more than a decade in practice with large US corporations and the US Federal government, I returned to academe, completed a Master's in CS from GSU in 2004. I began teaching online CS courses and later, teaching CS courses as a full time faculty at a local community college. Being a first generation college student motivated me to work in a community college with strong emphasis on education excellence. The merger of my institution and my Master's alma mater created an opportunity to enter the PhD program in CS at GSU. The Summer semester of 2016 initiated my full time status as a PhD student. Passing the qualifying exams in the Fall of 2017, leaves my remaining course requirements of a CS foundation course and one external departmental course. Fulfillment of one additional dissertation committee person is required before a thesis proposal submission. Completing time-line for these is Fall of 2019, and a target defense date is sometime in Fall 2020 or Spring 2021. My current project is analyzing the approved data of my institutional review board (IRB) for a study that compares performance of CS students in CS curriculum foundation courses based on a prerequisite fulfillment by either the discrete mathematics (MATH2420) or theoretical foundations of computer science (CSC2510). This work will be submitted to the ACM SIGCSE in August 2018, and will establish a basis for several related projects combining additional datasets within the university.

2 CONTEXT AND MOTIVATION

A preliminary data analysis shows an increase in population of transfer CS students at GSU and a trend to enroll in more CS courses per semester than native students. It also shows that transfer student performance is consistently different than that of native students, namely higher CS course fail rates and lower CS GPA scores. These detrimental findings [4], motivate me to investigate and identify other predictors of retention or discovery of performance attributes in the CS undergraduate program. My doctoral project will use graph data mining to find communities where behavioral outcome strategies like student-faculty relationships, cognitive and non-cognitive gains, and social network analysis can be applied and evaluated. Using these data-driven findings in my research, I can develop experimental models of predictive course sequencing, adaptive and targeted tutoring, and a student facing learning analytics reporting system to better understand the CS student perceptions and perceived effects of the models. These models along with improving the CS student experience, lowering attrition, and decreasing loss of time and resources are the motivating goals of my doctoral work.

3 BACKGROUND & RELATED WORK

Much research has focused on undergraduate student success factors resulting from flipped classrooms, hybrid learning, technology usage, and intuition-driven designs. Educational data mining (EDM) focuses on exploring this unique and large-scale research challenge with data-driven analysis to better understand students and their learning environments. [3] EDM is well positioned to analyze components of GSU's CS student digital avatar because they are mixed among sources of the university's learning management systems (LMS), CS courses, grades, demographics, socio-economic indicators, network usage data, and social networking interactions. According to New [5], achieving data-driven CS education systems are a result of four goals: 1) personalization, 2) evidence-based learning, 3) school efficiency, and 4) continuous innovation, all the while protecting the individual student privacy. The inclusion of data-driven education in CS starts with leveraging data to provide a more effective education system. An analysis of 240 EDM works over three years (2010 to 2013) by Penã-Ayla [6], shows that most common approaches to gage performance are student modeling and assessment function. Barker et al., found most higher education retention studies focus on the combining of STEM disciplines, giving an unclear picture of computer science. [2] My research will be completely focused in the CS program.

4 STATEMENT OF THESIS/PROBLEM

Producing bachelor degreed CS students to work in practice and academe is an increasing demand and is driving higher enrollments in colleges and universities in CS programs. Using EDM and learning analytics, a discovery of knowledge relating from student learning and behavior, demographics, academic advising, CS course sequencing, network usage/interactions will produce evidence based data, enabling higher retention and graduation pathways for these students. Using data mining and modeling to detect communities in the evidence based data, CS student prediction models can be made, tested, and improved through empirical research. Creating a learning analytics reporting model where CS students can see predictors of achievement, identification of skill deficits, and receive targeted and personalized intervention modalities, beyond the face-to-face or online interactions is the challenge in my research.

5 RESEARCH GOALS & METHODS

My research goals are:

- Analyze CS student data that fulfill a prerequisite from either MATH2420 or CSC2510 and:
  - Compare effective results on remaining core CS courses (CS grades, course failures, population behaviors)
  - Compare performance and job placement resulting from fulfillment of the prerequisite course (IT vs CS)
  - Currently under research with IRB-H18480
- Represent the CS student in/with graphical model(s) and use social network analysis of the data (clickstream) from our

LMS and the internal GSU network to discover relationships based on graph data mining and graph theory principles
- Compare transfer vs native CS student data in CS course loads per semester within course levels and student classifications
- Develop a position paper on transfer CS students addressing:
  - CS student's desire for lower cost of core courses at a 2-year college
  - Conflict of 2-year college's desire for their students to complete an AS degree, resulting in more classes at 2-year, leaving mostly CS courses with a 4-year university
  - And the desire for students to finish a BS degree within three years, post AS degree, with CS course overloading (>= 3 per semester) resulting in performance impacts

6 DISSERTATION STATUS

I have analyzed a cumulative data set of CS student data that compares transfer to native student performance impacts with results published at ACM SIGCSE. [4] In the summer of 2018, my plans include investigate the math versus CS prerequisite effect on remaining requirements of CS curriculum courses. GSU's managing group for our LMS has agreed to meet and discuss a protocol to incorporate data elements for a learning analytics study in the CSC4350, Software Engineering course, I will teach in Fall 2018. The thesis is currently in outline and my third year (Fall 2018, Spring 2019) will be used to complete the thesis proposal and defend it. The following years involve research and preparation for my dissertation defense.

7 EXPECTED CONTRIBUTIONS

The design of a framework or model for a student and faculty facing learning analytics reporting system to deliver advanced analysis of evidence data, LMS interactions, and student performance outcomes. Also, identify and compare communities of CS students through analysis of LMS data for improving the usage of and deeper integration into the undergraduate CS curriculum. Finally, I would like to design and present a common coding scheme or foundation grammar for evidence based education data to open new analysis and measurement instruments. These along with research data will be made available to other undergraduate STEM programs for education research.

REFERENCES

[1] *Assessing and Responding to the Growth of Computer Science Undergraduate Enrollments*. 2017. URL: https://www.nap.edu/catalog/24926, doi:10.17226/24926.
[2] L. Barker, C. L. Hovey, and L. D. Thompson. Results of a large-scale, multi-institutional study of undergraduate retention in computing. In *Frontiers in Education Conference (FIE), 2014 IEEE*, pages 1–8. IEEE, 2014.
[3] EDM Society. International Educational Data Mining Society. URL: http://jedm.educationaldatamining.org/index.php/JEDM.
[4] W. G. Johnson, R. Sunderraman, and A. G. Bourgeois. Performance Impact of Computer Science Course Load and Transfer Status. In *Proceedings of the 49th ACM Technical Symposium on Computer Science Education*, page 1076. ACM, 2018.
[5] J. New. Building a data-driven education system in the United States. *Center for Data Innovation, November*, 25, 2016.
[6] A. Peña-Ayala. Educational data mining: A survey and a data mining-based analysis of recent works. *Expert systems with applications*, 41(4):1432–1462, 2014.

What are they thinking? Student Conceptions about Important and Difficult Topics in Introductory Computer Science

Cazembe Kennedy
Clemson University
Clemson, South Carolina
cazembk@clemson.edu

ABSTRACT

Understanding student reasoning and identifying student misconceptions are important precursors to developing high quality pedagogical materials and approaches. In my work, I seek to build on prior work in the identification of important and difficult topics in computer science and in concept inventories that explore student reasoning about these topics. I wish to explore student reasoning and discover student misconceptions about important topics in introductory computer science, with the goal of informing the design and evaluation of interventions that improve teaching and learning of these topics.

I present here a summary of my work to date: a deep review of related work including the selection of important and difficult topics in introductory computer science, the creation of an exploratory instrument, the conduct of an initial, exploratory study using that instrument, and an analysis of a selected subset of the responses.

I present also my current plans in furtherance of my research goals: continued analysis of the responses to my initial study, the development of task-based interviews to gain clarification and deeper understanding of student reasoning and misconceptions, and the development and evaluation of interventions that both build on solid lines of students reasoning and address misconceptions.

CCS CONCEPTS

• **Social and professional topics** → **Computer science education**;

KEYWORDS

Computer science education, pedagogical content knowledge, misconceptions

ACM Reference format:
Cazembe Kennedy. 2018. What are they thinking? Student Conceptions about Important and Difficult Topics in Introductory Computer Science. In *Proceedings of 2018 International Computing Education Research Conference, Espoo, Finland, August 13–15, 2018 (ICER '18)*, 2 pages.
https://doi.org/10.1145/3230977.3231023

1 PROGRAM CONTEXT

I am currently a 4th year PhD student in the Human-Centered Computing program at Clemson University. I have completed all required coursework for the program and submitted my portfolio for review (equivalent to a comprehensive exam). I intend to propose my dissertation topic in the fall of 2018.

I have identified research questions that I seek to address, engaged in a deep review of related work, and identified some "important and difficult" topics in introductory computer science that have not yet been fully explored. I have designed and conducted an initial study and am engaged in the analysis of that data. I intend to conduct additional studies (described below) during the 2018-2019 academic year and to complete my dissertation in the summer or fall of 2019.

2 CONTEXT AND MOTIVATION

My work is in the area of Pedagogical Content Knowledge (PCK), which is "the blending of content and pedagogy into an understanding of how particular topics, problems or issues are organized, represented, and adapted to the diverse interests and abilities of learners, and presented for instruction[4]." I am seeking to expand Computer Science PCK by exploring student reasoning, identifying student misconceptions, and developing quality pedagogical content for important and difficult topics in computer science. Succeeding at this could lead to more engagement and higher retention rates for students within the CS field, especially underrepresented groups such as women and racial minorities. These are issues that are currently faced as there is an ever-growing need for people with a programming background in our technological world.

3 BACKGROUND & RELATED WORK

Pedagogical content knowledge for computer science (CS-PCK) is important, but is currently underdeveloped. Instructor knowledge of what students get wrong, their misconceptions and learning difficulties, is a critical piece of PCK.

STEM Researchers have studied misconceptions and how they can affect learning in various subjects. Confrey [1] states that even before formal study, people have "firmly held, descriptive, and explanatory systems" that are different than what is in the curriculum and "are resistant to change through traditional instruction." Tew and Guzdial posit that this may be less true for computer science, and that misconceptions in this domain may be more related to aspects of instruction rather than due to beliefs that students bring with them[5].

Work performed by Goldman et. al focused on the selection of topics the authors term "important and difficult" [2]. To identify these topics, they use a process that involves having a group of experts propose, rate, negotiate and re-rate a list of concepts in terms of importance and difficulty. Researchers have explored misconceptions in topics include propositional logic, memory models and assignment upon declaration, algorithms and data structures, looping strategies, BASIC programming statements, language-independent conceptual "bugs" in novice programming, and misconceptions and attitudes that interfere with learning to program.

A concept inventory is a criterion-referenced test, designed to help determine a student's knowledge of a specific set of concepts, and to expose misconceptions. Tew and Guzdial developed the FCS1[5], a validated instrument for CS1 that uses pseudocode in an effort to be applicable across a variety of pedagogies and programming languages. Beyond concept inventories, other assessments have sought to gauge if students' programming abilities are where they should be after completing introductory courses [3].

4 STATEMENT OF THESIS/PROBLEM

Research questions that I am interested to address include:

(1) What previously unexplored, important topics do introductory computer science students find difficult?
(2) How do students reason about these topics?
(3) What misconceptions do students hold regarding these topics?
(4) How can these misconceptions be addressed?

Answering these questions will allow me to contribute to the development of CS-PCK and to improve practices in teaching and learning about these topics.

5 RESEARCH GOALS & METHODS

Based on a review of prior work, an evaluation of CS1 curriculum, and interviews with instructors I selected a set of topics that are important and seemed likely to be difficult for students. I designed an assessment containing 21 questions that probe these topics. These questions are based on snippets of code and are either multiple choice or ask students about the result of the execution of that code. Each question then asks students to explain their reasoning. In the spring of 2018 I administered the assessment to 106 students in my university's CS2 course, which is taught in the C programming language.

I evaluated the correctness of the responses and used these quantitative results to select an initial set of topics that students appear to find difficult. Using a grounded theory approach, I have begun analyzing the text of the student responses with the goal of constructing a theory or framework that captures and explains student reasoning around these topics.

Through this evaluation, I have begun to notice interesting outcomes. When dealing with functions, students seem to have four distinct misconceptions which I have given codes that are explained below:

(1) Mistaking pass by value semantics with pass by reference semantics (**PBV**)
(2) Believing a global variable cannot be accessed by a calling function (**GlX**)

(3) A scope misconception in which students believed that a variable with the same name but in a different scope could be overwritten by a write to the local variable (**OW**)
(4) A more specific OW misconception in which students had the belief that a global variable could be overwritten by a local variable of the same name (**GlOW**)

Scope and visibility appear to play a significant part in students' misconceptions. The idea of variable shadowing is prominent in two of the four coded misconceptions (OW + GlOW). Scope and visibility also are relevant in the GlX misconception. PBV misconceptions may stem from cognitive overload exposing their fragile knowledge, over-reliance on function name, or simply not fully grasping pass by value semantics.

My plan after finishing analyzing and categorizing misconceptions is to develop a smaller, more detailed assessment that more precisely probes at key features of the emerging theory/framework and to use this in task-based interviews (think-aloud studies) that delve further into student reasoning around these topics. I will iterate on question refinement and interviewing until the theory/framework stabilizes. From this consortium, I hope to gain a better idea of the best way to use a grounded theory approach with data analysis, or have alternative methods suggested that may better suit my goals. Based on the theory I will design and evaluate an "intervention" (example, activity, diagram or computational tool) to aid in teaching and learning of these topics.

6 EXPECTED CONTRIBUTIONS

Through my research, I expect to gain a concrete understanding of some conceptions introductory students have that lead to incorrect reasoning in topics deemed important and difficult. For the topics and misconceptions identified, I intend to develop theories as to why they occur and suggest potential ways to teach the topics in a manner that builds on what students already know and allows them to understand why the misconceptions arise. If I am successful at developing a theory/theories that explain student reasoning and misconceptions around the identified topics, then this knowledge will inform the development of pedagogical innovations in CS. If time, resources, and evidence permits, I intend to develop interventions to allow teachers to address the misconceptions held and evaluate their effectiveness. Successful interventions/innovations could lead to greater engagement and higher retention rates for all CS students, and especially impact underrepresented groups.

REFERENCES

[1] J. Confrey. Chapter 1: A review of the research on student conceptions in mathematics, science, and programming. *Review of research in education*, 16(1):3–56, 1990.
[2] K. Goldman, P. Gross, C. Heeren, G. Herman, L. Kaczmarczyk, M. C. Loui, and C. Zilles. Identifying important and difficult concepts in introductory computing courses using a delphi process. *ACM SIGCSE Bulletin*, 40(1):256–260, 2008.
[3] M. McCracken, V. Almstrum, D. Diaz, M. Guzdial, D. Hagan, Y. B.-D. Kolikant, C. Laxer, L. Thomas, I. Utting, and T. Wilusz. A multi-national, multi-institutional study of assessment of programming skills of first-year cs students. In *Working group reports from ITiCSE on Innovation and technology in computer science education*, pages 125–180. ACM, 2001.
[4] L. Shulman. Knowledge and teaching: Foundations of the new reform. *Harvard educational review*, 57(1):1–23, 1987.
[5] A. E. Tew and M. Guzdial. The fcs1: a language independent assessment of cs1 knowledge. In *Proceedings of the 42nd ACM technical symposium on Computer science education*, pages 111–116. ACM, 2011.

The Collegiate Hackathon Experience

Brittany Ann Kos
ATLAS Institute
College of Engineering and Applied Sciences
University of Colorado Boulder
brittany.kos@colorado.edu

ABSTRACT

Collegiate hackathons are marathon-style, project building competitions where students can learn computing in an informal environment, build community, network with members of the technology industry, and be more productive members of the workforce. I am interested in understanding the social climate of hackathons and how it affects hackathon participants, particularly women and non-binary students, who only make up 23% of collegiate hackathon attendees. I will be exploring two lines of inquiry: (1) to explore the experiences of hackathon attendees to gain a deeper understanding about why participants do (or do not) participate in hackathons, what motivates them to attend, and what engages them at these events; and (2) to explore the ways collegiate hackathons can adapt their design practices to create an inclusive and equitable events for marginalized and minority students.

CCS CONCEPTS

• **Social and professional topics** → **Informal education**; *Women*;

KEYWORDS

collegiate hackathon; informal learning; gender; women; nonbinary

ACM Reference Format:

Brittany Ann Kos. 2018. The Collegiate Hackathon Experience. In *ICER '18: 2018 International Computing Education Research Conference, August 13–15, 2018, Espoo, Finland*. ACM, New York, NY, USA, 2 pages. https://doi.org/10.1145/3230977.3231022

1 PROGRAM CONTEXT

I am beginning the sixth and final year of my Ph.D. studies of an interdisciplinary degree program at the University of Colorado Boulder. This program has allowed me to combine my CS background with research methodologies and perspectives from multiple disciplines, including Computer Science, Education, the Learning Sciences, and Information Science.

2 CONTEXT AND MOTIVATION

Collegiate hackathons are informal learning environments where teams of college students build computing projects competitively. The events are 24 or 36 hours long and held on weekends at college campuses. Collegiate hackathons have been growing in popularity

over the last decade and are becoming more popular as the computing field grows in size and demand. In the 2016-2017 school year, over 200 collegiate hackathons were hosted in North America and Europe and over 65,000 students participated in these events [6]. These events are largely attended by computer science (CS) undergraduates [6] and many students go to these events to learn skills and practices of the computing field [1, 5], build community with fellow students and work on projects with friends [7, 10], networking with mentors and sponsors within the technology industry [1, 8], and become better prepared for the workforce and industry hackathons [4].

Despite the benefits that hackathons offer, we still see a disproportionate number of white and Asian men attending these events over women, non-binary students, and non-Asian students of color [6]. Collegiate hackathons can create an environment where marginalized students feel disinterested in attending or unwelcome at the events. I am interested in understanding the social climate of hackathons and how it affects hackathon participants, particularly women and non-binary students. I will explore two lines of inquiry: (1) to gain a deeper understanding about why participants do (or do not) participate in hackathons, what motivates them to attend, and what engages them at these events; and (2) to explore the design of hackathons with the end goal of creating inclusive and equitable events for all students.

3 BACKGROUND & RELATED WORK

There is a small, but growing body of work done on collegiate hackathons. Current work shows that collegiate hackathons are sites of informal learning [5, 8, 10] that impact students' perceptions of computing [9, 10] and may impact their retention in CS [7]. However there are hardly any studies about student experiences at these events, particularly women and non-binary students [10]. Overall, collegiate hackathons report that 23% [6] of their participants are female or non-binary and non-collegiate hackathons report that as little as 10% of their participants are female [3]. A handful of studies have researched why this gender gap exists and they have made some design recommendations for building events that are more inclusive for women. There is also an effort from the community of collegiate hackathon organizers across the US and Europe to build more diverse events, which includes changing design practices to be more inclusive as well as hosting female and non-binary focused collegiate hackathons. My work is positioned within these diversity and inclusion efforts and seeks to expand our understanding of hackathon attendees and build more equitable environments for all students. My dissertation will explore three lines of inquiry that build on the previous studies and add to the body of collegiate hackathon literature.

4 RESEARCH PROBLEM, GOALS & METHODS

This work is guided by two motivating questions: (1) what types of experiences do attendees (and non-attendees) have with collegiate hackathons; and (2) how can we design collegiate hackathons to be more inclusive and equitable for more types of students? I have three lines of inquiry that explore these motivating questions.

Study #1 will be a retrospective, design-based research project about the design of a female-focused hackathon called T9Hacks. Four years ago I founded T9Hacks and have worked as the lead event organizer for three iterations of T9Hacks events. While planning T9Hacks, my team and I were influenced by our experiences attending collegiate hackathons and a desire to create an inclusive event, we also tried to mimic best practices that we knew created equitable and welcoming environments for women in computing, all while trying to work within a standard collegiate hackathon model that was set by one of our event partners, Major League Hacking (MLH). I chose a design-based research study [2] because it is research that is conducted in real-life, ongoing contexts where the researcher is involved in the design of the project; these studies often result in producing theories that richly describe participant experiences and produce interventionist designs that iteratively improve the research context. This study has two goals: (1) to explore how the design practices of T9Hacks changed over four years; and (2) to show the tension between "scholarly" hackathon design recommendations and what the organizing team wants to do. By performing a retrospective analysis on my team's decision-making process, we can look at which design elements were the most impactful for students as well as what was resources were available or influential to the organizing team.

Study #2 is a two-part exploratory study that provides insight into the experiences of female-focused collegiate hackathon attendees. The first part of this study studies hackathon participants' sense of community at three types of hackathons: women-only (where only women and non-binary students are the focus and only they are allowed to attend), female-focused (here there is a focus on female and non-binary students, but students of all genders can attend), and traditional events (where there is no gender focus at the hackathon and all students can attend). The second part of this study explores the goals participants had and the different ways they engaged at T9Hacks. Findings show that students were motivated in attending T9Hacks for different reasons, had worked with other participants in multiple ways, and had different motivations for attending workshops. This study also shows how the design of the can support or restrict the trajectories these different students. These findings are important since they contradict the traditional hackathon narrative that researchers and popular student hackathon guides have provided in the past. These findings can inform future hackathons and show additional ways hackathons can be designed to be inclusive of different types of students.

Study #3 is under design. I hope to use the feedback from the ICER Doctoral Consortium to finalize the details of this study, since engaging in the ICER DC will allow me to better understand how my research can provide insight and value to the CS Education community. This study builds on Study #2 findings and delves deeper into participants' motivations and engagement with collegiate hackathons. This study will be a multi-part mixed-methods study. The first part of the study will be an intervention and design-based study of T9Hacks. I will be implementing design changes to the event that build inclusive events for the different types of participants found in Study #2. Another part of the study will be exploring how these design changes did (or did not) affect the hackathon participants. I intend to interview hackathon participants and non-participants to gain a deeper understanding of their experiences with collegiate hackathons and what pieces of the hackathon were most impactful or influential to them. The results will be used to gain a deeper understanding of female-focused hackathon participants and to suggest inclusive design practices that can be used at other collegiate hackathons.

5 DISSERTATION STATUS

My Ph.D. program requires students to complete three exams: Preliminary Exam, Comprehensive Exam (where a student becomes a candidate), and the final Dissertation Defense. I have completed the Preliminary Exam and will be completing the Comprehensive Exam in May of 2018. For my dissertation, I proposed three studies; Study #1 will be complete in Summer 2018, Study #2 is complete, and Study #3 will begin in Fall of 2018, after the ICER DC. I have a working outline for my dissertation and I will begin writing in Summer 2018. Completion of all dissertation work is anticipated for Spring of 2019.

6 EXPECTED CONTRIBUTIONS

My research and findings will be used to inform the design practices of collegiate hackathons and to create inclusive and equitable environments. Broadening participation at collegiate hackathons will allow all students to have the opportunity to engage in these events, learn computing in an informal environment, build community, network with members of the technology industry, and be more productive members of the workforce. Designing inclusive and equitable collegiate hackathons will benefit all students, but may have the most impact on female and non-binary students. Findings may also inform the design of industry hackathons and other informal learning environments.

REFERENCES

[1] C. Anslow, J. Brosz, F. Maurer, and M. Boyes. 2016. Datathons: An Experience Report of Data Hackathons for Data Science Education. In *SIGCSE '16*. ACM, 615–620.
[2] S. Barab and K. Squire. 2004. Design-Based Research: Putting a Stake in the Ground. *J. of the Learning Sciences* 13, 1 (Jan. 2004), 1–14.
[3] G. Briscoe and C. Mulligan. 2014. *Digital Innovation: The Hackathon Phenomenon*. Technical Report 6. Creativeworks London.
[4] The Economist. 2015. What the Hack? - The Rise of Hackathons. *The Economist* (Dec. 2015).
[5] A. Fowler. 2016. Informal STEM Learning in Game Jams, Hackathons and Game Creation Events. In *GJH&GC '16*. ACM, 38–41.
[6] MLH. 2016. HACKATHON DATA - Hackcon IV.
[7] D. Munro. 2015. Hosting Hackathons a Tool in Retaining Students with Beneficial Side Effects. *J. Comput. Sci. Coll.* 30, 5 (2015), 46–51.
[8] A. Nandi and M. Mandernach. 2016. Hackathons As an Informal Learning Platform. In *SIGCSE '16*. ACM, 346–351.
[9] G. T. Richard, Y. B. Kafai, B. Adleberg, and O. Telhan. 2015. StitchFest: Diversifying a College Hackathon to Broaden Participation and Perceptions in Computing. In *SIGCSE '15*. ACM, 114–119.
[10] J. Warner and P. J. Guo. 2017. Hack.Edu: Examining How College Hackathons Are Perceived By Student Attendees and Non-Attendees. In *ICER '17*. ACM, 254–262.

Fostering Computational Thinking
through Problem-Solving at School

Amelie Labusch
Paderborn University
Institute for Educational Science
Paderborn, Germany, 33098
amelie.labusch@upb.de

ABSTRACT

Computational thinking has recently gained more and more relevance as problem-solving competence of the 21st century. Taking Wing's [1] grand vision into account, each student should have certain skills in computational thinking in order to be able to participate adequately in social life and in his/her future profession. Thus, the International Computer and Information Literacy Study (ICILS 2018) does in addition to other student competences also measure their achievement in computational thinking [2]. In this internationally comparative large-scale assessment with a representative sample, a sound body of information is gathered that is used, among others, to explain variation in students' achievement in computational thinking. One field that represents a national extension in Germany is problem-solving. This paper presents a PhD project that focuses on this field and provides an analysis model that examines the relationship between students' self-perceived problem-solving skills and their computational thinking skills, taking into account further variables of influence and aims to explain variation in students' achievement of computational thinking.

CCS CONCEPTS

• **Social and professional topics** → **Computing education**; **Computational thinking**; **Computer science education**;

KEYWORDS

Computational thinking; problem-solving; ICILS 2018

ACM Reference Format:
Amelie Labusch. 2018. Fostering Computational Thinking through Problem-Solving at School. In *ICER '18: 2018 International Computing Education Research Conference, August 13–15, 2018, Espoo, Finland*. ACM, New York, NY, USA, 2 pages. https://doi.org/10.1145/3230977.3231019

1 PROGRAM CONTEXT

While I am currently in my second year as a PhD student, I am a research assistant at the professorship for school pedagogy of Prof. Dr. Birgit Eickelmann at the Institute for Educational Science at Paderborn University, Germany. As is often the case in Germany, I am enrolled as a doctoral student, but I do not participate in a

special university doctoral program. However, the professorship guarantees a closely meshed supervision program with regular doctoral conferences at which the latest status of the PhD thesis is presented and discussed.

2 CONTEXT AND MOTIVATION

In today's technological world, it is hard to find a job without at least a basic knowledge of IT. Moreover, the simple use of digital media is no longer enough, because more and more is regulated by automation and algorithms. If students do not have at least a basic knowledge of computational thinking at the end of their school years, it will be difficult for them to keep up with technological progress [3].

Education and thus the school as an educational institution can lay the foundation for an adequate acquisition of computational thinking competences. This is paid tribute above all in computer science lessons, where computational thinking is learnt through action in computational steps and algorithmic thinking. Nevertheless, if computational thinking is only learnt in computer science lessons and computer science is not a compulsory subject at school, not every student can benefit from it. This is why it makes sense to introduce students to problem-solving and algorithmic thinking as early as primary school level. This may also make it easier for computer science novices to get started, but above all, it ensures that all students have sufficient skills at the end of their schooling to keep up with technological progress. However, there are many hurdles on the way to integrating a new competence area into education systems and everyday school life [4].

To further develop initiatives in this area, it is necessary to know which competences in the field of computational thinking students already have and where similarities and differences to their general problem-solving skills emerge. Research in this context represents a great challenge because many aspects, such as the existence of different educational systems and the different conceptualization of computational thinking, have to be taken into account [5].

3 BACKGROUND & RELATED WORK

In recent years, research has focused on computational thinking as a relevant part of the 21st century student competences [6]. The resulting learning and teaching challenges are reflected in the discussion on how students can learn these skills in school. Since computational thinking is considered as a way of solving problems and thinking, previous research has proposed a high degree of congruence between problem-solving and computational thinking [7], but there are hardly any studies on this congruence on a solid empirical data basis under the control of other relevant determinants.

4 STATEMENT OF THESIS/PROBLEM

In view of the increasing importance of computational thinking for everyone, the question arises of what competences students should have in their future lives in this area. Since these are diverse, it is all the more important to examine the conceptualization of computational thinking in a problem-solving context. The core idea of the doctoral project is to take up current developments in computational thinking, to introduce a study that measures students' achievement in computational thinking in international comparison, and to provide an analytical model to investigate the relationship between computational thinking and problem-solving taking further influencing variables into account. It thus aims to explain variation in student's achievement in computational thinking. This results in the following research questions for the PhD project:

(1) To what extent are students' achievements in computational thinking related to their self-perceived general problem-solving skills?

(2) To what extent are students' achievements in computational thinking related to their cognitive abilities?

(3) Which other predictors at student and school level can explain variation in students' achievements in computational thinking?

5 RESEARCH GOALS & METHODS

Learning and teaching computational thinking is so crucial that the international comparative large-scale assessment ICILS 2018 (International Computer and Information Literacy Study) offers an international option to examine 8th Grade students' achievement in computational thinking with computer-based test modules and to gather further background data with questionnaires for students, teachers, principals, and ICT coordinators [2]. The international sample will be representative and the German sub-sample will comprise about 4,500 students. Nine education systems take advantage of this international option. However, the international part of ICILS 2018 does not take all factors into account that can possibly explain variation in students' achievement in computational thinking. This results in the need for national extensions, so that other influencing factors can be considered in the same sample. In the national extensions of ICILS 2018, problem-solving skills (on research question 1) and cognitive abilities (on research question 2), the background characteristics of students, their self-proficiency of computational thinking, the teaching activities of computational thinking and the attitude of teachers towards computational thinking (research question 3) serve to design an empirically verifiable theoretical analysis model. It is aimed to include all constructs necessary for answering research questions 1 to 3, using a multi-level

structural equation model. This model will be calculated using R, a free software environment for statistical computing and graphics.

6 DISSERTATION STATUS

I began my PhD thesis in 2017 and aim to complete it by 2020. Until now I have been working on the theoretical and methodological part of my dissertation and I have already presented my research approach at reputable conferences. So far, the theoretical and methodological parts have been written down to the current state of research; the theoretical part will be supplemented until the dissertation is submitted. As my PhD thesis is directly linked to my project work as a research assistant and thus to the International Computer and Information Literacy Study 2018 (ICILS 2018), I am bound to the international schedule and after this year's main survey, next year (2019) I will follow my data analyses and have the goal of submitting my dissertation in 2020.

7 EXPECTED CONTRIBUTIONS

The PhD project aims to provide a starting point for a deeper understanding of computational thinking by examining its relationship to a general understanding of problem-solving, taking into account other factors that can explain variation in students' achievement in computational thinking, and thus providing a holistic picture of computational thinking as 21st century competence. The big advantage of this approach is that all relationships are examined in the same sample and calculated in one model. By focusing on the relationship between computational thinking and problem solving, and if these two are strongly correlated, this will be of interest for the development of educational systems in so far as it would make it possible to work specifically on computational thinking in the coming years. Furthermore, the provided information could explain variation in students' achievement in computational thinking.

REFERENCES

[1] J.M. Wing. Computational thinking's influence on research and education for all. *Italian Journal of Educational Technology, 25*(2): 7–14, 2017.

[2] J. Fraillon, W. Schulz, T. Friedmann, D. Duckworth. Assessment Framework of ICILS 2018. Amsterdam: IEA, 2018, in press.

[3] B. Eickelmann. Computational Thinking als internationales Zusatzmodul zu ICILS 2018 – Konzeptionierung und Perspektiven für die empirische Bildungsforschung. [Computational Thinking as an international option in ICILS 2018 – the perspective of educational research]. *Tertium Comparationis. Journal für International und Interkulturell Vergleichende Erziehungswissenschaft, 23*(1): 47–61, 2017.

[4] B. Eickelmann. Measuring Secondary School Students' Competence in Computational Thinking in ICILS 2018 – Challenges, Concepts and Potential Implications for School Systems Around the World. In S. C. Kong & H. Abelson (Eds.), Computational Thinking Education, 2018, in press.

[5] A. Labusch, B. Eickelmann. Computational Thinking and Problem-Solving – a Research Approach in the Context of ICILS 2018. In E. Langran & J. Borup (Eds.), *Proceedings of Society for Information Technology & Teacher Education International Conference*, pages 3724–3729. Washington, D.C., United States: Association for the Advancement of Computing in Education (AACE), 2018.

[6] J. Voogt, P. Fisser, J. Good, P. Mishra, A. Yadav. Computational thinking in compulsory education: Towards an agenda for research and practice. *Education and Information Technologies, 20*(4): 715–728, 2015.

[7] A. Yadav, C. Stephenson, H. Hong. Computational Thinking for Teacher Education. *Communications of the ACM, 60*(4): 55–62, 2017.

Developing Students' Conceptual Design Skills for Software Engineering

T.G.Lakshmi
Inter-Disciplinary Programme in Educational Technology
Indian Institute of Technology Bombay
Mumbai, Maharashtra 400076, India
tglakshmi@iitb.ac.in

ABSTRACT

Conceptual design activity is described as a process in which the functional requirements of the design problem are extracted and transformed into descriptions of solution concepts. Peculiar characteristics of software design, such as dynamicity and intangibility makes this activity more challenging. It is a standard practice to create and integrate various standard representations of Unified Modeling Language (UML) into a comprehensive and cohesive software system. In the Software Engineering course, students learn about syntax, semantics and processes to create the formal (UML) representations. However when students encounter open-ended real world problems they are unable to use the formal representations. Current teaching-learning methods do not explicitly train students to overcome these difficulties. The Ph.D. work discussed in this paper aims at designing and evaluating an intervention for creating and integrating UML design. The theoretical foundation of the intervention is Function-Behaviour-Structure (FBS), i.e. extracting functions from the problem, simulating end user behaviours and associating them to structures thereby linking FBS together. By the end of the doctoral research I expect the following contributions: 1) an empirically evaluated intervention for learning to create and integrate UML design, 2) cognitive scaffolds for creating and integrating UML design based on FBS, 3) a validated assessment framework to evaluate FBS, UML design artifacts and processes and 4) a Technology Enhanced Learning Environment (TELE) which incorporates 1, 2 and 3. I am carrying out this research in the domain of software engineering and the target population is third year computer engineering undergraduates.

KEYWORDS

Conceptual Design; UML Design; Function-Behaviour-Structure; Software Design

ACM Reference Format:
T.G.Lakshmi. 2018. Developing Students' Conceptual Design Skills for Software Engineering. In *ICER '18: 2018 International Computing Education Research Conference, August 13-15, 2018, Espoo, Finland.* ACM, New York, NY, USA, 2 pages. https://doi.org/10.1145/3230977.3231008

1 PROGRAM CONTEXT

I am currently a full-time Ph.D. candidate in the Inter-disciplinary Program in Educational Technology at Indian Institute of Technology Bombay. I have successfully completed the academic credit requirements and enrolled as a full-time research scholar in teaching assistant category in July 2016, and I will graduate in the next 2-3 years.

The goals of my research are to create FBS based intervention and design a TELE to develop conceptual design skills for software engineering. The research methodology adopted for the same is Design Based Research (DBR). I have completed one cycle of DBR. In this cycle, I have explored how students create software conceptual design for open-ended design problems. I found that while creating software conceptual design students are unable to utilize basic formal representations like use case diagrams, component diagrams and state diagrams though they have formally completed the Software Engineering course in their curriculum. In the next cycles of DBR I will (i) design, implement, and evaluate a FBS based intervention to improve students' UML design, (ii) devise a rubric for assessment of UML design and (iii) build a TELE which incorporates (i) and (ii).

2 CONTEXT AND MOTIVATION

Conceptual design is an important phase in engineering design [5]. In the conceptual design phase the functional requirements are elicited and schematic descriptions of solution are generated [2]. In the context of software conceptual design, UML notations are a standard representation mechanism [4]. The standard UML notations are useful to represent the solution from different views and details. Students are unable to utilize the formal representation mechanism and connect them to create a software design. In my studies I have found, that the UML representations created by students are neither comprehensive (fulfilling all the functional requirements) nor are they cohesive (integrated).

So we would require an intervention for teaching learning of comprehensive and cohesive conceptual design. In the context of software engineering the learning intervention is aimed to help students create UML design that fulfills all the requirements of the design problem and is a logically coherent software design.

3 BACKGROUND AND RELATED WORK

Software design plays an important role in the development of software system [8]. It allows the developer to produce blueprint of solution, which then can be analyzed and evaluated against the requirements. The Unified Modeling Language (UML) is a family of design notations that is rapidly becoming a de facto standard software design language [4].

Traditional teaching learning of UML design is based on a combination of lectures for syntax/semantics and modeling tools [1]. However the current teaching-learning methods are unable to address the problems in students such as, inability to create basic UML representations for real world problems [6].Additionally, I have found that while creating software conceptual design students face the difficulties of fixation and cohesive integration [7].

4 STATEMENT OF THESIS PROBLEM

The broad research question (RQ) is - How to improve students conceptual design skills? The theoretical basis for the solution is the FBS framework. Function-Behaviour-Structure (FBS) is a framework that allows for effective reasoning about the functional and causal roles played by structural elements in a system by describing a systems components, their purpose in the system, and the mechanisms that enable their functions [3].

More specific research questions that I would be answering in this research are:

(1) What are the difficulties that students face during software conceptual design?
(2) What is a suitable intervention for students to learn to use FBS for UML design?
(3) How to assess students learning as a result of the FBS intervention?
(4) How effective is the TELE in developing conceptual design skills of students?

5 RESEARCH GOALS AND METHODS

Using the design-based research methodology the research has been broadly divided into three cycles. The specific goals and methods in each cycle are described below:

(1) *Cycle 1: Identifying students' difficulties to create software conceptual design for innovative design problems*- To get answers for this question, I performed qualitative exploratory studies. The exploratory studies had participants who were typical representation of learners from that age group with appropriate domain exposure. The study participants were given innovative design problem and were required to create software conceptual designs. While the participants created the software conceptual design their interaction with the tools and environment was video recorded. The video recording and artifacts created were analyzed from the FBS lens (content analysis). This analysis leads to the identification of the two most frequent difficulties-fixation and cohesive integration [7].
(2) *Cycle 2: Devising a suitable intervention to improve students UML design and measuring its effectiveness*- The phase-I of the intervention design, engages the learner to construct a 'FBS graph'. I have designed the phase-I of the intervention in the IHMC CMAP tool to utilize its affordances of graph construction. The FBS graph is an external representation of the function, structure, behaviour in the design solution and their corresponding relationship. Through the process

of construction of FBS graph the associated cognitive processes for conceptual design are triggered. I conducted a few exploratory studies to evaluate the activity design and identify tools and scaffolds in the learning environment. The assessment design is based on the FBS graph construction process as well as the final artifacts FBS graph and the UML diagrams. I would be conducting mixed method studies to further refine the learning strategy and assessment design in future DBR cycles.

(3) *Cycle 3: Evaluate the effectiveness of the TELE*- Based on the answers from cycle 1 and 2, the TELE would be built. I plan to conduct mixed method studies with third year computer engineering undergraduates using the TELE while they create software conceptual design for open-ended design problems.

6 DISSERTATION STATUS

The key findings from the studies conducted in cycle1 was that students were unable to use basic formal representation mechanisms like the UML class diagrams, use case diagram and component diagram. The students faced difficulty as they (i) fixated towards at least one of the FBS elements, (ii) lacked cohesive integration of FBS. The details of this study have been communicated for publication [7].The next goals of the research would be to devise a learning strategy and create a TELE.

From the ICER community I hope to discuss and receive feedback on the intervention design (RQ 2) and the evaluation framework for the intervention (RQ 3).

7 EXPECTED CONTRIBUTIONS

One of the key contributions of my research (till date) is the identification of problems faced by students while creating software conceptual design. By the completion of my thesis, I anticipate that I would have an empirically evaluated instructional strategy, assessment framework and an effective TELE to improve students' software conceptual design skills.

REFERENCES

[1] Seiko Akayama, Birgit Demuth, Timothy C Lethbridge, Marion Scholz, Perdita Stevens, and Dave R Stikkolorum. 2013. Tool Use in Software Modelling Education.. In *EduSymp@ MoDELS*.
[2] Amaresh Chakrabarti and Thomas P Bligh. 2001. A scheme for functional reasoning in conceptual design. *Design Studies* 22, 6 (2001), 493–517.
[3] Ashok K Goel, Spencer Rugaber, and Swaroop Vattam. 2009. Structure, behavior, and function of complex systems: The structure, behavior, and function modeling language. *Ai Edam* 23, 1 (2009), 23–35.
[4] Nenad Medvidovic, David S Rosenblum, David F Redmiles, and Jason E Robbins. 2002. Modeling software architectures in the Unified Modeling Language. *ACM Transactions on Software Engineering and Methodology (TOSEM)* 11, 1 (2002), 2–57.
[5] Gerhard Pahl and Wolfgang Beitz. 2013. *Engineering design: a systematic approach*. Springer Science & Business Media.
[6] Ven Yu Sien. 2011. An investigation of difficulties experienced by students developing unified modelling language (UML) class and sequence diagrams. *Computer Science Education* 21, 4 (2011), 317–342.
[7] Lakshmi T.G. and Iyer S. 2018. Exploring novice approach to conceptual design of software. In *13th International Conference of the Learning Sciences*.
[8] Guy Tremblay. 2001. Software Design. *SWEBOK* (2001), 35.

Progression of Student Reasoning about Concurrency

Extended Abstract

Aubrey Lawson
School of Computing
Clemson, SC
aubreyl@g.clemson.edu

ABSTRACT

In computing, concurrency refers to the notion that different parts or units of a program or algorithm may be executed out-of-order or in partial order, without affecting the final outcome. I seek to study how students conceptualize concurrency concepts and how these conceptualizations mature over the course of their undergraduate education. Thus far, I have designed an assessment that comprises two natural language problems and administered it to 110 undergraduate students at all four levels of the undergraduate program. I employed a grounded theory analysis to identify the emerging strategies and conceptions, performed open coding of student responses and abstracted emergent categories about student conceptions and problem-solving strategies. I compared these strategies and conceptions across grade levels to explore how student thinking around concurrency changes over the course of a CS education. This analysis will guide the design of a protocol for task-based interviews to further explore student reasoning. Longer term, the goal of my work is to inform the development of educational tools and strategies intended to promote the growth of student conceptions about concurrency.

CCS CONCEPTS

• **Social and professional topics** → **Computing education**; **Computational thinking**; Student assessment; • **Computing methodologies** → **Parallel computing methodologies**; **Concurrent computing methodologies**;

KEYWORDS

Applied computing, Education, Concurrency, Concurrent computing methodologies, Parallel computing methodologies, Grounded theory

ACM Reference Format:
Aubrey Lawson. 2018. Progression of Student Reasoning about Concurrency: Extended Abstract. In *ICER '18: 2018 International Computing Education Research Conference, August 13–15, 2018, Espoo, Finland.* ACM, New York, NY, USA, Article 4, 2 pages. https://doi.org/10.1145/3230977.3231024

1 PROGRAM CONTEXT

I am a fourth-year student in the Computer Science PhD program at Clemson University. I have completed the portfolio requirements for candidacy, and am currently engaged in a grounded theory study to investigate how students reason about concurrency. To study student conceptions of concurrency I designed an assessment that comprises two natural language problems, one for foundational, sequential logic and one for concurrency. This assessment was administered at the beginning of the Spring 2018 semester. I have analyzed student responses and derived emergent categories that represent the problem-solving strategies and solution features that I will focus on in subsequent task-based interviews. I will begin conducting task-based interviews during the Summer of 2018 and will be prepared to discuss the outcomes at the doctoral consortium. The outcomes of these task-based interviews will help me to refine my research questions. I expect to propose in the fall of 2018, conduct additional studies during the fall of 2018 and spring of 2019, and defend between May and December of 2019.

2 CONTEXT AND MOTIVATION

Concurrency is historically a difficult topic for students. Conventionally, topics of concurrency are presented later in the undergraduate course of study, after students have formed many conceptions and mental models of a notional machine. When confronted with non-deterministic systems, students are challenged to refine their reasoning about sequence, state, and what makes a program "correct". Concurrency-related problems utilize foundational knowledge, involve new vocabulary, and employ more rigorous testing methods than sequential problems. These factors may contribute to the production of successful or unsuccessful solutions, and the creation of knowledge that may be either fragile or firmly held. Instructors' understandings of student misconceptions affect their pedagogy and overall student performance [3]. As concepts in concurrency become a regular part of undergraduate curricula, instructors need pedagogical content knowledge (PCK) that addresses the unique challenges of concurrency topics. I am performing studies to elicit student conceptions and misconceptions about concurrency to inform a pedagogical tool specifically tailored to concurrency.

3 BACKGROUND & RELATED WORK

To study student conceptions of concurrency I designed an assessment that comprised two natural language problems, a sequential priming activity and one for concurrency–the Concert Tickets problem. The Concert Tickets problem, replicated from Lewandowski et al.[2], presents in natural language a real-world problem that requires concurrency for a sufficient solution. Students are asked to speculate about the possible problems and solutions of selling the best tickets to a high-demand concert with multiple sellers accessing the available seats. The primary goal of the activity is for students to discover the hidden issue of double booking and discuss the need for a critical section to encapsulate ticket sales.

Concurrency requires students to expand their models of computation beyond sequential execution, and I seek to elicit how students expand their models of notional machines [5] and discover misconceptions that develop in the process. Given that these topics are not addressed until the latter portion of a degree program, I will focus on constructivist pedagogy that seeks to work from these misconceptions to build stronger knowledge structures of both sequential and concurrent execution [4].

As my primary goal is to find emergent categories of student conceptions, I am using a grounded theory approach to analyze student responses and ground all results in the data collected[6]. As I continue with the data collection and analysis cycle, I will collect student responses from think-aloud interviews, as in[1].

4 STATEMENT OF THESIS/PROBLEM

With a grounded theory approach, I will identify and classify common student conceptions about concurrency by addressing the following questions:

- What is the nature of students' conceptions of concurrency concepts at each stage of CS education?
- How does students' thinking about CS concepts mature over the course of their undergraduate education?
- What interventions promote the growth of these student conceptions?

5 RESEARCH GOALS & METHODS

The goal of my research is to fully utilize a grounded theory approach to answer the research questions stated above. With this approach, no a priori hypotheses are applied to the data, and all data are iteratively and incrementally analyzed to derive emergent trends. My first data set was collected at the beginning of the Spring 2018 semester by administering the assessment with two natural language problems to students at each undergraduate course level. The problems were selected to minimize coding related barriers such as syntax knowledge and self-efficacy concerns.

Through line-by-line open coding, with the constant comparison method, I derived initial categories, sampling until each incident could be classified by the features of our categories. I searched for commonality in problem-solving strategies and conceptions between the Rainfall and Concert Tickets problems. Further theoretical sampling will focus on students currently taking courses that cover concurrency topics, and responses will be actively collected through think-aloud interviews informed by our initial analysis. The results of these analyses will lead to the development of a tool to facilitate student learning about concurrency.

6 DISSERTATION STATUS

My first data collection and analysis explored a natural language problem to observe how students reasoned about a real-world situation that required concurrency. I found that although most students acknowledge the issue of double booking, they actively tried to avoid concurrent solutions.

Three prominent trends that represent misconceptions about concurrency. The first trend was placing a focus on computing speed, i.e. a faster computer will avoid race conditions. The second trend was to create another state for tickets such that tickets could be marked as "reserved" or "pending" prior to "sold". This solution pushes the point of concurrency without ever addressing the issue. The third trend involved placing the responsibility on the sellers rather than the system. Seller-based solutions ranged from highly inefficient and error-prone seller-to-seller communication strategies to distributed solutions in which each seller is assigned a block of seats to sell, which is a differnt problem than was posed.

The next step will involve a task that overtly requires concurrency and active interaction with students to elicit the reasoning behind their chosen tactics. These task-based interviews will be conducted during the Summer 2018 semester in the context of an operating systems course. I will collect screen capture data and perform interview sessions to observe and elicit student reasoning when working in a technical environment that requires concurrency-related concepts.

I plan to propose my dissertation topic in September, and will include the results of the summer study. In the fall 2018 semester I will repeat the collection and analysis in the operating systems course. In the spring 2019 semester, a course will be taught with curriculum that focuses on three models of concurrency–threads, actors, and coroutines. In this context I will study student reasoning across multiple models of concurrency.

7 EXPECTED CONTRIBUTIONS

By collecting rich data sets from undergraduate students at each level of the computer science program I will derive a deep understanding of the the nature and development of student reasoning around three models of concurrency, which will provide a rich basis for the creation of appropriate pedagogical materials for these topics.

REFERENCES

[1] Holger Danielsiek, Wolfgang Paul, and Jan Vahrenhold. 2012. Detecting and Understanding Students' Misconceptions Related to Algorithms and Data Structures. In *Proceedings of the 43rd ACM Technical Symposium on Computer Science Education (SIGCSE '12)*. ACM, New York, NY, USA, 21–26.
[2] Gary Lewandowski, Dennis J. Bouvier, Robert McCartney, Kate Sanders, and Beth Simon. 2007. Commonsense Computing (Episode 3): Concurrency and Concert Tickets. In *Proceedings of the Third International Workshop on Computing Education Research (ICER '07)*. ACM, New York, NY, USA, 133–144.
[3] Alan Lightman and Philip M Sadler. 1993. Teacher predictions versus actual student gains. *The Physics Teacher* 31, 3 (1993), 162–167.
[4] John P Smith III, Andrea A Disessa, and Jeremy Roschelle. 1994. Misconceptions reconceived: A constructivist analysis of knowledge in transition. *The journal of the learning sciences* 3, 2 (1994), 115–163.
[5] Juha Sorva. 2013. Notional machines and introductory programming education. *ACM Transactions on Computing Education (TOCE)* 13, 2 (2013), 8.
[6] Anselm Strauss and Juliet Corbin. 1994. Grounded theory methodology. *Handbook of qualitative research* 17 (1994), 273–285.

The <1%: Black Women Obtaining PhDs in Computing

Amari Lewis

University of California, Irvine

Irvine, CA, 92697

amaril@ics.uci.edu

ABSTRACT

In 2016, 49 Black women in the United States and Canada were enrolled in computer science PhD programs. This is less than one percent of total enrollment. In the same year, only 8 Black women earned the PhD. Additionally, Black women achieving tenured and tenure-track positions are sorely lacking in computer science, computer engineering and informatics departments. In 2016, 3 black females were full professors, 14 were associate professors, and 11 were assistant professors. In comparison, white female faculty numbers included 219 full professors, 144 associate professors, and 118 assistant professors. This research studies two main factors that deter black women from pursuing and achieving PhDs in computer science through understanding and uncovering the statistics provided by the Computing Research Association's annual Taulbee survey. Additionally, we explore the misrepresentation of the "unknowns" in the statistics. The next phase of this work will include a more in-depth analysis of the personal experiences of Black and Brown women in doctoral programs in the computer sciences.

CCS CONCEPTS

• **Computing Education Programs** →**Computer Science Education**

KEYWORDS

Doctoral degrees; CRA Taulbee survey; Diversity

ACM Reference format:

Amari Lewis. 2018. <1% Black Women Obtaining PhDs in Computing. In *Proceedings of ACM International Computing Education Research Conference (ICER'18)*, August 13-15, 2018, Espoo, Finland. ACM, New York, NY. 2 pages. DOI: https://doi.org/10.1145/3230977.3231016

1 PROGRAM CONTEXT

I am finishing the second year of a PhD program in Computer Science at the University of California, Irvine (UCI). While earning an MS degree enroute to the PhD is not required, I will be awarded an MS degree at the end of this quarter. My primary

dissertation work concerns technologies for improving public transportation systems for elderly and disabled travelers (paratransit) but a secondary, but equally strong interest, of mine is increasing the participation of underrepresented students in PhD programs and later in academic careers. My dissertation supervisor is very supportive of my dual interests and is convinced that I will be able to contribute in both areas of inquiry. I began this research in early 2018 and completed a short paper. In collaboration with an ongoing study at UCI examining the experiences of Black women in doctoral and postdoctoral programs in computing and engineering, I hope to further investigate this topic and to use the data from that study to draw new conclusions. To date, I have analyzed the CRA's annual Taulbee survey results in regards to enrollment and attainment of Black women in doctoral programs in computing focusing on the data from 2013-2016.

My hope for the ICER doctoral consortium is that I will gain insights from other students and faculty about the process of writing and finishing a dissertation and that I will make long term connections with other researchers.

2 CONTEXT AND MOTIVATION

As a double minority, I encounter forms of oppression that other groups may not experience. This is true in academia, industry and in government. Anecdotal evidence suggests that the lack of black faculty in leading PhD programs is itself a barrier to increasing diversity in those programs. Faced with that fact and the clear lack of black student participation, qualified students chose the easier route -- a position in industry rather than a PhD or even an MS degree.

We live in a society where Black/African-American people comprise about 13% of the population, and according to the 2016 educational census about 14.8% received their bachelor's degree, 6.8% advanced degrees, 0.8% professional degrees and 0.9% Doctoral degrees. Additionally, the educational attainment database of the same year indicated that a total of 1,110,000 Black women over the age of 18 have obtained their master's degree and a total of 122,000 black women achieved have a doctoral degree. In comparison to white women with 8,865,000 master's degrees, and 1,274,000 doctoral degrees.

Computing jobs provide enormous career opportunities. However, groups are not benefiting equally from these opportunities. Faculty positions require a PhD or at least an MS degree, and most entry level positions require a Bachelor's degree in computer science or engineering.

The majority of doctoral programs in computing provide full funding to students and many provide students with subsidized housing, health insurance and other incentives. So why aren't more black women taking advantage of this opportunity? This research uncovers two primary factors that deter black women from pursuing PhDs in computing; 1) the GRE exam and 2) persistent discouragement and microaggressions experienced at many different levels. The Computing Research Association's (CRA) current and previous statistics are used to draw conclusions. The overarching goal of this research is to identify ways to increase representation by conducting a research study on the CRA's Taulbee survey statistics.

3 BACKGROUND AND RELATED WORK

In 2016, the premier of Theodore Melfi's film, *Hidden Figures* truly highlighted a hidden story of black women in STEM. The film showcases the contributions that several black women made in one of the greatest scientific achievements of the last fifty years. These women were engineers, scientists and computer scientists but, their story took over 50 years to be acknowledged.

Additionally, in February 2018, Marvel released a film called Black Panther which features a black female character who is an expert in technology. The princess of Wakanda, 'Shuri' designs technology for the technologically advanced country. While the film is fictional, black female technologists welcome the exposure. Although there is limited research on this topic, previous research suggests that there is positive correlation between women's confidence in completing their Computer Science and Engineering (CSE) degrees and self-ratings. Chao et al. investigates how academic self-ratings and contextual factors are associated with confidence for women in various phases of CSE doctoral study from the participants of the annual CRA-W grad cohort for women [3]. My hope is to model this research study by focusing on black women specifically, as well as expanding the pool by comparing the results from those who have attended the CRA-W and those who did not.

In 2008 Gilbert et al. present a model for broadening participation of African-Americans in computing. In doing so, the researchers conclude seven barriers including: stereotypes, role models, "helping" professions, financial concerns, inadequate advisement, lack of knowledge regarding advantages of having PhD, and employment opportunities [4].

"Intersectionality reminds us that oppression cannot be reduced to one fundamental type..." At Purdue University, the researchers took a theoretical approach to shed light on the experiences of black women throughout the engineering industry. Using the social identity and intersectionality theory to support their research [5].

At UCI the Neila project is a qualitative investigation of the experiences of Black women in pursuit of doctorates and post doctorate degrees in computing and engineering. It is a four-year collaborative research effort to improve the understanding of the dynamics and factors that black women may have on their academic persistence and overall well-being [1].

4 STATEMENT OF THESIS/PROBLEM

We posit that two primary factors that deter Black women from pursuing PhDs in computing are: 1) the GRE requirement and 2) persistent discouragement and microaggressions experienced at many different levels.

Within the last 25 years of the Taulbee survey, participating universities have varied. The highest percentage of representation was in 2000, with a record breaking 81%, or 173/214 participants. Surveys were sent to CRA members, the CRA Deans group members, and participants in the iSchools Caucus who met the criteria of granting PhDs and being located in North America.

Additionally, prior to 2008, departments of information (or informatics) were not accounted for. The CRA defines these programs as included here are Information Science, Information Systems, Information Technology, Informatics, and related disciplines with a strong computing component.

In 2016 268 departments of computer science, computer engineering and information across the U.S. and Canada were contacted and they received a 68% response rate. Although, there are a small number of HBCU's (three) that offer computing doctoral degrees, none of these universities are represented in the recent Taulbee survey.

5 RESEARCH GOALS AND METHODS

Our research goal is to analyze and understand the experiences of Black women in doctoral programs in computing. In order to reach the <1%, we will implement the snowball sampling method. This is a non-probabilistic sampling method in which survey participants recruit other qualified participants.

6 DISSERTATION STATUS

As mentioned above, this research is still in an early stage, but we hope to finish one or more papers in the next year.

7 EXPECTED CONTRIBUTIONS

We believe that our insights could be used to improve conditions for underrepresented minority students in computing PhD programs by promoting and understanding of the invisible barriers to success faced by these students.

8 ACKNOWLEDGMENTS

I would like to acknowledge and thank my PhD advisor professor Amelia Regan for her continual support and assistance. I would also like to thank professor Bonnie Ruberg from the informatics department at UCI for supporting this work.

9 REFERENCES

[1] Artis, S. The Niela Project. http://sites.uci.edu/thenielaproject
[2] Computing Research Association. *Taulbee Survey.* https://cra.org/resources/taulbee-survey/
[3] Chao, Jie, McGrath, C. (2010) Can I Really Complete This CSE Doctoral Degree? Women's Confidence and Self-Rated Abilities.
[4] Gilbert, Juan; J.J. (2008). African American researchers in computing science, a model for broadening participation. *Computing Research Association News.*
[5] Ross, Monique. (2015). Stories of Black Women in Engineering Industry- why they leave. Purdue University.

Developing Students' Cognitive Processes Required for Software Design Verification

Prajish Prasad
Inter-disciplinary Programme in Educational Technology
Indian Institute of Technology Bombay
Mumbai, Maharashtra, India
prajish.prasad@iitb.ac.in

ABSTRACT

Computer Science undergraduates are expected to design software solutions and also verify that the design satisfies the intended requirements. The Ph.D. work discussed in this paper aims at designing and evaluating a learning environment to train computer science undergraduates to effectively verify properties of a software system design. Literature on expertise in software design has shown that experts create rich mental models of the software design on which they perform mental simulations. I propose a model-based learning strategy in order to foster the cognitive processes of mental modeling and mental simulation. I hypothesize that by triggering the cognitive processes of mental modeling and mental simulation, students will be able to perform design verification better. By the end of my doctoral research I expect the following contributions: 1) Understanding how the cognitive processes of mental modeling and mental simulation aid in software design verification. 2) Application of a model-based learning strategy and creation of a learning environment in order to foster these cognitive processes.

KEYWORDS

software design verification; model-based learning; mental modeling; mental simulations

ACM Reference Format:
Prajish Prasad. 2018. Developing Students' Cognitive Processes Required for Software Design Verification. In *ICER '18: 2018 International Computing Education Research Conference, August 13–15, 2018, Espoo, Finland*. ACM, New York, NY, USA, 2 pages. https://doi.org/10.1145/3230977.3231011

1 PROGRAM CONTEXT

I am a third year PhD student in the Inter-disciplinary Programme in Educational Technology at the Indian Institute of Technology, Bombay(IIT Bombay), India. I joined the programme in July 2015. I have successfully completed the academic credit requirements and I am enrolled as a full-time research scholar in the teaching assistant category.

The goal of my research is to enable computer science undergraduates to effectively verify properties of a software system design. Such a task is known as a design verification task. I am using the

design-based research methodology for my research. The research has been broadly divided into three cycles. In the first cycle, I identified the cognitive processes involved in a design verification task and difficulties encountered while performing this task. In the second cycle, which is ongoing, I am designing and evaluating a model-based learning strategy required to foster the identified cognitive processes. I intend to incorporate this strategy in a learning environment(LE). In the third cycle, I plan to evaluate the LE.

2 CONTEXT AND MOTIVATION

Verifying software design is an important part of the design process. If the whole design episode is considered, experts spend significant time verifying their solutions[5]. Computer science undergraduates need to be taught not only to create design solutions but also correctly verify if the design is satisfying the intended requirements. Literature on expertise in software design has shown that experts create rich mental models of the software design, on which they perform mental simulations[7]. My thesis aims at designing and evaluating a learning environment to train students to perform a software design verification task.

3 BACKGROUND & RELATED WORK

Various teaching strategies have been employed in teaching-learning of software design. Project courses are a common strategy used[2]. Other strategies include teaching through games[1] and games in the classroom[4]. In such strategies, much emphasis has not been given in verifying the correctness of the created designs. Formal methods in software engineering can be used to address this gap. However, difficulties in integrating formal methods into the curriculum have been documented, such as insufficient mathematical background and less motivation to learn[6].

It is necessary to verify properties in the design stage, so that these errors are not propagated into the code in the implementation phase. Hence it is essential to teach students how to effectively verify the correctness of their designs before they proceed to implement their designs. An analysis of the literature shows that there is a lack of teaching-learning strategies which enable learners to effectively perform a design verification task.

4 STATEMENT OF THESIS/PROBLEM

The broad research goal of my thesis is to develop a learning environment(LE) which will enable final year computer science undergraduates to correctly verify properties of a software system design. Specific research questions which I wish to answer in the thesis are as follows -

(1) What difficulties do learners encounter while doing a software design verification task?
(2) What are the cognitive processes involved in a software design verification task?
(3) How can the proposed model-based learning strategy be used to
   a) Overcome difficulties identified in 1?
   b) Foster cognitive processes identified in 2?
(4) How effective is the LE in enabling learners to carry out a software design verification task?

5 RESEARCH GOALS & METHODS

The specific research goals, methods and findings in each cycle are described below -

Cycle 1[Completed] - I identified the cognitive processes involved in a design verification task. I conducted a qualitative study with two final year computer science undergraduates who were given a software design in the form of UML diagrams and were asked to verify certain properties of the design. Based on the analysis of the data, I identified that students

(1) **Construct** a model based on the properties, but focus on adding new functionalities which are not required to verify the given property.
(2) **Refine** the model based on the design provided but focus on checking whether all functions are used, rather than checking whether their model is consistent.
(3) **Verify** the model by simulating scenarios on the model, but do not simulate state change of variables and scenarios where the design violates the property.

Cycle 2[Ongoing] - I propose a model-based learning strategy in order to foster the identified cognitive processes. "Model-based learning" has been extensively studied and implemented in science and mathematics education[3]. The central tenet of model-based learning is that the process of constructing and manipulating mental models of a scientific phenomenon causes a deeper and integrated understanding of scientific concepts required to understand the phenomenon. Hence, teaching learners to effectively apply the model-based learning paradigm to design software systems can help learners
1. Perform mental modelling and simulation better
2. Develop an integrated and deep understanding of the design
Both these reasons are essential to effectively perform design verification.

The proposed strategy makes learners perform the following activities -

(1) **Construct** a model based on the properties to be verified by translating informal requirements into formal properties of the system and simulating scenarios where the property is satisfied. The model which the learner constructs is a simplified state diagram.
(2) **Refine** the model based on the UML diagrams by analyzing relevant behaviors of the system required to verify the property. Learners perform activities which help them progressively refine the state diagram based on the given design.

(3) **Verify** the model by simulating the state change of relevant data variables. Learners perform simulations on the state diagram and examine different values of variables at different states.

I aim to incorporate this strategy in an LE. I plan to collect data such as actions performed by learners in the LE and evolve the LE based on this analysis. I hypothesize that the features of progressive refinement of the state diagram and the ability to perform simulations on the state diagram foster the cognitive processes of mental modeling and mental simulations which are required for the design verification task.

Cycle 3 - I aim to evaluate the effect of the LE on learners' ability to effectively carry out a design verification task. I plan to conduct a mixed method study with final year computer science undergraduates. Performance in the post-test can help determine the effect of the LE on learning. Qualitative interviews with students can help uncover students' perception of learning as well as the usability and usefulness of the LE. These results will inform further refinement of the design of the LE.

From the ICER community, I would like feedback on the appropriateness of the proposed model-based learning strategy. I hope to gain insights on appropriate research methods to evaluate the effectiveness of this strategy. I would also appreciate feedback on how this strategy can be used by CS instructors in the context of a software engineering course.

6 EXPECTED CONTRIBUTIONS

The expected contributions which I anticipate will be useful to the CS Ed research community are

(1) Understanding how the cognitive processes of mental modeling and mental simulation aid in software design verification.
(2) Application of a model-based learning strategy in order to foster these cognitive processes.

The pedagogical features and scaffolds in the LE can be used by CS instructors in the context of a software engineering course, to help students verify their software design.

REFERENCES

[1] Alex Baker, Emily Oh Navarro, and Andre Van Der Hoek. 2005. An experimental card game for teaching software engineering processes. *Journal of Systems and Software* 75, 1-2 (2005), 3–16.
[2] Joe D Chase, Prem Uppuluri, Tracy Lewis, Ian Barland, and Jeff Pittges. 2015. Integrating live projects into computing curriculum. In *Proceedings of the 46th ACM Technical Symposium on Computer Science Education*. ACM, 82–83.
[3] David Hestenes. 2010. Modeling theory for math and science education. In *Modeling students' mathematical modeling competencies*. Springer, 13–41.
[4] Carlos Mario Zapata Jaramillo. 2014. Teaching software development by means of a classroom game: The software development game. *Developments in Business Simulation and Experiential Learning* 36 (2014).
[5] Thomas Mc Neill, John S Gero, and James Warren. 1998. Understanding conceptual electronic design using protocol analysis. *Research in Engineering Design* 10, 3 (1998), 129–140.
[6] Maria Spichkova and Anna Zamansky. 2016. Teaching of formal methods for software engineering. In *Proceedings of the 11th International Conference on Evaluation of Novel Software Approaches to Software Engineering*. SCITEPRESS-Science and Technology Publications, Lda, 370–376.
[7] Carmen Zannier, Mike Chiasson, and Frank Maurer. 2007. A model of design decision making based on empirical results of interviews with software designers. *Information and Software Technology* 49, 6 (2007), 637–653.

Using Computational Thinking to Transform Elementary Mathematics Instruction

Kathryn M. Rich
College of Education, Michigan State University
East Lansing, Michigan, USA
richkat3@msu.edu

ABSTRACT

Computer science (CS) education advocates argue that integration of computational thinking (CT) into instruction in other subjects has promise for providing a strong foundation in computer science ideas for elementary school students. Less attention has been given to the role that CT may play in improving learning in subjects other than computer science. This document summarizes my plans to study how teaching elementary level mathematics through computational thinking practices can improve mathematics learning.

CCS CONCEPTS

• **Social and professional topics** → **Computational thinking**; **K-12 education**;

KEYWORDS

Computational thinking; K–5; Mathematics

ACM Reference Format:
Kathryn M. Rich. 2018. Using Computational Thinking to Transform Elementary Mathematics Instruction. In *ICER '18: 2018 International Computing Education Research Conference, August 13–15, 2018, Espoo, Finland*. ACM, New York, NY, USA, 2 pages. https://doi.org/10.1145/3230977.3231010

1 PROGRAM CONTEXT

I am a Ph.D. student in the Educational Psychology and Educational Technology (EPET) program in the Michigan State University (MSU) College of Education. Before coming to MSU, I worked in a research-oriented job for ten years. I therefore entered the program with well-developed ideas of what I wanted to study. Through an NSF grant awarded to the University of Chicago (for which I was co-PI), I became interested in exploring the intersections between mathematical thinking and computational thinking and whether such intersections might be leveraged in bringing meaningful computer science instruction to students in elementary school.

I will be starting my second year in the EPET program in fall of 2018. Through a research assistantship on an NSF *CSForAll* grant awarded to MSU, I have been collaborating with experts in computer science, mathematics, and science education to develop sample activities that use CT to enhance mathematics and science instruction in grades 3–5. This *CSForAll* project, in which we plan to enact

ICER '18, August 13–15, 2018, Espoo, Finland
© 2018 Copyright held by the owner/author(s).
ACM ISBN 978-1-4503-5628-2/18/08.
https://doi.org/10.1145/3230977.3231010

several cycles of implementation, reflection, and improvement of these CT-infused lessons, will likely serve as the context for my dissertation study.

2 CONTEXT AND MOTIVATION

Ongoing efforts to bring computer science instruction to all K–12 students have included the development of programming environments (e.g., Scratch) and curricula (e.g., the code.org materials) aimed at elementary school. Although widely used, these materials tend to assume that CS will be taught as a stand-alone subject. Elementary school teachers, however, lack adequate preparation and do not always have time to teach CS as an additional subject in an already-full curriculum. Rather, integration of CS into other subject areas can be key to successful implementation [2]. Understanding how to integrate CS into a core subject in elementary school, such as mathematics, is thus a high priority for the CS education field.

Computational thinking (CT) has been proposed as a means for connecting computer science with other disciplinary subjects [1]. The similarities between CT and mathematics disciplinary practices makes mathematics a strong candidate for CT integration. Such integrated instruction, however, must do more than provide students with exposure to CT. Given the strong influence of high-stakes assessments, teachers and school administrators are highly concerned with supporting their students' mathematics achievement. To be widely taken up, integration of CT into mathematics must also serve to improve students' understanding of mathematics.

3 BACKGROUND & RELATED WORK

Teaching mathematics and computer science in an integrated manner is not a new idea. In his seminal 1980 book, *Mindstorms*, Seymour Papert [3] argued that teaching mathematics through simple programming environments would allow students to get to know mathematics concepts in a personal and meaningful way. More recently, developers of Bootstrap [5] have explored how programming activities can support middle- and high-school students' understanding of algebra. Despite many years of implementation of instruction that brings together mathematics and programming, evidence that such instruction improves mathematics performance is scant.

Although programming remains the dominate means of teaching students computer science, researchers' explorations of how to connect computing and mathematics have not been limited to programming. Weintrop et al. [6] developed a detailed taxonomy to define CT in the context of high school STEM disciplines. In my own work, I have explored how learning trajectories for CT concepts in K-8 could be shaped to support learning of mathematics [4]. These efforts approach both mathematics and CT broadly, aiming to provide an overall mapping between the fields. Minimal attention has been given to understanding how more focused aspects of mathematics and CT might mutually support each other.

4 STATEMENT OF THESIS/PROBLEM

The overall goal of my work is to understand how CT can be used as a frame for developing new approaches to solving enduring problems of elementary mathematics education, such as students' difficulty with conceptual understanding of fractions. Specifically, I hope to address the following questions:

- How can key CT ideas be applied to teaching and learning of elementary mathematics topics, such as fractions, that are challenging for many students?
- In what ways does teaching these mathematics topics through CT support conceptual understanding?
- In what ways does teaching these mathematics topics through CT build readiness for later CS courses?

5 RESEARCH GOALS & METHODS

I plan organize my research around three goals:

- Identify pervasive problems of practice related to mathematics teaching relevant to my teacher partners.
- Co-develop lessons addressing these problems of practice that apply CT ideas, such as abstraction, as thinking strategies for teachers and students.
- Measure the effectiveness of the CT-infused lessons on students' understanding of mathematics and computer science.

My tentative plan is to conduct three phases of work corresponding to the three goals above. In phase 1, to identify problems of practice, I will conduct interviews with the partner teachers focused on their mathematics teaching and the related challenges that most concern them. In phase 2, I will consult the mathematics education literature on the topics that teachers identify (e.g., fractions) and review it with attention to common misconceptions and other common hindrances to student understanding. In consultation with the teachers, I will develop activities that address these common difficulties using CT practices, such as decomposition of problems, as instructional strategies. Through quick cycles of design-based research, the teachers and I will adjust and improve the activities to suit the teachers' contexts.

Finally, in phase 3, ideally in a new school year, I will work with the teachers to implement the activities in their classrooms. Using a pre-post research design, I will administer assessments of mathematics (likely based on previously-created, standardized test items). Absent any available assessments of CT that become available, I will conduct focus groups with select groups of students to assess their CT understanding after the intervention.

6 DISSERTATION STATUS

I have not officially proposed a dissertation topic. Thus, I have a great deal of flexibility and also a great deal of work yet to do. I have half-time funding on a grant project that is closely connected to my research interests that I expect to continue through the completion of my degree. I plan to stay abreast — and to the extent that it is possible and appropriate, involved in the decision making — about the

data collected during the project's professional development efforts, lesson development, and implementation of classroom activities. In consultation with my advisor and with the feedback I receive from this ICER doctoral consortium, I will develop a research plan for my dissertation in the coming year. I hope to defend a dissertation proposal in fall of 2019, and complete the study by spring of 2021.

7 EXPECTED CONTRIBUTIONS

I expect the results of my dissertation work to be of use to researchers, teacher educators, and curriculum developers. From a research perspective, the results of my study could be used to advance our understanding of the ways in which mathematics and computational thinking can be mutually supportive in preparing elementary school students to opt into, and to succeed in, more rigorous coursework in both mathematics and computer science in later years. The results could also be used to inform professional development programs for in-service elementary school teachers as well as coursework in preservice teacher preparation programs. Finally, the results have potential aid in the development of educative curriculum materials designed around teaching elementary mathematics from a CT perspective.

8 DESIRED LEARNING FROM DOCTORIAL CONSORTIUM

I hope that the doctoral consortium will contribute to my thinking about the following issues:

- Rigorous and methodologically sound processes for conducting design-based research.
- Available assessments for computational thinking outside of a programming context, or how such assessments might be developed.
- Means of measuring student learning other than assessments, for example, through analysis of students' discourse around CT topics.
- Kinds of data that would constitute evidence of readiness for computer science in middle school.
- Venues for publishing research that straddles multiple disciplinary areas (in my case, mathematics education and computer science education).

REFERENCES

[1] Valerie Barr and Chris Stephenson. 2011. Bringing computational thinking to K-12: what is Involved and what is the role of the computer science education community? *ACM Inroads* 2, 1 (2011), 48–54.
[2] Maya Israel, Jamie N Pearson, Tanya Tapia, Quentin M Wherfel, and George Reese. 2015. Supporting all learners in school-wide computational thinking: A cross-case qualitative analysis. *Computers & Education* 82 (2015), 263–279.
[3] Seymour Papert. 1980. *Mindstorms: Children, computers, and powerful ideas.* Basic Books, Inc.
[4] Kathryn M Rich, Carla Strickland, T Andrew Binkowski, Cheryl Moran, and Diana Franklin. 2017. K-8 Learning Trajectories Derived from Research Literature: Sequence, Repetition, Conditionals. In *Proceedings of the 2017 ACM Conference on International Computing Education Research.* ACM, 182–190.
[5] Emmanuel Schanzer, Kathi Fisler, Shriram Krishnamurthi, and Matthias Felleisen. 2015. Transferring skills at solving word problems from computing to algebra through bootstrap. In *Proceedings of the 46th ACM Technical symposium on computer science education.* ACM, 616–621.
[6] David Weintrop, Elham Beheshti, Michael Horn, Kai Orton, Kemi Jona, Laura Trouille, and Uri Wilensky. 2016. Defining computational thinking for mathematics and science classrooms. *Journal of Science Education and Technology* 25, 1 (2016), 127–147.

Massive Open Online Courses in Programming: the Case of Estonia

Merilin Säde
Institute of Computer Science
University of Tartu
Tartu, 50409, Estonia
merilin.sade@ut.ee

ABSTRACT

Most of the related work describes the designing of MOOC (Massive Open Online Course) and the motivational aspects of the participants separately, but not in a combined way using motivational aspects and several support mechanisms. Programming MOOCs provided by the University of Tartu are characterized by a high percentage of graduates (50–70%), which is unusual for MOOCs and is mainly achieved through different automated and non-automated feedback, support systems and learning activities and the fact that these MOOCs are held in Estonian language [4]. The focus of my PhD study is to investigate the participants' motivation and the associations between the motivation, the accomplishment and using of support mechanisms in the courses. We also want to study the impact of the programming MOOCs in a society of Estonia by investigating participants' career choice after conducting MOOC.

CCS CONCEPTS

• **Social and professional topics** → *Computer science education*;

KEYWORDS

MOOC; motivation; programming

ACM Reference Format:
Merilin Säde. 2018. Massive Open Online Courses in Programming: the Case of Estonia. In *ICER '18: 2018 International Computing Education Research Conference, August 13–15, 2018, Espoo, Finland*. ACM, New York, NY, USA, 2 pages. https://doi.org/10.1145/3230977.3231017

1 PROGRAMM CONTEXT

I have completed my first year as CS student of the PhD program at the University of Tartu. I have worked on a study to understand what motivates people to enroll programming MOOCs provided by the University of Tartu in Estonia. I also started research to understand the impact of MOOCs in Estonia.

2 CONTEXT AND MOTIVATION

The context of this PhD research is a better understanding of participants' motivation in programming MOOCs that can help us to improve our courses and support participants' learning process.

ICER '18, August 13–15, 2018, Espoo, Finland
© 2018 Copyright held by the owner/author(s).
ACM ISBN 978-1-4503-5628-2/18/08.
https://doi.org/10.1145/3230977.3231017

Our motivation is to give suggestions for educators and policy-makers how the use of programming MOOCs can be a considerable part of future curricular innovation.

3 BACKGROUND AND RELATED WORK

Computer programming is a current topic of interest in Estonia as well as in other countries, and MOOCs offer a good opportunity for everyone to get acquainted with this subject [8] Traditionally there were two main kinds of MOOCs: cMOOC and xMOOC [1, 7]. However, there is a move away from the cMOOC/xMOOC division [1]. The MOOCs implemented in the Institute of Computer Science (CS) in Tartu are unique, as in addition to a forum the learners have an opportunity to ask about their programs, problems, etc via helpdesk provided by the organizers. MOOCs that used a helpdesk were rated extremely positive [9]. In our case, this opportunity resulted in a high completion rate (50–70%). Research has shown that the average completion rate for MOOCs is approximately 15% [2], the dropout rate is one of the challenges of MOOCs [7] and there are attempts to prevent dropout [11]. There are few studies investigating motivation on MOOCs. In studies both intrinsic and extrinsic reasons for starting a MOOC are studied [10]. Reasons for participating on MOOCs were analyzed both in qualitatively [5] and quantitatively [3] and in some studies [6] the main aim in MOOC was questioned in interviews. Different theories are used: self-regulated learning theory is mentioned [10], self-determination theory was used as the basis of motivational items in a study [13]. However, there are quite many studies without information about the motivational scale or relation to motivational theory. There are studies which list more important reasons for the enrollment in MOOCs. Three most marked reasons for choosing MOOC were: because MOOCs are free, refresh knowledge and interest in the topic [10]. Conducting of interviews by Zheng et al. [12] identified four broad types of learners' motivations for joining MOOCs: fulfilling current needs, preparing for the future (including getting certification), satisfying curiosity, and connecting with people. In our research we will also, list and investigate these intrinsic and extrinsic motives and combine them with the accomplishment in the programming MOOCs to investigate how much and in which way they are affected by the support mechanisms and using helpdesk.

4 STATEMENT OF THESIS/PROBLEM

The main aim of the study is to investigate the participants' motivation and its associations between accomplishment and using of support mechanisms in the courses and to describe the impact of programming MOOCs on participants' career choices. Research questions:

(1) Which are the reasons and motivational aspects to enter programming MOOCs?
(2) What motivational aspects in the programming MOOCs are affected by the support mechanisms?
(3) How do the programming MOOCs impact the participants and their future career choices after conducting a programming MOOC or several MOOCs?

5 RESEARCH GOALS AND METHODS

The PhD project will proceed in three phases according to research questions. First was to the design and implement an instrument to measure participants' motivation to enroll programming MOOCs in Estonia. This scale was based on Expectancy-Value motivation Theory. The second step is to conduct an instrument to measure participants' motivational aspects affected by support mechanisms used in programming MOOCs. The final phase is to survey participants' career choices after graduating programming MOOC.

6 DISSERTATION STATUS

I have analyzed related work and developed with colleagues a scale to measure motivation to enroll programming MOOCs. The next phase is to design an instrument to measure motivational aspect affected by support mechanisms. My goal is to complete my dissertation proposal in the winter of 2020 and graduate PhD studies in spring of 2021.

7 EXPECTED CONTRIBUTIONS

We will study the programming MOOCs participants' reasons and motivational aspects and mainly focus on the questionnaires, assessment tools, forums and helpdesk information, also developing and conducting interviews to evaluate the impact of the MOOCs. We also expect to find the extent to which the accomplishment in these MOOCs is affected by the support mechanisms and using helpdesk. We also plan, to give an overview of the participants' career choice after graduating programming MOOC. We will be able to give suggestions for educators and policy-makers how the use of programming MOOCs can be a considerable part in future curricular innovation. This research can improve the existing MOOCs, for example by making it accessible to a broader audience and also improve the cost-efficiency of MOOCs.

8 LEARNING FROM DC

I think that participating in ICER Doctoral Consortium will have a positive impact on my PhD studies. I am still at the beginning of my studies and a novice researcher. So, I think I have much to learn in Doctoral Consortium and hope to discuss different research methods and topics related students' motivation.

REFERENCES

[1] Wilfried Admiraal, Bart Huisman, and Olga Pilli. 2015. Assessment in Massive Open Online Courses. *Electronic Journal of e-Learning* 13, 4 (2015), 207 – 216.
[2] Katry Jordan. 2015. MOOC completion rates: The data. http://www.katyjordan.com/MOOCproject.html
[3] René F Kizilcec, Chris Piech, and Emily Schneider. 2013. Deconstructing disengagement: analyzing learner subpopulations in massive open online courses. In *Proceedings of the third international conference on learning analytics and knowledge*. ACM, New York, NY, USA, 170–179.
[4] Marina Lepp, Piret Luik, Tauno Palts, Kaspar Papli, Reelika Suviste, Merilin Säde, and Eno Tõnisson. 2017. MOOC in Programming: A Success Story. In *Proceedings of the International Conference on e-Learning (ICEL) 12th International Conference on e- Learning*. Academic Conferences International Limited, 138–147.
[5] Rhonda Jessen Paul Signorelli Maha Bali, Maureen Crawford and Mia Zamora. 2015. What makes a cMOOC community endure? Multiple participant perspectives from diverse cMOOCs. *Educational Media International* 52, 2 (2015), 100–115. https://doi.org/10.1080/09523987.2015.1053290
[6] Colin Milligan and Allison Littlejohn. 2016. How health professionals regulate their learning in massive open online courses. *The Internet and Higher Education* 31 (2016), 113 – 121. https://doi.org/10.1016/j.iheduc.2016.07.005
[7] George Siemens. 2013. *Massive open online courses: Innovation in education?* Chapter 1, 5–16.
[8] Arto Vihavainen, Matti Luukkainen, and Jaakko Kurhila. 2012. Multi-faceted support for MOOC in programming. In *Proceedings of the 13th annual conference on Information technology education*. ACM, New York, NY, USA, 171–176. https://doi.org/10.1145/2380552.2380603
[9] Joe Warren, Scott Rixner, John Greiner, and Stephen Wong. 2014. Facilitating human interaction in an online programming course. In *Proceedings of the 45th ACM technical symposium on Computer science education*. ACM, New York, NY, USA, 665–670. https://doi.org/10.1145/2538862.2538893
[10] Su White, Hugh Davis, Kate Dickens, Manuel León, and Ma Mar Sánchez-Vera. 2014. MOOCs: what motivates the producers and participants?. In *International Conference on Computer Supported Education*. Springer, 99–114.
[11] Diyi Yang, Tanmay Sinha, David Adamson, and Carolyn Penstein Rosé. 2013. "Turn on, tune in, drop out": Anticipating student dropouts in massive open online courses. In *Proceedings of the 2013 NIPS Data-driven education workshop*. 1–8.
[12] Saijing Zheng, Mary Beth Rosson, Patrick C Shih, and John M Carroll. 2015. Understanding student motivation, behaviors and perceptions in MOOCs. In *Proceedings of the 18th ACM conference on computer supported cooperative work & social computing*. ACM, 1882–1895.
[13] Mingming Zhou. 2016. Chinese university students' acceptance of MOOCs: A self-determination perspective. *Computers & Education* 92-93 (2016), 194 – 203. https://doi.org/10.1016/j.compedu.2015.10.012

Easing Learners into Data Science via Visualization of Concepts and Computations

Lovisa Sundin
University of Glasgow
Glasgow, United Kingdom
l.sundin.1@research.gla.ac.uk

ABSTRACT

In my research, I will explore the potential of adapting the literature on algorithm visualization and visual analogy to the teaching of concepts and computations in introductory data science. Using computerized tutorials informed by the extensive literature on multimedia principles already available, I will explore if a visual pseudo-code facilitates simulation and application of data algorithms, beyond the facilitation afforded by mathematical notation. The research will combine between-subject classroom interventions with distance learning and within-subject laboratory studies. The dissertation will give fine-grained evidence on which types are more effective and how it could be implemented in the community at large. I am primarily interested in discussing methodological issues relating to how to make comparisons in such a multi-dimensional design space.

KEYWORDS

Data Science; Statistical Reasoning; Graphical Aids; Algorithm Visualization

ACM Reference Format:
Lovisa Sundin. 2018. Easing Learners into Data Science via Visualization of Concepts and Computations . In *ICER '18: 2018 International Computing Education Research Conference, August 13–15, 2018, Espoo, Finland*. ACM, New York, NY, USA, 2 pages. https://doi.org/10.1145/3230977.3231026

1 PROGRAM CONTEXT

I have an undergraduate degree in Computing Science and Psychology at University of Glasgow and completed the first 7 months of my PhD at the same university.

2 CONTEXT & MOTIVATION

Across every discipline, from psychology to geology, drag-and-drop data analysis software like SPSS is being supplanted by programming languages like R [10]. Undergraduates all over the world scrabble for the programming skills expected from them. The prevalence of machine learning and big data has made members of the public curious and wary about its workings. To meet this demand for data literacy, the onus is on CS education researchers to adapt

and advance the insights into programming instruction to learners including - but also extending beyond - CS majors.

Algorithm visualization is one of the field's most investigated methods, but the field may not be as exhausted as previously thought. A review from 2010 analyzed more than 500 applets, revealing that the algorithms visualized are near-exclusively sorting algorithms and data structure manipulations [13]. This reflects the usual content of an introductory algorithmics course, but novice data analysts have little direct benefit from these concepts. Statistics does not seem to have a corresponding field: data visualization may be intensely researched, and interactive applets for experimenting with parameters may abound, but the data manipulations themselves remain unvisualized, its potential unexplored.

3 BACKGROUND & RELATED WORK

Statistics educators commonly distinguish between *computational* and *conceptual* understanding [2]. The former refers to the procedural skill of simulating and implementing algorithms, the latter to understanding its meaning and when to apply it. Quite like how CS students need to know conceptually when a data structure is appropriate, neither kind is useful without the other. Commentators have warned of the danger of ritualization of research, of following analysis recipes mindlessly and mechanically, causing statistical tests to be misapplied and leaving science on shaky ground [6]. Educators, therefore, need to address both.

Previous research has shown that representing equations in ways that make its meaning more salient also makes them easier to learn. Atkinson and Catrambone, for example, compared the definitional equation for sum of squares (used for t-tests and ANOVAs) with a more efficient but less intuitive one. They found that transfer was best when instruction used the conceptual variant [1].

This supports a wider body of work on how solution procedures are taught most effectively by breaking them down hierarchically into modules, defined by meaningful subgoals [4]. Given their sequential rather than nested nature, pseudo-code can achieve this more easily than equations, but students are often given the cognitive burden to translate the latter into the former on their own.

To expose the procedural nature of statistical concepts, one strategy could be to use visualization. The picture that is emerging from cognitive science is that reasoning involves representing abstract properties like magnitude in terms of spatial and geometrical metaphors such as line length and collection size [7]. Computer-based multimedia that shows mathematical computations in terms of number line position have led to improved performance [9].

In statistics, the idea is not without precedents either. Sedlmeier and Gigerenzer designed a tutorial for Bayesian reasoning where participants in one group plugged numbers into Bayes' rule and participants in another viewed a tree representation of natural frequencies. The representation condition outperformed the rule condition on immediate learning [12]. Others have likewise demonstrated how visualization aids Bayesian reasoning [11] [3] and more advanced concepts [5]. Crucially, however, none of these have visualized the computational *procedure* and calculations like ANOVAs and correlation coefficients have received little attention.

4 STATEMENT OF THESIS/PROBLEM

RQ. *How pedagogically effective are visualizations of data analytical procedures?*

(1) How do data algorithm visualizations perform compared with, or in interaction with, equations and pseudo-code?
  (a) Does it interact with spatial ability?
  (b) Does it interact with maths/statistics/test anxiety?
(2) Which type of visualization is more effective?
  (a) Are additional decorative graphics beneficial?
  (b) Are instructional booklets better than computerized tutorials?
  (c) Are visualizations that embed code and equations better than visualizations that separate them?
  (d) Are compressed visualizations contained within a single page or slide better than more airy ones spread across several pages?

5 RESEARCH GOALS & METHODS

Visualizations will be administered using e-learning platforms that collect learning analytics data such as session duration and interactions. Questionnaires assessing spatial ability and maths/statistics/test anxiety will be given to all participants. The studies will be conducted at three different levels, each of increasing internal validity, decreasing ecological validity, and coarser grain.

- The overall impact (RQ 1) will be assessed by a between-group study on classes in introductory statistics and data fundamentals courses. The cohorts will range from psychology to CS majors, and tested on their prior understanding, immediate learning effect and long-term learning. The intervention will take the form of 10-minute animations to be watched during lab hours. The control group will use traditional text, equations and diagrams that is informationally equivalent. This will be conducted in the upcoming academic year.
- In parallel with this, I will recruit people to learn one data science concept per week, using either a visualization or standard on-line instruction in counter-balanced order, and monitor the duration of their study sessions. This will give an idea of whether visualization accelerates the learning in a naturalistic setting.
- My final year will be dedicated to RQ2: the comparison between different visualization types, where the effect size is expected to be relatively small. Since between-group studies have less power, within-group designs will be used in a laboratory study. Subjects will be given a counter-balanced succession of the two types. Behavioral measures like prior and post-instruction performance will be accompanied by eye-tracking methodology, which has been used successfully

before to monitor extraneous cognitive load in multimedia research [8].

6 DISSERTATION STATUS

For the first 7 months of my PhD I have, alongside extensive literature research into the cognition of multimedia and procedural learning, completed a project that involved producing a A0 poster that visualizes the contents of the high school CS syllabus using a combination of concept maps and visual metaphors. To evaluate its reception as a classroom knowledge organizer, I conducted five focus groups among students (aged 15-17) that raised interesting questions of when complexity should be hidden or visually exposed. The rest of my PhD will examine this through a quantitative lens, with focus shifted to data science.

7 EXPECTED CONTRIBUTIONS

My dissertation work will produce a set of visualizations for data scientific concepts and algorithms, along with empirically examined guidelines and recommendations that are easy for other educators to implement. It will also illuminate how the efficacy interacts with traits like maths anxiety and spatial ability, indicating how applicable it will be to the diverse community of future data scientists.

REFERENCES

[1] Robert K Atkinson, Richard Catrambone, and Mary Margaret Merrill. 2003. Aiding Transfer in Statistics: Examining the Use of Conceptually Oriented Equations and Elaborations During Subgoal Learning. *Journal of Educational Psychology* 95, 4 (2003), 762.
[2] Carmen Batanero, Juan D Godino, A Vallecillos, DR Green, and P Holmes. 1994. Errors and difficulties in understanding elementary statistical concepts. *International Journal of Mathematical Education in Science and Technology* 25, 4 (1994), 527–547.
[3] Gary L Brase. 2009. Pictorial representations in statistical reasoning. *Applied Cognitive Psychology* 23, 3 (2009), 369–381.
[4] Richard Catrambone. 1998. The subgoal learning model: Creating better examples so that students can solve novel problems. *Journal of Experimental Psychology: General* 127, 4 (1998), 355.
[5] Richard William Farebrother and Michael Schyns. 2002. *Visualizing statistical models and concepts*. Vol. 166. CRC Press.
[6] Gerd Gigerenzer. 2004. Mindless statistics. *The Journal of Socio-Economics* 33, 5 (2004), 587–606.
[7] George Lakoff and Rafael Núñez. 2003. Where mathematics comes from. Santa Fe Institute.
[8] Richard E Mayer. 2010. Unique contributions of eye-tracking research to the study of learning with graphics. *Learning and instruction* 20, 2 (2010), 167–171.
[9] Roxana Moreno and Richard E Mayer. 1999. Multimedia-supported metaphors for meaning making in mathematics. *Cognition and instruction* 17, 3 (1999), 215–248.
[10] Robert A Muenchen. 2012. The popularity of data analysis software. *URL http://r4stats. com/popularity* (2012).
[11] Alvitta Ottley, Evan M Peck, Lane T Harrison, Daniel Afergan, Caroline Ziemkiewicz, Holly A Taylor, Paul KJ Han, and Remco Chang. 2016. Improving Bayesian reasoning: The effects of phrasing, visualization, and spatial ability. *IEEE transactions on visualization and computer graphics* 22, 1 (2016), 529–538.
[12] Peter Sedlmeier and Gerd Gigerenzer. 2001. Teaching Bayesian reasoning in less than two hours. *Journal of Experimental Psychology: General* 130, 3 (2001), 380.
[13] Clifford A Shaffer, Matthew L Cooper, Alexander Joel D Alon, Monika Akbar, Michael Stewart, Sean Ponce, and Stephen H Edwards. 2010. Algorithm visualization: The state of the field. *ACM Transactions on Computing Education (TOCE)* 10, 3 (2010), 9.

Using Program Analysis to Improve API Learnability

Kyle Thayer

Paul G. Allen School of Computer Science & Engineering

University of Washington

Seattle, WA

kthayer@cs.washington.edu

ABSTRACT

Learning from API documentation and tutorials is challenging for many programmers. Improving the learnability of APIs can reduce this barrier, especially for new programmers. We will use the tools of program analysis to extract key concepts and learning dependencies from API source code, API documentation, open source code, and other online sources of information on APIs. With this information we will generate learning maps for any user-provided code snippet, and will take users through each concept used in the code snippet. Users may also navigate through the most commonly used features of an API without providing a code snippet. We also hope to extend this work to help users find the features of an API they need and also help them integrate that into their code.

CCS CONCEPTS

• **Social and professional topics** → **Computer science education**; • **Software and its engineering** → *Software libraries and repositories*;

KEYWORDS

API learnability, program analysis, auto-generated documentation

ACM Reference Format:

Kyle Thayer. 2018. Using Program Analysis to Improve API Learnability. In *ICER '18: 2018 International Computing Education Research Conference, August 13–15, 2018, Espoo, Finland*. ACM, New York, NY, USA, 2 pages. https://doi.org/10.1145/3230977.3231009

1 PRELIMINARY WORK

I am a third-year PhD student in Paul G. Allen School of Computer Science & Engineering at the University of Washington. I have passed my Qualifying Evaluation and am now starting work toward my thesis proposal.

I have published one research project for publication: a qualitative study on barriers faced by coding bootcamp students. We found that, while bootcamps provided an alternate path into the software industry, students faced great personal costs and risks in taking this path, often including significant time, money and effort spent before, during, and after their bootcamps. To get software development jobs, students had to develop the ability to learn new

programming languages and libraries from documentation, tutorials and websites like StackOverflow. Many students said their bootcamp taught them this skill, though not all were happy with how this skill was taught.

I have started creating a theory of *key concepts* for this work, and I hope to get feedback on the scope and direction of my dissertation.

2 BACKGROUND AND MOTIVATION

Hearing about the challenge in using documentation, tutorials and other resources to learn new programming languages and the Application Programming Interfaces (APIs) of libraries and frameworks made us consider ways of reducing this barrier. In particular we are investigating how to use program analysis methods to create content that may help people who are learning APIs.

The challenges of using programming systems range from a programmer deciding what they want the computer to do regardless of the programming language or library, to the specific challenges of selecting programming interfaces, knowing how they work, and knowing the relevant concepts and terminology [1, 2]. Using API documentation provides specific challenges as well, such as navigating documentation, understanding how API designers intended their APIs to be use, matching specific scenario needs with API features [4]. To make good decisions on what API features to use and use them properly, programmers need to learn the API they are working with.

Existing methods of learning many large APIs consist of formatted code documentation (i.e., JavaDocs), sometimes with examples and a brief intro, and human-created tutorials. The raw documentation is often difficult for newcomers to navigate and the human-created tutorials take large amounts of effort and can go out of date when new versions of APIs are released. Our previous study on coding bootcamps showed the challenge of learning APIs and how the ability to learn from API documentation and other resources are seen as a valuable skill that was difficult to acquire.

Researchers have proposed generating on-demand documentation [5] and have made various attempts to make APIs easier to learn and use. These attempts include changes to APIs designs [8], and improved methods of searching API documentation [6] and other online resources [7]. These methods focus on improving the search for specific desired features instead of on explaining user-provided code snippets.

3 RESEARCH GOALS & METHODS

Given the importance of knowing relevant concepts and terminology in using APIs [2], our future research will focus on how to make it easier to learn the concepts and terminology used in arbitrary code. We will create *learning maps* for APIs which will be constructed from of *key concepts* and *learning dependencies*. By *key concepts* we mean the terminology, ideas, and patterns needed to perform tasks with an API, and by *learning dependencies* we mean the ways in which some *key concepts* can only be understood in relation to other *key concepts*.

These *learning maps* can be used by programmers wanting to understand code they've found or written and see how it can be expanded. They can also be used by tutorial creators in organizing their tutorials (saving time) or by newcomers as a guide for which concepts to learn (giving guidance). In particular, we believe newcomers will benefit from seeing a concise layout of *key concepts* which they can compare against their prior knowledge. The *learning maps* will provide paths to learning any *key concept* in an API. This will support learning one, some, or all features of the API.

In our research we will ask and attempt to answer the following research questions about *key concepts*, *learning dependencies*, and *learning maps*:

1) Can we extract *key concepts* and *learning dependencies* from available API code, documentation, open source repositories and question and answers sites?

To extract *key concepts* and *learning dependencies* from available code, we will first look at multiple APIs and tutorials. We will determine from the content and organization of tutorials what each one considers the *key concepts* of an API and what order those concepts can be presented in. These may not be the only *key concepts* a learner may need to know, but they will provide a baseline of concepts and APIs we will hope to recover through automated methods.

We will look at how *key concepts* and *learning dependencies* might be extracted from existing code, and other online resources, but most of the work in clarifying how to extract them will be done in conjunction with answering the next question.

Additionally, since there are many APIs, APIs change quickly, and new APIs are created, we want to use automated processes to do this work, so our second research question is:

2) Can we use program analysis to automatically extract *key concepts* and *learning dependencies* for an API?

Program analysis allows the automated extraction of features from computer programs, whether from code, execution information, or other resources. These analyses often provide information about how programs are expected to work, such as profiling, performance evaluation and bug detection [3]. We will instead use program analysis to identify *key concepts* and *learning dependencies* in APIs.

We will take the example APIs we looked at before and turn to what available code we can find for those APIs, such as: the API code, API documentation, open source code that uses the API and other resources on the API such as StackOverflow. We will then create definitions of *key concepts* and *learning dependencies* in terms of this available code and create program analyses that can extract them. As we iterate through this process we will come up with clearer definitions of our terms and better methods of automatically extracting these features.

3) How effective are *learning maps* generated from our automatically extracted *key concepts* and *learning dependencies*?

To test this, we will create an interface for learners that will give them a generated *learning map*. This interface may include automatically generated links to content for learning each concept or manually curated links for the concepts. We will then give learners tasks to complete with an API with the generated *learning map*, measure the effectiveness of these *learning maps* in terms of conceptual learning, problem solving ability, and perceived difficulty. Through this we hope to gain insights for improving to the underlying algorithms and the presentation of these *learning maps*.

4) Can we make *learning maps* based on provided code using an API?

To do this, detect which parts of an API are being used in the code and find the relevant sections of the *learning map*. We will then generate a tutorial that highlights concepts used in their code and also suggests possible extensions to the code.

5) Can we help developers search *learning maps* for the *key concepts* they need?

To do this, we will take user inputted searches and code, and find *key concepts* related to their input and their code while also considering how commonly used those concepts are. We can then help them integrate the *key concepts* into the code.

4 EXPECTED CONTRIBUTIONS

When this work has been completed, we will have created new analyses that extract newly defined factors from code bases: *key concepts* and *learning dependencies*. We will also have used these analyses to create new content and tools for API learners with specific code questions, newcomers to an API, and creators of API tutorials. Finally, we will have gained new understanding in how programmers learn APIs and what their needs are.

REFERENCES
[1] A.J. Ko, B.A. Myers, and H.H. Aung. 2004. Six Learning Barriers in End-User Programming Systems. In *2004 IEEE Symposium on Visual Languages and Human Centric Computing*. 199–206. https://doi.org/10.1109/VLHCC.2004.47

[2] A. J. Ko and Y. Riche. 2011. The role of conceptual knowledge in API usability. In *2011 IEEE Symposium on Visual Languages and Human-Centric Computing (VL/HCC)*. 173–176. https://doi.org/10.1109/VLHCC.2011.6070395

[3] Chi-Keung Luk, Robert Cohn, Robert Muth, Harish Patil, Artur Klauser, Geoff Lowney, Steven Wallace, Vijay Janapa Reddi, and Kim Hazelwood. 2005. Pin: Building Customized Program Analysis Tools with Dynamic Instrumentation. In *Proceedings of the 2005 ACM SIGPLAN Conference on Programming Language Design and Implementation (PLDI '05)*. ACM, New York, NY, USA, 190–200. https://doi.org/10.1145/1065010.1065034

[4] Martin P. Robillard and Robert DeLine. 2011. A field study of API learning obstacles. *Empirical Software Engineering* 16, 6 (Dec. 2011), 703–732. https://doi.org/10.1007/s10664-010-9150-8

[5] Martin P. Robillard, Andrian Marcus, Christoph Treude, Gabriele Bavota, Oscar Chaparro, Neil Ernst, Marco Aurĺlio Gerosa, Michael Godfrey, Michele Lanza, Mario Linares-Vásquez, and others. 2017. On-Demand Developer Documentation. *Software Maintenance and Evolution (ICSME)* (2017). http://www.inf.usi.ch/lanza/Downloads/Robi2017a.pdf

[6] J. Stylos, A. Faulring, Z. Yang, and B. A. Myers. 2009. Improving API documentation using API usage information. In *2009 IEEE Symposium on Visual Languages and Human-Centric Computing (VL/HCC)*. 119–126. https://doi.org/10.1109/VLHCC.2009.5295283

[7] J. Stylos and B. A. Myers. 2006. Mica: A Web-Search Tool for Finding API Components and Examples. In *Visual Languages and Human-Centric Computing (VL/HCC'06)*. 195–202. https://doi.org/10.1109/VLHCC.2006.32

[8] Jeffrey Stylos and Brad A. Myers. 2008. The Implications of Method Placement on API Learnability. In *Proceedings of the 16th ACM SIGSOFT International Symposium on Foundations of Software Engineering (SIGSOFT '08/FSE-16)*. ACM, New York, NY, USA, 105–112. https://doi.org/10.1145/1453101.1453117

Exploring Data-driven Worked Examples
for Block-based Programming

Rui Zhi
North Carolina State University
Raleigh, North Carolina
rzhi@ncsu.edu

ABSTRACT

Empirical studies show that worked examples (WEs) are effective in improving students' learning efficiency in a variety of domains. I aim to create and evaluate data-driven intelligent WEs for novices using the Snap! block-based programming environment. First, I will design and evaluate WEs with self-explanation prompts in Snap!. Then I will develop a data-driven method to generate WEs based on student solutions and compare it with manually-curated WEs.

KEYWORDS

block-based programming environment, data-driven, worked examples, self-explanation

ACM Reference Format:

Rui Zhi. 2018. Exploring Data-driven Worked Examples for Block-based Programming. In *ICER '18: 2018 International Computing Education Research Conference, August 13–15, 2018, Espoo, Finland.* ACM, New York, NY, USA, 2 pages. https://doi.org/10.1145/3230977.3231018

1 PROGRAM CONTEXT

I am a fourth year Ph.D. student in Computer Science at North Carolina State University. I will propose my dissertation in Fall 2018 and defend my dissertation in Fall 2019. I have led two studies investigating programming problems. In the first, I built and compared instructional designs for a programming game. In the second, I investigated the potential to algorithmically identify common features from student programs. Now I am developing the interface for worked examples (WEs) with self-explanation prompts in Snap! and will do a study to explore its effectiveness in this summer. I will refine the interface based on the study and evaluate this feature in a CS0 class with non-majors. I will also design algorithms to identify students' progress (i.e. to detect what parts of a problem a student has solved) and to generate data-driven WEs from student data.

2 CONTEXT AND MOTIVATION

My goal is to provide intelligent, data-driven support in blocked-based programming environments. My research is motivated by the effectiveness of worked examples (WEs) [6] and self explanations [5] in improving student learning in a variety of domains. However, WEs have not often been used for teaching programming, though

ICER '18, August 13–15, 2018, Espoo, Finland
© 2018 Copyright held by the owner/author(s).
ACM ISBN 978-1-4503-5628-2/18/08.
https://doi.org/10.1145/3230977.3231018

many software engineers learn from and adapt examples to solve problems as they work. I plan to explore the effectiveness of data-driven WEs in novice block-based programming environments. A recent study shows that novices have difficulty in using examples to solve programming problems in a block-based programming environment [2]. I want to understand how to derive effective WEs from data, how students might use them, and whether the WEs help student learn programming. Based on the results of this work, I plan to augment Snap! with data-driven methods to detect student progress and provide relevant, timely interventions. Ideally, when a student gets stuck, the system I envision can provide corresponding example code to help them make progress, and the student can learn from the example by running the example code, reflecting on the output, explaining the code, and adapting it to their own solutions.

3 BACKGROUND & RELATED WORK

Worked examples (WEs) are a common instructional support that helps novices learn more effectively than problem solving in various domains [6]. However, only a few studies explored how novices can effectively use WEs to learn block-based programming. In a pilot study for comparing different instructional designs in a programming game, we found that buggy WEs may be effective in helping students learn programming [7], but we had a small sample size. On the other hand, a study by Ichinco et al. shows that novices struggle to use WEs to solve block-based programming problems [2]. They found novices have difficulty in understanding the example and finding relevant blocks to finish the programming task. Along with WEs, self-explanation prompts help students foster greater understanding [5] and improve students' performance on problem solving [4]. Morrison et al. show that students who self-explained subgoal labels performed better than those who were not given subgoal labels [4]. Besides, the success of generating hints from student data motivates my research for leveraging the Hint Factory method [1] to generate WEs in block-based programming environments.

4 STATEMENT OF THESIS/PROBLEM

I will explore the effectiveness of WEs in helping novices learn block-based programming and develop a method to create data-driven WEs. My research questions are: **RQ1:** How effectively can students learn programming from WEs with self-explanation? **RQ2:** How can we generate data-driven WEs? **RQ3:** How do data-driven WEs compare with manually-curated WEs for student learning?

5 RESEARCH GOALS & METHODS

I will do 3 studies to answer my research questions. In **Study 1**, I will develop an interface that allows students to view, run, and annotate WEs, and I evaluate it in a high school summer camp. The study uses a switching replications design. In this design, both groups will take a concept-based pre-test, solve a programming problem, take an isomorphic post-test, solve another programming problem, take a second isomorphic post-test, and solve a third programming problem. However, group A will be given a series of WEs during the first problem, and group B will receive WEs on the second problem. This means the first portion of the study serves as a controlled experiment, while the second portion ensures all students have access to the intervention and allows us to investigate the impact of WEs' ordering on students' problem solving. I will compare participants' problem-solving performance and learning gains between pre-test and the two post-tests. The third programming problem serves as a performance post-test to evaluate how well the WEs supported student programming skill development.

In **Study 2**, I will analyze student data from 2016-2018 to design methods for generating data-driven WEs - creating them from prior student data. I led a study to determine the feasibility of automatically classifying student programs according to features that they do and do not include [8]. In this study, 3 experts extracted features from student solutions, with each feature indicating a subset of correct code, and used those features to represent a student's code status. We also designed a data-driven way to classify student programs based on their program features. Our results show that the data-driven feature space overlaps with the expert feature space both qualitatively and quantitatively, and that students take similar strategies to accomplish programming assignments. These results suggest that it is feasible to detect a student's progress towards completing a problem, and to break apart sample student code to generate WEs for desired features in an open-ended problem. Based on this work, I will develop an algorithm to detect students' progress and integrate it into Snap!. Specifically, when a student is programming, the system can detect the features that are completed. When the student gets stuck, the system will select code from another prior student solution to present a WE that achieves a needed feature(s). I will design an algorithm to identify prior student work that achieves certain features, and use program traces to identify when a feature first appears in a solution. In this way, I can derive WEs that students can self-explain to determine how a new feature is added to existing code. I hypothesize that data-driven WEs can help improve students' problem-solving performance and learning gains. I will conduct a controlled experiment to test my hypothesis.

In **Study 3**, I will evaluate the data-driven WEs and compare it with manually-curated WEs in a CS0 class in Spring 2019. I will collect data and evaluate the manually-curated WEs from this class in Fall 2018. After finishing **Study 2**, I will integrate the algorithm into Snap! and generate data-driven WEs. Before each programming assignment, students will take a test to evaluate their learning. When they use the system to finish assignments, they will be randomly assigned to either the control group (with manually-curated WEs) or the experiment group (with data-driven WEs). I will compare their problem-solving performance, learning gains between pre- and post-tests, and final exam scores. I hypothesize that students receiving data-driven WEs will perform similarly to those receiving manually-curated WEs in the time it takes for them to write

programs, and in learning gains. If successful, this will show that our system can use data to effectively select and present WEs.

6 DISSERTATION STATUS

I have gained an understanding of novices' programming behavior through a study to explore novices' debugging behavior in BOTS [3]. Our results show that students with higher scores on a self-explanation post-test made fewer code edits to fix a program. Recently, I led a study to explore the effect of WEs in BOTS [7]. In this study, we compared different instructional designs and our results suggest no difference of effectiveness on improving students' performance between WEs and instructional text, but participants using buggy WEs performed better. In addition to my previous work [8], the development of WEs with self-explanation prompts interface in Snap! is almost finished. I plan to propose my dissertation by the end of 2018 and finish my dissertation in December 2019. I hope the ICER doctoral consortium help me refine my proposal and research plan. In particular, I believe DC mentors will provide insight into how to best design the interface for WEs, and how to leverage WEs for novices in the context of solving a single problem and within the larger context of a semester-long programming course.

7 EXPECTED CONTRIBUTIONS

This work will provide insight into best practices for designing intelligent block-based programming environments. First, I will determine whether using WEs can help students learn programming concepts faster, and whether it helps them write programs to solve open-ended problems quicker. Second, I will investigate ways to derive relevant WEs from data, building on my work in using both expert and data-driven classification of the important aspects of student code solutions to open-ended problems. If successful, this will result in automatic detection of the features that students are working on and selection of prior student data that is similar to current student work. Third, I will compare the quality of data-driven WEs with that of manually-curated WEs in helping students learn programming.

REFERENCES

[1] Tiffany Barnes and John Stamper. 2010. Automatic hint generation for logic proof tutoring using historical data. *Journal of Educational Technology & Society* (2010), 3.

[2] Michelle Ichinco, Kyle J Harms, and Caitlin Kelleher. 2017. Towards Understanding Successful Novice Example User in Blocks-Based Programming. *Journal of Visual Languages and Sentient Systems* (2017), 101–118.

[3] Zhongxiu Liu, Rui Zhi, Andrew Hicks, and Tiffany Barnes. 2017. Understanding problem solving behavior of 6–8 graders in a debugging game. *Computer Science Education* (2017), 1–29.

[4] Briana B Morrison, Lauren E Margulieux, and Mark Guzdial. 2015. Subgoals, context, and worked examples in learning computing problem solving. In *ICER*. 21–29.

[5] Marguerite Roy and Michelene TH Chi. 2005. The self-explanation principle in multimedia learning. *The Cambridge handbook of multimedia learning* (2005), 271–286.

[6] John Sweller. 2006. The worked example effect and human cognition. *Learning and instruction* (2006), 165–169.

[7] Rui Zhi, Nicholas Lytle, and Thomas W Price. 2018. Exploring Instructional Support Design in an Educational Game for K-12 Computing Education. In *SIGCSE*. 747–752.

[8] Rui Zhi, Thomas W. Price, Nicholas Lytle, Yihuan Dong, and Tiffany Barnes. (in press). Reducing the State Space of Programming Problems through Data-Driven Feature Detection. In *EDM Workshop*.

Author Index